9.04

System Administration
and
Security

To George

Ubuntu 9.04: System Administration and Security

Richard Petersen

Surfing Turtle Press

Alameda, CA

www.surfingturtlepress.com

Please send inquires to: **editor@surfingturtlepress.com**

Library of Congress Control Number: 2009935453

ISBN   0-9841036-0-0

ISBN-13   978-0-9841036-0-7

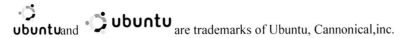

1005879724

Preface

This book is designed as a system administration and security reference. Administration tools are covered as well as the underlying configuration files and system implementations. The emphasis is on what administrators will need to know to perform key administration and security tasks. Topics covered include user management, time server settings, start up configuration, software management, kernel configuration, AppArmor, SELinux, devices, and file system management. System configuration tools are covered as well as the underlying configuration files. Topics covered include network connections, shell configuration files, Upstart service management, runlevels, and the Network Time Protocol..

The book is organized into four parts: system administration, security, and file system and device management, and shell configuration.

Part 1 focuses on administrative tasks such as managing users, managing software with APT, customizing the kernel, and setting up virtual systems.

Part 2 keys in on security tasks beginning with authorizations using PolicyKit. GPG encryption support with seahorse as well as the structure of public/private key encryption is covered. File and directory permissions, along with access controls are examined. SELinux tools and the format and command structure of SELinux configurations are discussed. SSH encryptions and Kerberos authentication are also examined. The security section ends with a detailed examination of IPtables firewalls and the firewall tools.

Part 3 deals with file systems and devices. File systems formats are discussed in detail along with mount and encryption operations. LVM and Linux RAID are covered. For devices, both HAL and udev are examined in detail. Backup applications for your file systems are then discussed.

Part 4 covers the shell interface in detail, including command line editing, shell scripts and programming, file and directory operations, jobs, regular expressions, shell configuration, and environment variables.

Overview

Part 1: System Administration

Part 2: Security

Part 3: Devices and File Systems

Part 4: Shells

Contents

Part 1

System Administration

Part 2

Security

Part 3

Devices and File Systems

17. Devices 419

Part 4
Shells

ubuntu

Part 1: System Administration

Introduction
Basic System Administration
System Startup and Services
Software Management
System Information
Managing Users
Kernel Administration
Virtualization

1. Ubuntu 9.04 Introduction

Ubuntu releases

Ubuntu Editions

Ubuntu 9.04

Landscape

Ubuntu Software

Ubuntu Linux Help and Documentation

Ubuntu Linux is currently one of the most popular end-user Linux distributions (**www.ubuntu.com**). Ubuntu Linux is managed by the Ubuntu foundation, which is sponsored by Cannonical, Ltd (**www.cannonical.com**), a commercial organization that supports and promotes open source projects. Ubuntu is based on Debian Linux, one of the oldest Linux distributions dedicated to incorporating cutting edge developments and features (**www.debian.org**). The Ubuntu project was initiated by Mark Shuttleworth, a South African and Debian Linux developer. Debian Linux is primarily a development Linux project, trying out new features. Ubuntu provides a Debian based Linux distribution that is stable, reliable, and easy to use.

Ubuntu is designed as a Linux operating system that can be used easily by everyone. The name Ubuntu means "humanity to others". As the Ubuntu project describes it: "Ubuntu is an African word meaning 'Humanity to others', or 'I am what I am because of who we all are'. The Ubuntu distribution brings the spirit of Ubuntu to the software world."

The official Ubuntu philosophy lists the following principles.

1. Every computer user should have the freedom to download, run, copy, distribute study, share, change, and improve their software for any purpose, without paying licensing fees.

2. Every computer user should be able to use their software in the language of their choice.

3. Every computer user should be given every opportunity to use software, even if they work under a disability.

The emphasis on language reflects Ubuntu's international scope. It is meant to be a global distribution, not focused on any one market. Language support has been integrated into Linux in general by its internationalization projects, denoted by the term i18n. These include sites like **www.li18nux.net** and **www.openi18n.org**.

Making software available to all users involves both full accessibility supports for disabled users as well as seamless integration of software access using online repositories, making massive amounts of software available to all users at the touch of a button. Ubuntu also makes full use of recent developments in automatic device detection, greatly simplifying installation as well as access to removable devices and attached storage.

Ubuntu aims to provide a fully supported and reliable, open source and free, easy to use and modify, Linux operating system. Ubuntu makes these promises about its distribution.

➤ Ubuntu will always be free of charge, including enterprise releases and security updates.

➤ Ubuntu comes with full commercial support from Canonical and hundreds of companies around the world.

➤ Ubuntu includes the very best translations and accessibility infrastructure that the free software community has to offer.

➤ Ubuntu CDs contain only free software applications; we encourage you to use free and open source software, improve it and pass it on.

Ubuntu releases

Ubuntu provides both long term and short term releases. Long term support releases (LTS) are released every two years. Ubuntu 8.04 is a long term release. Short term releases are provided every six months between the LTS versions. These are designed to make available the latest application and support for the newest hardware. Each has its own nickname, like Jaunty Jackalope for the 9.04 release. The long term releases are supported for three years for the desktop and five years for the servers, whereas short term releases are supported for 18 months. Canonical also provides limited commercial support for companies that purchase it.

Installing Ubuntu has been significantly simplified. A core set of applications are installed, and you add to them as you wish. Following installation, added software is taken from online repositories. Install screens have been reduced to just a few screens, moving quickly through default partitioning, user setup, and time settings. The hardware like graphics cards and network connections are now configured and detected automatically.

The Ubuntu distribution of Linux is available online at numerous sites. Ubuntu maintains its own site at **www.ubuntu.com/getubuntu** where you can download the current release of Ubuntu Linux.

Ubuntu Editions

Ubuntu is released in several editions, each designed for a distinct group of users or functions (see Table 1-1). Editions install different collections of software such as the KDE desktop, the XFce desktop, servers, educational software, and multimedia applications. Table 1-2 lists Web sites where you can download ISO images for these editions. ISO images can be downloaded directly or using a BitTorrent application like Transmission.

The Ubuntu Desktop edition provides standard functionality for end users. The standard Ubuntu release provides a Live CD using the GNOME desktop. Most users would install this edition. This is the CD image that you download from the Get Ubuntu download page at:

```
www.ubuntu.com/getubuntu/download
```

Those that want to run the Ubuntu Desktop edition on their netbook can download the Ubuntu Netbook Remix (UNR). This is a USB image file that can be copied to a USB drive. The USB drive can operate as an Ubuntu Live USB drive or be used to install Ubuntu Linux on your netbook. You can find out more about the Remix at:

```
http://www.canonical.com/projects/ubuntu/unr
```

You can download the Ubuntu Netbook Remix image file from:

```
http://www.ubuntu.com/getubuntu/download-netbook
```

Those that want to run Ubuntu just as a server, providing an Internet service like a Web site, would use the Server edition. The server edition also provides Cloud computer support. The Server edition provided only a simple command line interface; it does not install the desktop. It is designed to primarily run servers. Keep in mind that you could install the desktop first, and later download server software from the Ubuntu repositories, running them from a system that also has a desktop. You do not have to install the Server edition to install and run servers. The Server edition can be downloaded from the Ubuntu download page, like the Desktop edition.

Users that want more enhanced operating system features like RAID arrays, LVM file systems, or file system encryption would use the Alternate edition. The Alternate edition, along with the Desktop and Server editions, can be downloaded directly from.

```
releases.ubuntu.com/jaunty
releases.ubuntu.com/releases/9.04
```

Ubuntu Editions	Description.
Ubuntu Desktop	Live CD using GNOME desktop, **www.ubuntu.com/getubuntu**.
Server Install	Install server software (no desktop) **www.ubuntu.com/getubuntu**.
Alternate Install	Install enhanced features **http://releases.ubuntu.com**.
Netbook Remix	Install a netbook version. The netbooks remix is a Live USB image. **http://www.ubuntu.com/getubuntu/download-netbook**
Kubuntu	Live CD using the KDE desktop, instead of GNOME, **www.kubuntu.org**. kubuntu-desktop
Xubuntu	Uses the Xfce desktop instead of GNOME, **www.xubuntu.org**. Useful for laptops.
Edubuntu	Installs Educational software: Desktop, Server, and Server add-on CDs, **www.edubuntu.org**
goubuntu	Uses only open source software, no access to restricted software of any kind. See the **goubuntu** link at **http://www.ubuntu.com/products/whatisubuntu**
ubuntustudio	Ubuntu desktop with multimedia and graphics production applications, **www.ubuntustudio.org**. **ubuntustudio-desktop** (Meta Packages, universe)
mythbuntu	Ubuntu desktop with MythTV multimedia and DVR applications, **www.mythbuntu.org**. **mythbuntu-desktop** (Meta Packages, multiverse)

Table 1-1: Ubuntu Editions

Other editions use either a different desktop or a specialized collection of software for certain groups of users. Links to the editions are listed on the **http://www.ubuntu.com/products/whatisubuntu** Web page. From there you can download their live/install CDs. The KUbuntu edition used the KDE desktop instead of GNOME. Xubuntu uses the XFce desktop instead of GNOME. This is a stripped down highly efficient desktop, ideal for low power use on laptops and smaller computer. The Edubuntu edition provides educational software. It can also be used with a specialized Edubuntu server to provide educational software on a school network. The Goubuntu edition is a modified version of the standard edition that includes only open source software, with no access to commercial software of any kind, including restricted vendor graphics drivers. Only Xorg open source display drivers are used. The ubuntustudio edition is a new edition that provides a collection of multimedia and image production software. The mythbuntu edition is designed to install and run the MythTV software, letting Ubuntu operate like Multimedia DVR and Video playback system.

The Ubuntu Server, KUbuntu, and Edubuntu are all officially supported by Ubuntu. The Xubuntu, Goubuntu, Mythbuntu, and Ubuntu Studio editions are not supported, but are officially recognized. These are all considered derivatives of the original Ubuntu Desktop. You can find out more about these derivatives at: **http://www.ubuntu.com/products/whatisubuntu/derivatives**.

URL	Internet Site
www.ubuntu.com/getubuntu/download	Primary download site for Desktop and Server CDs
http://releases.ubuntu.com/jaunty	Download site for Desktop, Alternate, and Server CDs: also the Netbook USB (image files, jigdo, and BitTorrent)
http://cdimages.ubuntu.com/releases/jaunty/release/	Download site for Install/Live DVD and for MID USB (image files and BitTorrent).
http://releases.ubuntu.com	Download site for Ubuntu, along with KUbuntu and Edubuntu.
http://cdimages.ubuntu.com	Download site for all Ubuntu editions, including KUbuntu, XUbuntu, Edubuntu, mythbuntu, goubuntu, and ubuntustudio. Check also their respective Web sites.
http://launchpad.net	Ubuntu mirrors
http://torrent.ubuntu.com	Ubuntu BitTorrent site for BitTorrent downloads of Ubuntu distribution ISO images. Bittorrent files also available at **http://releases.ubuntu.com** and **http://cdimages.ubuntu.com**.
http://www.ubuntu.com/getubuntu/download-netbook	Netbook Remix live USB image

Table 1-2: Ubuntu CD ISO Image locations

All these editions can be downloaded from their respective Web sites, as well as from the **http://cdimages.ubuntu.com** site, and from links at **http://www.ubuntu.com/products/whatisubuntu**.

The Kubuntu and Edubuntu editions can be downloaded directly from both:

```
http://releases.ubuntu.com
http://www.ubuntu.com/getubuntu/
```

The Gobuntu, Mythbuntu, Xubuntu, and Ubuntu Studio are all available, along with all the other editions and Ubuntu releases, on the cdimage server, and from the Ubuntu Web site's whatisubuntu page.

```
http://cdimages.ubuntu.com
http://www.ubuntu.com/products/whatisubuntu
```

The **http://releases.ubuntu.com** and **http://cdimages.ubuntu.com** sites hold both BitTorrent and full image files for the editions they provide. The **http://releases.ubuntu.com** site also provides jigdo files for Jigsaw downloads from multiple mirrors.

Keep in mind that most of these editions are released as Live CDs or Live DVD install discs, for which there are two versions, a 32 bit x86 version and a 64 bit x86_64 version. Older computers may only support a 32 bit version, whereas most current computers will support the 64 bit versions. Check your computer hardware specifications to be sure. The 64 bit version should run faster, and most computer software is now available in stable 64 bit packages.

Note: In addition, Ubuntu provides different releases for different kinds of installation on hard drives. These include a Server disc for installing just servers, and an Alternate disc for supporting specific kinds of file systems and features during an installation, like RAID and LVM file systems.

Ubuntu 9.04 Server and Desktop Features

Check the Ubuntu Technical Overview for an explanation of changes.

`https://wiki.ubuntu.com/JauntyJackalope/TechnicalOverview`

For operational issues and bugs check the Ubuntu Release notes.

`http://www.ubuntu.com/getubuntu/releasenotes/9.04`

Ubuntu 9.04 includes the following features.

➢ The Ubuntu server edition provides support for Cloud computing. You can set up your own cloud with Ubuntu Enterprise Cloud, or use the public cloud provided by Amazon with Ubuntu on Amazon with EC2. The Amazon cloud is a commercial/fee service provided by Amazon.

➢ The dovecot-postfix meta package installs a complete Mail server using both the Postfix mail server and dovecot IMAP and POP3 mail servers.

➢ For netbooks, Ubuntu 9.04 provides the Ubuntu Netbook Remix (UNR), available as a USB image. See **http://www.canonical.com/projects/ubuntu/unr** for more information. Download from either **http://www.ubuntu.com/getubuntu/download-netbook** or **http://releases.ubuntu.com/jaunty/**. You can use the UNR to install Ubuntu on most netbooks, using a USB drive.

➢ The installation program (Ubiquity) has been reworked, with a new time zone selection screen supporting graphical map time zone selection. For the keyboard there is a detected default selected for you, and an added option for selecting the keyboard type yourself. There are also graphical representations for hard disk partition configuration. It also features an option for automatically logging in to the main user account.

➢ The default Ubuntu login screen, though functionally the same, has been redesigned with new artwork.

➢ The recovery menu adds options for fixing the GRUB boot loader and entering a root shell with networking.

➢ You use the User Switcher/Quit menu to shut down, logout, restart, suspend, and hibernate. Pressing your computer power button opens the Shut Down dialog with Shutdown, Restart, Hibernate, and Suspend options. The System menu no longer has Log Out and Shut Down entries.

➢ KUbuntu now uses KDE 4.2 with its new desktop including the Plasma desktop and panel, Dolphin file manager, Kickoff application launcher, and the Zoom User Interface (ZUI).

➢ The Synaptic Package Manager features a "Get Screenshot" capability, allowing you download a screenshot of the application and display it in the package description pane. Screen shots are not available for all packages.

➢ There is now a unified notification system that all messages use. The notification messages have been redesigned with a black background.

➢ Brasero is the integrated GNOME DVD/CD burner used to perform all disc burning tasks, including create, copy, erase, and check.

➢ Startup Applications Preferences has replaced the Sessions tool.

➢ Computer Janitor detects unused packages and lets you remove them. It can also perform configuration fixes, like those to your GRUB **menu.lst** file, reflecting any changes.

➢ Volume control features a tab for selecting PulseAudio sound themes. You can also choose to have no sound for your alerts.

➢ There are three new GNOME desktop themes for Ubuntu: Dust, Dust Sand, and New Wave.

➢ GNOME archiving and compression (File Roller, named Archive Manager), now supports LZMA compression which is more efficient and faster.

Ubuntu 8.10

Feature introduced previously with Ubuntu 8.10.

➢ The new version of NetworkManager is now used for configuring all network connections, even manually. The older GNOME network-admin has been dropped. You can also use NetworkManager to configure 3G wireless networks.

➢ The user switcher and Quit button on the desktop panel have been combined, displaying options for both other users to switch to, and entries to logout, restart, and shutdown.

➢ For users, Ubuntu provides a Private encrypted directory (**ecryptfs**). The Private directory is not accessible to other users or groups. Furthermore the directory remain unmount until you decide to access it. The **encryptfs-setup-private** command implements the Private directory.

➢ You can more easily create a USB install drive, letting you install Ubuntu using just a USB drive instead of a CD/DVD ROM disc. The tool to use is **usb-creator**.

➢ An improved hardware driver install tool (jockey) better locates and installs restricted (third party) drivers.

➢ Synaptic supports Quick searches, displaying results as you type in your query.

➢ GNOME Nautilus file manager supports tabs for displaying multiple folders in the same window, as well as a new compact view for listing files.

➢ Gufw provides a user interface for configuring the UFW default firewall on the GNOME desktop.

➢ GNOME Nautilus file manager provides an Eject button for removable media like USB drives and CD/DVD discs (similar to KDE 4). The Places view on the sidebar will display an Eject icon next to the mounted removable media. Just click the button to eject the media (or unmount in the case of USB drives so you can then remove it).

➤ The GNOME Archive Mounter allows you to access archives, displaying or extracting their contents. Works also on CD/DVD disc images (does not mount them as file systems).

➤ Adobe FLASH is included

➤ The GNOME Archive Manager (fileroller) supports additions archiving formats, ALZ, CAB, RZIP, and TAR.7Z. These are based on the p7zip archiving format.

➤ GNOME Archive Manager can now encrypt archives (password accessible)

➤ CompizFusion is fully integrated with the GNOME desktop with plugins like cube deformation (cylinder and sphere) and window thumbnails. KDE4's KWin provides similar desktop effects for workspace switching and window selection.

➤ OpenOffice 3.0 features support for MS Office 2007 files.

➤ Open Java 6 JRE and JDK are included as part of the main Ubuntu repository.

Ubuntu 8.04

Features introduced previously with Ubuntu 8.04.

➤ PolicyKit authorization for users, allowing limited controlled administrative access to users for administration tools, and for storage and media devices.

➤ Brasero GNOME CD/DVD burner

➤ Kernel-based Virtualization Machine (KVM) support is included with the kernel. KVM uses hardware virtualization enabled processors. Use the Virtual Machine Manager to manage and install KVM virtual machines.

➤ Applications like Transmission BitTorrent client, Vinagre Virtual Network Client, and the World Clock applet with weather around the world.

➤ Features automatic detection of removable devices like USB printers, digital cameras, and card readers. CD/DVD discs are treated as removable devices, automatically displayed and accessed when inserted.

➤ GNOME supports GUI access to all removable devices and shared directories on networked hosts, including Windows folders, using the GNOME Virtual File System, **gvfs**. Gvfs replaces gnomevfs.

➤ Any NTFS Windows file systems on your computer are automatically detected and mounted using **ntfs-3g**. Mounted file systems are located in the **/media** directory.

➤ The Update Manager automatically updates your Ubuntu system and all its installed applications, from the Ubuntu online repositories.

➤ Software management (Synaptic Package Manager) accesses and installs software directly from all your configured online Ubuntu repositories.

➤ Wine Windows Compatibility Layer lets you run most popular Windows applications directly on your Ubuntu desktop.

Ubuntu Software

For Ubuntu, you can update to the latest software from the Ubuntu repository using the update manager. The Ubuntu distribution provides an initial selection of desktop software. Additional applications can be downloaded and installed from online repositories, ranging from office and multimedia applications to Internet servers and administration services. Many popular applications are included in separate sections of the repository. During installation, your system is configured to access Ubuntu repositories.

All Linux software for Ubuntu is currently available from online repositories. You can download applications for desktops, Internet servers, office suites, and programming packages, among others. Software packages are primarily distributed in through Debian-enabled repositories, the largest of which is the official Ubuntu repository. Downloads and updates are handled automatically by your desktop software manager and updater.

A complete listing of software packages for the Ubuntu distribution, along with a search capability is located at.

`http://packages.ubuntu.com`

In addition, you could download from third-party sources software that is in the form of compressed archives or in DEB packages. DEB packages are those archived using the Debian Package Manager. Compressed archives have an extension such as **.tar.gz**, whereas Debian packages have a **.deb** extension. You could also download the source version and compile it directly on your system. This has become a simple process, almost as simple as installing the compiled DEB versions.

Due to licensing restrictions, multimedia support for popular operations like MP3, DVD, and DivX are included with Ubuntu in a separate section of the repository called multiverse. Ubuntu does include on its restricted repository Nvidia and ATI vendor graphics drivers. Ubuntu also provides as part of its standard installation, the generic X.org which will enable your graphics cards to work.

All software packages in different sections and Ubuntu repositories are accessible directly with the Install/Remove Applications and the Synaptic Package Manager.

Due to further licensing issues, added multimedia support for popular operations like DVD Video, as well as popular applications like Google Earth, Skype, and Adobe reader are provide by the **medibuntu.org** repository. This is a third party repository which does not have repository support initially configured. You have to implement repository support manually before you can access the software packages with the Synaptic Package Manager.

Managing Systems with Landscape

Landscape is Ubuntu's administration and monitoring management service accessed through a hosted Web interface. You can register online with Ubuntu for the Landscape service. With Landscape you can administer, monitor, and maintain machines on your network, as well as install and update hosts software. You can find out more about Landscape at:

`http://www.canonical.com/projects/landscape`

Machines can be organized into groups, letting you install packages on different groups. Your custom repository can be accessed directly with Landscape, using it to install software on your machines. You can also manage users and servers, adding and removing users, as well as starting an stopping servers.

Landscape also installs its own monitoring application on each machine, providing reports on usage, hardware status, and performance. You can also manage processes, detecting those that use the most resources.

Landscape also supports cloud computing, letting you manage instances of a system on a cloud as you would machines on your network. Landscape can manage Ubuntu instances on the Amazon EC2 cloud.

Cannonical provides a free trial (60 days for 5 machines) at:

```
www.canonical.com/landscape/register
```

Ubuntu Linux Help and Documentation

A great deal of help and documentation is available online for Ubuntu, ranging from detailed install procedures to beginners questions (see Table 1-3). The two major sites for documentation are help.ubuntu.com and the Ubuntu forums at **http://ubuntuforums.org**. In additions there are blog and news sites as well as the standard Linux documentation. Also helpful is the Ubuntu Guide Wiki at **www.ubuntuguide.org**. Links to Ubuntu documentation, support, blogs, and news are listed at **www.ubuntu.com/community**. Here you will also find links for the Ubuntu community structure including the code of conduct. A Contribute section links to sites where you can make contributions in development, artwork, documentation, support.

For mailing lists, check **http://lists.ubuntu.com**. There are lists for categories like Ubuntu announcements, community support for specific editions, and development for areas like the desktop, servers, or mobile implementation. For more specialized tasks like Samba support and LAMP server installation check **www.ubuntugeek.com**.

help.ubuntu.com

Ubuntu-specific documentation is available at **help.ubuntu.com**. Here on tabbed pages you can find specific documentation for different releases. Always check the release help page first for documentation. The documentation though may be sparse. It covers mainly changed areas. The Ubuntu release usually includes desktop, installation, server guides. The guides are very complete and will cover most topics. The desktop guide covers these main topics: text editing, using terminals, sudo administrative access, software management, music and video applications, Internet application including mail and instant messaging, office applications, graphics and photos, printing, and games. Advanced topics are covered like programming, partitions, and font management.

For the Ubuntu server, be sure to check the Ubuntu Server Guide, 9.04 version, at:

```
https://help.ubuntu.com/9.04/serverguide/C/index.html
```

The installation guide provides a very detailed discussion of install topics like system requirements, obtaining the CDs, boot parameters, partitioning, and automatic installs.

The short term support releases tend to have just a few detailed documentation topics like software management, desktop customization, security, multimedia and Internet applications, and printing. These will vary depending on what new features are included in the release.

Site	Description
http://help.ubuntu.com	Help pages
http://packages.ubuntu.com	Ubuntu software package list and search
http://ubuntuforums.org	Ubuntu forums
www.ubuntuguide.org	Guide to Ubuntu
http://fridge.ubuntu.com	News and developments
http://planet.ubuntu.com	Member and developer blogs
http://blog.canonical.com	Latest Canonical news
www.tldp.org	Linux Documentation Project Web site
www.ubuntuguide.org	All purpose guide to Ubuntu topics
www.ubuntugeek.com	Specialized Ubuntu modifications
www.ubuntu.com/community	Links to Documentation, Support, News, and Blogs
http://lists.ubuntu.com	Ubuntu mailing lists
www.ubuntugeek.com	Tutorials and guides for specialized tasks

Table 1-3: Ubuntu help and documentation

One of the most helpful pages is the last, Community Docs page. Here you will find detailed documentation on installation of all Ubuntu releases, using the desktop, installing software, and configuring devices. Always check the page for your Ubuntu release first. The page has these main sections:

> ➢ Getting Help: links to documentation and FAQs. The official documentation link displays the tabbed page for that release on **help.ubuntu.com**.

> ➢ Getting Ubuntu: Link to Install page with sections on desktop, server, and alternate installation. Also information on how to move from using other operating systems like Windows or Mac.

> ➢ Using and Customizing your System: Sections on managing and installing software, Internet access, configuring multimedia applications, and setting up accessibility, the desktop appearance (eye candy), server configuration, and development tools (programming).

> ➢ Maintain your Computer: Links to system administration, security, and trouble shooting pages. System administration cover topics like adding users, configuring the GRUB boot loader, setting the time and date, and installing software. The Security page covers much lower level issues like IPtables for firewalls and how GPG security works. Of particular interest is the LUKS encrypted file system howtos.

> ➢ Connecting and Configuring Hardware: Links to pages on drives and partitions, input devices, wireless configuration, printers. sound, video, and laptops.

ubuntuforums.org

Ubuntu forums provide detailed online support and discussion for users. An Absolute Beginner section provides an area where new users can obtain answers to questions. Sticky threads include both quick and complete guides to installation for the current Ubuntu release. You can use the search feature to find discussions on your topic of interest.

The main support categories section covers specific support areas like networking, multimedia, laptops, security, and 64 bit support.

Other community discussions cover ongoing work such as virtualization, art and design, gaming, education and science, Wine, assistive technology, and even testimonials. Here you will also find community announcements and news. Of particular interest are third party projects that include projects like Mythbuntu (MythTV on Ubuntu), Ubuntu Podcast forum, Ubuntu Women, and Ubuntu Gamers.

The forum community discussion is where you talk about anything else. The **http://ubuntuforums.org/** site also provides a gallery page for posted screenshots as well as RSS feeds for specific forums.

ubuntuguide.org

The Ubuntu Guide is a kind of all purpose HowTo for frequently asked questions. It is independent of the official Ubuntu site and can deal with topics like how to get DVD-video to work (**www.ubuntuguide.org**). Areas cover topics like popular add-on applications like Flash, Adobe Reader, and MPlayer. The Hardware section deals with specific hardware like Nvidia drivers and Logitech mice. Emulators like Wine and VMWare are also discussed.

Ubuntu news and blog sites

Several news and blog sites are accessible from the News pop-up menu on the **www.ubuntu.com** site.

➤ **fridge.ubuntu.com** The Fridge site lists the latest news and developments for Ubuntu. It features the Weekly newsletter, latest announcements, and upcoming events.

➤ **planet.ubuntu.com** Ubuntu blog for members and developers

➤ **blog.canonical.com** Canonical news

Linux documentation

Linux documentation has also been developed over the Internet. Much of the documentation currently available for Linux can be downloaded from Internet FTP sites. A special Linux project called the Linux Documentation Project (LDP), headed by Matt Welsh, has developed a complete set of Linux manuals. The documentation is available at the LDP home site at **www.tldp.org**. The Linux documentation for your installed software will be available at your **/usr/share/doc** directory.

2. Basic System Administration

Administrator Access

Terminal Window

Ubuntu Administration Tools

System Directories

Configuration Directories and Files

Grand Unified Bootloader (GRUB)

System Time and Date

Scheduling Tasks: cron

This chapter reviews a few administrative task and tools you may normally use. Most administrative configurations tasks are now performed for you automatically. Devices like printers, hard drive partitions, and graphics cards are now detected and set up for you automatically. There are cases where you may need to perform tasks manually like adding new users or trouble-shooting your display. Administrative operations can now be performed with user-friendly system tools. This chapter discusses a few system administration operations, and tells where to find out how to perform certain common tasks like adding new users and configured remote printers. Most administration tools can be found in System | Administration and System | Preferences menus.

Ubuntu Administration Menus	Description
System	Administration	Ubuntu menu for accessing administrative tools
System	Preferences	Ubuntu menu for desktop interface configuration like mouse or screen resolution
Applications	System Tools	Ubuntu menu for accessing specialized administrative applications and configuration tools

Ubuntu Administration Tools	Description
Synaptic Package Manager	Apt Software management using online repositories
Add/Remove Applications	Apt Software management, Add/Remove Applications
Update Manager	Update tool using Apt repositories
Network Manager	Configures your network interfaces (GNOME)
services-admin	Services tool, manages system and network services such as starting and stopping servers. (GNOME)
time-admin	Changes system time and date (GNOME)
users-admin	User and Group configuration tool
system-config-printer	Printer configuration tool (Fedora/Red Hat)
system-config-samba	Configures your Samba server (Fedora/Red Hat). User level authentication support.
gnome-language-selector	Selects a language to use
Gufw	Configures your network firewall
polkit-gnome-authorization	Sets authentication settings for devices and administration tasks, PolicyKit

Table 2-1: Administration Tools on System | Administration

TIP: If you have difficulties with your system configuration, check the **http://ubuntuforums.org** site for possible solutions. The site offers helpful forums ranging from desktop and install problems to games, browsers, and multimedia solutions. Also check the support link at **www.ubuntu.com** for documentation, live chat, and mailing lists.

Terminal Window

The Terminal window allows you to enter Linux commands on a command line (Applications | Accessories | Terminal) . It also provides you with a shell interface for using shell commands instead of your desktop. The command line is editable, allowing you to use the backspace key to erase characters on the line. Pressing any key will insert the key. You can use the left and right arrow keys to move anywhere on the line, and then press keys to insert characters, or use backspace to delete characters (see Figure 2-1). Folders, files, and executable files are color coded: black for files, blue for folders, and green for executable files. Shared folders are displayed with a green background.

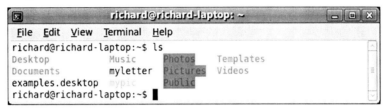

Figure 2-1: Terminal Window

The terminal window will remember the previous commands you entered. Use the up and down arrows to have those commands displayed in turn. Press the ENTER key to re-execute the currently displayed command. You can even edit a previous command before running it, allowing you to execute a modified version of a previous command.

The terminal window will display all your previous interactions and commands for that session. Use the scrollbar to see any previous commands you ran and their displayed results.

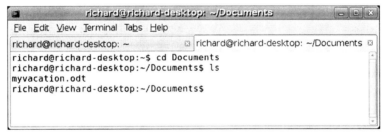

Figure 2-2: Terminal Window with tabs

You can open as many terminal windows as you want, each working in its own shell. Instead of opening a separate window for each new shell you may want, you can open several shells in the same window, using tabbed panels. Select Open Tab from the File menu to open a new tab window, (**Shift-Ctrl-t**). Each tab runs a separate shell, letting you enter different commands in each (see Figure 2-2). You can use the Tabs menu to move to different tabs, or just click on its panel to select it. The Tab menu is displayed on the toolbar only if multiple tabs are open. For a single window, the Tab menu is not displayed (see Figure 12-3).

The terminal window is also supports GNOME desktop cut/copy and paste operations. You can copy a line from a Web page and then paste it to the terminal window (you may have to use the Copy entry on the Terminal window's Edit menu). The command will appear and then you can press ENTER to execute the command. This is useful for command line operations that may be displayed on an instructional Web page. Instead of typing in a complex command yourself, just copy from the Web page directly, and then paste to the Terminal window. Perform any edits if needed.

Ubuntu Administration Tools

On Ubuntu, administration is handled by a set of separate specialized administrative tools, such as those for user management and printer configuration (see Table 2-1). To access the GUI-based administrative tools, you log in as a user that has administrative access. This is the user you created when you first installed Ubuntu.

On the GNOME desktop System administration tools are listed on the System | Administration menu. Here you will find tools to set the time and date, manage users, configure printers, and install software. Users and Groups lets you create and modify users and groups. Printing lets you install and reconfigure printers. All tools provide very intuitive GUI interfaces that are easy to use. On the Administration menu, tools are identified by simple descriptive terms, whereas their actual names normally begin with the terms like admin or system-config. For example, the printer configuration tool is listed as Printing, but its actual name is **system-config-printer**, whereas Users and Groups is **admin-users**. You can separately invoke any tool by entering its name in a terminal window. Table 2-2 shows some common system administration commands.

Command	Description
`su root`	Logs a superuser into the root from a user login. Root user access disabled by default on Ubuntu.
`sudo` *command*	Restricts administrative access to specified users.
`passwd` *login-name*	Sets a new password for the login name.
`gksu` *command*	Run graphical application with administrative access
`shutdown` *options time*	Shuts down the system.
`date`	Sets the date and time for the system.

Table 2-2: Administration commands

Ubuntu uses the GNOME administration tools, with KDE counterparts, administration tools adapted from the Fedora distribution supported by Red Hat Linux, and independent tools, like Firestarter for your firewall, PolicyKit for device authorizations, and the Synaptic Package Manager for software installation. The GNOME administrative tools are suffixed with the term **admin**, whereas the Fedora tools have the prefix **system-config**. Since Ubuntu 7.10, the Printing administrative tool is Fedora's **system-config-printer**, replacing the GNOME printer-admin tool used in previous Ubuntu releases. A Samba GUI tool is now available for Ubuntu, which is the Fedora **system-config-samba** tool. The Fedora **system-config-lvm** tool provides a simple and effective way to manage Logical Volume Manager (LVM) file systems, but is now available on the Ubuntu repository. In addition, Virus protection is handled by an entirely separate application like ClamAV (Universe repository).

Note: Many configuration tasks can also be handled on a command line, invoking programs directly. To use the command line, open a terminal window by selecting the Terminal entry in the Applications | Accessories menu. This opens a terminal window with a command line prompt. Commands like sudo and make discussed later will require a terminal window.

Controlled Administrative Access

To access administrative tools, you have to login as a user that have administrative permissions. The user that was created during installation is automatically granted administrative permissions. Log in as that user. When you attempt to use an administrative tool to use, like those in the System | Administration menu, you will be prompted in a window to enter your user password. This is the password for the user you logged in as. You can use the Users and Groups tool to grant or deny particular users administrative access.

To perform system administration operations, you must first have access rights enabling you to perform administrative tasks like add new users or set the time. There are several ways to gain such access, each with more refined access controls. In each case you have to login as a user who has been granted administrative access. The access methods are: logging in as the root user, login as a sudo supported user (gksu is the graphical version of sudo), and unlocking an administrative tool for access by a PolicyKit authorized users. PolicyKit is the preferred access method and is used for most administrative tools. The **sudo** access method was used in previous Ubuntu releases, and is still used for software upgrade and installation tasks (Synaptic and Update Manager), as well as performing any command line operation requiring administrative access (like editing system configuration files). **gksu** is the graphical version of **sudo**. The root user access was and is still discouraged, but provides complete control over the entire system.

- PolicyKit: Provides access only to specific applications and only to users with administrative access for that application. Requires that the specific application be configured for use by PolicyKit.

- **sudo** and **gksu**: Provides access to any application will full root level authorization. Given a time limit to reduce risk. The gsku command is used for graphical administrative tools like Synaptic Package Manager. You will still need to use **sudo** to perform any standard Unix commands at the root level like editing configuration files. You must use a valid administrative username and password to gain access to a any administrative tool and perform any operation on the system.

- **root** user access, **su**: Provides complete direct control over the entire system. This is the traditional method for accessing administrative tools. It is disabled by default on Ubuntu, but can be enabled. The **su** command will allow any user to login as the root user if they know the root user password. Logging in as the root user makes you the superuser.

PolicyKit

PolicyKit will let any user start an administrative tool, but restrict use to read only access. On the users-admin tool for managing users, you will be able to see the list of users on your system, but not make any changes to them, or even add new users. In effect, you are locked out. For PolicyKit controlled utilities, a Lock/Unlock button will appear in the lower right corner of the administrative tool's window. To gain full access, you need to unlock it. Click on the Unlock button to open a dialog where you can specify the authorized user you want to use, and password for that authorized users (see Figure 2-3). The list of authorized users is selectable from a pop-up menu. The user you created when you installed your system is an authorized user. Authorized users are those user granted administrative access when their account was set up. For single user systems, with just one user, this will default to user you logged in as.

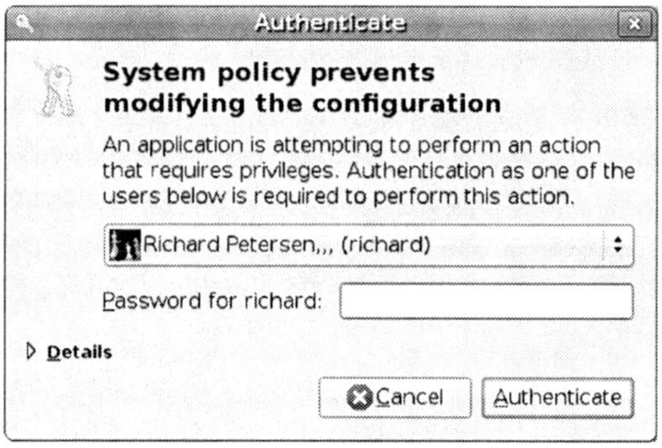

Figure 2-3: PolicyKit authorization window

With PolicyKit, you can login as a user with no administrative access, and then gain access to an administrative tool by selecting a user with that access and entering that user's password in the Authenticate dialog. Without PolicyKit, you would first have to login as an administrative user that would be able to access any administration application and be able perform any administrative task. With PolicyKit, you do not have to login as an administrative user, just use that user to access a particular administrative tool.

sudo and gksu

The sudo service provides administrative access to specific users. You have to be a user on the system with a valid username and password that has been authorized by the sudo service for administrative access. This allows other users to perform specific superuser operations without having full administrative level control. You use the **sudo** command to run a command with administrative access. The **gksu** tool is the graphical version of sudo used on the Ubuntu GNOME desktop.You can find more about sudo at **www.sudo.ws**.

gksu

You can use the **gksu** command in place of **sudo** to run graphical applications with administrative access. The **gksu** tool is a front end to sudo that does not require a terminal window (another name for **gksu** is **gksudo**). The gsku tool will prompt you to enter your password, assuming you are logged in as a user that has sudo authorized administrative access (See Figure 2-4).

You can enter the **gksu** command in a terminal window with the application as an argument, or set up an application launcher with **gksu** as the command. The following example will start up the Gedit editor with administrative access, allowing you to directly edit system configuration files (see Figure 2-5).

```
gksu gedit
```

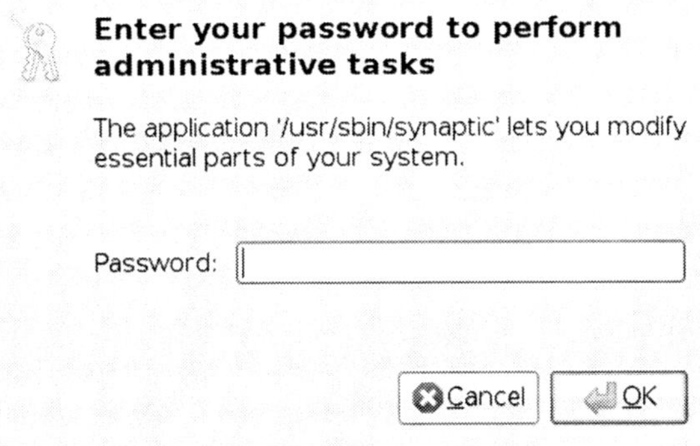

Enter your password to perform
administrative tasks

The application '/usr/sbin/synaptic' lets you modify
essential parts of your system.

Password: |

❌ Cancel   ⬅ OK

Figure 2-4: gksu prompt for access to administrative tools

The administrative tools on your desktop actually invoke their applications using gksu, as in **gksu synaptic**. You will see this command in the Launcher tab in the application's properties window. If you run **gksu** directly without any application specified, it will prompt you to enter the application. You could set up a GNOME or KDE application launcher for an application with the gksu command prefixing the application command.

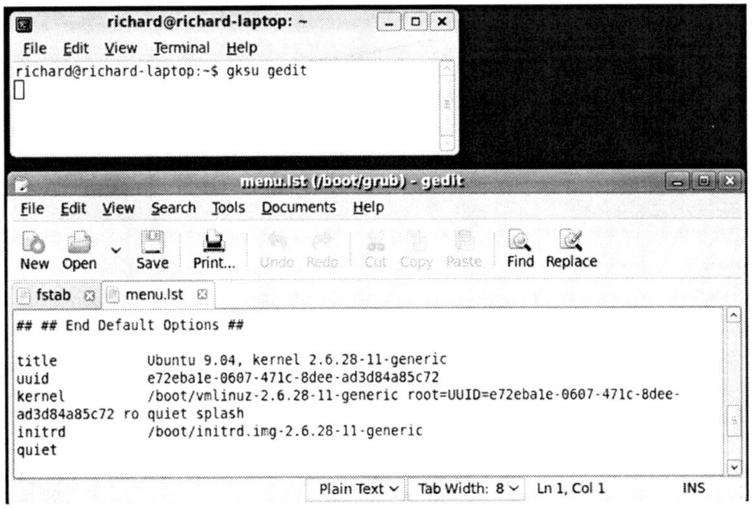

Figure 2-5: Invoking Gedit with gksu command

sudo command

Some administrative operations require access from the command line in the terminal window. For such operations you would use the **sudo** command, run from a terminal window. You can open a terminal window using the Terminal tool accessible from the Applications | Accessories window. For easier access, you can drag the menu entry for the Terminal tool to the desktop to create a desktop Terminal icon for creating a terminal window.

```
sudo
```

To use sudo to run an administrative command, the user precedes the command with the sudo command. The user is then prompted to enter their password. The user is issued a time-restricted ticket to allow access.

```
sudo date 0406145908
password:
```

From the terminal window, you would then enter the sudo command with the administrative program name as an argument. For example, to use Vi to edit system configuration files, you would have start Vi using the **sudo** command in a terminal window, with the **vi** command and the file name as its arguments. This starts up Vi with administrator privileges. The following example will allow you to edit the **/etc/fstab** file to add or edit file system entries for automatic mounting. You will be prompted for your user password.

```
sudo vi /etc/fstab
```

sudo configuration

Access is controlled by the /etc/sudoers file. This file lists users and the commands they can run, along with the password for access. If the NOPASSWD option is set, then users will not need a password. ALL, depending on the context, can refer to all hosts on your network, all root-level commands, or all users. See the Man page for **sudoers** for detailed information on all options.

To make changes or add entries, you have to edit the file with the special sudo editing command **visudo**. This invokes the Vi editor to edit the **/etc/sudoers** file. Unlike a standard editor, **visudo** will lock the **/etc/sodoers** file and check the syntax of your entries. You are not allowed to save changes unless the syntax is correct. If you want to use a different editor, you can assign it to the EDITOR shell variable.

A sudoers entry has the following syntax:

```
user    host=command
```

The host is a host on your network. You can specify all hosts with the ALL option. The command can be a list of commands, some or all qualified by options such as whether a password is required. To specify all commands, you can also use the ALL option. The following gives the user george full root-level access to all commands on all hosts:

```
george  ALL = ALL
```

To specify a group name, you prefix the group with a **%** sign, as in **%mygroup**. This lets you grant the same access to a group of users. By default sudo grants access to all users in the **admin** group, who are granted administrative access. The ALL=(ALL) ALL entry allows access by the **admin** group to all hosts as all users to all commands.

```
%admin   ALL=(ALL)   ALL
```

You can also allow members of a certain group access without requiring a password by using the NOPASSWD option. A commented configuration entry allowing permission for all members of the **sudo** group is provided in the **/etc/sudoers** file.

```
%admin   ALL=NOPASSWD   ALL
```

By default sudo will deny access to all users, including the root. For this reason, the default **/etc/sudoers** file sets full access for the root user to all commands. The ALL=(ALL) ALL entry allows access by the root to all hosts as all users to all commands.

```
root   ALL=(ALL)   ALL
```

Though on Ubuntu the sudo file is configured to allow **root** user access, Ubuntu does not create a **root** user password. This prevents you from logging in as the **root** user, rendering the sudo root permission useless.

In addition, you can let a user work as another user on a given host. Such alternate users are placed within parentheses in front of the commands. For example, if you want to give **george** access to the **beach** host as the user **mydns**, you use the following:

```
george beach = (mydns) ALL
```

To give **robert** access on all hosts to the date command, you would use

```
robert ALL=/usr/bin/time-admin
```

If a user wants to see what commands he or she can run, that user would use the sudo command with the **-l** option.

```
sudo -l
```

Full Administrative Access: root, su, and superuser

Ubuntu is designed to never to let anyone directly access the root user. The **root** user has total control over the entire system. Instead certain users are granted administrative access with which they can separately access administrative tools, performing specific administrative tasks. Even though a **root** user exists, a password for the root user is not defined, never allowing access to it.

You can, however, activate the root user by using the **passwd** command to create a root user password. Enter the **passwd** command with the root user name in a sudo operation.

```
sudo passwd root
```

You will be prompted for your administrative password, and then prompted by the **passwd** command to enter a password for the **root** user. You will then be prompted to re-enter the password.

```
Enter new UNIX password:
Retype new UNIX password:
passwd: password updated successfully
```

You can then log in with the **su** command as the root user, making you the superuser (you still cannot login as the root user from the GDM login window). Because a superuser has the power to change almost anything on the system, such a password is usually a carefully guarded secret, changed very frequently, and given only to those who manage the system. With the correct password, you can log in to the system as a system administrator and configure the system in various ways. You can also add or remove users, add or remove whole file systems, back up and restore files, and even designate the system's name and address.

```
su root
```

The **su** command alone with assume the root username.

```
su
```

The **su** command can actually be used to login to any user, provided you have that user's password.

It is possible to access the root user using the **sudo** command on the **su** command. The **su** command is the superuser command. Superuser is another name for **root** user. A user granted administrative access by **sudo**, could then become the **root** user. The following logs in as the root user.

```
sudo su
```

To exit from a **su** login operation, when you are finished working in that account, just enter the **exit** command.

```
exit
```

Tip: For security reasons, Linux distributions do not allow the use of `su` in a Telnet session to access the root user.

Editing User Configuration Files Directly

Although the administrative and preferences tools will handle all configuration settings for you, at times you will need to make changes by directly editing configuration files. These are usually text files in the **/etc** directory or user configuration files in a user home directory, like **.profile** (often called *dot files* because they are prefixed with a period). As noted, to change system files, you will need administrative access, invoking an editor using the **sudo** command.

You can use any standard editor such as Vi or Emacs to edit these files, though one of the easiest ways to edit them is to use the Gedit editor on the GNOME desktop. Select Text Editor from the Accessories menu. This opens a Gedit window. Click Open to open a file browser where you can move through the file system to locate the file you want to edit.

Caution: Be careful when editing your configuration files. Editing mistakes can corrupt your configurations. It is advisable to make a backup of any configuration files you are working on first, before making major changes to the original.

Gedit will let you edit several files at once, opening a tabbed pane for each. You can use Gedit to edit any text file, including ones you create yourself. Three commonly edited configuration files are **.profile**, **/boot/grub/grub.conf**, and **/etc/fstab**. The **.profile** file configures your login shell, **/etc/fstab** file lists all your file systems and how they are mounted, and **/boot/grub/grub.conf** file is the configuration file for your Grub boot loader.

To edit any of the system wide configuration files, like those in the **/etc** directory, you will first need root user access. Either login as the root user and run gedit, or, as any user with administrative access, run **gedit** from a terminal window using the **sudo** command. You will be prompted for the root user password. You could also login as the root user from a terminal window using the **su** command. Then enter the **gedit** command on that terminal line.

```
sudo -u root gedit
```

User configuration files, dot files, can be changed by individual users directly. They do not show up automatically on Gedit. Dot files like **.profile** have to be chosen from the file manager window, not from the Gedit open operation. First configure the file manager to display dot files by opening the Preferences dialog (select Preferences in the Edit menu of any file manager window) and then check the Show Hidden Files entry and close the dialog. This displays the dot files in your file manager window. Double-click to open one in Gedit.

Note: Most hardware configuration tasks are now handled by desktop preferences, like those in the System | Preferences menu. Here you can configure your mouse, keyboard, and sound card.

Editing files with the command line interface: text editors

If you are using the command line interface only, you will often have to edit configuration files directly to configure your system and servers. You will have to use a command line based editor to perform your editing tasks. Most command line editors provide a screen based interface that makes displaying and editing a file fairly simple. Two standard command line editors are installed by default on your system, **vi** and **nano**. Several common command line text editors are listed in Table 2-6. The commands you use to start the editors are also the editor names, in lower case, like **vi** for the Vi editor, **nano**, **joe**, and **emacs** for Emacs.

The **vi** editor is the standard editor used on most Linux and UNIX systems. It can be very difficult to use by people accustomed to a desktop editor. The **nano** editor is much more easy to use, featuring a screen-base interface that you can navigate with arrow keys. If you do not already know **vi**, you may want to use **nano** instead.

Editor	Description
vi	The Vi editor, difficult to use, considered the standard editor on Linux ad UNIX system, installed by default
nano	Easy to use screen based editor, installed by default
emacs	Powerful and complex screen-based editor, though easier to use than Vi, Ubuntu repository
vim	Easier to use version of vi, Ubuntu repository
joe	Simple screen based editor similar to Emacs, Universe repository
the	Screen based editor similar to Emacs, Universe repository
ne	Simple screen based editor similar to nano, Universe repository
aee	Simple screen based editor similar to nano, Universe repository
ae	Simple screen based editor, Universe repository
joe	Simple screen based editor, Universe repository
joe	Simple screen based editor, Universe repository

Table 2-3: Command line interface text editors

The nano editor is a simple screen-based editor that lets you visually edit your file, using arrow and page keys to move around the file. You use control keys to perform actions. **Ctrl-x** will exit and prompt you to save the file, **Ctrl-o** will save it.

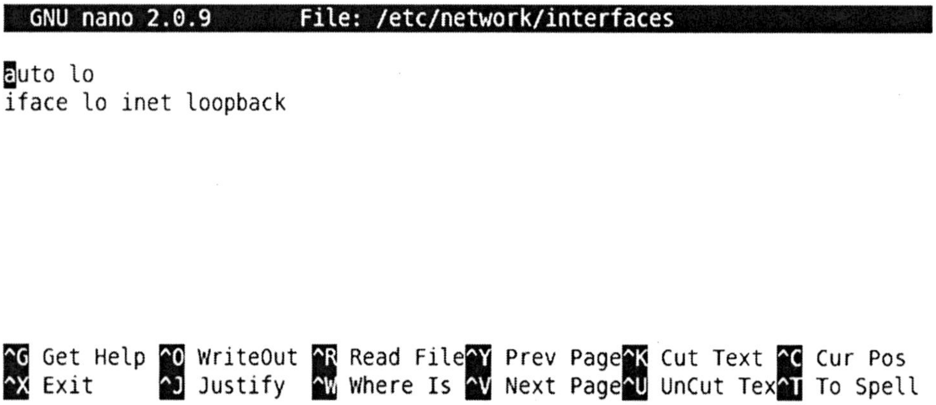

```
  GNU nano 2.0.9        File: /etc/network/interfaces

auto lo
iface lo inet loopback




^G Get Help ^O WriteOut ^R Read File^Y Prev Page^K Cut Text ^C Cur Pos
^X Exit     ^J Justify  ^W Where Is ^V Next Page^U UnCut Tex^T To Spell
```

Figure 2-6: Editing with nano

You start nano with the **nano** command. To edit a configuration file you will need administrative access. You would start nano with the **sudo** command. Figure 3-1 shows the nano editor being used to edit the **/etc/network/interfaces** file. To edit a configuration file like **/etc/network/interfaces** you would enter the following.

```
sudo nano /etc/network/interfaces
```

More powerful editors you may find helpful are vim and emacs. You will have to first install them. The **vim** editor provides a slightly easier interface for vi. Emacs provides an interface similar to **nano**, but much more complex.

Other simple screen-based editors you may find helpful are **joe**, **aee**, **ne**, and **the**. All are available on the Universe repository. **joe** and **the** are similar to Emacs. **ne** and **aee** are more like **nano**.

Administrative access from the file browser

You may want to perform file management operations on system directories or files, like editing system configuration files or creating new folders to mount new file systems onto. The file browser on your administrative user account, does not have permission to make changes to the system files or directories. To gain this kind of access, you can invoke the file browser with the **gksu** command from a terminal window. The name of the GNOME browser is nautilus. In a terminal window enter the following.

```
gksu nautilus
```

You will be prompted to enter your administrative user password. Then the GNOME nautilus file browser open up at the root user home directory. For easy access, you could create an application launcher with the previous command in the Launcher panel. Then just double click the launcher to start up the file browser with root access.

Tip: For easy access, you can create an application launcher using the gksu nautilus command in the Launcher panel. Then you can double-click the launcher from the desktop to start up the file browser with root access.

You can perform any administrative action on files you may wish, like changing permissions to folders and directories, creating new ones, or deleting old ones anywhere in the system. You can also edit any configuration files. Configuration files are usually found in the **/etc** directory, and are text files that can be edited by Gedit text editor. Double clicking on one will open the Gedit text editor, displaying the file and allowing you to edit it.

System Directories

Your Linux file system is organized into directories whose files are used for different system functions (see Table 2-4). For basic system administration, you should be familiar with the system program directories where applications are kept, the system configuration directory (**/etc**) where most configuration files are placed, and the system log directory (**/var/log**) that holds the system logs, recording activity on your system.

Directory	Description
/bin	System-related programs
/sbin	System programs for specialized tasks
/lib	System and application libraries
/etc	Configuration files for system and network services and applications
/home	User home directories and server data directories, such as web and FTP site files
/mnt	Where CD-ROM and floppy disk file systems are mounted
/var	System directories whose files continually change, such as logs, printer spool files, and lock files
/usr	User-related programs and files; includes several key subdirectories, such as **/usr/bin**, **/usr/X11**, and **/usr/doc**
/usr/bin	Programs for users
/dev	Dynamically generated directory for device files
/etc/X11	X Window System configuration files
/usr/share	Shared files
/usr/share/doc	Documentation for applications
/tmp	Directory for system temporary files
/var/log	Logging directory
/var/log/	System logs generated by **syslogd**
/var/log/audit	Audit logs generated by **auditd**

Table 2-4: System Directories

Program Directories

Directories with "bin" in the name are used to hold programs. The **/bin** directory holds basic user programs, such as login shells (BASH, TCSH, and ZSH) and file commands (cp, mv, rm, ln, and so on). The **/sbin** directory holds specialized system programs for such tasks as file system management (`fsck`, `fdisk`, `mkfs`) and system operations like shutdown and startup (`init`). The **/usr/bin** directory holds program files designed for user tasks. The **/usr/sbin** directory holds user-related system operations, such as `useradd` to add new users. The **/lib** directory holds all the libraries your system uses, including the main Linux library, `libc`, and subdirectories such as **modules**, which holds all the current kernel modules.

Configuration Files: /etc

When you configure different elements of your system, such as users, applications, servers, or network connections, you use configuration files kept in certain system directories. Configuration files are placed in the **/etc** directory.

The **/etc** directory holds your system, network, server, and application configuration files. Here you can find the **fstab** file listing your file systems, the **hosts** file with IP addresses for hosts on your system, and **/etc/profile**, the system wide default BASH shell configuration file. This directory includes various subdirectories, such as **/etc/apache** for the Apache web server configuration files, **/etc/X11** for the X Window System and window manager configuration files, and **/etc/udev** for rules to generate device files in **/dev**. You can configure many applications and services by directly editing their configuration files, though it is best to use a corresponding administration tool. Table 2-5 lists several commonly used configuration files found in the **/etc** directory.

File	Description
/etc/bashrc	Default shell configuration file Bash shell
/etc/group	A list of groups with configurations for each
/etc/fstab	File systems that are automatically mounted when you start your system
/boot/grub/menu.lst	The GRUB configuration file for the GRUB boot loader, linked to by /etc/menu.lst.
/etc/default	Directory holding service and application configuration parameters, options and variables set when the service or application starts up.
/etc/event.d	Upstart start up scripts
/etc/inittab	Dummy inittab file used for specifying default runlevel
/etc/profile	Default shell configuration file for users
/etc/modules	Modules on your system to be automatically loaded
/etc/motd	System administrator's message of the day
/etc/mtab	Currently mounted file systems
/etc/passwd	User password and login configurations
/etc/services	Services run on the system and the ports they use
/etc/shadow	User-encrypted passwords
/etc/shells	Shells installed on the system that users can use
/etc/sudoers	sudo configuration to control administrative access

/etc/termcap	A list of terminal type specifications for terminals that could be connected to the system
/etc/xinetd.conf	Xinetd server configuration
Directori	
/etc/cron.d	**cron** scripts
/etc/cups	CUPS printer configuration files
/etc/event.d	Configuration scripts for Upstart startup operations, replaces System V init.
/etc/init.d	Service scripts for distribution that support SysV Init scripts.
/etc/mail	Sendmail configuration files
/etc/openldap	Configuration for Open LDAP server
/etc/rc.*N*	Startup scripts for different runlevels
/etc/skel	Versions of initialization files, such as **.profile**, which are copied to new users' home directories
/etc/X11	X Window System configuration files
/etc/xinetd.d	Configuration scripts for services managed by Xinetd server
/etc/udev	Rules for generating devices
/etc/hal	Rules for generating removable devices

Table 2-5: Common System Configuration Files and Directories

Grand Unified Bootloader (GRUB)

The Grand Unified Bootloader (GRUB) is a multi-boot boot loader used for most Linux distributions. With GRUB, users can select operating systems to run from a menu interface displayed when a system boots up. Use arrow keys to move to an entry and press ENTER. Type **e** to edit a command, letting you change kernel arguments or specify a different kernel. The **c** command places you in a command line interface. Provided your system BIOS supports very large drives, GRUB can boot from anywhere on them. Linux and Unix operating systems are known as multi-boot operating systems and take arguments passed to them at boot time. Check the GRUB Man page for GRUB options. GRUB is a GNU project with its home page at **www.gnu.org/software/grub** and Wiki at **http://grub.enbug.org**.

Officially, the Grub configuration settings are held in the **/boot/grub/menu.lst** file. You only need to make your entries in the grub configuration file and GRUB will automatically read them when you reboot. There are several options you can set, such as the timeout period and the background image to use. Check the GRUB info documentation for a detailed description, `info grub`.

If you want to edit the **menu.lst** file, you will have to edit it with administrative access. Use **gksu gedit** or **sudo** with an editor like vi to edit the file with administrative access. You will be prompted to enter your user password.

```
gksu gedit /boot/grub/menu.lst
```

The **menu.lst** file generated by Ubuntu will initially list several commented GRUB options. Some will be uncommented, and thereby made active. You can activate others by editing the **menu.lst** file and removing the preceding #.

```
## default num
# Set the default entry to the entry number NUM. Numbering starts from 0, and
# the entry number 0 is the default if the command is not used.
default         0

## timeout sec
# Set a timeout, in SEC seconds, before automatically booting the default entry
# (normally the first entry defined).
timeout         3

## hiddenmenu
# Hides the menu by default (press ESC to see the menu)
hiddenmenu
```

The actual menu entries are located at the end of the file, beginning with the term title. Three options are already set for you: **default**, **timeout**, and **hiddenmenu**. The **default** option will specify the entry to run and will be set to the main kernel. If you have other operating systems that you want to make the default instead (such as Mac or Windows on a dual boot system), you could change the number to that entry (counting from 0). The **timeout** option is the time allotted before the default system is started up automatically. The **hiddenmenu** option hides the GRUB menu display, letting you display it if you press any key before the timeout.

The kernel option specifies the kernel to run. The kernel is located in the **/boot** directory and has the name **vmlinuz** with the kernel version number. You can have several kernels in the **/boot** directory and use GRUB to choose the one to use. After the kernel program you specify any options you want for the kernel. This includes an **ro** option, which initially starts the kernel as read only. On Ubuntu, the **uuid** line is used to specify the device on which your system was installed, your root directory. Ubuntu uses a special Universal Unique IDentifier (UUID) identifier for your boot partition. This identifier was created during installation.

```
title     Ubuntu 9.04, kernel 2.6.28-14-generic
uuid      dd4252ec-380e-4d00-9f89-857aba879b63
kernel    /boot/vmlinuz-2.6.28-14-generic  root=UUID=dd4252ec-380e-4d00-9f89-857aba879b63 \
          ro quiet splash apparmor.enabled=0 selinux=1
initrd    /boot/initrd.img-2.6.28-14-generic
quiet
```

If you installed your system on a Logical Volume Manager (LVM) disk, your root directory will be installed on a logical volume. On the **kernel** line, the **root** option references the logical volume on which your system is installed, instead of a UUID. The LVM volume is **/dev/mybuntugroup/mybuntu**, specifying firs the volume group (**myugrp**) and then the volume on that group where the system is installed (**mybuntu**).

```
kernel /boot/vmlinuz-2.6.22-14-generic root=/dev/myugrp/myubuntu ro quiet splash
```

You can specify a system to boot manually by creating a title entry for it, beginning with the term `title`. You then have to specify where the operating system kernel or program is located, which hard drive to use, and what partition on that hard drive. You can do this either by specifying the hard disk's UUID using the **uuid** line, or by specifying the actual hard disk and partition number on your system using the **root** line.

This hard disk and partition number is listed in parentheses following the **root** line. Numbering starts from 0, not 1, and hard drives are indicated with an **hd** prefix, whether they are IDE or SCSI hard drives. The entry **root(hd0,2)** references the first hard drive (**hda**) and the third partition on that hard drive (**hda3**). For Linux systems, you will also have to use the **kernel** option to indicate the kernel program to run, using the full pathname and any options the kernel may need. The RAM disk is indicated by the **initrd** option.

```
root      (hd0,1)
```

Disk and partition numbering requires that the drives position on your hardware system is not changed. It is not advisable for removable disks or for a system that has its disks changed or replaced frequently. In such cases the disk numbering could change and GRUB will not correctly locate the partition with your Ubuntu system on it. To avoid such problems, Ubuntu uses UUIDs instead of disk number. A UUID will always identify and locate a disk and its partition. UUIDs are ideal for systems where disk are being added and removed frequently.

For recovery you can start up in the single user mode. This provides administrative access without any services started up, services that could be failing. The following is an example of a recovery mode Grub entry. It is exactly the same as the main entry, but with the **single** option as the end of kernel line to indicate the single runlevel. Also the **splash** and **quiet** options are removed. The Upstart start up script, **/etc/event.d/rc-default**, is programmed to detect the single option, and then start up in runlevel **S**, single user mode using the telinit command.

```
title    Ubuntu 9.04, kernel 2.6.28-14-generic (recovery mode)
uuid     dd4252ec-380e-4d00-9f89-857aba879b63
kernel   /boot/vmlinuz-2.6.28-14-generic root=UUID=dd4252ec-380e-4d00-9f89-857aba879b63 \
         ro  single
initrd   /boot/initrd.img-2.6.28-14-generic
```

Following the main and recovery entries will be the main and recovery entries for your previously installed kernel. These are kept in case you have problems with the new kernel. You can always use Grub to boot to the old kernel. Should you have problems with the old kernel, you can boot to the recovery mode (single runlevel) for the old kernel.

In multi-boot systems, you can use Grub to book to another installed operating system, like Windows. For another non-Linux operating system such as Windows, you use the **rootnoverify** option to specify where Windows is installed. This option instructs GRUB not to try to mount the partition. Use the **chainloader+1** option to allow GRUB to access it. The **chainloader** option tells GRUB to use another boot program for that operating system. The number indicates the sector on the partition where the boot program is located—for example, **+1** indicates the first sector.

```
title    Windows Vista (loader)
rootnoverify (hd0,0)
savedefault
makeactive
chainloader  +1
```

Windows systems will all want to boot from the first partition on the first disk. This becomes a problem if you want to install several versions of Windows on different partitions or install Windows on a partition other than the first one. For Windows partitions on the same disk, GRUB lets you work around this by letting you hide other partitions in line, and then unhiding the one you want, making it appear to be the first partition. In this example, the first partition is hidden, and the second is unhidden. This assumes there is a Windows system on the second partition on the first hard drive (**hd0,1**). Now that the first partition is hidden, the second one appears as the first partition:

```
hide (hd0,0)
unhide (hd0,1)
rootnoverify (hd0,1)
```

For systems that have multiple hard drives, you may have Windows installed on a drive other than the first hard drive. GRUB numbers hard drives from 0, with **hd1** referencing the second hard drive, and **hd0** referencing the first hard drive. Windows will always want to boot from the first partition on the first hard drive. For a version of Windows installed on a hard drive other than the first one, GRUB lets you work around it by letting you renumber your drives with the **map** command. The first drive can be renumbered as another drive, and that drive can then ten be remapped as the first drive. In this example, the first drive is remapped as the second drive, and the second drive is mapped as the first drive. This example assumes there is a Windows system on the first partition on the second hard drive (**hd1,0**). Once the first drive is remapped as the second one, the second drive can operate as the first drive. However, the **chainloader** operation still detects the actual location of that Windows OS on the second hard drive, (**hd1,0)+1**, in this example on the first partition. GRUB will then boot the Windows partition on the second hard drive, as if it where located on a first hard drive.

```
map (hd0) (hd1)
map (hd1) (hd0)
chainloader (hd1,0)+1
```

A sample segment from a Grub configurations file (**menu.lst**) follows with entries for both Linux and Windows. The Windows system is installed on the first parttion (**hd0,0**).The Ubuntu kernels are refereneced using their UUIDs instead of a partition number. Keep in mind the the kernel entries are all one line, though they are displayed on two lines in this example, using the \ to quote the newline character. The UUID is shortend here to show the full line.

```
title    Ubuntu 9.04, kernel 2.6.28-14-generic
uuid     dd4252ec-380e-4d00-9f89-857aba879b63
kernel   /boot/vmlinuz-2.6.28-14-generic  root=UUID=dd4252ec-380e-4d00-9f89-857aba879b63 \
         ro quiet splash apparmor.enabled=0 selinux=1
initrd   /boot/initrd.img-2.6.28-14-generic
quiet

title    Ubuntu 9.04, kernel 2.6.28-14-generic (recovery mode)
uuid     dd4252ec-380e-4d00-9f89-857aba879b63
kernel   /boot/vmlinuz-2.6.28-14-generic root=UUID=dd4252ec-380e-4d00-9f89-857aba879b63 \
         ro  single
initrd   /boot/initrd.img-2.6.28-14-generic

title    Ubuntu 9.04, kernel 2.6.28-11-generic
uuid     dd4252ec-380e-4d00-9f89-857aba879b63
kernel   /boot/vmlinuz-2.6.28-11-generic root=UUID=dd4252ec-380e-4d00-9f89-857aba879b63 \
         ro quiet splash apparmor.enabled=0 selinux=1
initrd   /boot/initrd.img-2.6.28-11-generic
quiet

title    Ubuntu 9.04, kernel 2.6.28-11-generic (recovery mode)
uuid     dd4252ec-380e-4d00-9f89-857aba879b63
kernel   /boot/vmlinuz-2.6.28-11-generic root=UUID=dd4252ec-380e-4d00-9f89-857aba879b63 \
         ro  single
```

```
initrd    /boot/initrd.img-2.6.28-11-generic

title     Ubuntu 9.04, memtest86+
uuid      dd4252ec-380e-4d00-9f89-857aba879b63
kernel    /boot/memtest86+.bin
quiet

### END DEBIAN AUTOMAGIC KERNELS LIST

# This is a divider, added to separate the menu items below from the Debian
# ones.
title     Other operating systems:
root

# This entry automatically added by the Debian installer for a non-linux OS
# on /dev/sda1
title     Windows Vista (loader)
rootnoverify (hd0,0)
savedefault
makeactive
chainloader  +1
```

System Time and Date

You can set the system time and date using the shell **date** command, the GNOME clock applet, or the GNOME **time-admin** tool.. You probably set the time and date when you first installed your system. You should not need to do so again. However, if you entered the time incorrectly or are working in a different time zone, you can use this utility to change the time. Or perhaps you want to have your time checked and set automatically using the Network Time Protocol (NTP) time servers.

Using the time-admin Date and Time Utility

The preferred way to set the system time and date is to use the GNOME Date and Time utility (**time-admin**) or the world clock applet. To start **time-admin**, choose System | Administration | Date and Time. The time and date values will be displayed, but grayed out. The **time-admin** tool is controlled by PolicyKit. Click the Unlock button and enter an administrative user password to gain access.

In the Time and Date Settings dialog (Figure 2-7), the current time is shown in hours, minutes, and seconds. Use the arrow buttons to change these values. On the calendar, you can select the year, month, and day by using the arrow keys to move to the next or previous month or year. Clicking the Time Zone button at the top of the dialog displays the Time Zone dialog, which shows a map with location, along with a pop-up menu for specific cities. Select the city nearest you to set your time zone. Clicking the map zooms to that area.

The Configuration pop-up menu lets you choose to set the time manually or have a time server set it for you automatically. The Manual setting is the default. Alternatively, you can use time servers to set the time automatically. In this case, the Calendar and Time boxes will not be displayed (Figure 2-8). Time servers use the Network Time Protocol (NTP), which allows a remote server to set the date and time, instead of using local settings. NTP allows for the most accurate synchronization of your system's clock. It is often used to manage the time and date for networked systems, freeing the administrator from having to synchronize clocks manually. You can download current documentation and NTP software from **www.ntp.org**.

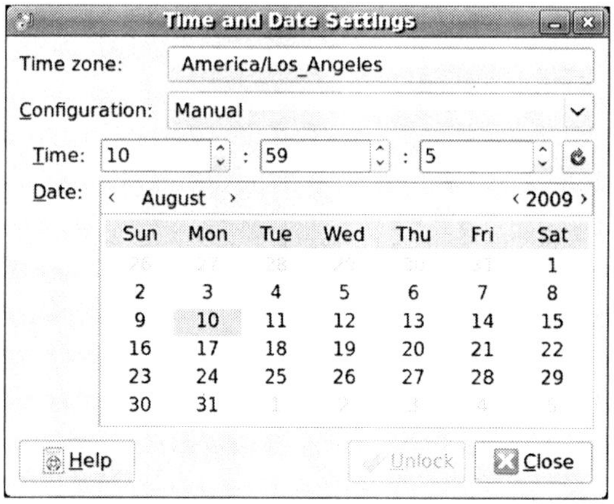

Figure 2-7: time-admin Time and Date Settings

Figure 2-8: time-admin NTP time server access

To use the NTP time servers, in the Configuration pop-up, select Keep Synchronized With Internet Servers. Initially, NTP support may not be installed. Ubuntu will prompt you to install it (just click Install NTP Support). Once installed, the Calendar and Time boxes are replaced by a Select Servers button.

NTP servers tend to be overworked, so you can choose more than one to access. Click the Select Servers button to display a list of NTP servers. The Ubuntu NTP server will already be selected, or you can select others in your area. You can even add NTP servers, as many local networks have their own. You can find out more about NTP servers at the NTP Public Services Project site (Time Servers link) at **http://ntp.isc.org**.

GNOME International Clock: Time, Date, and Weather

The international clock applet is located on the top panel to the right. It displays the current time and date for your region, but can be modified to display the weather, as well as the time, date, and weather of any location in the world.

To add a location, right-click on the time and select Preferences from the pop-up menu. The Clock Preferences window will display three tabs: General, Location, and Weather (see Figure 2-9). To add a new location, click on the Add button on the Locations tab. This opens a window where you can enter the name, timezone, and coordinates of the location. To specify a location, just start typing its name in the Location Name box. As you begin typing, a drop down menu appears automatically will possible completions. The listing of possible locations reduces the more you type, narrowing your choices. When the location you want is shown in the drop down menu, select it. The timezone, latitude, and longitude for that location will be added for you.

Figure 2-9: Selecting a location on the international clock

On the Weather panel, you can specify the temperature and wind measures to use. The General panel you can set the clocks display options for the locations, whether to show weather, temperature, date and seconds.

The Time Settings button opens a dialog where a user can manually set the time. A button on this dialog labeled System Time opens a dialog for setting system-wide time.

Note: Ubuntu provides several tools for configuring your GNOME desktop. These are listed in the System | Preferences menu. The Help button on each preference window will display detailed descriptions and examples. Some of the commonly used tools are discussed in the Desktop Operations section later in this chapter.

Once you set the location for your own location, you will see a weather icon appear next to the time on the panel, showing you your current weather (see Figure 3-19).

64 ℉   Wed Apr 30, 4:54 PM

Figure 2-10: International clock with weather icon

To see the locations you have selected, click on the time displayed on the top panel (see Figure 2-10). This opens a calendar, with Location label with an expandable arrow at the bottom.

Click this arrow to display all your locations, their time and weather (see Figure 2-11). You home location will have a house icon next to it. A world map will show all your locations as red dots, with a blue house icon for your current home location. When you click on a location entry, its corresponding dot will blink for a few seconds. Each location will have a small globe weather icon, indicating the general weather, like sun or clouds. To see weather details, move your mouse over the weather icon. A pop-up dialog will display the current weather, temperature, wind speed, and time for sunrise and sunset. The clock icons for each location will be dark, grey, or bright depending on the time of day at that location.

Figure 2-11: International clock, full display

You can easily change your home location, by click the Set button to the right the location you want made your home. You will see the home icon shift to the new location. This is helpful when traveling. Each location has a set button which will be hidden until you move your mouse over it, on the right side of the clock display

To make any changes, you can click the Edit button next to the Locations label. This opens the Clock Preferences window where you can configure the display or add and remove locations.

The calendar will show the current date, but you can move to different months and years using the month and year scroll arrows at the top of the calendar.

To set the time manually, right-click on the time and select Adjust Date & Time (also from the General panel of the Clock Preferences window, click the Time Settings button). This opens a Time Settings window where you can enter the time and set the date (see Figure 2-12). Use the month and year arrows on the calendar to change the month and year. To set the time for the entire system, click the Set System Time button which open **time-admin** (System | Administration | Time and Date).

To set the time for the entire system, click the Set System Time button. You will be prompted to authenticate by entering your password.

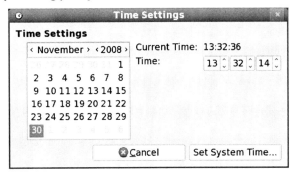

Figure 2-12: Manually setting the clock

Using the date Command

You can use the **date** command on your root user command line to set the date and time for the system. As an argument to **date**, you list (with no delimiters) the month, day, time, and year. In the next example, the date is set to 2:59 P.M., April 6, 2008 (04 for April, 06 for the day, 1459 for the time (2:59 PM), and 08 for the year 2008):

```
date 0406145908
Sun Apr 6 02:59:22 PST 2008
```

Gnome Power Manager

For power management, Ubuntu uses the GNOME Power Manager, **gnome-power-manager**, which makes use of ACPI support provided by a computer to manage power use.

The GNOME Power Manager will display an applet on the panel showing the current connection, battery (laptop), plug (desktop), or plugged in battery (laptop). On a Laptop, the battery icon displayed on the panel will show how much power you have left, as well as when the battery become critical. It will also indicate an AC connection, as well as when the battery has recharged. If you left-click on the icon, a menu will display the current battery charge. It will also lis Suspend and Hibernate entries for manually suspending or hibernating your system.

The GNOME Power manager is configured with the Power Management Preferences window (**gnome-power-preferences**), accessible from System | Preferences | Power Management menu, and by righ-clicking on the GNOME Power Management panel icon and selecting Preferences from the pop-up menu. Power management preferences can be used to configure both a desktop and a laptop.

For a desktop there are only two tabs, On AC Power and General. On the On AC Power tab you have two sleep options, one for the computer and one for the screen. You can put each to sleep after a specified interval of inactivity. On the General tab you set desktop features like actions to take when pressing the power button or whether to display the power icon. The AC power icon will show a plug image for desktops and a battery for laptops. The icon is displayed on the top panel.

A laptop will also have an On Battery Power tab where you can set additional option for the battery and display, such as shutting down if the battery is too low, or dimming the display when the system is idle (see Figure 2-13).

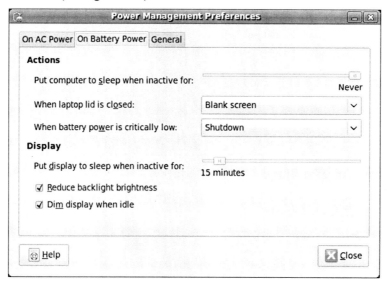

Figure 2-13: GNOME Power Manager

To see how your laptop or desktop is performing with power, you can use Power statistics. This is accessible either from the Applications | System Tools | Power Statistics menu, or by righ-clicking on the GNOME Power Management panel icon and selecting "Power history" from the pop-up menu. The Power Statistics window will display a sidebar listing you different power devices. A left pane will show tabs with power use information for a selected device. The Laptop battery will device will display three tabs: Details, History, and Statitistics. History will show your recent use, with options for Time to empty (time left) and Time to ful (recharging). Statistics tab can show charge and discharge graphs.

Tip: With the GNOME Screensaver Preferences you can control when the computer is considered idle and what screen saver to use if any. You can also control whether to lock the screen or not, when idle. Access the Screensaver Preferences from System | Preferences | Screensaver. You can turn off the Screensaver by unchecking the "Activate screensaver when computer is idle" box.

Scheduling Tasks: cron and GNOME schedule

Scheduling regular maintenance tasks is managed by the **cron** service on Linux, and implemented by a **cron** daemon. A daemon is a continually running server that constantly checks for certain actions to take. These tasks are listed in the **crontab** file. The **cron** daemon constantly checks the user's **crontab** file to see if it is time to take these actions. Any user can set up a

crontab file of his or her own. The root user can set up a **crontab** file to perform system administrative actions, such as backing up files at a certain time each week or month.

The easiest way to schedule tasks is to use the desktop **cron** tool. In KDE you can use the KCRON tool and for GNOME you can use GNOME Schedule. Both let you choose the month, date, and time for a process, though you will have to manually enter the command you want run, as if on a command line. A listing of **cron** entries lets you modify or delete tasks. If you have an open ended operation, be sure to also schedule a command to shut it down.

GNOME Schedule

GNOME Schedule is a more recent tool that also creates and easy to use interface for managing scheduled tasks (See Figure 2-14). It is currently part of the Universe repository, though part of the GNOME desktop release. Once installed (**gnome-schedule** package) you can access it from the Applications | System Tools menu as Scheduled Tasks.

Figure 2-14: GNOME Schedule

Figure 2-15: Schedule new task

Use the New button to schedule a task. You are first asked if you want to create the task as a recurrent item, one time task, or from a template. The Create a New Scheduled Task window then open where you can specify the time and date, and whether to repeat weekly or monthly (see Figure 2-15). You can use the Basic button to set defaults for Hourly, Daily, Weekly, or Monthly entries. Then click Advanced to specify a time.

The template feature lets you set up a new schedule with information for a previous one, using the same or similar commands but different time. Click the Template button to add a new template. This opens a window similar to the Create task window in Figure 2-14. Once you have created the template you can use it to create scheduled tasks. When creating a task, from the initial menu, choose "A task from a predefined template. This opens the Choose template window (see Figure 12-15). Clicking the Use template button opens the Create task window where you can modify your task.

Once you have created the template you can use it to create scheduled tasks. When creating a task, from the initial menu, choose "A task from a predefined template". This opens the Choose template window (see Figure 2-16). Select the template to use. Clicking the Use template button opens the Create task window where you can modify your task, changing its name or time as needed, and then clicking the Apply button to create the task.

To delete a task, just select the entry in the Scheduled Tasks window and click the Delete button. To run a task immediately, select and click the Run task button.

On the Scheduled Tasks window you can click the Advanced button to see the actual cron entries created by GNOME Schedule.

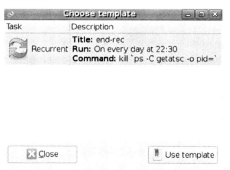

Figure 2-16: Schedule templates

KCron (KDE4)

KCron which creates and easy to use interface for creating scheduled commands. It is part of the Ubuntu main repository and is maintained by Ubuntu. KCron is a KDE desktop tool and will require installation of supporting KDE libraries (selected automatically for you when you install KCron). To run KCron, login to the KDE desktop. Use the New entry in the Edit menu to schedule a command, specifying the time and date, and whether to repeat weekly or monthly.

The crond Service

The name of the **cron** daemon is crond. Normally it is started automatically when your system starts up. You can set this feature using services-admin

You can also start and stop the **crond** service manually, which you may want to do for emergency maintenance or during upgrades. Use the **service** command and the **stop** option to shut down the service, and the **start** option to run it again, and **restart** to restart it:

```
service crond stop
```

crontab Entries

Cron task schedules are kept in **crontab** files, like **/etc/crontab**. An entry has six fields: the first five are used to specify the time for an action, while the last field is the action itself.

- The first field specifies minutes (0–59)T

- he second field specifies the hour (0–23)

- The third field specifies the day of the month (1–31)

- The fourth field specifies the month of the year (1–12, or month prefixes like *Jan* and *Sep*),

- The fifth field specifies the day of the week (0–6, or day prefixes like *Wed* and *Fri*), starting with 0 as Sunday.

In each of the time fields, you can specify a range, a set of values, or use the asterisk to indicate all values. For example, **1-5** for the day-of-week field specifies Monday through Friday. In the hour field, **8, 12, 17** would specify 8 A.M., 12 noon, and 5 P.M. An ***** in the month-of-year field indicates every month. The format of a cron field follows:

```
minute  hour  day-month  month  day(s)-week  task
```

The following example backs up the **projects** directory at 2:00 A.M. every weekday:

```
0 2 * * 1-5   tar cf /home/backp /home/projects
```

The same entry is listed here again using prefixes for the month and weekday:

```
0 2 * * Mon-Fri tar cf /home/backp /home/projects
```

To specify particular months, days, weeks, or hours, you can list them individually, separated by commas. For example, to perform the previous task on Sunday, Wednesday, and Friday, you could use **0,3,5** in the day-of-week field, or their prefix equivalents, **Sun,Wed,Fri**.

```
0 2 * * 0,3,5   tar cf /home/backp /home/projects
```

Cron also supports comments. A comment is any line beginning with a **#** sign.

```
# Weekly backup for Chris's projects
0 2 * * Mon-Fri  tar cf /home/backp /home/projects
```

Environment Variables for cron

The **cron** service also lets you define environment variables for use with tasks performed. Ubuntu defines variables for **SHELL**, **PATH**, **HOME**, and **MAILTO**. **SHELL** designates the shell to use tasks, in this case the bash shell. **PATH** lists the directories where programs and scripts can be found. This example lists the standard directories, **/usr/bin** and **/bin**, as well as the system directories reserved for system applications, **/usr/sbin** and **/sbin**. **MAILTO** designates to who the results of a task are to be mailed. By default, these are mailed to the user who schedules it, but you can have the results sent to a specific user, such as the administrator's e-mail address, or an account on another system in a network. **HOME** is the home directory for a task, in this case the top directory.

```
SHELL=/bin/bash
PATH=/sbin:/bin:/usr/sbin:/usr/bin
MAILTO=root
HOME=/
```

The cron.d Directory

On a heavily used system, the **/etc/crontab** file can become crowded easily. There may also be instances where certain entries require different variables. For example, you may need to run some task under a different shell. To help you organize your cron tasks, you can place entries in files within the **cron.d** directory. The files in the **cron.d** directory all contain entries of the same format as those used in **/etc/crontab**. They may be given any name. They are treated as added `crontab` files, with **cron** checking them for tasks to run.

The crontab Command

You use the `crontab` command to install your entries into a **crontab** file. To do this, first create a text file and type your `crontab` entries. Save this file with any name you want, such as **mycronfile**. Then, to install these entries, enter **crontab** and the name of the text file. The `crontab` command takes the contents of the text file and creates a **crontab** file in the **/var/spool/cron** directory, adding the name of the user who issued the command. In the following example, the root user installs the contents of **mycronfile** as the root's **crontab** file.

```
sudo crontab mycronfile
```

This creates a file called **/var/spool/cron/root**. If a user named justin installed a **crontab** file, it would create a file called **/var/spool/cron/justin**. You can control use of the `crontab` command by regular users with the **/etc/cron.allow** file. Only users with their names in this file can create **crontab** files of their own. Conversely, the **/etc/cron.deny** file lists those users denied use of the **cron** tool, preventing them for scheduling tasks. If neither file exists, access is denied to all users. If a user is not in a **/etc/cron.allow** file, access is denied. However, if the **/etc/cron.allow** file does not exist, and the **/etc/cron.deny** file does, then all users not listed in **/etc/cron.deny** are automatically allowed access.

Editing in cron

Never try to edit your **crontab** file directly. Instead, use the `crontab` command with the -e option. This opens your **crontab** file in the **/var/spool/cron** directory with the standard text editor, such as **vi**. `crontab` uses the default editor as specified by the **EDITOR** shell environment variable. To use a different editor for `crontab`, change the default editor by assigning the editor's program name to the `EDITOR` variable and exporting that variable. Normally, the editor variable is set in the **/etc/profile** script.

Running `crontab` with the `-1` option displays the contents of your **crontab** file, and the `-r` option deletes the entire file. Invoking `crontab` with another text file of `crontab` entries overwrites your current **crontab** file, replacing it with the contents of the text file.

Organizing Scheduled Tasks

You can organize administrative **cron** tasks into two general groups: common administrative tasks that can be run at regular intervals and specialized tasks that need to be run at a unique time. Unique tasks can be run as entries in the **/etc/crontab** file, as described in the next section. Common administrative tasks, though they can be run from the **/etc/crontab** file, are better organized into specialized **cron** directories. Within such directories, each task is placed in its own shell script that will invoke the task when run. For example, there may be several administrative tasks that all need to be run each week on the same day, say if maintenance for a system is scheduled on a Sunday morning. For these kinds of task, **cron** provides several specialized directories for automatic daily, weekly, monthly, and yearly tasks. Each contains a **cron** prefix and a suffix for the time interval. The **/etc/cron.daily** directory is used for tasks that need to be performed every day, whereas weekly tasks can be placed in the **/etc/cron.weekly** directory. The **cron** directories are listed in Table 2-6.

cron Files and Directories	Description
/etc/crontab	System `crontab` file, accessible only by the root user
/etc/cron.d	Directory containing multiple `crontab` files, accessible only by the administrative user
/etc/cron.hourly	Directory for tasks performed hourly
/etc/cron.daily	Directory for tasks performed daily
/etc/cron.weekly	Directory for tasks performed weekly
/etc/cron.monthly	Directory for tasks performed monthly
/etc/cron.yearly	Directory for tasks performed yearly
/etc/cron.hourly	Directory for tasks performed hourly
/etc/cron.allow	Users allowed to submit **cron** tasks
/etc/cron.deny	Users denied access to **cron**

Table 2-6: Cron Files and Directories

Running cron Directory Scripts

Each directory contains scripts that are all run at the same time. The scheduling for each group is determined by an entry in the **/etc/crontab** file. The actual execution of the scripts is performed by the **/usr/bin/run-parts** script, which runs all the scripts and programs in a given directory. Scheduling for all the tasks in a given directory is handled by an entry in the **/etc/crontab** file. Ubuntu provides entries with designated times, which you may change for your own needs.

The default Ubuntu **crontab** file is shown here, with times for running scripts in the different **cron** directories. Here you can see that most scripts are run at about 4 A.M. either daily (4:02), Sunday (4:22), or first day of each month (4:42). Hourly ones are run one minute after the hour.

```
SHELL=/bin/bash
PATH=/sbin:/bin:/usr/sbin:/usr/bin
MAILTO=root
HOME=/
# run-parts
01 * * * * root run-parts /etc/cron.hourly
02 4 * * * root run-parts /etc/cron.daily
22 4 * * 0 root run-parts /etc/cron.weekly
42 4 1 * * root run-parts /etc/cron.monthly
```

Tip: Scripts within a **cron** directory are run alphabetically. If you need a certain script to run before any others, you may have to alter its name. One method is to prefix the name with a numeral. For example, in the **/cron.weekly** directory, the **anacron** script is named **0anacron** so that it will run before any others.

Keep in mind though that these are simply directories that contain executable files. The actual scheduling is performed by the entries in the **/etc/crontab** file. For example, if the weekly field in the `cron.weekly crontab` entry is entry is changed to * instead of 0, and the monthly field to 1 (`22 4 1 * *` instead of `22 4 * * 0`), tasks in the **cron.weekly** file would end up running monthly instead of weekly.

Cron Directory Names

The names used for these directories are merely conventions. They have no special meaning to the **cron** daemon. You could, in fact, create your own directory, place scripts within it, and schedule **run-parts** to run those scripts at a given time. In the next example, scripts placed in the **/etc/cron.mydocs** directory will run at 12 noon every Wednesday.

```
* 12 * * 3 root run-parts /etc/cron.mydocs
```

Anacron

For a system that may normally be shut down during times that **cron** is likely to run, you may want to supplement **cron** with **anacron**. **anacron** activates only when scheduled tasks need to be executed. For example, if a system is shut down on a weekend when **cron** jobs are scheduled, then the jobs will not be performed; **anacron**, however, checks to see what jobs need to be performed when the system is turned on again, and then runs them. It is designed only for jobs that run daily or weekly.

For **anacron** jobs, you place `crontab` entries in the **/etc/anacrontab** file. For each scheduled task, you specify the number of intervening days when it is executed (7 is weekly, 30 is monthly), the time of day it is run (numbered in minutes), a description of the task, and the command to be executed. For backups, the command used would be **tar** operation. You can use services-admin to turn on the **anacron** service or have it start up automatically at boot time.

3. System Startup and Services

Upstart

Upstart and Runlevels: event.d and init.d

System Startup files and scripts

System Runlevels: telinit, inittab, and shutdown

Managing Services

System start up is now managed by the Upstart service. The original System V init format for start individual services is still in place, but now connected to Upstart, which performs the actual work. A single Linux system can provide several different kinds of services, ranging from security to administration and including more obvious Internet services like web and FTP sites, e-mail, and printing. Security tools such as SSH and Kerberos run as services, along with administrative network tools such as DHCP and LDAP. The network connection interface is itself a service that you can restart at will. Each service operates as a continually running daemon looking for requests for its particular services.

Upstart

Linux systems traditionally used the Unix System V init daemon to manage services by setting up runlevels at which they could be started or shutdown. Ubuntu has since replaced the SystemV init daemon with the Upstart init daemon, while maintaining the System V init runlevel structure for compatibility purposes. Whereas the System V init daemon would start certain services when the entire system started up or shutdown, Upstart is entirely event driven. When an event occurs invoking the need for a service, then the service is started. This even oriented approach is designed to work well with removable devices. When a device is added or removed, this change becomes an event that the Upstart daemon detects and then runs any appropriate associated scripts. System V init daemon only ran scripts when its runlevels changed. It saw only runlevels, not events.

Structurally, Upstart can detect and respond to any event. Eventually it may implement scheduled events, replacing cron, atd, an anacron schedulers, as well as support for on demand service now managed by xinetd and inetd. You can find out more about Upstart at:

```
upstart.ubuntu.com
```

Upstart will detect events, and run scripts in the **/etc/event.d** directory for those events. These scripts define jobs that Upstart can then run. Jobs that can be performed by Upstart are defined in scripts in Upstart event directory, **/etc/event.d**. Here you will finds Upstart job scripts for emulating runlevels like the rc2 script, as well as system services like TTY terminal connections. In effect, Upstart jobs replace the entries that used to be in the SysVinit's **/etc/inittab** file.

Upstart operates by running jobs. These jobs are defined in job definition files located in the **/etc/event.d** directory. Jobs are already defined for System V init runlevel emulation, TTY system services, and for certain tasks like Ctrl-Alt-Delete event to restart your system. A job script will specify an event, the action to take for that event, and any commands to run for that event. The commands can be either a single command run by an exec operation, or a set of command encased in **script** and **end script** stanza.

Note: An Upstart job definition script does not have to have a **start on** directive. I could just be started manually with the **start** command.

To have a job started automatically when a certain event occurs you place a **start on** directive in its job file, specifying the event. You can use a stop on directive to stop the event automatically. You can have several start on directives, each for different events. The **start on** directive for the control-alt-delete job is shown here.

```
start on control-alt-delete
```

In the control-alt-delete job, you have a control-alt-delete event that runs the **shutdown** command with the **-r** option to restart. The **exec** command is used to run a shell command directly. The full pathname for the b command is specified, and a message is passed to the **shutdown** command saying that the Ctrl-Alt-Del keys have been pressed.

```
start on control-alt-delete
    exec /sbin/shutdown -r -now  "Control-Alt-Delete pressed"
```

Many jobs defined both a start on and stop on directive, for starting and stopping the job. The event can also take an argument. In the **rc2** job definition which control runlevel 2 emulation has start and stop event as shown here:

```
start on runlevel 2
stop on runlevel [!2]
```

The rc2 job will start when a runlevel event occurs with the argument 2. It will stop when any runlevel even occurs that has an number other than 2, **[!2]**.

A **stopped** or **started** event indicates when some other job has been started or stopped. The following start on directive would star its job whenever the **myjob** job started.

```
start on started myjob
```

The **startup** event indicates system startup. The **rcS** job (single user mode) will be started up initially whenever you system starts up. In its **/etc/event.d/rcS** job definition file you will find:

```
start on startup
```

The **rc-default** job is started when the **rcS** job stops.

```
start on stopped rcS
```

The **tty1** job used for terminal services will have several start and stop directives, automatically starting when rc2, rc3, rc4, and rc5 events have stopped, and stopping on runlevel 0, 1, and 6 events.

```
start on stopped rc2
start on stopped rc3
start on stopped rc4
start on stopped rc5

stop on runlevel 0
stop on runlevel 1
stop on runlevel 6

respawn
exec /sbin/getty 38400 tty1
```

The **tty2** through **tty6** jobs will start only on runlevel 2 and 3, stopping at all other runlevels. The script for tty2 is shown here. Scripts tty2 through tty6 are the same except for the **exec** operation which runs the respective tty terminal.

```
start on runlevel 2
start on runlevel 3

stop on runlevel 0
stop on runlevel 1
stop on runlevel 4
stop on runlevel 5
stop on runlevel 6

respawn
exec /sbin/getty 38400 tty2
```

To run several commands you encase the command in a **script** stanza. A script stanza begins with the **script** keyword and ends with **end script**. Most complex jobs use a the script stanza. The **rc2** job script shown here will start on a runlevel event with the 2 argument. Then the commands in the script structure are run, setting the runlevel to 2 with the runlevel command. Then the **/etc/init.d/rc** script is run with the 2 argument to start up any **/etc/init.d** service scripts for runlevel 2, emulating a runlevel change to 2. The **rc2** job is started when **telinit** triggers a runlevel event with a 2 argument. For any runlevel events that are not 2, the **rc2** job will be stopped. The **console** directive specifies where the job output goes, usually to the console (**output**).

```
start on runlevel 2
stop on runlevel [!2]

console output
script
    set $(runlevel --set 2 || true)
    if [ "$1" != "unknown" ]; then
        PREVLEVEL=$1
        RUNLEVEL=$2
        export PREVLEVEL RUNLEVEL
    fi

    exec /etc/init.d/rc 2
end script
```

You can think of the Upstart daemon managing a set of jobs, much like the shell can manage background jobs. With the **start** and **stop** commands you can start and stop any job. Use status to find out the **status** of a job.

The **initctl** command with the **list** option will display a complete list of current Upstart jobs. You can add a pattern to search or a particular job. The **initctl** command also has **start**, **stop**, and **status** options for managing jobs.

```
sudo initctl list
```

You could also use the **emit** command to manually trigger an event that would run a certain job.

```
$ sudo stop tty1
tty1 (stop) running, process 5109
tty1 (stop) pre-stop, (main) process 5109
tty1 (stop) stopping, process 5109
tty1 (stop) killed, process 5109
tty1 (stop) post-stop
tty1 (stop) waiting
$ sudo start tty1
tty1 (start) waiting
tty1 (start) starting
tty1 (start) pre-start
tty1 (start) spawned, process 8457
tty1 (start) post-start, (main) process 8457
tty1 (start) running, process 8457
$ sudo status tty1
tty1 (start) running, process 8457
```

Upstart and Runlevels: event.d and init.d

Ubuntu still maintain SysVinit startup and shutdown scripts in the **/etc/init.d** directory which Upstart uses to start and stop services. You can run these scripts directly to start and stop a service. Upstart will also use the SysVinit links in the runlevel directories (**/etc/rc*N*.d**) to start and stop services. In effect, the supporting structure for runlevels remains the same, though in fact services are now handled by Upstart. SysVinit compatibility scripts, directory structure, and tools, like **telinit** and **runlevel** equivalents, are held in the **upstart-compat-sysv** package.

You can start up your system at different levels with certain capabilities. For example, you can run your system at an administrative level, locking out user access. Normal full operations are activated by simply running your system at a certain level of operational capability such as supporting multi-user access or graphical interfaces. These levels (also known as states or modes) are referred to as *runlevels,* the level of support that you are running your system at.

Note: You can select certain services to run and the runlevel at which to run them. Most services are servers like a web server or proxy server. Other services provide security, such as SSH or Kerberos. On Ubuntu you can **services-admin** (System | Administration | Services) to turn on and off services, specifying the runlevel. The default is runlevel 2.

Runlevels

Traditionally, a Linux system has several runlevels, numbered from 0 to 6. Support for these is now emulated by Upstart. When you power up your system, you enter the default runlevel. Runlevels 0, 1, and 6 are special runlevels that perform specific functions. Runlevel 0 is the power-down state and is invoked by the **halt** command to shut down the system. Runlevel 6 is the reboot state—it shuts down the system and reboots. Runlevel 1 is the single-user state, which allows access only to the superuser and does not run any network services. This enables you, as the administrator, to perform administrative actions without interference from others.

Other runlevels reflect how you want the system to be used. Ubuntu uses runlevel 2 for graphical logins and the remainder as user defined, also using graphical logins.

Tip: You can use the single-user runlevel (1) as a recovery mode state, allowing you to start up your system without running startup scripts for services like DNS. This is helpful if your system hangs when you try to start such services. Networking is disabled, as well as any multi-user access. You can also use `linux -s` at the boot prompt to enter runlevel 1. If you want to enter the single-user state and also run the startup scripts, you can use the special **s**, **single**, or s runlevel. The Recovery entry on the Grub boot menu will start the system in single user mode using the **single** option.

Runlevels in event.d directory

Runlevels are managed by the Upstart service, but the Upstart service does not actually implement runlevels, it simulates them. To maintain compatibility with System V compliant Linux and Unix applications, Upstart does provide a runlevel compatibility scripts in the **/etc/event.d** directory that emulate System V init. To start up a runlevel, it uses **telinit** with the runlevel number to. When your system starts up, it uses the default runlevel as specified by the **rc-default** script in the **/etc/event.d** directory. There are runlevel scripts for each runlevel in the **/etc/event.d** directory. The default runlevel is 2, which will run the **/etc/event.d/rc2** script ,which in turn invokes **telinit** with the argument **2**.

default runlevel

The default runlevel is 2. You can change this default runlevel, to either 3, 4, or 5 if you wish. To actually change the default runlevel safely, you can create an **/etc/inittab** file and place and **initdefault** entry in it (use **vi** or **emacs** if editing from a command line interface).

```
gksu gedit /etc/inittab
```

This file would be just a dummy file used only by **rc-default** to read the default entry. A sample default entry is shown here, changing the default to runlevel 3. Your **/etc/inittab** file would have only this line.

```
id:3:initdefault:
```

rc-default script

The default runlevel is actually implemented by the /etc/event.d/rc-default script. This is the script that reads the inittab file and then starts the designated runlevel using the **telinit** command. It also determines and starts the default runlevel, runlevel 2, should the **/etc/event.d/inittab** file be missing or the parsing fails. It will also read the Grub command line at boot for a **-s**, **single**, or S option for starting the single user runlevel.

In the **rc-default** script, the first the Grub command line is checked for a **-s**, **single**, or S option, and, if present, then telinit starts up the single user runlevel; the **s**, **single**, or S options. The recovery entry in the **/etc/grub/menu.lst** file has the **single** option.

```
if grep -q -w -- "-s\|single\|S" /proc/cmdline; then
    telinit S
```

A copy of the **rc-default** script is shown here.

```
# rc - runlevel compatibility
#
# This task guesses what the "default runlevel" should be and starts the
# appropriate script.

start on stopped rcS

script
    runlevel --reboot || true

    if grep -q -w -- "-s\|single\|S" /proc/cmdline; then
        telinit S
    elif [ -r /etc/inittab ]; then
        RL="$(sed -n -e "/^id:[0-9]*:initdefault:/{s/^id://;s/:.*//;p}"
/etc/inittab || true)"
        if [ -n "$RL" ]; then
         telinit $RL
        else
         telinit 2
        fi
    else
        telinit 2
    fi
end script
```

If there is no **S**, **single**, or **-s** option, then the **/etc/inittab** file is read and parsed, checking for the runlevel number. This is then assigned to the RL variable, whose value telinit used to start the appropriate runlevel.

```
    elif [ -r /etc/inittab ]; then
        RL="$(sed -n -e "/^id:[0-9]*:initdefault:/{s/^id://;s/:.*//;p}"
/etc/inittab || true)"
        if [ -n "$RL" ]; then
         telinit $RL
```

If the parsing of the **/etc/inittab** file fails, or if the **/etc/inittab** file does not exist, then **telinit** starts with runlevel 2. Runlevel 2, in effect, becomes the default runlevel.

```
    elif [ -r /etc/inittab ]; then
        # commands to parse inittab file
        if [ -n "$RL" ]; then
         telinit $RL   #parsing succeeds
      else
         telinit 2   #parsing fails
        fi
    else
        telinit 2    #inittab does not exist
    fi
```

Using telinit

Once logged in, you can open a terminal window and use the use the **telinit** command with the runlevel number to change to another runlevel directly. You can choose from runlevels 2, 3, 4, and 5. These are all set up as standard multi-user graphical runlevels. The **single** runlevel (S) is reserved for recovery use. The **telinit** command just triggers a runlevel event for Upstart, which then uses the **/etc/init.d/rc** script to emulate a runlevel change. The **telinit** command is now just a wrapper for an Upstart runlevel event, not the **telinit** command used in previous releases with System V init.

The multi-user runlevels are initially all configured the same, though you could make changes in each, such as running different services at different runlevels (use **services-admin**, **update-rc.d**, or **sysv-rc-conf** to make these changes). You could then use **telinit** to start up at that runlevel.

```
sudo telinit 4
```

With the Upstart emulation, you can now only boot directly to the **single** user runlevel from Grub menu. A recovery mode Grub boot entry is set up to do just that. For all other runlevels you have to login first as runlevel 2, the default, or S (single) and then use the **telinit** command to enter a new runlevel. Alternatively you could carefully edit the **rc-default** file to detect other runlevel numbers on the GRUB command line other than single, and invoke the corresponding runlevel with **telinit**. You could then make Grub entries for these runlevels or just edit the Grub kernel line to add the runlevel number. Editing **rc-default** is risky (back it up first), and requires a competency in shell programming.

Command line runlevel

On other distributions, like Fedora, some runlevels are designed for special behavior. On Fedora, runlevel 3 will run just the command line, without the graphical interface. This is not the case with Ubuntu. On Debian, Ubuntu, and similar distributions, the desktop version invokes the X server at all primary runlevels. To run the command line interface as the primary interface for a runlevel, you need to shut down the display managers (your login screen). To set up a particular runlevel to use just the command line, you would have to instruct its startup service for the X Server (**/etc/init.d/gdm**) to stop. To set up runlevel 3 to run just the command line interface when you start up your system, you would use the sysv-rc-conf, update-rc.d, or admin-users tool to have the GDM service to stop at runlevel 3, instead of start. This will put a stop link in the **/etc/rc3.d** directory for the GDM service, like K01gdm, replacing the start link, **S30gdm**. The **K01gdm** link would invoke the **gdm init.d** script with the **stop** option, shutting down the X server. You can then change to runlevel 3 with the telnet command and the argument 3. The screen will blank and start up the command line interface.

```
sudo telinit 3
```

Upon startup in runlevel 3, press ENTER display the login prompt (also from GRUB, remove splash option for kernel).

Tip: If you used **/etc/inittab** to change the default runlevel, and you want to change quickly back to using runlevel 2 as the default without having to edit the **/etc/inittab** file, you can just remove the **/etc/inittab** file. The **rc-start** script will start runlevel 2 if there is no **/etc/inittab** file, **sudo rm /etc/inittab**.

The runlevel Command

Use the `runlevel` command to see what state you are currently running in. It lists the previous state followed by the current one. If you have not changed states, the previous state will be listed as N, indicating no previous state. This is the case for the state you boot up in. In the next example, the system is running in state 3, with no previous state change:

```
runlevel
N 2
```

System Startup files and scripts

Each time you start your system, the Upstart init daemon starts up services defined in startup scripts. Currently most services still use the older System V init method for starting up services using runlevels. Upstart will use its event based init daemon to emulate the System V init structure, allowing many services to run as if they were using a System V init daemon. Eventually, service applications will be rewritten to use Upstart directly, without the need for a System V init emulation.

Upstart emulates the System V startup procedure by running a series of startup script from system service scripts located in your **/etc/init.d** directory. It uses links in directories with the name **rc***N***.d**, to determine what service scripts to run. The *N* in the name is a number from 1 to 6 indicating a runlevel, like **rc2.d** for runlevel 2. These initialization files are organized according to different tasks. You should not have to change any of these files (see Table 3-1).

File	Description
/etc/event.d	Upstart job files that actually start services and processes.
/etc/rc*N***.d**	Directories that holds system startup and shutdown files, where *N* is the runlevel. The directories hold links to scripts in the **/etc/init.d** directory.
/etc/rc.local	Initialization file for your own commands; you can freely edit this file to add your own startup commands; this is the last startup file executed.
/etc/init.d	Directory that holds system service scripts
/etc/init.d/rc	Runlevel emulation by Upstart. Upstart runs this script to emulate runlevel changes.

Table 3-1: System Startup Files and Directories

rc.local

The **/etc/rc.local** file is the last initialization file executed. You can place commands of your own here. When you shut down your system, the system calls the **halt** file, which contains shutdown commands. The files in **init.d** are then called to shut down daemons, and the file systems are unmounted. **halt** is located in the **init.d** directory.

/etc/init.d

The **/etc/init.d** directory is designed primarily to hold scripts that start up and shut down different specialized daemons, such as network and printer daemons and those for font and web servers. These files perform double duty, starting a daemon when the system starts up and shutting down the daemon when the system shuts down. The files in **init.d** are designed in a way to make it easy to write scripts for starting up and shutting down specialized applications. Many of these files are set up for you automatically. You shouldn't need to change them. If you do change them, be sure you know how these files work first.

When your system starts up, several programs are automatically started and run continuously to provide services, such as a website or print servers. Depending on what kind of services you want your system to provide you can add or remove items in a list of services to be started automatically. For example, the web server is run automatically when your system starts up. If you are not hosting a website, you have no need for the web server. You can prevent the service from starting, removing an extra task the system does not need to perform, freeing up resources, and possibly reducing potential security holes. Several of the servers and daemons perform necessary tasks. The **sendmail** server enables you to send messages across networks, and the **cupsd** server performs printing operations.

/etc/init.d/rc

The **/etc/init.d/rc** script is used by Upstart to emulate System V runlevel changes. The script takes as its argument a runlevel. It then checks the **/etc/rc*N*.d** links for the runlevel to determine what services to start or stop.

/etc/event.d

In the **/etc/event.d** directory, Upstart maintains event scripts for different runlevels, **rc*N***. For runlevel 2, there is an **rc2** script. This script simply runs the **/etc/init.d/rc** script with the number 2 as its argument. The **/etc/init.d/rc** script will then search the **/etc/rc2.d** directory for links specifying which service script to start and which to stop.

When your system starts, the **/etc/event.d/rc.default** script is run which will start up with runlevel 2 or the runlevel specified in an **/etc/inittab** dummy file. For runlevel 2 it will invoke the **/etc/init.d/rc** script with the argument 2.

Service Script	Description
networking	Operations to start up or shut down your network connections
policykit	Policy authentication tool
xinetd	Operations to start up or shut down the **xinetd** daemon
cupsys	The CUPS printer daemon (see Chapter 10)
apache2	Apache web server (see Chapter 8)
innd	Internet News service (see Chapter 9)
nfs	Network Filesystem (see Chapter 11)
postfix	Postfix mail server (see Chapter 6)
samba	Samba for Windows hosts (see Chapter 12)
squid	Squid proxy-cache server (see Chapter 14)
vsftpd	Very Secure FTP server (see Chapter 7)

Table 3-2: Selection of Service Scripts in /etc/init.d

Note: Keep in mind that the System V runlevel system does not exist on Ubuntu though its service management structure does. Instead, Upstart emulates System V runlevels using the **/etc/init.d/rc** script and the same service links and startup scripts in the **/etc/init.d** and **/etc/rc*N*.d** directories.

/etc/default

The **/etc/default** directory holds configuration parameters and variables set when a service or applications starts up. Configuration files include **/etc/default/samba** for the Samba server, and **/etct/default/ufw** for the UFW firewall, **/etc/default/ssh** for the SSH service, and **/etc/default/hddtemp** for an hard drive temperature sensor. Configuration files tend to be short, with a few parameters set to configure the service when it starts.

Service Scripts: /etc/init.d

You can manage the startup and shutdown of server daemons with special service scripts located in the **/etc/init.d** directory. These scripts often have the same name as the service's program. For example, for the **/usr/sbin/apache2** web server program, the corresponding script is called `/etc/init.d/apache2`. This script starts and stops the web server. This method of using **init.d** service scripts to start servers is called *SysV Init,* after the method used in Unix System V. Some of the more commonly used service scripts are listed in Table 3-2.

The service scripts in the **/etc/init.d** directory can be executed automatically whenever you boot your system. Be careful when accessing these scripts, however. These start essential programs, such as your network interface and your printer daemon. These init scripts are accessed from links in subdirectories set up in the **/etc** directory for each possible runlevel. These directories have names with the format **rc*n*.d**, where *n* is a number referring to a runlevel (see Table 3-3).

Runlevel	Directory	Description
0	**rc0.d**	Halts (shuts down) the system
1	**rc1.d**	Single-user mode (limited capabilities)
2	**rc2.d**	Multi-user mode with graphical login (full operation mode, X server started automatically)
3	**rc3.d**	Multi-user mode with graphical login (full operation mode, X server started automatically)
4	**rc4.d**	Multi-user mode with graphical login (full operation mode, X server started automatically)
5	**rc5.d**	Multi-user mode with graphical login (full operation mode, X server started automatically)
6	**rc6.d**	Reboots system
S	**rcS.d**	Single user mode

Table 3-3: Emulated System Runlevels for Ubuntu distributions

The `rc` script detects the runlevel in which the system was started and then executes only the service scripts specified in the subdirectory for that runlevel. When you start your system, the `rc` script executes the service scripts designated default start up directory like in **rc1.d** (graphical login for Debian and Ubuntu). The **rc*n*.d** directories hold symbolic links to certain service scripts in the **/etc/init.d** directory. Thus, the `apache2` script in the **/etc/init.d** directory is actually called through a symbolic link in an **rc*n*.d** directory. The symbolic link for the `/etc/init.d/apache2` script in the **rc3.d** directory is **S91apache2**.

The *S* prefixing the link stands for "startup"; thus, the link calls the corresponding `init.d` script with the `start` option. The number indicates the order in which service scripts are run; lower numbers run first. `S91apache2` invokes `/etc/init.d/apache2` with the option `start`. If you change the name of the link to start with a *K*, the script is invoked with the `stop` option, stopping it. Such links are used in the runlevels 0 and 6 directories, **rc6.d** and **rc0.d**. Runlevel 0 halts the system, and runlevel 6 reboots it. You can use the `runlevel` command to find out what runlevel you are currently operating at. A listing of runlevels is shown in Table 3-3.

Services

A *service* is a daemon that runs concurrently with your other programs, continually looking for a request for its services, either from other users on your system or from remote users connecting to your system through a network. When a server receives a request from a user, it starts up a *session* to provide its services. For example, if users want to download a file from your system, they can use their own FTP client to connect to your FTP server and start up a session. In the session, they can access and download files from your system. Your server needs to be running for a user to access its services. For example, if you set up a website on your system with HTML files, you must have the **apache2** web server program running before users can access your website and display those files.

Managing Services Directly

You can use service scripts to start and stop your server manually. These scripts are located in the **/etc/init.d** directory and have the same names as the server programs. For example, the `/etc/init.d/apache2` script with the `start` option starts the web server. Using this script with the `stop` option stops it, and the `restart` option restarts it. Instead of using the complete pathname for the script, you can use the `service` command and the script name, provided you have installed the **sysvconfig** package. Any of the service management tools will also work, like services-admin and rrconf. The services-admin tool in installed initially and is accessible from the System | Administration | Services menu. The following commands are equivalent:

```
sudo /etc/init.d/apache2 stop
sudo service apache2 stop
```

To see if your server is running, you can use the `status` option.

```
sudo /etc/init.d/apache2 status
sudo service apache2 status
```

Alternatively, you can use the `ps` command with the `-aux` option to list all currently running processes. You should see a process for the server program you started. To refine the list, you can add a `grep` operation with a pattern for the server name you want. The second command lists the process for the web server.

```
ps -aux
ps -aux | grep 'apache2'
```

You can just as easily check for the **apache2** process on the GNOME System Monitor.

Service Management: services-admin, rrconf, sysv-rc-conf, and update-rc.d

Instead of manually executing all the server programs each time you boot your system, you can have your system automatically start the servers for you. You can do this in two ways, depending on how you want to use a server. You can have a server running continuously from the time you start your system until you shut it down, or you can have the server start only when it receives a request from a user for its services. If a server is being used frequently, you may want to have it running all the time. If it is used rarely, you may want the server to start only when it receives a request. For example, if you are hosting a website, your web server is receiving requests all the time from remote users on the Internet. For an FTP site, however, you may receive requests infrequently, in which case you may want to have the FTP server start only when it receives a request. Of course, certain FTP sites receive frequent requests, which would warrant a continuously running FTP server.

A server that starts automatically and runs continuously is referred to as a *standalone* server. The SysV Init procedure can be used to start servers automatically whenever your system boots. This procedure uses service scripts for the servers located in the **/etc/init.d** directory. Most Linux systems configure the web server to start automatically and to run continuously by default. A script for it called **apache2** is in the **/etc/init.d** directory.

Though there is no distribution-independent tool for managing servers, most distributions use the **services-admin** (GNOME), **rcconf** (Debian), **sysv-rc-conf**, or **update-rc.d** tools. The **rcconf** and **update-rc.d** tools were developed by Debian and is used on Debian, Ubuntu, and similar distributions. The **sysv-rc-conf** tool is a generic tool that can be used on all distributions. The **services-admin** tool is part of GNOME system tools and is installed with Ubuntu

The tools provide simple interfaces you can use to choose what servers you want started up and how you want them to run. You use these tools to control any daemon you want started up, including system services such as **cron**, the print server, remote file servers for Samba and NFS, authentication servers for Kerberos, and, of course, Internet servers for FTP or HTTP. Such daemons are referred to as *services,* and you should think of these tools as managing these services. Any of these services can be set up to start or stop at different runlevels.

If you add a new service, **services-admin, rcconf**, or **sysv-rc-conf** can manage it. As described in the following section, services are started up at specific runlevels using service links in various runlevel directories. These links are connected to the service scripts in the **init.d** directory. Runlevel directories are numbered from 0 to 6 in the **/etc/** directory, such as **/etc/rc2.d** for runlevel 2 and **/etc/rc5.d** for runlevel 5. Removing a service from a runlevel only changes its link in the corresponding runlevel directory. It does not touch the service script in the **init.d** directory.

services-admin

GNOME's services-admin tool lets you turn services on or off as well as specify runlevels and the actions to take (see Figure 3-1). It provides a GUI interface on GNOME, usually accessible from the System | Administration menu as the Services entry. Every service has a checkbox. Those checked will be started at boot time, those unchecked will not. To turn on a service, scroll to its entry and click the checkbox next to it, if empty. To turn off a service, click its checkbox again.

Note: The Boot Up Manager (**bum**) provides a simple desktop interface for turning services on and off. Its features are similar to **rrconf**.

Figure 3-1: services-admin tool, System | Administration | Service

Figure 3-2: services-admin tool runlevel selection

To turn a service on or off for a specific runlevel. right-click on the service to display a small pop-up menu with a Properties entry (see Figure 3-2). Click on this entry to display a window with the runlevels listed and whether to the service will be started or stopped. To change or set a stop or start action for a runlevel, click and hold down on a specific runlevel. This displays a pop-up menu with start and stop options. Select the one you want.

rcconf and sysv-rc-conf

On Ubuntu, to turn services on or off for different runlevels, you can also use **rcconf** or **sysv-rc-conf** (Universe repository). Both tools are run from a terminal window on the command line. Both provide an easy cursor based interface for using arrow keys and the spacebar to turn services on or off. The **rcconf** tool is a more limited Debian tool that turns services on or all for the default runlevels, whereas **sysv-rc-conf** is more refined, allowing you to select specific runlevels.

The **sysv-rc-conf** tool displays a cursor-based screen where you can check which services to run or stop, and at which runlevel (see Figure 3-3). The runlevels will be listed from 0 to 6 and S. Use the arrow keys to position to the cell for your service and runlevel. Then use the spacebar to turn a service on or off. You can set the particular runlevel at which to start and stop services.

The **sysv-rc-conf** tool is part of the Universe repository. Once installed, you can start it up entering the following command in a terminal window. It is a cursor-based keyboard applications run entirely within the terminal window.

```
sudo sysv-rc-conf
```

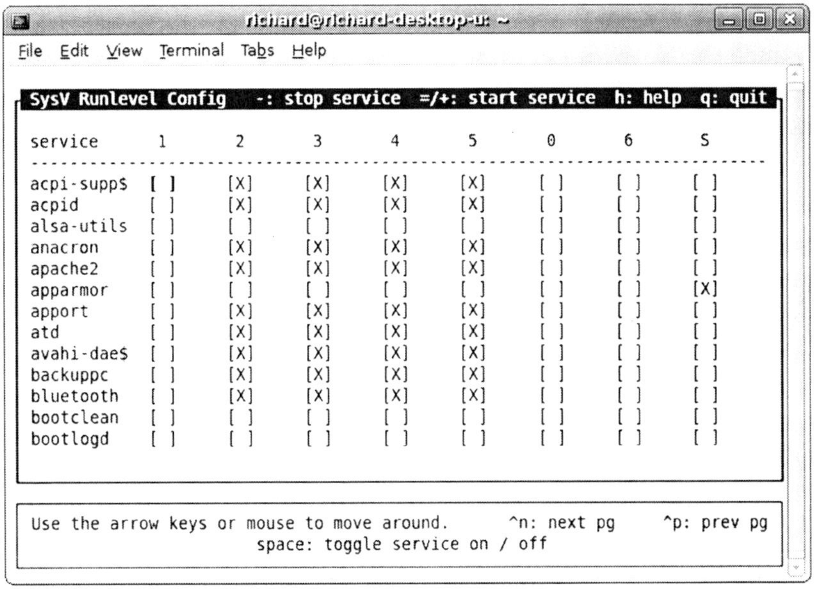

Figure 3-3: The sysv-rc-conf service management with runlevels

update-rc.d

The **update-rc.d** tool is a lower level tool that can install or remove runlevel links. It is usually used when installing service packages to create default runlevel links. You can use it to configure your own runlevels for a service, but requires detailed understanding of how runlevel links for services are configured.

The `update-rc.d` tool does not affect links that are already installed. It only works on links that are not already present in the runlevel directories. In this respect, it cannot turn a service on or off directly like **sysv-rc-conf** can. To turn off a service you would first have to remove all runlevel links in all the rc*n*.d directories using the **remove** option, and then add in the ones you want with the **start** or **stop** options. This makes turning services on an off using the **update-rc.d** tool much more complicated.

You use **start** and **stop** options along with the runlevel to set the runlevels at which to start or stop a service. You will need to provide a link number for ordering the sequence in which it will be run. You the enter the runlevel followed by a period. You can specify more than one runlevel. The following will start the web server on runlevel 5. The order number used for the link name is 91. The link name will be **S91apache**. Be sure to include the **sudo** command.

```
sudo update-rc.d apache start 91 5 .
```

The stop number is always 100 minus the start number. So the stop number for service with a start number of 91 would be 09.

```
sudo update-rc.d apache stop 09 6 .
```

The **start** and **stop** options can be combined.

```
update-rc.d apache 99 start 5 . stop 09 6 .
```

A **defaults** option will start and stop the service at predetermined runlevel. This option can be used to quickly set standard start and stop links for all runlevels. Startup links will be set in runlevels 2, 3, 4, and 5. Stop entries are set in runlevels 0, 1, and 6.

```
update-rc.d apache defaults
```

The following command performs the same operation with the stop and start options.

```
update-rc.d apache 99 start 2 3 4 5 . stop 09 0 1 6 .
```

The **multi-user** options will start entries at 2, 3, 4 , 5 and stop them at 1.

```
update-rc.d apache multiuser
```

To remove a service you use the remove option. The links will not be removed if the service script is still present in the **init.d** directory. Use the **-f** option to force removal of the links without having to remove the service script. The following removes all web service startup and shutdown entries from all runlevels.

```
update-rc.d -f apache  remove
```

To turn off a service at a given runlevel that is already turned on, you would have to first remove all its runlevel links and the add in the one's you want. So to turn off the apache server at runlevel 3, but still have it turned on at runlevels 2, 4, and 5 you would use the following commands.

```
update-rc.d -f apache remove
update-rc.d apache 99 start 2 4 5 . stop 09 0 1 3 6 .
```

Keep in mind that the **remove** option removes all stop links as well as start ones. So you have to restore the stop links for 0, 1, and 6.

Tip: On Debian and Ubuntu you can use file-rc instead of sysv-rc. The file-rc tool uses a single configuration file instead of links in separate runlevel directories.

Services Daemon (openbsd-inetd)

If your system averages only a few requests for a specific service, you don't need the server for that service running all the time. You need it only when a remote user is accessing its service. The OpenBSD Internet Services Daemon (**openbsd-inetd**) manages Internet servers, invoking them only when your system receives a request for their services. **openbsd-inetd** checks continuously for any requests by remote users for a particular Internet service; when it receives a request, it then starts the appropriate server daemon.

Certain services on Ubuntu are still configured to use **inetd**, like the SWAT configuration tool for CUPS print servers. These will use the **openbsd-inetd** package. The **xinetd** and **openbsd-inetd** packages are incompatible. You must use one or the other.

For **inetd** you would use the **openbsd-inetd** script.

```
sudo /etc/init.d/openbsd-inetd restart
```

When you install the openbsd-inetd package, the **openbsd-inetd** server will be configured to start automatically at runlevels 2, 3, 4, and 5. Whenever you start up your system, the **openbsd-inetd** server will be running.

If you add, change, or delete server entries in the **/etc/inetd.conf** file, you will have to restart the **inetd** daemon for these changes to take effect. The openbsd-inetd service is managed by the **/etc/init.d/openbsd-inetd** script. The following command will have the effect of restarting all the supported inetd servers.

```
sudo service openbsd-inetd restart
```

You can also reference the openbsd-inetd script directly, as shown here:

```
sudo /etc/init.d/openbsd-inetd restart
```

openbsd-inetd configuration:/etc/inetd.conf

The openbsd-inetd configuration file is **/etc/inetd.conf**. The file holds single line entries for each server configured. An entry holds the server name, socket type, protocol, wait options, owner, and the run of the server program using the tcpd daemon. The tcpd daemon provides TCP wrapper security when running the server (see following section on TCP wrappers). The wait option is applied to most stream servers that have to process all messages on the same socket, whereas nowait servers support multiple connections and do not have to wait. An attached argument specifies the maximum number of times the server can be invoked in a minute (400 for the swat server). The entries for the CUPS swat and tftp (trivial ftp) services are shown where.

```
swat stream tcp  nowait.400  root   /usr/sbin/tcpd  /usr/sbin/swat
tftp dgram  udp   wait        nobody /usr/sbin/tcpd  /usr/sbin/in.tftpd /srv/tftp
```

The server is invoked with the **tcpd** daemon.

```
/usr/sbin/tcpd  /usr/sbin/swat
```

See the man page for **inetd** for more information.

Extended Internet Services Daemon (xinetd)

The Extended Internet Services Daemon (**xinetd**) also manages Internet servers, invoking them only when your system receives a request for their services. Like **openbsd-inetd**, **xinetd** checks continuously for any requests by remote users for a particular Internet service; when it receives a request, it then starts the appropriate server daemon.

The **xinetd** program is designed to be a replacement for **inetd** (**openbsd-inetd**), providing security enhancements, logging support, and even user notifications. For example, with **xinetd** you can send banner notices to users when they are not able to access a service, telling them why. **xinetd** security capabilities can be used to prevent denial-of-service attacks, limiting remote hosts' simultaneous connections or restricting the rate of incoming connections. **xinetd** also incorporates TCP, providing TCP security without the need to invoke the **tcpd** daemon. Furthermore, you do not have to have a service listed in the **/etc/services** file. **xinetd** can be set up to start any kind of special-purpose server.

As previously noted, the **xinetd** and **openbsd-inetd** packages are incompatible. You must use one or the other. To install **xinetd**, the **openbsd-inetd** package will be removed, and to install **openbsd-inetd**, **xinetd** will be removed.

When you install the xinetd package, the **xinetd** server will be configured to start automatically at runlevels 2, 3, 4, and 5. Whenever you start up your system, the **xinetd** server will be running.

If you add, change, or delete server entries in the **/etc/xinetd** files, you will have to restart the **xinetd** daemon for these changes to take effect. On distributions that support SysV Init scripts, you can restart the **xinetd** daemon using the **/etc/init.d/xinetd** script with the `restart` argument, as shown here:

```
sudo /etc/init.d/xinetd restart
```

You can also use the **service** command.

```
sudo service xinetd restart
```

You can also use the `xinetd` script to start and stop the **xinetd** daemon. Stopping effectively shuts down all the servers that the **xinetd** daemon manages (those listed in the **/etc/xinetd.conf** file or the **xinetd.d** directory).

```
sudo service xinetd stop
sudo service xinetd start
```

You can also directly restart **xinetd** by stopping its process directly. To do this, you use the `killall` command with the `-HUP` signal and the name `xinetd`.

```
killall -HUP xinetd
```

Keep in mind that the xinetd and inetd servers are incompatible. You cannot have both installed. If one is already installed, and you choose to install the other, then the currently installed one will be removed. If **xinetd** is installed, and you choose to install **openbsd-inetd**, the **xinetd** package will be removed.

xinetd Configuration: /etc/xinetd.conf

The **xinetd.conf** file contains settings for your xinetd server, such as logging and security attributes. This file can also contain server configuration entries, or they may be placed into separate configuration files located in the **/etc/xinetd.d** directory. The **includedir** attribute specifies this directory:

```
includedir /etc/xinetd.d
```

You can find a detailed listing of all **xinetd.conf** configuration options and attributes in the **xinetd.conf** man page.

```
man xinetd.conf
```

Logging xinetd Services

You can further add a variety of other attributes such as logging information about connections and server priority (**nice**). In the following example, the **log_on_success** attribute logs the duration (**DURATION**) and the user ID (**USERID**) for connections to a service, **log_on_failure** logs the users that failed to connect, and **nice** sets the priority of the service to 10.

```
log_on_success += DURATION USERID
log_on_failure += USERID
nice = 10
```

The default attributes defined in the defaults block often set global attributes such as default logging activity and security restrictions: **log_type** specifies where logging information is to be sent, such as to a specific file (**FILE**) or to the system logger (**SYSLOG**), **log_on_success** specifies information to be logged when connections are made, and **log_on_failure** specifies information to be logged when they fail.

```
log_type = SYSLOG daemon info
log_on_failure = HOST
log_on_success = PID HOST EXIT
```

xinetd Network Security

For security restrictions, you can use **only_from** to restrict access by certain remote hosts. The **no_access** attribute denies access from the listed hosts, but no others. These controls take IP addresses as their values. You can list individual IP addresses, a range of IP addresses, or a network, using the network address. The **instances** attribute limits the number of server processes that can be active at once for a particular service. The following examples restrict access to a local network 192.168.1.0 and the localhost, deny access from 192.168.1.15, and use the **instances** attribute to limit the number of server processes at one time to 60.

```
only_from = 192.168.1.0
only_from = localhost
no_access = 192.168.1.15
instances = 60
```

The **xinetd** program also provides several internal services, including **time**, **services**, **servers**, and **xadmin**: **services** provides a list of currently active services, and **servers** provides information about servers; **xadmin** provides **xinetd** administrative support.

xinetd Service Configuration Files: /etc/xinetd.d Directory

Instead of having one large **xinetd.conf** file for all services, the service configurations are split it into several configuration files, one for each service. The directory is specified in **xinetd.conf** file with an **includedir** option. In the following example, the **xinetd.d** directory holds **xinetd** configuration files for services like SWAT. This approach has the advantage of letting you add services by just creating a new configuration file for them. Modifying a service involves editing only its configuration file, not an entire **xinetd.conf** file.

Configuring Services: xinetd Attributes

Entries in an **xinetd** service file define the server to be activated when requested along with any options and security precautions. An entry consists of a block of attributes defined for different features, such as the name of the server program, the protocol used, and security restrictions. Each block for an Internet service such as a server is preceded by the keyword `service` and the name by which you want to identify the service. A pair of braces encloses the block of attributes. Each attribute entry begins with the attribute name, followed by an assignment operator, such as =, and then the value or values assigned. A special block specified by the keyword `default` contains default attributes for services. The syntax is shown here:

```
service <service_name>
{
<attribute> <assign_op> <value> <value> ...
 ...
}
```

Most attributes take a single value for which you use the standard assignment operator, =. Some attributes can take a list of values. You can assign values with the = operator, but you can also add or remove items from these lists with the =+ and =- operators. Use =+ to add values and =- to remove values. You often use the =+ and =- operators to add values to attributes that may have an initial value assigned in the default block.

Attributes are listed in the **xinetd.conf** man page. Certain attributes are required for a service. These include `socket_type` and `wait`. For a standard Internet service, you also need to provide the `user` (user ID for the service), the `server` (name of the server program), and the `protocol` (protocol used by the server). With `server_args`, you can also list any arguments you want passed to the server program (this does not include the server name). If `protocol` is not defined, the default protocol for the service is used.

Disabling and Enabling xinetd Services

You can turn services on or off manually by editing their **xinetd** configuration file. Services are turned on and off with the `disable` attribute in their configuration file. To enable a service, you set the disable attribute to `no`, as shown here:

```
disable = no
```

You then have to restart **xinetd** to start the service.

```
sudo service xinetd restart
```

If you want to turn on a service that is off by default, you can set its `disable` attribute to **no** and restart **xinetd**. The entry for the time service is shown here. The `disable` attribute is set to yes, turning it off by default.

```
service time
{
        disable         = yes
        type            = INTERNAL
        id              = time-stream
        socket_type     = stream
        protocol        = tcp
        user            = root
        wait            = no
}
```

Note: You can also use `xinetd` to implement SSH port forwarding, should your system be used to tunnel connections between hosts or services.

TCP Wrappers

TCP wrappers add another level of security to **xinetd** and **inetd** managed servers. In effect, the server is wrapped with an intervening level of security, monitoring connections and controlling access. A server connection made through **xinetd** is monitored, verifying remote user identities and checking to make sure they are making valid requests. Connections are logged with the **syslogd** daemon and may be found in **syslogd** files such as **/var/log/secure**. With TCP wrappers, you can also restrict access to your system by remote hosts. Lists of hosts are kept in the **hosts.allow** and **hosts.deny** files. Entries in these files have the format `service:hostname:domain`. The domain is optional. For the service, you can specify a particular service, such as FTP, or you can enter **ALL** for all services. For the hostname, you can specify a particular host or use a wildcard to match several hosts. For example, **ALL** will match on all hosts. Table 3-4 lists the available wildcards. In the following example, the first entry allows access by all hosts to the web service, **http**. The second entry allows access to all services by the **pango1.train.com** host. The third and fourth entries allow FTP access to **rabbit.trek.com** and **sparrow.com**:

```
http:ALL
ALL:pango1.train.com
ftp:rabbit.trek.com
ftp:sparrow.com
```

The **hosts.allow** file holds hosts to which you allow access. If you want to allow access to all but a few specific hosts, you can specify **ALL** for a service in the **hosts.allow** file but list the ones you are denying access to in the **hosts.deny** file. Using IP addresses instead of hostnames is more secure because hostnames can be compromised through the DNS records by spoofing attacks where an attacker pretends to be another host.

TCP wrappers for the **openbsd-inetd** service are managed by the **tcpd** daemon. The **inetd.conf** entry for a server will invoked the **tcpd** daemon. The **tcpd** Man pages (`man tcpd`) provide more detailed information about **tcpd**.

Wildcard	Description
ALL	Matches all hosts or services.
LOCAL	Matches any host specified with just a hostname without a domain name. Used to match on hosts in the local domain.
UNKNOWN	Matches any user or host whose name or address is unknown.
KNOWN	Matches any user or host whose name or address is known.
PARANOID	Matches any host whose hostname does not match its IP address.
EXCEPT	An operator that lets you provide exceptions to matches. It takes the form of *list1* **EXCEPT** *list2* where those hosts matched in *list1* that are also matched in *list2* are excluded.

Table 3-4: TCP Wrapper Wildcards

The **xinetd** has integrated support for TCP wrappers into its own program. For the **xinetd** service, when **xinetd** receives a request for an FTP service, a TCP wrapper monitors the connection and starts up the **in.ftpd** server program. By default, all requests are allowed. To allow all requests specifically for the FTP service, you enter the following in your **/etc/hosts.allow** file. The entry **ALL:ALL** opens your system to all hosts for all services:

```
ftp:ALL
```

Network Time Protocol, NTP

For servers to run correctly, they need to always have the correct time. Internet time servers worldwide provide the time in the form of the Universal Time Coordinated (UTC). Local time is then calculated using the local systems local time zone. The time is obtained from Internet time servers from an Internet connection. You have the option of using a local hardware clock instead, though this may be much less accurate.

Normally, the time on a host machine is kept in a Time of Year chip (TOY) that maintains the time when the machine is off. Its time is used when the machine is rebooted. A host using the Network Time Protocol, then adjusts the time using the time obtained from an Internet time server. If there is a discrepancy of more than 1000 seconds (about 15 minutes), the system administrator is required to manually set the time. Time servers in the public network are organized in stratum levels, the highest being 1. Time servers from a lower stratum obtain the time from those in the next higher level.

For servers on your local network, you may want to set up your own time server, insuring that all your servers are using a synchronized time. If all your servers are running on a single host system that is directly connected to the Internet and accessing an Internet time server, you will not need to set up a separate time server. You can use the **ntpdate** command to update directly from an Internet time server.

```
sudo ntpdate ntp.ubuntu.com
```

If the servers are on different host systems, then you may want a time server to insure their times are synchronized. Alternatively, you could just use the **ntpdate** command to update those hosts directly at given intervals. You could set up a cron job to perform the **ntpdate** operation automatically.

There are packages on the Ubuntu repository for both the NTP server and its documentation. You can install them with **apt-get**, **aptitutde**, or (from the desktop) Synaptic.

```
ntp
ntp-docs
```

The documentation will be located in the /usr/share/doc/ntp-doc directory in Web page format.

```
/usr/share/doc/ntp-doc/html/index.html
```

The ntp server

The NTP server name is **ntpd** and is managed by the **/etc/init.d/ntp** script. Use the start, stop, and restart options to mange the server

```
sudo /etc/init.d/ntp start
```

Your host systems can then be configured to use NTP and access your NTP time server.

To check the status of your time server, you can use the **ntpq** command. With the **-p** option is displays the current status.

```
ntpq -p
```

The ntp.conf configuration file

The NTP server configuration file is **/etc/ntp.conf**. This file lists the Internet time servers that your own time server used to deterring the time. Check the **ntp.conf** Man page for a complete listing of the NTP server configuration directives.

In the **ntp.conf** file, the server directive specifies the Internet time server's Internet address that your NTP server uses to access the time. There is a default entry for the Ubuntu time server, but you can add more server entries for other time servers.

```
server ntp.ubuntu.com
```

NTP access controls

Access control to the NTP server is determined by the restrict directives. An NTP server is accessible from the Internet, anyone can access it. You can specify access options and the addresses of hosts allowed access. The **default** option lets you specify the set of default options. The **noquery**, **notrust**, **nopeer**, and **nomodify** option deny all access. The notrust option will not trust hosts unless specifically allowed access. The nomodify option prevents any modification of the time server. The **noquery** option will not even allow queries from other hosts, unless specifically allowed.

```
restrict -4 default kod notrap nomodify nopeer noquery
```

Then the local user, users on the same host that is running the NTP server, are allowed to access the NTP server. Addresses are specified for both IPv4 and IPv6 local host, **127.0.0.1** and **::1**.

```
restrict 127.0.0.1
restrict ::1
```

The default **ntp.conf** file is shown here.

```
#/etc/ntp.conf, configuration for ntpd: see ntp.conf(5) for help
driftfile /ver/lib/ntp/ntp.drift

#Enable this if you want statistics to be logged.
#statsdir /var/log/ntpstats/

statistics loopstats peerstats clockstats
filegen loopstats file loopstats type day enable
filegen peerstats file peerstats type day enable
filegen clockstats file clockstats type day enable

# You do need to talk to an NTP server or two (or three).
server ntp.ubuntu.com

# Access control configuration; see
# /usr/share/doc/ntp-doc/html/accopt.html for
# details.  The web page
# <http://support.ntp.org/bin/view/Support/AccessRestrictions>
# might also be helpful.
#
# Note that "restrict" applies to both servers and clients, so a
# configuration that might be intended to block requests from certain
# clients could also end up blocking replies from your own upstream
# servers.

# By default, exchange time with everybody,
# but don't allow configuration.
restrict -4 default kod notrap nomodify nopeer noquery
restrict -6 default kod notrap nomodify nopeer noquery

# Local users may interrogate the ntp server more closely.
restrict 127.0.0.1
restrict ::1

# Clients from this (example!) subnet have unlimited access, but only if
# cryptographically authenticated.
#restrict 192.168.123.0 mask 255.255.255.0 notrust

# If you want to provide time to your local subnet, change the next
# line. (Again, the address is an example only.)
#broadcast 192.168.123.255

# If you want to listen to time broadcasts on your local subnet,
# de-comment the next lines. Please do this only if you trust everybody
# on the network!
#disable auth
#broadcastclient
```

To allow access from hosts on a private local network, you can use the restrict directive to specify the local network address and mask. The following allows access to a local network,

192.168.123, with a network mask of 255.255.255.0 to determine the range of allowable host addresses.

```
restrict 192.168.123.0 mask 255.255.255.0
```

If you want to require the use of encrypted keys for access, add the **notrust** option. Use **ntp-keygen** to generate the required public/private keys.

You can also run the time server in broadcast mode where the time is broadcasted to your network clients (this can involve security risks). Use the broadcast directive and your network's broadcast address. Your host systems need to have the **broadcastclient** setting set, which will listen for time broadcasts.

```
broadcast 192.168.123.255
```

NTP clock support

You can also list a reference to the local hardware clock, and have that clock used should your connection to the Internet time server fail. The hardware clock is references by the IP address that has the prefix 127.127 followed by the clock type and instance, as in 127.127.1.1. The type for the local clock is 1.

```
server 127.127.1.1
```

The **fudge** directive is used to specify the time for a hardware clock, passing time parameters for that clock's driver.

4. Installing and Updating Software

Installing software is an administrative function performed by a user with administrative access. Unless you chose to install all your packages during your installation, only some of the many applications and utilities available for users on Linux were installed on your system. On Ubuntu, you can easily install or remove software from your system with the Add/Remove Applications tool, the Synaptic Package Manager, or the **apt** command. Alternatively, you can install software by downloading and compiling its source code.

APT (Advanced Package Tool) is integrated as the primary install packages tool. When you install a package with Package Manager or with Synaptic, APT will be invoked and it will automatically select and download the package from the appropriate online repository. This is a major change that users may not be aware of at first glance. After having installed your system, when you then want to install additional packages, the install packages tool will now use APT to install from an online repository, though it will check your CD or DVD ROM first if you wish. This will include the entire Ubuntu online repository, including the main repository as well as Universe and Multiverse ones.

A DEB software package includes all the files needed for a software application. A Linux software application often consists of several files that must be installed in different directories. The program itself is most likely placed in a directory called **/usr/bin**, online manual files go in another directory, and library files go in yet another directory.

When you select a package for download, APT will install any additional dependent (required) packages. With Ubuntu 9.04, APT will also install all recommended packages by default. Many software applications have additional features that rely on recommended packages.

Note: Be careful not to mix distributions. The distribution segments of all your **sources.list** entries should be the same: jaunty if you are using Ubuntu 9.04, gutsy for 7.10, edgy for 7.05, dapper for 6.06, and so on.

Ubuntu Package Management Software

Though all Ubuntu software packages have the same DEB format, they can be managed and installed using different package management software tools. The primary software management tool is APT. Some tools will operate on the command line interface, while other only work on the desktop.

Check the Ubuntu Server Guide | Package Management for basic command line software operations and repository configuration.

```
https://help.ubuntu.com/9.04/serverguide/C/package-management.html
```

Command Line interface tools

If you installed the Ubuntu Server CD, you will only have access to the following command line interface based tools.

> **tasksel** Cursor-based screen for selecting package groups and particular servers. This tool will work on the command-line interface installed by the Ubuntu Server CD. You can also run it in a terminal window on a desktop. Use arrow keys to move to and entry, the spacebar to select it, the Tab key to move to the OK button. Press ENTER on the OK button to perform your installs.

> **aptitude** Front end for tools like dpkg or apt-get, screen based, uses own database, **/var/lib/aptitude**

> **apt-get** primary command line tool to install, update, and remove software, uses own database, **/var/lib/apt/**, repository info at **/var/cache/apt**

> **dpkg** older command line tool to install, update, remove, and query software packages. Uses own database, **/var/lib/dpkg**, , repository info at **/var/cache/apt**, same as APT

Desktop tools

If you installed the Ubuntu Desktop CD or one of its variations like KUbuntu, you will have access to the following desktop interface tools, as well as using a terminal window to run the previously listed command line interface tools.

> **Gdebi** Simple package installation for installing single packages. Uses a GNOME interface.

> APT (Advanced Package Tool): Synaptic, Package Manager, update-manager, dpkg and apt-get are front ends for APT.

> Synaptic Package Manager: Graphical front end for managing packages, repository info at **/var/cache/apt**, same as APT

> Update Manager: Ubuntu graphical front end for updating installed software uses APT.

> Add/Remove Applications tool, **gnome-app-install**: GNOME Graphical front end for managing packages, repository info at **/var/cache/apt**, same as APT

> KPackageKit: KDE4 software manager, graphical front end for APT.

Ubuntu Software Repositories

There are four main components or sections to the Ubuntu repository: main, restricted, universe, and multiverse. These components are described in detail at:

`www.ubuntu.com/ubuntu/components`

To see a listing of all packages in the Ubuntu repository see **http://packages.ubuntu.com**. To see available repositories and their sections, open Synaptic, click Repositories from Settings menu.

In addition, there is a third-party repository called **medibuntu.org** which provides several popular codecs and applications like Skype and the DVD Video codec. This repository has to be manually configured. It is not configured on your Ubuntu system automatically.

Repository Sections

The repository sections for the main Ubuntu repository are as follows:

> **main**: Officially supported Ubuntu software (canonical), includes gstreamer good.

> **restricted**: Commonly used and required for many applications, but not open source or freely licensed, like proprietary graphics card drivers from Nvidia and ATI. Needed for hardware support, because not open source, they are not guaranteed to work.

> ➢ **universe**: All open source Linux software not directly supported by Ubuntu would include Gstreamer bad.

> ➢ **multiverse**: Linux software that does not meet licensing requirements. But is not considered essential. It may not necessarily work. For example, the Gstreamer ugly package is in this repository. see **www.ubuntu.com/community/ubuntustory/licensing**.

Repositories

In addition to the main repository, Ubuntu maintains several other repositories, primarily for maintenance and support for existing packages. The updates repository holds updated packages for a release. The security updates repository contains critical security package updates every system will need.

> ➢ **Main** repository: Collection of Ubuntu compliant software packages for releases.

> ➢ **Updates**: Corresponding updates for packages in the main repository, both main and restricted sections. Universe and Multiverse sections are not updated.

> ➢ **Backports**: Software under development for the next Ubuntu release, but packaged for use in the current one. Not guaranteed or fully tested.

> ➢ **Security updates**: security fixes for main software.

In addition, the backports repository provides un-finalized or development versions for new or current software. They are not guaranteed to work, but may provide needed features.

There is also a third-party repository called **Medibuntu.org (www.medibuntu.org)** that is commonly used for multimedia and Web applications that have licensing issues, like the DVD Video **libdvdcss** codec for commercial DVD Video, the Adobe Acrobat Reader, and Google Earth. You first have to configure access to this repository. Once setup, packages from this repository will be listed in the Synaptic Packages Manager, which you then use to install them.

> ➢ **Medibuntu.org**   Third-party repository for software and codecs with licensing issues.

Note: for added repositories be sure your have installed the correct signature key as well as a valid URL for the repository.

TIP: Though it is possible to add the Debian Linux distribution repository, it is not advisable. Packages are designed for specific distributions. Combining them and lead to irresolvable conflicts.

Ubuntu Repository Configuration file: sources.list and sources.list.d

Repository configuration is managed by APT using configuration files in the **/etc/apt** directory. The **/etc/apt/sources.list** file holds repository entries. The main and restricted sections are enabled by default. An entry consists of a single line with the following format:

```
format URI    distribution    component
```

The format is normally **deb**, for Debian package format. The URI (universal resource identifier) provides the location of the repository, such as an FTP or Web URL. The distribution is the official name of a particular Ubuntu distribution like dapper or gutsy. Ubuntu 9.04 has the name jaunty. The component can be one or more terms that identify a section in that distribution repository, like main for the main repository and restricted for the restricted section. You can also list individual packages if you want.

```
deb http://archive.ubuntu.com/ubuntu/   jaunty   main restricted
```

Corresponding source code repositories will have a **deb-src** format.

```
deb-src http://us.archive.ubuntu.com/ubuntu/ jaunty main restricted
```

Update sections of a repository are referenced by the **-updates** suffix, as jaunty-updates.

```
deb http://archive.ubuntu.com/ubuntu/   jaunty-updates   main restricted
```

Security sections for a repository have the suffix **-security**.

```
deb http://archive.ubuntu.com/ubuntu/   jaunty-security   main restricted
```

Both Universe and Multiverse repositories should already be enabled. Each will have an updates repository as well as corresponding source code repositories, like those shown here for Universe.

```
deb http://us.archive.ubuntu.com/ubuntu/ jaunty universe
deb-src http://us.archive.ubuntu.com/ubuntu/ jaunty universe
deb http://us.archive.ubuntu.com/ubuntu/ jaunty-updates universe
deb-src http://us.archive.ubuntu.com/ubuntu/ jaunty-updates universe
```

Comments begin with a # mark. You can add comments of your own if you wish. Commenting an entry effectively disables that component of a repository. Placing a # mark before a repository entry will effectively disable it.

Commented entries are included for the backports and Cannonical partners repositories. Backports holds applications being developed for future Ubuntu releases and may not work. Partners include companies like Vmware and Parallels. To activate these repositories, just edit the **/etc/apt/sources.list** file using any text editor, and then remove the # at the beginning of the line.

```
# deb http://us.archive.ubuntu.com/ubuntu/ jaunty-backports \
     main restricted universe multiverse
```

Certain entries like third-party entries for Ubuntu partners can be managed using Software Sources. Others, like backports, require that you edit the **sources.list** file. You can edit the file directly with the following command.

```
gksu gedit /etc/apt/sources.list
```

Repository information does not have to be added to the **sources.list** file directly. It can also be placed in a file in the **/etc/apt/sources.list.d** directory, which APT will read as if part of the **sources.list** file.

Software Management with Tasksel, DEB, APT, and DKPG

Both the Debian distribution and Ubuntu use the Debian package format (DEB) for their software packages. Two basic package managers are available for use with Debian packages: the Advanced Package Tool (APT) and the Debian Package tool (dpkg). APT is designed to work with repositories and is used to install and maintain all your package installations on Ubuntu. Though you can install packages directly as single files with just dpkg, it is always advisable to use APT.

Information and package files for Ubuntu compliant software can be obtained from **packages.ubuntu.com**.

You can also download source code versions of applications and then compile and install them on your system. Where this process once was complex, it has been significantly streamlined with the addition of *configure scripts.* Most current source code, including GNU software, is distributed with a configure script. The configure script automatically detects your system configuration and generates a *Makefile,* which is used to compile the application and create a binary file that is compatible with your system. In most cases, with a few Makefile operations you can compile and install complex source code on any system.

Installing from source code requires that supporting development libraries and source code header files be installed. You can to this separately for each major development platform like GNOME, KDE, or just the kernel. Alternatively you can run the APT metapackage **build-essential** for all the Ubuntu development packages. You will only have to do this once.

```
sudo apt-get install build-essential
```

DEB Software Packages

A Debian package will automatically resolve dependencies, installing any other needed packages instead of simply reporting their absence. Packages are named with the software name, the version number, and the **.deb** extension. Check **www.debian.org/doc** for more information. File name format is as follows:

> ➢ the package name

> ➢ version number

> ➢ distribution label and build number. Packages created specifically for Ubuntu will have the ubuntu label here. Attached to it will be the build number, the number of times the package was built for Ubuntu.

> ➢ architecture   The type of system the package runs on, like i386 for Intel 32 bit x86 systems, or amd64 for both Intel and AMD 64 bit systems, x86_64.

> ➢ package format. This is always deb

For example, the package name for 3dchess is 3dchess, with a version and build number 0.0.1-13, and an architecture amd64 for a 64 bit system.

```
3dchess_0.0.1-13_amd64.deb
```

The following package has an Ubuntu label, a package specifically created for Ubuntu. The version number is 1.2 and build number is 4, with the Ubuntu label ubuntu2. The architecture is i386 for a 32 bit system.

```
spider_1.2-4ubuntu2_i386.deb
```

Installing and Removing Software with tasksel

The easiest way to install server packages it to use tasksel. The **tasksel** tool will display a list of all your server metapackages as well as all other meta-packages on your configured repositories. To run **tasksel**, enter the **tasksel** command at the shell prompt. If you are using a desktop, open a terminal window and enter the tasksel command.

```
sudo tasksel
```

Should you want to quit tasksel without installing or removing any software, press the ESC key. The tasksel application will end, and you will return to the shell prompt.

A keyboard based screen interface is displayed listing the server and meta packages (see Figure 4-1). Those already installed with have a asterisk next to their entries. Use the arrow keys to move to an entry and the spacebar to select it. When you have made all your selections, use the Tab key to move to the OK button. Then press the ENTER key to install the selected software.

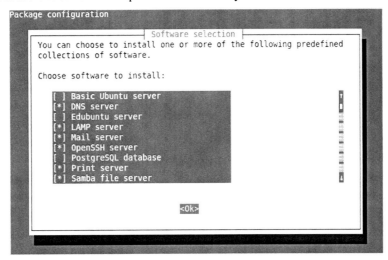

Figure 4-1: Tasksel server and meta package installation

You can also use tasksel to uninstall packages. Installed packages will have an asterisk next to them. Move to the package you want to remove and press the spacebar. The asterisk will disappear, leaving you with empty brackets. Tab to the OK button and press Enter. An installation window will be displayed, and the de-selected meta package will be removed.

The last entry in the tasksel is Manual Page Selection. Selecting this entry will open the Aptitude package manager (discussed in the next section), which provides you with a screen based interface to install, remove, and update individual packages.

If you already know the name of the server or meta package you want to install, you can use the install option and the package name to install the package directly. You would not have to use the screen interface. The package names are usually the same as those listed on the screen interface, but in lower case with a dash connecting the words, as in samba-server for Samba server. The option **--list-tasks** lists the server and meta package names with their associated descriptions used on the screen interface. The following command directly installs the Samba server.

```
sudo tasksel install samba-server
```

You can use the remove option to remove server or meta package. Check the tasksel Man page for a complete set of options.

```
sudo tasksel remove dns-server
```

Managing software with Aptitude

The Aptitude software tool provides a keyboard based screen interface on command line interfaces for managing software. Because of its easy to use screen interface, Aptitude is an very effective package management tool for Ubuntu server installs that do not have a desktop. Check the Ubuntu Server Guide | Package Management | Aptitude for basic operations.

```
https://help.ubuntu.com/9.04/serverguide/C/aptitude.html
```

Key	Description
Ctrl-t	Access menu, the Ctrl-t will toggle between the menu and the main screen. Menu entries will also show equivalent key operations.
Arrow and Page up/down	Move to a selection
ENTER	Expand a category or open a package description
q	Quit the current screen. If only one screen is open, quit Aptitude
+	Mark a package for installation
-	Mark a package for removal
g g	Install and removed marked packages, the first g displays a preview showing what packages will be installed and removed. Pressing g again performs the actual install and remove operations. Press **q** on the preview screen to leave the preview and not perform any install and remove operations.
/	Search for a package, the Find operation
u	Update the package list
U	Mark packages to be updated for updating, use **g g** to perform the actual update.
?	Display the list of key commands
F6 and F7	Move forward and backward between tabs (screens)

Table 4-1: Aptitude key commands

A menu bar at the top lets you use your arrow keys to select menus and entries for package management, searching, and views (see Figure 4-2). You use the **Ctrl-t** keys to access the menu. To quit aptitude, just press the **q** key if only one screen is open. Aptitude can have several screens open at the same time, though only one is shown at a time. The tabs for the screens are listed under the menubar. As you open a new screen, its label will be displayed be low the menu. Pressing the **q** key will close the current screen, and, if there is only one screen open, will quit from Aptitude. To move from one tab screen to another, use the F6 and F7 keys. To see a listing of all the key commands, press the **?** key. Several commonly used key commands are listed in Table 4-1.

You start Aptitude by entering the **sudo aptitude** command on the command line. On desktops open a terminal window.

```
sudo aptitude
```

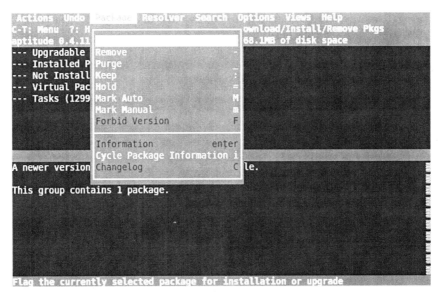

Figure 4-2: Aptitude package manager

The screen will have two main views, the top one listing packages by category, and the bottom one displaying information about a selected package or category. On the top view, use the arrow keys to move to an entry, and then press the ENTER key to expand an entry. Categories will expand to a package listing, and packages will open a detailed description along with a listing of dependent packages. Use the + key to mark a package for installation, and the - key to mark an installed package for removal. You can also use the Package menu's Install and Remove entries.

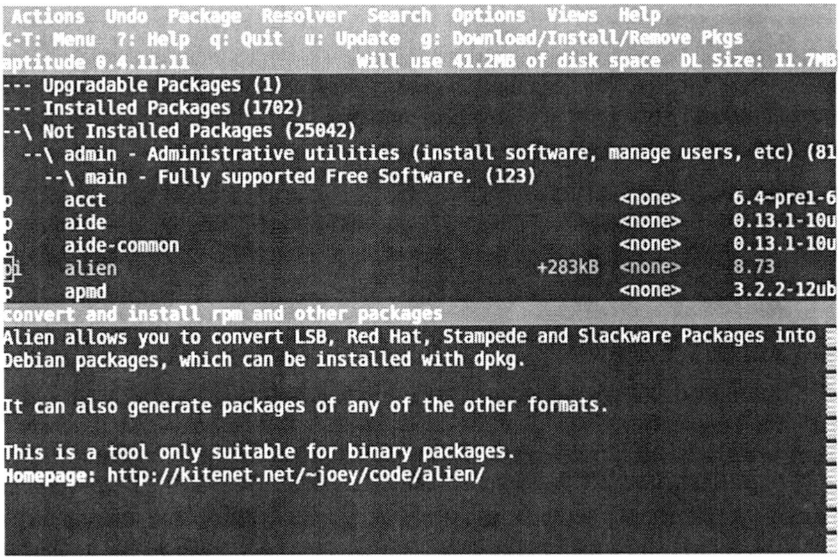

Figure 4-3: Aptitude: selecting packages

Each package entry begins with a letter denoting the package state. Uninstalled packages will be labeled with a **p** indicating a purged package, one not on the system. Installed packages will have the letter **i**. Packages marked for installation or removal will have an additional letter indicating an action yet to be taken. When a package is marked for installation it will have both a **p** and **i** (see Figure 4-3), as shown her for the **alien** package entry.

```
pi    alien                              +283kB  <none>     8.73
```

Once you have selected packages for installation (or removal), press the **g** key. A preview of the packages to be installed and removed will be listed (see Figure 4-4). Then press the **g** key again. Basically, press **g** twice to install. Aptitude will change to the shell interface, displaying the download, unpack, and setup messages as packages are being installed. You are then prompted to press return (the ENTER key), to return to the Aptitude interface. To install you could also select the Actions | Install/remove packages menu entry twice.

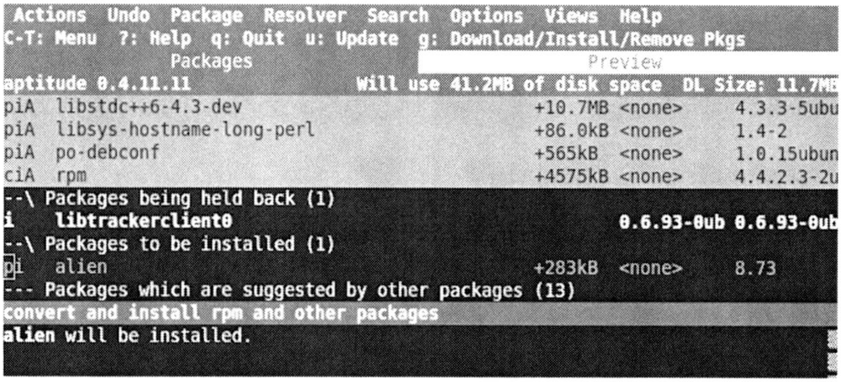

```
Actions  Undo  Package  Resolver  Search  Options  Views  Help
C-T: Menu  ?: Help  q: Quit  u: Update  g: Download/Install/Remove Pkgs
           Packages                            Preview
aptitude 0.4.11.11              Will use 41.2MB of disk space  DL Size: 11.7MB
piA  libstdc++6-4.3-dev                       +10.7MB <none>    4.3.3-5ubu
piA  libsys-hostname-long-perl                +86.0kB <none>    1.4-2
piA  po-debconf                               +565kB  <none>    1.0.15ubun
ciA  rpm                                      +4575kB <none>    4.4.2.3-2u
--\ Packages being held back (1)
i    libtrackerclient0                        0.6.93-0ub 0.6.93-0ub
--\ Packages to be installed (1)
pi   alien                                    +283kB  <none>     8.73
--- Packages which are suggested by other packages (13)
convert and install rpm and other packages
alien will be installed.
```

Figure 4-4: Aptitude: installing packages

If you know the package name, you can search for it to locate it more easily. To open a search window, press the / key (or from the menubar (**Ctrl-t**) use the right arrow key to move to the Search menu and select Find). Type in your search and press ENTER. The selected package will be listed and highlighted.

In Figure 4-4, you will also see that two tabs (screens) are actually open, Packages and Preview. The Preview tab is currently displayed. You can use the F7 and F6 keys to move to the other tab (Packages) and back again. Use the q key to close a tab. With the Preview tab open, pressing **q** will quit and close the Preview screen.

Managing software with APT

APT is designed to work with repositories, and will handle any dependencies for you. It uses **dpkg** to install and remove individual packages, but can also determine what dependent packages need to be installed, as well as query and download packages from repositories. There are several popular front ends for APT that let you manage your software easily, like synaptic, gnome-apt (Add/Remove Applications), aptitude, and deselect. Synaptic and gnome-apt rely on a desktop interface like GNOME. If you are using the command line interface, you can use **apt-get** to manage packages. Using the **apt-get** command on the command line you can install, update, and remove packages. Check the **apt-get** man page for a detailed listing of **apt-get** commands (see Table 4-2).

```
apt-get   command   package
```

Command	Description
update	Download and resynchronize the package listing of available and updated packages for APT supported repositories. APT repositories updated are those specified in **/etc/apt/sources.list**
upgrade	Update packages, install new versions of installed packages if available.
dist-upgrade	Update (upgrade) all your installed packages to a new release
install	Install a specific package, using its package name, not full package file name.
remove	Remove a software package from your system.
source	Download and extract a source code package
check	Check for broken dependencies
clean	Removes the downloaded packages held in the repository cache on your system. Used to free up disk space.

Table 4-2: apt-get commands

The **apt-get** tool takes two arguments: the command to perform and the name of the package. Other APT package tools follow the same format. The command is a term such as `install` for installing packages or `remove` to uninstall a package. Use the **install**, **remove**, or **update** commands respectively. You only need to specify the software name, not the package's full file name. APT will determine that. To install the MPlayer package you would use:

```
sudo apt-get install mplayer
```

To make sure that apt-get has current repository information, use the **apt-get update** command.

```
sudo apt-get update
```

To remove packages, you use the **remove** option.

```
sudo apt-get remove mplayer
```

You can use the **-s** option to check the remove or install first, especially to check if there are any dependency problems. For remove operations you can use **-s** to find out first what dependent packages will also be removed.

```
sudo apt-get remove -s mplayer
```

The **apt-get** command can be very helpful if your X Windows System server ever fails (your display driver). For example, if you installed a restricted vendor display driver, and then your desktop fails to start, you can start up the recover mode, drop to the root shell, and use apt-get to remove the restricted display driver. The following would remove the ATI (AMD) restricted display driver.

```
sudo apt-get remove fglrx*
```

Your former X open source display drivers would be automatically restored.

A complete log of all install, remove, and update operations are kept in the **/var/log/dpkg.log** file. You can consult this file to find out exactly what files were installed or removed.

Configuration for APT is held in the **/etc/apt** directory. Here the **sources.list** file lists the distribution repositories from where packages are installed. Source lists for additional third party repositories (like that for Wine) are kept in the **/etc/sources.list.d** directory. GPG database files hold validation keys for those repositories. Specific options for apt-get are kept in either a **/etc/apt.conf** file or in various files located in the **/etc/apt.conf.d** directory.

Updating (Upgrading) packages with apt-get and unattended-upgrades

The apt-get tool also lets you easily update your entire system at once. The terms update and upgrade are used differently from other software tools. The update command just updates your package listing, checking for packages that may need to install newer version, but not installing those versions. Technically it updates the package list that APT uses to determine what packages need updated. The term upgrade is used to denote the actual update of a software package; a new version is downloaded and installed. What is referred to at updating by apt-get, other package managers refer to a obtaining the list of software packages to be updated. In apt-get, upgrading is what other package managers refer to as performing updates.

TIP: The terms **update** and **upgrade** can be confusing when used with apt-get. The **update** operation updates the Apt package list only, whereas **upgrade** downloads and installs all the packages for a new release.

Upgrading is a simple matter of using the `upgrade` command. With no package specified, apt-get with the `upgrade` command will upgrade your entire system, downloading from an FTP site or copying from a CD-ROM and installing packages as needed. Add the **-u** option to list packages as they are upgraded. First make sure your repository information (package list) is up to date with the **update** command.

```
sudo apt-get update
sudo apt-get -u upgrade
```

You can implement automatic updates using the **unattended-upgrades** package. If you choose "Install security updates automatically" during installation, then this package is already installed and configured to upgrade security updates.

The configuration file for unattended-upgrades is **/etc/apt/apt.conf.d/50unattended-upgrades**. The configuration is organized into blocks specifying certain options. The Unattended-Upgrade::Allowed-Origins block lists the repositories for which updating (upgrading) is allowed. Ubuntu jaunty-security will be configured, with comments removed. To enable Ubuntu updates, remove the comment characters, //, from the Ubuntu jaunty-update entry. An entry will reference a repository with both an origin and archive name, as in Ubuntu and jaunty-updates. These values are taken from the repository's Release file, using the Origin and Suite headers.

```
// Automatically upgrade packages from these (origin, archive) pairs
Unattended-Upgrade::Allowed-Origins {
        "Ubuntu jaunty-security";
//      "Ubuntu jaunty-updates";
};
```

The Package-Blacklist block lets you list packages for which you do not want automatic updates performed. The Mail directive specifies the address to which upgrade and problems are sent. Messages are logged to **/var/log/unattended-upgrades**.

```
//Unattended-Upgrade::Mail "root@localhost";
```

The unattended -upgrades service is enabled in the **/etc/apt/apt.conf.d/periodic10** file, using the following two entries. The first may already be present. These entries also set the period for checking, with 1 being one day.

```
APT::Periodic::Update-Package-Lists "1";
APT::Periodic::Unattended-Upgrade-Lists "1";
```

Command Line Search and Information :dpkg-query and apt-cache tools

The **dpkg-query** command lets you list detailed information about your packages. They operate on the command line (terminal window). **dpkg-query** with the **-l** option will list all your packages.

```
dpkg-query -l
```

The dpkg command can operate as a front end for dpkg-query, detecting its options to perform the appropriate task. The previous command could also be run as:

```
dpkg -l
```

To list a particular package requires and exact match on the package name, unless you use pattern matching operators. The following lists the **wine** package (Windows Compatibility Layer).

```
dpkg-query -l wine
```

A pattern matching operator, like *, placed after a patter will display any packages beginning with that pattern. The pattern with operators needs to be quoted to prevent an attempt by the shell to use the pattern to match on filenames on your current directory. The following example finds all packages beginning with the pattern "wine". This would include packages line **wine-doc** and **wine-utils**.

```
dpkg-query -l 'wine*'
```

You can further refine the results by using **grep** to perform an additional search. The following operation first outputs all packages beginning with **wine**, and from those results, the **grep** operations lists only those with the pattern *utils* in their name, like **wine-utils**.

```
dpkg -l 'wine*' | grep 'utils'
```

Use the **-L** option to just list the files that a package has installed.

```
dpkg-query -L wine
```

To see the status information about a package, including its dependencies and configuration files, use the **-s** option. Fields will include Status, Section, Architecture, Version, Depends (dependent packages), Suggests, Conflicts (conflicting packages), and Conffiles (configuration files).

```
dpkg-query -s wine
```

The status information will also provide suggested dependencies. These are packages not installed, but like to be used. For the wine package, the **msttcorefonts** Windows fonts package is suggested.

```
dpkg-query  -s  wine | grep Suggests
```

Use the **-S** option to find what package a particular file belongs to.

```
dpkg-query  -S  filename
```

You can also obtain information with the **apt-cache** tool. Use the search command with **apt-cache** to perform a search.

```
apt-cache search wine
```

To find dependencies for a particular package, use the **depends** command.

```
apt-cache depends wine
```

To just display the package description use the **show** command.

```
apt-cache show wine
```

Note: If you have installed aptitude, you can use the **aptitude** command with the **search** and **show** options to find and display information about packages.

Source code files

Though you can install source code files directly, the best way to install one is to use **apt-get**. Use the **source** command with the package name. Packages will be downloaded and extracted.

```
sudo apt-get source mplayer
```

The **--download** option lets you just download the source package without extracting it. The **--compile** option will download, extract, compile, and package the source code into a Debian binary package, ready for installation.

No dependent packages will be downloaded. If you have a software packages that requires any dependent packages to run, you will have to download and compile those also. To obtain needed dependent files, you use the **build-dep** option. All your dependent files will be located and downloaded for you automatically.

```
sudo apt-get build-dep mplayer
```

Managing Software from the Ubuntu Desktop

If you have install the Ubuntu desktop (either from the Server install or directly from a Desktop CD), you can use desktop-based software management tools for installing, updating, and removing software.

Software Sources managed from Ubuntu Desktop

If you have installed a desktop interface, you can manage your repositories with the Software Sources tool. With the Software Sources you can enable or disable repository sections, as well as add new entries. This tool edits the **/etc/apt/sources.list** file directly. Choose System | Administration | Software Sources entry. This opens the Software Sources window with four tabs:

Ubuntu Software, Third-Party Software, Updates, Authentication, and Statistics (see Figure 4-5). The Ubuntu Software tab will list all your current repository section entries. These include the main repository, universe, restricted, and multiverse, as well as source code. Those that are enabled will be checked. All of them, except the source code, will initially be enabled. You can enable or disable a repository section by simply checking or uncheck it entry. From a pop-up menu you can select the server to use. To install from a CD/DVD disc, just insert it.

Figure 4-5: Software Sources Ubuntu Software repository sections.

On the Third-Party Software tab, you can add repositories for third party software. The repository for Ubuntu Software Partners will already be listed, but not checked. Check that entry if you want access software from the Partners. To add a third party repository click the Add button. This opens a dialog window where you enter the complete APT entry, starting with the deb format, followed by the URL, distribution, and components or packages. This is the line as it will appear in the **/etc/apt/sources.list** file. Once entered, click the Add Channel button.

The Updates tab lets you configure how updates are handled (see Figure 4-6). The tab specifies both your update sources and how automatic updates are handled. You have the option to install security (jaunty-security), recommended (jaunty-updates, pre-released (jaunty-proposed), and unsupported (jaunty-backports) updates. The security and recommended updates will already be selected. These cover updates for the entire Ubuntu repository. Pre-released and unsupported updates useful if you have installed any packages from the backports or development repositories.

Your system is already configured to check for updates automatically on a daily basis. You can opt to not check for updates at all by un-checking the Check or updates box. You also have options for how updates are to be handled.

You can install any security updates automatically, without confirmation. You can download updates in the background. Or you can just be notified of available updates, and then manually choose to install them when you wish. The options are exclusive. The Authentication tab shows the repository software signature keys that are installed on your system (see Figure 4-7).

Signature keys will already be installed for Ubuntu repositories, including your CD/DVD-ROM. If you are adding a third party repository, you will need to add its signature key. Click Import Key File button to browse for and locate a downloaded signature key file. Ubuntu requires a signature key for any package that it installs. Signature keys for all the Ubuntu repositories are already installed, and will be listed on this tab. For third party repositories you will have to locate their signature key on their Web site, download it to a file, and then import that file.

Figure 4-6: Software Sources Update configuration

Figure 4-7: Software Sources Authentication, package signature keys

Most repositories will provide a signature key file for you to download and import. Click the Import Key File to open a file browser where you can select the downloaded key file. This procedure is the same as the **apt-key add** operation. Both add keys that APT then uses to verify DEB software packages downloaded from repositories before it installs them.

The Statistics package lets you provide Ubuntu with software usage information, letting them know what software is being used.

After you have made changes and click the Close button, the Software Sources tool will notify you that your software package information is out of date, displaying a Reload button. Click on the Reload button to make the new repositories or components available on your package managers like the Synaptic Package Manager. If you do not click Reload, you can run apt-get update or perform the Check operation on the Synaptic Package Manager to reload the repository configuration.

Medibuntu.org repository quick configuration

Though not likely for a server, if you are running a desktop, there may be certain third-party multimedia codecs and applications you may want to install. These codecs and applications are held in the Medibuntu.org repository. This repository holds many non-free multimedia codec and proprietary applications like Skype. Configuring access requires special operations. A **medibuntu.list** repository file, which holds the Medibuntu repository references, has to be added to the **/etc/apt/sources.list.d** directory. In addition the Medibuntu software key has to be installed on your system. These tasks are usually performed on a command line in a terminal window. See the Medibuntu help page for details:

```
https://help.ubuntu.com/community/Medibuntu
```

To quickly configure access to the Medibuntu repository, you can copy the command line from the Web page and paste it directly to a terminal window, without having to type anything. First, locate the "Adding the Repositories" section on the Web page, and within it the Jaunty section. Then click and drag to select the following line.

```
sudo wget http://www.medibuntu.org/sources.list.d/jaunty.list --output-
document=/etc/apt/sources.list.d/medibuntu.list
```

From the Web browser Edit menu, select Copy.

Open a terminal window, Applications | Accessories | Terminal.

Select the terminal window, then click on the Edit menu for the terminal window and select the Paste entry. The selected text from the Web page will be pasted to the terminal window. Make sure it was copied correctly. Then press the Enter key.

Follow the same copy and paste procedure for the GPG key (further down the Web page). Copy and paste the following to a terminal window and press enter.

```
sudo apt-get update && sudo apt-get install medibuntu-keyring && sudo apt-get
update
```

You can then start up the Synaptic Package Manager. The first time you start after configuring Medibuntu.org, click the Reload button so that Synaptic will scan and load the Medibuntu.org package list. The Synaptic Package Manage to list and install Medibuntu packages like Skype or **libdvdcss** for DVD Video support.

Synaptic Package Manager

The Synaptic Package Manager provides more control over all your packages. Packages are listed by name and include supporting packages like libraries as well as system critical packages. You can start up Synaptic from System | Administration | Synaptic Package Manager entry.

The Synaptic Package Manager window display three panes, a side pane for listing software categories and buttons, a top pane for listing software packages, and a bottom pane for displaying a selected package's description. When a package is selected, description pane will also display a Get Screenshot button. Clicking this button will download and display an image of the application, if there is one (see Figure 4-8).

Buttons on the lower left of the Synaptic Package Manager window provide options for organizing and refining the list of packages shown (see Figure 4-8). Five options are available: Sections, Status, Origin, Custom Filters, and Search results. The dialog pane above the buttons will change depending on which option you choose. Clicking on the Sections button will list section categories for your software such as Base System, Communications, or Development. The Status button will list options for installed and not installed software. The Origin button shows entries for different repositories, as well as those locally installed (manual or disk based installations). Custom filters lets you choose a filter to use for listing packages. You can create your own filter and use it to display selected packages. Search results will list your current and previous searches, letting you move from one to the other.

Synaptic supports a quick search option. Enter the pattern to be searched for in the Quick search box and the results will appear. In Figure 4-8 the scribus pattern is used to locate the Scribus desktop publishing software.

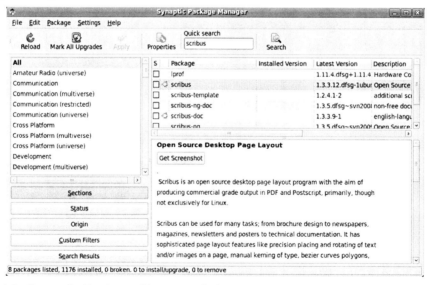

Figure 4-8: Synaptic Package Manager: Quick search

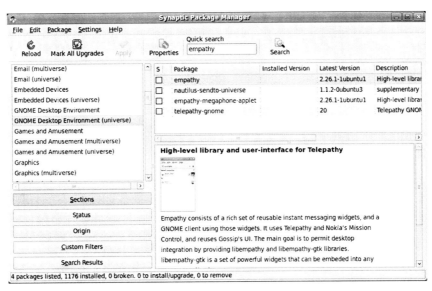

Figure 4-9: Synaptic Package Manager: Sections

The Sections option is selected by default. You can choose to list all packages, or refine your listing using categories provided in the pane. The All entry in this pane will list all available packages. Packages are organized into categories like Base System, Cross Platform, and Communications. Each category is in turn subdivided by multiverse, universe, and restricted software.

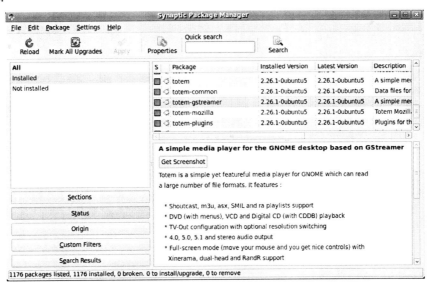

Figure 4-10: Synaptic Package Manager: Status

Quick searches will be performed within selected sections. In Figure 4-9, the empathy instant messenger package is searched for in the GNOME Desktop Environment (Universe) section. Selecting different sections will automatically apply your quick search pattern to the packages in that section. Clicking on the Graphics section with an empathy search pattern would give no results, since empathy is not a graphics package.

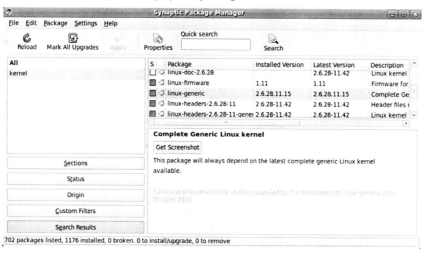

Figure 4-11: Synaptic Package Manager: Search

Status entries further refine installed software as auto-removable or as local or obsolete (see Figure 4-10). Local software consists of packages you download and install manually

With the Origins options, Ubuntu compliant repositories may further refine access according to multiverse, universe, and restricted software. A main entry selects Ubuntu supported software. Both the Ubuntu and Ubuntu security repositories are organized this way.

To perform more detailed searches, you can use the Search tool. To perform a search, click the Search button on the toolbar. This opens a Search dialog with a text box where you can enter your search terms. A pop-up menu lets you specify what features of a package to search. The "Description and Name" feature is used most commonly. You can search other package features like just the Name, the maintainer name, the package version, packages it may depend on, or provided (associated) packages.

A list of searches will be displayed in Search Results. You can move back and forth between search results by clicking on the search entries in this listing (see Figure 4-11).

Properties

To find out information about a package, select the package and click the properties button. This opens a window with panels for Common, Dependencies, Installed files, Versions, and Description. The Common pane provides section, versions, and maintainer information. The Installed files panel show you exactly what files are installed, useful for finding the exact location and names for configuration files as well as commands. Description information displays a detailed paragraph about the software. Dependencies will show all dependent software packages needed by this software, usually libraries.

Installing packages

Before installing software, you should press the Reload button to reload to load the most recent package lists from the active repositories

To install a package, click on its entry to display a pop-up menu and select the Mark for installation entry. Should there be any dependent packages, a dialog opens listing those packages. Click the Mark button to also mark those packages for installation. The package entry will then have its checkbox marked.

Once you have selected the packages you want to install, click the Apply button on the toolbar to begin the installation process. A Summary dialog opens up showing all the packages to be installed. You have the option to just download the package files. The number of packages to be installed is listed, along with the size of the download and the amount of disk space used. Click Apply button on the dialog to download and install the packages. A download window will appear showing the progress of your package installations. You can choose to show the progress of individual packages, which opens a terminal window listing each package as it is downloaded and installed.

Once downloaded, the dialog changes to Installing Software label. You can choose to close the dialog automatically when finished.

Sometimes installation requires user input to set up a configuration for the software. You will be prompted to enter the information.

On the submenu that opens when you right-click, you also have the options to Mark Suggested for Installation or Mark Recommended for Installation. These will mark applications that can enhance your selected software, though they are not essential.

Certain software, like desktops or office suites that require a significant number of packages, can be selected all at once using metapackages. A metapackage has configuration files that select, download, and configure the range of packages needed for such complex software like a desktop.

Removing packages

To remove a package, just locate it. Then right-click and select the "Mark package for removal" entry. This will leave configuration files untouched. Alternatively, you can mark a package for complete removal which will also remove any configuration files. Dependent packages will not be removed.

Once you have marked packages for removal, click the Apply button. A summary dialog will display the packages for removal. Click Apply to remove them.

Synaptic may not remove dependent packages, especially shared libraries that might or might not be used by other applications. This means that your system could eventually have installed packages that are never being used. Their continued presence will not harm anything, but if you want to conserve space, you can clean them out using the **deborphan** tool. **deborphan** will output a listing of packages no longer needed by other packages or no longer used. You can then use this list to remove the packages.

Search filters

You can further refine your search for packages by creating search filters. The Filters window will show two components, a filter list on the left, and a set of three tabbed panels on the right, showing a selected Filter's status, repository section, and properties. To create a new filter, click on the New button located just below the filter listing.

Click on the New Filter 1 entry in the filter list on the left panel. On the Status panel you can refine your search criteria according to a package's status. You can search just uninstalled packages, or include installed ones. Include or exclude those marked for removal. Or just search or those that are new in the repository. Initially all criteria are selected. Uncheck those you do not want included in your search.

Updating Ubuntu with Update Manager

New updates are continually being prepared for particular software packages as well as system components. These are posted as updates you can download from software repositories and install on your system. These include new versions of applications, servers, and even the kernel.

Such updates may range from single software packages to whole components. Updating your Ubuntu system has become a very simple procedure, using the Update Manager tool. For Ubuntu, you can update your system by accessing software repositories supporting Apt update methods. To update your packages, you now use the Update Manager. Update Manager is a graphical update interface for Apt, which now performs all updates.

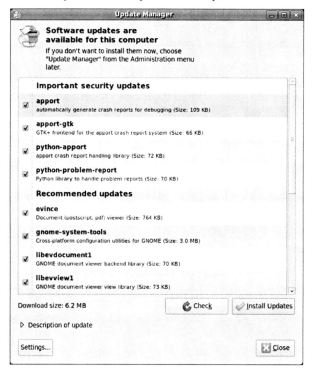

Figure 4-12: Update Manager with selected packages

Update Manager makes use of the Update Manager applet on your GNOME panel, which will automatically check for updates whenever you log in. If updates are detected, Update Manager icon will flash its icon on the panel and display a message telling you that updates are available and how many there are. Click the Update Manager button to start Update Manager. You can also select Update Manager manually from its Updater Manager entry in the System | Administration menu, and click the Check button to check current repository package listings for updates.

With Ubuntu 9.04, you are notified of security updates daily, but for recommended updates you are notified only once a week. You can restore the update notification behavior used in previous Ubuntu releases by turning off the update-notifier auto_launch option.

```
gconftool -s --type bool /apps/update-notifier/auto_launch false
```

All needed updates will be selected automatically when Update Manager starts up (see Figure 4-12). The check boxes for each entry let you deselect any particular packages you may not want to update. Packages are organized according to importance, beginning with Important security updates and followed by Recommended updates. You should always perform the security updates.

Click the Install Updates button to start updating. The packages will be downloaded from their appropriate repository. Once downloaded, the packages are updated. All the Apt-compatible repositories that are configured on your system will be checked.

Figure 4-13: Detailed Update information

To see a detailed description of an update, select the update and then click on the "Description of update" arrow at the bottom of the window (see Figure 4-13). Two panes are displayed, Changes and Description. Changes list detailed update information, whereas description provides information about the software.

When downloading and installing, a dialog will first appear that shows the download and install progress (see Figure 4-14). You can choose to show progress for individual files. A window will open up that lists each file and its progress.

Once downloaded, the updates are installed. Click details for see install messages for particular software packages.

Figure 4-14: Download and install updates

When the download completes, Update Manager will display a message saying that your system is up-to-date.

Managing Packages with Add/Remove Applications

To perform simple install and removal of software you use the Add/Remove Applications tool located in the Applications menu. This is the **gnome-app-install** application designed for simple package installation and removal. For more detailed and extensive installation such as libraries and kernel packages, you would use the Synaptic Package Manager.

To use Add/Remove Applications tool you select the Add/Remove Applications entry from the Applications menu. Add/Remove Applications tool will start up by gathering information on all your packages (see Figure 4-15).

You then have different ways to display applications. A pop-up menu labeled Show will list of applications organized by their kind of source. To access just applications maintained for Ubuntu you would select "Canonical-maintained applications" (see Figure 4-15). Other options are: All open source applications, All available applications, Third party applications, or Installed applications. If you just want to remove a package, you could select Installed applications to narrow your search.

The pane on the left will let you list software for different categories, like Office, Graphics, or Programming, further refining your search.

You can also perform a search using the Search box. If you have selected a category in the left pane, the search will be performed just on application in that category. Clicking on different categories will apply your current search entry to that category automatically. A search on "ink" in Graphics displays Inkscape, but in Accessories it only displays the Tomboy Notetaker.

An uninstalled package will have an empty checkbox to the left of its entry, whereas installed packages will have a check mark in its box. To install a package just click its empty checkbox. The Apply Changes button on the bottom right will become active. Click it to install the selected package. You can check several packages first and then click Apply Changes to install them all at once.

Figure 4-15: Add/Remove Applications package manager

To uninstall a package, click its check box. You will see its check mark disappear. Then click Apply Changes to perform the removal. You can uncheck several before clicking Apply Changes, and the remove them all at once.

APT is integrated as the primary install packages tool. When you install a package with Add/Remove Applications, APT will be invoked and it will automatically select and download the package from the appropriate online repository.

The packages listed in Add/Remove Applications are set up using the app-install-data packages. These are accessibly through the Synaptic Package Manager. The app-install-data and app-install-data-partner packages will already be installed. These list the commonly used packages on the Ubuntu repository. In addition you can install the app-install-data-edubuntu package to list edubuntu educational packages. If you have set up Medibuntu.org repository access, you can install the **app-install-data-medibuntu** package to list software applications on the Medibuntu.org repository.

Gdebi

Gdebi is designed to perform an installation of a single DEB software package. These are usually packages that are downloaded directly from a Web site and have few or no dependent packages. When you use your browser to download a particular package, you will be prompted to open it with Gdebi when the download is finished. Gdebi will install the package for you; displaying information about the package and checking to see if it is compatible with your system (see Figure 4-16). It is advisable to always use Gdebi to install a manually downloaded package.

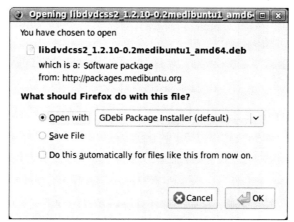

Figure 4-16: Web browser prompt with Gdebi selected

You could also first download the package, and then later select it from your GNOME nautilus window. Double clicking should open the package with Gdebi. You can also right-click and choose to open it with Gdebi. Gdebi can be started directly from Applications | System Tools | Gdebi Package Installer (this menu item is turned off by default, use System | Preferences | Main Menu to have it displayed).

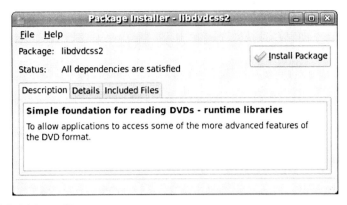

Figure 4-17: Gdebi installer

In Figure 4-17, The Gdebi tool is opened for a download of the **libdvdcss2** library, the codec for DVD Video. The package is part of the Medibuntu.org repository, but if you did not configure access to that repository, you can use your Web browser to download and install packages directly with Gdebi (**http://packages.medibuntu.org/jaunty/**).

Once downloaded Gdebi display the package name and status. There are tabs for Description, Details, and Included Files. Status will indicate if any dependent files are needed. You can then click the Install Package button to install the package. The package file will first be downloaded, along with any dependent packages, and then installed (see Figure 4-18). With some packages, like Google Earth, the terminal segment will open and prompt you to access the license. Once installed, the If you did previously configure access to that repository, you will be warned to use that software channel instead, using **apt-get** or the Synaptic Package Manager to install.

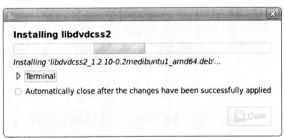

Figure 4-18: Gdebi install progress

Computer Janitor

The Computer Janitor application is designed to detect unused software packages on your system. These are usually packages installed as additional dependent packages that where selected automatically when you installed a particular package. If you later remove a package, not all the dependent packages may also be removed. As your install and remove packages, unused dependent package may pile up, remaining on your system and using space, while no longer needed. Computer Janitor is also useful if you upgrade your system instead of performing a clean install. Computer Janitor will detect the unused packages from the previous release, letting you remove them easily.

Computer janitor will detect unused packages and let you remove them (see Figure 4-19). It will also suggest any configuration changes, fixing configuration files like the GRUB **menu.lst** file. For example, you may have removed old kernels without updating the menu.lst file to remove their entries. Computer Janitor will correctly edit your **menu.lst** file for you, removing the old kernel entries. When editing the **menu.lst** file, Computer Janitor will not edit the default number. If you had previously changed this to make a specific kernel or other operating system your default, you may have to edit your **menu.lst** file to change the default number so that it lines up again, taking into account the kernel entries that Computer Janitor removed for you.

You can access Computer Janitor from System | Administration | Computer Janitor. You will be prompted to enter your password.

The packages detected for removal will be listed. You can un-check the ones you want to keep. All will be selected initially. If you are unsure of a package, uncheck it. Click the Cleanup button to remove the selected packages.

Figure 4-19: Computer Janitor

Before the packages are removed, you are prompted to re-consider, warning you that removing needed packages can break some of your system's capability. Use this tool carefully. If there are not that many unused packages on your system, you may want to leave them alone.

Software Package Types

Ubuntu uses Debian compliant software packages (DEB) that will have a **.deb** extension. Other packages, such as those in the form of source code that you need to compile, may come in a variety of compressed archives. These commonly have the extension **.tar.gz**, **.tgz**, or **.tar.bz2**. Packages with the **.rpm** extension are Red Hat Package software packages used on Red Hat, Fedora, SuSE and other Linux distributions that use RPM packages. They are not compatible directly with Ubuntu. You can use the alien command to convert most RPM packages to DEB packages that you can then install. Table 4-3 lists several common file extensions that you will find for the great variety of Linux software packages available to you. You can download any Ubuntu compliant deb package as well as the original source code package, as single files, directly from **packages.ubuntu.com**.

Extension	Package type
.deb	A Debian/Ubuntu Linux package
.gz	A **gzip**-compressed file (use **gunzip** to decompress)
.bz2	A **bzip2**-compressed file (use **bunzip2** to decompress; also use the **j** option with **tar**, as in **xvjf**)
.tar	A tar archive file (use **tar** with **xvf** to extract)
.tar.gz	A **gzip**-compressed **tar** archive file (use **gunzip** to decompress and **tar** to extract; use the **z** option with **tar**, as in **xvzf**, to both decompress and extract in one step)
.tar.bz2	A **bzip2**-compressed **tar** archive file (extract with **tar -xvzj**)
.tz	A **tar** archive file compressed with the **compress** command
.Z	A file compressed with the **compress** command (use the **decompress** command to decompress)
.bin	A self-extracting software file
.rpm	A software package created with the Red Hat Software Package Manager, used on Fedora, Red Hat, Centos, and SuSE distributions

Table 4-3: Linux Software Package File Extensions

Managing non-repository packages with dpkg

You can use **dpkg** to install a software package you have already downloaded directly, not with an APT enabled software tool like **apt-get** or **Synaptic**. In this case you are not installing from a repository. Instead, you have manually downloaded the package file from a Web or FTP site to a folder on your system. Such a situation would be rare, reserved for software not available on the Ubuntu or any APT enabled repository. Keep in mind that most software is already on your Ubuntu or an APT enabled repository. Check there first before performing a direct download and install with **dpkg**. The **dpkg** configuration files are located in the **/etc/dpkg** directory. Configuration is held in the **dpkg.cfg** file. See the **dpkg** man page for a detailed listing of **dpkg** options.

One situation where you would use dpkg, is for packages you have built yourself, like those created when converting a package in another format to a Debian package. This is the case when converting a RPM package (Red Hat Package Manager) to a Debian package format.

For **dpkg**, you use the **-i** option to install a package and **-r** to remove it.

```
sudo dpkg -i package.deb
```

The major failing for **dpkg** is that it provides no dependency support. It will inform you of needed dependencies, but you will have to install them separately. **dpkg** installs only the specified package. It is ideal for packages that have no dependencies.

You use the **-I** option to obtain package information directly from the DEB package file.

```
sudo dpkg -I package.deb
```

To remove a package you use the **-r** option with the package software name. You do not need version or extension information like **.386** or **.deb**. With **dpkg**, when removing a package with dependencies, you first have to remove all its dependencies manually. You will not be able to uninstall the package until you do. Configuration files are not removed.

```
sudo dpkg -r packagename
```

If you install a package that requires dependencies, and then fail to also install these dependencies, then your install database will be marked as having broken packages. In this case APT will not allow new packages to be installed until the broken packages are fixed. You can enter the **apt-get** command with the **-f** and install options. This will fix all broken packages at once.

```
sudo apt-get -f install
```

Installing Software from Compressed Archives: .tar.gz

Linux software applications in the form of source code are available at different sites on the Internet. You can download any of this software and install it on your system. Recent releases are often available in the form of compressed archive files. Applications will always be downloadable as compressed archives if they don't have an RPM version. This is particularly true for the recent versions of GNOME or KDE packages. RPM packages are only intermittently generated.

Decompressing and Extracting Software in One Step

Though you can decompress and extract software in separate operations, you will find that the more common approach is to perform both actions with a single command. The `tar` utility provides decompression options you can use to have `tar` first decompress a file for you, invoking the specified decompression utility. The `z` option automatically invokes `gunzip` to unpack a `.gz` file, and the `j` option unpacks a `.bz2` file. Use the `z` option for `.z` files. For example, to combine the decompressing and unpacking operation for a `tar.gz` file into one `tar` command, insert a `z` option to the option list, `xzvf` (see the later section "Extracting Software" for a discussion of these options). The next example shows how you can combine decompression and extraction in one step:

```
tar xvzf antigrav_0.0.3.orig.tar.gz
```

For a `.bz2`-compressed archive, you use the `j` option instead of the `z` option.

```
tar xvjf antigrav_0.0.3.orig.tar.bz2
```

Decompressing Software Separately

Many software packages under development or designed for cross-platform implementation may not be in an RPM format. Instead, they may be archived and compressed. The filenames for these files end with the extension **.tar.gz**, **.tar.bz2**, or **.tar.Z**. The different extensions indicate different decompression methods using different commands: `gunzip` for **.gz**, `bunzip2` for **.bz2**, and `decompress` for **.Z**. In fact, most software with an RPM format also has a corresponding **.tar.gz** format. After you download such a package, you must first decompress it and then unpack it with the `tar` command. The compressed archives can hold either source code that you then need to compile or, as is the case with Java packages, binaries that are ready to run.

A *compressed archive* is an archive file created with `tar` and then compressed with a compression tool like `gzip`. To install such a file, you must first decompress it with a decompression utility like `gunzip` utility and then use `tar` to extract the files and directories making up the software package. Instead of the `gunzip` utility, you could also use `gzip -d`. The next example decompresses the **antigrav_0.0.3.orig.tar.gz** file, replacing it with a decompressed version called **antigrav_0.0.3.orig.tar**:

```
ls
 antigrav_0.0.3.orig.gz
gunzip antigrav_0.0.3.orig.tar.gz
ls
 antigrav_0.0.3.orig.tar
```

You can download compressed archives from many different sites, including those mentioned previously. Downloads can be accomplished with FTP clients such as NcFTP and gFTP or with any web browser. Once downloaded, any file that ends with **.Z**, **.bz2**, **.zip**, or **.gz** is a compressed file that must be decompressed.

For files ending with **.bz2**, you use the `bunzip2` command. The following example decompresses a **bz2** version:

```
ls
 antigrav_0.0.3.orig.tar.bz2
bunzip2 antigrav_0.0.3.orig.tar.bz2
ls
antigrav_0.0.3.orig.tar
```

Files ending with **.bin** are self-extracting archives. Run the bin file as if it were a command. You may have to use `chmod` to make it executable.

Selecting an Install Directory

Before you unpack the archive, move it to the directory where you want it. Source code packages are often placed in a directory like **/usr/local/src**, and binary packages go in designated directories. When source code files are unpacked, they generate their own subdirectories from which you can compile and install the software. Once the package is installed, you can delete this directory, keeping the original source code package file (**.tar.gz**).

Packages that hold binary programs ready to run, like Java, are meant to be extracted in certain directories. Usually this is the **/usr/local** directory. Most archives, when they unpack, create a subdirectory named with the application name and its release, placing all those files or directories making up the software package into that subdirectory. For example, the file **antigrav_0.0.3.orig.tar** unpacks to a subdirectory called **antigrav_0.0.3.orig**. In certain cases, the software package that contains precompiled binaries is designed to unpack directly into the system subdirectory where it will be used.

Extracting Software

First, use `tar` with the `t` option to check the contents of the archive. If the first entry is a directory, then when you extract the archive, that directory is created and the extracted files are placed in it. If the first entry is not a directory, you should first create one and then copy the archive file to it. Then extract the archive within that directory. If no directory exists as the first entry, files are extracted to the current directory. You must create a directory yourself to hold these files.

```
tar tvf antigrav_0.0.3.orig.tar
```

Now you are ready to extract the files from the tar archive. You use `tar` with the `x` option to extract files, the `v` option to display the pathnames of files as they are extracted, and the `f` option, followed by the name of the archive file:

```
tar xvf antigrav_0.0.3.orig.tar
```

You can also decompress and extract in one step using the **-z** option for **gz** files and **-j** for **bz2** files.

```
tar xvzf antigrav_0.0.3.orig.tar.gz
```

The extraction process creates a subdirectory consisting of the name and release of the software. In the preceding example, the extraction created a subdirectory called **antigrav_0.0.3.orig**. You can change to this subdirectory and examine its files, such as the **README** and **INSTALL** files.

```
cd antigrav_0.0.3.orig
```

Installation of your software may differ for each package. Instructions are usually provided along with an installation program. Be sure to consult the **README** and **INSTALL** files, if included. See the following section on compiling software for information on how to create and install the application on your system.

Compiling Software

Some software may be in the form of source code that you need to compile before you can install it. This is particularly true of programs designed for cross-platform implementations. Programs designed to run on various Unix systems, such as Sun, as well as on Linux, may be distributed as source code that is downloaded and compiled in those different systems. Compiling such software has been greatly simplified in recent years by the use of configuration scripts that automatically detect a given system's hardware and software configuration and then allow you to compile the program accordingly. For example, the name of the C compiler on a system could be `gcc` or `cc`. Configuration scripts detect which is present and select it for use in the program compilation.

Note: Some software will run using scripting languages like Python, instead of programming language code like C++. These may require only a setup operation (a setup command), not compiling. Once installed, they will run directly using the scripting language interpreter, like Python.

A configure script works by generating a customized Makefile, designed for that particular system. A Makefile contains detailed commands to compile a program, including any preprocessing, links to required libraries, and the compilation of program components in their proper order. Many Makefiles for complex applications may have to access several software subdirectories, each with separate components to compile. The use of configure and Makefile scripts vastly automates the compile process, reducing the procedure to a few simple steps.

First, change to the directory where the software's source code has been extracted:

```
# cd /usr/local/src/antigrav_0.0.3.orig
```

Before you compile software, read the **README** or **INSTALL** files included with it. These give you detailed instructions on how to compile and install this particular program.

Most software can be compiled and installed in three simple steps. Their fist step is the `./configure` command, which generates your customized Makefile. The second step is the **make** command, which uses a Makefile in your working directory (in this case, the Makefile you just generated with the `./configure` command) to compile your software. The final step also uses the **make** command, but this time with the `install` option. The Makefile generated by the `./configure` command also contains instructions for installing the software on your system. Using the `install` option runs just those installation commands. To perform the installation, you have to be logged in as the root user, giving you the ability to add software files to system directories as needed. If the software uses configuration scripts, compiling and installing usually involves only the following three simple commands:

```
./configure
make
make install
```

In the preceding example, the `./configure` command performs configuration detection. The **make** command performs the actual compiling, using a Makefile script generated by the `./configure` operation. The **make install** command installs the program on your system, placing the executable program in a directory, such as **/usr/local/bin**, and any configuration files in **/etc**. Any shared libraries it created may go into **/usr/local/lib**.

Once you have compiled and installed your application, and you have checked that it is working properly, you can remove the source code directory that was created when you extracted the software. You can keep the archive file (**tar**) in case you need to extract the software again. Use **rm** with the **-rf** options so that all subdirectories will be deleted and you do not have to confirm each deletion.

Tip: Be sure to remember to place the period and slash before the **configure** command. The `./` references a command in the current working directory, rather than another Linux command with the same name.

Configure Command Options

Certain software may have specific options set up for the `./configure` operation. To find out what these are, you use the `./configure` command with the `--help` option:

```
./configure --help
```

A useful common option is the `-prefix` option, which lets you specify the install directory:

```
./configure -prefix=/usr/bin
```

Tip: Some older X applications use `xmkmf` directly instead of a configure script to generate the needed Makefile. Although `xmkmf` has been officially replaced, in this case, enter the command `xmkmf` in place of `./configure`. Be sure to consult the **INSTALL** and **README** files for the software.

Development Libraries

If you are compiling an X, GNOME, or KDE-based program, be sure their development libraries have been installed. For X applications, be sure the `xmkmf` program is also installed. If you chose a standard install when you installed your distribution system, these most likely were not installed. For distributions using RPM packages, these come in the form of a set of development RPM packages, usually with the word "development" or "develop" in their names. You need to install those using `rpm`. GNOME, in particular, has an extensive set of RPM packages for development libraries. Many X applications need special shared libraries. For example, some applications may need the `xforms` library or the `qt` library. Some of these you may need to obtain from online sites.

Shared and Static Libraries

Libraries can be static, shared, or dynamic. A *static* library is one whose code is incorporated into the program when it is compiled. A *shared* library, however, has its code loaded for access whenever the program is run. When compiled, such a program simply notes the libraries it needs. Then when the program is run, that library is loaded and the program can access its functions. A *dynamic* library is a variation on a shared library. Like a shared library, it can be loaded when the program is run. However, it does not actually load until instructions in the program tell it to. It can also be unloaded as the program runs, and another library can be loaded in its place. Shared and dynamic libraries make for much smaller code. Instead of a program including the library as part of its executable file, it only needs a reference to it.

Libraries made available on your system reside in the **/usr/lib** and **/lib** directories. The names of these libraries always begin with the prefix **lib** followed by the library name and a suffix. The suffix differs, depending on whether it is a static or shared library. A shared library has the extension **.so** followed by major and minor version numbers. A static library simply has the **.a** extension. A further distinction is made for shared libraries in the old **a.out** format. These have the extension **.sa**. The syntax for the library name is the following:

```
libname.so.major.minor
libname.a
```

The *name* can be any string, and it uniquely identifies a library. It can be a word, a few characters, or even a single letter. The name of the shared math library is **libm.so.5**, where the math library is uniquely identified by the letter **m** and the major version is **5**, and **libm.a** is the static math library. The name of the X Window library is **libX11.so.6**, where the X Window library is uniquely identified with the letters **X11** and its major version is 6.

Most shared libraries are found in the **/usr/lib** and **/lib** directories. These directories are always searched first. Some shared libraries are located in special directories of their own. A listing of these is placed in the **/etc/ld.conf** configuration file. These directories will also be searched for a given library. By default, Linux first looks for shared libraries, then static ones. Whenever a shared library is updated or a new one installed, you need to run the `ldconfig` command to update its entries in the **/etc/ld.conf** file as well as links to it (if you install from an RPM package, this is usually done for you).

Checking Software Package Digital Signatures

One very effective use for digital signatures is to verify that a software package has not been tampered with. A software package could be intercepted in transmission and some of its system-level files changed or substituted. Software packages from your distribution, as well as those by reputable GNU and Linux projects, are digitally signed. The signature provides modification digest information with which to check the integrity of the package. The digital signature may be included with the package file or posted as a separate file. To import a key that APT can use to check a software package, you use the **apt-key** command. APT will automatically check for digital signatures. To check the digital signature of a software package file that is not part of the APT repository system, you use the `gpg` command with the `--verify` option. These would include packages like those made available as compressed archives, **.tar.gz**, whereas APT can check all DEB packages itself.

Importing Software Public keys with apt-key

First, however, you will need to make sure that you have the signer's public key. The digital signature was encrypted with the software distributor's private key; that distributor is the signer. Once you have that signer's public key, you can check any data you receive from them. In the case of third party software repositories, you have to install their public key. Once the key is installed, you do not have to install it again.

Ubuntu includes and installs its public keys with its distribution. For any packages on the Ubuntu repositories, the needed public keys are already installed and checked by APT automatically. For other sites, like Wine (the Linux Windows emulator), you may need to download the public key from their site and install it (**www.winehq.org**). You may also have to add repository support to access their Ubuntu compatible software. The Wine public key is available from winhq.org, with the public key for Ubuntu located at **wine.budgetdedicated.com/apt/387EE263.gpg** You could download the public key and then install it on your system with the apt-key command.

```
wget -q http://wine.budgetdedicated.com/apt/387EE263.gpg
```

Once downloaded you can then use the **apt-key** command to install the pubic key for use by APT in software verification. Ubuntu uses the **apt-key** command to maintain public keys for software packages. Use the **apt-key** command with the **add** option to add the key.

```
sudo apt-key add 387EE263.gpg
```

You can combine both operations into one as:

```
wget -q http://wine.budgetdedicated.com/apt/387EE263.gpg -O- | sudo apt-key add -
```

To actually access the software repository you would have to also install its APT configuration file in the **/etc/apt/sources.list.d** directory. For wine this is named **winehq.ist**. Check the Wine site for download instructions.

Checking Software Compressed Archives

Many software packages in the form of compressed archives, **.tar.gz** or **tar.bz2**, will provide signatures in separate files that end with the **.sig** extension. To check these, you use the `gpg` command with the `--verify` option. For example, the most recent Sendmail package is distributed in the form of a compressed archive, **.tar.gz**. Its digital signature is provided in a separate **.sig** file. First you download and install the public key for Sendmail software obtained from the Sendmail website (the key may have the year as part of its name). Sendmail has combined all its keys into one armored text file, **PGPKEYS**.

```
gpg --import PGPKEYS
```

You can also use the **gpg** command with the **--search-key** and **--keyserver** options to import the key. Keys matching the search term will be displayed in a numbered list. You will be prompted to enter the number of the key you want. The 2007 Sendmail key from the results from the following example would be 7. This is the key used for 2007 released software.

```
gpg  --keyserver pgp.mit.edu  --search-keys Sendmail
```

Instead of using **gpg**, you could use Encryptions and Password Keys application to find and import the key (Applications | Accessories | Encryption and Password Keys).

To check a software archive, a **tar.gz**, file, you need to also download its digital signature files. For the compressed archive (**.tar.gz**) you can use the **.sig** file ending in **.gz.sig**, and for the uncompressed archive use **.tar.sig**. Then, with the `gpg` command and the `--verify` option, use the digital signature in the **.sig** file to check the authenticity and integrity of the software compressed archive.

```
$ gpg --verify sendmail.8.14.2.tar.gz.sig sendmail.8.14.2.tar.gz
gpg: Signature made Wed 31 Oct 2007 08:23:07 PM PDT using RSA key ID 7093B841
gpg: Good signature from "Sendmail Signing Key/2007 <sendmail@Sendmail.ORG>"$
```

You can also specify just the signature file, and `gpg` will automatically search for and select a file of the same name, but without the **.sig** or **.asc** extension.

```
gpg --verify sendmail.8.14.2.tar.gz.sig
```

In the future, when you download any software from the Sendmail site that uses this key, you just have to perform the `--verify` operation. Bear in mind, though, that different software packages from the same site may use different keys. You will have to make sure that you have imported and signed the appropriate key for the software you are checking.

Tip: You can use the `--fingerprint` option to check a key's validity if you wish. If you are confident that the key is valid, you can then sign it with the `--sign-key` command.

Installing Source Code Applications

Many programs are available for Linux in source code format. These programs are stored in a compressed archive that you need to decompress and then extract. The resulting source code can then be configured, compiled, and installed on your system. The process has been simplified to the extent that it involves not much more than installing an RPM package. The following example shows the common method to extract, compile, and install software, in this case the freeciv program, a linux game. Always check the included README and INSTALL files that come with the source code to check the appropriate method for creating and installing that software.

Tip: Be sure that you have installed all development packages onto your system. Development packages contain the key components such as the compiler, GNOME and KDE headers and libraries, and preprocessors. You cannot compile source code software without them.

First you locate the software—in this example, from **www.linuxgames.com**—and then you download it to your system. freeciv is downloaded in a file named - **freeciv-2.1.8.tar.bz2**. Then decompress and extract the file either with the Archive Manager on the desktop, or with the `tar` command in a terminal window.

Extracting the Archive: Archive Manager (File Roller)

The easiest way to extract compressed archives is to use the Archive Manager (Applications | Accessories | Archive Manager) on GNOME (Archive Manager is the fileroller application). Either double-click the compressed archive file, or right-click and select Open With "Archive Manager". This displays the top-level contents of the archive, which you can browse if you wish, even reading text files like README and INSTALL files. You can also see what files will actually be installed. Use the button to navigate and double-click a directory to open it. Nothing is extracted at this point. To extract the archive, click Extract. You will be able to select what directory to extract to, the default will be a subdirectory in the current one (see Figure 4-20).

Archive Manager will let you actually read text files in the archive directly. Just select and double click the text file from its listing in the Archive manager window. Archive Manager will extract the file on the fly and display it in window (see Figure 4-21). The file is not actually extracted anywhere at this point.

You can also use Archive manager to create your own archives, creating an archive with the New button and then selecting files and folders for it with the Add File and Add Folder buttons.

Alternatively, on a command line, you can use the `tar` command to extract archives. To use the `tar` command, first open a terminal window (right-click on the desktop and select Open Terminal). At the prompt, enter the `tar` command with the **xvjf** options (**j** for **bz2** and **z** for **gz**), as shown here:

```
tar xvjf freeciv-2.1.8.tar.bz2
```

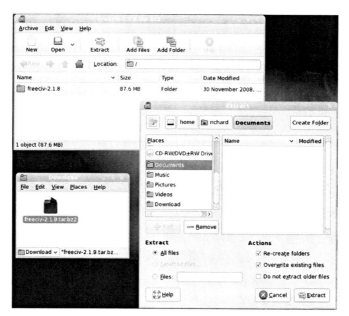

Figure 4-20: Archive Manager (File Roller) to exact software archive.

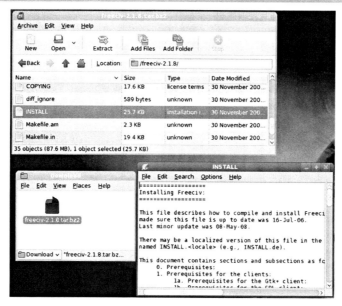

Figure 4-21: Archive Manager displaying archive text file.

Configure, Compile, and Install

Extracting the archive will create a directory with the name of the software, in this case **freeciv-2.1-4**. Once it is extracted, you have to configure, compile, and install the software. This usually needs to be done from a terminal window.

Change to the software directory with the **cd** command:

```
cd freeciv-2.1-4
```

Issue the command **./configure**. This generates a compiler configuration for your particular system (creates a custom Makefile).

```
./configure
```

Compile the software with the **make** command:

```
make
```

Then install the program with the **make install** command:

```
make install
```

Most KDE and GNOME supported software will also place an entry for the program in the appropriate menus—for example, a freeciv entry will be placed in the KDE Applications menu. You can then run freeciv from the menu entry. You could also open a terminal window and enter the program's name.

5. System Information

System Logs: /var/log and rsyslogd

GNOME Log Viewer

The Linux Auditing System: auditd

Disk Usage Analyzer

GNOME System Monitor

Managing Proceses

Performance Analysis Tools and Processes

Information about your system is provided by system logs and performance analysis tools. These include the new Reliable and Extended Syslog logging application and a variety of performance tools like the GNOME System Monitor and the Disk Usage Analyzer.

System Logs: /var/log and rsyslogd

Various system logs for tasks performed on your system are stored in the **/var/log** directory. Here you can find logs for mail, news, and all other system operations, such as Web server logs. The **/var/log/messages** file is a log of all system tasks not covered by other logs. This usually includes startup tasks, such as loading drivers and mounting file systems. If a driver for a card failed to load at startup, you find an error message for it here. Logins are also recorded in this file, showing you who attempted to log in to what account. The **/var/log/maillog** file logs mail message transmissions and news transfers.

System logging is handled by the Reliable and Extended Syslog service, using the **rsyslogd** daemon. This replaces the older syslogd service. Configuration is now in the **/etc/rsyslog.conf** file. See **www.rsyslog.com** and the rsyslog documentation in **/usr/share/doc/rsyslog***. This documentation folder contains extensive Web page documentation on rsyslog.

GNOME Log Viewer

To view these logs you can use the GNOME Log Viewer, System | Administration | Log File Viewer. A side panel lists different logs. Selecting one will display the log on the panel to the right.   For **/var/log/messages**, select **messages**. You can also choose to display messages in this file just for a specific date (see Figure 5-1).

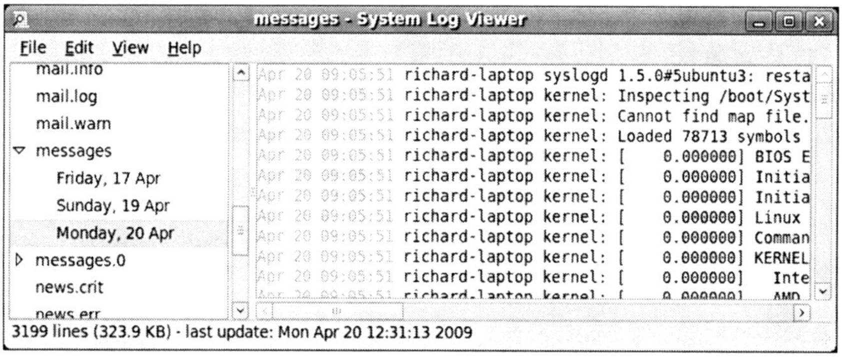

Figure 5-1: GNOME System Log Viewer

rsyslogd and /etc/rsyslog.conf

The **rsyslogd** daemon manages all the logs on your system, as well as coordinating with any of the logging operations of other systems on your network. Configuration information for **rsyslogd** is held in the **/etc/rsyslog.conf** file, which contains the names and locations for your system log files. Here you find entries for **/var/log/messages** and **/var/log/maillog**, among others. Whenever you make changes to the rsyslog.conf file, you need to restart the **rsyslogd** daemon using the following command (or use services-admin, System | Administration | Services):

```
service syslog restart
```

Facilities	Description
`auth-priv`	Security/authorization messages (private)
`cron`	Clock daemon (cron and at) messages
`daemon`	Other system daemon messages
`kern`	Kernel messages
`lpr`	Line printer subsystem messages
`mail`	Mail subsystem messages
`news`	Usenet news subsystem messages
`syslog`	Syslog internal messages
`user`	Generic user-level messages
`uucp`	UUCP subsystem messages
`local0` through `local7`	Reserved for local use
priorities	**Description**
`debug`	7, Debugging messages, lowest priority
`info`	6, Informational messages
`notice`	5, Notifications, normal, but significant, condition
`warning`	4, Warnings
`err`	3, Error messages
`crit`	2, Critical conditions
`alert`	1, Alerts, action must be taken immediately
`emerg`	0, Emergency messages, system is unusable
Operators	**Description**
`*`	Matches all facilities or priorities in a sector
`=`	Restrict to a specified priority
`!`	Exclude specified priority and higher ones
`/`	A file to save messages to
`@`	A host to send messages to
`|`	A FIFO pipe to send messages to

Table 5-1: rsyslogd Facilities, Priorities, and Operators

Entries in rsyslogd.conf

An entry in **rsyslog.conf** consists of two fields: a *selector* and an *action* (rsyslog uses the same selectors as the older syslog, maintaining compatibility). The selector is the kind of service to be logged, such as mail or news, and the action is the location where messages are to be placed. The action is usually a log file, but it can also be a remote host or a pipe to another program. The kind of service is referred to as a *facility.* The **rsyslogd** daemon has several terms it uses to specify certain kinds of service (see Table 5-1). A facility can be further qualified by a priority. A *priority* specifies the kind of message generated by the facility; **rsyslogd** uses several designated terms to indicate different priorities. A *selector* is constructed from both the facility and the priority, separated by a period. For example, to save error messages generated by mail systems, you use a sector consisting of the `mail` facility and the `err` priority, as shown here:

```
mail.err
```

To save these messages to the **/var/log/maillog** file, you specify that file as the action, giving you the following entry:

```
mail.err /var/log/maillog
```

The **rsyslogd** daemon also supports the use of * as a matching character to match either all the facilities or all the priorities in a sector: `cron.*` would match on all **cron** messages no matter what the priority, `*.err` would match on error messages from all the facilities, and `*.*` would match on all messages. The following example saves all mail messages to the **/var/log/maillog** file and all critical messages to the **/var/log/mycritical** file:

```
mail.* /var/log/maillog
*.crit /var/log/mycritical
```

Priorities

When you specify a priority for a facility, all messages with a higher priority are also included. The `err` priority also includes the `crit`, `alert`, and `emerg` priorities. If you just want to select the message for a specific priority, you qualify the priority with the = operator. For example, `mail.=err` will select only error messages, not `crit`, `alert`, or `emerg` messages. You can also restrict priorities with the ! operator. This will eliminate messages with the specified priority and higher. For example, `mail.!crit` will exclude `crit` messages, as well as the higher `alert` and `emerg` messages. To specifically exclude all the messages for an entire facility, you use the `none` priority; for instance, `mail.none` excludes all mail messages. This is usually used when you're defining several sectors in the same entry.

You can list several priorities or facilities in a given sector by separating them with commas. You can also have several sectors in the same entry by separating them with semicolons. The first example saves to the **/var/log/messages** file all messages with `info` priority, excluding all mail and authentication messages (`authpriv`). The second saves all `crit` messages and higher for the **uucp** and **news** facilities to the **/var/log/spooler** file:

```
*.info;mail.none;news.none;authpriv.none /var/log/messages
uucp,news.crit /var/log/spooler
```

Actions and Users

In the action field, you can specify files, remote systems, users, or pipes. An action entry for a file must always begin with a / and specify its full pathname, such as **/var/log/messages**. To log messages to a remote host, you simply specify the hostname preceded by an @ sign. The following example saves all kernel messages on **rabbit.trek.com**:

```
kern.*  @rabbit.trek.com
```

To send messages to users, you list their login names. The following example will send critical news messages to the consoles for the users **chris** and **aleina**:

```
news.=crit chris,aleina
```

You can also output messages to a named pipe (FIFO). The pipe entry for the action field begins with a |. The following example pipes kernel debug messages to the named pipe **|/usr/adm/debug**:

```
kern.=debug |/usr/adm/debug
```

An Example for /etc/rsyslog.conf

The default **/etc/rsyslog.conf** file for Ubuntu systems is shown here. Messages are logged to various files in the **/var/log** directory.

/etc/rsyslog.conf

```
# Log all kernel messages to the console.
kern.*                          /dev/console
# Log anything (except mail) of level info or higher.
# Don't log private authentication messages!
*.info;mail.none;news.none;authpriv.none;cron.none      /var/log/messages

# The authpriv file has restricted access.
authpriv.*                      /var/log/secure
# Log all the mail messages in one place.
mail.*                          /var/log/maillog
# Log cron stuff.
cron.*                          /var/log/cron
# Everybody gets emergency messages
*.emerg                                 *
# Save mail and news errors of level err and higher in a special file.
uucp,news.crit                  /var/log/spooler
# Save boot messages also to boot.log
local7.*                        /var/log/boot.log
```

The Linux Auditing System: auditd

The Linux Auditing System provides system call auditing. The auditing is performed by a server called **auditd**, with logs saved to the **/var/log/audit** directory. It is designed to compliment SELinux which saves its messages to the **auditd** log in **/var/log/audit/audit.log** file. The audit logging service provides specialize logging for services like SELinux. Logs are located at

/var/log/audit. To refine the auditing, you can create audit rules to check certain system calls like those generated by a specific user or group.

You can use **/etc/init.d/auditd** service script to start up and shutdown the **auditd** server. Use services-admin or the **service** command to start and stop the server.

```
sudo service auditd start
```

Configuration for auditd is located in both the **/etc/audit/auditd.conf** and the **/etc/sysconfig/auditd** files. Primary configuration is handled with **/etc/audit/auditd.conf** where options like the log file name, log format, the maximum size of log files, and actions to take when disk space diminishes. See the auditd.conf man page for a detailed description of all options. The **/etc/sysconfig/auditd** file sets server start up options and locale location like **en_US**.

The audit package includes the auditd server and three commands: **autrace**, **ausearch**, and **auditctl**. You use **ausearch** to query the audit logs. You can search by various ids, process, user, group, or event, as well as by filename or even time or date. Check the **ausearch** man page for a complete listing. autrace is a specialized tool that lets you trace a specific process. It operates similar to strace, recording the system calls and actions of a particular process.

You can control the behavior of the **auditd** server with the **auditctl** tool. With **auditctl** you can turn auditing on an off., check the status, and add audit rules for specific events. Check the **auditctl** man page for a detailed description.

Audit rules are organized into pre-determined lists with a specific set of actions for system calls. Currently there are three lists: task, entry, and exit, and three actions: never, always, and possible. When adding a rule, the list and action are paired, separated by a comma, as in:

```
exit,always
```

To add a rule you use the **-a** option. With the **-S** option you can specify a particular system call, and with the **-F** option specify a field. There are several possible fields you can use such as loginuid (user login id), pid (process id), and exit (system call exit value). For a field you specify a value, such as **longinuid=510** for the user with a user login id of 510. The following rule, as described in the documentation, checks all files opened by a particular user.

```
auditctl -a exit,always  -S open -F loginuid=510
```

Place rules you want loaded automatically in the **/etc/audit/auditd.rules**. The **sample.rules** file in **/usr/share/doc/auditd*** directory lists rule examples. You can also create a specific file of audit rules and use **auditctl** with the **-R** option to read the rules from it.

GNOME System Monitor

Ubuntu provides the GNOME System Monitor for displaying system information and monitoring system processes, accessible from System | Administration | System Monitor. There are four panels; one for system information, one for processes, one for resources, and one for file systems (see Figure 12-1). The System panel shows the amount of memory, available disk space, and the type of CPU on your system. The Resources panel displays graphs for CPU, Memory and Swap memory, and Network usage.

Your File Systems panel lists your file systems, where they are mounted, and their type, as well as the amount of disk space used and how much is free. The Processes panel lists your processes, letting you sort or search for processes. You can use field buttons to sort by name, process ID, user, and memory. The View pop-up menu lets you select all processes, just your own, or active processes. You can easily stop any process by selecting it and then clicking the End Process button. Right-clicking an item displays actions you can take on the process such as stopping or hiding it. The Memory Maps display, selected from the View menu, shows information on virtual memory, inodes, and flags.

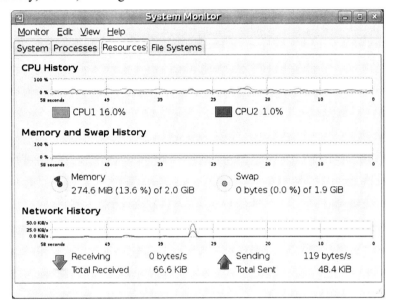

Figure 5-3: GNOME System Monitor: Resources

The Resources tab displays graphs for CPU, Memory and Swap memory, and Network usage. Your File Systems panel lists your file systems, where they are mounted, and their type, as well as the amount of disk space used and how much is free. The Processes tab lists your processes, letting you sort or search for processes. You can use field buttons to sort by name, process ID, user, and memory. The View pop-up menu lets you select all processes, just your own, or active processes. You can easily stop any process by selecting it and then clicking the End Process button. Right-clicking an item displays actions you can take on the process such as stopping or ending it. The Memory Maps display, selected from the View menu, shows information on virtual memory, inodes, and flags.

Managing Processes

Should you have to force a process or application to quit, you can use the Gnome System Monitor Processes tab to find, select, and stop the process. You should be sure of the process you want to stop. Ending a critical process could cripple your system. Application processes will bear the name of the application, and you can use those to force an application to quit. Ending processes manually is usually preformed for open ended operations that you are unable to stop normally. In Figure 5-4, the firefox application has been selected. Clicking the End Process button on the lower right will then force the Firefox Web browser to end (you can also right-click on the entry and select End process from the pop-up menu).

The Edit menu provides several other options for managing a selected process. You can also right-click on a process entry to display a pop-up menu with the same options. There are corresponding keyboard keys for each option. The options are: stop, continue, end, kill, and change priority. The stop and continue operations work together. You can stop (pause) and process, and then later start it again with the continue option. The end process stops a process safely, whereas a kill option forces an immediate end to the process. The end process option is preferred, but if it does not work, you can use the kill process option. Change priority can give a process a lower or higher priority, letting run faster or slower.

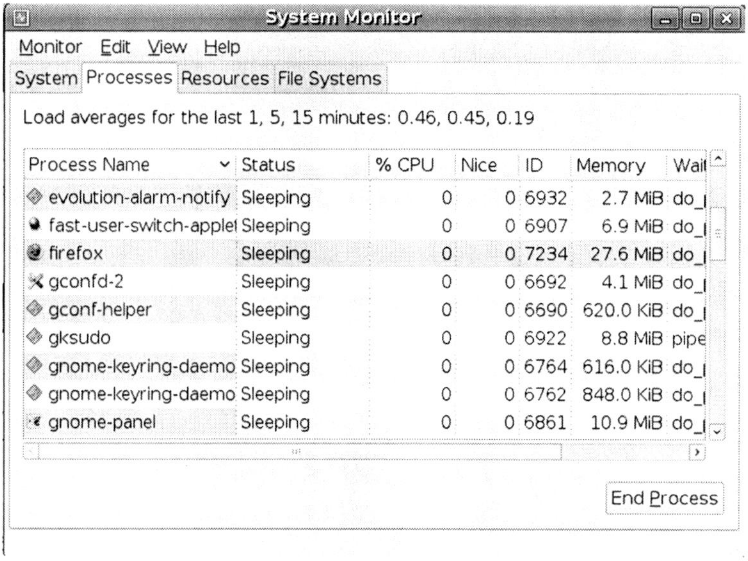

Figure 5-4: GNOME System Monitor, Processes tab

You can also use the kill command in a terminal window to end a process. The **kill** command takes as its argument a process number. Be sure you obtain the correct one. Use the **ps** command to display a process id. Entering in the incorrect process number could also cripple your system. The **ps** command with the **-C** option searches for a particular application name. The **-o** **pid=** will display only the process id, instead of the process id, time, application name, and tty. Once you have the process id, you can use the kill command with the process id as its argument to end the process.

```
$ ps -C firefox -o pid=
5555
$ kill 5555
```

One way to insure the correct number is to use the **ps** command to return the process number directly as an argument to a **kill** command. In the following example, an open ended process was started to record a program from channel 12 from a digital video broadcast device, using the **getatsc** command.

```
getatsc -dvb 0 12 > my.ts
```

The process is then stopped by first executing the **ps** command to obtain the process id for the **getatsc** process (backquotes), and then using that process id in the **kill** command to end the process.v The **-o pid=** option displays only the process id.

```
kill `ps -C getatsc -o pid=`
```

With the **-aux** option, you can list all processes. Piping the output to a `grep` command with a pattern enables you to search for a particular process. A pipe funnels the output of a preceding command as input to a following command. The following command lists all X Window System processes:

```
ps -aux | grep 'X'
```

Disk Usage Analyzer

The disk usage analyzer lets you see how much disk space is used and available on all your mounted hard disk partitions (see Figure 5-2). Applications | Accessories | Disk Usage Analyzer. It will also check all LVM and RAID arrays. Usage is shown in simple graph, letting you see how much overall space is available and where it is. You can scan your home directory (Scan Home), your entire file system (Scan Filesystem), a particular folder (Scan Folder), or a remote folder (Scan Remote Folder). When you scan a directory or the file system, disk usage for your directories is analyzed and displayed in the left pane along with a representational graph for the disk usage on the right pane. In the left listing, each files system is first shown with a graph for its usage, as well as its size and number of top-level directories and files. Then the directories are shown, along with their size and contents (files and directories).

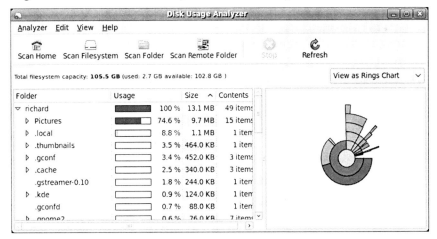

Figure 5-2: Disk Usage Analyzer, Applications | Accessories | Disk Usage Analyzer

On the right pane, the graph can be either a Ring Chart or a Treemap. The Ring Chart is the default. Choose the one you want from the View as drop down menu. For the Ring Chart, directories are show, starting with the top level directories at the center and moving out to the subdirectories. Passing your mouse over a section in the graph will display its directory name and disk usage, as well as all its subdirectories. The Treemap chart shows a box representation, with greater disk usage in larger boxes, and subdirectories encased within directory boxes.

Performance Analysis Tools and Processes

Linux treats each task performed on your system as a process, which is assigned a number and a name. You can examine these processes and even stop them. Ubuntu provides several tools for examining processes as well as your system performance. Easy monitoring is provided by the GNOME System Monitor (Applications | System Tools | System Monitor). Other tools are also available, such as GKrellM and KSysguard.

A number of utilities on your system provide detailed information on your processes, as well as other system information such as CPU and disk use (see Table 5-2). Although these tools were designed to be used on a shell command line, displaying output in text lines, several now have KDE and GNOME versions that provide a GUI interface for displaying results and managing processes.

Performance Tool	Description
`vmstat`	Performance of system components
`top`	Listing of most CPU-intensive processes
`free`	Listing of free RAM memory
`sar`	System activity information
`iostat`	Disk usage
GNOME System Monitor	System monitor for processes and usage monitoring (System | Administration | System Monitor)
GKrellM	Stackable, flexible, and extensible monitoring tool
KDE Performance Monitor	KDE system monitor for processes and usage monitoring
Frysk	Monitoring tool for system processes
System Tap	Tool to analyze performance bottlenecks
Gnome Power Manager	Manage power efficiency features of your system
cpuspeed	Implement CPU speed reduction (AMD Cool and Quiet).

Table 5-2: Performance Tools

vmstat, free, top, iostat, Xload, and sar

The `vmstat` command outputs a detailed listing indicating the performance of different system components, including CPU, memory, I/O, and swap operations. A report is issued as a line with fields for the different components. If you provide a time period as an argument, it repeats at the specified interval—usually a few seconds. The `top` command provides a listing of the processes on your system that are the most CPU intensive, showing what processes are using most of your resources. The listing is in real time and updated every few seconds. Commands are provided for changing a process's status, such as its priority.

The `free` command lists the amount of free RAM memory on your system, showing how much is used and how much is free, as well as what is used for buffers and swap memory. `Xload` is an X Window System tool showing the load, CPU, and memory, `iostat` displays your disk usage, and `sar` shows system activity information.

System Tap

System Tap is a diagnostic tool for providing information about complex system implementations. It essentially analyzes performance bottlenecks, letting you hone in on where a problem could be located. System Tap relies on Kprobes (Kernel Dynamic Probes) which allows kernel modules to set up simple probes.

KDE Task Manager and Performance Monitor (KSysguard)

Ubuntu also provides the KDE Task Manager and Performance Monitor, KSysguard, accessible from the System Tools menu as KDE System Guard only on the KDE desktop. This tool allows you to monitor the performance of your own system as well as remote systems. KSysguard can provide simple values or detailed tables for various parameters. A System Load panel provides graphical information about CPU and memory usage, and a Process Table list current processes using a tree format to show dependencies. You can design your own monitoring panels with worksheets, showing different types of values you want to display and the form you want to display them in, like a bar graph or digital meter. The Sensor Browser pane is an expandable tree of sensors for information like CPU System Load or Memory's Used Memory. There is a top entry for each host you are connected to, including your own, localhost. To design your own monitor, create a worksheet and drag and drop a sensor onto it.

6. Managing Users

You can add or remove users, as well as add and remove groups, and you can modify access rights and permissions for both users and groups. You also have access to system initialization files you can use to configure all user shells, and you have control over the default initialization files copied into a user account when it is first created. You can decide how new user accounts should be configured initially by configuring these files.

User Management with users-admin

Currently, the easiest and most effective way to add new users is to use the users-admin. tool. You can access it from the GNOME Desktop menu, System | Administration menu | Users and Groups entry. You will be prompted to enter you administrative password. The users-admin tool opens up with a Users Settings window listing users with their full name, login name, and home directory.

When you start up the users-admin application (System | Administration | Users and Groups), only read access is allowed, letting you scroll through the list of users, but not make any changes or add new ones (see Figure 6-1).

Read only access is provided to all users; before you can use **users-admin**, you have to unlock it. User entries will be grayed out. Users will be able to see the list of users on your system, but they cannot modify their entries, add new ones, or delete current users. Administrative access is required to perform these operations. Administrative access for the **users-admin** tool is controlled by PolicyKit. Click the Unlock button at the bottom of the window. This opens a prompt for you to enter your user password (see Figure 6-2). Then click the Authenticate button. User entries will no longer be grayed out.

After you unlock the users-admin, the Unlock button is grayed out, and you can now make changes (see Figure 6-3). The User Settings window will list users according with their icon, full name, and login name. The icon is the image each user chooses with their About Me tool in the System | Preferences menu. To the right are buttons for adding new users, deleting users, editing a user's properties, and managing groups. With administrative access granted, the bottom Unlock button will be grayed out.

New Users

To create a new user, click Add User in the Users Settings window. This opens a New user account window that displays four tabs, Account, Contact, User Privileges, and Advanced (see Figure 6-4). The Account has entries for the Username, Real Name, Profile, and password. The Read Name is the user's full name. The Profile entry is a pop-up menu listing Desktop user, Administrator, and Unprivileged. Administrator will allow the user to perform system wide configuration tasks. These users can use the administration tools and the sudo command to perform system-wide administration tasks. Desktop users do not have any kind of administration access. Unprivileged denies access to most resources, though online access is allowed. If operates much like a dumb terminal.

On the Contacts tab, you can add basic contact information if you wish for an office address, as well as work and home phones.

Figure 6-1: Users and Groups locked

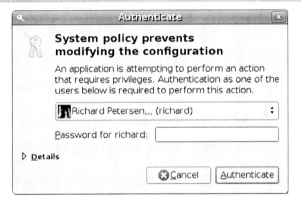

Figure 6-2: Policykit unlock prompt

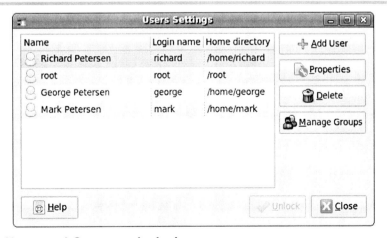

Figure 6-3: Users and Groups unlocked

On the User Privileges tab you can control device access as well as administrative access (see Figure 6-5). Here you can restrict or allow access to CD-ROMs, scanners, and external storage like USB drives. You can also determine if the user can perform administrative tasks. The "Administer the System" entry is left unchecked by default. If you want to allow the user to perform administration tasks, be sure to check this box.

The Advanced tab lets you select a home directory, the shell to use, a main group, and a user ID. Defaults will already be chosen for you. A home directory in the name of the new user will be specified and the shell used will be the BASH shell. Normally you would not want to change these settings, though you might prefer a different shell, like the C-Shell. For the group, the user will have a group with its own user name. In addition, the user will have access to all system resource groups like cdrom, audio, video, and scanner.

Figure 6-4: Users and Groups: Create New User

To later change settings, select the User in the User Settings window and click the Properties button. A four tabbed Account Properties window opens with the same Account, Contact, User Privileges, and Advanced tabs. To delete a user, select it and click the Delete button.

Alternatively, you can use the `useradd` command in a terminal window or command line to add user accounts and the `userdel` command to remove them. The following example adds the user **dylan** to the system:

```
$ useradd Dylan
```

Groups

To manage groups, click on the Manage Groups button. This opens a Group Settings window that lists all groups (see Figure 6-6). To add users to a group, select it and click Properties. In the Properties window, users will be listed and you can select the ones you want to add.

To add a new group, click on the Add Group button to open a New Group window where you can specify the group name, its id, and select users to add to the group.

To later add or remove users to or from a group, click on the group name in the Group settings window and click Properties. You can then check or uncheck users from the Group Members listing.

If you want to remove a user as member, click the check box to remove its check. Click OK to effect your changes. If you want to remove a group, just select its entry in the Groups panel and then click the Delete button.

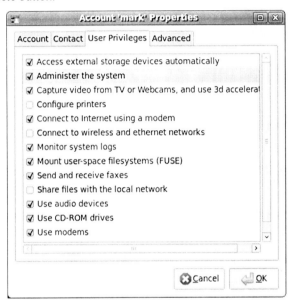

Figure 6-5: Users and Groups: User Privileges

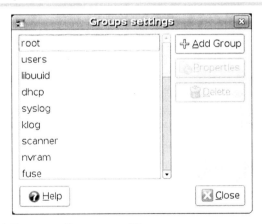

Figure 6-6: Users and Groups: Groups settings

You can also add groups to a user by selecting the user in the Users panel, and opening their Properties window. Then select the Groups panel (see Figure 6-7). Select the groups you wan that user to belong to.

Figure 6-7: Group Properties: Group Users panel

Note: On KDE, the KDE User Manager (KUser) lets you manage both users and groups. The KDE User Manager window displays two panels, one for users and the other for groups. The Users panel lists users user login, full name, home directory, and login shell, along with either user ID. On the toolbar there are Add, Edit, and Delete buttons for both users and groups, as well as Users and Groups menus with corresponding entries. Initially all system users and groups will also be displayed. Select Hide system users/groups from the Settings menu to display just normal users and groups.

Tip: Every file is owned by a user who can controls access to it. System files are owned by the root user and accessible by the root only. Services like FTP are an exception to this rule. Though accessible by the root, a service's files are owned by their own special user. For example, FTP files are owned by an **ftp** user. This provides users with access to a service's files without also having root user access.

User Configuration Files

Any utility to manage a user, such as GNOME's users-admin KDE's Kuser, makes use of certain default files, called *configuration files,* and directories to set up the new account. A set of pathnames is used to locate these default files or to indicate where to create certain user directories. Table 6-1 has a list of the pathnames.

Tip: You can find out which users are currently logged in with the **w** or **who** command. The **w** command displays detailed information about each connected user, such as from where they logged in and how long they have been inactive, and the date and time of login. The **who** command provides less detailed data.

Directory and Files	Description
/home	The user's own home directory
/etc/shells	The supported login shells
/etc/passwd	The password for a user
/etc/group	The group to which the user belongs
/etc/shadow	Encrypted password file
/etc/gshadow	Encrypted password file for groups
/etc/login.defs	Default login definitions for users

Table 6-1: Paths for User Configuration Files

The Password Files

A user gains access to an account by providing a correct login and password. The system maintains passwords in password files, along with login information like the username and ID. Tools like the `passwd` command let users change their passwords by modifying these files; **/etc/passwd** is the file that traditionally held user passwords, though in encrypted form. However, all users are allowed to read the **/etc/passwd** file, which allows access by users to the encrypted passwords. For better security, password entries are now kept in the **/etc/shadow** file, which is restricted to the root user.

/etc/passwd

When you add a user, an entry for that user is made in the **/etc/passwd** file, commonly known as the *password file.* Each entry takes up one line that has several fields separated by colons. The fields are as follows:

- ➢ **Username**   Login name of the user
- ➢ **Password**   Encrypted password for the user's account
- ➢ **User ID**   Unique number assigned by the system
- ➢ **Group ID**   Number used to identify the group to which the user belongs
- ➢ **Comment**   Any user information, such as the user's full name
- ➢ **Home directory**   The user's home directory
- ➢ **Login shell**   Shell to run when the user logs in; this is the default shell, usually **/bin/bash**

Depending on whether or not you are using shadow passwords, the password field (the second field) will be either an **x** or an encrypted form of the user's password. Linux implements shadow passwords by default, so these entries should have an **x** for their passwords. The following is an example of an **/etc/passwd** entry. For such entries, you must use the `passwd` command to create a password. Notice also that user IDs in this particular system start at 500 and increment by one. The group given is not the generic User, but a group consisting uniquely of that user. For example, the **dylan** user belongs to a group named **Dylan**, not to the generic **User** group.

```
dylan:x:500:500:Dylan:/home/dylan:/bin/bash
chris:x:501:501:Chris:/home/chris:/bin/bash
```

Tip: If you turn off shadow password support, entries in your **passwd** file will display encrypted passwords. Because any user can read the **/etc/passwd** file, intruders can access and possibly crack the encrypted passwords.

Note: Although it is technically possible to edit entries in the **/etc/passwd** file directly, it is not recommended. In particular, deleting an entry does not remove any other information, permissions, and data associated with a user, which opens a possible security breach whereby an intruder could take over the deleted user's ID or disk space.

/etc/shadow and /etc/gshadow

The **/etc/passwd** file is a simple text file and is vulnerable to security breaches. Anyone who gains access to the **/etc/password** file might be able to decipher or crack the encrypted passwords through a brute-force crack. The shadow suite of applications implements a greater level of security. These include versions of **useradd**, **groupadd**, and their corresponding update and delete programs. Most other user configuration tools support shadow security measures. With shadow security, passwords are no longer kept in the **/etc/password** file. Instead, passwords are kept in a separate file called **/etc/shadow**. Access is restricted to the root user.

The following example shows the **/etc/passwd** entry for a user.

```
chris:x:501:501:Chris:/home/chris:/bin/bash
```

A corresponding password file, called **/etc/gshadow,** is also maintained for groups that require passwords.

Password Tools

To change any particular field for a given user, you should use the user management tools provided, such as the **passwd** command, **usermod**, **useradd**, and **chage**, discussed in this chapter. The **passwd** command lets you change the password only. Other tools not only make entries in the **/etc/passwd** file, but also create the home directory for the user and install initialization files in the user's home directory.

These tools also let you control users' access to their accounts. You can set expiration dates for users or lock them out of their accounts. Users locked out of their accounts will have a their password in the **/etc/shadow** file prefixed by the invalid string, !!. Unlocking the account removes this prefix.

Changing Passwords

One common operation performed from the command line is to change a password. The easiest way to change your password on the GNOME desktop is to use the About Me utility (System | Preferences | Personal | About Me). Click on the Change Password button. A dialog opens up in which you enter your current password, and then the new password twice.

Alternatively you can use the **passwd** command. If you are using GNOME or KDE you first have to open a terminal window (Applications | System Tools | Terminal). Then, at the shell prompt, enter the `passwd` command. The command prompts you for your current password. After entering your current password and pressing ENTER, you are then prompted for your new password. After entering the new password, you are asked to reenter it. This is to make sure you actually entered the password you intended to enter.

```
$ passwd
Old password:
New password:
Retype new password:
$
```

Managing User Environments

Each time a user logs in, two profile scripts are executed, a system profile script that is the same for every user, and a user login profile script that can be customized to each user's needs. When the user logs out, a user logout script is run. In addition, each time a shell is generated, including the login shell, a user shell script is run. There are different kinds of scripts used for different shells. The default shell commonly used is the BASH shell. As an alternative, users can use different shells such as TCSH or the Z shell.

Profile Scripts

For the BASH shell, each user has his or her own BASH login profile script named **.profile** in the user's home directory. The system profile script is located in the **/etc** directory and named **profile** with no preceding period. The BASH shell user shell script is called **.bashrc**. The **.bashrc** file also runs the **/etc/bashrc** file to implement any global definitions such as the `PS1` and `TERM` variables. The **.profile** file runs the **.bashrc** file, and through it, the **/etc/bashrc** file, implementing global definitions.

As a superuser, you can edit any of these profile or shell scripts and put in any commands you want executed for each user when that user logs in. For example, you may want to define a default path for commands, in case the user has not done so. Or you may want to notify the user of recent system news or account changes.

/etc/login.defs

System wide values used by user and group creation utilities such as **useradd** and **usergroup** are kept in the **/etc/login.defs** file. Here you will find the range of possible user and group IDs listed. `UID_MIN` holds the minimum number for user IDs and `UID_MAX` the maximum number. Various password options control password controls—such as `PASS_MAX_DAYS`, which determines the maximum days allowable for a password. Many password options, like password lengths, are now handled by Pluggable Authentication Modules (PAM). Samples of these entries are shown here:

```
UID_MIN     1000
MAIL_DIR    /var/mail
PASS_MAX_DAYS   99999
```

Controlling User Passwords

Once you have created a user account, you can control the user's access to it. The **passwd** tool lets you lock and unlock a user's account. You use the **passwd** command with the **-l** option to lock an account, invalidating its password, and you use the **-u** option to unlock it.

You can also force a user to change his or her password at given intervals by setting an expiration date for that password. The **chage** command let you specify an expiration limit for a user's password. A user can be required to change his or her password every month, every week, or at a given date. Once the password expires, the user is prompted to enter a new one. You can issue a warning beforehand, telling the user how much time is left before the password expires.

If there is an account that you want to close, you can permanently expire a password. You can even shut down accounts that are inactive too long. In the next example, the password for the **chris** account will stay valid for only seven days. The **-M** option with the number of days sets the maximum time that a password can be valid. In the next example, the password for the **chris** account will stay valid for seven days.

```
chage -M 7  chris
```

To set a particular date for the account to expire, use the **-E** option with the date specified mm/dd/yyyy.

```
chage -E 07/30/2003  chris
```

To find out what the current expiration settings are for a given account, use the **-l** option.

```
chage -l chris
```

You can also combine your options into one command,

```
chage -M 7 -E 07/30/2003  chris
```

A listing of the **chage** options appears in Table 6-2.

Option	Description
-m	Minimum number of days a user must go before being able to change his password
-M	Maximum number of days a user can go without changing her password
-d	The last day the password was changed
-E	Specific expiration date for a password, date in format in yyyy-mm-dd or in commonly used format like mm/dd/yyyy
-I	Allowable account inactivity period (in days), after which password will expire
-W	Warning period, number of days before expiration when the user will be sent a warning message
-l	Display current password expiration controls

Table 6-2: Options for the chage Command

Adding and Removing Users and Groups with useradd, usermod, and userdel

Linux also provides the `useradd`, `usermod`, and `userdel` commands to manage user accounts. All these commands take in their information as options on the command line. If an option is not specified, they use predetermined default values. These are command line operations. To use them on your desktop you first need to open a terminal window (right-click the desktop and select Open Terminal), and then enter the commands at the shell prompt.

Tool	Description
`users-admin`	GNOME desktop tool for adding, removing, and modifying users and groups, primary Ubuntu desktop user management tool.
`Kuser`	K Desktop tool for adding, removing, and modifying users and groups
`useradd` *username options*	Adds a user
`userdel` *username*	Deletes a user
`usermod` *username options*	Modifies a user properties
`groupadd` *groupname options*	Adds a group
`groupdel` *groupname*	Deletes a group
`groupmod` *groupname options*	Modifies a group name

Table 6-3 User and Group Management Tools

If you are using a desktop interface, you should use GUI tools to manage user accounts. Each Linux distribution usually provides a tool to manage users. In addition you can use the K DE KUser tool or the GNOME users-admin tool. See Table 6-3 for a listing of user management tools.

Note: On KDE, KUser lets you manage both users and groups. The KDE User Manager window displays two tabs for Users and Groups. The Users tab lists user login, full name, home directory, login shell, and user ID. On the toolbar, Add, Edit, and Delete buttons can be used for both users and groups, and Users and Groups menus offer corresponding entries. Initially, all system users and groups will also be displayed. Choose Settings | Hide System Users/Groups to display normal users and groups.

useradd

With the `useradd` command, you enter values as options on the command line, such as the name of a user, to create a user account. It then creates a new login and directory for that name using all the default features for a new account.

```
useradd chris
```

The `useradd` utility first checks the **/etc/login.defs** file for default values for creating a new account. For those defaults not defined in the **/etc/login.defs** file, `useradd` supplies its own. You can display these defaults using the `useradd` command with the `-D` option. The default values include the group name, the user ID, the home directory, the **skel** directory, and the login shell.

Values the user enters on the command line will override corresponding defaults. The group name is the name of the group in which the new account is placed. By default, this is **other**, which means the new account belongs to no group. The user ID is a number identifying the user account. The **skel** directory is the system directory that holds copies of initialization files. These initialization files are copied into the user's new home directory when it is created. The login shell is the pathname for the particular shell the user plans to use.

Option	Description
-d *dir*	Sets the home directory of the new user.
-D	Displays defaults for all settings. Can also be used to reset default settings for the home directory (-b), group (-g), shell (-s), expiration date (-e), and password expirations (-f).
-e *mm/dd/yy*	Sets an expiration date for the account (none, by default). Specified as month/day/year.
-f *days*	Sets the number of days an account remains active after its password expires.
-g *group*	Sets a group.
-m	Creates user's home directory, if it does not exist.
-m -k *skl-dir*	Sets the skeleton directory that holds skeleton files, such as .profile files, which are copied to the user's home directory automatically when it is created; the default is /etc/skel.
-M	Does not create user's home directory.
-p *password*	Supplies an encrypted password (crypt or MD5). With no argument, the account is immediately disabled.
-s *shell*	Sets the login shell of the new user. This is /bin/bash by default, the BASH shell.
-u *userid*	Sets the user ID of the new user. The default is the increment of the highest number used so far.

Table 6-4: Options for useradd **and** usermod

The **useradd** command has options that correspond to each default value. Table 6-4 holds a list of all the options you can use with the **useradd** command. You can use specific values in place of any of these defaults when creating a particular account. The login is inaccessible until you do. In the next example, the group name for the **chris** account is set to **intro1** and the user ID is set to 578:

```
useradd chris -g intro1 -u 578
```

Once you add a new user login, you need to give the new login a password. Password entries are placed in the **/etc/passwd** and **/etc/shadow** files. Use the **passwd** command to create a new password for the user, as shown here. The password you enter will not appear on your screen. You will be prompted to repeat the password. A message will then be issued indicating that the password was successfully changed.

```
$ passwd chris
Changing password for user chris
New UNIX password:
```

```
Retype new UNIX password:
passwd: all authentication tokens updated successfully
```

usermod

The **usermod** command enables you to change the values for any of these features. You can change the home directory or the user ID. You can even change the username for the account. The **usermod** command takes the same options as **useradd**, listed previously in Table 6-4.

userdel

When you want to remove a user from the system, you can use the **userdel** command to delete the user's login. With the **-r** option, the user's home directory will also be removed. In the next example, the user **chris** is removed from the system:

```
# userdel -r chris
```

Managing Groups

You can manage groups using either shell commands or GUI utilities. Groups are an effective way to manage access and permissions, letting you control several users with just their group name.

/etc/group and /etc/gshadow

The system file that holds group entries is called **/etc/group**. The file consists of group records, with one record per line and its fields separated by colons. A group record has four fields: a group name, a password, its ID, and the users who are part of this group. The Password field can be left blank. The fields for a group record are as follows:

➢ **Group name**   The name of the group, which must be unique

➢ **Password**   With shadow security implemented, this field is an **x**, with the password indicated in the **/etc/gshadow** file (this field can be left blank)

➢ **Group ID**   The number assigned by the system to identify this group

➢ **Users**   The list of users that belong to the group, separated by commas

Here is an example of an entry in an **/etc/group** file. The group is called **engines**, the password is managed by shadow security, the group ID is 100, and the users who are part of this group are **chris**, **robert**, **valerie**, and **aleina**:

```
engines:x:100:chris,robert,valerie,aleina
```

As in the case of the **/etc/passwd** file, it is best to change group entries using a group management utility like **groupmod** or **groupadd**. All users have read access to the **/etc/group** file. With shadow security, secure group data such as passwords are kept in the **/etc/gshadow** file, to which only the root user has access.

User Private Groups

A new user can be assigned to a special group set up for just that user and given the user's name. Thus the new user **dylan** is given a default group also called **dylan**. The group **dylan** will also show up in the listing of groups. This method of assigning default user groups is called the User Private Group (UPG) scheme. The supplementary groups are additional groups that the user may want to belong to. Traditionally, users were all assigned to one group named **users** that subjected all users to the group permission controls for the **users** group. With UPG, each user has its own group, with its own group permissions.

Group Directories

As with users, you can create a home directory for a group. To do so, you simply create a directory for the group in the **/home** directory and change its home group to that group and allow access by any member of the group. The following example creates a directory called **engines** and changes its group to the **engines** group:

```
mkdir /home/engines
chgrp engines /home/engines
```

Then the read, write, and execute permissions for the group level should be set with the **chmod** command.

```
chmod g+rwx /home/engines
```

Any member of the **engines** group can now access the **/home/engines** directory and any shared files placed therein. This directory becomes a shared directory for the group. You can, in fact, use the same procedure to make other shared directories at any location on the file system.

Files within the shared directory should also have their permissions set to allow access by other users in the group. When a user places a file in a shared directory, the user needs to set the permissions on that file to allow other members of the group to access it. A read permission will let others display it, write lets them change it, and execute lets them run it (used for scripts and programs). The following example first changes the group for the **mymodel** file to **engines**. Then it copies the **mymodel** file to the **/home/engines** directory and sets the group read and write permission for the **engines** group:

```
$ chgrp engines mymodel
$ cp mymodel /home/engines
$ chmod g+rw /home/engines/mymodel
```

Managing Groups Using groupadd, groupmod, and groupdel

You can also manage groups with the **groupadd**, **groupmod**, and **groupdel** commands. These command line operations let you quickly manage a group from a terminal window.

groupadd and groupdel

With the **groupadd** command, you can create new groups. When you add a group to the system, the system places the group's name in the **/etc/group** file and gives it a group ID number. If shadow security is in place, changes are made to the **/etc/gshadow** file. The **groupadd** command only creates the group category. You need to add users to the group individually. In the following example, the **groupadd** command creates the **engines** group:

```
# groupadd engines
```

You can delete a group with the **groupdel** command. In the next example, the **engines** group is deleted:

```
# groupdel engines
```

groupmod

You can change the name of a group or its ID using the `groupmod` command. Enter `groupmod -g` with the new ID number and the group name. To change the name of a group, you use the `-n` option. Enter `groupmod -n` with the new name of the group, followed by the current name. In the next example, the **engines** group has its name changed to **trains**:

```
# groupmod -n trains engines
```

Disk Quotas

You can use disk quotas to control how much disk space a particular user makes use of on your system. On your Linux system, unused disk space is held as a common resource that each user can access as he or she needs it. As users create more files, they take the space they need from the pool of available disk space. In this sense, all the users are sharing a single resource of unused disk space. However, if one user were to use up all the remaining disk space, none of the other users would be able to create files or even run programs. To counter this problem, you can create disk quotas on particular users, limiting the amount of available disk space they can use.

Quota Tools

Quota checks can be implemented on the file system of a hard disk partition mounted on your system (**quota** package, Ubuntu main repository). The quotas are enabled using the `quotacheck` and `quotaon` programs. They are executed in the **/etc/init.d/quota** script, which can be run whenever you start up your system. Each partition needs to be mounted with the quota options, `usrquota` or `grpquota`. `usrquota` enables quota controls for users, and `grpquota` works for groups. These options are usually placed in the mount entry in the **/etc/fstab** file for a particular partition. For example, to mount the **/dev/hda6** hard disk partition mounted to the **/home** directory with support for user and group quotas, you require a mount entry like the following:

```
/dev/hda6 /home ext2 defaults,usrquota,grpquota 1 1
```

You also need to create **quota.user** and **quota.group** files for each partition for which you enable quotas. These are the quota databases that hold the quota information for each user and group. You can create these files by running the `quotacheck` command with the `-a` option or the device name of the file system where you want to enable quotas.

The quota service script will perform both a quota check and turns on the quota service for all file systems. It will also use quotacheck to create **quota.user** and **quota.group** files for new file systems. You can run this script manually to start, stop, and restart the service. The following command will start the quota service, running quotacheck and quotaon with the following command.

```
sudo /etc/init.d/quota start
```

You can also use **quotacheck** directly to check quota files for a particular file systems. The following example creates the quota database on the hda1 hard disk partition:

```
sudo quotacheck /dev/hda1
```

Though the **quota** script can be used to turn the quota service on or off (start, stop, and restart options), you can also manually turn the quota service on directly with the **quotaon** command. Using just **quotaon** lets you turn the service on without having to perform a quotacheck operation. You can turn quotas off using the `quotaoff` command.

```
sudo quotaon  -aug
```

When you start up your system, the **quota** script will use `quotacheck` to check the quota databases, and then `quotaon` to turn on quotas.

Note: The quotarpc service enables remote quota controls.

edquota

You can set disk quotas using the `edquota` command. With it, you can access the quota record for a particular user and group, which is maintained in the disk quota database. You can also set default quotas that will be applied to any user or group on the file system for which quotas have not been set. `edquota` will open the record in your default editor, and you can use your editor to make any changes. To open the record for a particular user, use the **-u** option and the username as an argument for `edquota` (see Table 6-5). The following example opens the disk quota record for the user **larisa**:

```
sudo edquota -u larisa
```

edquota Option	Description
-u	Edits the user quota. This is the default.
-g	Edits the group quota.
-p	Duplicates the quotas of the typical user specified. This is the normal mechanism used to initialize quotas for groups of users.
-t	Edits the soft time limits for each file system.

Table 6-5: Options for edquota

The limit you set for a quota can be hard or soft. A hard limit will deny a user the ability to exceed his or her quota, whereas a soft limit will just issue a warning. For the soft limit, you can designate a grace period during which time the user has the chance to reduce their disk space below the limit. If the disk space still exceeds the limit after the grace period expires, the user can be denied access to their account. For example, a soft limit is typically 75MB, whereas the hard limit could be 100MB. Users who exceed their soft limit can have a 48-hour grace period.

The quota record begins with the hard disk device name and the blocks of memory and inodes in use. The limits segments have parameters for soft and hard limits. If these entries are 0, there are no limits in place. You can set both hard and soft limits, using the hard limit as a firm restriction. Blocks in Linux are currently about 1,000 bytes. The inodes are used by files to hold information about the memory blocks making up a file. To set the time limit for a soft limit, use the `edquota` command with the **-t** option. The following example displays the quota record for **larisa**:

```
Quotas for user larisa:
/dev/hda3: blocks in use: 9000, limits (soft = 40000, hard = 60000)
 inodes in use: 321, limits (soft = 0, hard = 0)
```

repquota and quota

As the system administrator, you can use the `repquota` command to generate a summary of disk usage for a specified file system, checking to see what users are approaching or exceeding quota limits. `repquota` takes as its argument the file system to check; the `-a` option checks all file systems.

```
repquota /dev/hda1
```

Individual users can use the `quota` command to check their memory use and how much disk space they have left in their quota (see Table 6-7).

quota Option	Description
`-g`	Prints group quotas for the group of which the user is a member.
`-u`	Prints the user's quota.
`-v`	Displays quotas on file systems where no storage is allocated.
`-q`	Prints information on file systems where usage is over quota.

Table 6-6: Options for quota

Pluggable Authentication Modules

Pluggable Authentication Modules (PAM) is an authentication service that lets a system determine the method of authentication to be performed for users. In a Linux system, authentication has traditionally been performed by looking up passwords. When a user logs in, the login process looks up their password in the password file. With PAM, users' requests for authentication are directed to PAM, which in turn uses a specified method to authenticate the user. This could be a simple password lookup or a request to an LDAP server, but it is PAM that provides authentication, not a direct password lookup by the user or application. In this respect, authentication becomes centralized and controlled by a specific service, PAM. The actual authentication procedures can be dynamically configured by the system administrator. Authentication is carried out by modules that can vary according to the kind of authentication needed. An administrator can add or replace modules by simply changing the PAM configuration files. See the PAM website at **http://kernel.org/pub/linux/libs/pam** for more information and a listing of PAM modules. PAM modules are located in the **/lib/security** directory.

PAM modules will usually have their own Man pages. This will list options that can be used for particular modules. Some of the more commonly used are pam_unix (password check), pam_deny (lock out), pam_env (PAM environment variables), and pam_group (check group membership). The following command in a terminal window will display the Man page for pam_unix.

```
man pam_unix
```

Lightweight Directory Access Protocol

The Lightweight Directory Access Protocol (LDAP) is designed to implement network-accessible directories of information. In this context, the term directory is defined as a database of primarily read-only, simple, small, widely accessible, and quickly distributable information. It is not designed for transactions or updates. It is primarily used to provide information about users on a network, providing information about them such as their e-mail address or phone number. Such directories can also be used for authentication purposes, identifying that a certain user belongs to a specified network. You can find out more information on LDAP at **www.ldapman.org**.

You can think of an LDAP directory for users as an Internet-accessible phone book, where anyone can look you up to find your e-mail address or other information. In fact, it may be more accurate to refer to such directories as databases. They are databases of user information, accessible over networks like the Internet. Normally, the users on a local network are spread across several different systems, and to obtain information about a user, you would have to know what system the user is on, and then query that system. With LDAP, user information for all users on a network is kept in the LDAP server. You only have to query the network's LDAP server to obtain information about a user. For example, Sendmail can use LDAP to look up user addresses. You can also use Firefox or Netscape to query LDAP.

Note: LDAP is a directory access protocol to an X.500 directory service, the OSI directory service.

Numerous LDAP packages are available on the Ubuntu repository that provide specific LDAP support. LDAP support packages include those for Java, Kerberos, Asterisk, Cyrus mail, DBmail, Mozilla SDK, nagios, NSS and PAM, Perl, ProFTPP, Ruby, Samba, and Wine.

For documentation of the LDAP server on Ubuntu check the OpenLDAP Server entry for your distribution on the **http://help.ubuntu.com** site.

LDAP Clients and Servers

LDAP directories are implemented as clients and servers, where you use an LDAP client to access an LDAP server that manages the LDAP database. Ubuntu uses OpenLDAP, an open-source version of LDAP (you can find out more about OpenLDAP at **http://openldap.org**). OpenLDAP provides an LDAP server (`slapd`), an LDAP replication server (`slurpd`), an LDAP client, and LDAP utilities.

On Ubuntu, you install the LDAP packages using the **ldap-auth-config** meta package. This package will also select and install the **ldap-auth-client**, **libpam-ldap**, and **libnss-ldap** packages. For the LDAP server you select the **slapd** package. If you are running Postfix mail server, you may want **postfix-ldap**.

When installing ldap-auth-config you will be prompted to enter in the URI for the LDAP server, distinguishing name of the search base, and the version to use. You are then prompted to specify if the administrator on your system has administrative access to the LDAP server and if the LDAP database requires a login. Then specify the LDAP account for the root, and the LDAP root account password.

For documentation of the LDAP server on Ubuntu, check the OpenLDAP Server entry for your distribution at **https://help.ubuntu.com**.

LDAP Configuration Files

All LDAP configuration files are kept in the **/etc/openldap** directory. These include **slapd.conf**, the LDAP server configuration file, and **ldap.conf**, the LDAP clients and tools configuration file. To enable the LDAP server, you have to manually edit the **slapd.conf** file, and change the domain value (dc) for the suffix and rootdn entries to your own network's domain address. This is the network that will be serviced by the LDAP server.

To enable LDAP clients and their tools, you have to specify the correct domain address in the **ldap.conf** file in the BASE option, along with the server's address in the URI option (domain name or IP address). For clients, this is the configuration information you entered when installing the **ldap-auth-config** package. You can also edit the **ldap.conf** file directly. See the **ldap.conf** Man entry for detailed descriptions of LDAP options.

If you installed the LDAP server, you can start, stop, and restart the LDAP service using the slapd script.

```
sudo service slapd start
```

You can also have the LDAP servers started when your system starts up by checking the LDAP Server entry in the **services-admin** tool, choose System | Administration | Services.

Tip: Keep in mind that the **/etc/ldap.conf** and **/etc/ldap/ldap.conf** files are not the same: **/etc/ldap.conf** is used to configure LDAP for the Nameservice Switch and PAM support, whereas **/etc/ldap/ldap.conf** is used for all LDAP clients.

Configuring the LDAP server: /etc/slapd.conf

You configure the LDAP server with the /etc/**slapd.conf** file. Here you will find entries for loading schemas and for specifying access controls, the database directory, and passwords. The file is commented in detail, with default settings for most options, although you will have to enter settings for several. First you need to specify your domain suffix and root domain manager. The default settings are shown here:

```
suffix          "dc=my-domain,dc=com"
rootdn          "cn=Manager,dc=my-domain,dc=com"
```

In this example, the **suffix** is changed to **mytrek**, for **mytrek.com**. The **rootdn** remains the same.

```
suffix          "dc=mytrek,dc=com"
rootdn          "cn=Manager,dc=mytrek,dc=com"
```

Next you will have to specify a password with **rootpw**. There are entries for both plain text and encrypted versions. Both are commented. Remove the comment for one. In the following example the plain text password option is used, **secret**:

```
rootpw          secret
# rootpw        {crypt}ijFYNcSNctBYg
```

For an encrypted password, you can first create the encrypted version with **slappasswd**. This will generate a text encryption string for the password. Then copy the generated encrypted string to the **rootpw** entry. On GNOME you can simply cut and paste from a terminal window to the **/etc/slapd.conf** file in Text Editor (Accessories). You can also redirect the encrypted string to a file and read it in later. SSHA encryption will be used by default.

```
$ sudo slappasswd
Enter password:
Re-enter new password:
{SSHA}0a+szaAwElK57Y8AoD5uMULSvLfCUfg5
```

The **rootpw** root password entry should then look like this:

```
rootpw      {SSHA}0a+szaAwElK57Y8AoD5uMULSvLfCUfg5
```

Use the password you entered at the **slappasswd** prompt to access your LDAP directory.

The configuration file also lists the schemas to be used. Schemas are included with the **include** directive.

```
include          /etc/openldap/schema/core.schema
include          /etc/openldap/schema/cosine.schema
include          /etc/openldap/schema/inetorgperson.schema
include          /etc/openldap/schema/nis.schema
```

LDAP directory database: ldif

A record (also known as entry) in an LDAP database begins with a name, known as a *distinguishing name,* followed by a set of attributes and their values. The distinguishing name uniquely identifies the record. For example, a name could be a username and the attribute would be the user's e-mail address, the address being the attribute's value. Allowable attributes are determined by schemas defined in the **/etc/openldap/schema** directory. This directory will hold various schema definition files, each with a **schema** extension. Some will be dependent on others, enhancing their supported classes and attributes. The basic core set of attributes are defined in the **core.schema** file. Here you will find definitions for attributes like country name and street address. Other schemas, like **inetorgperson.schema**, specify **core.schema** as a dependent schema, making its attributes available to the classes. The inetOrgPerson schema will also define its own attributes such as jpegPhoto for a person's photograph.

Schema Attributes and Classes

Attributes and classes are defined officially by RFC specifications that are listed with each attribute and class entry in the schema files. These are standardized definitions and should not be changed. Attributes are defined by an **attributetype** definition. Each is given a unique identifying number followed by a name by which it can be referenced. Fields include the attribute description (DESC), search features such as EQUALITY and SUBSTR, and the object identifier (SYNTAX). See the OpenLDAP administrative guide for a detailed description.

```
attributetype ( 2.5.4.9 NAME ( 'street' 'streetAddress' )
    DESC 'RFC2256: street address of this object'
    EQUALITY caseIgnoreMatch
    SUBSTR caseIgnoreSubstringsMatch
    SYNTAX 1.3.6.1.4.1.1466.115.121.1.15{128} )
```

A class defines the kind of database (directory) you can create. This will specify the kinds of attributes you can include in your records. Classes can be dependent, where one class becomes and extension of another. The class most often used for LDAP databases is inetOrgPerson, defined in the **inetOrgPerson.schema** file. The term inetOrgPerson stands for Internet Organization Person, as many LDAP directories perform Internet tasks. The class is derived from the organizationalPerson class defined in **core.schema**, which includes the original attributes for commonly used fields like street address and name.

```
# inetOrgPerson
# The inetOrgPerson represents people who are associated with an
```

```
# organization in some way. It is a structural class and is derived
# from the organizationalPerson which is defined in X.521 [X521].
objectclass ( 2.16.840.1.113730.3.2.2
    NAME 'inetOrgPerson'
      DESC 'RFC2798: Internet Organizational Person'
    SUP organizationalPerson
    STRUCTURAL
     MAY (
            audio $ businessCategory $ carLicense $ departmentNumber $
            displayName $ employeeNumber $ employeeType $ givenName $
            homePhone $ homePostalAddress $ initials $ jpegPhoto $
            labeledURI $ mail $ manager $ mobile $ o $ pager $
            photo $ roomNumber $ secretary $ uid $ userCertificate $
            x500uniqueIdentifier $ preferredLanguage $
            userSMIMECertificate $ userPKCS12 )
     )
```

You can create your own classes, building on the standard ones already defined. You can also create your own attributes. But each attribute will require a unique object identifier (OID).

Distinguishing Names

Data in an LDAP directory is organized hierarchically, from general categories to specific data. An LDAP directory could be organized starting with countries, narrowing to states, then organizations and their subunits, and finally individuals. Commonly, LDAP directories are organized along the lines of Internet domains. In this format, the top category would be the domain name extension, for instance **.com** or **.ca**. The directory would then break down to the network (organization), units, and finally users.

This organization is used to help define distinguishing names that will identify the LDAP records. In a network-based organization, the top-level organization is defined by a domain component specified by the dcObject class, which includes the domainComponent (dc) attribute. Usually you define the network and extension as domain components to make up the top-level organization that becomes the distinguishing name for the database itself.

```
dc=mytrek, dc=com
```

Under the organization name is an organizational unit, such as users. These are defined as an organizationalUnitName (ou), which is part of the organizationalUnit class. The distinguishing name for the user's organizational unit would be.

```
ou=users, dc=mytrek, dc=com
```

Under the organizational unit you could then have individual users. Here the user name is defined with the commonName (cn) attribute, which is used in various classes, including Person, which is part of organizationalPerson, which in turn is part of inetOrgPerson. The distinguishing name for the user **dylan** would then be:

```
cn=dylan,ou=users,dc=mytrek,dc=com
```

LDIF Entries

Database entries are placed in an LDAP Interchange Format (LDIF) file. This format provides a global standard that allows a database to be accessed by any LDAP-compliant client. An

LDIF file is a simple text file with an **.ldif** extension, placed in the **/etc/openldap** directory. The entries for an LDIF record consist of a distinguishing name or attribute, followed by a colon, and its list of values. Each record begins with a distinguishing name to uniquely identify the record. Attributes then follow. You can think of the name as a record and the attributes as fields in that record. You end the record with an empty line.

Initially you create an LDIF file using any text editor. Then enter the records. In the following example, the **mytrek.ldif** LDIF file contains records for users on the network.

First you create records defining your organization and organization units. These distinguishing names will be used in user-level records. You will also have to specify a manager for the database, in this case simply Manager. Be sure to include the appropriate object classes. The organization uses both the dcObject (domain component object) and organization objects. The Manager uses organizationalRole, and users use the organizationalUnit. Within each record you can have attribute definitions, like the organization attribute, o, in the first record, which is set to MyTrek.

```
dn: dc=mytrek,dc=com
objectclass: dcobject
objectclass: organization
dc: mytrek
o: MyTrek

dn: cn=Manager,dc=mytrek,dc=com
cn: Manager
objectclass: organizationalRole

dn: ou=users,dc=mytrek,dc=com
objectclass: organizationalUnit
ou: users
```

Individual records then follow, such as the following for **dylan**. Here the object classes are organizationalPerson and inetOrgPerson. Attributes then follow, like common name (cn), user ID (uid), organization (o), surname (sn), and street.

```
dn: cn=dylan,ou=users,dc=mytrek,dc=com
objectclass: organizationalPerson
objectclass: inetOrgPerson
cn: dylan
uid: dylan
o: MyTrek
sn: shark
street: 77777 saturn ave
```

An example of an LDIF file is shown here. The organization is **mytrek.com**. There are two records, one for **dylan** and the other for **chris**:

mytrek.ldif

```
dn: dc=mytrek,dc=com
objectclass: dcobject
objectclass: organization
dc: mytrek
o: MyTrek
```

```
dn: cn=Manager,dc=mytrek,dc=com
cn: Manager
objectclass: organizationalRole

dn: ou=users,dc=mytrek,dc=com
objectclass: organizationalUnit
ou: users

dn: cn=dylan,ou=users,dc=mytrek,dc=com
objectclass: organizationalPerson
objectclass: inetOrgPerson
cn: dylan
uid: dylan
o: MyTrek
sn: shark
street: 77777 saturn ave

dn: cn=chris,ou=users,dc=mytrek,dc=com
objectclass: organizationalPerson
objectclass: inetOrgPerson
cn: chris
uid: chris
o: MyTrek
sn: dolphin
street: 99999 neptune way
```

Adding the Records

Once you have created your LDIF file, you can then use the **ldapadd** command to add the records to you LDAP directory. Use the **-D** option to specify the directory to add the records to, and the **-f** option to specify the LDIF file to read from. You could use **ldapadd** to enter fields directly. The **-x** option says to use simple password access, the **-W** will prompt for the password, and the **-D** option specifies the directory manager.

```
$ ldapadd -x -D "cn=Manager,dc=mytrek,dc=com" -W -f mytrek.ldif

Enter LDAP Password:
adding new entry "dc=mytrek,dc=com"
adding new entry "cn=Manager,dc=mytrek,dc=com"
adding new entry "ou=users,dc=mytrek,dc=com"
adding new entry "cn=dylan,ou=users,dc=mytrek,dc=com"
adding new entry "cn=chris,ou=users,dc=mytrek,dc=com"
```

Be sure to restart the LDAP server to have your changes take effect.

Searching LDAP

Once you have added your records, you can use the **ldapsearch** command to search your LDAP directory. The **-x** and **-w** options provide simple password access, and the **-b** option will specify the LDAP database to use. Following the options are the attributes to search for, in this case the street attribute.

```
# ldapsearch -x -W -D 'cn=Manager,dc=mytrek,dc=com' -b 'dc=mytrek,dc=com' street
Enter LDAP Password:
# extended LDIF
#
# LDAPv3
# base <dc=mytrek,dc=com> with scope sub
# filter: (objectclass=*)
# requesting: street

# dylan, users, mytrek.com
dn: cn=dylan,ou=users,dc=mytrek,dc=com
street: 77777 saturn ave

# chris, users, mytrek.com
dn: cn=chris,ou=users,dc=mytrek,dc=com
street: 99999 neptune way

# search result
search: 2
result: 0 Success

# numResponses: 6
# numEntries: 5
```

If you want to see all the records listed in the database, you can use the same search command without any attributes.

LDAP Tools

To actually make or change entries in the LDAP database, you use the **ldapadd** and **ldapmodify** utilities (**openldap-clients** package). With **ldapdelete**, you can remove entries. Once you have created an LDAP database, you can then query it, through the LDAP server, with **ldapsearch**. For the LDAP server, you can create a text file of LDAP entries using the LDAP Data Interchange Format (LDIF). Such text files can then be read in all at once to the LDAP database using the **slapadd** tool. The **slapcat** tool extracts entries from the LDAP database and saves them in an LDIF file. To reindex additions and changes, you use the **slapindex** utility. See the LDAP Howto at the Linux documentation project for details on using and setting up LDAP databases such as address books (**www.tldp.org**).

LDAP and the Name Service Switch Service

With the **libnss_ldap** library, LDAP can also be used in the Nameservice Switch (NSS) service along with NIS and system files for system database services like passwords and groups (**nss_ldap** package). Clients can easily enable LDAP for NSS by using the System Settings Authentication tool and selecting Enable LDAP Support in the User Information panel. You also need to make sure that the LDAP server is specified. You could also manually add **ldap** for entries in the **/etc/nsswitch.conf** file.

Tip: To better secure access to the LDAP server, you should encrypt your LDAP administrator's password. The LDAP administrator is specified in the **rootdn** entry, and its password in the **rootpw** entry. To create an encrypted password, use the `slappasswd` command. This prompts you for a password and displays its encrypted version. Copy that encrypted version in the `rootpw` entry.

Enabling LDAP on Thunderbird

In Thunderbird, open the address book, then select File | New, and choose the LDAPD directory. Here you can enter the LDAP server. This displays a panel where you can enter the address book name, the host name of LDAP server, the Base DN to search, and the port number, 389 on Ubuntu.

Note: LDAP supports the Simple Authentication and Security Layer (SASL) for secure authentication with methods like MD5 and Kerberos.

7. Kernel Administration

Kernel Versions

Kernel Tuning: Kernel Runtime Parameters

Installing a New Kernel Version

Creating a Customized Ubuntu Kernel

Compiling the Kernel from Source Code

Important Kernel Configuration Features

Compiling and Installing the Kernel

GRUB Boot Loader Configurations

initramfs RAM filesystems

The *kernel* is the operating system, performing core tasks such as managing memory and disk access, as well as interfacing with the hardware that makes up your system. For example, the kernel makes possible such standard Linux features as multitasking and multiuser support. It also handles communications with devices like your CD-ROM or hard disk. Users send requests for access to these devices through the kernel, which then handles the lower-level task of actually sending appropriate instructions to a device. Given the great variety of devices available, the kind of devices available to a Linux system will vary. When Linux is installed, the kernel is appropriately configured for available devices. However, if you add a rarely used or unsupported device, you may have to enable support for it in the kernel. This involves reconfiguring the existing kernel to support the new device through a procedure that is often referred to as *building* or *compiling the kernel.* In addition, new versions of the kernel are continuously made available that provide improved support for your devices, as well as support for new features and increased reliability for a smoother-running system. You can download, compile, and install these new versions on your system.

Kernel Versions

The version number for a Linux kernel consists of four segments: the major, minor, revision, and bug-fix numbers. The major number and minor numbers increment with major releases of the kernel. As new features are introduced, new revisions of a kernel are released. For example, kernel **2.6.28** has a major number of 2 and a minor number of 6, with a revision number of 28.

As bugs are discovered and corrected new kernel versions are released specified with a fourth number, the security/bug fix number. Distributions often add another number that refers to a specific set of patches applied to the kernel for that distribution. This distribution bug fix is indicated by a dashed number at the end. For Ubuntu, the two are combined. For the Ubuntu kernel **2.6.28-14-generic**, the Ubuntu security and bug fix number is **-14**. The current kernel version is displayed on the System tab on the GNOME System Monitor (Applications | System Tools | System Monitor). The original kernel source package, available from www.kernel.org, will list the security-bug fix number as the fourth number delineated by a period, as in **2.6.28.10**.

You could have more than one version of the kernel installed on your system. To see which one is running currently, you use the **uname** command with the **-r** option (the **-a** option provides more detailed information).

```
uname -r
```

New features first appear in the development versions. New development versions will first appear as release candidates, which will have an **rc** in the name. If you're concerned about stability, you should wait for the stable version. A development kernel may have numerous revisions. The release candidate version would have a name like **2.6.31-rc8**. Often development kernels, though unstable, include support for the most recent hardware and software features. However, unless you are experimenting with kernel development, you should always install a stable version of the kernel.

The Linux kernel is being worked on constantly, and new versions are released when they are ready. Distributions may include different kernel versions. Ubuntu includes the most up-to-date stable kernel in its releases. Linux kernels are available at **www.kernel.org**. Also, RPM packages for a new kernel are often available at distribution update sites. One reason you may need to upgrade your kernel is to provide support for new hardware or for features not supported by your distribution's version. For example, you may need support for a new device not provided in your distribution's version of the kernel. Certain features may not be included in a distribution's version because they are considered experimental or a security risk.

Note: In many cases, you don't need to compile and install a new kernel just to add support for a new device. Kernels provide most device support in the form of loadable modules, of which only those needed are installed with the kernel. Most likely, your current kernel has the module you need; you simply have to compile it and install it.

Tip: Many modules can be separately compiled using sources provided by vendors, such as updated network device drivers. For these you only need the Kernel headers, which are already installed in the **/usr/lib/modules/***version***/source** directory, where *version* is an installed kernel version. In these cases, you do not have to install the full kernel source to add or modify modules.

References

You can learn more about the Linux kernel from **www.kernel.org**, the official repository for the current Linux kernels. The most current source code, as well as documentation, is there. The Ubuntu also provides online documentation for installing and compiling the kernel on its systems, **https://help.ubuntu.com/community/Kernel/Compile**. Several Linux HOW-TOs also exist on the subject. The kernel source code software packages also include extensive documentation. Kernel source code files should always be installed in a local user directory (the **/usr/src/kernels** directory is used for library headers, not the kernel source). The source itself will be in a directory labeled **linux-***version,* where *version* is the kernel release, as in **linux-2.6.27**. In this directory, you can find a subdirectory named **/Documentation,** which contains an extensive set of files and directories documenting kernel features, modules, and commands. The following listing of kernel resources also contains more information:

> ➤ **www.kernel.org** The official Linux kernel Web site. All new kernels originate from here

> ➤ **www.linuxhq.com** Linux headquarters, kernel sources, and patches

> ➤ **http://kernelnewbies.org** Linux kernel sources and information

> ➤ **http://en.tldp.org/** Linux Documentation Project

> ➤ **https://help.ubuntu.com/community/Kernel/Compile** Ubuntu help site for instructions for configurateur and building kernels on Ubuntu.

> ➤ **http://kernel-handbook.alioth.debian.org/** Debian kernel handbook

Kernel Tuning: Kernel Runtime Parameters

Several kernel features, such as IP forwarding or the maximum number of files, can be turned on or off without compiling and installing a new kernel or module. These tunable parameters are controlled by the files in **/proc/sys** directory. Parameters that you set are made in the **/etc/sysctl.conf** file. Ubuntu installs this file with basic configuration entries such as those for IP forwarding and debugging control. You use the **sysctl** command directly. The **-p** option causes `sysctl` to read parameters from the **/etc/sysctl.conf** file (you can specify a different file). You can use the **-w** option to change specific parameters. You reference a parameter with its key. A key is the parameter name prefixed with its **proc** system categories (directories), such as **net.ipv4.ip_forward** for the **ip_forward** parameter located in **/proc/sys/net/ipv4/**. To display the value of a particular parameter, just use it's key. The **-a** option lists all available changeable parameters. In the next example, the user changes the domain name parameter, referencing it with the **kernel.domainname** key (the **domainname** command also sets the **kernel.domainname** parameter):

```
sysctl -w kernel.domainname="mytrek.com"
```

The following example turns on IP forwarding:

```
sysctl -w net.ipv4.ip_forward=1
```

If you use just the key, you display the parameter's current value:

```
sysctl net.ipv4.ip_forward
 net.ipv4.ip_forward = 1
```

Installing a New Kernel Version

To install a new kernel, you need to download the software packages for that kernel to your system. You can install a new kernel either by downloading a binary version from your distribution's Web site and installing it or by downloading the source code, compiling the kernel, and then installing the resulting binary file along with the modules. The binary version of the kernel is provided in an DEB package. You can install a new kernel, just as you would any other DEB software package.

The easiest way to install a new kernel on Ubuntu is to use the Synaptic Package Manager. The name of a Linux kernel package begins with the term **linux**. The Synaptic Package Manager will automatically download and install a new kernel. The installation will create a GRUB entry so that when you boot, the new kernel will be listed as one of the options, usually the default.

The kernel source code for Ubuntu is available in the **linux-source** package. This package will include Ubuntu patches (modifications) to the original linux kernel.

The original Linux kernel source code version is also available for download directly from **www.kernel.org**.

CPU Kernel Packages

Ubuntu provides different kernel packages optimized 32 bit and 64 bit CPUs. The one appropriate for your machine is included with the distribution CD spin. All the kernels include multi-processor support. The 32-bit spin will include the x86 versions, and the 64-bit spin will hold the x86_64 versions.

Ubuntu provides three kernel packages types optimized for different operations: generic, server, and virtual. The generic kernel package is used for desktops, the server is optimized for use with servers, and the virtual package is designed for use with systems running virtual machines. The virtual and server kernels are incompatible. If you install one, the other will be removed. Both, however, will work with the generic kernel.

A system running the generic kernel can switch easily to the server or virtual kernel, provided the system is not making use of vendor graphics drivers. You could install a desktop system which used the generic kernel (**linux-image**), and then decide to run it as a server. Just use the Synaptic Package Manager to install the **linux-image-server** package and then use Grub to select that as the kernel to use instead of the generic kernel. You could use the generic kernel to run the servers, but the generic kernel is not optimized for server operation and would work much more slowly. The server is optimized for supporting the command line interface. It will work with the X server drivers, but may not always work with proprietary video hardware drivers (Nvidia and AMD).

You can do the same for systems running virtual machines. On a system where you have already installed the linux-generic kernel, you can install the **linux-virtual** meta-package and then, from Grub, choose to run it. Keep in mind that if the server kernel is installed, the server kernel will be removed.

A **linux** kernel metapackage, like **linux-generic**, installs the **linux-image** meta package which will install the recent kernel image package. It will also install any needed supporting kernel module packages like the restricted modules for non-free applications and codecs. The kernel meta packages are shown here.

```
linux-generic
linux-server
linux-virtual
```

If, for some reason, you want to just install the kernel image file, you can use the kernel image meta packages. These begin with **linux-image**. They will install the latest version of the kernel.

```
linux-image-generic
linux-image-server
linux-image-virtual
```

The actual kernel package name will include the kernel version, like that show here for the generic kernel.

```
linux-image-2.6.28-14-generic
```

Should you have problems for some reason with the newest kernel version, you can choose to install an earlier one. From the Synaptic Package Manager, select the earlier kernel version package, like the one shown here. An entry for choosing it will be placed in the Grub menu, which you can then choose to run when your system starts up.

```
linux-image-2.6.28-11-generic
```

As new kernels are installed, the previous one will be retained, allowing you to go back to using the previous kernel should you have problems with the new one. Entries for the previous and current kernel will be listed on your Grub menu at start up.

For each kernel, there are corresponding kernel header packages (also known as builds), denoted with the term **linux-headers**, that contain only the kernel headers. These are used for compiling kernel modules or software applications that do not need the full kernel source code, just the headers. The headers for your current kernel are already installed. The kernel headers will be installed in the **/usr/src/linux-***version* directory with a **build** link to it in the kernel's **/lib/modules** directory. The kernel headers package will also have the version name.

```
linux-headers-2.6.28-14-generic
```

You can also install the Backports kernel modules package that provides backport support for the latest development software. .

```
linux-backports-modules-jaunty
```

The Backports kernel modules also has its own headers package.

```
linux-headers-lbm-version
```

Update kernel packages

The Update Manager will automatically download and install new kernels as they become available, selecting the version appropriate for your system. Normally you do not have to do anything to have the latest kernels installed, except to approve the install. They will be installed for you by the Update Manager. The previous kernel will remain installed, in case you have problems with the new kernel. In the event of problems, you can select the older kernel from the GRUB menu and use that instead.

The GRUB boot loader configuration file will be automatically edited for you to boot the new kernel. An entry for the new kernel will be placed in the **/boot/grub/menu.lst** file, keeping the entry for the previous kernel. All other entries and configurations will remain. Only the entry for the new kernel is added.

Boot Loader configuration

Installation of a kernel package will automatically create a GRUB boot loader entry for the new kernel. You will be able to select it on startup. Entries for your older kernel will remain. Should you create a customized version of the current kernel, while keeping the original versions as a backup, you would then need to specify the **append-to-version** option to create a new name for the new kernel. It will then be installed as an added kernel.

Creating a Custom Kernel from Ubuntu Kernel Source

Instead of installing already-compiled binary versions of the kernel, you can install the Ubuntu kernel source code on your system, modify it using kernel configuration tools, and use it to create customized kernel binary files yourself. Kernel source code files are compiled with the gcc compiler just as any other source code files are. One advantage to compiling the kernel is that you can enhance its configuration, adding support for certain kinds of devices.

Be sure to consult the Ubuntu documentation on building a kernel at:

```
https://help.ubuntu.com/community/Kernel/Compile
```

If you want to modify your kernel configuration and build a new one, you should be sure to give the kernel a different name. This way you current kernel will not be overwritten. As a precaution, you could make a backup copy of your current kernel. In case something goes wrong with your modified version, you can always boot from the copy you kept. You do not have to worry about this happening if you are installing a new version of the kernel. New kernels are given different names, so the older one is not overwritten.

Compiling and packaging the Ubuntu kernel source requires two supporting packages, the **kernel-package** and **fakeroot** packages. The **kernel-package** package contains the **make-kpkg** used to both compile the kernel and create the kernel DEB package. The fakeroot package allows you to create DEB packages whose files can be installed with administrative access (root user). Use apt-get or the Synaptic Package Manager to install them.

```
sudo apt-get kernel-package fakeroot
```

Installing Ubuntu Kernel Sources

You can obtain the kernel source code package for Ubuntu as the **linux-source** package. You can download it from the Ubuntu repository using the Synaptic Package Manager. The linux-source package is a meta-package that will install the latest kernel source version.

```
linux-source-2.6.28
```

Using **apt-get** you would add the source option to specify as source package and the build-dep option to add any dependent packages the source package may need. Install the dependent packages first.

```
sudo apt-get build-dep linux-source
sudo apt-get source linux-source
```

To obtain the kernel source for a particular kernel version you would specify the linux-image file.

```
sudo apt-get build-dep linux-image-2.6.28-11-generic
sudo apt-get source linux-image-2.6.28-11-generic
```

This package will download a compressed archive to the **/usr/src** directory.

```
linux-source-2.6.28.tar.bz2
```

You can use the **tar -xvjf** command to extract it. It creates a directory with the prefix **linux-source** where the source files are placed. The following example extracts the 2.6.28 kernel to a **linux-source-2.6.28** subdirectory.

```
cd /usr/src
sudo tar -xvjf linux-source-2.6.28.tar.bz2
```

The kernel source file will be extracted to a directory named **/usr/src/linux-2.6.28**.

```
cd  /usr/src/linux-source-2.6.28
```

It is advisable to work with the kernel source in a local directory instead of the /usr/src directory. You can create a local directory and then copy the tar.bz2 file to it. Then extract it in the local directory.

```
mkdir mykernel
sudo cp /usr/src/linux-source-2.6.28.tar.bz2 mykernel
cd mykernel
sudo tar -xvjf linux-source-2.6.28.tar.bz2
cd linux-source-2.6.28
```

Configuring the Kernel

Once the source is installed, you can configure the kernel. Configuration consists of determining the features for which you want to provide kernel-level support. These include drivers for different devices, such as sound cards and SCSI devices. You can configure features as directly included in the kernel itself or as modules the kernel can load as needed. You can also specifically exclude features. Features incorporated directly into the kernel make for a larger kernel program. Features set up as separate modules can also be easily updated. Documentation for many devices that provide sound, video, or network support can be found in the **/usr/share/doc** directory.

Kernel Configuration File: .config

You configure your kernel by generating a .config file in your kernel directory that holds the settings for kernel options. When you first download and install your kernel source package, there will be no .config file in your kernel source directory. It is advisable to set up a an initial **.config** kernel depending on the kind of kernel you want to create. If you do not, then most of the kernel options will be selected by default, generating a larger kernel with options you do not need.

Once you run a kernel configuration tool like **gconfig** or **xconfig**, and then save, the configuration is saved to your **.config** file. The previous version is copied to the **.config.old** file, in case to need to restore it (just rename it as **.config**).

The **.config** file is a dot hidden file. To list is use the **ls** command with the **-a** option.

```
ls -a
```

Customizing the current kernel using the current kernel configuration file

If there is not .config configuration file present, the kernel configuration tools (gconfig, menuconfig, and xconfig) will automatically read the kernel configuration file for the currently running kernel from the **/boot** directory. When you save your configuration, a **.config** file will be generated and written.

Should you want to first manually create a **.conf** file for the currently running kernel, you can copy it from the **/boot** directory and use the **uname -r** command to specify the current kernel version. You would copy it as a **.config**, a dot file, into the directory where you have expanded your kernel source, **linux-2.6.28** in this case. Using the current example, the following command would copy the **/boot/config-2.6.28-14-generic** to **/home/richard/mykernel/linux-2.6.28/.config**.

```
cd linux-2.6.28
cp /boot/config-`uname  -r` .config
```

If you want to generate a customized version based on an installed kernel that is not your currently running kernel, you can copy the kernel from that kernel's configuration file directly from the **/boot** directory. The installed kernel configuration files will have the prefix **config**. The following example uses the configuration file for the **2.6.28-11-generic** installed kernel.

```
cp /boot/config-2.6.28-11-gneeric .config
```

Kernel configuration files for other architectures

If you want to create a kernel for an architecture other than your own, like an arm, x86, powerpc, or ia64, you can use the configuration defaults for those architectures. These are located in the respective **configs** subdirectories for those architectures. The kernel architecture sources are located a the **arch** directory. Within most architecture directories there is a **configs** subdirectory that holds the configuration files. For example, the x86 architecture directory has a config subdirectory with i386_defconfig and x86_64_defconfig for 32 bit and 64it versions.

```
cp  arch/i86/configs/i386_defconfig  .config
```

Kernel Configuration Tools

You can configure the kernel using one of several available configuration tools: `config`, `menuconfig`, `xconfig` (qconf), and `gconfig` (gkc). You can also edit the configuration file directly. These tools perform the same configuration tasks but use different interfaces. The `config` tool is a simple configure script providing line-based prompts for different configuration options. The `menuconfig` tool provides a cursor-based menu, which you can still run from the command line. Menu entries exist for different configuration categories, and you can pick and choose the ones you want. To mark a feature for inclusion in the kernel, move to it and press the SPACEBAR. An asterisk appears in the empty parentheses to the left of the entry. If you want to make it a module, press M and an *M* appears in the parentheses. The `xconfig` option runs qconf, the QT (KDE)–based GUI kernel configuration tool, and requires that the QT libraries (KDE) be installed first. The `gconfig` option runs the **gkc** tool, which uses a GTK interface, requiring that GNOME be installed first. Both **qconf** and **gkc** provide expandable menu trees, selectable panels, and help windows. Selectable features include check buttons you can click.

Instead of using a configuration tool, you could simply edit the **.config** file directly with any text editor and make changes to the listed kernel options. You can set a kernel option to **y** (include in the kernel), **m** (include as a module), and n (do not include). For example, the following line enables ext4 file system support directly in the kernel.

```
CONFIG_EXT4_FS=y
```

Options that have not been set will be commented out with a preceding # sign with an added note saying that it is not set.

```
#CONFIG_EXT4DEV_COMPAT is not set
```

You start a configuration tool by preceding it with the **make** command. Be sure you are in the kernel directory (either the **/usr/src** directory you are using for an Ubuntu kernel package, or the local directory you used for the compressed archive, such as **tar.gz**). The process of starting a configuration tool is a **make** operation that uses the Linux kernel Makefile. The `xconfig` and `gconfig` tools should be started from a terminal window on your window manager. The `menuconfig` and `config` tools are started on a shell command line. You will still need administrative access to modify the files, even though they may reside in a local directory. The files will still need to have **root** user (administrative) access. The following example lists commands to start `xconfig`, `gconfig`, `menuconfig`, and `config`:

```
make gconfig
make xconfig
make menuconfig
make config
```

To run the kernel configuration tools be sure the required development libraries are installed.

> ➤ menuconfg Requires the ncurses development libraries.
> **libncurses5**
> **libncurses5-dev**
> **lib32curses5-dev**

> ➤ gconfig Requires the GTK+ and Glade development libraries.
> **liblibgtk2.0-dev**
> **libglade2-dev**

> ➤ xonfig Requires the QT3 development libraries
> **libqwt5-qt3**
> **libqwt5-qt3-dev**
> **libqt3-mt-dev**

gconfig (gkc)

The GTK kernel configuration tool (**gkc**) is invoked with the **gconfig** option. This uses a GNOME-based interface that is similar to **xconfig** (**qconf**). Be sure the GTK+ development library package is installed, **liblibgtk2.0-dev**. Start the gconfig tool with following command.

```
make gconfig
```

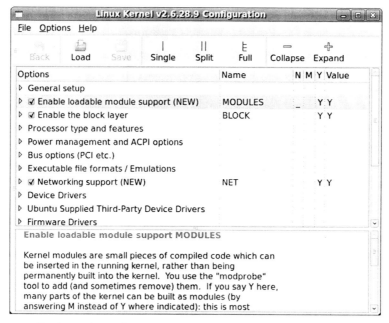

Figure 7-1: gconfig kernel configuration (make gconfig)

The **gkc** tool opens a Linux Kernel Configuration window with expandable submenus like those for qconf (see Figure 7-1). Many categories are organized into a few major headings, with many now included under the Device Drivers menu. The Load and Save buttons and File menu entries can be used to save the configuration or to copy it to a file. Single, Split, and Full view buttons let you display menus in one window, in a display panel with another panel to containing an expandable tree to select entries, or as a single expandable tree of entries. The Expand button will expand all heading and subheading, whereas Collapse will let you expand only those you want displayed. Use the down and side triangles for each entry to expand or collapse subentries.

Clicking an entry opens a window that lists different features you can include. Entries are arranged in columns listing the option, its actual name, its range (yes, module, or no), and its data (yes, no, or module status), see Figure 7-2. Entries in the Options menu let you determine what columns to display: Name for the actual module name; Range for the selectable yes, no, and module entries; and Data for the option status, titled as Value.

The Options column will include a status showing whether the option is included directly (check mark), included as a module (line mark), or not included at all (empty). To quickly select or deselect an entry, double-click the option name in the Options field. You will see its check box checked, lined (module), or empty. Corresponding N, M, and Y entries for no inclusion, module, or kernel inclusion are selected. The default preference for either module or direct kernel inclusion for that option is selected automatically. You can change it manually if you wish.

The Range entries are titled N, M, and Y and are used to select whether not to include an option (N), to load it as a module (M), or to compile it directly into the kernel (Y). Entries that you can select will display an underscore. Clicking the underscore will change its entry to Y for module or direct kernel inclusion, and N for no inclusion. The Value column will show which is currently selected.

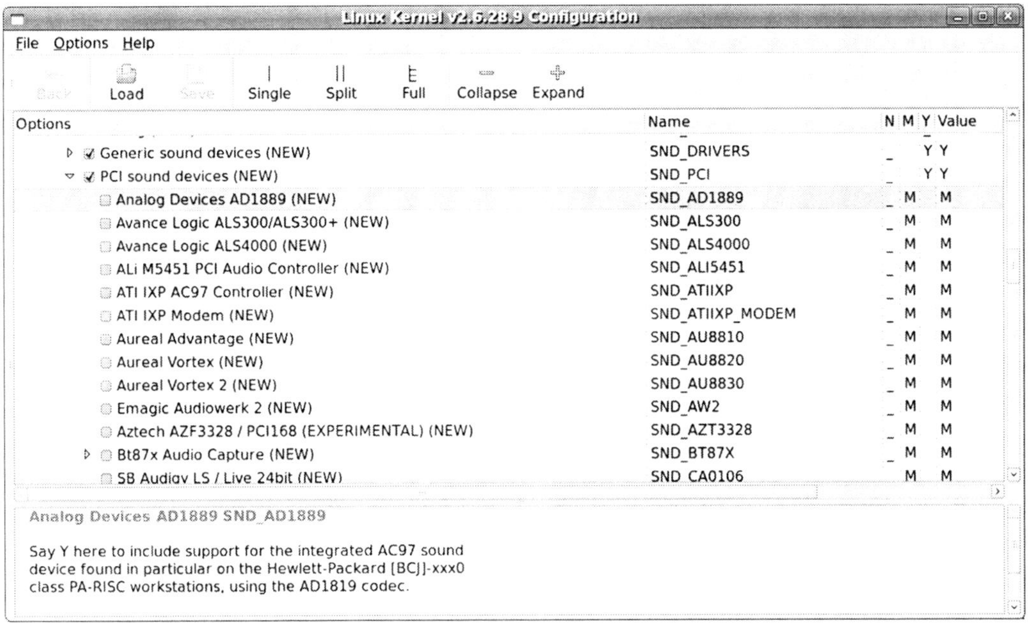

Figure 7-2: gconfig kernel configuration selection

Clicking the Split view will open a sidebar with an expandable tree of all the compiler options (see Figure 7-3). It is an easy way to locate and select a feature. The selected entry will be displayed on the right pane.

Figure 7-3: gconfig kernel configuration split view

menuconfig

The **menuconfig** option generates a cursor based text menu. You can use arrow, tab, and enter keys to move to different menus and entries (see Figure 7-4). Use the spacebar to select or deselect an entry. Be sure you have installed the ncurses development library package, **libncurses5-dev** for 64bit systems, and **lib32curses5-dev** for 32bit systems.

```
make menuconfig
```

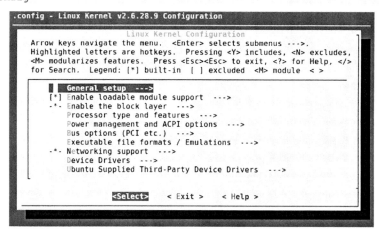

Figure 7-4: menuconfig kernel configuration (make menuconfig)

xconfig (qconf)

The **xconfig** option invokes the qconf tool, which is based on KDE QT libraries. KDE support has to first be installed. The qconf tool opens a Linux Kernel Configuration window listing the different configuration categories. Like gconfig it has a split window option (see Figure 7-5). It has a slightly simpler interface, without the columns for module and source status that `gconfig` has. You use checkboxes next to each feature to select them.

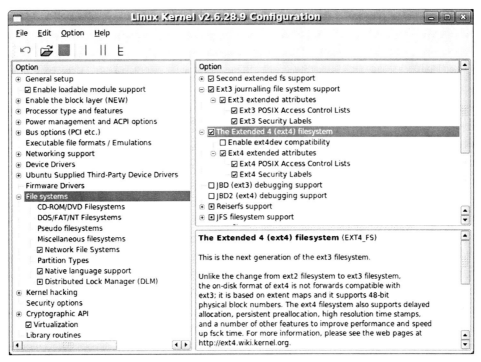

Figure 7-5: kernel configuration (make xconfig)

Be sure to first install the QT3 runtime and development packages, **libqwt5-qt3** and **libqwt5-qt3-dev**.

Important Kernel Configuration Features

The `xconfig`, `menuconfig`, and `gconfig` tools provide excellent context-sensitive help for each entry. To the right of each entry is a Help button. Click it to display a detailed explanation of what that feature does and why you would include it either directly or as a module, or even exclude it. When you are in doubt about a feature, always use the Help button to learn exactly what it does and why you would want to use it. Many of the key features are described here. The primary category for a feature is listed in parentheses.

Tip: As a rule, features in continual use, such as network and file system support, should be compiled directly into the kernel. Features that could easily change, such as sound cards, or features used less frequently should be compiled as modules. Otherwise, your kernel image file may become too large and slower to run.

> **Enable Loadable Module Support (General Setup)**   In most cases, you should make sure your kernel can load modules. Click the Loadable Module Support button to display a listing of several module management options. Make sure Enable Loadable Module

Support is checked. This feature allows your kernel to load modules as they are needed. Kernel Module Loader should also be set to Yes, because this allows your daemons, such as your Web server, to load any modules they may need.

> **Processor Type And Features**   Processor Type And Features entries allow you to set up support for your particular system. Here, you select the type of processor you have and processor features.

> **Power Management and ACPI Options**   Enable power management support like CPU scaling and ACPI.

> **Device Drivers**   The Devices Drivers lists entries that enable support for your SATA, SCSI, video, sound, and USB devices among others

> **Multi-Device Support (RAID and LVM) (Device Drivers)**   Multi-Device Support lists entries that enable the use of RAID devices. You can choose the level of RAID support you want. Here you can also enable Logical Volume Management support (LVM), which lets you combine partitions into logical volumes that can be managed dynamically.

> **SCSI Device Support (Device Drivers)**   If you have any SCSI devices on your system, make sure the entries in the SCSI Support window are set to Yes. You enable support for SCSI disks, tape drives, and CD-ROMs here. The SCSI Low-Level Drivers window displays an extensive list of SCSI devices currently supported by Linux. Be sure the ones you have are selected.

> **Network Device Support (Device Drivers)**   The Network Device Support window lists several general features for network device support. There are entries here for windows that list support for particular types of network devices, including Ethernet (10 or 100Mb) devices, token ring devices, WAN interfaces, and AppleTalk devices. Many of these devices are created as modules you can load as needed. You can elect to rebuild your kernel with support for any of these devices built directly into the kernel.

> **Multimedia Devices (Device Drivers)**   Multimedia devices provide support for various multimedia cards like DVB as well as Video4Linux.

> **File Systems**   The File Systems window lists the different types of file systems Linux can support. These include the Windows file system VFAT (Windows 95/98), but not NTFS (this managed by the ntfs3g module). DVD/CD-ROM file systems such as ISO and UDF are listed. UDF support is configured as a module that needs to be loaded. Network File Systems lists entries like NFS, CIFS (Samba), and NCP (NetWare) are included> Miscellaneous file systems HFS (Macintosh).

> **Sound Card Support (Device Drivers)**   For Sound you can select the Advanced Linux Sound Architecture sound support, expanding it to the drivers for particular sound devices (the Open Sound System is also included, though deprecated).

> **Kernel Hacking**   The Kernel Hacking window lists features of interest to developers who work at the kernel level and need to modify the kernel code. You can have the kernel include debugging information, and also provide some measure of control during crashes.

> **Cryptographic API**   Cryptographic listed supported encryption ciphers.

> ➤ **Virtualization**   Virtualization lists support for KVM, processor built-in virtualization support.

Once you set your options, save your configuration. Select the Save entry on the File menu to overwrites your **.config** configuration file. The Save as option lets you save your configuration to a particular file.

Kernels will be configured to include debugging info, useful for development kernels. However they make kernel modules much larger than they need to be. For kernels you want to use regularly, you may want to have the debugging information left out. In the Kernel Hacking category de-select the "Compile the kernel with debug info" entry.

Compiling an Ubuntu DEB Packaged Kernel: make-kpkg and fakeroot

Kernels you are modifying can be compiled and installed by creating an DEB kernel package that will contain the new kernel binaries. You then simply install that DEB package to install the new kernel.

First make sure you have installed the **kernel-package** package. This contains the **make-kpkg** used to both compile the kernel and create the kernel DEB package.

```
sudo apt-get kernel-package
```

See the man page for **make-kpkg** for a complete description of its use and options.

The configuration file for **make-kpkg** is **/etc/kernel-pkg.conf** for system wide configuration and **.kernel-pkg.conf** for user level configuration. If a **.kernel-pkg.conf** file is present it will take precedence. The **/etc/kernel-pkg.conf** file will already have entries for maintainer and email which you can change to your own name and email. User modifiable options are described in the **make-kpkg.conf** man page. To create a .kernel-pkg file you can start by copying the /etc/kernel-pkg.conf file to your home directory. You can then modify it as you wish.

```
cp /etc/kernel-pkg.conf  .kernel-pkg.conf
```

If you have a multi-core processor, one helpful variable to set would be CONCURRENCY_LEVEL, which specifies the number of cores to use (2, 3, or 4). This will significantly speed up compile time. Variable assignments use the := operator.

```
CONNCURRENCY_LEVEL:=3
```

The kernel files will have root permissions. The **fakeroot** command is used to allow a user with no root user permission build a package with files that have root permission. Be sure to install the **fakeroot** package.

Before you compile the kernel, if want to start with a clean build, you need to run the **make-kpkg** command with the **clean** target. This will remove any compiled files from a previous kernel compilation you may have performed. Your **.config** file will remain.

```
make-kpkg clean
```

You then both generate the kernel binary and package it into an DEB package for installation. Use the **make-kpkg** command with the **-initrd** option to include the **initrd** image. Precede the **make-kpkg** command with the **fakeroot** command. The option **kernel-image** creates the kernel image file.

You can name your kernel version with the **--append-to-version** option. You can use any distinctive number or name you wish (no uppercase). The options names the kernel binaries and its library directory with the linux version with the appended name and number you specified.

```
fakeroot make-kpkg -initrd --append-to-version=version  kernel-image  kernel-headers
```

This creates the deb package and places it in the parent directory for your **linux-source** directory. Then install with Gdebi or dpkg.

```
dpkg -i linux-image-version.deb
```

The following example creates a kernel package with the version name and number **5mymedia**.

```
fakeroot make-kpkg -initrd -- append-to-version=5mymedia kernel-image
```

The kernel binary will have the name.

```
vmlinuz- 2.6.28.9.5mymedia
```

The appended revision number is added after the linux version number, in this case **linux-image-2.6.28.9**, and before the architecture specification, like **_amd64** for 64 bit..

```
linux-image-2.6.28.9_5mymedia_amd64.deb
```

As the kernel compiles you will see compile messages, many indicating access to the kernel architecture directory for the kernel you are generating, like **arch/x86/kernel** for the Intel x86 systems. The kernel image file will then be changed to be owned by the **root** user, and **dpkg** will then build the kernel package. The package will be placed in the parent directory for the **linux-source** directory.

You can add the option **kernel-headers** to include the kernel development headers.

```
fakeroot make-kpkg -initrd --revision=mykernel  kernel-image  kernel-headers
```

There is a **--rootcmd** option which can be used to specify **fakeroot**, **--rootcmd fakeroot**, but it will not work when creating binary versions. For binary packages you need to run **make-kpkg** under **fakeroot**, preceding the **make-kpkg** command with **fakeroot**.

You can then install that kernel package using the Gdebi or dpkg commands. If you place it on a Ubuntu enabled repository, you can install it with **apt-get** or the Synaptic Package Manager.

To review, a sample set of steps to compile a Ubuntu kernel package are shown here:

```
make gconfig
make-kpkg clean
fakeroot make-kpkg -initrd --revision=mykernel kernel-image kernel-headers
```

If you wanted to also generate the documentation, manual, and kernel source packages, you can use the buildpackage target. This target will also perform a **make-kpkg** clean operation.

```
fakeroot make-kpkg -initrd --revision=mykernel buildpackage kernel-image kernel-headers
```

To give your kernel a new revision number, you would use the **--revision** option. You can append a name to the number, but a number is required. The number is appended to the kernel version. For the **--revision** option to work, you first have to run **make-kpkg** with the **clean** target.

This will allow the **make-kpkg** to correctly specify your kernel revision. The commands for a simple compilation and installation are shown here:

```
make-kpkg clean
fakeroot make-kpkg -initrd --revision=number kernel-image
```

The following example creates a kernel package with the revision number **33**.

```
fakeroot make-kpkg -initrd --revision=33 kernel-image
```

The revision number is added after the linux version number, in this case **linux-image-2.6.28.9**, and before the architecture specification, like **_amd64** for 64 bit..

```
linux-image-2.6.28.9_33_amd64.deb
```

Ubuntu Kernel Repository: GIT

To use the latest kernels for professional kernel development, you use the GIT revision control system. With GIT you can access the Ubuntu development kernel sources from **kernel.ubuntu.com**. See the KernelGitGuide and the man page for **gittutorial** for more information about GIT. Also check the Ubuntu help kernel compile page for information on how to use GIT to compile your kernel.

```
https://wiki.ubuntu.com/KernelTeam/KernelGitGuide
man gittutorial
https://help.ubuntu.com/community/Kernel/Compile
```

The Ubuntu kernel repository is located at:

```
http://kernel.ubuntu.com/git/
```

Here you will find subdirectories for the GIT repositories including the various Ubuntu releases.

Before using git, first install the GIT software, the **git-core** package. You will also need the **kernel-wedge** and **makedumpfile** packages.

To download a kernel repository you use the **git** command with the **clone** option and specify the Ubuntu release, in this case **ubntu-jaunty.git**. GIT has its own protocol, **git://**. This is a large repository of several hundred MB.

```
git clone git://kernel.ubuntu.com/ubuntu/ubuntu-jaunty.git
```

The download will first count and compress objects, and then download the repository objects showing the percentage and amount of the download progress with the speed (the repository size is about 1 GIG). Once downloaded the source files are checked out of the repository.

You then change to your GIT directory, in this case **ubuntu-jaunty**. By default the current kernel is extracted.

You can use the kernel configuration tools like **menuconfig** and **gconfig** to configure your kernel source.

The boot kernel configuration file for the running kernel will be used by default if no **.config** file is present. To use another configuration file, copy it from the /boot directory as the

.confg file, or, for a different architecture, copy the **defconfig** file from the architecture's **configs** directory (**arch** directory). You can also copy the default GIT kernel configuration files located in the **debian.master/config** subdirectory.

First make sure the build is clean. Run **debian/rules** with the **clean** option. You will have to use the **sudo** command as the build subdirectories are owned by the root user.

```
sudo debian/rules clean
```

You may also need to clean your GIT tree using the **git** command and **clean** target with the **-xdf** options.

```
git clean -xdf
```

Then compile using the **rules** script in the **debian** directory, **debian/rules**. This needs to be run under **fakeroot**.

```
AUTOBUILD=1 fakeroot debian/rules binary-debs
```

For a specific kernel use the binary-*flavor* option where *flavor* is the type of kernel like generic or server. The skipabi option will ignore ABI errors.

```
AUTOBUILD=1 NOEXTRAS=1 skipabi=true fakeroot debian/rules binary-generic
```

If you have a multi-core processor on your system, you can speed up compiling by using **CONCURRENCY_LEVEL** to specify the number of processors to use.

```
CONCURRENCY_LEVEL=2 NOEXTRAS=1 skipabi=true fakeroot debian/rules binary-generic
```

The compiled package will be placed in a DEB package in your GIT directory's parent directory. Both image and headers packages will be created. Examples are shown here.

```
linux-image-2.6.28-15-generic_2.6.28-15.52_amd64.deb
linux-headers-2.6.28-15-generic_2.6.28-15.52_amd64.deb
```

Keep your GIT repository updated by running the **git fetch** command.

```
git fetch
```

If you want to use a different kernel, you can check it out from the repository. To find out the available versions use the **git tag** command and pipe the output to **grep Ubuntu***..

```
git tag | grep Ubuntu*
```

Then checkout (extract) the kernel version you want, an example is shown here.

```
git checkout Ubntu-2.6.28-11
```

Then reset the GIT tree to the checked out kernel. Use the **reset** command with the **--hard** option. Then clean the GIT tree with the **git** command and **clean** target with the **-xdf** options.

```
git reset --hard
git clean -xdf
```

Note: To use the GIT repository to build an original source kernel see:
https://wiki.ubuntu.com/KernelTeam/GitKernelBuild.

Compiling and Installing the original Kernel using the original kernel compile and install commands

Though not recommended, you can, instead, compile and install the kernel using the original standard kernel compile and install commands. You will, however, have to manually configure the GRUB boot loader to access your new kernel.

If you want to remove a configuration entirely, you can use the `mrproper` option to remove the **.config** file and any binary files, starting over from scratch.

```
make mrproper
```

By default, when you configured the kernel with a configuration tool, the configuration file for the currently running kernel is used. To use a specific installed kernel, you can copy its configuration file from the **/boot** directory as the **.config** file.

If you want to use a **.config** file from a kernel you configured previously, you can use the **make** command with the **oldconfig** option. The previous **.config** is copied to **.old.config**.

```
make oldconfig
```

You configure the kernel using the kernel configuration tools as described in the previous section. Use the **make** command with the **gconfig**, **xconfig**, or **menuconfig** options to start a configuration interface.

```
make gconfig
```

To compile and install a kernel using the original kernel commands, you run a series of **make** operations, first to compile the kernel and then to install it and its modules. Now that the configuration is ready, you can compile your kernel. You can display the options available with the help option.

```
make help
```

You also have to clean up any object and dependency files that may remain from a previous compilation. Use the following command to remove such files:

```
make clean
```

You can use several options to compile the kernel (see Table 7-1).

Option	Description
install	Creates the kernel and installs it on your system.
bzImage	Creates the compressed kernel file and calls it **bzImage**.
isoimage	Creates the kernel and installs it on a CD-ROM disk (creates a boot disk).
vmlinuz	Creates the bare kernel image file.
fdimage	Creates floppy disk image with the kernel, 1.44 MB (bootable).
fdimage288	Creates floppy disk 2.88 image with the kernel (bootable).

Table 7-1: Original Compiling Options for Kernel make command

The **bzImage** option simply generates a kernel file called **bzImage** and places it in the **arch** directory. For Intel and AMD systems, you find **bzImage** in the **86/boot** subdirectory, **arch/86/boot**. For a kernel source, this would be in **arch/86/boot**. A kernel type directory will also be generated in the **arch** directory like **i686** or **x86_64**, which will hold the **boot** directory only with a link named **bzImage** to the **arch/86/boot/bzImage** file. The **bzImage** option is the default so you can simply enter **make** with no arguments.

```
make
```

The options in Table 7-1 create the kernel, but not the modules—those features of the kernel to be compiled into separate modules. To compile your modules, use the **make** command with the **modules** argument.

```
make modules
```

To install your modules, use the **make** command with the **modules_install** option. This installs the modules in the **/lib/modules/***version-num* directory, where *version-num* is the version number of the kernel. You should make a backup copy of the old modules before you install the new ones.

```
make modules_install
```

The **install** option both generates the kernel files and installs them on your system as **vmlinuz**, incorporating the **make bzImage** step. This operation will place the kernel files such as **bzImage** in the **/boot** directory, giving them the appropriate names and kernel version number.

```
make install
```

The commands for a simple compilation and installation are shown here:

```
make clean
make
make modules_install
make install
```

If you want, you could enter these all on fewer lines, separating the commands with semicolons, as shown here:

```
make clean; make; make modules_install; make install
```

A safer way to perform these operations on single lines is to make them conditionally dependent on one another, using the **&&** command. In the preceding method, if one operation has an error, the next one will still be executed. By making the operations conditional, the next operation is run only if the preceding one is successful.

```
make clean && make && make modules_install &&  make install
```

You will also have to create a module ram disk image and add an entry for the new kernel in the GRUB bootloader configuration file, **/etc/grub/grub.conf**.

Module RAM Disks: initramfs

If your system uses certain block devices unsupported by the kernel, such as some SCSI, RAID, or IDE devices, you will need to load certain required modules when you boot. Such block device modules are kept on a RAM disk that is accessed when your system first starts up (RAM disks are also used for diskless systems). For example, if you have a SCSI hard drive or CD-ROMs, the SCSI drivers for them are often held in modules that are loaded whenever you start up your system. These modules are stored in a RAM disk from which the startup process reads. If you create a new kernel that needs to load modules to start up, you must create a new RAM disk for those modules. You need to create a new RAM disk only if your kernel has to load modules at startup. If, for example, you use a SCSI hard drive but you incorporated SCSI hard drive and CD-ROM support (including support for the specific model) directly into your kernel, you don't need to set up a RAM disk (support for most IDE hard drives and CD-ROMs is already incorporated directly into the kernel).

RAM disks are created automatically with the **--initrd** option for the **make-kpkg** command when you created our Ubuntu kernel.

RAM disks are now implemented as **initramfs** file systems, replacing the older cramfs initrd disks.

To manage the initrd RAM disk images on your system, you use the **mkinitramfs-update** command (see the man page for **mkinitramfs-update** for all options). With mkinitramfs-update you can modify, replace, or remove RAM disk on your system. Appropriate changes are made to GRUB. Options for the RAM disk are specified in the **initramfs-tools** configuration directory, **/etc/initramfs-tools**. In the modules file you can specify specific modules to add. For example, if you want to add RAID support your kernel RAM disk, you would enter the raid module name in the **/etc/initramfs-tools/modules** file, then use **mkinitramfs**-update to make the changes to your kernel initrd img file, the RAM disk. With no specific kernel specified, the command will update the latest kernel, as shown here.

```
mkinitramfs-update -u
```

For a specific kernel, specify the kernel version with the **-k** option.

```
mkinitramfs-update -u  -k 2.6.28-11
```

To create a new RAM disk for a kernel version use the **-c** option.

```
mkinitramfs-update -c  -k 2.6.28-11
```

The **/etc/initramfs-tools/initramfs-update.conf** file configures basic capabilities for the **mkinitramfs-update** command. You can set the initramfs-update option in this file to **yes** (allow updating), **all** (update all RAM disk files), or **no** (disable RAM disk updating). You can also enable backups.

```
initramfs-update=yes
```

The **/etc/initramfs-tools/initramfs.conf** file configures how your RAM disk are created. The MODULES directive specifies the collection of modules in general to include (**most** for all modules, **list** for just those specified, **netbook** for only network and basic modules without block devices, and **dep** to try and guess what modules are needed).

```
MODULES=most
```

If you need to create a RAM disk image to save separately (like one you want to install on another system), you can use the `mkinitramfs` command. See the Man page for `mkinitramfs` for more details. The `mkinitramfs` command takes as its argument the kernel that the modules are taken from. The **-o** option specifies the file to output to. In the following example, a RAM disk image called **initrd-2.6.***version***.img** is created in the **/boot** directory, using modules from the 2.6.28-14 kernel. The 2.6.28-14 kernel must already be installed on your system and its modules created.

```
mkinitramfs -o initrd-2.6.version.img     2.6.28-14
```

To have kernel modules added to the initramfs RAM disk created by **mkinitramfs**, you specify them in the **/etc/initramfs-tools/modules** file.

GRUB Boot Loader Configurations

For the boot loader GRUB, you can configure your system to enable you to start any of your installed kernels. When you install a new kernel versions, a new entry is created for it in the /boot/grub/menu.lst file. From the GRUB boot menu you can then select the kernel you want to use. Entries are added every for customized kernels installed with Gdebi or dpkg. It is possible for you to manually add new Grub entries for specific kernels not automatically installed.

Kernel Boot Disks

You can also install a kernel on a boot disk or CD-ROM and boot your system from that disc. You can either install your Ubuntu kernel with **bootcdwrite**, or use make options to install a kernel generated using the original kernel make operations.

bootcdwrite

To make a boot CD using your current Ubuntu kernel, you use the **bootcdwrite** command. Configuration for **bootcdwrite** is in the **/etc/bootcd** directory. The **bootcdwrite.conf** file holds configuration setting for creating the boot CD such as the kernel to use and kernel label. Be sure to also install the **boot-mkinitramfs** package. The bootcdwrite command will start a series of checks and questions like cleaning up the APT repository.

```
sudo bootcdwrite
```

Original Kernel make Operations

Instead of installing the kernel on your system, you can simply place it on a boot disk or CD-ROM and boot your system from that disc. For an original kernel compile, you can generate a boot disk using kernel **make** options. For a DVD/CD-ROM you can use the **isoimage** option. For a floppy disk image you can create either a 1.44 or 2.88 image (which will hold the 2.6 kernel). Use the **fdimage** option for a 1.44 image and **fdimage288** for the 1.88 image. Both fdimage and fdimage288 create corresponding floppy disk images in the in the **arch/i386/boot** directory. The **fdimage288** image is often used for virtual users.

```
make isoimage
make fdimage
make fdimage288
```

8. Virtualization

Virtual Machine Manager: virt-manager

Kernel-based Virtualization Machine (KVM)

Xen Virtualization

Though Linux provides support to two methods of virtualization: the paravirtualization implementation employed by Xen to the hardware acceleration used by the Kernel-based Virtual Machine (KVM) for Intel and AMD processors with hardware virtualization support. However only the Kernel-based Virtual Machine (KVM) is currently implemented in the kernel. On Ubuntu 9.04 you can only use KVM to run virtual machines, requires that your system processor have hardware virtualization support built in.

Virtual Machines can be installed and managed with the Virtual Machine Manager (**virt-manager**), a GNOME-based tool that provides a simple GUI for managing your virtual machines and installing new ones. Linux also provides the GNOME VM applet, **gnome-applet-vm**, a panel applet that can monitor your virtual machines. See Table 8-1 for a listing of virtualization resources. See **http://virt.kernelnewbies.org** for general virtualization links and overview.

Resource	Description
http://virt-manager.et.redhat.com/	Virtual Machine Manager, virt-manager.
http://bellard.org/qemu/	QEMU software virtualization
http://kvm.qumranet.com/kvmwiki	KVM hardware virtualization
http://libvirt.org/	libvirt tool kit for accessing Linux virtualization capabilities.
http://sourceforge.net/projects/kvm	Kernel Virtual Machine (KVM) Web site
http://kraxel.fedorapeople.org/xenner/	Xenner Xen emulation using KVM

Table 8-1: Virtualization Resources

Virtual Machine Manager: virt-manager

You can easily manage and set up KVM or Xen virtual machines using the Virtual Machine Manager (virt-manager). Be sure that virt-manager is installed. Select Virtual Machine Manager from the Applications | System Tools menu. This will display a window listing your virtual machines (see Figure 8-1). Features like the machine ID, name, status, CPU and memory usage will be displayed. You can use the View menu to determine what features to display. Click the Help entry in the Help menu to show a detailed manual for Virtual Machine Manager.

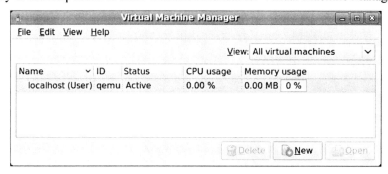

Figure 8-1: The Virtual Machine Manager

Initially, you should be connected to the localhost virtual host. If not, to access the host, right-click on its entry in the Virtual Machine Manager window and select connect from the pop-up menu. Once connected, the several of the buttons at the bottom of the widow become active. You can use the New button to create a new virtual machine on that host. The Delete button will remove it.

You could have several hosts, with machine running on remote hosts. To connect, select the Add Connection entry from the File menu. This opens an Add Connection window where you can specify the Hypervisor (QEMU/KVM or Xen) and the connection like "Remote tunnel over SSH". Specify the host and then click Connect.

Xen is currently not supported on Ubuntu. When it becomes supported, a Xen virtual machine will be listed as a Xen host. To access the host, right-click on its entry in the Virtual Machine Manager window, and select connect from the pop-up menu. Once connected, the several of the buttons at the bottom of the widow become active. You can use the New button to create a new virtual machine.

Virtual Host Details and Preferences

For detailed information about the host machine, click Host Details from the Edit menu to open the Host Details window (see Figure 8-2). The Overview tab will show information like the host name, the number of CPUs it has, and the kind of hypervisor it can launch. The Virtual Network tab shows your virtual networks, listing IPv4 connection information, the device name, and the network name. A default virtual network will already be set up. To add a new network, click the plus (+) button. This opens a series of dialogs for adding a new virtual network device. The device is then displayed on the Virtual Networks tab.

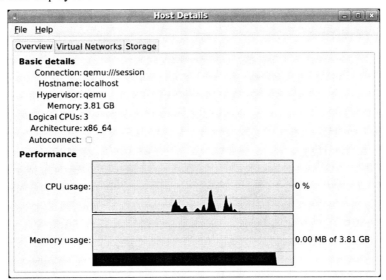

Figure 8-2: Host Details: Overview

Virtual Storage

The Storage tab lists the external storage available to your virtual machine (See Figure 8-3). Initially it will be empty and the only active button will be the plus sign at the lower left corner.

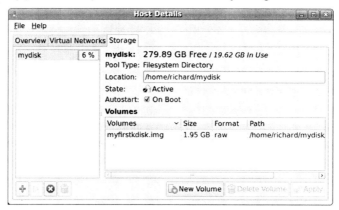

Figure 8-3: Storage pool with virtual volumes (disk images)

First you create a storage pool using an external storage device. Click the plus button (+) in the lower left corner to open an Add a New Storage Pool dialog where you first select the type of storage you want to use and provide a name for it (see Figure 8-4). The device type can be a directory where a file system is mounted, a physical hard disk, are preformatted block device like a USB drive, ISCSI device, an LVM device, or are remote NFS directory. On the Add Storage Pool dialog you specify the target path, format, host name, source path depending on the type of storage to select. Once the storage pool is created you can then create image files on it that you can then use on your virtual machine.

Figure 8-4: Add storage pool

The easiest way to access your own hard disk to use for additional storage is to first create a directory to use for the virtual pool. Make sure you have permission to access it. A simple method is to set up a virtual pool on your home directory. To make a virtual pool accessible to other virtual machines, you could set it up in a shared directory. On the Add a New Storage Pool dialog select the first entry for the type, dir: Filesystem Directory. For the name specify the name of the directory you created for the storage pool (see Figure 8-5). On the next dialog specify the target path for your directory. This will default to /var/lib/libvirt/images/ with the name you gave to the storage pool attached as a subdirectory. You will not initially have permission to access to this directory. Either provide permission (read/write access by other users) or select another directory for which you have access. In this example the **mydisk** directory in the user home folder is used instead. The Browse button is clicked to select that directory. You can use the Browse button to locate and use any other directory. Once the directory is selected, click the Forward button to create your pool.

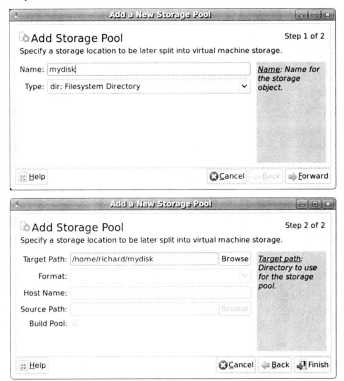

Figure 8-5: Add storage pool using directory on local hard disk

The new storage pool will be created and listed on the Storage tab (see Figure 8-3). To create additional storage, select the storage pool to create the storage one. The New Volume button become active, click on it. This opens a New Storage Volume window where you can create a new disk image file, specifying its size and name (see Figure 8-6). For the size you can specify a maximum and allocated size. The allocated size can be smaller and the image file will grow to the maximum as needed. To delete a disk image, select the disk image entry can click the Delete Volume button.

Host Preferences

Virtual machine preferences can be set by selecting Preferences from the Edit menu to open the Preferences window (see Figure 8-7). The Stats tab lets you set update options and features to display. The VM Details tab provides settings for console opening, keyboard input, and audio device install.

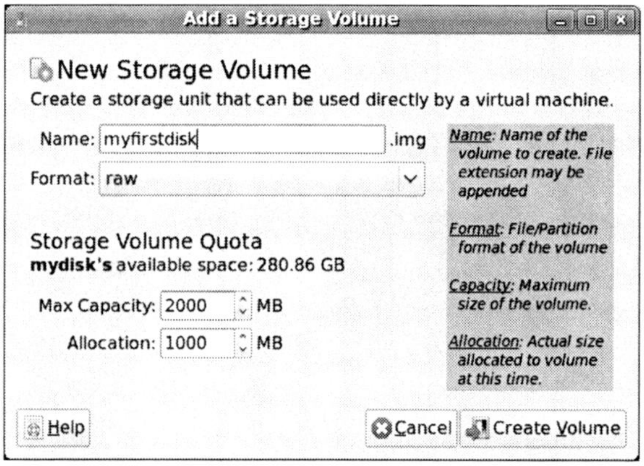

Figure 8-6: Add a storage volume (image file) on a storage pool

Figure 8-7: Virtual Machine Manager Preferences

Creating a Virtual Machine

To create a virtual machine, first select a virtual host. Initially a localhost virtual host will be set up for you and selected. Should you have several virtual hosts, first select the one you want to create the new virtual machine on.

You can have several hosts. This is the case if you have installed both Xen and KVM support. KVM will show a qemu host and Xen will show a Xen host. Initially the hosts are disconnected. Your first have to connect to the host to access or create its virtual machines. To access a host, right-click on its entry in the Virtual Machine Manager window, and select connect from the pop-up menu. Once connected, the several of the buttons at the bottom of the widow become active. You can use the New button to create a new virtual machine.

Once the virtual host is selected, to create a new virtual machine on that host, either select New Machine from the File menu or click the New button. This will start up virt-install wizard.

You will be prompted for name and type of install location, the location of the Operating System install disk or files, the storage to use for the virtual machine, and the amount of system memory to allocate for the guest OS.

On the first dialog you enter a name for your virtual machine (see Figure 8-8).

Figure 8-8: Create a new virtual machine: Name

After entering a name, you then choose your virtualization method (see Figure 8-9). If you are running a standard kernel, you will only have the option to use a fully virtualized method. On systems with Intel VT and AMD SVM processors you will also have the option to enable hardware acceleration. This means using KVM (kernel-based virtual machine) support that will provide processor-level hardware virtualization. For processors without hardware virtualization support, software emulation is used.

Figure 8-9: Create a new virtual machine: virtualization method

You then choose the installation method, whether from local media (iso image file or CD-ROM disk) or a network source (FTP, HTTP, NFS, or PXE), see Figure 8-10. An ISO disk image is preferred. You also choose the type of operation system. From the OS Type menu you can choose an OS type such as Linux or Windows. From the OS Variant menu you can choose the particular OS like Fedora 11 or Windows XP. The options vary depending upon the OS Type you choose.

Figure 8-10: Create a new virtual machine: installation method

Figure 8-11 Create a new virtual machine: installation media

You then choose the location of the OS install media (see Figure 8-11). For a fully virtualized OS, this can either be a disk image or a CD/DVD-ROM, like a Windows install disk.

You then choose the type of operating system you are installing, first selecting a category like Linux or Windows, and then a particular distribution or version like Centos Linux or Windows XP.

You then choose the storage method (see Figure 8-12). This can be either an existing partition or a file. If you choose a file, you can either set a fixed size (like a fixed partition), or have the file expand as needed. Should the file be on partition with a great deal of free space, this may not be an issue. Initially the file will be 4 GB, though you may want to make it larger to allow for regular use.

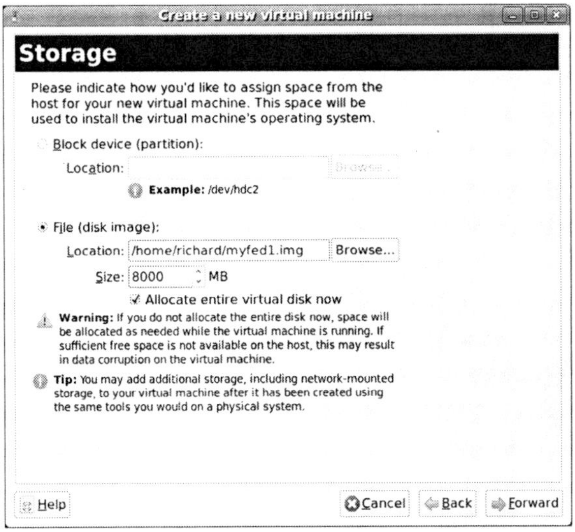

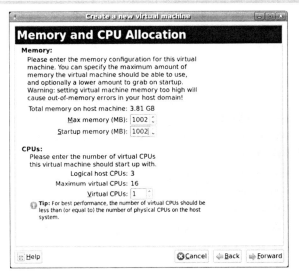

Figure 8-12: Create a new virtual machine: Storage

Figure 8-13: Create a new virtual machine: memory and CPU allocation

You then choose the amount of physical ram to use and the number of CPUs (see Figure 8-13). 512 MB is usually the default, though, if you have the memory, you should increase this to at least 1GB, 1002 MB. Your machine will run much more smoothly. Still, keep in mind you many virtual machines you want to run at once and how much memory you have.

A final screen displays all your configuration information for the new virtual machine before you start installation (see Figure 8-14). You can still cancel at this point. The Advanced button will open further options like the network connection to use and the architecture. Be careful to check that the correct architecture is selected. By default the architecture of the Ubuntu system running the Virtual Machine Manager is selected, like x86_64 for a 64 bit system. Should you want to run a i386 (32 bit) operating system on the virtual machine, be sure to change the architecture to i686.

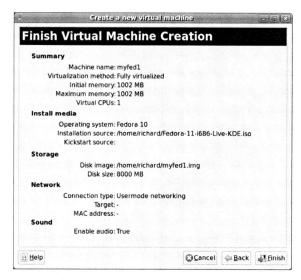

Figure 8-14: Create a new virtual machine: Finish

The Virtual Machine window is then opened to the Console tab, and the install process for that operating system begins (see Figure 8-15). You install as you normally would. To use your mouse on for installing the operating system, pass the mouse over the Virtual Machine Console window. It will be captured and you can use it on the operating system install dialogs. To return the mouse to your Ubuntu desktop, press Ctrl-Alt and move the mouse away from the Virtual Machine Console.

Once you have finished your installation, that operating system will try to reboot. You man have to click the Run button on the Virtual Machine window to have it restart. There are buttons to run, pause, and shutdown the new operating system (see Figure 8-15).

Figure 8-15: The Virtual Machine Console (installation)

Your installed virtual machines will now be listed under its host in the Virtual Machine Manager window (See Figure 8-16)

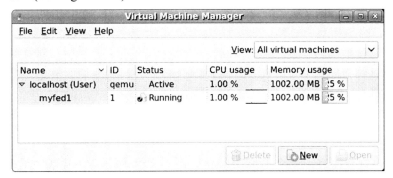

Figure 8-16: The Virtual Machine Console with Virtual Machines

Once restarted the operating system will start as it normally would with its own login interface. Once logged in, you will have a fully functional operating system, like the one shown in Figure 8-17 for Ubuntu.

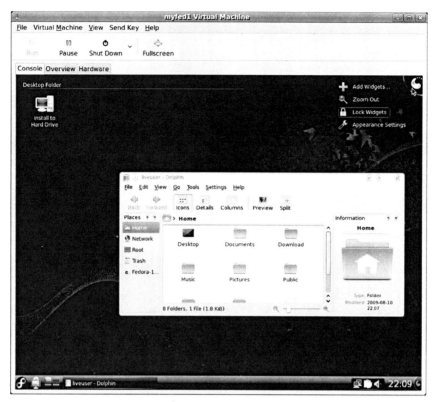

Figure 8-17: The Virtual Machine Console (running os)

To shut down, you should use the operating system's shut down commands, not the Virtual Machine Windows's Shutdown button.

Should your system crash or fail to shut down completely, the virtual machine will still continue to run. To force a shutoff you select the Shut Down menu's Force Off entry. The Shut Down menu is available on the Virtual Machine Console toolbar (drop-down menu next to the Shut Down icon) and also on the Virtual Machine Manager window (select and right-click on the virtual machine entry in the Virtual Machine Manager window and select the Shut Down menu, to open submenu with options to Reboot, Shut Down, and Force Off). Select the Force Off entry to shutdown the system.

Virtual Machine Window

The Virtual Machine window will display a toolbar with buttons for Run, Pause, Shut Down, and Fullscreen. Next to the Shut Down icon is a drop-down menu with options to Reboot, Shut Down, and Force Off. Use these to force shutdown if needed.

The menu bar lists menus for File, Virtual Machine, View, Send Key, and Help. The Virtual Machine menu has the same entries as the toolbar, with an added entry to Save the current state of the virtual machine. The View menu lets you scale the display and move to full screen. The Send Key menu lets you send special key sequences like Ctrl-Alt-Delete to reboot.

The Virtual Machine Window has three tabs: Console, Overview, and Hardware. The Console tab is used for running the virtual machine, displaying the interactive desktop interface as you would have on any system. The Over view tab provides monitoring information, and the Hardware tab lets you manage the hardware device tasks, like setting the boot device, inserting a CD-ROM virtually, or even adding new disk partitions or image files.

Monitoring your virtual machine: Overview tab

To monitor your virtual machine click the Overview tab (see Figure 8-18). This Overview tab shows basic details including the virtual machine name and UUID, as well as performance information showing graphs of the machine's real time CPU and Memory usage (see Figure 8-12).

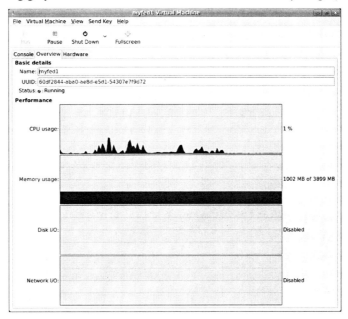

Figure 8-18: The Virtual Machine window: Overview tab

Managing virtual devices: Hardware tab

The Hardware tab lists the machine's hardware devices on a left side scrollable window. Selecting an entry displays its associated pane on the right side (see Figure 8-16). You can use the Memory pane to change the amount of memory allocated for the virtual machine and the Processor pane to set the number of CPUs to use (must be less than the physical number on your system).

Boot Options lets you select the device to boot from, like a hard disk or CD-ROM. Disk **hdc** is the CD-ROM device. Here you can connect to a CD/DVD disc image file, effectively inserting the disc to the virtual CD/DVD drive.

The Disk **vda** pane is the virtual disk you are booting form. The NIC entry is for setting your network card device. There are also settings panes for your Mouse, Display, Sound device, and Serial device.

Panes for devices will have a Remove button at the lower right corner (see Figure 8-19). Be careful not to click this button unless you really want to remove the device. For the CD/DVD device, you use the Disconnect and Connect button to insert and eject a CD/DVD-ROM ISO image file. The Remove button would be similar to remove the actual CD/DVD drive from your computer.

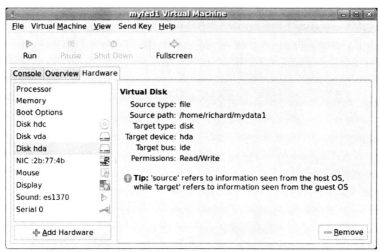

Figure 8-19: The Virtual Machine window: Hardware tab

You can also add devices by clicking the Add Hardware button. This opens an Add Virtual Hardware window (see Figure 8-20). From the drop-down menu you first select the hardware type.

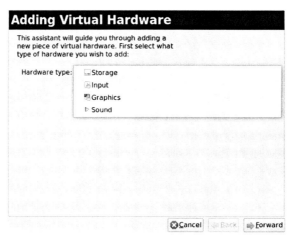

Figure 8-20: Add Virtual Hardware

For the Storage type, a Storage dialog opens where you select either a physical partition or previously created disk image file (See Figure 8-21). You also select the Device type which can be IDE disk, CD-ROM, SCSI disk, Floppy disk, or USB disk.

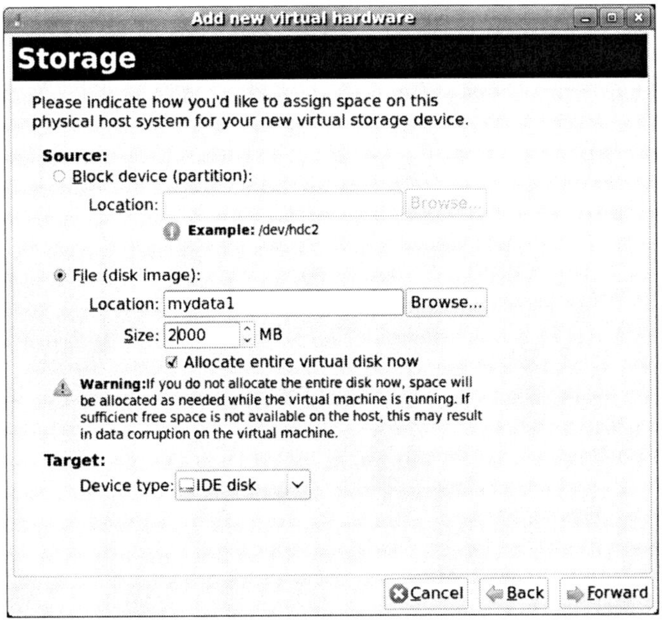

Figure 8-21: Add Virtual Storage

Should you accidently remove your CD/DVD device, you can use the Add Hardware dialogs to restore it. Select Storage as the type, and then on the Storage dialog, change the Device Type to CD-ROM. Then select Block Device and click the Browse button. On the Choose Volume window, click the Browse Local button. This opens a listing of devices in the /dev directory. Choose the **cdrom** entry.

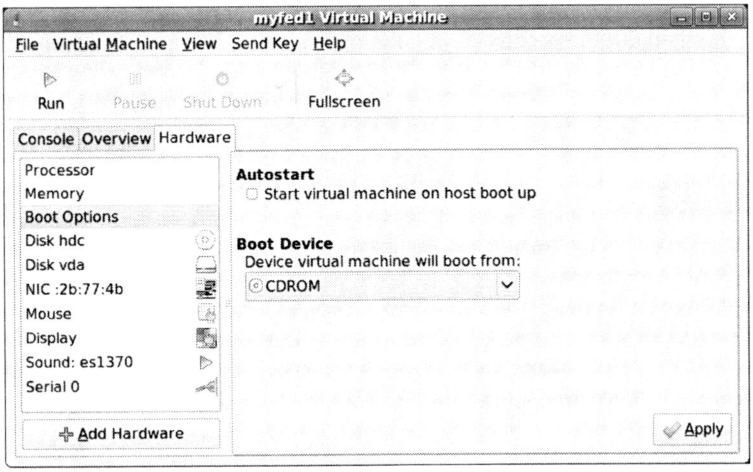

Figure 8-22: Virtual Boot Options

Managing virtual boot operations

You can use the Boot and CD-ROM device panes to set up your virtual machine to boot from a CD/DVD disc or disc ISO image file, instead of from your virtual hard drive. This is helpful if you want to install another operating system on your virtual machine, recover using a CD-ROM, or run a Live CD, like a Fedora or Ubuntu Live CD. You would first select Boot Options and change the Boot Device to CDROM using the drop-down menu, as shown in Figure 8-22. Be sure to click the Apply button to have the change take effect.

Then on the CD-ROM device pane (Disk hdc), use the Connect button to select the CD/DVD disk ISO image (see Figure 8-23). This effectively inserts the CD/DVD-ROM in the virtual CD/DVD drive. When you Run your virtual machine, it will boot from the CD/DVD disk ISO image instead of the hard drive.

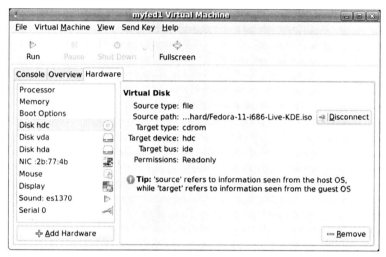

Figure 8-23: Virtual CD-ROM insertion

To one again boot form the hard drive, just change the Boot Device back to hard disk on the Boot Options pane, and click Apply.

virt-install and virsh

You can also install a virtual machine from the command using the **virt-install** script. It currently can only install from a remote network location using an **http://**, **nfs://**, or **ftp://** prefix. This script will now allow you to use less than 256MB for each virtual machine. If you want to use less memory, say for a scaled down version of Ubuntu, you will have to us the configuration files directly as described in the previous section. The script supports virtual hosts using either KVM or Xen (when Xen support becomes available).

If you have a limited amount of RAM memory, you may need to limit the amount the **domain 0** virtual machine is using. You can reduce this to the recommended 256MB with the following command.

```
xm mem-set 0 256
```

To start **virt-install** script, open a terminal window and enter the script name.

```
virt-install
```

You will be prompted to set different parameters, and then a configuration file will be automatically generated. You will first be prompted to name the virtual machine. This is your host name. Then you are asked how much RAM to allocate.

You are then prompted for the disk path for the virtual machine image file. Enter the path with the image file name. You are then prompted for the size of the image file in Gigabytes. Virtual machines use an image file where its entire system is kept. Finally you are prompted for the location of installation files for the operating system you want to install. Here you can enter an FTP, Web, or NFS site, such as the online Fedora repository. The online Fedora 11 directory is shown in the next example.

```
# virt-install
What is the name of your virtual machine? my-newvm1
 How much RAM should be allocated (in megabytes)? 1002
 What would you like to use as the disk (path)? /home/my-newvm1
  How large would you like the disk to be (in gigabytes)? 8
Would you like to enable graphics support?(yes or no) yes
What is the install location?
http://download.fedora.redhat.com/pub/fedora/linux/releases/11/i386/os/
```

Once the files have been downloaded, the text-based install interface will start up, asking for keyboard and language. If you enabled graphics support, the standard graphical install will start up.

Once installed, you can use the **virsh** command to manage and access your virtual machine form the command line. Check the virsh man page for details on how to use virsh. To connect to a QEMU (KVM) virtual host as use in the previous examples you would use the virsh command with the connect option and the qemu:///session URI.

```
sudo virsh connect qemu:///session
```

The **virsh** command can be used as single commands for as a shell within which you can run virsh commands.

```
sudo virsh
Welcome to virsh, the virtualization interactive terminal.

virsh # connect qemu:///session
```

Kernel-based Virtualization Machine (KVM): Hardware Virtualization

With kernel version 2.6.21, hardware virtualization is now directly supported in the kernel (pervious versions used a kernel module). Hardware virtualization is implemented by Intel and AMD as Hardware Virtual Machine abstraction layer. Intel processors that have hardware virtualization support are labeled VT (Virtualization Technology), and AMD processors are labeled SVM (Secure Virtual Machine). An HVM system has the capability to provide full virtualization, not requiring a specially modified version of an OS kernel like Xen's para-virtualization method uses. You can even run Windows XP directly from Linux using the HVM capability. KVM is an open source project developed by Qumranet, **http://kvm.qumranet.com/kvmwiki**. The KVM applications are included in the Ubuntu **kvm** package.

Kernel-based Virtual Machine (KVM) uses the hardware virtualization in a processor to run virtual machine directly from hardware. There is no underlying software translation. KVM operates directly with the processor.

Hardware requirements are as follows:

➢ An Intel (VT) or AMD (SVM) virtualization enabled processor (like AMD AM2 socket processors or Intel Core2Duo processors). You may need to enable virtualization support in your motherboard. Some motherboards will work better than others. In some cases you may have to disable ACPI support in the motherboard BIOS to allow Windows XP to run.

➢ At least 1 GIG of system memory to allow space for the virtual OS to run. The hardware virtual OS requires its own memory.

KVM is launched as a process directly from the Linux kernel, as if booting to a new OS. As a process is can be managed like any Linux process. KVM adds a quest process mode with its own user and kernel mode. This is in addition to the Linux kernel and user modes. KVM uses the kernel modules kvm-intel or kvm-amd to interface with the processor's virtualization hardware. A modified version of a software emulator QEMU is used to run the OS guest. QEMU was originally designed as an emulator and is also available as such for processors without hardware virtualization. See **http://fabrice.bellard.free.fr/qemu** form more information on QEMU. Both the KVM and QEMU projects have now merged.

Note: KVM is run with a modified version of QEMU which has limited virtual device support, like the graphics driver.

Start the Virtual Machine Manager on your Gnome desktop (Applications | System Tools | Virtual Machine Manager). Choose New Machine for the File menu. This starts the virt-install wizard. When choosing the type of virtualization to use, select Fully Virtualized and make sure hardware acceleration is selected (Enabled kernel/hardware acceleration). You are then prompted for various features like the name, the amount of system memory to use, whether to use a given partition or an image file along with the file size, graphics support, and where the install image is located (this can be a CD/DVD-ROM disk, though a disk image is preferred for Windows).

Note: KVM now supports direct PCI device access (graphics cards are not supported). Direct PCI device access requires that the virtual host run entirely in memory. It cannot be run on a different machine.

Once installed, you can use the Virtual Machine Manager to start up your guest OS at any time. Your guest OK is run in a virtual machine console.

Note: To access data directly on your virtual disks or files, you can use **lomount** or **kpartx**.

Xen Virtualization Kernel

Xen Virtualization technology allows you to run different operating systems on a Linux system, as well as running virtual versions of the kernel to test new applications. Xen is an open source project run by the University of Cambridge Computer Laboratory in coordination with the Open Source Development Labs and several Linux distributors, including Ubuntu. You can find more about Xen at **www.cl.cam.ac.uk/Research/SRG/netos/xen**. Ubuntu integrates Xen support into all its kernels (there are no separate Xen kernel packages).

Xen is designed so that on a single Xen server you can run several virtual machines to run different operating systems at the same time. Xen is a para-virtualized system, meaning that the guest operation system has to be modified to run on Xen. It cannot run without modification as it could on a fully virtualized system like VMware. Xen is designed to use a para-virtualization approach to increase efficiency, giving its virtual machines nearly the same level of efficiency as the native kernel. For an operating system to work on Xen, it must be configured to access the Xen interface. Currently only UNIX and Linux operating systems are configured to be Xen compatible, though work is progressing on Windows.

The Xen support is now integrated into all kernel packages, but is not fully supported yet (you have to use QEMU/KVM for now). In addition you can download install Xen tools and documentation packages. Detailed documentation will be in **/usr/share/xen-2**. Configuration files will be placed in **/etc/xen** directory, and corresponding kernels in the **/boot** and **/lib/modules** directories. In the **/etc/xen** directory you will find the **xend-config** file for configuring the Xen **xend** server, as well as example Xen configuration files.

```
xen
xen-hypervisor
xen-runtime
xen-watch
```

Xen sets up separate virtual machines called domains. When the Xen kernel starts up, it is designed to set up a primary domain, domain0, which manages your system and sets up virtual machines for other operating systems. The virtual machines it managers are domain U domains which provide user unprivileged access. Management of the virtual machines is handled by the **xend** server. Your native kernel would be installed on domain0, which will handle most of the hardware devices for all the other virtual machines. Xen is designed to use two kinds of domains, domain 0 (xen0) as a server and controller of other virtual systems, and domain U for unprivileged (xenU), user access. In Ubuntu 9.04, domain 0, the controller, is not supported. Only domain U, the unprivileged user operation, is supported. Xen can run as a virtual guest machine, but not as a controller or server.

You control the domains with the **xend** server. **xend** messages are placed in the **/var/log/xend.log** file. The xend server should automatically be started when you start up with the Xen kernel. There is a **xend** service script on Ubuntu letting you start the xend server manually with the following command. You can also manage xend from **services-admin**:

```
/sbin/service xend start
```

Xenner

You can run Xen as a domain U, guest system, by using Xenner to emulate a Xen domain 0 controller. Xenner actually runs KVM, which requires hardware virtualization support in the CPU. Xenner uses KVM to emulate a Xen domain 0 server. It runs KVM but with Xen support. Xenner is still in development and may not be that reliable. You first enable and run Xenner as a service, which makes sure that KVM is loaded, and then rung several xenner emulation daemons for KVM.

```
service xenner start
```

You then use the xenner application to run a Xen virtual machine.

Should domain 0 support be integrated into the kernel by later releases, you would no longer need Xenner.

Hardware Virtual Machine: hvm

Xen also provides support for the Hardware Virtual Machine, hvm. This is the Hardware Virtual Machine abstraction layer that Intel is implementing in its new processors as Intel VT-x. AMD will implement hvm as SVM. An hvm system has the capability to provide full virtualization, not requiring a specially modified Xen compatible version of an OS kernel. Theoretically you could even run Windows XP on Xen using the hvm capability (the Windows XP installer throws up other complications unrelated to virtualization). Intel's virtualization for the Itanium processors is called VT-i. VT-x is for x86 processors.

Xen can support a system with an hvm capable processor. Example configuration file for hvm in the /etc/xen directory has the extension **.hvm**. In this file, options are set to detect and use hvm. The xenguest-install also checks for hvm.

Managing Virtual Machines: xm

After you have installed the system, you can then create a connection to it with **xm** command (**xen-utils** package). To access a particular domain, use the `console` option and the domain name.

```
xm console my-newvml
```

If the domain no longer exists, you have to also create it and then connect.

```
xm create -c my-newvml
```

Check the **xm** options on the **xm** man page for other operations you can perform on your virtual machines.

To access domains, you use the `xm` command. The **list** option lists your domains. The listing will include detailed information such as its domain ID, the CPU time used, memory used, and the domain state. The following lists your domains:

```
xm list
```

The `xm` `save` and `restore` options can be used to suspend and restart a domain.

Block devices such as partitions and CD-ROMs can be exported from the main domain to virtual domains. This allows a given virtual domain to use a particular partition. You can even share block devices between domains, though such shared devices should be read only.

Part 2: Security

Authorization: Policykit

Encryption

File and Directory Access

AppArmor and SE Linux

SSH and Kerberos

Firewalls

9. Authorization

Controlled Access with Policykit: Authorizations

Pluggable Authentication Modules

Authorization, encryption, and permissions are all methods for controlling access. Authorizations can control access to administrative tools, making sure only valid and trusted users make changes to your system setup. Encryption can protect messages and files you may send, and digital signatures can confirm the source of a message or file. Users can also place their own access controls on their files using permissions and access control lists (ACLs). You can even encrypt entire file systems, making them accessible only with a valid key.

Certain security packages control access to resources such as devices, messages, directories, and file systems. PolicyKit provides controls for accessing devices and administrative tools by users. It is designed to permit limited administrative access to particular users, instead of allowing full root user access.

You can use encryption, integrity checks, and digital signatures to protect data transmitted over a network. For example, the GNU Privacy Guard (GPG) encryption as supported by Seahorse encryption management lets you encrypt your e-mail messages or files you want to send, as well as letting you sign them with an encrypted digital signature authenticating that the message was sent by you. The digital signature also includes encrypted modification digest information that provides an integrity check, allowing the recipient to verify that the message received is the original and not one that has been changed or substituted.

Permissions can be set on file and directories allowing access to just the owner, members of a group, or to all other users. This is the traditional method of controlling access to files. You can also use access control lists to add further restrictions. Access control lists provide more refined access, but are more difficult to manage. You can also encrypt entire file systems, using the same Public Key encryption method used for messages and archives.

Controlled Access with PolicyKit: Authorizations

Designed by the Freedesktop.org project, PolicyKit allows ordinary users and applications access to administrative-controlled applications and devices. Currently it works primarily with Hardware Abstraction Layer (HAL)–enabled devices and some GNOME desktop tasks. Though its functions could be accomplished with other operations such as group permissions, PolicyKit aims to provide a simple and centralized interface for granting users access to administration controlled devices and tools. PolicyKit is used to grant access to most of the devices on your system, including removable devices. It is also used to control access to several administrative tools such as **users-admin** and **services-admin** (GNOME administration tools). It is not used for access for other administrative tools such as Synaptic Package Manager or the login window. For these uses, you would use sudo and gksu. PolicyKit also controls access to the GNOME desktop clock applet.

For administrative tools, read-only access is granted to everyone, but the application is locked to prevent any changes. To gain full access, you click a Lock button in the lower-right corner of the application. You are then prompted to enter your administrative password, as you would for sudo or gksu. The application will unlock, allowing full access and displaying an Unlock button.

PolicyKit can also allow more refined access. Instead of an all-or-nothing approach, in which a user had to gain full root level control over the entire system just to access a specific administration tool, PolicyKit can allow access to a specific administrative application (currently only the GNOME clock is supported). All other access can be denied. Without PolicyKit, this kind of access could be configured in a limited way for some devices, such as while mounting and unmounting CD/DVD discs but not for applications. A similar kind of refined control is provided on Ubuntu with sudo and gksu, allowing access to specific administrative applications; administrative password access is still required, and root level access, though limited to that application, is still granted. You can find out more about PolicyKit at **http://hal.freedesktop.org/docs/PolicyKit/**.

A listing of applications and devices controlled by PolicyKit are shown here.

world-clock-applet	allow setting the time and date
Network Manager	Network detection
Power Management	shut down and reboot
PackageKit	Software Management
GNOME System Monitor	managing processes
PulseAudio	Sound device interface
storage devices	mount and unmount fixed and removable devices
device access	video, sound, scanners, PDA, DVB, CD/DVD-RW/ROM, firewire

Using PolicyKit, administrator controlled devices and applications are set up to communicate with ordinary users, allowing them to request certain actions. If the user is allowed to perform the action, the request is authorized and the action is performed. In the case of devices, which are now controlled and managed by HAL, the request can be sent to HAL, which then can authorize the action. Technically, all devices and administrative tools are considered mechanism to which requests are sent by user PolicyKit agents. Administration mechanisms use a shared library called **policykit** to decide whether to grant access. Users and application requests are validated by a **libpolkit-grant** shared library. The **policykit** library will check the validations provided by **libpolkit-grant** and allow access accordingly.

Authentication can be required for the user (user password) or for an administrator (root user password). On Ubuntu, no root user access is defined, unless you first set up a root user password. You would be given user level access requiring only your user password, as is the case for sudo. Access can further be controlled by time limits: indefinite, for the rest of the current session, or as long as the process is active.

PolicyKit Agent

To gain access, a user makes use of an authentication agent. The PolicyKit GNOME agent is installed with PolicyKit and can be run by any administration-enabled user by choosing System | Administration | Authorization. Both the **policykit** and **gnome-policykit** packages are part of the Ubuntu main repository and installed by default. This runs the **polkit-gnome-authorization** tool with which you can set PolicyKit access.

You can also run the PolicyKit agent from the terminal window by entering the following command.

```
polkit-gnome-authorization
```

Figure 9-1: PolicyKit sidebar, collapsed

The PolicyKit GNOME agent will be displayed. When you try to make any changes, an Authenticate dialog will open, prompting you to enter the **root** user password. This will give **root** user authorization to make the change. You can choose to remember authorization. Click the Authenticate button to make the change.

PolicyKit sidebar

The PolicyKit agent will display a window with a sidebar showing and expandable tree of supported PolicyKit devices and applications. Collapsing the tree gives you a better view of what is available (Figure 9-1). There are main entries for **gnome** and **freedesktop**. The **freedesktop** entry holds freedesktop-supported tools including **hal** and **policykit**, as well as **systemtoolsbackends** for administrative tool support.

Application entries let you control access to certain tasks. The PolicyKit entry lets you control access for installing, removing, and updating software, as well as changing repository configuration. The clock applet entry controls changes to the system time and time zone. The System Monitor entry has controls for processes (ending and priority changes). The Network Manager entry controls access to the modification of the network connections.

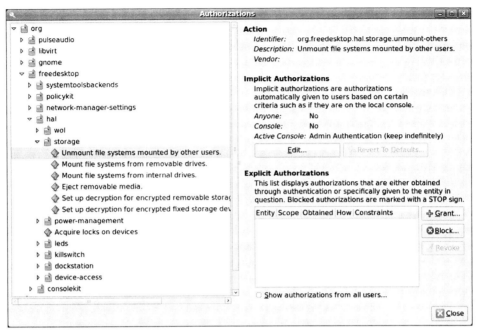

Figure 9-2: storage devices in hal

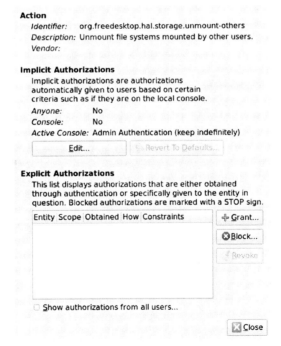

Figure 9-3: PolicyKit Implicit and Explicit Authorizations

The **hal** entry lets you control access to devices, with subsections for storage devices, device access to other devices, and power management, among others (see Figure 9-2). The **storage** section lets you control mounting for internal and removable drives, as well as encryption configuration.

PolicyKit Implicit and Explicit Authorizations

A selected entry will display its PolicyKit configuration on the right panel. This is divided into three segments: Action, Implicit Authorizations, and Explicit Authorizations (see Figure 9-3).

Implicit Authorizations are applied to the device or tool for all users. These are set for Anyone, Console, and Active Console. For single user systems like most laptops, the logged in user will be the active console. Console and Anyone would cover remote users. The Yes entry allows complete automatic access, and the NO entry denies all access. You can use the Edit button to change the settings (see Figure 9-4). You have the choice to restrict access to administrative users or users that provide their password, as well as limiting authorization to the duration of the session.

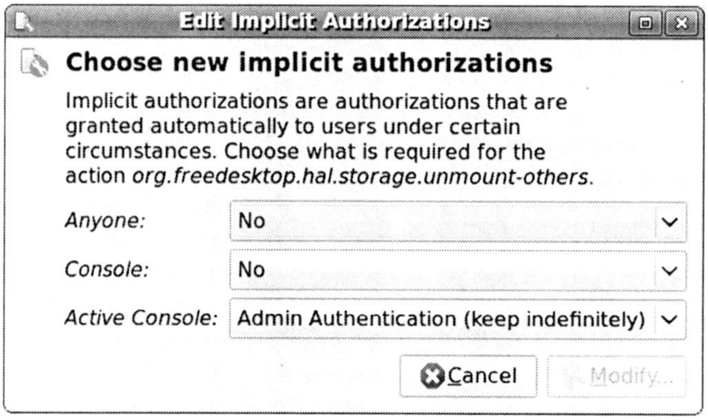

Figure 9-4: Implicit Authorization

Menu of possible authorizations for the Implicit authorizations is shown in Figure 9-5.

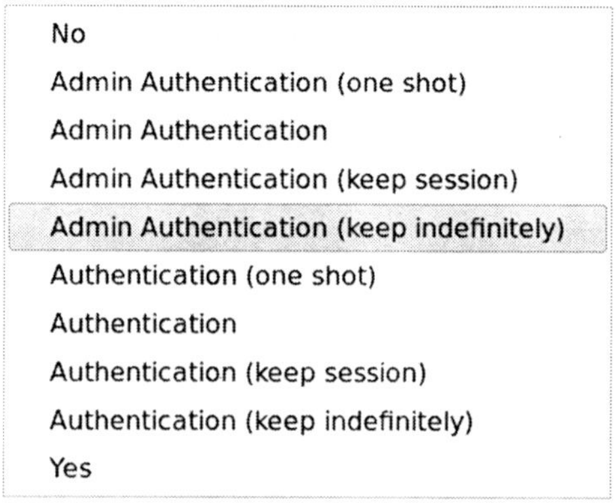

Figure 9-5: Implicit Authorization options

To grant access to specific users, click on the Grant button on the Explicit Authorizations section. This opens the Grant Authorization dialog where you can select a user and then specify the level of access (see Figure 9-6).

In the **device access** section under **hal** you can permit access by remote users to certain devices such as video, sound, and DVB devices. In this case, the implicit authorizations could be modified to allows access by anyone. Or you could allow access to specific users.

In the **freedesktop** entry, you can use entries under **policykit** to configure PolicyKit authorization. Here you can specify who can revoke, read, modify, or grant PolicyKit authorizations.

Figure 9-6: Explicit Authorization, Grant access

For administrative tools such as user, services, and networking, you use the **freedesktop | systemtoolsbackends | manage system configuration** entry. Implicit authorizations are set for the active console only with administrative authentication (see Figure 9-6). There are no explicit authorizations. You can use the Grant and Block buttons in the Explicit Authorizations section to grant or block access for particular users.

PolicyKit configuration files and tools

For devices and administrative applications to make use of PolicyKit, they have to be modified to access it. Currently HAL, which controls access to most devices, provides PolicyKit control for devices. On GNOME, the clock applet is configured for PolicyKit control. PolicyKit for devices and applications are configured using XML files with the extension **.policy** in the **/usr/share/PolicyKit/policy** directory. Here you will find **.policy** files for the gnome-clock-applet as well as several for HAL and one for PolicyKit.

The **/etc/PolicyKit/PolicyKit.conf** file is used to permit overriding any PolicyKit authorizations for users. Currently the configuration file is set up to always allow access to the root user and to any users with administrative access (admin group). It can be configured for specific users.

Though you would use polkit-gnome-authorization to configure PolicyKit, several command line tools are available. These include **polkit-auth** to mange authorization, **polkit-action** to list and modify allowed actions, **polkit-policy-file-validate** to validate a PolicyKit policy file, and **polkit-config-file-validate** to validate the PolicyKit configuration file. Should you make changes directly to the **PolicyKit.conf** file, you should run **polkit-config-file-validate** to make sure the file is valid. If you add or modify any of the .policy files, you can run **polkit-policy-file-validate** on them to verify that they are correctly configured.

Pluggable Authentication Modules

Pluggable Authentication Modules (PAM) is an authentication service that lets a system determine the method of authentication to be performed for users. In a Linux system, authentication has traditionally been performed by looking up passwords. When a user logs in, the login process looks up the user's password in the password file. With PAM, users' requests for authentication are directed to PAM, which in turn uses a specified method to authenticate the user. This could be a simple password lookup or a request to an LDAP server, but it is PAM that provides authentication, not a direct password lookup by the user or application. In this respect, authentication becomes centralized and controlled by a specific service, PAM. The actual authentication procedures can be dynamically configured by the system administrator. Authentication is carried out by modules that can vary according to the kind of authentication needed. An administrator can add or replace modules by simply changing the PAM configuration files. See the PAM Web site at **http://kernel.org/pub/linux/libs/pam** for more information and a listing of PAM modules. PAM modules are located in the **/lib/security** directory.

PAM Configuration Files

PAM uses different configuration files for different services that request authentication. Such configuration files are kept in the **/etc/pam.d** directory. For example, you have a configuration file for logging into your system (**/etc/pam.d/login**), one for the graphical login (**/etc/pam.d/gdm**), and one for accessing your Samba server (**/etc/pam.d/samba**). A default PAM configuration file, called **/etc/pam.d/other**, is invoked if no services file is present. The **system-auth** file contains standard authentication modules for system services, and is invoked in many of the other configuration files. In addition, Ubuntu sets up an authentication for its configuration tools, such as services-admin and system-config-printer.

PAM Modules

A PAM configuration file contains a list of modules to be used for authentication. They have the following format:

```
module-type control-flag module-path module-args
```

The *module-path* is the module to be run, and *module-args* are the parameters you want passed to that module. Though there are a few generic arguments, most modules have their own specific ones. The *module-type* refers to different groups of authentication management: account, authentication, session, and password. The account management performs account verification, checking such account aspects as whether the user has access, or whether the password has expired.

Authentication (`auth`) verifies who the user is, usually through a password confirmation. Password management performs authentication updates such as password changes. Session management refers to tasks performed before a service is accessed and before it is shut down. These include tasks like initiating a log of a user's activity or mounting and unmounting home directories.

Tip: As an alternative to the **/etc/pam.d** directory, you could create one configuration file called the **/etc/pam.conf** file. Entries in this file have a service field, which refers to the application that the module is used for. If the **/etc/pam.d** directory exists, **/etc/pam.conf** is automatically ignored.

The *control-flag* field indicates how PAM is to respond if the module fails. The control can be a simple directive or a more complicated response that can specify return codes like `open_err` with actions to take. The simple directives are `requisite`, `required`, `sufficient`, and `optional`. The `requisite` directive ends the authentication process immediately if the module fails to authenticate. The `required` directive only ends the authentication after the remaining modules are run. The `sufficient` directive indicates that success of this module is enough to provide authentication unless a previous required module has failed. The `optional` directive indicates the module's success is not needed unless it is the only authentication module for its service. If you specify return codes, you can refine the conditions for authentication failure or success. Return codes can be given values such as `die` or `ok`. The `open_err` return code could be given the action `die`, which would stop all authentication operations and return failure.

On Ubuntu, commonly used PAM module entries are placed in the PAM files prefixed with the **common** term. These include **common-account**, **common-auth**, **common-password**, and **common-session**. The **common-account** modules are used to verify that the user has a valid account on the system. The **common-session** modules provide support for login sessions. The **common-auth** modules provide system authentication. The **common-password** modules check passwords.

The **common-account** modules include **pam_unix.so** (Unix password authentication), **pam_permit.so** (allow anyone access), and **pam_deny.so** (deny access). The **pam_permit** module is listed last as a last resort. It will allow access to anyone and should be used with caution.

```
account   [success=1 default=ignore]   pam_unix.so nullok_secure
account   requisite                    pam_deny.so
account   required                     pam_permit.so
```

The **common-password** modules will also include options like checking password strength (obscure) and providing encryption (sha512). Check the man pages for each module to see their options (man pam_unix). .The optional entry lists the Samba password module, **pam_smbpass.so**.

```
password   [success=1 default=ignore    pam_unix.so obscure sha512
password   requisite                    pam_deny.so
password   required                     pam_permit.so
password   optional                pam_smbpass.so nullok use_authtok use_first_pass
```

A common PAM file is included in a PAM configuration file with the **@include** command:

```
@include   common-account
```

The **/etc/pam.d/vsftpd** configuration file for the FTP server is shown next. The **pam_listfile** module allows a particular file to be used for authentication, in this case, **/etc/ftpusers**. The **deny** setting for the **sense** option will set up **/etc/ftpusers** to deny access to any users listed there. The **pam_shells** module checks for a valid login shell. See the man pages for each for more details and options.

```
auth   required   pam_listfile.so item=user sense=deny file=/etc/ftpusers
          onerr=succeed
@include common-account
@include common-session
@include common-auth
auth   required pam_shells.so
```

10. Encryption

Public-Key Encryption

Managing keys with Seahorse

GNU Privacy Guard: gpg

Using GnuPG

Encrypting and decrypting data with gpg command

Signing Messages

Encrypting data is the only sure way to secure data transmitted over a network. Encrypt data with a key, and the receiver or receivers can later decrypt it. To fully protect data transmitted over a network, you should not only encrypt it, but also check that it has not been modified, as well as confirm that it was actually created by the claimed author. An encrypted message could still be intercepted and modified and then re-encrypted. Integrity checks such as modification digests make sure that the data was not altered. Though encryption and integrity checks protect the data, they do not authenticate it. You also need to know that the person who claimed to send a message actually is the one who sent it, rather than an imposter. To authenticate a message, the author can sign it using a digital signature. This signature can also be encrypted, allowing the receiver to validate it. Digital signatures ensure that the message you receive is authentic.

This type of encryption was originally implemented with Pretty Good Privacy (PGP). Originally a privately controlled methodology, it was handed over to the Internet Engineering Task Force (IETF) to support an open standard for PGP called OpenPGP (see Table 10-1). Any project can use OpenPGP to create encryption applications, such as GnuPG. Commercial products for PGP are still developed by the PGP Corporation, which also uses the OpenPGP standard.

Website	Description
http:// gnupg.org	GnuPG, Gnu Privacy Guard
http:// openpgp.org	IETF open standard for Pretty Good Privacy (PGP)
www.pgp.com	PGP Corporation, Pretty Good Privacy commercial products

Table 10-1: PGP Sites

Public-Key Encryption

Encryption uses a key to encrypt data in such a way that a corresponding key can decrypt it. In the past, older forms of encryption used the same key to both encrypt and decrypt a message. This, however, involved providing the receiver with the key, opening up the possibility that anyone who obtained the key could decrypt the data. Public-key encryption uses two keys to encrypt and decrypt a message, a private key and a public key. The *private* key you always keep and use to decrypt messages you have received. The *public* key you make available to those you send messages to. They then use your public key to encrypt any message they want to send to you. The private key decrypts messages, and the public key encrypts them. Each user has a set of private and public keys, securely kept in keyrings.

Reciprocally, if you want to send messages to another user, you first obtain that user's public key and use it to encrypt the message you want to send to the user. The user then decrypts the messages with their private key. In other words, your public key is used by others to encrypt the messages you receive, and you use other users' public keys to encrypt messages you send to them. All the users on your Linux system can have their own public and private keys. They will use the gpg program to generate them and keep their private key in their own keyrings.

Digital Signatures

A *digital signature* is used to both authenticate a message and provide an integrity check. Authentication guarantees that the message has not been modified—that it is the original message sent by you—and the integrity check verifies that it has not been changed. Though usually combined with encrypted messages to provide a greater level of security, digital signatures can also be used for messages that can be sent in the clear. For example, you would want to know if a public notice of upgrades of a Ubuntu release was actually sent by Ubuntu and not by someone trying to spread confusion. Such a message still needs to be authenticated and checked to see if it was actually sent by the sender or, if sent by the original sender, was not somehow changed en route. Verification like this protects against modification or substitution of the message by someone pretending to be the sender.

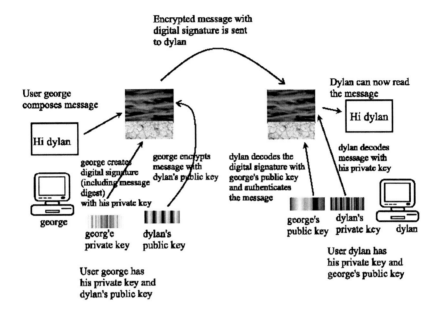

Figure 10-1: Public-key encryption and digital signatures

Integrity Checks

Digitally signing a message involves generating a checksum value from the contents of the message using an encryption hash algorithm such as the SHA2 modification digest algorithm. This is a unique value that accurately represents the size and contents of your message. Any changes to the message of any kind will generate a different value. Such a value provides a way to check the integrity of the data. The value is commonly known as the MD5 value, reflective of the MD5 hash algorithm that was used encrypt the value. The MD5 algorithm has since been replaced by the more secure SHA2 algorithms.

The MD5 value is then itself encrypted with your private key. When the user receives your message, they decrypt your digital signature with your public key. The user then generates an MD5 value of the message received and compares it with the MD5 value you sent. If they are the same, the message is authenticated—it is the original message sent by you, not a false one sent by a user pretending to be you. The user can use GnuPG to decrypt and check digital signatures.

Combining Encryption and Signatures

Normally, digital signatures are combined with encryption to provide a more secure level of transmission. The message is encrypted with the recipient's public key, and the digital signature is encrypted with your private key. The user decrypts both the message (with their private key) and then the signature (with your public key). The user then compares the signature with one that user generates from the message to authenticate it. When GnuPG decodes a message, it will also decode and check a digital signature automatically. Figure 10-1 shows the process for encrypting and digitally signing a message.

Managing keys with Seahorse

For GPG and SSH encryption, signing, and decryption of files and text, GNOME provides Seahorse. With Seahorse you can manage your encryption keys stored in keyrings as well as SSH keys and passphrases. You can import keys, sign keys, search for remote keys, and create your own keyrings, as well as specify keyserver to search and publish to. All these operations can also be performed using the **gpg** command described later in this chapter.

Figure 10-2: Seahorse First Time Use

Passwords and Encryption Keys: Seahorse

To import, sign, and locate keys, you use the Seahorse encryption key manager. On the GNOME desktop, Seahorse is referred to as "Passwords and Encryption Keys". Choose Applications | Accessories | Passwords And Encryption Keys. This entry will run the **seahorse** command that will display the "Passwords And Encryption Keys" window. This window shows four tabs: My Personal Keys, Trusted Keys, Other Collected Keys, and Passwords. When you first start up the utility, it will display three buttons on the lower part of the panel: Help, Import, and New (see Figure 10-2).

Figure 10-3: Choose Encryption key type

Creating a new private key

Click the New button (or choose Key | Create New Key), to create your own private/public keys. Keep in mind that before you can perform any encryption, you first have to set up your own GPG key pair, private and public. You first choose whether to set up a PGP or SSH key. The PGP entry sets up a GPG key (GPG is the GNU version of PGP). Choose the PGP Key entry and click Continue (see Figure 10-3).

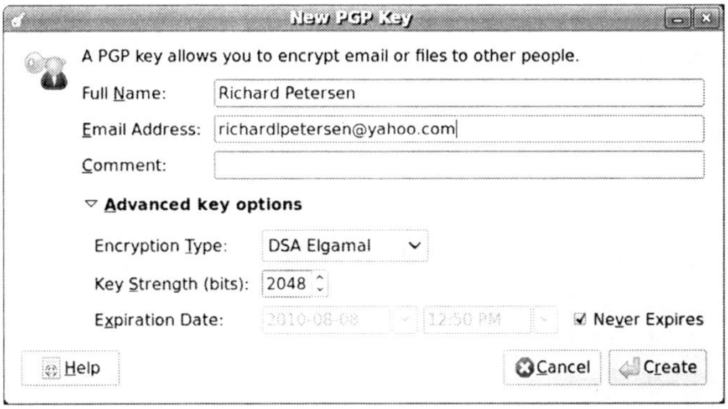

Figure 10-4: Create Encryption key

This opens a New PGP Key window where you enter your name and email address. Click the Advanced key options drop-down arrow to set Encryption type (DSA, or RSA), Key strength, and Expiration Date (see Figure 10-4). Then click the Create button.

You are then asked to enter a passphrase (password) for the encryption key (see Figure 10-5). This passphrase will allow you to decrypt any data encrypted by your key.

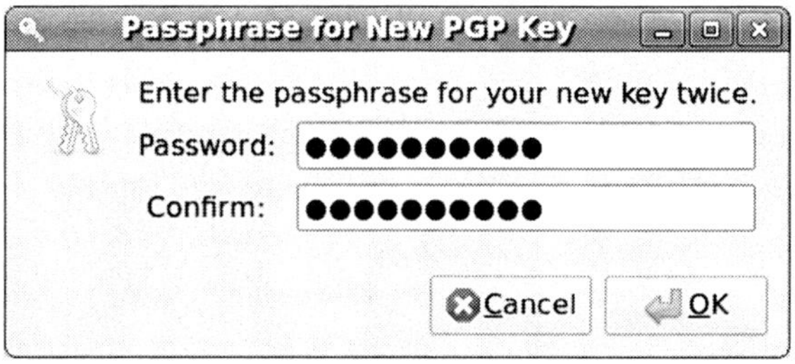

Figure 10-5: Passphrase for encryption key

The key is then generated. This can take some time. During the generation process, a busy notification will let you know the generation is still in process (see Figure 10-6).

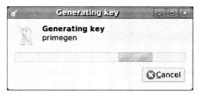

Figure 10-6: Generating encryption key

Once you key is created, it will appear in the My Personal Keys tab of the Passwords And Encryption Keys window (See Figure 10-7).

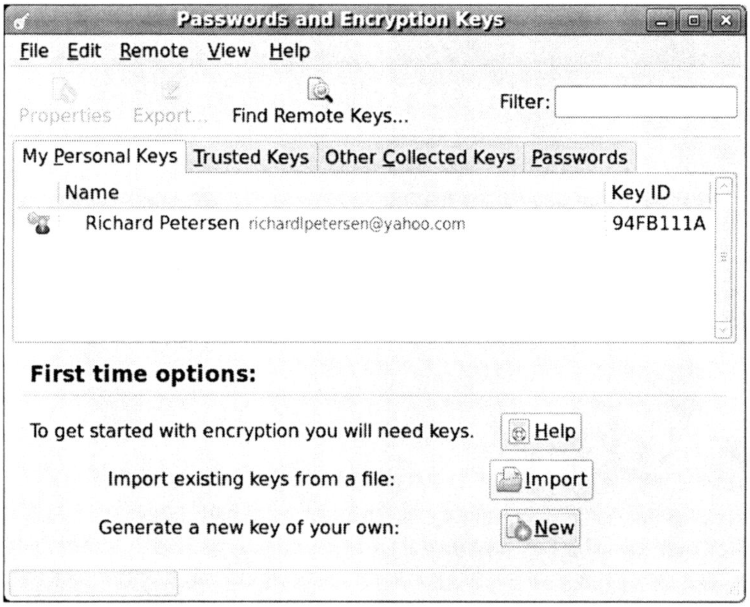

Figure 10-7: My Personal Keys

Importing Public Keys

In the Passwords And Encryption Keys window, click Use the Import button (or choose Import from the Key menu) to import any public keys you may downloaded. If you know the name of the key file, you can try searching the key servers for it. Choose Find Remote Keys from the Remote menu to open the Find Remote Keys dialog where you can enter a search string for the key (see Figure 10-8). The search term is treated as a prefix, matching on all possible completions. An expandable tree lists you key servers, letting you choose which ones to search. Results are then listed in a new window. Select the one you want, and then either click Import to import the key directly, or click Save Key As to save the key as an asc key file that you can later import. To see information about a key, select it and click the Properties button. Information about the owner and the key is displayed.

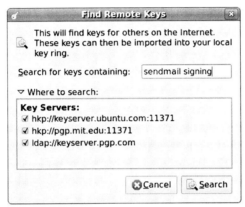

Figure 10-8: Searching for keys

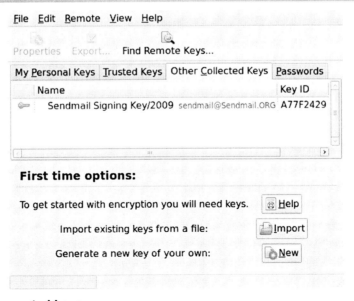

Figure 10-9: Imported keys

Once you have imported the key, it will appear in the Other Collected Keys tab in the Passwords And Encryption Keys window (see Figure 10-9). If you know that you can trust the key, you can sign it, making it a trusted key. Right-click on its entry and choose Sign to open a signing dialog, or click the Sign button. You are asked to specify how carefully you have checked this key (Not at all, Casually, and Very Carefully). The key will be moved from the Other Collected Keys tab to the Trusted Keys tab. It will then appear in the Trusted Keys tab.

When you created your own private key, you also generated a corresponding public key that other can use to decrypt data encrypted with that key. To make you public key available to others, you can export it to a file to send directly other users, automatically share it with other uses on your system, or publish on a keyserver. To export your public key to file, select your key in the "My Personal Keys" tab, and click the Export Public Key button. You can do this for your public keys also.

Seahorse integrates support for GPG. Should you import a key with the **gpg** command, it will appear in the Other Collected Keys tab. Also, you can sing a key using the **gpg** command with the **--sign-key** option and the key will appear in the Trusted Key tab.

Seahorse Settings

To manage and configure key support, you use the seahorse-preferences utility (System | Preferences | Encryption and Keyrings). The Password and Encryption Settings window opens with two tabs: Encryption and PGP Passphrases. On the Encryption tab you can select the default keyring. On the Passphrases tab you can set remembrance options, like setting a time period in which to remember the passphrases, or to remember them whenever you are logging in.

Figure 10-10: Seahorse Settings: System | Preferences | Encryption and Keyrings

GNU Privacy Guard: gpg

To protect messages and text files, Ubuntu, like most Linux distributions, provides GNU Privacy Guard (GnuPG) encryption and authentication (**www.gnupg.org**). GnuPG is the GNU open source software that works much like Pretty Good Privacy (PGP) encryption. It is the OpenPGP encryption and signing tool (OpenPGP is the open source version of PGP). With GnuPG, you can both encrypt and digitally sign your messages and files—protecting the message or file and authenticating that it is from you.

To protect messages that you send by e-mail, Evolution and KMail both support GnuPG encryption and authentication, along with Thunderbird with added GPG plugins. On Evolution, you can select PGP encryption and signatures from the Security menu to use GnuPG (the PGP options use GnuPG). On KMail, you can select the encryption to use on the Security panel in the Options window. For Thunderbird you can use the **enigmail** extension to support OpenGPG and PGP encryption (**http://enigmail.mozdev.org**). Be sure to always send a copy of your encrypted message to yourself. This way you can decrypt the message and read them as sent messages.

You can encrypt text files using GEdit as well as your Nautilus file manager. Other applications like Openoffice.org will support digital signatures, authenticating your files.

GNU Privacy Guard (GnuPG) operations are carried out with the **gpg** command, which uses both commands and options to perform tasks. Commonly used commands and options are listed in Table 10-2. Some commands and options have short forms that use only one hyphen. Normally, two hyphens are used. If you just want to verify the validity of a digital signature, you can use **gpgv** instead. This is a stripped-down version of **gpg** used just for signature verification.

For managing your encryption keys, you can use the GNOME Seahorse encryption management tool (Applications | Accessories | Passwords and Encryption Keys), instead of **gpg** commands directly (see the previous section). Encryption for text files and GEdit text editor are provided by the Seahorse plugin. Other applications, like Evolution, support encrypt directly.

The first time you use **gpg**, a **.gnupg** directory is created in your home directory with a file named **options**. The **.gnupg/gpg.conf** file contains commented default options for GPG operations. You can edit this file and uncomment or change any default options you want implemented for GPG. You can use a different options file by specifying it with the **--options** parameter when invoking **gpg**. Helpful options include keyserver entries. The **.gnupg** directory will also hold encryption files such as **secring.gpg** for your secret keys (secret keyring), **pubring.gpg** for your public keys (public keyring), and **trustdb.gpg**, which is a database for trusted keys.

Generating your public key with gpg

Before you can use GnuPG, you will have to generate your private and public keys. You can do this with the Passwords and Encryption Keys utility as described in the previous section, or with the **gpg** command entered in a terminal window, as described here. On the command line (terminal window), enter the **gpg** command with the **--gen-key** command. The **gpg** program will then prompt with different options for creating your private and public keys. You can check the **gpg** Man page for information on using the **gpg** program.

```
gpg --gen-key
```

GPG Commands	Description
`-s, --sign`	Signs a document, creating a signature. May be combined with `--encrypt`.
`--clearsign`	Creates a clear-text signature.
`-b, --detach-sign`	Creates a detached signature.
`-e, --encrypt`	Encrypts data. May be combined with `--sign`.
`--decrypt` [*file*]	Decrypts file (or **stdin** if no file is specified) and writes it to **stdout** (or the file specified with `--output`). If the decrypted file is signed, the signature is verified.
`--verify` [[*sigfile*] [*signed-files*]]	Verifies a signed file. The signature can be either contained with the file or a separate detached signature file.
`-k, --list-keys` [*names*], `--list-public-keys` [*names*]	Lists all keys from the public keyrings or those specified.
`-K, --list-secret-keys` [*names*]	Lists your private (secret) keys.
`--list-sigs` [*names*]	Lists your keys along with any signatures they have.
`--check-sigs` [*names*]	Lists keys and their signatures and verifies the signatures.
`--fingerprint` [*names*]	Lists fingerprints for specified keys.
`--gen-key`	Generates a new set of private and public keys.
`--edit-key` *name*	Edits your keys. Commands perform most key operations, such as `sign` to sign a key or `passwd` to change your passphrase.
`--sign-key` *name*	Signs a public key with your private key. Same as `sign in --edit-key`.
`--delete-key` *name*	Removes a public key from the public keyring.
`--delete-secret-key` *name*	Removes private and public keys from both the secret and public keyrings.
`--gen-revoke`	Generates a revocation certificate for your own key.
`--export` [*names*]	Exports a specified key from your keyring. With no arguments, exports all keys.
`--send-keys` [*names*]	Exports and sends specified keys to a keyserver. The option `--keyserver` must be used to give the name of this keyserver.
`--import` [*files*]	Imports keys contained in files into your public keyring.

GPG Options	Description
`-a, --armor`	Creates ASCII armored output, ASCII version of encrypted data.
`-o, --output` *file*	Writes output to a specified file.
`--default-key` *name*	Specifies the default private key to use for signatures.
`--keyserver` *site*	Looks up public keys not on your keyring.
`-r, --recipient` *names*	Encrypts data for the specified user, using that user's public key.
`--default-recipient` *names*	Specifies the default recipient to use for encrypting data.

Table 10-2: GPG Commands and Options

You are first asked to select the kind of key you want. Normally, you just select the default entry, which you can do by pressing the ENTER key.

Then you choose the key size, usually the default 1024.

You then specify how long the key is to be valid—usually, there is no expiration.

You are then asked to enter a user ID, a comment, and an e-mail address. Press ENTER to be prompted for each in turn. These elements, any of which can be used as the key's name, identify the key. You use the key name when performing certain GPG tasks such as signing a key or creating a revocation certificate. For example, the following elements create a key for the user richlp with the comment "author" and the e-mail address **richlp@turtle.mytrek.com**:

```
Richard Petersen (author) <richlp@turtle.mytrek.com>
```

You can use any unique part of a key's identity to reference that key. For example, the string "Richard" would reference the preceding key, provided there are no other keys that have the string "Richard" in them. The string "richlp" would also reference the key, as would "author". Where a string matches more than one key, all those matched would be referenced.

After you have entered your user ID, comment, and email address, the elements are displayed along with a menu is which will allow you change any element.

```
Change (N)ame, (C)omment, (E)mail or (O)kay/(Q)uit?
```

Enter **o** to approve and accept the key.

The gpg program will then ask you to enter a passphrase, used to protect your private key. Be sure to use a real phrase, including spaces, not just a password.

gpg then generates your public and private keys and places them in the **.gnupg** directory. This may take a few minutes.

The private keys are kept in a file called **secring.gpg** in your **.gnupg** directory. The public key is placed in the **pubring.gpg** file, to which you can add the public keys of other users. You can list these keys with the `--list-keys` and **--list-public-keys** commands.

```
gpg --list-keys
```

To list your private keys you would use the **--list-secret-keys** command.

```
gpg --list-secret-keys
```

If you need to change your keys later, you can create a revocation certificate to notify others that the public key is no longer valid. For example, if you forget your password or someone else discovers it, you can use the revocation certificate to tell others that your public key should no longer be used. In the next example, the user creates a revocation certificate for the key richlp and places it in the file **myrevoke.asc**:

```
gpg --output myrevoke.asc --gen-revoke richlp
```

Importing Public Keys

To decode messages from other users, you will need to have their public keys. Either they can send them to you or you can download them from a keyserver. Save the message or web page containing the public key to a file. You will then need to import the key, and you should also verify and sign the key. Use the file you received to import the public key to your **pubring** file. As noted previously, you can also use the Seahorse Passwords and Encryptions Keys utility (Applications | Accessories | Passwords and Encryption Keys) to import and sign keys. In the following example, the user imports George's public key, which he has received as the file **georgekey.asc**.

```
gpg --import georgekey.asc
```

You can also use the **gpg --search-key** and **--keyserver** options to import the key. Keys matching the search term will be displayed in a numbered list. You will be prompted to enter the number of the key you want. The 2007 Sendmail key from the results from the following example would be 7. This is the key used for 2007 released software.

```
$ gpg  --keyserver pgp.mit.edu  --search-keys Sendmail

gpg: searching for "Sendmail" from hkp server pgp.mit.edu
(1)     Sendmail Signing Key/2008 <sendmail@Sendmail.ORG>
          1024 bit RSA key F6B30729, created: 2008-01-18
. . . . . .
(7)     Sendmail Signing Key/2007 <sendmail@Sendmail.ORG>
          1024 bit RSA key 7093B841, created: 2006-12-16
Enter number(s), N)ext, or Q)uit > 7
gpg: requesting key 7093B841 from hkp server pgp.mit.edu
gpg: key 7093B841: public key "Sendmail Signing Key/2007 <sendmail@Sendmail.ORG>"
imported
gpg: 3 marginal(s) needed, 1 complete(s) needed, PGP trust model
gpg: depth: 0  valid:   1  signed:   0  trust: 0-, 0q, 0n, 0m, 0f, 1u
gpg: Total number processed: 1
gpg:                 imported: 1  (RSA: 1)
```

Note: You can remove any key, including your own private key, with the `--delete-key` and `--delete-secret-key` commands.

Signing Your Public Keys

If you trust the imported key, you can then sign it, making it a trusted key (these will show up in the Trusted Keys tab of the Passwords and Encryption Keys window). To sign a key, you use the `gpg` command with the `--sign-key` command and the key's name.

```
gpg --sign-key george@rabbit
```

Alternatively, you can edit the key with the **--edit-key** command to start an interactive session in which you can enter the command **sign** to sign the key and **save** to save the change. Signing a key involves accessing your private key, so you will be prompted for your passphrase. When you are finished, leave the interactive session with the **quit** command.

In this example, the e-mail address is used for the key name. You are prompted to make sure you want to sign it. Then you have to enter the passphrase for your own GPG key.

```
$ gpg --sign-key sendmail@Sendmail.ORG
pub  1024R/7093B841  created: 2006-12-16  expires: never       usage: SCEA
                     trust: unknown      validity: unknown
[ unknown] (1). Sendmail Signing Key/2007 <sendmail@Sendmail.ORG>
pub  1024R/7093B841  created: 2006-12-16  expires: never       usage: SCEA
                     trust: unknown      validity: unknown
 Primary key fingerprint: D9 FD C5 6B EE 1E 7A A8  CE 27 D9 B9 55 8B 56 B6
      Sendmail Signing Key/2007 <sendmail@Sendmail.ORG>
Are you sure that you want to sign this key with your
key "Richard Petersen <richard@somedomain>" (0108D72C)
Really sign? (y/N) y
You need a passphrase to unlock the secret key for
user: "Richard Petersen <richard@somedomain>"
1024-bit DSA key, ID 0108D72C, created 2008-03-26
```

For public keys in your keyrings, you can set different trust levels. GPG supports several trust levels, including marginal, full trust, and ultimate. You use the **--edit-key** command with the **trust** option to set the trust level.

```
gpg --edit-key george@rabbit trust
```

This will display a menu of several options

```
1 = I don't know or won't say
2 = I do NOT trust
3 = I trust marginally
4 = I trust full
5 = I trust ultimately
m = back to main menu
```

The **--edit-key** command actually runs a shell in which you can enter a variety of different key modification operations, like **trust** to set the trust level, **keyserver** to tell where the key can be found, and **sign** to sign the key. Use the **quit** command to leave the edit-key shell.

You can also check the fingerprint of the key for added verification. To manually check that a public key file was not modified in transit, you can check its fingerprint. This is a hash value generated from the contents of the key, much like a modification digest. Using the **--fingerprint** option, you can generate a hash value from the key you installed, and then contact the sender and ask them what the hash value should really be. If they are not the same, you know the key was tampered with in transit.

Tip: You can use the **--fingerprint** option to check a key's validity if you wish. If you are confident that the key is valid, you can then sign it with the **--sign-key** command.

You do not have to check the fingerprint to have gpg operate. This is just an advisable precaution you can perform on your own. The point is that you need to be confident that the key you received is valid. Normally you can accept most keys from public servers or known sites as valid, though it is easy to check their posted fingerprints. Once assured of the key's validity, you can then sign it with your private key. Signing a key notifies gpg that you officially accept the key.

Publishing keys

You can use the **gpg** command with the **-keyserver** option and **--send-key** command to send keys directly to a keyserver. The **--send-key** command takes as its argument your e-mail address. You need to send to only one keyserver, as it will share your key with other keyservers automatically. The following command publishes a key to the **pgp.mit.edu** keyserver

```
gpg --keyserver pgp.mit.edu:11371 --send-key chris@turtle.mytrek.com
```

If you want to send your key directly to another user, you should generate an armored text version of the key that you can then e-mail. You do this with the **--armor** and **--export** options, using the **--output** option to specify a file to place the key in. The **--armor** option will generate an ASCII text version of the encrypted file so that it can be e-mailed directly, instead of as an attached binary. Files that hold an ASCII-encoded version of the encryption normally have the extension **.asc**, by convention. Binary encrypted files normally use the extension **.gpg**. You can then e-mail the file to users you want to send encrypted messages.

```
# gpg --armor --export richlp@turtle.mytrek.com --output richlp.asc
# mail -s 'mypubkey' george@rabbit.mytrek.com < richlp.asc
```

Many companies and institutions post their public key files on their websites, where they can be downloaded and used to verify encrypted software downloads or official announcements.

Note: Some commands and options for GPG have both long and short forms. For example, the **--armor** command can be written as **-a**, **--output** as **-o**, **--sign** as **-s**, and **--encrypt** as **-e**. Most others, like **--export**, have no short form.

Using GnuPG

GnuPG encryption is currently supported by most mail clients, including KMail, Thunderbird, and Evolution. You can use the gpg command to manually encode and decode messages, including digital signatures. Seahorse provides several GPG encryption plugins for use with Evolution and Gedit.

Encrypting and decrypting data with gpg command

The gpg command provides several options for managing secure messages. The **e** option encrypts messages, the **a** option generates an armored text version, and the **s** option adds a digital signature. Email applications will use this option. You will need to specify the recipient's public key, which you should already have imported into your **pubring** file. It is this key that is used to encrypt the message. The recipient will then be able to decode the message with their private key. Use the **--recipient** or **-r** option to specify the name of the recipient key. You can use any unique substring in the user's public key name. The e-mail address usually suffices. You use the **d** option to decode received messages. In the following example, the user encrypts (**e**) and signs (**s**) a file generated in armored text format (**a**). The **-r** option indicates the recipient for the message (whose public key is used to encrypt the message).

```
gpg e -s -a -o myfile.asc -r george@rabbit.mytrek.com myfile
# mail george@rabbit.mytrek.com < myfile.asc
```

You can leave out the ASCII armor option if you want to send or transfer the file as a binary attachment. Without the **--armor** or **-a** option, **gpg** generates an encoded binary file, not an encoded text file. This is the method used for encryption by Nautilus. A binary file can be transmitted through e-mail only as an attachment. As noted previously, ASCII armored versions usually have an extension of **.asc**, whereas binary version use **.gpg**.

When the other user receives the file, they can save it to a file named something like **myfile.asc** and then decode the file with the **-d** option. The **-o** option will specify a file to save the decoded version in. GPG will automatically determine if it is a binary file or an ASCII armored version.

```
gpg -d -o myfile.txt myfile.asc
```

To check the digital signature of the file, you use the **gpg** command with the **--verify** option. This assumes that the sender has signed the file.

```
gpg --verify myfile.asc
```

Note: You can use **gpgsplit** to split a GPG message into its components to examine them separately.

As you perform GPG tasks, you will need to reference the keys you have using their key names. Bear in mind that you need only a unique identifying substring to select the key you want. GPG performs a pattern search on the string you specify as the key name in any given command. If the string matches more than one key, all those matching keys will be selected.

Seahorse plugins: Choose Recipients

Plug-ins are provided for Gedit editor to encrypt text files, the Epiphany Web browser for text phrases, and Nautilus to perform encryption from the context menu. A panel applet lets you encrypt, sign, and decrypt clipboard content.

The Seahorse plugin opens a Choose Recipients window in which you can choose the key to use for encryption (see Figure 10-10). A pop-up menu lets you use all keys, just selected recipients, or search results. A search box lets you search for keys, selecting them based on a pattern you enter. Available keys will be listed in the window by name and key ID. You also have the option to sign the message, selecting signatures from the Sign Message As pop-up menu. Once you make your selection, you will be prompted to enter the passphrase for that encryption key.

Encrypting and decrypting files with Nautilus

Nautilus will generate an encrypted copy of a file, giving that copy the extension **.gpg**. It operates like gpg with just the **-e** option, and no **-a** option. To encrypt a file from Nautilus, select the file and then right-click to open the Nautilus pop-up menu. On this menu select the Encrypt option. You can also select the file and then choose Encrypt from the Edit menu (Edit | Encrypt). The Choose Recipients window then opens letting you select the encryption keys and digital signature to use (see Figure 10-11). Select the encryption key. You will be prompted to enter the key's passphrase. Then an encrypted copy of the file will be generated with the extension **.pgp**. The original is left untouched.

Figure 10-11: Choose Recipients window.

If you just want to sign a file, you can select the Sign entry in the Edit menu, Edit | Sign (or right-click on the filename/icon and choose Sign from). This opens a dialog with a pop-up menu listing digital signatures you can use.

To decrypt the encrypted .pgp file, simply double-click on it or right-click and choose Open With to select Decrypt File. This opens the file with the decrypt tool which will generate a decrypted copy of the file. A "Choose decrypted file name" dialog will then open where you can enter the name for the copy and the directory to save it in. You are then prompted for the passphrase.

Encrypting data with GEdit

GEdit is designed to create armored text encrypted files, the kind you would send as an email. It will change the original text file, transforming the text into an encoded armor ASCII equivalent, with BEGIN and END entries for the encoded data. You could then send the text directly as a message. To decode, be sure to select the entire encoded text, including the BEGIN and END lines. You will be prompted for the passphrase for the key. If signed, the signature will also be checked.

To encrypt files with GEdit, you first have to enable encryption. Open Gedit and select preferences from the Edit menu. On the Preferences window select the Plugins tab. Scroll down the list of active plugins ad click the checkbox for Text Encryption. Now, on the Gedit Edit menu, you will see entries for Sign, Decrypt/Verify, and Encrypt. Choose Encrypt to encrypt the message, Sign to just sign it. When you choose Encrypt, the Choose Recipients dialog opens where you can select the encryption keys to use. If you choose Sign, a small dialog appears with a pop-up menu listing digital signatures you can use. To decrypt or verify, first select the text and then select the Decrypt/Verify entry.

Decrypting a Digital Signature

You will need to have the signer's public key to decode and check the digital signature. If you do not have the key, you will receive a message saying that the public key was not found. In this case, you will first have to obtain the signer's public key. You can access a keyserver that you think may have the public key or request the public key directly from a website or from the signer. Then import the key as described earlier.

Signing Messages

Most applications that handle text and data files provide the ability to sign those files. For the Gedit editor and Nautilus file browser, a window opens with a pop-up menu letting you choose the key to use to sign the file. On Evolution you can select the PGP signature entry from the Security menu in the Compose message window.

Note: One very effective use for digital signatures is to verify that a software package has not been altered. A software package could be intercepted in transmission and some of its system-level files changed or substituted. Software packages for Ubuntu, as well as those by reputable GNU and Linux projects, are digitally signed. The signature provides modification digest information with which to check the integrity of the package.

You do not have to encrypt a file to sign it. A digital signature is a separate component. You can either combine the signature with a given file or generate one separately. To combine a signature with a file, you generate a new version that incorporates both. Use the **--sign** or **-s** option to generate a version of the document that includes the digital signature. In the following example, the **mydoc** file is digitally signed with **mydoc.gpg** file containing both the original file and the signature.

```
gpg -o mydoc.gpg  --sign mydoc
```

If, instead, you want to just generate a separate signature file, you use the **--detach-sig** command. This has the advantage of not having to generate a complete copy of the original file. That file remains untouched. The signature file usually has an extension such as **.sig**. In the following example, the user creates a signature file called **mydoc2.sig** for the **mydoc2** file.

```
gpg -o mydoc2.sig --detach-sig mydoc2
```

To verify the file using a detached signature, the recipient user specifies both the signature file and the original file.

```
gpg --verify mydoc2.sig  mydoc2
```

To verify a trusted signature you can use **gpgv**.

You can also generate a clear sign signature to be used in text files. A *clear sign* signature is a text version of the signature that can be attached to a text file. The text file can be further edited by any text editor. Use the **--clearsign** option to create a clear sign signature. The following example creates a clear signed version of a text file called **mysignotice.txt**.

```
gpg -o mysignotice.txt --clearsign mynotice.txt
```

11. File and Directory Access

File System Access: remote shares

Permissions: Discretionary Access Control

Access Control Lists: FACL

Encrypted File Systems

Access to files and directories can be directly controlled by permissions and access controls. Permissions are the traditional method for controlling access. They limit access by a broad set of restrictions for owner, group, or anyone else. For more refined access, like specifying access by particular users, you can use Access Control Lists (ACL). Permissions are common used on most Unix and Linux systems and remain the simplest way to control access. ACLs require more maintenance, but offer many more access options.

Another level of control can be applied to file systems using file system encryption. Administrators can block any access to a file system, except to authorized users. In effect, encryption implements password protected file system.

File System Access

Various file systems can be accessed on Ubuntu easily. Any additional internal hard drive partitions on your system, both Linux and Windows NTFS, will be automatically detected and can be automatically mounted, providing immediate and direct access from your desktop. In addition you can access remote Windows shared folders and make your own shared folders accessible.

Access Linux File Systems on Internal Drives

Other Linux file systems on internal hard drives will be detect by Ubuntu automatically. Icons for them will be displayed on Computer window. Initially they will not be mounted. You will have to first validate your authorization to mount a disk. To mount a file system for the first time, double click on its icon. A PolicyKit authorization window will appear. You then enter your user password. The option to Remember authorization is checked, keeping the authorization indefinitely. Whenever you start up your system again, the file system will be mounted for you automatically.

Your file system is then mounted, displaying its icon both in the Computer window and the desktop. The file system will be mounted under the **/media** directory and given folder with the name of the file system label, or, if unlabeled, with the device name like **sda3** for the third partition on the first SATA drive.

Once granted, authentication access will remain in place for a limited time, allowing you to mount other file systems without having to enter your password. These file systems will then be automatically mounted also, provided you had left the Remember Authorization checked in the Authenticate window.

Any user with administrative access on the primary console is authorized to mount file systems. You can use PolicyKit agent to expand or restrict this level of authorization, as well as enabling access for specific users.

In addition, your partitions will automatically be displayed on the desktop and in the computer window as disks. Select Computer from the Places menu.

Access to Windows NTFS File Systems on Internal Drives

If you have installed Ubuntu on a dual-boot system with Windows XP, NT, or 2000, or otherwise need access to NTFS partitions, Linux NTFS file system support is installed automatically. Your NTFS partitions are mounted using FUSE, file system in user space. The same authentication control used for Linux file systems applies to NTFS file systems. Icons for the NTFS partitions will be displayed in the Computer window (Computer in Places menu). The first time you access the file system, you may be asked to provide authorization, as in Figure 11-1. Your NTFS file system is then mounted with icons displayed in the Computer widow and on the desktop. Whenever you start up your system, they will be automatically mounted for you. The partitions will be mounted under the **/media** directory with their labels used as folder names. If they have no labels, then they are given the name **disk**, and then numbered as **disk0, disk1**, and so on for additional partitions (unlabeled removable devices may also share these names). The NTFS partitions are mounted using **ntfs-3g** drivers.

Access to Local Network Shared File Systems (Windows)

Shared Windows folders and printers on any of the computers connected to your local network are automatically accessible from your Ubuntu desktop. The DNS discovery service (Ahavi) automatically detects hosts on your home or local network and will let you access directly any of their shared folders.

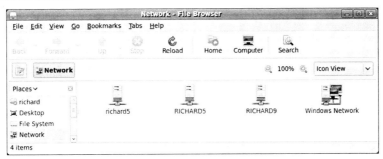

Figure 11-1: Network Places

Once selected, the shared folders will be shown.

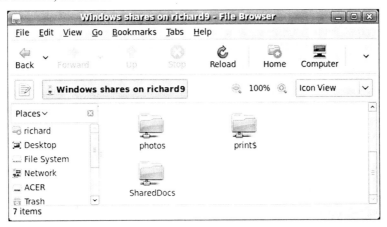

Figure 11-2: Remote shares

To access the shared folders, select Network from the Places menu to open the Network Places window (see Figure 11-1). Your connected computers will be listed. If you know the name of the Windows computer you want to access, just click on its icon, otherwise, click on the Windows network icon to see just the Windows machines (see Figure 11-2).

Figure 11-3: Mount remote Windows ShareDocs

You can then access a shared folder and it will be automatically mounted on your desktop. The Places sidebar will show an entry for the folder with an Eject button for unmounting it if you wish. You can also right-click on the desktop icon and select unmount volume. Figure 11-3 shows the ShareDocs shared folder on a Windows systems mounted on the Ubuntu desktop.

However, local systems cannot access your shared folders until you install a sharing server, Samba for Windows systems and NFS for Linux/Unix systems. Should you attempt to share a directory; an error notice will be displayed asking you to install Samba or NFS.

Shared Folders for your network

To share a folder on your local network, right-click on it and select Sharing options. This opens a window where you can allow sharing, and whether to permit modifying, adding, or deleting files in the folder (see Figure 11-4). You can also use the Share panel on the file's properties dialog (see Figure 11-6). You can also allow access to anyone who does not also have an account on your system (guest). Once you have made your selections, click the Create Share button. You can later change the sharing options if you wish.

Figure 11-4: Folder Sharing Options

To allow access by other users, permissions on the folder will have to be changed. You will be prompted to allow Nautilus to make these changes for you. Just click the "Add the permissions automatically button" (see Figure 11-5).

Figure 11-5: Folder Sharing permissions prompt

Folders that are shared will display a sharing emblem next to their icon on a file manager window.

Figure 11-6: Prompt to install sharing service (Samba and NFS)

To allow others to access your folders be sure the sharing servers are installed, Samba for Windows systems and NFS for Linux/Unix systems. The serves will be automatically configured for you and run. You will not be able to share folders until these servers are installed. If your sharing servers are not installed, you will be prompted to install them (see Figure 11-6). Click the Install service button. The Samba servers will be downloaded and installed. You are then prompted to restart your GNOME session. Click the Restart session button.

To later change the sharing permissions for a folder, open the folder's Properties window and then select the Share tab. When you make a change, a Modify Share button will be displayed. Click it to make the changes. In Figure 11-7 Guest access is added to the Photos folder.

To share folders (directories) with other Linux systems on your network, you use the NFS service (**nfs-kernelserver**). For Windows systems you use the Samba service (**samba**). It is possible to use the older **system-config-samba** tool to set up access. For more complex Samba configuration you can use SWAT or system-config-samba tools.

Figure 11-7: Folder Share panel

Permissions on GNOME

On GNOME, you can set a directory or file permission using the Permissions panel in its Properties window (see Figure 11-8). For Files, right-click the file or directory icon or entry in the file manager window and select Properties. Then select the Permissions panel. Here you will find pop-up menus for read and write permissions, along with rows for Owner, Group, and Other. You can set owner permissions as Read Only or Read And Write. For the group and others, you can also set the None option, denying access. The group name expands to a pop-up menu listing different groups; select one to change the file's group. If you want to execute this as an application (say, a shell script) check the Allow Executing File As Program entry. This has the effect of setting the execute permission.

The Permissions panel for directories operates much the same way, but it includes two access entries, Folder Access and File Access (see Figure 11-9). The Folder Access entry controls access to the folder with options for List Files Only, Access Files, and Create And Delete Files. These correspond to the read, read and execute, and read/write/execute permissions given to directories. The File Access entry lets you set permissions for all those files in the directory. They are the same as for files: for the owner, Read or Read and Write; for the group and others, the entry adds a None option to deny access. To set the permissions for all the files in the directory accordingly (not just the folder), click the Apply Permissions To Enclosed Files button.

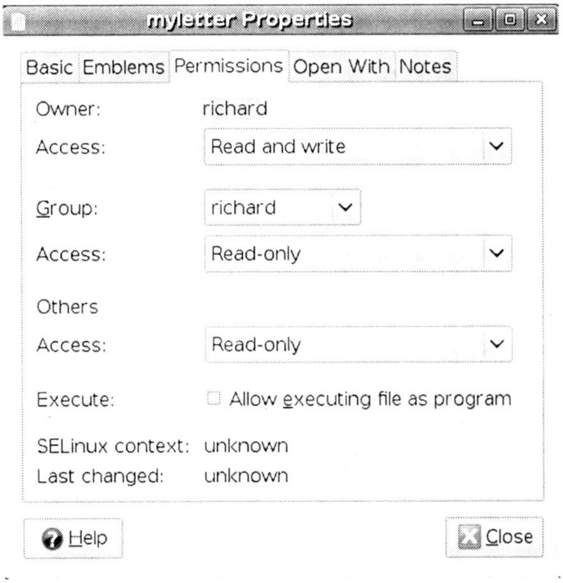

Figure 11-8: File Permissions

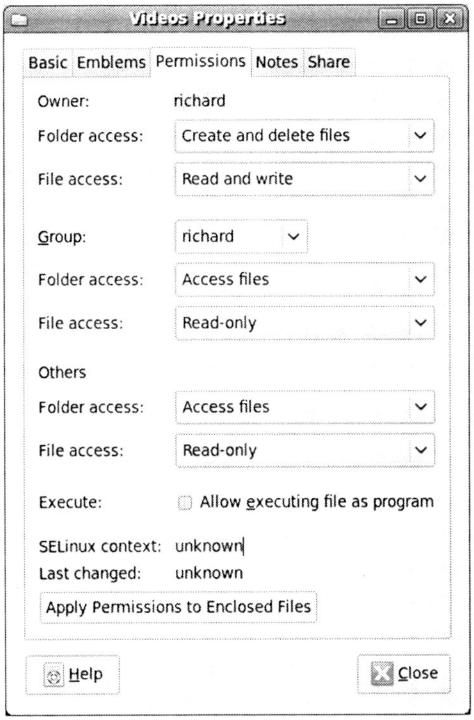

Figure 11-9: Folder Permissions

Permissions on KDE

On KDE, you can set a directory or file permission using the Permissions tab in its Properties window. Right-click the file or directory entry in the file manager window and select Properties. Then select the Permissions tab. Here you will find pop-up menus for Owner, Group, and Others. Options include Can Read, Can Read and Write, and Forbidden. For more refined access, click on the Advanced Permissions button to display a table for checking read, write, and execute access (**r**, **w**, **x**) for owner, group, and others. You can also set the sticky bit and user and group ID permissions. The Add Entry button lets you set up ACL access, specifying certain users or groups that can or cannot have access to the file.

Directories have slightly different options: Can View Content and Can View and Modify Content which are the read and write permissions. You have the option to apply changes to all subdirectories and the files in them. Clicking on the Advanced Permissions button displays the same read, write, and execute table for owner, group, and others. Click a table entry to toggle a permission on or off. The selected permissions are shown in the Effective column. Use the Add Entry button to add ACL entries to control access by specific users and groups.

Permissions: Discretionary Access Control

Each file and directory in Linux contains a set of permissions that determine who can access it and how. These are known as Discretionary Access Controls (DACs). You set these permissions to limit access in one of three ways: you can restrict access to yourself alone, you can allow users in a pre-designated group to have access, or you can permit anyone on your system to have access. You can also control how a given file or directory is accessed.

read, write, and execute

A file or directory may have read, write, and execute permissions. When you create a file, you, as the creator and owner, are automatically given read and write permissions for the owner, enabling you to display and modify the file. You may change these permissions to any combination you want. A file can also have read-only permission, which prevents any modifications.

Tip: From GNOME and KDE desktops you can change permissions easily by right-clicking on a file or directory icon and selecting Properties. On the Properties window's Permissions tab you will see options for setting Owner, Group, and Other permissions.

Three different categories of users can have access to a file or directory: the owner, the group, and all others not belonging to that group. The owner is the user who created the file. Any file you create, you own. You can also permit a group to have access to a file. Users are often collected into groups. For example, all the users for a given class or project can be formed into a group by the system administrator. A user can grant access to a file to the members of a designated group. Finally, you can also open up access to a file to all other users on the system. In this case, every user not part of the file's group can have access to that file. In this sense, every other user on the system makes up the "others" category. If you want to give the same access to all users on your system, you set the same permissions for both the group and the others. That way, you include both members of the group (group permission) and all those users who are not members (others permission).

Each category has its own set of read, write, and execute permissions. The first set controls the user's own access to his or her files—the owner access. The second set controls the access of the group to a user's files. The third set controls the access of all other users to the user's files. The three sets of read, write, and execute permissions for the three categories—owner, group, and other—make a total of nine types of permissions.

The `ls` command with the `-l` option displays detailed information about the file, including the permissions. In the following example's second line, the first set of characters on the left is a list of the permissions set for the **mydata** file:

```
$ ls -l mydata
-rw-r--r-- 1 chris weather 207 Feb 20 11:55 mydata
```

An empty permission is represented by a dash, `-`. The read permission is represented by `r`, write by `w`, and execute by `x`. There are ten positions for ten characters. The first character indicates the file type. In a general sense, a directory can be considered a type of file. If the first character is a dash, it means a file is being listed. If the first character is `d`, information about a directory is being displayed.

The next nine characters are arranged according to the different user categories. The first set of three characters is the owner's set of permissions for the file. The second set of three characters is the group's set of permissions for the file. The last set of three characters is the other users' set of permissions for the file.

chmod

You use the `chmod` command to change different permission configurations. `chmod` takes two lists as its arguments: permission changes and filenames. You can specify the list of permissions in two different ways. One way uses permission symbols and is referred to as the *symbolic method.* The other uses what is known as a "binary mask" and is referred to as either the absolute or the relative method. Table 11-1 lists options for the `chmod` command.

Ownership

Files and directories belong to both an owner and a group. A group usually consists of a collection of users, all belonging to the same group. In the following example, the **mydata** file is owned by the user **robert** and belongs to the group **weather**:

```
-rw-r--r-- 1 robert weather 207 Feb 20 11:55 mydata
```

A group can also consist of one user, normally the user who creates the file. Each user on the system, including the root user, is assigned his or her own group of which he or she is the only member, ensuring access only by that user. In the next example, the report file is owned by the **robert** user and belongs to that user's single user group, **robert**:

```
-rw-r--r-- 1 robert robert 305 Mar 17 12:01 report
```

The root user, the system administrator, owns most of the system files that also belong to the root group, of which only the root user is a member. Most administration files, like configuration files in the **/etc** directory, are owned by the root user and belong to the root group. Only the root user has permission to modify them, whereas normal users can read and, in the case of programs, also execute them. In the next example, the root user owns the **fstab** file in the **/etc** directory, which also belongs to the root user group.

```
-rw-r--r-- 1 root root 621 Apr 22 11:03 fstab
```

Command or Option	Execution
`chmod`	Changes the permission of a file or directory.
Options	
`+`	Adds a permission.
`-`	Removes a permission.
`=`	Assigns entire set of permissions.
`r`	Sets read permission for a file or directory. A file can be displayed or printed. A directory can have the list of its files displayed.
`w`	Sets write permission for a file or directory. A file can be edited or erased. A directory can be removed.
`x`	Sets execute permission for a file or directory. If the file is a shell script, it can be executed as a program. A directory can be changed to and entered.
`u`	Sets permissions for the user who created and owns the file or directory.
`g`	Sets permissions for group access to a file or directory.
`o`	Sets permissions for access to a file or directory by all other users on the system.
`a`	Sets permissions for access by the owner, group, and all other users.
`s`	Sets User ID and Group ID permission; program owned by owner and group.
`t`	Sets sticky bit permission; program remains in memory.
Commands	
`chgrp` *groupname filenames*	Changes the group for a file or files.
`chown` *user-name filenames*	Changes the owner of a file or files.
`ls -l` *filename*	Lists a filename with its permissions displayed.
`ls -ld` *directory*	Lists a directory name with its permissions displayed.
`ls -l`	Lists all files in a directory with its permissions displayed.

Table 11-1: File and Directory Permission Operations

Certain directories and files located in the system directories are owned by a service, rather than the root user, because the services need to change those files directly. This is particularly true for services that interact with remote users, such as Internet servers. Most of these files are located in the **/var** directory. Here you will find files and directories managed by services like the Squid proxy server and the Domain Name Server (named). In this example, the Squid proxy server directory is owned by the **squid** user and belongs to the **squid** group:

```
drwxr-x--- 2 squid squid 4096 Jan 24 16:29 squid
```

Note: When a program is owned by the root, setting the user ID permission will give the user the ability to execute the program with root permissions. This can be a serious security risk for any program that can effect changes—such as **rm**, which removes files.

Changing a File's Owner or Group: chown and chgrp

Although other users may be able to access a file, only the owner can change its permissions. If, however, you want to give some other user control over one of your file's permissions, you can change the owner of the file from yourself to the other user. The **chown** command transfers control over a file to another user. This command takes as its first argument the name of the other user. Following the username, you list the files you are transferring. In the next example, the user gives control of the **mydata** file to user **robert**:

```
$ chown robert mydata
$ ls -l mydata
-rw-r--r-- 1 robert weather 207 Feb 20 11:55 mydata
```

You can also, if you wish, change the group for a file, using the **chgrp** command. **chgrp** takes as its first argument the name of the new group for a file or files. Following the new group name, you list the files you want changed to that group. In the next example, the user changes the group name for **today** and **weekend** to the **forecast** group. The **ls -l** command then reflects the group change.

```
$ chgrp forecast today weekend
$ ls -l
-rw-rw-r-- 1 chris forecast 568 Feb 14 10:30 today
-rw-rw-r-- 1 chris forecast 308 Feb 17 12:40 weekend
```

You can combine the **chgrp** operation with the **chown** command by attaching a group to the new owner with a colon.

```
$ chown george:forecast tomorrow
-rw-rw-r-- 1 george forecast 568 Feb 14 10:30 tomorrow
```

Setting Permissions: Permission Symbols

The symbolic method of setting permissions uses the characters **r**, **w**, and **x** for read, write, and execute, respectively. Any of these permissions can be added or removed. The symbol to add a permission is the plus sign, **+**. The symbol to remove a permission is the minus sign, **-**. In the next example, the **chmod** command adds the execute permission and removes the write permission for the **mydata** file for all categories. The read permission is not changed.

```
$ chmod +x-w mydata
```

Permission symbols also specify each user category. The owner, group, and others categories are represented by the **u**, **g**, and **o** characters, respectively. Notice the owner category is represented by a **u** and can be thought of as the user. The symbol for a category is placed before the plus and minus sign preceding the read, write, and execute permissions. If no category symbol is used, all categories are assumed, and the permissions specified are set for the user, group, and others. In the next example, the first **chmod** command sets the permissions for the group to read and write. The second **chmod** command sets permissions for other users to read. Notice no spaces are between the permission specifications and the category. The permissions list is simply one long phrase, with no spaces.

```
$ chmod g+rw mydata
$ chmod o+r mydata
```

A user may remove permissions as well as add them. In the next example, the read permission is set for other users, but the write and execute permissions are removed:

```
$ chmod o+r-wx mydata
```

Another permission character exists, **a**, which represents all the categories. The **a** character is the default. In the next example, the two commands are equivalent. The read permission is explicitly set with the **a** character denoting all types of users: other, group, and user.

```
$ chmod a+r mydata
$ chmod +r mydata
```

One of the most common permission operations is setting a file's executable permission. This is often done in the case of shell program files. The executable permission indicates a file contains executable instructions and can be directly run by the system. In the next example, the file **lsc** has its executable permission set and then executed:

```
$ chmod u+x lsc
$ lsc
main.c lib.c
$
```

Absolute Permissions: Binary Masks

Instead of using the permission symbols shown in Table 11-1, many users find it convenient to use the absolute method. The *absolute method* changes all the permissions at once, instead of specifying one or the other. It uses a *binary mask* that references all the permissions in each category. The three categories, each with three permissions, conform to an octal binary format. Octal numbers have a base 8 structure. When translated into a binary number, each octal digit becomes three binary digits. A binary number is a set of 1 and 0 digits. Three octal digits in a number translate into three sets of three binary digits, which is nine altogether—and the exact number of permissions for a file.

You can use the octal digits as a mask to set the different file permissions. Each octal digit applies to one of the user categories. You can think of the digits matching up with the permission categories from left to right, beginning with the owner category. The first octal digit applies to the owner category, the second to the group, and the third to the others category. The actual octal digit you choose determines the read, write, and execute permissions for each category. At this point, you need to know how octal digits translate into their binary equivalents.

Calculating Octal Numbers

A simple way to calculate the octal number makes use of the fact that any number used for permissions will be a combination derived from adding in decimal terms the numbers 4, 2, and 1.

Use 4 for read permission, 2 for write, and 1 for execute. The read, write, execute permission is simply the addition of 4 + 2 + 1 to get 7. The read and execute permission adds 4 and 1 to get 5. You can use this method to calculate the octal number for each category. To get 755, you would add 4 + 2 + 1 for the owner read, write, and execute permission, 4 + 1 for the group read and execute permission, and 4 + 1 again for the other read and execute permission.

Binary Masks

When dealing with a binary mask, you need to specify three digits for all three categories, as well as their permissions. This makes a binary mask less versatile than the permission symbols. To set the owner execute permission on and the write permission off for the **mydata** file and retain the read permission, you need to use the octal digit 5 (binary 101). At the same time, you need to specify the digits for group and other user's access. If these categories are to retain read access, you need the octal number 4 for each (100). This gives you three octal digits, 544, which translate into the binary digits 101 100 100.

```
$ chmod 544 mydata
```

Execute Permissions

One of the most common uses of the binary mask is to set the execute permission. You can create files that contain Linux commands, called *shell scripts.* To execute the commands in a shell script, you must first indicate that the file is executable—that it contains commands the system can execute. You can do this in several ways, one of which is to set the executable permission on the shell script file. Suppose you just completed a shell script file and you need to give it executable permission to run it. You also want to retain read and write permission but deny any access by the group or other users. The octal digit 7 (111) will set all three permissions, including execute (you can also add 4-read, 2-write, and 1-execute to get 7). Using 0 for the group and other users denies them access. This gives you the digits 700, which are equivalent to the binary digits 111 000 000. In this example, the owner permission for the **myprog** file is set to include execute permission:

```
$ chmod 700 myprog
```

If you want others to be able to execute and read the file but not change it, you can set the read and execute permissions and turn off the write permission with the digit 5 (101). In this case, you use the octal digits 755, having the binary equivalent of 111 101 101.

```
$ chmod 755 myprog
```

Directory Permissions

You can also set permissions on directories. The read permission set on a directory allows the list of files in a directory to be displayed. The execute permission enables a user to change to that directory. The write permission enables a user to create and remove his or her files in that directory. If you allow other users to have write permission on a directory, they can add their own files to it. When you create a directory, it is automatically given read, write, and execute permission for the owner. You may list the files in that directory, change to the directory, and create files in it.

Like files, directories have sets of permissions for the owner, the group, and all other users. Often, you may want to allow other users to change to and list the files in one of your directories but not let them add their own files to the directory. In this case, you set read and execute permissions on the directory but you don't set a write permission. This allows other users to change to the directory and list the files in it but not to create new files or to copy any of their files into it. The next example sets read and execute permissions for the group for the **thankyou** directory but removes the write permission. Members of the group may enter the **thankyou** directory and list the files there, but they may not create new ones.

```
$ chmod g+rx-w letters/thankyou
```

Just as with files, you can also use octal digits to set a directory permission. To set the same permissions as in the preceding example, you use the octal digits 750, which have the binary equivalents of 111 101 000.

```
$ chmod 750 letters/thankyou
```

Displaying Directory Permissions

The **ls** command with the **-l** option lists all files in a directory. To list only the information about the directory itself, add a **d** modifier. In the next example, **ls -ld** displays information about the **thankyou** directory. Notice the first character in the permissions list is **d**, indicating it is a directory:

```
$ ls -ld thankyou
drwxr-x--- 2 chris 512 Feb 10 04:30 thankyou
```

Parent Directory Permissions

If you want other users to have access to a file, you not only need to set permissions for that file, you also must make sure the permissions are set for the directory in which the file is located. To access your file, a user must first access the file's directory. The same applies to parents of directories. Although a directory may give permission to others to access it, if its parent directory denies access, the directory cannot be reached. Therefore, you must pay close attention to your directory tree. To provide access to a directory, all other directories above it in the directory tree must also be accessible to other users.

Ownership Permissions

In addition to the read/write/execute permissions, you can also set ownership permissions for executable programs. Normally, the user who runs a program owns it while it is running, even though the program file itself may be owned by another user. The Set User ID permission allows the original owner of the program to own it always, even while another user is running the program. For example, most software on the system is owned by the root user but is run by ordinary users. Some such software may have to modify files owned by the root. In this case, the ordinary user needs to run that program with the root retaining ownership so that the program can have the permissions to change those root-owned files. The Group ID permission works the same way, except it applies to groups. Programs owned by a group retain ownership, even when run by users from another group. The program can then change the owner group's files. There is a potential security risk involved in that you are essentially giving a user some limited root-level access.

Ownership Permissions Using Symbols

To add both the User ID and Group ID permissions to a file, you use the **s** option. The following example adds the User ID permission to the **pppd** program, which is owned by the root user. When an ordinary user runs **pppd**, the root user retains ownership, allowing the **pppd** program to change root-owned files.

```
# chmod +s /usr/sbin/pppd
```

The Set User ID and Set Group ID permissions show up as an **s** in the execute position of the owner and group segments. Set User ID and Group ID are essentially variations of the execute permission, **x**. Read, write, and User ID permission are **rws** instead of just **rwx**.

```
# ls -l /usr/sbin/pppd
-rwsr-sr-x 1 root root 184412 Jan 24 22:48 /usr/sbin/pppd
```

Ownership Permissions Using the Binary Method

For the ownership permissions, you add another octal number to the beginning of the octal digits. The octal digit for User ID permission is 4 (100) and for Group ID, it is 2 (010) (use 6 to set both—110). The following example sets the User ID permission to the **pppd** program, along with read and execute permissions for the owner, group, and others:

```
# chmod 4555 /usr/sbin/pppd
```

Sticky Bit Permissions

One other special permission provides for greater security on directories, the *sticky bit.* Originally the sticky bit was used to keep a program in memory after it finished execution to increase efficiency. Current Linux systems ignore this feature. Instead, it is used for directories to protect files within them. Files in a directory with the sticky bit set can only be deleted or renamed by the root user or the owner of the directory.

Sticky Bit Permission Using Symbols

The sticky bit permission symbol is **t**. The sticky bit shows up as a **t** in the execute position of the other permissions. A program with read and execute permissions with the sticky bit has its permissions displayed as **r-t**.

```
# chmod +t /home/dylan/myreports
# ls -l /home/dylan/myreports
-rwxr-xr-t 1 root root 4096 /home/dylan/myreports
```

Sticky Bit Permission Using the Binary Method

As with ownership, for sticky bit permissions, you add another octal number to the beginning of the octal digits. The octal digit for the sticky bit is 1 (001). The following example sets the sticky bit for the **myreports** directory:

```
# chmod 1755 /home/dylan/myreports
```

The next example sets both the sticky bit and the User ID permission on the **newprogs** directory. The permission 5755 has the binary equivalent of 101 111 101 101:

```
# chmod 5755 /usr/bin/newprogs
# ls -l /usr/bin/newprogs
drwsr-xr-t 1 root root 4096  /usr/bin/newprogs
```

Permission Defaults: umask

Whenever you create a file or directory, it is given default permissions. You can display the current defaults or change them with the **umask** command. The permissions are displayed in binary or symbolic format as described in the following sections. The default permissions include any execute permissions that are applied to a directory. Execute permission for a file is turned off by default when you create it because standard data files do not use the executable permissions (to make a file executable like a script, you have to manually set it's execute permission). To display the current default permissions, use the **umask** command with no arguments. Use the **-s** option for the symbolic format.

```
$ umask -S
u=rwx,g=rx,o=rx
```

This default umask provides **rw-r--r--** permission for standard files and adds execute permission for directories, **rwxr-xr-x**.

You can set a new default by specifying permissions in either symbolic or binary format. To specify the new permissions, use the **-s** option. The following example denies others read permission, while allowing user and group read access, which results in permissions of **rwxr-x---:**

```
umask -S  u=rwx,g=rx,o=
```

When you use the binary format, the mask is the inverse of the permissions you want to set. To set both the read and execute permission on and the write permission off, you use the octal number 2, a binary 010. To set all permissions on, you use an octal 0, a binary 000. The following example shows the mask for the permission defaults rwx, rx, and rx (rw, r, and r for files):

```
$ umask
0022
```

To set the default to only deny all permissions for others, you use 0027, using the binary mask 0111 for the other permissions.

```
$ umask 0027
```

Access Control Lists: ACL

Users can provide more refined control of their files and directories by using Access Control Lists (ACL). Access Control Lists maintains lists of users and groups and the rights they have to access certain files and directories. ACLs allow for much more refined access to directories, instead of just the all or nothing approach of owners, groups, and other. With ACLs only specific users could be granted write access to a file, while some others could be given just read access. Instead of opening a file up to all members of a group or everyone else on the system or network, an ACL could limit access to just a few specified users, regardless of their group membership. Like permissions, ACLs are controlled by the user, allowing users to setup access to a file by particular individuals or groups.

On Ubuntu, ACL support can be installed with the **acl** package (universe repository). Check the man pages for **acl**, **setfacl**, and **getfacl** for detailed descriptions and examples.

ACL entries have the three fields: a type (user, group, other, mask), a qualifier (specific user or group), and the discretionary access permissions (read, write, execute). The fields are separated by colons. The type can be u, **g**, **o**, and **m** referencing user, group, other, and mask, respectively. For the qualifier you can enter a user or group. Instead of a name you can use a user or group ID, UID or GID. Permissions can be read, write, or execute: **r**, **w**, or **x**. The permissions can be managed with binary or symbolic methods. In a standard binary method, the **rwx** permissions are positional, with read being first, write second, and execute third. If a dash (-) appears in any of these positions, it is denying that kind of access. **r-x** would allow read and execute permission, but deny write access. With a symbolic method, you use a + or ^ symbol to specify a permission you want to add or remove. **+r^w+x** would add read and execute permissions, and remove write permission.

The entry **u:chris:rw** would allow the user chris to have read and write permissions for the specified file. You can list several entries on the same line, separated by commas, or place each entry in a file on its own line.

ACL for file systems

File systems need to be mounted with the **acl** option. The ACL tools (acl package) include **setfacl** and **getfacl** commands to set permissions. See **setfacl** and **getfacl** Man pages for more information.

Once permissions are set for a file system, you can use the **mount** command with the **acl** option to mount it. With Ubuntu 9.04, be sure the file system is labeled.

```
sudo mount  -o acl  LABEL=myvideos /myvideo1
```

To have the device automatically mounted with the ACL options, add the acl option to its entry in the **/etc/fstab** file.

```
LABEL=myvideos    /myvideo1    ext3       defaults,acl   0    0
```

Displaying ACL controls

Once the file system has been mounted with ACL attributes enabled, you can then use the **getfacl** command to display the ACL attributes for particular files and directories. The **getfacl** command will list the file name, owner, and group. It will then list permissions for user, group, mask, and other. The permission entry will have three fields, the first being the type (user, group, mask, or other). The second is a list of users and groups that are permitted access. And the third is the permission granted to the listed users and groups. You can have several permissions of the same type, listing users and groups that would have different permissions. Default permissions are initially listed with empty user and group lists (empty second field). The following command will show the ACL settings for the **myfirstvid** file.

```
getfacl  myfirstvid
```

To see the ACL for the current working directory, use the period as the argument.

```
getfacl .
```

When you use the **ls** command with the **–l** option on and ACL file or directory, a + will appear at the end of the permissions field indicating that ACLs are in effect.

```
ls -l myfirstvid
```

To copy an ACL file you use the **–p** permission (the move/rename operation, **mv**, will preserve the ACL permissions).

```
cp -p myfirstvid  myvidback
```

ACL settings

With the **setfacl** command you can control access by specific users, setting read, write, and execute permissions. Use the **-m** option to add new permissions and change current ones (**-x** removes a setting). As noted previously, users and permissions are referenced with a colon separate list with permissions specified using the **r**, **w**, and x options, and **u**, **g**, and **o** referencing user, group, and other categories. The argument **u:chris:rw** would allow the user chris to have read and write permissions for the specified file

```
setfacl  -m u:chris:rw  myfirstvid
```

The **getfacl** operation will then display added permission entry.

```
getfacl  myfirstvid
```

Tip: You can install and use the **eiciel** tool to provide a graphical user interface for setting ACL controls on files and directories.

To change a particular entry, use the **–m** option.

```
setfacl  -m u:chris:r  myfirstvid
```

To remove an entire entry, use the –x option. Specify just the type and the user or group name.

```
setfacl  -x u:chris  myfirstvid
```

Tip: You can also use chacl command to change ACL settings.

Note: Instead of repeating the same ACL entries for each file, you can create a file that holds the entries and then read them to your file.

For each file ACL an effective mask is set up whenever you add a new entry. The effective rights mask is calculated by the **setfacl** command as the union of all other permissions already in specified for ACL entries, and the current one specified. In effect, when you use the **setfacl** command with the **-m** option to add an ACL entry, a mask entry is calculated by **setfacl** and added to the operation. You can turn off this implied calculation with the **-n** option. You would then have to explicitly set the effective rights mask.

```
setfacl -n -m u:chris:r,m::rw  myfirstvid
```

Should you use **chmod** to changes permissions on an ACL file, you are changing the mask entry. The mask entry takes precedence over all other entries. If you change a mask to just read only for all permissions, all other entries are overridden. This is indicated by an effective comment displayed after the entry, showing the actual permission allowed. The original entries remain, they are just not effective. There has been no modification of the original entry. This feature lets you shut off access to all users and groups, without having to change all the particular entries. You can then use **chmod** or change the mask entry directly to turn access back on for all the original entries.

Encrypted File Systems

Ubuntu lets you encrypt nonroot and swap file systems, allowing access only to those users with the appropriate encrypted password. You can apply encryption to both fixed and removable file systems such as USB devices. It is recommended that you use the LUKS (Linux Unified Key Setup) encryption tools to encrypt file systems. Ubuntu supports encrypted file systems during installation using the Alternate install disc.

To set up an encrypted file system is to use **cryptsetup** tool. You first use the **cryptsetup** command with the **luksFormat** option to initialize and create an encrypted volume. You will be prompted to specify a key (or add the key file as an argument). You will be prompted for the passphrase (or use **--keyfile** to specify the file with the passphrase). You can then format the file system, specifying its name and type.

Be sure the file system is not mounted. The default system type is **vfat**. Use the **-t** option to specify one. Be sure to specify the file system, the encryption cipher and passphrase, and the file system type and name. The **crypsetup** tool sets up the encrypted file system and you can use it directly, later formatting it with **mkfs**. Encryption is often used for removable devices like USB drives.

Once your encrypted file system is setup and formatted, restart your system. You can then access the encrypted partition or removable drive. For a USB drive or disk, from the file system window double-click the USB drive icon. This opens a window in which you are prompted for a password with the option to forget, remember for the session, or always remember. A message tells you the device is encrypted. Once you enter your password, you can then mount and access the device (double-click it again). The volume name will appear with an icon on your desktop. HAL will handle all mounting and access for removable media. Use the same procedure for fixed partitions. Instead of restarting your system after the initialization and format, you can use **crypsetup** with the **luksOpen** option to open the encrypted file system.

HAL manages access to encrypted file systems with the **15-lstorage-uks.fdi** file in the **/usr/share/hal/fdi/policy/10osverndor** directory. This file uses the **hal-luks-setup** and the **hal-luks-teardown** scripts to manage encrypted file systems.

If you want to manage fixed drives manually, you can place entries in the **/etc/crypttab** and **/etc/fstab** files for them.

The **cryptsetup** tool is installed as part of the **cryptsetup** package. Check **/usr/share/doc/cryptsetup** for HOWTOs and example for managing encrypted partitions. Support for encrypted file systems is provided by the **/etc/init.d/cryptdisks** script. Default options are set in the **/etc/default/cryptdisks** file which enable encrypted disk support.

If you did not use Luks, you will have to specify a encryption method with the **cipher** option. Use the **--cipher** option with **cryptsetup** in the **/etc/crypttab** entry. For an Encrypted Salt-Sector Initialization Vector (ESSIV) cipher, you use **aes-cbc-essiv:sha256**. For a plain cipher, you use **aes-cbc-plain**.

Intrusion Detection: Tripwire and AIDE

When an attacker breaks into a system, he will usually try to gain control by making his own changes to system administration files, such as password files. He can create his own user and password information, allowing him access at any time, or he can simply change the root user password. He can also replace entire programs, such as the login program, with his own version. One method of detecting such actions is to use an integrity checking tool such as Tripwire or Advanced Intrusion Detection Environment (AIDE) to detect any changes to system administration files. AIDEI is a free and enhanced alternative to Tripwire (Ubuntu main repository). It provides easy configuration and detailed reporting.

An integrity checking tool works by first creating a database of unique identifiers for each file or program to be checked. These can include features such as permissions and file size, but more important, they can also include checksum numbers generated by encryption algorithms from the file's contents. Default identifiers are checksum numbers created by algorithms such as the SHA2 modification digest algorithm. An encrypted value that provides such a unique identification of a file is known as a *signature*. In effect, a signature provides an accurate snapshot of the contents of a file. Files and programs are then periodically checked by generating their identifiers again and matching them with those in the database. The intrusion detection application will generate signatures of the current files and programs and match them against the values previously generated for its database. Any differences are noted as changes to the file, and you are notified of the changes.

12. AppArmor and Security Enhanced Linux

AppArmor security

Ubuntu installs AppArmor as its default security system. AppArmor is designed as an alternative to SELinux. It is much less complicated but makes use of the same kernel support provided for SELinux. AppArmor is a simple method for implementing MAC for specified Linux applications. AppArmor is used primarily to control network servers such as Web, FTP, Samba, and Common UNIX Printing System (CUPS) servers. In this respect, it is much more limited in scope than SELinux, which tries to cover every object. Instead of labeling each object, as SELinux does, AppArmor identifies an object by its pathname. The object does not have to be affected by AppArmor. Originally developed by Immunix and later supported for a time by Novell (OpenSUSE), AppArmor is available under the GNU Public License. You can find out more about AppArmor at **http://en.opensuse.org/Apparmor**. Ubuntu will install the **apparmor** and **apparmor-utils** packages (Ubuntu main repository). Also available are the **apparmor-profiles** and **apparmor-doc** packages (universe repository).

AppArmor works by setting up a profile for supported applications. The profile is a security policy that is similar to SELinux policies. A profile defines what an application can access and use on the system.

AppArmor is started with the **/etc/init.d/apparmor** script. You can use the service command or services-admin to stop and restart AppArmor. As you modify profiles, you may need to stop or restart AppArmor. The following would restart AppArmor

```
sudo service apparmor restart
```

Most servers have profiles, like the Apache Web server, or the Samba Windows file sharing server. Initially there are two profiles loaded, both for the CUPS printer server, controlling access to the system printers. The **apparmor-profiles** package will install many pre-configured profiles for use on Ubuntu. There are profiles for most servers such as the vsftp FTP server, the Apache Web server, and Squid proxy server, and the Postfix mail server.

AppArmor can apply either an enforce or a complain mode to a particular profile. In the enforce mode, a profile's restrictions are executed, denying access to processes or user not permitted to access the profiled application. In the complain mode, restrictions are not executed. Warning messages are issued instead.

AppArmor utilities

The **apparmor-utils** packages installs several AppArmor tools, including **enforce**, which enables AppArmor to enforce restrictions on a profile, and **complain**, which instructs AppArmor to onlyissues warning messages for a profile. The **unconfined** tool lists applications that have no AppArmor profiles. The **audit** tool turns on AppArmor message logging for an application (uses enforce mode). The **apparmor_status** tool displays current profile information. The **--complaining** option lists only those applications that are in complain mode, and the **--enforced** option lists applications that are in enforcing mode. The following show the current status for apparmor, showing what profiles are loaded and what mode is applied to it.

```
sudo apparmor_status
```

The **logprof** tool will analyze AppArmor logs to determine if any changes are needed in any of the application profile. Suggested changes will be presented and the user can allow (**A**) or deny them (**D**). In complain mode, allow is the default, and in enforce mode, deny is the default.

You can also make your own changes with the new (**N**) option. Should you want the change applied to all files and directories in a suggested path, you can select the glob option (**G**), essentially replacing the last directory or file in a path with the b global file matching symbol.

Utility	Description
apparmor_status	Status information about AppArmor policies.
audit *applications*	Enable logging for AppArmor messages for specified applications
complain	Set AppArmor to complain mode
enforce	Set AppArmor to enforce mode
autodep *application*	Generate a basic profile for new applications
logprof	Analyzes AppArmor complain messages for a profile, and suggests profile modifications.
genprof *application*	Generate profile for an application
unconfined	Lists applications not controlled by AppArmor (no profiles)

Table 12-1: AppArmor Utilities

The **autodep** tool will generate a basic AppArmor profile for a new or unconfined application. If you want a more effective profile, you can use **genprof** to analyze the applications use and generate profile controls accordingly.

The **genprof** tool will update or generate a detailed profile for a specified application. genprof will first set the profile to complain mode. You then starts up the application and uses it, generating complain mode log messages on that use. Then **genprof** prompts you to either scan the complain messages to refine the profile (**S**) further, or to finish (**F**). When scanned, violations are detected and you are prompted to allow or deny recommended controls. You can then repeat the scan operation until you think the profile is acceptable. Select finish (**F**) to finalize the profile and quit.

AppArmor configuration

AppArmor configuration is located in the **/etc/apparmor** directory. Configurations for different profiles are located in the **/etc/apparmor.d** directory. Loaded profile configuration files have as their name their pathname, using periods instead of slashes to separate directory names. The profile file for the **smbd** (Samba) application is **usr.sbin.smbd**. For CUPS (**cupsd**) it is **usr.sbin.cupsd**. Additional profiles like the Samba profile are installed with the **apparmor-profiles** package (not installed by default).

Configuration rules for AppArmor profiles consist of a path and permissions allowable on that path. A detailed explanation of AppArmor rules and permissions can be found in the apparmor.d Man page, including a profile example. A path ending in a * matching symbol will select all the files in that directory. The ** selects all file in the parent directory. All file matching operations are supported (*, ||, ?). Permissions include **r** (read), **w** (write), **x** (execute), and **l** (link). The **u** permission allows unconstrained access. The following entry allows all the files in the **/var/log/samba/cores/smdb** directory to be written to.

```
/var/log/samba/cores/smbd/** rww,
```

The abstractions subdirectory has files with profile rules that are common to different profiles. Rules from these files are read into actual profiles using the include directive. There are abstractions for applications like gnome, samba, and ftp. Some abstractions will include yet other more general abstractions, like those for the X server or GNOME. For example, the profile for the Samba smbd server, usr.sbin.smbd, will have a include directive for the samba abstraction. This abstraction holds rules common to both the smbd and nmbd servers, both used by the Samba service. The <> used in an include directive indicate the **/etc/arpparmor.d** directory. A list of abstraction files can be found in the apparmor.d Man page. The include line for Samba is shown here.

```
#include <abstractions/samba>
```

In some cases, such as with the Web server profile, a profile may need access to particular files in a directory to which it normally should not have access. In such a case, the application may need to use a subprofile to allow access. In effect, the application changes hats, taking on permissions is does not have in the original profile.

The **apparmor-profiles** package will also provide profile default files for numerous applications in the **/usr/share/doc/apparmor-profiles/extras** directory. It can also be used to activate several commonly used profiles, setting up profile files for them in the **/etc/apparmor.d** directory, such as those for samba (**nmbd** and **smbd**), **avahi**, and the network time protocol daemon (**ntpd**).

SELinux

Although numerous security tools have existed for protecting specific services, user information, and data, no tool has been available for protecting the entire system at the administrative level—at least not until SELinux, which provides built-in administrative protection for aspects of your Linux system. Instead of relying on users to protect their files or on a specific network program to control access, security measures are built into SELinux's basic file management system and network access methods. All controls can be managed directly by an administrator as part of Linux system administration.

Resource	Location
NSA SELinux	http://www.nsa.gov/selinux
NSA SELinux FAQ	http://www.nsa.gov/selinux/info/faq.cfm
SELinux at sourceforge.net	http://selinux.sourceforge.net
NSA SELinux Documentation	http://www.nsa.gov/selinux/info/docs.cfm
Configuring SELinux Policy	www.nsa.gov/selinux/papers/policy2-abs.cfm
SELinux Reference Policy Project	http://oss.tresys.com/projects/refpolicy

Table 12-2: SELinux Resources

SELinux was developed and is maintained by the U.S. National Security Agency (NSA), which chose Linux as its platform for implementing a secure operating system. Most Linux distributions have embraced SELinux and incorporated it as a standard feature. Detailed documentation is available from resources listed in Table 12-2, including sites provided by the

NSA and SourceForge. In addition, check your Linux distribution's Web site for any manuals, FAQs, or documentation on SELinux.

Linux and Unix systems normally use a discretionary access control (DAC) method for restricting access. In this approach users and the objects they own, such as files, determine permissions. The user has completed discretion over the objects it owns. The weak point in many Linux/Unix systems has been the user administrative accounts. If an attacker managed to gain access to an administrative account, they would have complete control over the service the account managed. Access to the root user would give control over the entire system, all its users, and any network services it was running. To counter this weakness, the NSA set up a mandatory access control (MAC) structure. Instead of an all-or-nothing set of privileges based on accounts, services and administrative tasks are compartmentalized and separately controlled with policies detailing what can and cannot be done. Access is granted not just because one is an authenticated user, but when specific security criteria are met. Users, applications, processes, files, and devices can be given just the access they need to do their job, and nothing more.

Ubuntu SE Linux Packages and Policies

Though Ubuntu provides shared library support for SELinux, it does not include SELinux as part of the main repository. Instead, SELinux is made available as part of the universe repository. Though not integrated into Ubuntu, SELinux is still a critically important and powerful security service. You can use the Synaptic Package Manager to search for, download, and install SELinux packages.

Select the **selinux** metapackage to install required packages. The **selinux** package itself installs the service script for selinux. It will install the SELinux reference policy package (**selinux-policy-ubuntu**) and supporting tools packages including **policycoreutils**, **selinux-utils**, and **selinux-basic**.

Should you want to generate your own SE linux modules you would install the **selinux-policy-ubuntu-dev** package which contains SE Linux header files (SELinux Refernece Policy), and **checkpolicy** which will compile selinux modules.

The **selinux-policy-ubuntu** package installs the SE Linux reference policy, tailored for use on Ubuntu. Should you want to use the targeted or strict policies provided in previous releases, you would install the **selinux-policy-default** package. This package installs the targeted policy by default. Removing the unconfined module will, in effect, implement a strict policy. Policy files are installed at **/etc/selinux/default**. For Multi-level security you would install **selinux-policy-mls**.

The SE Linux reference policy not compatible with the default (strict and targeted) and mls policies. If you install the **selinux-policy-default** or **selinux-policy-mls** packages, then the **selinux-policy-ubuntu** package will be removed, and visa versa. The default and mls policies provide an added level of organization to control access to confidential files. In the default policy this is known as mandated multi-catgory security (MMCS), and for the mls policy this is referred to as multi-level security. MLS offers a very high level of security and is usually used in the military. For development header files for the default and mls policies, install the **selinux-policy-dev** package.

Documentation is installed by the **selinux-doc** and **selinux-policy-ubuntu-doc** packages.

If you want to create a customized policy, generating a SE Linux policy from the SE Linux source, you would install the **selinux-policy-src** package. This package will install a compressed archive of the SE Linux Referenc Policy source files, **selinux-policy-src.tar.gz**, to the **/usr/src** directory. Copy the file to a local directory, then decompress and extract the archive. The **selinux-policy-src** directory will hold the **.te** and **.fi** files that you can then modify.

Flask Architecture

The Flux Advanced Security Kernel (Flask) operating system security architecture provides support for security policies. It organizes OS components and data into subjects and objects, for which a security context is defined. *Subjects* are processes: applications, drivers, and system tasks that are currently running. *Objects* are fixed components such as files, directories, sockets, network interfaces, and devices. A *security context* is a set of security attributes that determines how a subject or object can be used. This approach provides very fine-grained control over every element in the OS as well as all data on your computer.

The attributes designated for the security contexts and the degree to which they are enforced are determined by an overall *security policy*, which is enforced by a *security server*. Distributions may provide different preconfigured policies from which to work.

SELinux uses a combination of the Type Enforcement (TE), Role-based Access Control (RBAC), and Multilevel Security (MLS) security models. TE focuses on objects and processes such as directories and applications. For the TE model, the security attributes assigned to an object are known as either *domains* or *types*. Types are used for fixed objects such as files, and domains are used for processes such as running applications.

For user access to processes and objects, SELinux makes use of the RBAC model. When new processes or objects are created, transition rules specify the type or domain to which they belong in their security contexts. With the RBAC model, users are assigned roles for which permissions are defined. The roles restrict what objects and processes a user can access. The security context for processes include a role attribute, controlling what objects it can assess. The new MLS adds a security level that contains both a sensitivity and capability value.

Users are given separate SELinux user identities. Normally these correspond to the user IDs set up under the standard Linux user creation operations. Though the separate user IDs may use the same names, they are not the same identifiers. Standard Linux identities can be easily changed with commands such **setuid** and **su**. Changes to the Linux user ID will not affect the SELinux ID, however. This means that even if a user changes her ID, SELinux will still be able to track it, maintaining control over that user.

System Administration Access

It is critically important that you make sure you have system administrative access under SELinux before you enforce its policies. This is especially true if you are using a strict or MLS policy, which imposes restrictions on administrative access. You should always use SELinux in permissive mode first and check for any messages denying access. With SELinux enforced, it may no longer matter whether you can access the root user or not. What matters is whether your user, even the root user, has **sysadm_r** role and **sysadm_t** object access and an administrative security level. You may not be able to use the **su** command to access the root user and expect to have root user administrative access. Recall that SELinux keeps its own security identities that are not the same as Linux user IDs. Although you may change your user ID with **su**, you will not have changed your security ID.

The targeted approach to policy implementation will set up rules that allow standard system administrator access using normal Linux procedures. The root user will be able to access the root user account normally. In the strict policy, however, the root user needs to access her account using the appropriate security ID. Both are now part of a single reference policy. If you want administrative access through the **su** command (from another user), you first use the **su** command to log in as the root user. You then have to change your role to the **sysadm_r** role—however, you must already be configured by SELinux policy rules to be allowed to take on the **sysadm_r** role. A user can be allowed to assume several possible roles. To change a role, the user can use the **newrole** command with the **-r** option:

```
newrole -r sysadm_r
```

Terminology

SELinux uses several terms that have different meanings in other contexts. The terminology can be confusing because some of the terms, such as *domain*, have different meanings in other, related, areas. For example, a *domain* in SELinux is a *process* as opposed to an *object*, whereas in networking the term refers to network DNS addresses. A *policy* is a set of rules used to determine the relationships between users, roles, and types or domains. These rules state what types a role can access and what roles a user can have.

Identity

SELinux creates *identities* that are used to control access. Identities are not the same as traditional user IDs. Although each SELinux user normally has an user ID, identities and user IDs are not linked. Therefore, operations that affect a user do not affect the corresponding SELinux identity.

SELinux can set up a separate corresponding identity for each user, though on less secure policies, such as unconfined (targeted) policies, general identities are used. A general user identity is used for all normal users, restricting users to user-level access, whereas administrators are assigned administrative identities. You can further define security identities for particular users.

The identity makes up part of a security context that determines what a user can or cannot do. Should a user change her user ID, that user's security identity will not change. A user will always have the same security identity. In traditional Linux systems, a user can use commands such as **su** to change her user ID, becoming a different user. On SELinux, even though a user can still change her Linux user ID, the user still retains the same original security ID. You always know what a particular person is doing on your system, no matter what user ID that person may assume.

The security identity can have limited access. So even though a user may use the Linux **su** command to become the root user, the user's security identity could prevent her from performing any root user administrative commands. As noted, to gain an administrative access, the role for the user's security identity would have to change as well.

Security identities have roles that control what they can do. Use **id -Z** to see the security context for your security identity, what roles you have, and what kinds of objects you can access. This command lists the user security context that starts with the security ID, followed by a colon, and then the roles the user has and the objects the user can control. A user role is **user_r**, and a system administration role is **system_r**. The general security identity is **user_u**, whereas a particular security identity will normally use the username. The following example shows the security context for a standard user with the general security identity:

```
$ id -Z
 user_u:user_r:user_t
```

In this example the user has a security identity called george:

```
$ id -Z
 george:user_r:user_t
```

You can use the `newrole` command to change the role a user is allowed. Changing to a system administrative role, the user can then have equivalent root access.

```
$ newrole -r sysadm_r
$ id -Z
 george:sysadm_r:sysadm_t
```

Domains

Domains are used to identify and control processes. Each process is assigned a domain within which it can run. A domain sets restrictions on what a process can do. Traditionally, a process was given a user ID to determine what it could do, and many processes required a root user ID to gain access to the full file system. A process with a root user ID could be used to gain full administrative access over the entire system. A domain, on the other hand, can be tailored to access some areas but not others. Attempts to break into another domain such as the administrative domain would be blocked. For example, the administrative domain is **sysadm_t**, whereas the DNS server uses only **named_t**, and users have a **user_t** domain.

Types

Whereas domains control processes, *types* control objects such as files and directories. Files and directories are grouped into types that can be used to control who can have access to them. The type names use the same format used by the domain names, ending with a **_t** suffix. Unlike domains, types reference objects, including files, devices, and network interfaces.

Roles

Types and domains are assigned to roles. Users (security identities) with a given role can access types and domains assigned to that role. For example, most users can access user_t type objects, but not sysadm_t objects. The types and domains a user can access are set by the role entry in configuration files. The following example allows users to access objects with the user password type:

```
role user_r types user_passwd_t
```

Security Context

Each object has a *security context* that sets its security attributes, such as identity, role, domain, or type. A file will have a security context listing the kind of identity that can access it, the role under which it can be accessed, and the security type to which it belongs. Each component adds its own refined level of security. Passive objects are usually assigned a generic role, **object_r**, which has no effect, as such objects cannot initiate actions.

A normal file created by a user in his own directory will have an identity, role, and type, as shown next. The *identity* is a user and the *role* is that of an object. The *type* is the user's home directory. This type is used for all subdirectories and their files created within a user's home directory.

```
user_u:object_r:user_home_t
```

A file or directory created by that same user in a different part of the file system will use a different type. For example, the type for files created in the **/tmp** directory will be **tmp_t**:

```
user_u:object_r:tmp_t
```

Transition: Labeling

A *transition,* also known as labeling, assigns a security context to a process or file. For a file, the security context is assigned when it is created, whereas for a process the security context is determined when the process is run.

Making sure every file has an appropriate security context is called *labeling.* Adding another file system would require that you label (add security contexts) to the directories and files on it. Labeling varies, depending on the policy you use. Each policy may have different security contexts for objects and processes. Relabeling is carried out using the **fixfiles** command in the policy source directory.

```
fixfiles relabel
```

Policies

A *policy* is a set of rules to determine the relationships between users, roles, and types or domains. These rules state what types a role can access and what roles a user can have.

Labeling

One of the most common administrative tasks for controlling access is relabeling a file's security context. A file with a certain context may deny access to an application that is set up to access files of a different kind of access. You use the commands **chcon**, **semanage** with the fcontext option, and **restorecon** to change a file's security context. The **setfiles** command is used for relabeling.

> ➤ **chcon**   Changes contexts, but does not persist if a relabel or restore operation is performed.

> ➤ **restorecon**   Restores the default security context of a file.

> ➤ **semanage fcontext**   Change the security context of a file. This change is persistent through any relabel or restore operations. Changes are added to the active policy's **file_contexts** configuration file, like **/etc/selinux/targeted/contexts/files/file_contexts** for the targeted policy.

For example, in the case of user Web site directories, the Web server, which is designed to access files with Web contexts, will try to access files that have a user context. The user Web site files are created in a user's home directory by the user and are thereby given the user_home_t context type. The Web server can only access files with the httpd_sys_content_t type.

Using the chcon command would change the type to **httpd_sys_content_t**, but any restore or relabel operations would change it back to the default **user_home_t** type. Use the **-t** option to indicate the file context type. You can add the **-R** option for changing any files and subdirectories already in the directory.

```
chcon -Rt httpd_sys_content_t public_html
```

To make the change persistent you have to add an entry for in the policy's **file_contexts** file. Use **semanage** with the **fcontext** directive and the **-a** (add) and **-t** (type) options. The file_contexts configuration file is read by the restorecon command. Once you add a new entry, run restorecon to make the actual change. Be sure to use full pathnames for file and directory names.

```
semanage  fcontext -a -t httpd_sys_content_t /home/robert/public_html
restorecon  /home/robert/public_html
```

Any later relabeling or restore operations will use that new file context configuration for this file.

Also, any files or directories you create will inherit the security context of the parent directory. In this example, any files and subdirectories created later in the **public_html** directory will also have the context type **httpd_sys_content_t**. Any previous files or directories will not.

TIP: The tar command does not retain security context when creating an archive of files and directories. Use the **tar** command with the **--selinux** option to retain the file contexts for files in the archive in the archive.

To change any files and subdirectories already in the directory, you use file matching regular expressions, **(/.*)**, for the fcontext configuration. Be sure to quote the entire name including the expression. When you run the **restorecon** command to make the change add the **-R** option (recursive) to change any files and subdirectories also. Changes are made to the directory and to any of its files and subdirectories.

```
semanage  fcontext -a -t "httpd_sys_content_t /home/robert/public_html(/.*)"
restorecon  -v -R /home/robert/public_html
```

To return to the default context, you would first remove the configuration entry, and then run restorecon. Use **semanage fcontext** with the **-d** option to delete a file's context. If the entry uses regular expressions, like (/.*), be sure to quote the entire file or directory name, including the expression.

```
semanage fcontext -d "/home/robert/public_html(/.*)"
restorecon -R /home/robert/public_html
```

NFS, Samba, and mount

A similar issue occurs commonly with NFS mounted file systems. NFS file systems use the **nfs_t** file context by default. If you want to make that file systems part of a Web server's Web site files, you would have to change the type to **httpd_sys_content_t**. NFS though is a remote system, and on its remote system will have its own file contexts. You would want to change the context only temporarily when the file system is mounted by your system. To do this you would use the context option for the **mount** command.

```
mount mynfs:/myrw/  /myweb/myw/  -o  context="system_u:object_r:httpd_sys_context_t:s0"
```

To make the operation automatic, add an entry for it in the **/etc/fstab** file.

```
mynfs:/myrw/  /myweb/myw/  nfs  context="system_u:object_r:httpd_sys_context_t:s0" 0  0
```

In the case of Samba, problems can occur when you create a new file or directory on a mounted Samba share. By default the new file would have the context type **default_t**. The Samba server though expects a context type of **samba_share_t**. When a Samba share is mounted, all its files and directories are given the **samba_share_t** context type. To overcome this problem, you can set the default context type when the file system is mounted. Then, any new files will have this context type. For Samba shares you can set the default context type to **samba_share_t**. Use the defcontext type with the mount option to se the default context type.

```
mount /dev/sd4 /mywin1 -o defcontext="system_u:object_r:samba_share_t:s0"
```

To make the operation automatic, add an entry for it in the **/etc/fstab** file.

```
/dev/sd4 /mywin1 ntfs context="system_u:object_r:samba_share_t:s0" 0 0
```

Copy and Moving Files: cp and mv

When copying or moving files you can choose to change or not change the original file's contexts.

By default the cp command will use the parent directory's contexts for the new created copies, not the contexts from the original copies. This is in keeping with the policy of newly created files and directories inheriting their contexts from their parent directory. If you are overwriting files, then the context of the overwritten file is used, not the original files.

If you want to retain the original file's contexts in the copies, use the **--preserve=context** option.

```
cp --preserve=context
```

If you want to change the copies to a particular file context, you can use the -Z option.

```
cp -Z system_u:object_r:httpd_sys_context:s0 /mytest/test1  /myweb/test.html
```

A move operation, **mv**, will retain the original context. The move operation is literally just a rename. The physical files are the same.

Management Operations for SELinux

Certain basic operations such as checking the SELinux status, checking a user's or file's security context, or disabling SELinux at boot can be very useful for managing SELinux.

Activating SELinux

SELinux is activated by adding the kernel parameter selinux=1 to the GRUB invocation of the Ubuntu kernel. In the GRUB menu.lst file the parameter will be placed on the Ubuntu kernel line. In the following example, Apparmor has been disabled and SELinux is enabled.

```
kernel        /boot/vmlinuz-2.6.28-14-generic root=UUID=dd4252ec-380e-4d00-9f89-
857aba879b63 ro quiet splash apparmor.enabled=0 selinux=1
```

The GRUB **menu.lst** file is modified by the **selinux-activate** script installed by the selinux-basic package. You can activate SELinux directly by running the **selinux-activate** script, which will add the **selinux=1** parameter to the GRUB menu.lst kernel entries.

```
sudo selinux-activate
```

Turning off SELinux

To turn off SELinux permanently, you can set the **SELINUX** variable in the **/etc/selinux/config** file to **disabled**.

```
SELINUX=disabled
```

You can also use the **selinux-activate** script with the **disable** option to remove the selinux option from the GRUB menu.lst kernel entry.

```
sudo selinux-activate disable
```

To turn off (permissive mode) SELinux temporarily without rebooting, use the **setenforce** command with the 0 option; use 1 to turn it back on (enforcing mode). You can also use the terms permissive or enforcing at the arguments instead of 0 or 1. You must first have the sysadm_r role, which you can obtain by logging in as the root user.

```
setenforce 1
```

Permissive and Enforcing Modes

To set the permissive or enforcing modes you can use selinux-config-enforcing. Use the permissive argument to set the permissive mode, turning of the enforcing mode.

```
sudo selinux-config-enforcing permissive
```

Use selinux-config-enforcing without any arugment to restore enforcement.

```
sudo selinux-config-enforcing
```

Modifcations are made to the **/etc/selinux/config** file directly.

Load Policy and Relabel using init script for SELinux

The selinux service script can be used to load the current policy and relabel if needed, **/etc/init.d/selinux**. The **start** opton will reload the current policy.

```
sudo service selinux start
```

A **stop** option will perform a stop SELinux and perform a relabel if needed.

```
sudo service selinux stop
```

The selinux script has a **relabel** option, but this option only requests that a relabel be performed when the system shuts down or the selinux script is run with the stop option.

```
sudo service selinux relabel
```

Relabeling can also be handled by the **selinux-basics** service script, which uses the start option to perform a relabel. It detects if a partial or complete relabeling is needed. You are then prompted to restart.

```
sudo service selinux-basics start
```

Checking Status and Statistics

To check the current status of your SELinux system, you can use **sestatus** . Add the **-v** option will also display process and file contexts, as listed in **/etc/sestatus.conf**. The contexts will specify the roles and types assigned to a particular process, file, or directory.

```
sestatus -v
```

Use the **seinfo** command to display your current SELinux statistics.

 # seinfo
```
Statistics for policy file: /etc/selinux/targeted/policy/policy.21
Policy Version & Type: v.21 (binary, MLS)
```

Classes:	55	Permissions:	206
Types:	1043	Attributes:	85
Users:	3	Roles:	6
Booleans:	135	Cond. Expr.:	138
Sensitivities:	1	Categories:	256
Allow:	46050	Neverallow:	0
Auditallow:	97	Dontaudit:	3465
Role allow:	5	Role trans:	0
Type_trans:	987	Type_change:	14
Type_member:	0	Range_trans:	10
Nodecon:	8	Initial SIDs:	0

Checking Security Context

The **-z** option used with the **ls**, **id**, and **ps** commands can be used to check the security context for files, users, and processes respectively. The security context tells you the roles that users must have to access given processes or objects. In the following, the first line list files with their security context, the second lists a user's security context, and the last will list the security context for processes.

```
ls -lZ
id -Z
ps -eZ
```

SELinux Management Tools

SELinux provides a number of tools that let you manage your SELinux configuration and policy implementation, including **semanage** to configure your policy (**policycoreutils** and **setools**). The **setools** collection provides SELinux configuration and analysis tools including **apol**, the Security Policy Analysis tool, for domain transition analysis; **sediffx** for policy differences; and **seaudit** to examine the audit logs (see Table 12-3). The command line user management tools, **useradd**, **usermod**, and **userdel**, all have SELinux options that can be applied when SELinux is installed. In addition, the **audit2allow** tool will convert SELinux denial messages into policy modules that will allow access.

Command	Description
seinfo	Display policy statistics
sestatus	Check status of SELinux on your system, including the contexts of processes and files
sesearch	Search for type enforcement rules in policies
seaudit	Examine SELinux log files
sediffx	Examine SELinux policy differences
setroubleshoot	SELinux GUI troubleshooting tool
autid2allow	Generate policy allow rules for modules using audit AVC denial messages.
apol	SELinux Policy Analysis
checkpolicy	The SELinux policy compiler
fixfiles	Check file systems and set security contexts
restorecon	Set security features for particular files
newrole	New role
setfiles	Set security context for files
chcon	Change context
chsid	Change security ID

Table 12-3: SELinux Tools

With the modular version of SELinux, policy management is no longer handled by editing configuration files directly. Instead you use the SELinux management tools such as the command line tool semanage.

semanage

semanage lets you change your SELinux configuration without having to edit selinux source files directly. It covers several major categories including users, ports, file contexts and logins. Check the man page for semanage for detailed descriptions. Options let you modify specific security features such as **-s** for the user name, **-R** for the role, -t for the type, and -r for an MLS security range. The following example adds a user with role user_r.

```
semanage user -a -R user_r  justin
```

semange is configured with the **/etc/selinux/semanage.conf** file where you can configure semange to write directly on modules (the default) or work on the source.

apol, The Security Policy Analysis Tool

The SE Linux Policy Analysis tool, **apol**, provides a complex and detailed analysis of a selected policy (**setools** package). Select the SELinux Policy Analysis entry in the Applications | System Tools menu to start it. You will also have to locate and open the SELinux policy file in **/etc/selinux/** directory. You could also use the SELinux Policy Difference tool to compare policies, and the SELinux Audit Log Analysis tool for log analysis. These are third party tools, though, and not directly supported by Ubuntu.

Checking SELinux Messages: seaudit

SELinux AVC messages are saved in the **/var/log/audit/audit.log** file. These entries are particularly important if you are using the permissive mode to test a policy you want to later enforce. You need to find out if you are being denied access where appropriate and afforded control when needed. To see just the SELinux messages, you can use the seaudit tool (System | Administration | SELinux Audit Log Analysis). Start up messages for the SE Linux service are logged in **/var/log/messages**.

Allowing access: chcon and audit2allow

Whenever SELinux denies access to a file or application, the kernel issues an AVC Denial notice. In many cases, the problem can be fixed simply by renaming the security context of a file to allow access. You use the **chcon** command to change a file's security context. To rename the security context of a file, access needs to be granted to the Samba server for a **log.richard3** file in the **/var/lib/samba** directory, as shown here:

```
chcon -R -t samba_share_t log.richard3
```

More complicated problems, especially ones that are unknown, may require that you create a new policy module using the AVC messages in the audit log. To do this, you can use the **audit2allow** command. The command will take an audit AVC messages and generate commands to allow SELinux access. The audit log is **/var/log/audit/audit.log**. This log is output to **audit2allow** which then can use its **-M** option to create a policy module. I

```
cat /var/log/audit/audit.log | audit2allow -M local
```

You then use the **semodule** command to load the module.

```
semodule -i local.pp
```

If you wan to first edit the allowable entries, you can use the following to create a **.te** file of the local module, **local.te**, which you can then edit.

```
audit2allow -m local -i /var/log/audit/audit.log > local.te
```

Once you have edited the **.te** file, you can then use **checkmodule** to compile the module, and then **semodule_package** to create the policy module, **local.pp**. Then you can install it with **semodule**. You first create a **.mod** file with **checkmodule**, and then **.pp** file with **semodule_package**.

```
checkmodule -M -m -o local.mod local.te
semodule_package -o local.pp -m local.mod
semodule -i local.pp
```

In this example the policy module is just called **local**. If you later want to create a new module with **audit2allow**, you should either use a different name or just append the output to the **.te** file using the **-o** option.

Tip: On Ubuntu you can use the SELinux troubleshooter (setroubleshooter) to detect SELinux access problems.

SELinux Troubleshooting

Ubuntu includes the SELinux troubleshooter which notifies problems that SELinux detects. Whenever SELinux denies access to a file or application, the kernel issue an AVC notice. These are analyzed by SELinux troubleshooter to detect problems that users may have to deal with. When a problem is detected, the SELinux troubleshooter notification will be displayed in the desktop notification area along with the troubleshooter icon. Clicking on the icon or notice will open the SELinux troubleshooter window. You can also access it at any time from System | Administration | SELinux troubleshooter. You can find out more information about SELinux troubleshooter at **http://hosted.fedoraproject.org/projects/setroubleshoot**.

The SELinux troubleshooter window will display a list of notices, along with their date, the number of times it has occurred, its category, and brief explanation. The Filter entry lets you turn off future notification of this event. Selecting and entry will display detailed information about the notice in four sections: Summary, Detailed Description, Allowing Access, and Additional Information (see Figure 12-1)

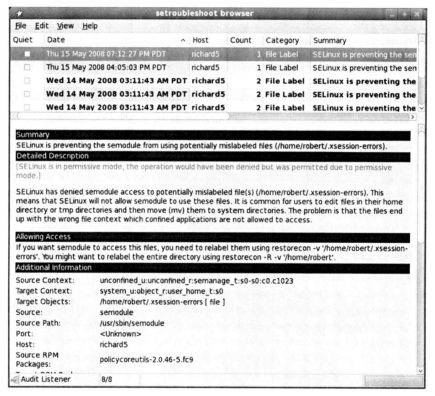

Figure 12-1: SELinux troubleshooter

In many cases the problem may be simple to fix, as shown in the Allowing Access section in Figure 12-4. Often, the security context of a file has to be renamed to allow access. You use the **chcon** command to change a file's security context. In this rename access needs to be granted to the Samba server for a **log.richard3** file in the **/var/lib/samba** directory. The SELinux troubleshooter will take no action of its own. Instead it recommends possible actions. In this example, the user just issues the following **chcon** command.

```
chcon -R -t samba_share_t log.richard3
```

The SE Linux reference policy

A SELinux operating system is secured using a *policy*. SELinux provides a single policy, called the *Reference Policy*. The SELinux Reference Policy project aims to provide a basic policy that can be easily adapted and expanded as needed. The SELinux Reference Policy configures SELinux into modules that can be handled separately. You can still have strict and targeted policies provided in previous releases, but they are variations on a basic reference policy. The SE Linux Referenc policy is installed by default with the **selinux-policy-ubuntu** package.

Should you want to install a strict or targeted policy, used in previous releases, you would install the **selinux-policy-default** package. It is not compatible with the SE Linux Reference Policy and will remove the **selinux-policy-ubuntu** package if already installed. The default policy installs the targeted policy by default. On Ubuntu, you can implement a strict policy by removing the unconfined module from the default policy. The targeted approach is used to control specific services, such as network and Internet servers such as Web, DNS, and FTP servers. It also can control local services with network connections. The policy will not affect only the daemon itself, but all the resources it uses on your system. The strict policy provides complete control over your system. It is with this kind of policy that users and even administrators can be inadvertently locked out of the system. A strict policy needs to be carefully tested to make sure access is appropriately denied and granted.

Policies are implemented in policy files, binary files that are compiled from source files. The policy binary files are in policy subdirectories in the **/etc/selinux** configuration directory, **/etc/selinux/ubuntu**. For example, the policy file for the refpolicy policy is **/etc/selinux/ubuntu/policy/policy.23**.

The reference development files that hold the interface header files are installed at **/usr/share/selinux/ubuntu/include.** You can use the development files to create your own policy modules that you can then load. Be sure to install the **selinux-policy-ubuntu-dev** package. For the default and mls policies, install the **selinux-policy-dev** package.

Multi-level Security (MLS)

Multi-level security (MLS) adds a more refined security access method. MLS adds a security level value to resources. Only users with access to certain levels can access the corresponding files and applications. Within each level access can be further controlled with the use of categories. Categories work much like groups, allowing access only to users cleared for that category. Access becomes more refined, instead of an all or nothing situation.

You can install the MLS policy with the **selinux-policy-mls** package. The policy will be installed to the **/etc/selinux/mls** directory, with modules placed in the **/usr/share/selinux/mls** directory.

Multi-category Security (MCS) and Mandated Multi-category Security (MMCS)

Multi-category security (MCS) extends SE Linux not only to use by administrators, but also by users. Users can set categories that restrict and control access to their files and applications. Though based on MLS, MCS uses only categories, not security levels. Users can select a category for a file, only the administrator can create a category and determine what users can access it. Though similar in concept to a ACL (access control list), it differs in that it makes use of the SE Linux security structure, providing user-level control enforced by SE Linux.

Mandated Multi-category security (MMCS) also provides control over access to files, but access is controlled by an administrator, not by a user. The default policy (strict and targeted) are implemented with MMCS controls, restricting access to servers and administration files.

You can install the default policy with the **selinux-policy-default** package. The policy will be installed to the **/etc/selinux/default** directory, with modules placed in the **/usr/share/selinux/default** directory.

Policy Methods

Operating system services and components are categorized in SELinux by their type and their role. Rules controlling these objects can be type based or role based. Policies are implemented using two different kinds of rules, type enforcement (TE) and role-based access control (RBAC). Multi-layer security (MLS) is an additional method further restricting access by security level. Security context now feature both the role of an object such as a user, and that object's security level.

Type Enforcement

With a type structure, the operating system resources are partitioned off into types, with each object assigned a type. Processes are assigned to domains. Users are restricted to certain domains, allowed to use only objects accessible in those domains.

Role-Based Access Control

A role-based approach focuses on controlling users. Users are assigned roles, which define what resources they can use. In a standard system, file permissions, such as those for groups, can control user access to files and directories. With roles, permissions become more flexible and refined. Certain users can have more access to services than others.

SELinux Users

Users will retain the permissions available on a standard system. In addition, SELinux can set up its own controls for a given user, defining a role for that user. General security identities created by SELinux include:

system_u The user for system processes

user_u To allow normal users to use a service

root For the root user

Policy Files

Policies are implemented in policy files. These are binary files compiled from source files. For a pre-configured targeted policy file, the policy binary files are in policy subdirectories in the **/etc/selinux** configuration directory, **/etc/selinux/targeted**. For example, the policy file for the targeted policy is

```
/etc/selinux/targeted/policy/policy.20
```

The targeted development files that hold the interface files are installed at **/usr/share/selinux**.

```
/usr/share/selinux/targeted
```

You can use the development files to create your own policy modules that you can then load.

SELinux Configuration

Configuration for general SELinux server settings is carried out in the **/etc/selinux/config** file. Currently, only two settings are available: the state and the policy. You set the **SELINUX** variable to the state, such as **enforcing** or **permissive**, and set the **SELINUXTYPE** variable to the kind of policy you want. Set the SELINUX variable to **disabled** to turn off the SELinux. A sample config file is shown here:

```
# This file controls the state of SELinux on the system.
# SELINUX= can take one of these three values:
# enforcing - SELinux security policy is enforced.
# permissive - SELinux prints warnings instead of enforcing.
# disabled - No SELinux policy is loaded.
SELINUX=permissive
# SELINUXTYPE= can take one of these two values:
# default - equivalent to the old strict and targeted policies
# mls     - Multi-Level Security (for military and educational use)
# src     - Custom policy built from source
SELINUXTYPE=default

# SETLOCALDEFS= Check local definition changes
SETLOCALDEFS=0
```

SELinux Policy Rules

Policy rules can be made up of either type (Type Enforcement) or rbac (Role Based Access Control) statements, along with security levels (Multi-level Security). A type statement can be a type or attribute declaration, or a transition, change, or assertion rule. The rbac statements can be role declarations or dominance or allow roles. A security level specifies a number corresponding to the level of access permitted. Policy configuration can be difficult, using extensive and complicated rules. For this reason, many rules are implemented using M4 macros in **fi** files that will in turn generate the appropriate rules (Sendmail uses M4 macros in a similar way). You will find these rules in files in the SE Linux reference policy source code package which you need to download and install. The reference policy package is **selinux-policy**. See the following section on SELinux configuration files.

Type and Role Declarations

A type declaration starts with the keyword **type**, followed by the type name (identifier) and any optional attributes or aliases. The type name will have a _t suffix. Standard type definitions are included for objects such as files. The following is a default type for any file, with attributes **file_type** and **sysadmfile**:

```
type file_t, file_type, sysadmfile;
```

The root will have its own type declaration.

```
type root_t, file_type, sysadmfile;
```

Specialized directories such as the boot directory will also have their own type.

```
type boot_t, file_type, sysadmfile;
```

More specialized rules are set up for specific targets like the Amanda server. The following example is the general type definition for **amanda_t** objects, those objects used by the Amanda backup server, as listed in the targeted policy's **src/program/amanda.te** file.

```
type amanda_t, domain, privlog, auth, nscd_client_domain ;
```

A role declaration determines the roles that can access objects of a certain type. These rules begin with the keyword **role** followed by the role and the objects associated with that role. In this example, the amanda objects (amanda_t) can be accessed by a user or process with the system role (system_r).

```
role system_r types amanda_t;
```

A more specific type declaration is provided for executables, such as the following for the Amanda server (amanda_exec_t). This defines the Amanda executable as a system administration–controlled executable file.

```
type amanda_exec_t, file_type, sysadmfile, exec_type;
```

Associated configuration files often have their own rules.

```
type amanda_config_t, file_type, sysadmfile;
```

In the targeted policy an general unconfined type is created that user and system roles can access, giving complete unrestricted access to the system. More specific rules will restrict access to certain targets like the Web server.

```
type unconfined_t, domain, privuser, privhome, privrole, privowner, admin,
auth_write, fs_domain, privmem;
role system_r types unconfined_t;
role user_r types unconfined_t;
role sysadm_r types unconfined_t;
```

Types are also set up for the files created in the user home directory.

```
type user_home_t, file_type, sysadmfile, home_type;
type user_home_dir_t, file_type, sysadmfile, home_dir_type;
```

File Contexts

File contexts associate specific files with security contexts. The file or files are listed first, with multiple files represented with regular expressions. Then the role, type, and security level are specified. The following creates a security context for all files in the **/etc** directory (configuration files). These are accessible from the system user (system_u) and are objects of the etc_t type with a security level of 0, s0.

```
/etc(/.*)?              system_u:object_r:etc_t:s0
```

Certain files can belong to other types, for instance, the **resolve.conf** configuration file belongs to the **net_conf** type.

```
/etc/resolv.conf.*    --    system_u:object_r:net_conf_t:s0
```

Certain services will have their own security contexts for their configuration files.

```
/etc/amanda(/.*)?           system_u:object_r:amanda_config_t:s0
```

File contexts are located in the **file_contexts** file in the policy's contexts directory, such as **/etc/selinux/targeted/contexts/files/file_contexts**. The version used to create or modify the policy is located in the policy modules active directory, as in **targeted/modules/active/file_contexts**.

User Roles

User roles define what roles a user can take on. Such as role begins with the keyword **user** followed by the user name, then the keyword **roles**, and finally the roles it can use. You will find these rules in the selinux reference policy source code files. The following example is a definition of the system_u user:

```
user system_u roles system_r;
```

If a user can have several roles, then they are listed in brackets. The following is the definition of the standard user role in the targeted policy, which allows users to take on system administrative roles.

```
user user_u roles { user_r sysadm_r system_r };
```

The strict policy lists only the user_r role.

```
user user_u roles { user_r };
```

Access Vector Rules: allow

Access vector rules are used to define permissions for objects and processes. The **allow** keyword is followed by the object or process type, and then the types it can access or be accessed by and the permissions used. The following allows processes in the amanda_t domain to search the Amanda configuration directories (any directories of type **amanda_config_t**).

```
allow amanda_t amanda_config_t:dir search;
```

The following example allows Amanda to read the files in a user home directory:

```
allow amanda_t user_home_type:file { getattr read };
```

The next example allows Amanda to read, search, and write files in the Amanda data directories:

```
allow amanda_t amanda_data_t:dir { read search write };
```

Role Allow Rules

Roles can also have allow rules. Though they can be used for domains and objects, they are usually used to control role transitions, specifying whether a role can transition to another role. These rules are listed in the rbac configuration file. The following entry allows the user to transition to a system administrator role:

```
allow user_r sysadm_r;
```

Transition and Vector Rule Macros

The type transition rules set the type used for rules to create objects. Transition rules also require corresponding access vector rules to enable permissions for the objects or processes. Instead of creating separate rules, macros are used that will generate the needed rules. The following example sets the transition and access rules for user files in the home directory using the **file_type_auto_trans** macro:

```
file_type_auto_trans(privhome, user_home_dir_t, user_home_t)
```

The next example sets the Amanda process transition and access rules for creating processes:

```
domain_auto_trans(inetd_t, amanda_inetd_exec_t, amanda_t)
```

Constraint Rules

Restrictions can be further placed on processes such as transitions to ensure greater security. These are implemented with constraint definitions in the constraints file. Constraint rules are often applied to transition operations, such as requiring that, in a process transition, user identities remain the same, or that process 1 be in a domain that has the privuser attribute and process 2 be in a domain with the userdomain attribute. The characters **u**, **t**, and **r** refer to user, type, and role.

```
constrain process transition
    ( u1 == u2 or ( t1 == privuser and t2 == userdomain )
```

SE Linux Policy Configuration Files

Configuration files are normally changed using **.te** an **.fc** files. These are missing from the module headers in **/usr/share/selinux**. If you are adding a module you will need to create the .te and .fc files for it. Then you can create a module and add it as described in the next section. If you want to create or modify your own policy, you will need to download and install the source code files for the SE Linux reference policy as described a following section. The reference policy code holds the complete set of **.te** and **.fc** configuration files.

Compiling SE Linux Modules

Instead of compiling the entire source each time you want to make a change, you can just compile a module for the area you changed. The modules directory holds the different modules. Each module is built from a corresponding .te file. The **checkmodule** command is used to create a **.mod** module file from the **.te** file, and then the **semanage_module** command is use to create the loadable **.pp** module file as well as a **.fc** file context file. As noted in the SE Linux documentation, if you need to just change the configuration for **rsyslogd**, you would first use the following to create a **rsyslogd.mod** file using **rsyslogd.te**. The -M option specifies support for MLS security levels.

```
checkmodule -M -m rsyslogd.te  -o rsyslogd.mod
```

Then use the **semanage_module** command to create a **rsyslogd.pp** file from the rsyslogd.mod file. The **-f** opton specifies the file context file.

```
semanage_module -m rsyslogd.mod  -o rsyslogd.pp -f rsyslogd.fc
```

To add the module you use semodule and the -i option. You can check if a module is loaded with the **-l** option.

```
semodule -i rsyslogd.pp
```

Changes to the base policy are made to the **policy.conf** file which is compiled into the **base.pp** module.

Using SE Linux Source Configuration

To perform you own configuration, you will have to install the source package for SE Linux, **selinux-policy-src**, available on the Ubuntu Universe repository. The **.te** files used for configuring SE Linux are not part of the SE Linux binary packages. This package will install a compressed archive of the SE Linux Referenc Policy source files, **selinux-policy-src.tar.gz**, to the **/usr/src** directory. Copy the file to a local directory, then decompress and extract the archive. The **selinux-policy-src** directory will hold the **.te** and **.fi** files that you can then modify.

The rules are held in configuration files located in various subdirectories in a policy's **selinux-policy-src** directory. Within this directory you will find a **policy/modules** subdirectory. There, organized into several directories like admin and apps you will find the **.tc**, **.fc**, and .if configuration files.

You will have configuration files for both type enforcement and security contexts. Type enforcement files have the extension **.te**, whereas security contexts have an **.sc** extension.

Reflecting the fine-grained control that SELinux provides, you have numerous module configuration files for the many kinds of objects and processes on your system. The primary configuration files and directories are listed in Table 12-4, but several expand to detailed listing of subdirectories and files.

InterfaceFiles

File *interface* files allow management tools to generate policy modules. They define interface macros for your current policy. The refpolicy SE Linux source file will hold .if files for each module, along with .te and .fc files. Also, .if files in the **/usr/share/selinux/devel** directory which can be used to generate modules.

Types Files

In the targeted policy, the modules directory that defines types holds a range of files, including **nfs.te** and **network.te** configuration files. Here you will find type declarations for the different kinds of objects on your system. The .te files are no longer included with your standard SE Linux installation. Instead you have to download and install the serefpolicy source package. This is the original source and allows you to completely reconfigure your SE Linux policy, instead of managing modules with management tools like **semanage**. The modules directory will hold .te files for each module listing their TE rules.

Directories and Files	Description
assert.te	Access vector assertions
config/appconfig-*	Application runtime configuration files
policy/booleans.conf	Tunable features
file_contexts	Security contexts for files and directories
policy/flask	Flask configuration
policy/mcs	Multi-category security (MCS) configuration
doc	Policy documentation support
policy/modules	Security policy modules
policy/modules.conf	Module list and use
policy/modules/admin	Administration modules
policy/modules/apps	Application modules
policy/modules/kernel	Kernel modules
policy/modules/services	Services and server modules
policy/modules/system	System modules
policy/rolemap	User domain types and roles
policy/users	General users definition
config/local.users	Define your own SELinux users
policy/constraints	Additional constraints for role transition and object access
policygentool	Script to generate policies
policy/global_tunables	Defines policy tunables for customization
policy/mls	Multilevel security (MLS) configuration

Table 12-4: SELinux Policy Configuration Files

Module Files

Module files are located among several directories in the policy/modules directory. Here you will find three corresponding files for each application or service. There will be a **.te** file that contains the actual type enforcement rules, an **.fi**, for interface, file that allows other applications to interact with the module, and the **.fc** files that define the file contexts.

Security Context Files

Security contexts for different files are detailed in security context files. The **file_contexts** file holds security context configurations for different groups, directories, and files. Each configuration file has an **.fc** extension. The **types.fc** file holds security contexts for various system files and directories, particularly access to configuration files in the **/etc** directory. In the SE Linux source, each module will have its own .fc file, along with corresponding .te and .if files. The **distros.fc** file defines distribution-dependent configurations. The **homedir_template** file defines security contexts for dot files that may be set up in a user's home directory, such as **.mozilla**, **.gconf**, and **.java**.

A modules directory has file context files for particular applications and services. For example, **apache.fc** has the security contexts for all the files and directories used by the Apache Web server, such as **/var/www** and **/etc/httpd**.

User Configuration: Roles

Global user configuration is defined in the policy directory's **users** file. Here you find the user definitions and the roles they have for standard users (user_u) and administrators (admin_u). To add your own users, you use the **local.users** file. Here you will find examples for entering your own SELinux users. Both the strict and targeted policies use the general user_u SELinux identity for users. To set up a separate SELinux identity for a user, you would define that user in the **local.users** file.

The **rbac** file defines the allowed roles one role can transition to. For example, can the user role transition to an system administration role? The targeted policy has several entries allowing a user to freely transition to an administrator, and vice versa. The strict policy has no such definitions.

Role transitions are further restricted by rules in the **constraints** file. Here the change to other users is controlled, and changing object security contexts (labeling) is restricted.

Policy module tools

To create a policy module and load it, you use several policy module tools. First the **checkmodule** command is used to create **.mod** file from a **.te** file. Then the **semodule_package** tool takes the **.mod** file and any supporting **.fc** file and generates a module policy package file, **.pp**. Finally the **semodule** tool can take the policy package file and install it as part of your SE Linux policy.

Application Configuration: appconfig

Certain services and applications are security aware and will request default security contexts and types from SELinux (see also the upcoming section "Runtime Security Contexts"). The configuration is kept files located in the **policy/config/appconfig-*** directory. The **default_types** file holds type defaults; **default_contexts** holds default security contexts. The **initrc_context** file has the default security context for running **/etc/rc.d** scripts. A special **root_default_contexts** file details how the root user can be accessed. The **removable_context** file holds the security context for removable devices, and **media** lists media devices, such as cdrom for CD-ROMs. Runtime values can also be entered in corresponding files in the policy contexts directory, such as **/etc/selinux/targeted/contexts**.

Creating an SELinux Policy: make and checkpolicy

If you want to create an entirely new policy, you use the SE Linux reference policy source, **/etc/selinux/serefpolicy**. Once you have configured your policy you can create it with the `make policy` and `checkpolicy` commands. The `make policy` command generates a policy.conf file for your configuration files, which `checkpolicy` can then use to generate a policy binary file. A policy binary file will be created in the **policy** subdirectory with a numeric extension for the policy version, such as **policy.20**.

You will have to generate a new policy **policy.conf** file. To do this you enter the following command in the policy src directory, which will be **/etc/selinux/serefpolicy/src/policy**.

```
make policy
```

Then you can use **checkpolicy** to create the new policy.

Instead of compiling the entire source each time you want to make a change, you can just compile a module for the area you changed. In the previous SE Linux version you always had to recompile the entire policy every time you made a change. The modules directory holds the different modules. Each module is built from a corresponding .te file. The **checkmodule** command is used to create a .mod module file from the **.te** file, and then the **semanage_module** command is use to create the loadable policy package **.pp** module file. As noted in the SE Linux documentation, if you need to just change the configuration for **rsyslogd**, you would first use the following to create an **rsyslogd.mod** file using **rsyslogd.te**. The **-M** option specifies support for MLS security levels.

```
checkmodule -M  -m rsyslogd.te  -o rsyslogd.mod
```

Then use the **semanage_module** command to create an **rsyslogd.pp** file from the rsyslogd.mod file. The **-f** option specifies the file context file.

```
semanage_module -m rsyslogd.mod  -o rsyslogd.pp -f rsyslogd.fc
```

To add the module you use semodule and the **-i** option. You can check if a module is loaded with the **-l** option.

```
semodule -i rsyslogd.pp
```

Changes to the base policy are made to the **policy.conf** file which is compiled into the **base.pp** module.

To perform you own configuration, you will now have to download the source code files. The **.te** files used for configuring SE Linux are no longer part of the SE Linux binary packages. Once installed the source will be in the **sefepolicy** directory in **/etc/selinux**.

For **fixfiles**, you use:

```
fixfiles relabel
```

SELinux: Administrative Operations

There are several tasks you can perform on your SELinux system without having to recompile your entire configuration. Security contexts for certain files and directories can be changed as needed. For example, when you add a new file system, you will need to label it with the appropriate security contexts. Also, when you add users, you may need to have a user given special attention by the system. For detecting and fixing problems you can use **setroubleshoot**.

Using Security Contexts: fixfiles, setfiles, restorecon, and chcon

Several tools are available for changing your objects' security contexts. The `fixfiles` command can set the security context for file systems. You use the `relabel` option to set security contexts, and the `check` option to see what should be changed. The `fixfiles` tool is a script that uses `setfiles` and `restorecon` to make actual changes.

The `restorecon` command will let you restore the security context for files and directories, but `setfiles` is the basic tool for setting security contexts. It can be applied to individual files or directories. It is used to label the file when a policy is first installed.

With `chcon`, you can change the permissions of individual files and directories, much as `chmod` does for general permissions.

Adding New Users

If a new user needs no special access, you can generally just use the generic SELinux user_u identity. If, however, you need to allow the user to take on roles that would otherwise be restricted, such as a system administrator role in the strict policy, you need to configure the user accordingly. To do this, you add the user to the **local.users** file in the policy users directory, as in **/etc/selinux/targeted/policy/users/local.users**. Note that this is different from the **local.users** file in the src directory which compiled directly into the policy. The user rules have the syntax

```
user username roles { rolelist };
```

The following example adds the sysadm role to the **george** user:

```
user george roles { user_r sysadm_r };
```

Once the role is added, you have to reload the policy.

```
make reload
```

Runtime Security Contexts and Types: contexts

Several applications and services are security aware and will need default security configuration information such as security contexts. Runtime configurations for default security contexts and types are kept in files located in the policy context directory, such as **/etc/selinux/targeted/contexts**. Types files will have the suffix **_types**, and security context files will use **_context**. For example, the default security context for removable files is located in the **removable_context** file. The contents of that file are shown here.

```
system_u:object_r:removable_t
```

The **default_context** file is used to assign a default security context for applications. In the strict policy it is used to control system admin access, providing it where needed, for instance, during the login process.

The following example sets the default roles for users in the login process:

```
system_r:local_login_t user_r:user_t
```

This would allow users to log in either as administrators or as regular users.

```
system_r:local_login_t sysadm_r:sysadm_t user_r:user_t
```

This next example is for remote user logins, where system administration is not included:

```
system_r:remote_login_t user_r:user_t staff_r:staff_t
```

The **default_types** file defines default types for roles. This file has role/type entries, and when a transition takes place to a new role, the default type specified here is used. For example, the default type for the sysadm_r role is sysadm_t.

```
sysadm_r:sysadm_t
user_r:user_t
```

Of particular interest is the **initrc_context** file, which sets the context for running the system scripts in the **/etc/rc.d** directory. In the targeted policy these are open to all users.

```
user_u:system_r:unconfined_t
```

In the strict policy these are limited to the system user.

```
system_u:system_r:initrc_t
```

users

Default security contexts may also need to be set up for particular users such as the root user. In the **sesuers** file you will find a root file that lists roles, types, and security levels the root user can take on, such as the following example for the su operation:

```
sysadm_r:sysadm_su_t  sysadm_r:sysadm_t  staff_r:staff_t  user_r:user_t
```

context/files

Default security contexts for your files and directories are located in the **contexts/files** directory. The **file_contexts** directory lists the default security contexts for all your files and directories as set up by your policy. The **file_context.homedirs** directory sets the file contexts for user home directory files as well as the root directory, including dot configuration files like **.mozilla** and **.gconf**. The media file sets the default context for media devices such as CD-ROMs and disks.

```
cdrom system_u:object_r:removable_device_t
floppy system_u:object_r:removable_device_t
disk system_u:object_r:fixed_disk_device_t
```

13. SSH, Kerberos, and IPsec

To protect remote connections from hosts outside your network, transmissions can be encrypted (see Table 13-1). For Linux systems, you can use the Secure Shell (SSH) suite of programs to encrypt and authenticate transmissions, preventing them from being read or modified by anyone else, as well confirming the identity of the sender. The SSH programs are meant to replace the remote tools such as **rsh** and **rcp**, which perform no encryption and include security risks such as transmitting passwords in clear text. SSH is available on the Ubuntu repository. It is considered an integral part of the Ubuntu distribution.

User authentication can be controlled for certain services by Kerberos servers. Kerberos authentication provides another level of security whereby individual services can be protected, allowing use of a service only to users who are cleared for access. Kerberos is provided as part of the universe repository.

Website	Description
www.openssh.org	OpenSSH open source version of SSH
www.ssh.com	SSH Communications Security, commercial SSH version
http://web.mit.edu/kerberos	Kerberos authentication

Table 13-1: SSH and Kerberos Resources

The Secure Shell: OpenSSH

Although a firewall can protect a network from attempts to break into it from the outside, the problem of securing legitimate communications to the network from outside sources still exists. A particular problem is one of users who want to connect to your network remotely. Such connections could be monitored, and information such as passwords and user IDs used when the user logs in to your network could be copied and used later to break in. One solution is to use SSH for remote logins and other kinds of remote connections such as FTP transfers. SSH encrypts any communications between the remote user and a system on your network.

Two different implementations of SSH currently use what are, in effect, two different and incompatible protocols. The first version of SSH, known as SSH1, uses the original SSH protocol. Version 2.0, known as SSH2, uses a completely rewritten version of the SSH protocol. Encryption is performed in different ways, encrypting different parts of a packet. SSH1 uses server and host keys to authenticate systems, whereas SSH2 uses only host keys. Furthermore, certain functions, such as sftp, are supported only by SSH2.

Note: A commercial version of SSH is available from SSH Communications Security, whose website is **www.ssh.com**. SSH Communications Security provides an entirely commercial version called SSH Tectia, designed for enterprise and government use. The older noncommercial SSH package is still freely available, which you can download and use.

The SSH protocol has become an official Internet Engineering Task Force (IETF) standard. A free and open source version is developed and maintained by the OpenSSH project, currently supported by the OpenBSD project. OpenSSH is the version supplied with most Linux distributions, including Ubuntu. You can find out more about OpenSSH at **www.openssh.org**.

SSH Encryption and Authentication

SSH secures connections by both authenticating users and encrypting their transmissions. The authentication process is handled with public key encryption. Once authenticated, transmissions are encrypted by a cipher agreed upon by the SSH server and client for use in a particular session. SSH supports multiple ciphers. Authentication is applied to hosts and users. SSH first authenticates a particular host, verifying that it is a valid SSH host that can be securely communicated with. Then the user is authenticated, verifying that the user is who they say they are.

SSH uses strong encryption methods, and their export from the United States may be restricted. Currently, SSH can deal with the following kinds of attacks:

➤ IP spoofing, in which a remote host sends out packets that pretend to come from another, trusted host

➤ IP source routing, where a host can pretend an IP packet comes from another, trusted host

➤ DNS spoofing, where an attacker forges name server records

➤ Interception of clear-text passwords and other data by intermediate hosts

➤ Manipulation of data by people in control of intermediate hosts

➤ Attacks based on listening to X authentication data and spoofed connections to the X11 server

Encryption

The public key encryption used in SSH authentication makes use of two keys: a public key and a private key. The *public key* is used to encrypt data, while the *private key* decrypts it. Each host or user has its own public and private keys. The public key is distributed to other hosts, who can then use it to encrypt authentication data that only the host's private key can decrypt. For example, when a host sends data to a user on another system, the host encrypts the authentication data with a public key, which it previously received from that user. The data can be decrypted only by the user's corresponding private key. The public key can safely be sent in the open from one host to another, allowing it to be installed safely on different hosts. You can think of the process as taking place between a client and a server. When the client sends data to the server, it first encrypts the data using the server's public key. The server can then decrypt the data using its own private key.

It is recommended that SSH transmissions be authenticated with public-private keys controlled by passphrases. Unlike PGP, SSH uses public-key encryption for the authentication process only. Once authenticated, participants agree on a common cipher to use to encrypt transmission. Authentication will verify the identity of the participants. Each user who intends to use SSH to access a remote account first needs to create the public and private keys along with a passphrase to use for the authentication process. A user then sends their public key to the remote account they want to access and installs the public key on that account. When the user attempts to access the remote account, that account can then use the user's public key to authenticate that the user is who they claim to be. The process assumes that the remote account has set up its own SSH private and public key. For the user to access the remote account, they will have to know the remote account's SSH passphrase. SSH is often used in situations where a user has two or more accounts located on different systems and wants to be able to securely access them from each other.

In that case, the user already has access to each account and can install SSH on each, giving each its own private and public keys along with their passphrases.

Authentication

The mechanics of authentication in SSH version 1 and version 2 differ slightly. However, the procedure on the part of users is the same. Essentially, a user creates both public and private keys. For this you use the **ssh-keygen** command. The user's public key then has to be distributed to those users that the original user wants access to. Often this is an account a user has on another host. A passphrase further protects access. The original user will need to know the other user's passphrase to access it.

SSH version 1 uses RSA authentication. When a remote user tries to log in to an account, that account is checked to see if it has the remote user's public key. That public key is then used to encrypt a challenge (usually a random number) that can be decrypted only by the remote user's private key. When the remote user receives the encrypted challenge, that user decrypts the challenge with its private key. SSH version 2 can use either RSA or DSA authentication. The remote user will first encrypt a session identifier using its private key, signing it. The encrypted session identifier is then decrypted by the account using the remote user's public key. The session identifier has been previously set up by SSH for that session.

SSH authentication is first carried out with the host, and then with users. Each host has its own host keys, public and private keys used for authentication. Once the host is authenticated, the user is queried. Each user has their own public and private keys. Users on an SSH server who want to receive connections from remote users will have to keep a list of those remote user's public keys. Similarly, an SSH host will maintain a list of public keys for other SSH hosts.

SSH Packages, Tools, and Server

SSH is implemented on Linux systems with OpenSSH. The full set of OpenSSH packages includes the OpenSSH meta-package (ssh), the OpenSSH server (openssh-server), and the OpenSSH client (openssh-clients). These packages also require OpenSSL (openssl), which installs the cryptographic libraries that SSH uses.

The SSH tools are listed in Table 13-2. They include several client programs such as **scp**, **ssh**, as well as the **ssh** server. The **ssh** server (**sshd**) provides secure connections to anyone from the outside using the **ssh** client to connect. Several configuration utilities are also included, such as ssh-add, which adds valid hosts to the authentication agent, and ssh-keygen, which generates the keys used for encryption.

For SSH2, names of the actual tools have a *2* suffix. SSH1 tools have a *1* as their suffix. During installation, however, links are set for each tool to use only the name with the suffix. For example, if you have installed version 2, there is a link called **scp** to the **scp2** application. You can then use the link to invoke the tool. Using **scp** starts **scp2**. Table 13-2 specifies only the link names, as these are the same for each version. Remember, though, some applications, such as sftp, are available only with SSH2.

Application	Description
ssh	SSH client
sshd	SSH server (daemon)
sftp	SSH FTP client, Secure File Transfer Program. Version 2 only. Use ? to list sftp commands(SFTP protocol)
sftp-server	SSH FTP server. Version 2 only (SFTP protocol)
scp	SSH copy command client
ssh-keygen	Utility for generating keys. **-h** for help
ssh-keyscan	Tool to automatically gather public host keys to generate ssh_known_hosts files
ssh-add	Adds RSD and DSA identities to the authentication agent
ssh-agent	SSH authentication agent that holds private keys for public key authentication (RSA, DSA)
ssh-askpass	X Window System utility for querying passwords, invoked by **ssh-add** (openssh-askpass)
ssh-askpass-gnome	GNOME utility for querying passwords, invoked by **ssh-add**
ssh-signer	Signs host-based authentication packets. Version 2 only. Must be suid root (performed by installation)
slogin	Remote login (version 1)

Table 13-2: SSH Tools

You can configure the Openssh server (sshd) to start up automatically using **services-admin** (System | Administration | Services) and selecting **sshd**. You can start, stop, and restart the server manually with the **/etc/init.d/sshd** script.

```
sudo service sshd restart
```

You must configure your firewall to allow access to the **sshd** server. The SSH server is normally accessed on port 22. You can configure a different port to use in the **/etc/ssh/shd_config** file if you want and then open that port on the firewall. If you are using a **ufw** firewall, simply allow access on port 22:

```
sudo ufw allow 22/tcp
```

If you are using Firestarter (System | Administration | Firestarter) , on the Policy tab, select the Inbound menu item and then right-click the Services pane to add a rule. On the Add New Inbound Rule window, select SSH from the Name pop-up menu, and the 22 port will be selected for you. The SSH rule will show up in the Allow Service section of the Policy Inbound panel.

If you are managing your IPTables firewall directly, you could manage access directly by adding the following IPtables rule. This accepts input on port 22 for TCP/IP protocol packages.

```
iptables -A INPUT -p tcp --dport 22 -j ACCEPT
```

SSH Setup

Using SSH involves creating your own public and private keys and then distributing your public key to other users you want to access. These can be different users or simply user accounts of your own that you have on remote systems. Often people remotely log in from a local client to an account on a remote server, perhaps from a home computer to a company computer. Your home computer would be your client account, and the account on your company computer would be your server account. On your client account, you need to generate your public and private keys and then place a copy of your public key in the server account. You can do this by simply e-mailing the key file or copying the file from a floppy disk or USB drive. Once the account on your server has a copy of your client user's public key, you can access the server account from your client account. You will be also prompted for the server account's passphrase. You will have to know this to access that account. Figure 13-1 illustrates the SSH setup that allows a user **george** to access the account **cecelia**.

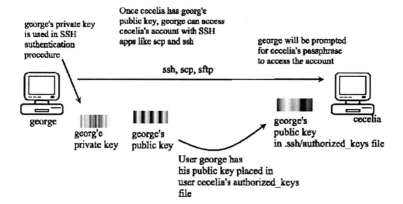

Figure 13-1: SSH setup and access

To allow you to use SSH to access other accounts:

➢ You must create public and private keys on your account along with a passphrase. You will need to use this passphrase to access your account from another account.

➢ You must distribute your public key to other accounts you want to access, placing them in the **.ssh/authorized_keys** file.

➢ Other accounts also have to set up public and private keys along with a passphrase.

➢ You must know the other account's passphrase to access it.

Creating SSH Keys with ssh-keygen

You create your public and private keys using the `ssh-keygen` command. You need to specify the kind of encryption you want to use. You can use either DSA or RSA encryption. Specify the type using the `-t` option and the encryption name in lowercase (`dsa` or `rsa`). In the following example, the user creates a key with the RSA encryption:

```
ssh-keygen -t rsa
```

The **ssh-keygen** command prompts you for a passphrase, which it will use as a kind of password to protect your private key. The passphrase should be several words long. You are also prompted to enter a filename for the keys. If you do not enter one, SSH will use its defaults. The public key will be given the extension **.pub**. The **ssh-keygen** command generates the public key and places it in your **.ssh/id_dsa.pub** or **.ssh/id_dsa.pub** file, depending on the type of key you specified; it places the private key in the corresponding **.ssh/id_dsa.pub** or **.ssh/id_rsa.pub** file.

If you need to change your passphrase, you can do so with the **ssh-keygen** command and the **-p** option. Each user will have their own SSH configuration directory, called **.ssh**, located in their own home directory. The public and private keys, as well as SSH configuration files, are placed here. If you build from the source code, the **make install** operation will automatically run **ssh-keygen**. Table 13-3 lists the SSH configuration files.

File	Description
$HOME/.ssh/known_hosts	Records host keys for all hosts the user has logged in to (that are not in **/etc/ssh/ssh_known_hosts**).
$HOME/.ssh/random_seed	Seeds the random number generator.
$HOME/.ssh/id_rsa	Contains the RSA authentication identity of the user.
$HOME/.ssh/ id_dsa	Contains the DSA authentication identity of the user.
$HOME/.ssh/id_rsa.pub	Contains the RSA public key for authentication. The contents of this file should be added to **$HOME/.ssh/authorized_keys** on all machines where you want to log in using RSA authentication.
$HOME/.ssh/id_dsa.pub	Contains the DSA public key for authentication.
$HOME/.ssh/config	The per-user configuration file.
$HOME/.ssh/authorized_keys	Lists the RSA or DSA keys that can be used for logging in as this user.
/etc/ssh/ssh_known_hosts	Contains the system-wide list of known host keys.
/etc/ssh/ssh_config	Contains the system-wide configuration file. This file provides defaults for those values not specified in the user's configuration file.
/etc/ssh/sshd_config	Contains the SSH server configuration file.
/etc/ssh/sshrc	Contains the system default. Commands in this file are executed by ssh when the user logs in just before the user's shell (or command) is started.
$HOME/.ssh/rc	Contains commands executed by ssh when the user logs in just before the user's shell (or command) is started.

Table 13-3: SSH Configuration Files

Authorized Keys

A public key is used to authenticate a user and its host. You use the public key on a remote system to allow that user access. The public key is placed in the remote user account's

.ssh/authorized_keys file. Recall that the public key is held in the **.ssh/id_dsa.pub** file. If a user wants to log in remotely from a local account to an account on a remote system, they would first place their public key in the **.ssh/authorized_keys** file in the account on the remote system they want to access. If the user **larisa** on **turtle.mytrek.com** wants to access the **aleina** account on **rabbit.mytrek.com**, **larisa**'s public key from **/home/larisa/.ssh/id_dsa.pub** first must be placed in **aleina**'s **authorized_keys** file, **/home/aleina/.ssh/authorized_keys**. User **larisa** can send the key or have it copied over. A simple cat operation can append a key to the authorized key file. In the next example, the user adds the public key for **aleina** in the **larisa.pub** file to the authorized key file. The **larisa.pub** file is a copy of the **/home/larisa/.ssh/id_dsa.pub** file that the user received earlier.

```
cat larisa.pub >>  .ssh/authorized_keys
```

Note: You can also use seahorse to create and manage SSH keys.

Note: The **.ssh/identity** filename is used in SSH version 1; it may be installed by default on older distribution versions. SSH version 2 uses a different filename, **.ssh/id_dsa** or **.ssh/id_rsa**, depending on whether RSA or DSA authentication is used.

Loading Keys

If you regularly make connections to a variety of remote hosts, you can use the `ssh-agent` command to place private keys in memory where they can be accessed quickly to decrypt received transmissions. The `ssh-agent` command is intended for use at the beginning of a login session. For GNOME, you can use the openssh-askpass-gnome utility, invoked by `ssh-add`, which allows you to enter a password when you log in to GNOME. GNOME will automatically supply that password whenever you use an SSH client.

Although the `ssh-agent` command enables you to use private keys in memory, you also must specifically load your private keys into memory using the `ssh-add` command. `ssh-add` with no arguments loads your private key from your **.ssh/id_dsa** or **.ssh/id_rsa.pub** file. You are prompted for your passphrase for this private key. To remove the key from memory, use `ssh-add` with the `-d` option. If you have several private keys, you can load them all into memory. `ssh-add` with the `-1` option lists those currently loaded.

SSH Clients

SSH was originally designed to replace remote access operations, such as rlogin, rcp, and Telnet, which perform no encryption and introduce security risks such as transmitting passwords in clear text. You can also use SSH to encode X server sessions as well as FTP transmissions (sftp). The ssh-clients package contains corresponding SSH clients to replace these applications. With slogin or ssh, you can log in from a remote host to execute commands and run applications, much as you can with rlogin and rsh. With scp, you can copy files between the remote host and a network host, just as with rcp. With sftp, you can transfer FTP files secured by encryption.

ssh

With **ssh** you can remotely log in from a local client to a remote system on your network operating as the SSH server. The term *local client* here refers to one outside the network, such as your home computer, and the term *remote* refers to a host system on the network to which you are connecting. In effect, you connect from your local system to the remote network host. It is designed to replace rlogin, which performs remote logins, and rsh, which executes remote commands. With ssh, you can log in from a local site to a remote host on your network and then send commands to be executed on that host. The **ssh** command is also capable of supporting X Window System connections. This feature is automatically enabled if you make an ssh connection from an X Window System environment, such as GNOME or KDE. A connection is set up for you between the local X server and the remote X server. The remote host sets up a dummy X server and sends any X Window System data through it to your local system to be processed by your own local X server.

The ssh login operation function is much like the `rlogin` command. You enter the **ssh** command with the address of the remote host, followed by a `-l` option and the login name (username) of the remote account you are logging in to. The following example logs in to the **aleina** user account on the **rabbit.mytrek.com** host:

```
ssh rabbit.mytrek.com -l aleina
```

You can also use the username in an address format with ssh, as in

```
ssh aleian@rabbit.mytrek.com
```

The following listing shows how the user **george** accesses the **cecelia** account on **turtle.mytrek.com**:

```
[george@turtle george]$ ssh turtle.mytrek.com -l cecelia
cecelia@turtle.mytrek.com's password:
[cecelia@turtle cecelia]$
```

A variety of options are available to enable you to configure your connection. Most have corresponding configuration options that can be set in the configuration file. For example, with the -c option, you can designate which encryption method you want to use, for instance, `idea`, `des`, `blowfish`, or `arcfour`. With the `-i` option, you can select a particular private key to use. The `-C` option enables you to have transmissions compressed at specified levels (see the **ssh** Man page for a complete list of options).

scp

You use **scp** to copy files from one host to another on a network. Designed to replace rcp, scp uses ssh to transfer data and employs the same authentication and encryption methods. If authentication requires it, scp requests a password or passphrase. The scp program operates much like rcp. Directories and files on remote hosts are specified using the username and the host address before the filename or directory. The username specifies the remote user account that scp is accessing, and the host is the remote system where that account is located. You separate the user from the host address with an @, and you separate the host address from the file or directory name with a colon. The following example copies the file **party** from a user's current directory to the user **aleina**'s **birthday** directory, located on the **rabbit.mytrek.com** host:

```
scp party aleina@rabbit.mytrek.com:/birthday/party
```

Of particular interest is the `-r` option (recursive) option, which enables you to copy whole directories. See the **scp** Man page for a complete list of options. In the next example, the user copies the entire **reports** directory to the user **justin**'s **projects** directory:

```
scp -r reports justin@rabbit.mytrek.com:/projects
```

In the next example, the user **george** copies the **mydoc1** file from the user **cecelia**'s home directory:

```
[george@turtle george]$ scp cecelia@turtle.mytrek.com:mydoc1  .
cecelia@turtle.mytrek.com's password:
mydoc1      0% |                                 |   0 --:--
ETA
mydoc1    100% |*****************************|  17 00:00
[george@turtle george]$
```

From a Windows system, you can also use **scp** clients such as **winscp**, which will interact with Linux scp-enabled systems.

sftp and sftp-server

With **sftp**, you can transfer FTP files secured by encryption. The **sftp** program uses the same commands as **ftp**. This client, which works only with ssh version 2, operates much like **ftp**, with many of the same commands. Use **sftp** instead of **ftp** to invoke the sftp client.

To use the sftp client to connect to an FTP server, that server needs to be operating the **sftp-server** application. The ssh server invokes sftp-server to provide encrypted FTP transmissions to those using the sftp client. The **sftp** server and client use the SSH File Transfer Protocol (SFTP) to perform FTP operations securely.

Port Forwarding (Tunneling)

If, for some reason, you can connect to a secure host only by going through an insecure host, ssh provides a feature called port forwarding. With *port forwarding,* you can secure the insecure segment of your connection. This involves simply specifying the port at which the insecure host is to connect to the secure one. This sets up a direct connection between the local host and the remote host, through the intermediary insecure host. Encrypted data is passed through directly. This process is referred to as tunneling, creating a secure tunnel of encrypted data through connected servers.

You can set up port forwarding to a port on the remote system or to one on your local system. To forward a port on the remote system to a port on your local system, use **ssh** with the **-R** option, followed by an argument holding the local port, the remote host address, and the remote port to be forwarded, each separated from the next by a colon. This works by allocating a socket to listen to the port on the remote side. Whenever a connection is made to this port, the connection is forwarded over the secure channel, and a connection is made to a remote port from the local machine. In the following example, port 22 on the local system is connected to port 23 on the **rabbit.mytrek.com** remote system:

```
ssh -R 22:rabbit.mytrek.com:23
```

To forward a port on your local system to a port on a remote system, use the **ssh -L** command, followed by an argument holding the local port, the remote host address, and the remote port to be forwarded, each two arguments separated by a colon. A socket is allocated to listen to the port on the local side. Whenever a connection is made to this port, the connection is forwarded over the secure channel and a connection is made to the remote port on the remote machine. In the following example, port 22 on the local system is connected to port 23 on the **rabbit.mytrek.com** remote system:

```
ssh -L 22:rabbit.mytrek.com:23
```

You can use the LocalForward and RemoteForward options in your **.ssh/config** file to set up port forwarding for particular hosts or to specify a default for all hosts you connect to.

SSH Configuration

The SSH configuration file for each user is in their **.ssh/config** file. The **/etc/ssh/ssh_config** file is used to SSH client set site-wide defaults. In the configuration file, you can set various options, as listed in the **ssh_config** Man document. The configuration file is designed to specify options for different remote hosts to which you might connect. It is organized into segments, where each segment begins with the keyword **HOST**, followed by the IP address of the host. The following lines hold the options you have set for that host. A segment ends at the next **HOST** entry. Of particular interest are the **User** and **Cipher** options. Use the **User** option to specify the names of users on the remote system who are allowed access. With the **Cipher** option, you can select which encryption method to use for a particular host. Encryption methods include IDEA, DES (standard), triple-DES (3DES), Blowfish (128 bit), Arcfour (RSA's RC4), and Twofish. The following example allows access from **larisa** at **turtle.mytrek.com** and uses Blowfish encryption for transmissions:

```
Host turtle.mytrek.com
    User larisa
    Compression no
    Cipher blowfish
```

Most standard options, including ciphers are already listed as commented entries. Remove the # to activate.

```
#   Ciphers aes128-cbc,3des-cbc,blowfish-cbc,cast128-cbc,arcfour,aes192-
cbc,aes256-cbc
```

To specify global options that apply to any host you connect to, create a **HOST** entry with the asterisk as its host, **HOST ***. This entry must be placed at the end of the configuration file because an option is changed only the first time it is set. Any subsequent entries for an option are ignored. Because a host matches on both its own entry and the global one, its specific entry should come before the global entry. The asterisk (*****) and the question mark (**?**) are both wildcard matching operators that enable you to specify a group of hosts with the same suffix or prefix.

```
Host *
  FallBackToRsh yes
  KeepAlive no
  Cipher 3des
```

The protocol option lets you specify what version of SSH to use, 1, 2, or both. By default, both protocols are acceptable, for backward compatibility. You can restrict use to just the more advanced and secure SSH2 protocol by changing the Protocol option to just 2.

```
Protocol 2
```

You use the **/etc/ssh/sshd_config** file to configure an SSH server. Here you will find server options like the port to use, password requirement, and PAM usage.

Kerberos

User authentication can further be controlled for certain services by Kerberos servers, discussed in this chapter. Kerberos authentication provides another level of security whereby individual services can be protected, allowing use of a service only to users who are cleared for access. Kerberos servers are all enabled and configured with **authconfig-gtk** (Authentication in the System | Administration menu).

Kerberos is a network authentication protocol that provides encrypted authentication to connections between a client and a server. As an authentication protocol, Kerberos requires a client to prove its identity using encryption methods before it can access a server. Once authenticated, the client and server can conduct all communications using encryption. Whereas firewalls protect only from outside attacks, Kerberos is designed to also protect from attacks from those inside the network. Users already within a network could try to break into local servers. To prevent this, Kerberos places protection around the servers themselves, rather than an entire network or computer. A free version is available from the Massachusetts Institute of Technology at **http://web.mit.edu/kerberos** under the MIT Public License, which is similar to the GNU Public License. The name *Kerberos* comes from Greek mythology and is the name of the three-headed watchdog for Hades. Be sure to check the **http://web.mit.edu/kerberos** site for recent upgrades and detailed documentation, including FAQs, manuals, and tutorials.

You can install the Kerberos server and several Kerberos clients using the krb5 packages. The Kerberos configuration files are installed by the **krb5-config** package. The server is **krb5-kdc**, which will install the kdc server and the krb5 libraries. The **krb5-admin-server** will install Kerberos administration server for managing the Kerberos kdc server. The **krb5-clients** package includes the Kerberos secured replacements for **rsh**, **rcp**, **telnet**, and the **ftp** client. The **krb5-user** package provides user tools like kinit. In addition, the **krb5-ftpd** and **krb5-rsh-server** packages install FTP and **rsh** (remote login and execution) Kerberos supported servers. Kerberos secured server plugins and libraries are also available for PAM, Python, LDAP, Perl, and Ruby. The LDAP plugin would be needed to operate a secure LDAP server (**krb5-kdc-ldap**).

Instead of running Kerberos server as a standalone server, you can run it on an on-demand basis using xinetd. This version of the Kerberos server is installed with the **kerberos-workstation-server** package.

Tip: The Kerberos V5 workstation clients package includes its own versions of network tools such as Telnet, RCP, FTP, and RSH. These provide secure authenticated access by remote users. The tools operate in the same way as their original counterparts. The package also contains a Kerberos version of the `su` administrative login command, `ksu`.

Kerberos Servers

The key to Kerberos is a Kerberos server through which all requests for any server services are channeled. The Kerberos server then authenticates a client, identifying the client and validating the client's right to use a particular server. The server maintains a database of authorized users. Kerberos then issues the client an encrypted ticket that the client can use to gain access to the server. For example, if a user needs to check their mail, a request for use of the mail server is sent to the Kerberos server, which then authenticates the user and issues a ticket that is then used to access the mail server. Without a Kerberos-issued ticket, no one can access any of the servers.

Originally, this process required that users undergo a separate authentication procedure for each server they wanted to access. However, users now only need to perform an initial authentication that is valid for all servers.

This process involves the use of two servers, an authentication server (AS) and a ticket-granting server (TGS). Together they make up what is known as the key distribution center (KDC). In effect, they distribute keys used to unlock access to services. The authentication server first validates a user's identity. The AS issues a ticket called the ticket-granting ticket (TGT) that allows the user to access the ticket-granting server. The TGS then issues the user another ticket to actually access a service. This way, the user never has any direct access of any kind to a server during the authentication process. The process is somewhat more complex than described. An authenticator using information such as the current time, a checksum, and an optional encryption key is sent along with the ticket and is decrypted with the session key. This authenticator is used by a service to verify a user's identity.

Note: You can view your list of current tickets with the `klist` command.

Authentication Process

The authentication server (AS) validates a user using information in its user database. Each user needs to be registered in the authentication server's database. The database will include a user password and other user information. To access the authentication server, the user provides the username and the password. The password is used to generate a user key with which communication between the AS and the user is encrypted. The user will have their own copy of the user key with which to decrypt communications. The authentication process is illustrated in Figure 13-2.

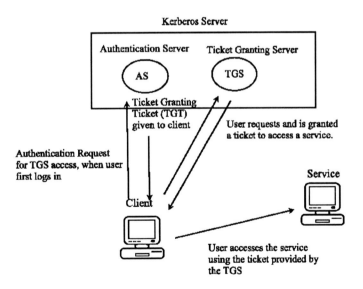

Figure 13-2: Kerberos authentication

Accessing a service with Kerberos involves the following steps:

1. The user has to be validated by the authentication server (AS) and granted access to the ticket-granting server with a ticket access key. You do this by issuing the `kinit` command, which will ask you enter your Kerberos username and then send it on to the authentication server (the Kerberos username is usually the same as your username).

2. The AS generates a ticket-granting ticket (TGT) with which to access the ticket-granting server (TGS). This ticket will include a session key that will be used to let you access the TGS. The TGT is sent back to you encrypted with your user key (password).

3. The `kinit` program then prompts you to enter your Kerberos password, which it then uses to decrypt the TGT. You can manage your Kerberos password with the `kpasswd` command.

4. Now you can use a client program such as a mail client program to access the mail server, for instance. When you do so, the TGT accesses the TGS, which then generates a ticket for accessing the mail server. The TGS generates a new session key for use with just the mail server. This is provided in the ticket sent to you for accessing the mail server. In effect, there is a TGT session key used for accessing the TGS, and a mail session key used for accessing the mail server. The ticket for the mail server is sent to you encrypted with the TGS session key.

5. The client then uses the mail ticket received from the TGS to access the mail server.

6. If you want to use another service such as FTP, when your FTP client sends a request to the TGS for a ticket, the TGS will automatically obtain authorization from the authentication server (AS) and issue an FTP ticket with an FTP session key. This kind of support remains in effect for a limited period of time, usually several hours, after which you again have to use `kinit` to undergo the authentication process and access the TGS. You can manually destroy any tickets you have with the `kdestroy` command.

Note: With Kerberos V5 (version 5), a Kerberos login utility is provided whereby users are automatically granted ticket-granting tickets when they log in normally. This avoids the need to use `kinit` to manually obtain a TGT.

Kerberized Services

Setting up a particular service to use Kerberos (known as Kerberizing) can be a complicated process. A Kerberized service needs to check the user's identity and credentials, check for a ticket for the service, and if one is not present, obtain one. Once they are set up, use of Kerberized services is nearly transparent to the user. Tickets are automatically issued and authentication carried out without any extra effort by the user. The **/etc/services** file should contain a listing of specific Kerberized services. These are services such as **kpasswd**, **kshell**, and **klogin** that provide Kerberos password, superuser access, and login services.

Kerberos also provides its own Kerberized network tools for **ftp**, **rsh**, **rcp**, and **rlogin**. These are located at **/usr/bin** and use the same names as the original network tools with the prefix **krb5-**, as in **krb5-ftp** for the command line FTP client. The **/usr/bin/ftp** entry become a link to the

/etc/alternatives/ftp item, which in turn is a link to **/usr/bin/krb5-ftp**. The **rsh**, **rcp**, an **rlogin** commands have the same kind of links. The telnet command will link to **/usr/bin/telnet.krb5**.

Kerberos Servers and Clients

Installing and configuring a Kerberos server is also a complex process. Carefully check the documentation for installing the current versions. Some of the key areas are listed here. In the Kerberos configuration file, **krb5.conf**, you can set such features as the encryption method used and the database name. When installing Kerberos, be sure to carefully follow the instructions for providing administrative access. To run Kerberos, you start the Kerberos server with `service` command and the `krb5-kdc` and `krb5-admin-server` scripts.

Tip: Check the Red Hat Linux Reference Manual for more detailed instructions on setting up Kerberos servers and clients on your system.

Consult the Red Hat Linux Reference Guide for detailed instructions on how to install and configure Kerberos on Red Hat. You will need to configure the server for your network, along with clients for each host (**krb5-dkc** package for servers and **krb5-clients** for clients).

To configure your server, you first specify your Kerberos realm and domain by manually replacing the lowercase `example.com` and the uppercase `EXAMPLE.COM` entries in the **/etc/krb5.conf** and **/var/kerberos/krb5kdc/kdc.conf** files with your own domain name. Maintain the same case for each entry. Realms are specified in uppercase, and simple host and domain names are in lowercase.

You will need to configure the server for your network, along with clients for each host (the **krb5-kdc** package for servers and **krb5-clients** for clients). To configure your server, you first specify your Kerberos realm and domain. You then create a database with the `kdb5_util` command and the `create` option. You will be prompted to enter a master key.

```
kdb5_util create -s
```

You then need to add a local principal, a local user with full administrative access from the host the server runs on. Start the **kadmin.local** tool and use the `addprincipal` command to add the local principal. You can then start your **krb5-kdc**,and **krb5-admin-server** servers.

On each client host, use the **kadmin** tool with the `addprincipal` command to add a principal for the host. Also add a host principal for each host on your network with **host/** qualifier, as in **host/rabbit.mytrek.com**. You can use the `-randkey` option to specify a random key. Then save local copies of the host keys, using the `ktadd` command to save them in its **/etc/krb5.keytab** file. Each host needs to also have the same **/etc/krb5.conf** configuration file on its system, specifying the Kerberos server and the kdc host.

Note: When you configure Kerberos with the Authentication tool, you will be able to enter the realm, kdc server, and Kerberos server. Default entries will be displayed using the domain "example.com." Be sure to specify the realm in uppercase. A new entry for your realm will be made in the realms segment of the **/etc/krb5.conf**, listing the kdc and server entries you made.

Internet Protocol Security: IPsec

The Internet Security Protocol, IPsec, incorporates security for network transmission into the Internet Protocol (IP) directly. IPsec is integrated into the new IPv6 protocol (Internet Protocol version 6). It can also be used with the older IPv4 protocol. IPsec provides methods for both encrypting data and authenticating the host or network it is sent to. The process can be handled manually or automated using the IPsec **racoon** key exchange tool. With IPsec, the kernel can automatically detect and decrypt incoming transmissions, as well as encrypt outgoing ones. You can also use IPsec to implement virtual private networks, encrypting data sent over the Internet from one local network to another. Though IPsec is a relatively new security method, its integration into the Internet Protocol will eventually provide it wide acceptance. Check the IPsec Howto for a detailed explanation of IPsec implementation on Linux, **www.ipsec-howto.org**. The Red Hat Linux Enterprise Security Guide provides a helpful description on using IPsec on Red Hat system in its Virtual Private Network section. The Guide can be found at the Red Hat Linux Enterprise Documentation page on the Red Hat site, **www.redhat.com**.

Several projects currently provide development and implementation of IPsec tools (see Table 13-4). The original IPsec tools were provided by the KAME project, whose efforts have since been integrated into Linux and BSD Unix. The **ipsec-tools** package, which includes raccoon, is available on the Ubuntu repository. Other IPsec tool projects include the Open Secure/Wide Area Network project (Openswan) at **www.openswan.org**, which provides a Linux implementation of IPsec tools, and the VPN Consortium (VPNC) at **www.vpnc.org**, which supports Windows and Macintosh versions. Openswan is now included with Ubuntu. Documentation will be located at **/usr/doc/openswan-***version*. Detailed documentation is held in the **openswan-doc** package, which will be installed at **/usr/doc/openswan-doc-***version*.

Web Site	Project
www.openvpn.org	Open Secure/Wide Area Network project (Ubuntu)
www.openswan.org	Open Secure/Wide Area Network project (Ubuntu)
www.vpnc.org	VPN Consortium
www.ipsec-howto.org	IPsec Howto documentation

Table 13-4: VPN Resources

Note: On Ubuntu you can also use OpenVPN to implement a virtual private network (VPN). OpenVPN uses the Web's SSL secure connections (Secure Socket Layer) and a server to manage connections. Set up and management is very easy. Check **www.openvpn.org** for more details.

IPsec Protocols

IPsec is made up of several protocols that provide authentication (AH), encryption (ESP), and the secure exchange of encryption keys (IKE). The Authentication Header protocol (AH) confirms that the packet was sent by the sender, and not by someone else. IPsec also includes an integrity check to detect any tampering in transit. Packets are encrypted using the Encapsulating Security Payload (ESP). Encryption and decryption are performed using secret keys shared by the sender and the receiver. These keys are themselves transmitted using the Internet Key Exchange protocol, which provides a secure exchange. ESP encryption can degrade certain compression transmission methods, such as PPP for dial-up Internet connections. To accommodate these compression methods, IPsec provides the IP Payload Compression Protocol (IPComp), with which packets can be compressed before being sent.

Encrypted authentication and integrity checks are included using Hash Methods Authentication Codes (HMAC) generated from hash security methods like SHA2 using a secret key. The HMAC is the included in the IPsec header, which the receiver can then check with the secret key. Encryption of transmitted data is performed by symmetric encryption methods like 3DES, Blowfish, and DES.

The AH, ESP, and IPComp protocols are incorporated into the Linux kernel. The IKE protocol is implemented as a separate daemon. It simply provides a way to share secret keys, and can be replaced by other sharing methods.

Note: You can now quickly and effectively configure IPsec connections using Network Manager.

IPsec Modes

You can use IPsec capabilities for either normal transport or packet tunneling. With normal transport, packets are encrypted and sent to the next destination. The normal transport mode is used to implement direct host-to-host encryption, where each host handles the IPsec encryption process. Packet tunneling is used to encrypt transmissions between gateways, letting the gateways handle the IPsec encryption process for traffic directed to or from an entire network, rather than having to configure IPsec encryption for each host. With packet tunneling, the packets are encapsulated with new headers for a specific destination, enabling you to implement virtual private networks (VPNs). Packets are directed to VPN gateways, which encrypt and send on local network packets.

Note: You can choose to encrypt packets for certain hosts or for those passing through specific ports.

IPsec Security Databases

The packets you choose to encrypt are designated by the IPsec Security Policy Database (SPD). The method you use to encrypt them is determined by the IPsec Security Association Database (SAD). The SAD associates an encryption method and key with a particular connection or kind of connection. The connections to be encrypted are designated in the Security Policy Database.

IPsec Tools

Several IPsec tools are provided with which you can manage your IPsec connections. These are included in the Ubuntu **ipsec-tools** package. With **setkey**, you can manage both the policy and association databases. The **racoon** tool configures the key exchange process to implement secure decryption key exchanges across connections. To administer your IPsec connections you can use **racoonctl**. For example, the **show-sa** option will display your security associations and the **vpn-connect** will establish a VPN connection.

14. Firewalls

Gufw and Firestarter

Firewalls: IPtables, NAT, and ip6tables

Packet Filtering

Network Address Translation (NAT)

Packet Mangling: the Mangle Table

IPtables Scripts

IP Masquerading

Most systems currently connected to the Internet are open to attempts by outside users to gain unauthorized access. Outside users can try to gain access directly by setting up an illegal connection, by intercepting valid communications from users remotely connected to the system, or by pretending to be a valid user. Firewalls, encryption, and authentication procedures are ways of protecting against such attacks. A *firewall* prevents any direct unauthorized attempts at access, *encryption* protects transmissions from authorized remote users, and *authentication* verifies that a user requesting access has the right to do so. The current Linux kernel incorporates support for firewalls using the Netfilter (IPtables) packet filtering package (the previous version, IP Chains, is used on older kernel versions). To implement a firewall, you simply provide a series of rules to govern what kind of access you want to allow on your system. If that system is also a gateway for a private network, the system's firewall capability can effectively help protect the network from outside attacks.

Web Site	Security Application
www.netfilter.org	Netfilter project, Iptables, and NAT
www.netfilter.org/ipchains	IP Chains firewall
www.openssh.org	Secure Shell encryption
www.squid-cache.org	Squid Web Proxy server
web.mit.edu/Kerberos	Kerberos network authentication

Table 14-1: Network Security Applications

To provide protection for remote communications, transmission can be simply encrypted. For Linux systems, you can use the Secure Shell (SSH) suite of programs to encrypt any transmissions, preventing them from being read by anyone else. Kerberos authentication provides another level of security whereby individual services can be protected, allowing use of a service only to users who are cleared for access. Outside users may also try to gain unauthorized access through any Internet services you may be hosting, such as a Web site. In such a case, you can set up a proxy to protect your site from attack. For Linux systems, use Squid proxy software to set up a proxy to protect your Web server. Table 14-1 lists several network security applications commonly used on Linux.

Firewalls management tools

You can choose from several different popular firewall management tools (see Table 14-2). Ubuntu now provides its own firewall configuration tool called the Uncomplicated Firewall (ufw). IPtables and ufw are on the Ubuntu main repository, all others are in the Universe repository. You can also choose to use other popular management tools like Firestarter or Fwbuilder. Firestarter provides a desktop interface whereas ufw is command line only. Both ufw and Firestarter are covered in this chapter, along with the underlying IPTables firewall application. Search Synaptic Package Manager for firewall to see a more complete listing.

Setting up a firewall with ufw

The Uncomplicated Firewall, ufw, is now the official firewall application for Ubuntu. It provides a simple firewall that can be managed with a few command-line operations. Like all firewall applications, ufw uses IPTables to define rules and run the firewall. The ufw application is just a management interface for IPTables. Default IPtables rules are kept in before and after files, with added rules in user files. The IPtables rule files are held in the **/etc/ufw** directory. Firewall configuration for certain packages will be placed in the **/usr/share/ufw.d** directory. The ufw firewall is started up at boot using the **/etc/init.d/ufw** script. You can find out more about ufw at the Ubuntu Firewall site at **http://wiki.ubuntu.com/UbuntuFirewall** and at the Ubuntu firewall section in the Ubuntu Server Guide at **https://help.ubuntu.com/9.04/serverguide/C/firewall.html**. The Server Guide also shows information on how to implement IP Masquerading on ufw.

Firewall	Description
IPTables	IPTables: netfilter, NAT, and mangle. **netfilter.org** (Main repository)
ufw	Uncomplicated Firewall, ufw. **wiki.ubuntu.com/UbuntuFirewall** (Ubuntu Main repository), also see Ubuntu Server Guide at **doc.ubuntu.com**.
Gufw	GNOME interface for Uncomplicated Firewall, ufw. **wiki.ubuntu.com/UbuntuFirewall**
Firestarter	Firestarter firewall configuration tool, **www.fs-secruity.com** (Universe repository)
Fwbuilder	Firewall configuration tool, allow for more complex configuration **www.fwbuilder.org** (Universe repository)
Shorewall	Shoreline firewall (Universe repository)
guarddog	KDE firewall configuration tool **www.simonzone.com/software/guarddog** (Universe repository)

Table 14-2: Ubuntu Firewall configuration tools

You can now manage the ufw firewall with either the standard ufw command or using the new Gufw configuration tool. You can quickly enable or disable the firewall by right-clicking on the Gufw icon and selecting Enable/Disable Firewall.

ufw commands

IPtables firewall rules can be set up using **ufw** commands entered on a command line in a Terminal window. Most users may only need to use **ufw** commands to allow or deny access by services like the Web server or Samba server. To check the current firewall status, listing those services allowed or blocked, use the status command.

```
sudo ufw status
```

If the firewall is not enabled, you will have to first enable it with the enable command.

```
sudo ufw enable
```

You can restart the firewall, reloading your rules, using the **/etc/init.d/ufw** script.

```
sudo /etc/init.d/ufw restart
```

You can then add rules using allow and deny commands and their options as listed in Table 14-3. To allow a service, use the allow command and the service name. This is the name for the service listed in the /etc/services file. The following allows the ftp service.

```
sudo ufw allow ftp
```

If the service you want is not listed in /etc/services, and you know the port and protocol it uses, can specify the port and protocol directly. For example, the Samba service uses port 137 and protocol tcp.

```
sudo ufw allow 137/tcp
```

The status operation will then show what services are allowed.

```
sudo ufw status
To                 Action         From
21:tcp             ALLOW          Anywhere
21:udp             ALLOW          Anywhere
137:tcp            ALLOW          Anywhere
```

To remove a rule, prefix it with the **delete** command.

```
sudo ufw delete allow 137/tcp
```

Commands	Description
**enable	disable**	Turn the firewall on or off
status	Display status along with services allowed or denied.
**logging on	off**	Turn logging on or off
**default allow	deny**	Set the default policy, allow is open, whereas deny is restrictive
allow *service*	Allow access by a service. Services are defined in **/etc/services** which specify the ports for that service.
allow *port-number/protocol*	Allow access on a particular port using specified protocol. The protocol is optional.
deny *service*	Deny access by a service
delete *rule*	Delete an installed rule, use **allow**, **deny**, or **limit** and include rule specifics.
proto *protocol*	Specify protocol in **allow**, **deny**, or **limit** rule
from *address*	Specify source address in **allow**, **deny**, or **limit** rule
to *address*	Specify destination address in **allow**, **deny**, or **limit** rule
port *port*	Specify port in **allow**, **deny**, or **limit** rule for **from** and **to** address operations

Table 14-3: UFW firewall operations

More detailed rules can be specified using address, port, and protocol commands. These are very similar to the actual IPTables commands. Packets to and from particular networks, hosts, and ports can be controlled. The following denies SSH access (port 22) from host 192.168.03.

```
sudo ufw deny proto tcp from 192.168.03 to any port 22
```

UFW also supports connection rate limiting. Use the **limit** option in place of **allow**. With **limit**, connections are limited to 6 per 30 seconds on the specified port. It is meant to protect against brute force attacks.

The rules you add are placed in the **/var/lib/ufw/user.rules** file as IPTables rules. ufw is just a front end for **iptables-restore** which will read this file and set up the firewall using **iptables** commands. **ufw** will also have **iptables-restore** read the **before.rules** and **after.rules** files in the **/etc/ufw** directory. These files are considered administrative files that include needed supporting rules for your IPTables firewall. Administrators can add their own IPTables rules to these files for system specific features like IP Masquerading.

The **before.rules** file will specify a table with the * symbol, as in *****filter** for the netfilter table. For the NAT table you would use *****nat**. At the end of each table segment, a COMMIT command is needed to instruct ufw to apply the rules. Rules use **-A** for allow and **-D** for deny, assuming the **iptables** command. The following would implement IP Forwarding when placed at the end of the **before.rules** file (see Ubuntu firewall server documentation). This particular rule works on the first Ethernet device (eth0) for a local network (192.168.0.0/24).

```
# nat Table rules
*nat
:POSTROUTING ACCEPT [0:0]
# Forward traffic from eth1 through eth0.
-A POSTROUTING -s 192.168.0.0/24 -o eth0 -j MASQUERADE
# don't delete the 'COMMIT' line or these nat table rules won't be processed
COMMIT
```

Default settings for ufw are placed in **/etc/default/ufw**. Here you will find the default INPUT, OUTPUT, and FORWARD policies. A **default deny** command will set the default INPUT to DROP and OUTPUT to ACCEPT, whereas a **default allow** will set both INPUT and OUTPUT defaults to ACCEPT. FORWARD will always be drop. To allow IP Masquerading, FORWARD would have to be set to ACCEPT. Any user rules you have set up would not be affected. You would have to change these manually.

Gufw

Gufw provides an easy to use GNOME interface for managing your ufw firewall. A simple interface lets you add rules, both custom and standard. Help entry in the Gufw Help menu will open the Gufw manual, which provides a very detailed explanation of Gufw features and use, including screenshots and examples.

Gufw is in the Ubuntu Universe repository, currently given Ubuntu development support. You will have to install it with Synaptic, System Administration (Universe). Once installed, you can access Gufw from the System | Administration | Firewall configuration menu entry. Gufw preferences will let you display the Gufw icon on the panel, letting you easily access the Gufw interface.

Gufw will initially open with the firewall disabled with no ports configured. All components, except the check box labeled Firewall enabled. That check box will be empty. Above the checkbox a large Disabled label will be displayed. To enable the firewall, just click the Enabled check box. The Disabled label will be replaced by a green Enabled label. Figure 14-1 shows the firewall enabled, as well as the SSH port configured (22).

Figure 14-1: Gufw

Figure 14-2: Gufw Preconfigured rules

Gufw has three sections, Current Configuration, Add a new rule, and Rules. The Current Configuration has two options, Deny or Allow incoming traffic. By default, incoming traffic will be denied. Rules will make exceptions, allowing only certain traffic in. Should you select the Allow incoming traffic option, the firewall, though active, becomes ineffective, allowing all connections.

Gufw has three tabs for managing rules in the Add a new rules section: Simple, Preconfigured, and Advanced. On the Simple tab you can specify a port to allow. The Preconfigured tab provides a pop-up menu listing services by name for which Gufw will enter the port for you. To allow connection for trusted services like SSH or NFS, you just select their entry from the pop-up menu and then click the Add button. A port entry will then appear in the Rules segment. In Figure 14-2 the netbios-ssn discovery service has been selected and then added, showing up in the Rules section as "139/tcp ALLOW Anywhere". There is a corresponding rule for the udp protocol. Also in the Rules section is the SSH entry for port 22.

Services can also be blocked. To prevent FTP service, you could select the FTP entry, but then changed the Allow entry to Deny.

Figure 14-3: Gufw Simple rules

Besides Allow and Deny, you can also choose a Limit option. The Limit option will enable connection rate limiting, restricting connections to no more than 6 every 30 seconds for a given port. This is meant to protect against brute force attacks.

Should there be no preconfigured entry, you can use the Simple tab to allow access to a port. Currently, you have to do this to allow Samba access, port 137. You may also have to do this to allow access on BitTorrent ports for BitTorrent applications. In Figure 14-3 Samba access is allowed by adding a rule for port 137.

On the Advanced tab you can enter more complex rules. You can set up allow or deny rules for tcp or udp protocols, and specify the host and port (see Figure 14-4).

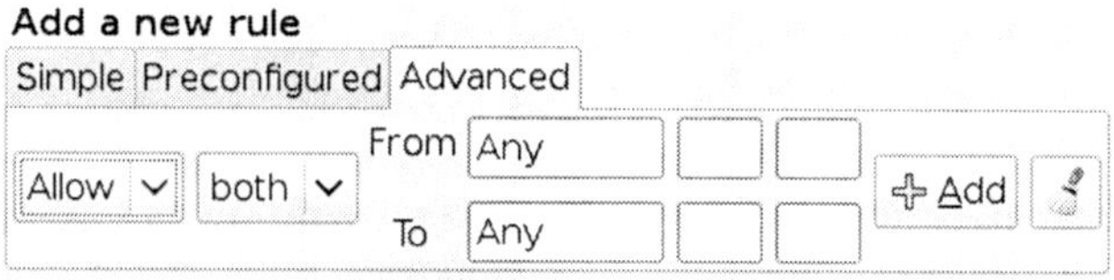

Add a new rule

Simple	Preconfigured	Advanced

Allow ∨	both ∨	From	Any			✛ Add	🖌
		To	Any				

Figure 14-4: Gufw Advanced rules

If you should want to remove a rule, select it in the Rules section and then click the Remove button. To clear out all rules, click the Select all button and then the Remove button.

Setting Up Your Firewall with Firestarter

Ubuntu also provides the Firestarter firewall configuration tool with which you can set up your firewall. Firestarter, though popular, is located in the Universe repository. You should use either Gufw or Firestarter, but not both at the same time.

To access Firestarter select Firestarter from the System | Administration menu. The first time you start up Firestarter the Firewall Wizard starts up which will prompt you for your network device and Internet connection sharing information (see Figure 14-5). Much of the configuration is automatic. If you are using a local home or work network, you may have to add rules for services like Samba Windows network access or the network address of your local network. After the Welcome screen, the Network device setup panel lets you select your network device, like an Ethernet connection or modem, as well as whether to use DHCP to detect your address information

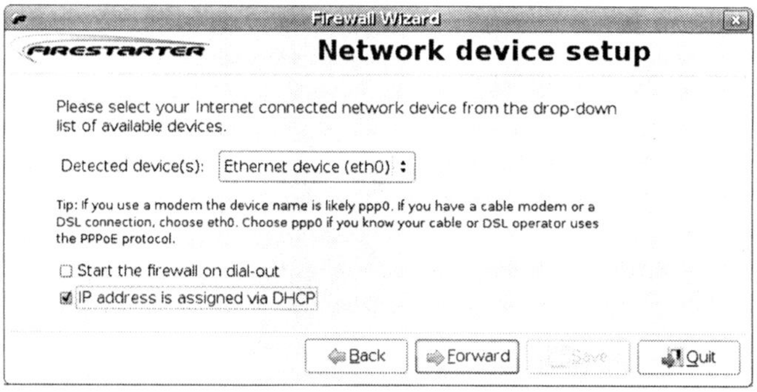

Firewall Wizard

FIRESTARTER   **Network device setup**

Please select your Internet connected network device from the drop-down list of available devices.

Detected device(s):   Ethernet device (eth0) ⬍

Tip: if you use a modem the device name is likely ppp0. if you have a cable modem or a DSL connection, choose eth0. Choose ppp0 if you know your cable or DSL operator uses the PPPoE protocol.

☐ Start the firewall on dial-out
☑ IP address is assigned via DHCP

⬅ Back   ➡ Forward   Save   🚪 Quit

Figure 14-5: Firestarter setup wizard

The Internet connection sharing setup panel is rarely used. You will most likely just skip it. It is used only for local networks where your computer is being used as a gateway to the Internet, letting other computer on your local network to access the Internet through your computer. There is usually a second Ethernet device connected to the local network as well as a local DHCP server controlling local network addressing. Again, this is rarely used, as most Internet gateways are now handled by dedicated routers, not computers. A final screen prompts you to start the firewall now, with a button to save your configuration. Click the SAVE button.

Firestarter will then start up with a window titled with your computer name. There are three panels: Status, Events, and Policy (see Figure 14-6). The toolbar entries will change with each panel selected. The Status panel lets you start and stop your firewall using the Stop/Start Firewall button in the toolbar. Its status is shown as a play or stop icon in the Status segment of the Status panel. The Events segment of this panel shows inbound and outbound traffic, and the Network segment lists your network devices along with device information like the number of packets received, sent, and average activity. Usually there will be only one device listed (a computer functioning as a gateway will have several). An expansion list will show Active connections. Here you can see what kind of connection is active, like Samba or Internet connections.

The Events panel will list any rejected connections, Blocked Connections. The Save, Clear, and Reload buttons on the toolbar let you save the event log, clear it, or reload to see the latest events.

The Policy panel shows rules for allowing host and service connections (see Figure 14-7). A pop-up menu lets you show Inbound traffic or Outbound traffic policies. On this panel you can add your own simplified rules for inbound or outbound hosts. The toolbar shows Add Rule, Remove Rule, Edit Rule, and Apply Rule buttons.

Figure 14-6: Firestarter Firewall

For Inbound Traffic, when you can set up rules for connections, services, or forwarding. There will be segments for each. Click on the segment first, and then click on the Add Rule button.

The dialog is different depending on the type of rule you are setting up. For a connection, the Add Rule dialog will let you enter the host, IP address, or network from which you can receive connections.

For a service, you can select the service to allow from a pop-up menu, along with the port, as well as whether to allow access by anyone or from a specific host or network (see Figure 14-8). By default all inbound traffic is denied, unless explicitly allowed by a rule. If you are setting up a firewall for just your personal computer connected to a network, you would enter a rule for the local network address. You could also set up rules to allow access by services like Samba or BitTorrent. Though Firestarter does have a preconfigured entry for Samba, it does not have a separate one for Netbios-ssn, port 139. You would have to add one manually.

The Outbound Traffic is more complex. Here you can set either a permissive or restrictive policy. There are entries for each to select which. The permissive is selected by default. The permissive entry will still reject blacklisted hosts and services, and the restrictive entry will allow white listed hosts and services. Each has both a connection and service segment, just like the Inbound connections, with the same options.

Figure 14-7: Firestarter Policy panel

Figure 14-8: Firestarter, choosing a service to permit

If permissive is selected, you will allow all outbound traffic, except those you specifically deny. For this configuration, you can create Deny rules for certain hosts and services. When setting up a Deny rule for a service you can choose a service from a pop-up menu, and specify its port. You can then reject either anyone using this service, or specify a particular host or network. For a connection, you simply specify the host, IP address, or network that can connect. The connection rules act like your own blacklist, listing hosts or network you will not allow yourself or others on your network to connect to.

If restrictive, you deny all outbound traffic, except those you specifically allow. In this case, you can set up Allow rules to allow connections by certain hosts and services, rejecting everything else. The restrictive option is not normally used, as it would cut off any connections from your computer to the Internet, unless you added a rule to permit the connection.

To configure your Firestarter firewall, click on the Preferences button. This opens a Preference window where you can set either Interface or Firewall settings.

For the Interface settings you can set either the Events logged or the Policy. The Events panel lets you eliminate logging of unwanted events, like redundant events or events from specific hosts or ports. The Policy panel has an option to let you apply changes immediately.

For Firewall Settings, you have panels for Network Settings, ICMP Filtering, ToS Filtering, and Advanced Options. Network Settings just selects your network device. Here you could change your network device between Ethernet, wireless, or modem. The ICMP filtering panel blocks ICMP packet attacks. Options allow certain ICMP packets through, like Unreachable to notify you of an unknown site. The Type of Service panel lets you prioritize your packets by both the kind of service and maximized efficiency. For the kind of service you can choose either workstations, servers, or the X Window System. For maximized efficiency you can choose reliability, throughput, or interactivity. Workstations and throughput are selected by default.

The Advanced options panel lets you select the drop method (silent or error reported), the Broadcast traffic rejection policy for internal and external connections (External broadcasts are blocked by default), and traffic validation block reserved addresses

IPtables, NAT, Mangle, and ip6tables

A good foundation for your network's security is to set up a Linux system to operate as a firewall for your network, protecting it from unauthorized access. You can use a firewall to implement either packet filtering or proxies. *Packet filtering* is simply the process of deciding whether a packet received by the firewall host should be passed on into the local network. The packet-filtering software checks the source and destination addresses of the packet and sends the packet on, if it's allowed. Even if your system is not part of a network but connects directly to the Internet, you can still use the firewall feature to control access to your system. Of course, this also provides you with much more security.

With proxies, you can control access to specific services, such as Web or FTP servers. You need a proxy for each service you want to control. The Web server has its own Web proxy, while an FTP server has an FTP proxy. Proxies can also be used to cache commonly used data, such as Web pages, so that users needn't constantly access the originating site. The proxy software commonly used on Linux systems is Squid.

An additional task performed by firewalls is network address translation (NAT). Network address translation redirects packets to appropriate destinations. It performs tasks such as redirecting packets to certain hosts, forwarding packets to other networks, and changing the host source of packets to implement IP masquerading.

Note: The IP Chains package is the precursor to IPtables that was used on Linux systems running the 2.2 kernel. It is still in use on many Linux systems. The Linux Web site for IP Chains, which is the successor to ipfwadm used on older versions of Linux, is currently **www.netfilter.org/ipchains**. IP Chains is no longer included with many Linux distributions.

The Netfilter software package implements both packet filtering and NAT tasks for the Linux 2.4 kernel and above. The Netfilter software is developed by the Netfilter Project, which you can find out more about at **www.netfilter.org**.

IPtables

The command used to execute packet filtering and NAT tasks is `iptables`, and the software is commonly referred to as simply IPtables. However, Netfilter implements packet filtering and NAT tasks separately using different tables and commands. A table will hold the set of commands for its application. This approach streamlines the packet-filtering task, letting IPtables perform packet-filtering checks without the overhead of also having to do address translations. NAT operations are also freed from being mixed in with packet-filtering checks. You use the `iptables` command for both packet filtering and NAT tasks, but for NAT you add the `-nat` option. The IPtables software can be built directly into the kernel or loaded as a kernel module, **iptable_filter.o**.

ip6tables

The ip6tables package provides support for IPv6 addressing. It is identical to IPtables except that it allows the use of IPv6 addresses instead of IPv4 addresses. Both filter and mangle tables are supported in ip6tables, but not NAT tables. The filter tables support the same options and commands as in IPtables. The mangle tables will allow specialized packet changes like those for IPtables, using PREROUTING, INPUT, OUTPUT, FORWARD, and POSTROUTING rules. Some extensions have ipv6 labels for their names, such as ipv6-icmp, which corresponds to the IPtables icmp extension. The ipv6headers extension is used to select IPv6 headers.

Modules

Unlike its predecessor, IP Chains, Netfilter is designed to be modularized and extensible. Capabilities can be added in the form of modules such as the state module, which adds connection tracking. Most modules are loaded as part of the IPtables service. Others are optional; you can elect to load them before installing rules. The IPtables modules are located at /usr/lib/*kernel-version*/kernel/net/ipv4/netfilter, where *kernel-version* is your kernel number. For IPv6 modules, check the **ipv6/netfilter** directory. Modules that load automatically will have an **ipt_** prefix, and optional ones have just an **ip_** prefix. If you are writing you own iptables script, you would have to add **modprobe** commands to load optional modules directly.

Packet Filtering

Netfilter is essentially a framework for packet management that can check packets for particular network protocols and notify parts of the kernel listening for them. Built on the Netfilter framework is the packet selection system implemented by IPtables. With IPtables, different tables of rules can be set up to select packets according to differing criteria. Netfilter currently supports three tables: filter, nat, and mangle. Packet filtering is implemented using a filter table that holds rules for dropping or accepting packets. Network address translation operations such as IP masquerading are implemented using the NAT table that holds IP masquerading rules. The mangle table is used for specialized packet changes. Changes can be made to packets before they are sent out, when they are received, or as they are being forwarded. This structure is extensible in that new modules can define their own tables with their own rules. It also greatly improves efficiency. Instead of all packets checking one large table, they access only the table of rules they need to.

IP table rules are managed using the `iptables` command. For this command, you will need to specify the table you want to manage. The default is the filter table, which need not be specified. You can list the rules you have added at any time with the `-L` and `-n` options, as shown here. The `-n` option says to use only numeric output for both IP addresses and ports, avoiding a DNS lookup for hostnames. You could, however, just use the `-L` option to see the port labels and hostnames:

```
iptables -L -n
```

Chains

Rules are combined into different chains. The kernel uses chains to manage packets it receives and sends out. A *chain* is simply a checklist of rules. These rules specify what action to take for packets containing certain headers. The rules operate with an if-then-else structure. If a packet does not match the first rule, the next rule is then checked, and so on. If the packet does not match any rules, the kernel consults chain policy. Usually, at this point the packet is rejected. If the packet does match a rule, it is passed to its target, which determines what to do with the packet. The standard targets are listed in Table 14-4. If a packet does not match any of the rules, it is passed to the chain's default target.

Targets

A *target* could, in turn, be another chain of rules, even a chain of user-defined rules. A packet could be passed through several chains before finally reaching a target. In the case of user-defined chains, the default target is always the next rule in the chains from which it was called. This sets up a procedure- or function call–like flow of control found in programming languages. When a rule has a user-defined chain as its target, when activated, that user-defined chain is executed. If no rules are matched, execution returns to the next rule in the originating chain.

Tip: Specialized targets and options can be added by means of kernel patches provided by the Netfilter site. For example, the SAME patch returns the same address for all connections. A patch-o-matic option for the Netfilter make file will patch your kernel source code, adding support for the new target and options. You can then rebuild and install your kernel.

Target	Function
ACCEPT	Allow packet to pass through the firewall.
DROP	Deny access by the packet.
REJECT	Deny access and notify the sender.
QUEUE	Send packets to user space.
RETURN	Jump to the end of the chain and let the default target process it.

Table 14-4: IPtables Targets

Firewall and NAT Chains

The kernel uses three firewall chains: INPUT, OUTPUT, and FORWARD. When a packet is received through an interface, the INPUT chain is used to determine what to do with it. The kernel then uses its routing information to decide where to send it. If the kernel sends the packet to another host, the FORWARD chain is checked. Before the packet is actually sent, the OUTPUT chain is also checked. In addition, two NAT table chains, POSTROUTING and PREROUTING, are implemented to handle masquerading and packet address modifications. The built-in Netfilter chains are listed in Table 14-5.

Chain	Description
INPUT	Rules for incoming packets
OUTPUT	Rules for outgoing packets
FORWARD	Rules for forwarded packets
PREROUTING	Rules for redirecting or modifying incoming packets, NAT table only
POSTROUTING	Rules for redirecting or modifying outgoing packets, NAT table only

Table 14-5: Netfilter Built-in Chains

Adding and Changing Rules

You add and modify chain rules using the `iptables` commands. An `iptables` command consists of the command `iptables`, followed by an argument denoting the command to execute (see Table 14-6). For example, `iptables -A` is the command to add a new rule, whereas `iptables -D` is the command to delete a rule. The `iptables` commands are listed in Table 14-4. The following command simply lists the chains along with their rules currently defined for your system. The output shows the default values created by `iptables` commands.

```
iptables -L -n
Chain input (policy ACCEPT):
Chain forward (policy ACCEPT):
Chain output (policy ACCEPT):
```

To add a new rule to a chain, you use `-A`. Use `-D` to remove it, and `-R` to replace it. Following the command, list the chain to which the rule applies, such as the INPUT, OUTPUT, or FORWARD chain, or a user-defined chain. Next, you list different options that specify the actions you want taken (most are the same as those used for IP Chains, with a few exceptions). The `-s` option specifies the source address attached to the packet, `-d` specifies the destination address, and the `-j` option specifies the target of the rule. The ACCEPT target will allow a packet to pass. The `-i` option now indicates the input device and can be used only with the INPUT and FORWARD chains. The `-o` option indicates the output device and can be used only for OUTPUT and FORWARD chains. Table 14-5 lists several basic options.

Option	Function
`-A` *chain*	Appends a rule to a chain.
`-D` *chain* [*rulenum*]	Deletes matching rules from a chain. Deletes rule *rulenum* (1 = first) from *chain*.
`-I` *chain* [*rulenum*]	Inserts in *chain* as *rulenum* (default 1 = first).
`-R` *chain rulenum*	Replaces rule *rulenum* (1 = first) in *chain*.
`-L` [*chain*]	Lists the rules in *chain* or all chains.
`-E` [*chain*]	Renames a chain.
`-F` [*chain*]	Deletes (flushes) all rules in *chain* or all chains.
`-R` *chain*	Replaces a rule; rules are numbered from 1.
`-Z` [*chain*]	Zero counters in *chain* or all chains.
`-N` *chain*	Creates a new user-defined chain.
`-X` *chain*	Deletes a user-defined chain.
`-P` *chain target*	Changes policy on *chain* to *target*.

Table 14-6: IPtables Commands

IPtables Options

The IPtables package is designed to be extensible, and there are number of options with selection criteria that can be included with IPtables (see Table 14-7). For example, the TCP extension includes the `--syn` option that checks for SYN packets. The ICMP extension provides the `--icmp-type` option for specifying ICMP packets as those used in ping operations. The limit extension includes the `--limit` option, with which you can limit the maximum number of matching packets in a specified time period, such as a second.

Note: In IPtables commands, chain names have to be entered in uppercase, as with the chain names INPUT, OUTPUT, and FORWARD.

In the following example, the user adds a rule to the INPUT chain to accept all packets originating from the address 192.168.0.55. Any packets that are received (`INPUT`) whose source address (`-s`) matches 192.168.0.55 are accepted and passed through (`-j ACCEPT`):

```
iptables -A INPUT -s 192.168.0.55 -j ACCEPT
```

Accepting and Denying Packets: DROP and ACCEPT

There are two built-in targets, DROP and ACCEPT. Other targets can be either user-defined chains or extensions added on, such as REJECT. Two special targets are used to manage chains, RETURN and QUEUE. RETURN indicates the end of a chain and returns to the chain it started from. QUEUE is used to send packets to user space.

```
iptables -A INPUT -s www.myjunk.com -j DROP
```

You can turn a rule into its inverse with an `!` symbol. For example, to accept all incoming packets except those from a specific address, place an `!` symbol before the `-s` option and that address. The following example will accept all packets except those from the IP address 192.168.0.45:

```
iptables -A INPUT -j ACCEPT ! -s 192.168.0.45
```

You can specify an individual address using its domain name or its IP number. For a range of addresses, you can use the IP number of their network and the network IP mask. The IP mask can be an IP number or simply the number of bits making up the mask. For example, all of the addresses in network 192.168.0 can be represented by 192.168.0.0/225.255.255.0 or by 192.168.0.0/24. To specify any address, you can use 0.0.0.0/0.0.0.0 or simply 0/0. By default, rules reference any address if no `-s` or `-d` specification exists. The following example accepts messages coming in that are from (source) any host in the 192.168.0.0 network and that are going (destination) anywhere at all (the `-d` option is left out or could be written as `-d 0/0`):

```
iptables -A INPUT -s 192.168.0.0/24   -j ACCEPT
```

The IPtables rules are usually applied to a specific network interface such as the Ethernet interface used to connect to the Internet. For a single system connected to the Internet, you will have two interfaces, one that is your Internet connection and a loopback interface (**lo**) for internal connections between users on your system. The network interface for the Internet is referenced using the device name for the interface. For example, an Ethernet card with the device name **/dev/eth0** would be referenced by the name **eth0**. A modem using PPP protocols with the device name **/dev/ppp0** would have the name **ppp0**. In IPtables rules, you use the `-i` option to indicate the input device; it can be used only with the INPUT and FORWARD chains. The `-o` option indicates the output device and can be used only for OUTPUT and FORWARD chains. Rules can then be applied to packets arriving and leaving on particular network devices. In the following examples, the first rule references the Ethernet device **eth0**, and the second, the localhost:

```
iptables -A INPUT -j DROP -i eth0 -s 192.168.0.45
iptables -A INPUT -j ACCEPT  -i lo
```

User-Defined Chains

With IPtables, the FORWARD and INPUT chains are evaluated separately. One does not feed into the other. This means that if you want to completely block certain addresses from passing through your system, you will need to add both a FORWARD rule and an INPUT rule for them.

```
iptables -A INPUT -j DROP -i eth0 -s 192.168.0.45
iptables -A FORWARD -j DROP -i eth0 -s 192.168.0.45
```

A common method for reducing repeated INPUT and FORWARD rules is to create a user chain that both the INPUT and FORWARD chains feed into. You define a user chain with the **-N** option. The next example shows the basic format for this arrangement. A new chain is created called incoming (it can be any name you choose). The rules you would define for your FORWARD and INPUT chains are now defined for the incoming chain. The INPUT and FORWARD chains then use the incoming chain as a target, jumping directly to it and using its rules to process any packets they receive.

```
iptables -N incoming

iptables -A incoming -j DROP -i eth0 -s 192.168.0.45
iptables -A incoming -j ACCEPT  -i lo

iptables -A FORWARD -j incoming
iptables -A INPUT -j incoming
```

Option	Function
-p [!] *proto*	Specifies a protocol, such as TCP, UDP, ICMP, or ALL.
-s [!] *address*[/*mask*] [!] [*port*[:*port*]]	Source address to match. With the *port* argument, you can specify the port.
--sport [!] [*port*[:*port*]]	Source port specification. You can specify a range of ports using the colon, *port:port*.
-d [!] *address*[/*mask*] [!] [*port*[:*port*]]	Destination address to match. With the *port* argument, you can specify the port.
--dport [!] [*port*[:*port*]]	Destination port specification.
--icmp-type [!] *typename*	Specifies ICMP type.
-i [!] *name*[+]	Specifies an input network interface using its name (for example, **eth0**). The + symbol functions as a wildcard. The + attached to the end of the name matches all interfaces with that prefix (**eth+** matches all Ethernet interfaces). Can be used only with the INPUT

	chain.
`-j` *target* `[port]`	Specifies the target for a rule (specify `[port]` for REDIRECT target).
`--to-source` < *ipaddr*>`[`-< *ipaddr*>`] [`: *port- port*`]`	Used with the SNAT target, rewrites packets with new source IP address.
`--to-destination` < *ipaddr*>`[`-< *ipaddr*>`] [`: *port- port*`]`	Used with the DNAT target, rewrites packets with new destination IP address.
`-n`	Numeric output of addresses and ports, used with `-L`.
`-o [!]` *name*`[+]`	Specifies an output network interface using its name (for example, `eth0`). Can be used only with FORWARD and OUTPUT chains.
`-t` *table*	Specifies a table to use, as in `-t nat` for the NAT table.
`-v`	Verbose mode, shows rule details, used with `-L`.
`-x`	Expands numbers (displays exact values), used with `-L`.
`[!] -f`	Matches second through last fragments of a fragmented packet.
`[!] -V`	Prints package version.
`!`	Negates an option or address.
`-m`	Specifies a module to use, such as state.
`--state`	Specifies options for the state module such as NEW, INVALID, RELATED, and ESTABLISHED. Used to detect packet's state. NEW references SYN packets (new connections).
`--syn`	SYN packets, new connections.
`--tcp-flags`	TCP flags: SYN, ACK, FIN, RST, URG, PS, and ALL for all flags.
`--limit`	Option for the limit module (`-m limit`). Used to control the rate of matches, matching a given number of times per second.
`--limit-burst`	Option for the limit module (`-m limit`). Specifies maximum burst before the limit kicks in. Used to control denial-of-service attacks.

Table 14-7: IPtables Options

ICMP Packets

Firewalls often block certain Internet Control Message Protocol (ICMP) messages. ICMP redirect messages, in particular, can take control of your routing tasks. You need to enable some ICMP messages, however, such as those needed for ping, traceroute, and particularly destination-unreachable operations. In most cases, you always need to make sure destination-unreachable packets are allowed; otherwise, domain name queries could hang. Some of the more common ICMP packet types are listed in Table 14-8. You can enable an ICMP type of packet with the `--icmp-type` option, which takes as its argument a number or a name representing the message. The following examples enable the use of echo-reply, echo-request, and destination-unreachable messages, which have the numbers 0, 8, and 3:

```
iptables -A INPUT -j ACCEPT  -p icmp -i eth0 --icmp -type  echo-reply -d 10.0.0.1
iptables -A INPUT -j ACCEPT  -p icmp -i eth0 --icmp-type  echo-request -d 10.0.0.1
iptables -A INPUT -j ACCEPT -p icmp -i eth0 --icmp-type destination-unreachable -d 10.0.0.1
```

Their rule listing will look like this:

```
ACCEPT     icmp --  0.0.0.0/0              10.0.0.1              icmp type 0
ACCEPT     icmp --  0.0.0.0/0              10.0.0.1              icmp type 8
ACCEPT     icmp --  0.0.0.0/0              10.0.0.1              icmp type 3
```

Ping operations need to be further controlled to avoid the ping-of-death security threat. You can do this several ways. One way is to deny any ping fragments. Ping packets are normally very small. You can block ping-of-death attacks by denying any ICMP packet that is a fragment. Use the `-f` option to indicate fragments.

```
iptables -A INPUT -p icmp -j DROP -f
```

Number	Name	Required By
0	echo-reply	ping
3	destination-unreachable	Any TCP/UDP traffic
5	redirect	Routing if not running routing daemon
8	echo-request	ping
11	time-exceeded	traceroute

Table 14-8: Common ICMP Packets

Another way is to limit the number of matches received for ping packets. You use the limit module to control the number of matches on the ICMP ping operation. Use `-m limit` to use the limit module, and `--limit` to specify the number of allowed matches. `1/s` will allow one match per second.

```
iptables -A FORWARD -p icmp --icmp-type echo-request -m limit --limit 1/s -j ACCEPT
```

Controlling Port Access

If your system is hosting an Internet service, such as a Web or FTP server, you can use IPtables to control access to it. You can specify a particular service by using the source port (`--sport`) or destination port (`--dport`) options with the port that the service uses. IPtables lets you use names for ports such as **www** for the Web server port. The names of services and the ports they use are listed in the **/etc/services** file, which maps ports to particular services. For a domain name server, the port would be **domain**. You can also use the port number if you want, preceding the number with a colon. The following example accepts all messages to the Web server located at 192.168.0.43:

```
iptables -A INPUT -d 192.168.0.43 --dport www -j ACCEPT
```

You can also use port references to protect certain services and deny others. This approach is often used if you are designing a firewall that is much more open to the Internet, letting users make freer use of Internet connections. Certain services you know can be harmful, such as Telnet and NTP, can be denied selectively. For example, to deny any kind of Telnet operation on your firewall, you can drop all packets coming in on the Telnet port, 23. To protect NFS operations, you can deny access to the port used for the portmapper, 111. You can use either the port number or the port name.

```
# deny outside access to portmapper port on firewall.
iptables -A arriving  -j DROP -p tcp -i eth0  --dport 111
# deny outside access to telnet port on firewall.
iptables -A arriving  -j DROP -p tcp -i eth0  --dport telnet
```

The rule listing will look like this:

```
DROP      tcp  --  0.0.0.0/0    0.0.0.0/0    tcp dpt:111
DROP      tcp  --  0.0.0.0/0    0.0.0.0/0    tcp dpt:23
```

Common ports checked and their labels are shown here:

Service	Port Number	Port Label
Auth	113	auth
Finger	79	finger
FTP	21	ftp
NTP	123	ntp
Portmapper	111	sunrpc
Telnet	23	telnet
Web server	80	www

One port-related security problem is access to your X server ports that range from 6000 to 6009. On a relatively open firewall, these ports could be used to illegally access your system through your X server. A range of ports can be specified with a colon, as in 6000:6009. You can also use x11 for the first port, x11:6009. Sessions on the X server can be secured by using SSH, which normally accesses the X server on port 6010.

```
iptables -A arriving  -j DROP -p tcp -i eth0  --dport 6000:6009
```

Packet States: Connection Tracking

One of the more useful extensions is the state extension, which can easily detect tracking information for a packet. Connection tracking maintains information about a connection such as its source, destination, and port. It provides an effective means for determining which packets belong to an established or related connection. To use connection tracking, you specify the state module first with `-m state`. Then you can use the `--state` option. Here you can specify any of the following states:

State	Description
NEW	A packet that creates a new connection
ESTABLISHED	A packet that belongs to an existing connection
RELATED	A packet that is related to, but not part of, an existing connection, such as an ICMP error or a packet establishing an FTP data connection
INVALID	A packet that could not be identified for some reason
RELATED+REPLY	A packet that is related to an established connection, but not part of one directly

If you are designing a firewall that is meant to protect your local network from any attempts to penetrate it from an outside network, you may want to restrict packets coming in. Simply denying access by all packets is unfeasible because users connected to outside servers—say, on the Internet—must receive information from them. You can, instead, deny access by a particular kind of packet used to initiate a connection. The idea is that an attacker must initiate a connection from the outside. The headers of these kinds of packets have their SYN bit set on and their FIN and ACK bits empty. The state module's NEW state matches on any such SYN packet. By specifying a DROP target for such packets, you deny access by any packet that is part of an attempt to make a connection with your system. Anyone trying to connect to your system from the outside is unable to do so. Users on your local system who have initiated connections with outside hosts can still communicate with them. The following example will drop any packets trying to create a new connection on the **eth0** interface, though they will be accepted on any other interface:

```
iptables -A INPUT -m state --state NEW -i eth0 -j DROP
```

You can use the `!` operator on the **eth0** device combined with an ACCEPT target to compose a rule that will accept any new packets except those on the **eth0** device. If the **eth0** device is the only one that connects to the Internet, this still effectively blocks outside access. At the same time, input operation for other devices such as your localhost are free to make new connections. This kind of conditional INPUT rule is used to allow access overall with exceptions. It usually assumes that a later rule such as a chain policy will drop remaining packets.

```
iptables -A INPUT -m state --state NEW ! -i eth0 -j ACCEPT
```

The next example will accept any packets that are part of an established connection or related to such a connection on the **eth0** interface:

```
iptables -A INPUT -m state --state ESTABLISHED,RELATED -j ACCEPT
```

Tip: You can use the iptstate tool to display the current state table.

Specialized Connection Tracking: ftp, irc, Amanda, tftp.

To track certain kinds of packets, IPtables uses specialized connection tracking modules. These are optional modules that you have to have loaded manually. To track passive FTP connections, you would have to load the ip_conntrack_ftp module. To add NAT table support, you would also load the ip_nat_ftp module. For IRC connections, you use ip_conntrack_irc and ip_nat_irc. There are corresponding modules for Amanda (the backup server) and TFTP (Trivial FTP).

If you are writing your own iptables script, you would have to add **modprobe** commands to load the modules.

```
modprobe ip_conntrack ip_conntrack_ftp ip_nat_ftp
modprobe ip_conntrack_amanda ip_nat_amanda
```

Network Address Translation (NAT)

Network address translation (NAT) is the process whereby a system will change the destination or source of packets as they pass through the system. A packet will traverse several linked systems on a network before it reaches its final destination. Normally, they will simply pass the packet on. However, if one of these systems performs a NAT on a packet, it can change the source or destination. A packet sent to a particular destination could have its destination address changed. To make this work, the system also needs to remember such changes so that the source and destination for any reply packets are altered back to the original addresses of the packet being replied to.

NAT is often used to provide access to systems that may be connected to the Internet through only one IP address. Such is the case with networking features such as IP masquerading, support for multiple servers, and transparent proxying. With IP masquerading, NAT operations will change the destination and source of a packet moving through a firewall/gateway linking the Internet to computers on a local network. The gateway has a single IP address that the other local computers can use through NAT operations. If you have multiple servers but only one IP address, you can use NAT operations to send packets to the alternate servers. You can also use NAT operations to have your IP address reference a particular server application such as a Web server (transparent proxy). NAT tables are not implemented for ip6tables.

Adding NAT Rules

Packet selection rules for NAT operations are added to the NAT table managed by the **iptables** command. To add rules to the NAT table, you have to specify the NAT table with the -t option. Thus to add a rule to the NAT table, you would have to specify the NAT table with the **-t nat** option as shown here:

```
iptables -t nat
```

With the **-L** option, you can list the rules you have added to the NAT table:

```
iptables -t nat -L -n
```

Adding the **-n** option will list IP addresses and ports in numeric form. This will speed up the listing, as iptables will not attempt to do a DNS lookup to determine the hostname for the IP address.

Nat Targets and Chains

In addition, there are two types of NAT operations: source NAT, specified as SNAT target, and destination NAT, specified as DNAT target. SNAT target is used for rules that alter source addresses, and DNAT target, for those that alter destination addresses.

Three chains in the NAT table are used by the kernel for NAT operations. These are PREROUTING, POSTROUTING, and OUTPUT. PREROUTING is used for destination NAT (DNAT) rules. These are packets that are arriving. POSTROUTING is used for source NAT (SNAT) rules. These are for packets leaving. OUTPUT is used for destination NAT rules for locally generated packets.

As with packet filtering, you can specify source (**-s**) and destination (**-d**) addresses, as well as the input (**-i**) and output (**-o**) devices. The **-j** option will specify a target such as MASQUERADE. You would implement IP masquerading by adding a MASQUERADE rule to the POSTROUTING chain:

```
iptables -t nat -A POSTROUTING -o eth0 -j MASQUERADE
```

To change the source address of a packet leaving your system, you would use the POSTROUTING rule with the SNAT target. For the SNAT target, you use the **--to-source** option to specify the source address:

```
iptables -t nat -A POSTROUTING -o eth0 -j SNAT --to-source 192.168.0.4
```

To change the destination address of packets arriving on your system, you would use the PREROUTING rule with the DNAT target and the **--to-destination** option:

```
iptables -t nat -A PRETROUTING -i eth0 -j DNAT --to-destination 192.168.0.3
```

Specifying a port lets you change destinations for packets arriving on a particular port. In effect, this lets you implement port forwarding. In the next example, every packet arriving on port 80 (the Web service port) is redirected to 10.0.0.3, which in this case would be a system running a Web server.

```
iptables -t nat -A PRETROUTING -i eth0 -dport 80 -j DNAT --to-destination 10.0.0.3
```

With the TOS and MARK targets, you can mangle the packet to control its routing or priority. A TOS target sets the type of service for a packet, which can set the priority using criteria such as normal-service, minimize-cost, or maximize-throughput, among others.

The targets valid only for the NAT table are shown here:

SNAT	Modify source address, use **--to-source** option to specify new source address.
DNAT	Modify destination address, use **--to-destination** option to specify new destination address.
REDIRECT	Redirect a packet.
MASQUERADE	IP masquerading.
MIRROR	Reverse source and destination and send back to sender.
MARK	Modify the Mark field to control message routing.

Nat Redirection: Transparent Proxies

NAT tables can be used to implement any kind of packet redirection, a process transparent to the user. Redirection is communing used to implement a transparent proxy. Redirection of packets is carried out with the REDIRECT target. With transparent proxies, packets received can be automatically redirected to a proxy server. For example, packets arriving on the Web service port, 80, can be redirected to the Squid Proxy service port, usually 3128. This involves a command to redirect an packet, using the REDIRECT target on the PREROUTING chain:

```
# iptables -t nat -A PREROUTING -i eth1 --dport 80 -j REDIRECT --to-port 3128
```

Packet Mangling: the Mangle Table

The *packet mangling* table is used to actually modify packet information. Rules applied specifically to this table are often designed to control the mundane behavior of packets, like routing, connection size, and priority. Rules that actually modify a packet, rather than simply redirecting or stopping it, can be used only in the mangle table. For example, the TOS target can be used directly in the mangle table to change the Type of Service field to modifying a packet's priority. A TCPMSS target could be set to control the size of a connection. The ECN target lets you work around ECN black holes, and the DSCP target will let you change DSCP bits. Several extensions such as the ROUTE extension will change a packet, in this case, rewriting its destination, rather than just redirecting it.

The mangle table is indicated with the `-t mangle` option. Use the following command to see what chains are listed in your mangle table:

```
iptables -t mangle  -L
```

Several mangle table targets are shown here:

TOS	Modify the Type of Service field to manage the priority of the packet.
TCPMSS	Modify the allowed size of packets for a connection, enabling larger transmissions.
ECN	Remove ECN black hole information.
DSCP	Change DSCP bits.
ROUTE	Extension TARGET to modify destination information in the packet.

Note: The IPtables package is designed to be extensible, allowing customized targets to be added easily. This involves applying patches to the kernel and rebuilding it. See **www.netfilter.org** for more details, along with a listing of extended targets.

IPtables Scripts

Though you can enter IPtables rules from the shell command line, when you shut down your system, these commands will be lost. You will most likely need to place your IPtables rules in a script that can then be executed directly. This way you can edit and manage a complex set of rules, adding comments and maintaining their ordering.

An IPtables Script Example: IPv4

You now have enough information to create a simple IPtables script that will provide basic protection for a single system connected to the Internet. The following script, **myfilter**, provides an IPtables filtering process to protect a local network and a Web site from outside attacks. This example uses IPtables and IPv4 addressing. For IPv6 addressing you would use ip6tables, which has corresponding commands, except for the NAT rules, which would be implemented as mangle rules.

The script configures a simple firewall for a private network (check the IPtables HOWTO for a more complex example). If you have a local network, you could adapt this script to it. In this configuration, all remote access initiated from the outside is blocked, but two-way communication is allowed for connections that users in the network make with outside systems. In this example, the firewall system functions as a gateway for a private network whose network address is 192.168.0.0 (see Figure 14-9). The Internet address is, for the sake of this example, 10.0.0.1. The system has two Ethernet devices: one for the private network (**eth1**) and one for the Internet (**eth0**). The gateway firewall system also supports a Web server at address 10.0.0.2. Entries in this example that are too large to fit on one line are continued on a second line, with the newline quoted with a backslash.

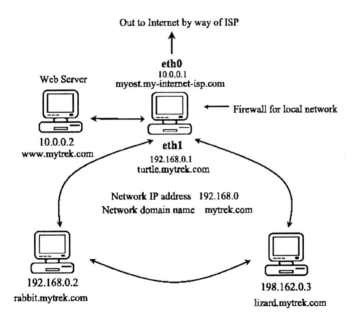

Figure 14-9: A network with a firewall

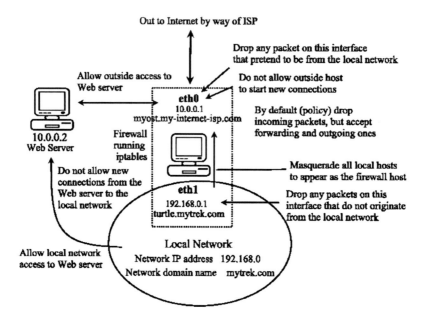

Out to Internet by way of ISP

Drop any packet on this interface
that pretend to be from the local network

Allow outside access to
Web server

Do not allow outside host
to start new connections

eth0
10.0.0.1
myost.my-internet-isp.com

By default (policy) drop
incoming packets, but accept
forwarding and outgoing ones

10.0.0.2
Web Server

Firewall
running
iptables

Masquerade all local hosts
to appear as the firewall host

Do not allow new
connections from the
Web server to the
local network

eth1
192.168.0.1
turtle.mytrek.com

Drop any packets on this
interface that do not originate
from the local network

Allow local network
access to Web server

Local Network
Network IP address   192.168.0
Network domain name   mytrek.com

Figure 14-10: Firewall rules applied to a local network example

The basic rules as they apply to different parts of the network are illustrated in Figure 14-10.

Initially, in the script you would clear your current IPtables with the flush option (**-F**), and then set the policies (default targets) for the non-user-defined rules. IP forwarding should also be turned off while the chain rules are being set:

```
echo 0 > /proc/sys/net/ipv4/ip_forward
```

Drop Policy

First, a DROP policy is set up for INPUT and FORWARD built-in IP chains. This means that if a packet does not meet a criterion in any of the rules to let it pass, it will be dropped. Then both IP spoofing attacks and any attempts from the outside to initiate connections (SYN packets) are rejected.

Outside connection attempts are also logged. This is a very basic configuration that can easily be refined to your own needs by adding IPtables rules.iptables -P

```
INPUT DROP
iptables -P OUTPUT ACCEPT
iptables -P FORWARD ACCEPT
```

myfilter

```
# Firewall Gateway system IP address is 10.0.0.1 using Ethernet device eth0
# Private network address is 192.168.0.0 using Ethernet device eth1
# Web site address is 10.0.0.2
# turn off IP forwarding
echo 0 > /proc/sys/net/ipv4/ip_forward
# Flush chain rules
iptables -F INPUT
iptables -F OUTPUT
iptables -F FORWARD
# set default (policy) rules
iptables -P INPUT DROP
iptables -P OUTPUT ACCEPT
iptables -P FORWARD ACCEPT

# IP spoofing, deny any packets on the internal network that have an external source address
iptables -A INPUT -j LOG  -i eth1 \! -s 192.168.0.0/24
iptables -A INPUT -j DROP  -i eth1 \! -s 192.168.0.0/24
iptables -A FORWARD -j DROP  -i eth1 \! -s 192.168.0.0/24
# IP spoofing, deny any outside packets (any not on eth1) that have the
# source address of the internal network
iptables -A INPUT -j DROP \! -i eth1 -s 192.168.0.0/24
iptables -A FORWARD -j DROP \! -i eth1 -s 192.168.0.0/24
# IP spoofing, deny any outside packets with localhost address
# (packets not on the lo interface (any on eth0 or eth1) that have source address localhost)
iptables -A INPUT -j DROP  -i \! lo  -s  127.0.0.0/255.0.0.0
iptables -A FORWARD -j DROP  -i \! lo  -s  127.0.0.0/255.0.0.0

# allow all incoming messages for users on your firewall system
iptables -A INPUT -j ACCEPT  -i lo

# allow  communication to the Web server (address 10.0.0.2), port www
iptables -A INPUT  -j ACCEPT -p tcp -i eth0  --dport www -s 10.0.0.2
# Allow  established connections from Web servers to internal network
iptables -A INPUT -m state --state ESTABLISHED,RELATED -i eth0 -p tcp  --sport www -s
10.0.0.2 -d 192.168.0.0/24  -j ACCEPT
# Prevent new  connections from Web servers to internal network
iptables -A OUTPUT -m state --state  NEW -o eth0 -p tcp --sport www -d 192.168.0.0/24 -j DROP

# allow established and related outside communication to your system
# allow outside communication to the firewall, except for ICMP packets
iptables -A INPUT -m state --state ESTABLISHED,RELATED -i eth0 -p \! icmp -j ACCEPT
# prevent outside initiated connections
iptables -A INPUT -m state --state NEW -i eth0 -j DROP
iptables -A FORWARD -m state --state NEW -i eth0 -j DROP
# allow all local communication to and from the firewall on eth1  from the local network
iptables -A INPUT -j ACCEPT -p all -i eth1 -s 192.168.0.0/24

# Set up masquerading to allow internal machines access to outside network
iptables -t nat -A POSTROUTING -o eth0 -j MASQUERADE

# Accept ICMP Ping and Destination unreachable messages
# Others will be rejected by INPUT and OUTPUT DROP policy
iptables -A INPUT -j ACCEPT  -p icmp -i eth0 --icmp-type  echo-reply -d 10.0.0.1
iptables -A INPUT -j ACCEPT  -p icmp -i eth0 --icmp-type  echo-request -d 10.0.0.1
iptables -A INPUT -j ACCEPT -p icmp -i eth0 --icmp-type  destination-unreachable -d 10.0.0.1
# Turn on IP Forwarding
echo 1 > /proc/sys/net/ipv4/ip_forward
```

IP Spoofing

One way to protect the private network from the IP spoofing of any packets is to check for any outside addresses on the Ethernet device dedicated to the private network. In this example, any packet on device **eth1** (dedicated to the private network) whose source address is not that of the private network (**! -s 192.168.0.0**) is denied. Also, check to see if any packets coming from the outside are designating the private network as their source. In this example, any packets with the source address of the private network on any Ethernet device other than for the private network (**eth1**) are denied. The same strategy can be applied to the local host.

```
# IP spoofing, deny any packets on the internal network
# that has an external source address.
iptables -A INPUT -j LOG  -i eth1 \! -s 192.168.0.0/24
iptables -A INPUT -j DROP  -i eth1 \! -s 192.168.0.0/24
iptables -A FORWARD -j DROP  -i eth1 \! -s 192.168.0.0/24
# IP spoofing, deny any outside packets (any not on eth1)
# that have the source address of the internal network
iptables -A INPUT -j DROP \! -i eth1 -s 192.168.0.0/24
iptables -A FORWARD -j DROP \! -i eth1 -s 192.168.0.0/24
# IP spoofing, deny any outside packets with localhost address
# (packets not on the lo interface (any on eth0 or eth1)
# that have the source address of localhost)
iptables -A INPUT -j DROP  -i \! lo  -s  127.0.0.0/255.0.0.0
iptables -A FORWARD -j DROP  -i \! lo  -s  127.0.0.0/255.0.0.0
```

Then, you would set up rules to allow all packets sent and received within your system (localhost) to pass.

```
iptables -A INPUT -j ACCEPT  -i lo
```

Server Access

For the Web server, you want to allow access by outside users but block access by anyone attempting to initiate a connection from the Web server into the private network. In the next example, all messages are accepted to the Web server, but the Web server cannot initiate contact with the private network. This prevents anyone from breaking into the local network through the Web server, which is open to outside access. Established connections are allowed, permitting the private network to use the Web server.

```
# allow  communication to the Web server (address 10.0.0.2), port www
iptables -A INPUT  -j ACCEPT -p tcp -i eth0  --dport www -s 10.0.0.2
# Allow  established connections from Web servers to internal network
iptables -A INPUT -m state --state ESTABLISHED,RELATED -i eth0 \
   -p tcp  --sport www -s 10.0.0.2 -d 192.168.0.0/24  -j ACCEPT
# Prevent new  connections from Web servers to internal network
iptables -A OUTPUT -m state --state  NEW -o eth0 -p tcp \
  --sport www -d 192.168.0.1.0/24  -j DROP
```

Firewall Outside Access

To allow access by the firewall to outside networks, you allow input by all packets except for ICMP packets. These are handled later. The firewall is specified by the firewall device, **eth0**. First your firewall should allow established and related connections to proceed, as shown here. Then you would block outside access as described later.

```
# allow outside communication to the firewall,
# except for ICMP packets
iptables -A INPUT -m state --state ESTABLISHED,RELATED \
         -i eth0 -p \! icmp -j ACCEPT
```

Blocking Outside Initiated Access

To prevent outsiders from initiating any access to your system, create a rule to block access by SYN packets from the outside using the **state** option with NEW. Drop any new connections on the **eth0** connection (assumes only **eth0** is connected to the Internet or outside network).

```
# prevent outside initiated connections
iptables -A INPUT -m state --state NEW -i eth0 -j DROP
iptables -A FORWARD -m state --state NEW -i eth0 -j DROP
```

Local Network Access

To allow interaction by the internal network with the firewall, you allow input by all packets on the internal Ethernet connection, **eth1**. The valid internal network addresses are designated as the input source.

```
iptables -A INPUT -j ACCEPT -p all -i eth1 -s 192.168.0.0/24
```

Listing Rules

A listing of these **iptables** options shows the different rules for each option, as shown here:

```
$ iptables -L
Chain INPUT (policy DROP)
target    prot opt source          destination
LOG       all  -- !192.168.0.0/24  anywhere         LOG level warning
DROP      all  -- !192.168.0.0/24  anywhere
DROP      all  -- 192.168.0.0/24   anywhere
DROP      all  -- 127.0.0.0/8      anywhere
ACCEPT    all  -- anywhere         anywhere
ACCEPT    tcp  -- 10.0.0.2         anywhere         tcp dpt:http
ACCEPT    tcp  -- 10.0.0.2         192.168.0.0/24   state RELATED,ESTABLISHED tcp spt:http
ACCEPT    !icmp -- anywhere        anywhere         state RELATED,ESTABLISHED
DROP      all  -- anywhere         anywhere         state NEW
ACCEPT    all  -- 192.168.0.0/24   anywhere
ACCEPT    icmp -- anywhere         10.0.0.1         icmp echo-reply
ACCEPT    icmp -- anywhere         10.0.0.1         icmp echo-request
ACCEPT    icmp -- anywhere         10.0.0.1         icmp destination-unreachable
Chain FORWARD (policy ACCEPT)
target    prot opt source          destination
DROP      all  -- !192.168.0.0/24  anywhere
DROP      all  -- 192.168.0.0/24   anywhere
DROP      all  -- 127.0.0.0/8      anywhere
DROP      all  -- anywhere         anywhere         state NEW

Chain OUTPUT (policy ACCEPT)
target    prot opt source          destination
DROP       tcp  -- anywhere        192.168.0.0/24   state NEW tcp spt:http
```

```
$ iptables -t nat -L
Chain PREROUTING (policy ACCEPT)
target      prot opt source          destination
Chain POSTROUTING (policy ACCEPT)
target      prot opt source          destination
MASQUERADE  all  --  anywhere        anywhere
Chain OUTPUT (policy ACCEPT)
target      prot opt source          destination
```

User-Defined Rules

For more complex rules, you may want to create your own chain to reduce repetition. A common method is to define a user chain for both INPUT and FORWARD chains, so that you do not have to repeat DROP operations for each. Instead, you would have only one user chain that both FORWARD and INPUT chains would feed into for DROP operations. Keep in mind that both FORWARD and INPUT operations may have separate rules in addition to the ones they share. In the next example, a user-defined chain called arriving is created. The chain is defined with the **-N** option at the top of the script:

```
iptables -N arriving
```

A user chain has to be defined before it can be used as a target in other rules. So you have to first define and add all the rules for that chain, and then use it as a target. The arriving chain is first defined and its rules added. Then, at the end of the file, it is used as a target for both the INPUT and FORWARD chains. The INPUT chain lists rules for accepting packets, whereas the FORWARD chain has an ACCEPT policy that will accept them by default.

```
iptables -N arriving
iptables -F arriving
# IP spoofing, deny any packets on the internal network
# that has an external source address.
iptables -A arriving -j LOG  -i eth1 \! -s 192.168.0.0/24
iptables -A arriving -j DROP  -i eth1 \! -s 192.168.0.0/24
iptables -A arriving -j DROP \! -i eth1 -s 192.168.0.0/24
.......................
# entries at end of script
iptables -A INPUT -j arriving
iptables -A FORWARD -j arriving
```

A listing of the corresponding rules is shown here:

```
Chain INPUT (policy DROP)
target      prot opt source          destination
arriving    all  --  0.0.0.0/0         0.0.0.0/0
Chain FORWARD (policy ACCEPT)
target      prot opt source          destination
arriving    all  --  0.0.0.0/0         0.0.0.0/0
Chain arriving (2 references)
target      prot opt source          destination
LOG         all  --  !192.168.0.0/24  0.0.0.0/0      LOG flags 0 level 4
DROP        all  --  !192.168.0.0/24  0.0.0.0/0
DROP        all  --  192.168.0.0/24   0.0.0.0/0
```

For rules where chains may differ, you will still need to enter separate rules. In the **myfilter** script, the FORWARD chain has an ACCEPT policy, allowing all forwarded packets to the local network to pass through the firewall. If the FORWARD chain had a DROP policy, like the INPUT chain, then you may need to define separate rules under which the FORWARD chain could accept packets. In this example, the FORWARD and INPUT chains have different rules for accepting packets on the **eth1** device. The INPUT rule is more restrictive. To enable the local network to receive forwarded packets through the firewall, you could enable forwarding on its device using a separate FORWARD rule, as shown here:

```
iptables -A FORWARD -j ACCEPT -p all -i eth1
```

The INPUT chain would accept packets only from the local network.

```
iptables -A INPUT -j ACCEPT -p all -i eth1 -s 192.168.0.0/24
```

Masquerading Local Networks

To implement masquerading, where systems on the private network can use the gateway's Internet address to connect to Internet hosts, you create a NAT table (**-t nat**) POSTROUTING rule with a MASQUERADE target.

```
iptables -t nat -A POSTROUTING -o eth0 -j MASQUERADE
```

Controlling ICMP Packets

In addition, to allow ping and destination-reachable ICMP packets, you enter INPUT rules with the firewall as the destination. To enable ping operations, you use both echo-reply and echo-request ICMP types, and for destination unreachable, you use the destination-unreachable type.

```
iptables -A INPUT -j ACCEPT  -p icmp -i eth0 --icmp-type echo-reply -d 10.0.0.1
iptables -A INPUT -j ACCEPT  -p icmp -i eth0 --icmp-type echo-request -d 10.0.0.1
iptables -A INPUT -j ACCEPT -p icmp -i eth0 --icmp-type destination-unreachable -d 10.0.0.1
```

At the end, IP forwarding is turned on again.

```
echo 1 > /proc/sys/net/ipv4/ip_forward
```

Simple LAN Configuration

To create a script to support a simple LAN without any Internet services like Web servers, you would just not include rules for supporting those services. You would still need FORWARD and POSTROUTING rules for connecting your local hosts to the Internet, as well as rules governing interaction between the hosts and the firewall. To modify the example script to support a simple LAN without the Web server, just remove the three rules governing the Web server. Leave everything else the same.

LAN Configuration with Internet Services on the Firewall System

Often, in the same system that functions as a firewall is also used to run Internet servers, like Web and FTP servers. In this case the firewall rules are applied to the ports used for those services. The example script dealt with a Web server running on a separate host system. If the Web server were instead running on the firewall system, you would apply the Web server firewall rules to the port that the Web server uses. Normally the port used for a Web server is 80. In the following example, the IPtables rules for the Web server have been applied to port www, port 80, on the firewall system. The modification simply requires removing the old Web server host address references, 10.0.0.2.

```
# allow  communication to the Web server, port www (port 80)
iptables -A INPUT  -j ACCEPT -p tcp -i eth0  --dport www
# Allow  established connections from Web servers to internal network
iptables -A INPUT -m state --state ESTABLISHED,RELATED -i eth0 \
   -p tcp  --sport www -d 192.168.0.0/24  -j ACCEPT
# Prevent new  connections from Web servers to internal network
iptables -A OUTPUT -m state --state  NEW -o eth0 -p tcp \
  --sport www -d 192.168.0.1.0/24 -j DROP
```

Similar entries could be set up for an FTP server. Should you run several Internet services, you could use a user-defined rule to run the same rules on each service, rather than repeating three separate rules per service. Working from the example script, you would use two defined rules, one for INPUT and one for OUTPUT, controlling incoming and outgoing packets for the services.

```
iptables -N inputservice
iptables -N outputservice
iptables -F inputservice
iptables -F outputservice


# allow  communication to the service
iptables -A inputservice  -j ACCEPT -p tcp -i eth0
# Allow  established connections from the service to internal network
iptables -A inputservice -m state --state ESTABLISHED,RELATED -i eth0 \
   -p tcp  -d 192.168.0.0/24  -j ACCEPT
# Prevent new  connections from service to internal network
iptables -A outputservice -m state --state  NEW -o eth0 -p tcp \
  -d 192.168.0.1.0/24 -j DROP
......................
# Run rules for the Web server, port www (port 80)
iptables -A INPUT  --dport www -j inputservice
iptables -A INPUT  --dport www -j outputservice
# Run rules for the FTP server, port ftp (port 21)
iptables -A OUTPUT  --dport ftp -j inputservice
iptables -A OUTPUT  --dport ftp -j outputservice
```

IP Masquerading

On Linux systems, you can set up a network in which you can have one connection to the Internet, which several systems on your network can use. This way, using only one IP address, several different systems can connect to the Internet. This method is called *IP masquerading,* where a system masquerades as another system, using that system's IP address. In such a network, one system is connected to the Internet with its own IP address, while the other systems are connected on a local area network (LAN) to this system. When a local system wants to access the network, it masquerades as the Internet-connected system, borrowing its IP address.

IP masquerading is implemented on Linux using the IPtables firewall tool. In effect, you set up a firewall, which you then configure to do IP masquerading. Currently, IP masquerading supports all the common network services—as does IPtables firewall—such as Web browsing, Telnet, and ping. Other services, such as IRC, FTP, and RealAudio, require the use of certain modules. Any services you want local systems to access must also be on the firewall system because request and response actually are handled by services on that system.

You can find out more information on IP masquerading at the IP Masquerade Resource Web site at **ipmasq.webhop.net**. In particular, the Linux IP Masquerade mini-HOWTO provides a detailed, step-by-step guide to setting up IP masquerading on your system. IP masquerading must be supported by the kernel before you can use it. If your kernel does not support it, you may have to rebuild the kernel, including IP masquerade support, or use loadable modules to add it. See the IP Masquerade mini-HOWTO for more information.

With IP masquerading, as implemented on Linux systems, the machine with the Internet address is also the firewall and gateway for the LAN of machines that use the firewall's Internet address to connect to the Internet. Firewalls that also implement IP masquerading are sometimes referred to as *MASQ gates*. With IP masquerading, the Internet-connected system (the firewall) listens for Internet requests from hosts on its LAN. When it receives one, it replaces the requesting local host's IP address with the Internet IP address of the firewall and then passes the request out to the Internet, as if the request were its own. Replies from the Internet are then sent to the firewall system. The replies the firewall receives are addressed to the firewall using its Internet address. The firewall then determines the local system to whose request the reply is responding. It then strips off its IP address and sends the response on to the local host across the LAN. The connection is transparent from the perspective of the local machines. They appear to be connected directly to the Internet.

Masquerading Local Networks

IP masquerading is often used to allow machines on a private network to access the Internet. These could be machines in a home network or a small LAN, such as for a small business. Such a network might have only one machine with Internet access, and as such, only the one Internet address. The local private network would have IP addresses chosen from the private network allocations (10., 172.16., or 192.168.). Ideally, the firewall has two Ethernet cards: one for an interface to the LAN (for example, **eth1**) and one for an interface to the Internet, such as **eth0** (for dial-up ISPs, this would be **ppp0** for the modem). The card for the Internet connection (**eth0**) would be assigned the Internet IP address. The Ethernet interface for the local network (**eth1**, in this example) is the firewall Ethernet interface. Your private LAN would have a network address like 192.168.0. Its Ethernet firewall interface (**eth1**) would be assigned the IP address 192.168.0.1. In effect, the firewall interface lets the firewall operate as the local network's gateway. The firewall is then configured to masquerade any packets coming from the private network. Your LAN needs to have its own domain name server, identifying the machines on your network, including your firewall. Each local machine needs to have the firewall specified as its gateway. Try not to use IP aliasing to assign both the firewall and Internet IP addresses to the same physical interface. Use separate interfaces for them, such as two Ethernet cards, or an Ethernet card and a modem (**ppp0**).

Masquerading NAT Rules

In Netfilter, IP masquerading is a NAT operation and is not integrated with packet filtering as in IP Chains. IP masquerading commands are placed on the NAT table and treated separately from the packet-filtering commands. Use IPtables to place a masquerade rule on the NAT table. First reference the NAT table with the -t nat option. Then add a rule to the

POSTROUTING chain with the **-o** option specifying the output device and the **-j** option with the MASQUERADE command.

```
iptables -t nat -A POSTROUTING -o eth0 -j MASQUERADE
```

IP Forwarding

The next step is to turn on IP forwarding, either manually or by setting the **net.ipv4.ip_forward** variable in the **/etc/sysctl.conf** file and running **sysctl** with the **-p** option. IP forwarding will be turned off by default. For IPv6, use **net.ipv6.conf.all.forwarding**. The **/etc/sysctl.conf** entries are shown here:

```
net.ipv4.ip_forward = 1
net.ipv6.conf.all.forwarding = 1
```

You then run **sysctl** with the **-p** option.

```
sysctl -p
```

You can directly change the respective forwarding files with an **echo** command as shown here:

```
echo 1 > /proc/sys/net/ipv4/ip_forward
```

For IPv6, you would to use the forwarding file in the corresponding **/proc/sys/net/ipv6** directory, **conf/all/forwarding**.

```
echo 1 > /proc/sys/net/ipv6/conf/all/forwarding
```

Masquerading Selected Hosts

Instead of masquerading all local hosts as the single IP address of the firewall/gateway host, you could use the NAT table to rewrite addresses for a few selected hosts. Such an approach is often applied to setups where you want several local hosts to appear as Internet servers. Using the DNAT and SNAT targets, you can direct packets to specific local hosts. You would use rules on the PREROUTING and POSTROUTING chains to direct input and output packets.

For example, the Web server described in the previous example could have been configured as a local host to which a DNAT target could redirect any packets originally received for 10.0.0.2. Say the Web server was set up on 192.168.0.5. It could appear as having the address 10.0.0.2 on the Internet. Packets sent to 10.0.0.2 would be rewritten and directed to 192.168.0.5 by the NAT table. You would use the PREROUTING chain with the **-d** option to handle incoming packets and POSTROUTING with the **-s** option for outgoing packets.

```
iptables -t nat -A PREROUTING -d 10.0.0.2 --to-destination 192.168.0.5 -j DNAT
iptables -t nat -A POSTROUTING -s 192.168.0.5 --to-source 10.0.0.2 -j SNAT
```

Tip: Bear in mind that with IPtables, masquerading is not combined with the FORWARD chain, as it is with IP Chains. So, if you specify a DROP policy for the FORWARD chain, you will also have to specifically enable FORWARD operation for the network that is being masqueraded. You will need both a POSTROUTING rule and a FORWARD rule.

ubuntu

Part 3: File Systems and Devices

File System Management

RAID and LVM

Devices

Archives, Compression, and Backups

Printing

Network Connections

15. File System management

File Systems

Filesystem Hierarchy Standard

Journaling

Mounting File Systems Automatically: /etc/fstab

Mounting File Systems Manually: mount and umount

Creating File Systems: mkfs, mke2fs, mkswap, parted, and fdisk

CD-ROM and DVD ROM Recording

Mono and .NET Support

Files reside on physical storage devices such as hard drives, CD-ROMs, or floppy disks. The files on each storage device are organized into a file system. The storage devices on your Linux system are presented as a collection of file systems that you can manage. When you want to add a new storage device, you need to format it as a file system and then attach it to your Linux file structure. Hard drives can be divided into separate storage devices called *partitions,* each of which has its own file system. You can perform administrative tasks on your file systems, such as backing them up, attaching or detaching them from your file structure, formatting new devices or erasing old ones, and checking a file system for problems.

To access files on a device, you attach its file system to a specified directory. This is called *mounting* the file system. For example, to access files on a USB drive, you first mount its file system to a particular directory. With Linux, you can mount a number of different types of file systems. You can even access a Windows hard drive partition or tape drive, as well as file systems on a remote server.

Linux file systems support *journaling,* which allows your system to recover from a crash or interruption easily. The ext3, ReiserFS, XFS, and JFS (IBM) file systems maintain a record of file and directory changes, called a *journal,* which can be used to recover files and directories in use when a system suddenly fails due to unforeseen events such as power interruptions. Most distributions currently use the **ext3** file system as their default, though you also have the option of using ReiserFS or JFS, an independently developed journaling system. Also available is the new **ext4** file system which provides better access to very large files like video.

Your Linux system is capable of handling any number of storage devices that may be connected to it. You can configure your system to access multiple hard drives, partitions on a hard drive, CD-ROM discs, DVDs, floppy disks, and even tapes. You can elect to attach these storage components manually or have them automatically mount when you boot. Automatic mounts are handled by configuring the **/etc/fstab** file. For example, the main partitions holding your Linux system programs are automatically mounted whenever you boot, whereas a floppy disk can be manually mounted when you put one in your floppy drive, though even these can also be automatically mounted. Removable storage devices like CD-ROMs, as well as removable devices like USB cameras and printers, are now handled by udev and the Hardware Abstract Layer (HAL), as described in Chapter 17 and partially discussed here. HAL and udev also will automatically mount any Windows **ntfs** file systems on your local hard drives. Remote files systems are mounted using Samba and NFS servers. All your mounted file systems will be browsable from your GNOME and KDE desktops.

File Systems

Although all the files in your Linux system are connected into one overall directory tree, parts of that tree may reside on different storage devices such as hard drives or CD-ROMs. Files on a particular storage device are organized into what is referred to as a *file system.* A file system is a formatted device, with its own tree of directories and files. Your Linux directory tree may encompass several file systems, each on different storage devices. On a hard drive with several partitions, you would have a file system for each partition. The files themselves are organized into one seamless tree of directories, beginning from the root directory. For example, if you attach a CD-ROM to your system, a pathname will lead directly from the root directory on your main root hard disk partition's file system to the files in the CD-ROM file system.

A file system has its files organized into its own directory tree. You can think of this as a subtree that must be attached to the main directory tree. The tree remains separate from your system's directory tree until you specifically connect it. For example, a floppy disk with Linux files has its own tree of directories. You need to attach this subtree to the main tree on your hard drive partition. Until they are attached, you cannot access the files on your floppy disk.

Directory	Function
/	Begins the file system structure—called the root.
/boot	Holds the kernel image files and associated boot information and files.
/home	Contains users' home directories.
/sbin	Holds administration-level commands and any commands used by the root user.
/dev	Holds dynamically generated file interfaces for devices such as the terminal and the printer (see "udev: Device Files" in Chapter 17).
/etc	Holds system configuration files and any other system files.
/etc/opt	Holds system configuration files for applications in **/opt**.
/etc/X11	Holds system configuration files for the X Window System and its applications.
/bin	Holds the essential user commands and utility programs.
/lib	Holds essential shared libraries and kernel modules.
/lib/modules	Holds the kernel modules.
/media	Used to hold directories for mounting media-based removable file systems, like CD-ROMs, floppy disks, USB card readers, and digital cameras.
/mnt	Used to hold directories for additional file systems such as hard disks.
/opt	Holds added software applications (for example, KDE on some distributions).
/proc	Process directory, a memory-resident directory containing files used to provide information about the system.
/sys	The sysfs file system for kernel objects, listing supported kernel devices and modules.
/tmp	Holds temporary files.
/usr	Holds those files and commands used by the system; this directory breaks down into several subdirectories.
/var	Holds files that vary, such as mailbox, Web, and FTP files.

Table 15-1: Linux File System Directories

Filesystem Hierarchy Standard

Linux organizes its files and directories into one overall interconnected tree, beginning from the root directory and extending down to system and user directories. The organization and layout for the system directories are determined by the file system hierarchy standard (FHS). The FHS provides a standardized layout that all Linux distributions should follow in setting up their system directories. For example, there must be an **/etc** directory to hold configuration files and a **/dev** directory for device files. You can find out more about FHS, including the official documentation, at **http://proton.pathname.com/fhs**. Linux distributions, developers, and administrators all follow the FHS to provide a consistent organization to the Linux file system.

Linux uses a number of specifically named directories for specialized administrative tasks. All these directories are at the very top level of your main Linux file system, the file system root directory, represented by a single slash, /. For example, the **/dev** directory holds device files, and the **/home** directory holds the user home directories and all their user files. You have access to these directories and files only as the system administrator (though users normally have read-only access). You need to log in as the root user, placing yourself in a special root user administrative directory called **/root**. From here, you can access any directory on the Linux file system, both administrative and user.

Root Directory: /

The subdirectories held in the root directory, /, are listed in Table 15-1, along with other useful subdirectories. Directories that you may commonly access as an administrator are the **/etc** directory, which holds configuration files; the **/dev** directory, which holds dynamically generated device files; and the **/var** directory, which holds server data files for DNS, Web, mail, and FTP servers, along with system logs and scheduled tasks. For managing different versions of the kernel, you may need to access the **/boot** and **/lib/modules** directories as well as **/usr/src/linux**. The **/boot** directory holds the kernel image files for any new kernels you install, and the **/lib/modules** directory holds modules for your different kernels.

Tip: With Linux you can mount file systems of different types, including those created by other operating systems, including Windows, Unix, and OSX. Within Linux a variety of file systems are supported, including several journaling systems like ReiserFS and ext3.

System Directories

Your Linux directory tree contains certain directories whose files are used for different system functions. For basic system administration, you should be familiar with the system program directories where applications are kept, the system configuration directory (**/etc**) where most configuration files are placed, and the system log directory (**/var/log**) that holds the system logs, recording activity on your system. Table 15-2 lists the system directories.

Program Directories

Directories with **bin** in the name are used to hold programs. The **/bin** directory holds basic user programs, such as login, shells (BASH, TCSH, and zsh), and file commands (`cp`, `mv`, `rm`, `ln`, and so on). The **/sbin** directory holds specialized system programs for such tasks as file system management (`fsck`, `fdisk`, `mkfs`) and system operations like shutdown and startup (`init`). The

/usr/bin directory holds program files designed for user tasks. The **/usr/sbin** directory holds user-related system operation, such as `useradd` for adding new users. The **/lib** directory holds all the libraries your system makes use of, including the main Linux library, **libc**, and subdirectories such as **modules**, which holds all the current kernel modules. It will also hold some system controlled configuration files, like **/lib/udev**.

Directory	Description
/bin	System-related programs
/sbin	System programs for specialized tasks
/lib	System libraries
/etc	Configuration files for system and network services and applications
/home	The location of user home directories and server data directories, such as Web and FTP site files
/media	The location where removable media file systems like CD-ROMs and floppy disks are mounted
/var	The location of system directories whose files continually change, such as logs, printer spool files, and lock files
/usr	User-related programs and files. Includes several key subdirectories, such as **/usr/bin**, **/usr/X11**, and **/usr/share/doc**
/usr/bin	Programs for users
/dev	Device files
/sys	The sysfs file system with device information for kernel-supported devices on your system
/usr/X11	X Window System configuration files
/usr/share	Shared files
/usr/share/doc	Documentation for applications
/usr/share/hal	Configuration for HAL removable devices
/etc/udev /lib/udev	Configuration for device files, udev
/tmp	Directory for system temporary files

Table 15-2: System Directories

Configuration Directories and Files

When you configure different elements of your system, such as user accounts, applications, servers, or network connections, you make use of configuration files kept in certain system directories. Configuration files are placed in the **/etc** directory.

The /usr Directory

The **/usr** directory contains a multitude of important subdirectories used to support users, providing applications, libraries, and documentation. The **/usr/bin** directory holds numerous user-accessible applications and utilities; **/usr/sbin** hold user-accessible administrative utilities. The **/usr/share** directory holds architecture-independent data that includes an extensive number of subdirectories, including those for documentation, such as **man**, **info**, and **doc** files. Table 15-3 lists the subdirectories of the **/usr** directory.

Directory	Description
/usr/bin	Holds most user commands and utility programs.
/usr/sbin	Holds administrative applications.
/usr/lib	Holds libraries for applications, programming languages, desktops, and so on.
/usr/games	Holds games and educational programs.
/usr/include	Holds C programming language header files (**.h**).
/usr/local	Holds locally installed software.
/usr/share	Holds architecture-independent data such as documentation.
/usr/src	Holds source code, including the kernel source code.

Table 15-3: /usr Directories

The /media Directory

The **/media** directory is used for mountpoints (the directories in the file structure to which the new file systems are attached) for removable media like CD-ROM, DVD, floppy, or Zip drives, as well as for other media-based file systems such as USB card readers, cameras, and MP3 players. These are file systems you may be changing frequently, unlike partitions on fixed disks. Most Linux systems use the Hardware Abstraction Layer (HAL) to dynamically manage the creation, mounting, and device assignment of these devices. As instructed by HAL, this tool will create floppy, CD-ROM, storage card, camera, and MP3 player subdirectories in **/media** as needed. The default subdirectory for mounting is **/media/disk**. Additional drives have an number attached to their name, like **disk-1**. CD/DVD-ROMs will use the **/media/cdrom** subdirectory. When you mount a Windows partition automatically from your GNOME or KDE desktop, the Windows partition will be mounted at the **/media** directory as **disk** subdirectories.

The /mnt Directory

The **/mnt** directory is usually used for mountpoints for other mounted file systems such as Windows partitions. You can create directories for any partitions you want to mount,

The /home Directory

The **/home** directory holds user home directories. When a user account is set up, a home directory is set up here for that account, usually with the same name as the user. As the system administrator, you can access any user's home directory, and so you have control over that user's files.

The /var Directory

The **/var** directory holds subdirectories for tasks whose files change frequently, such as lock files, log files, web server files, or printer spool files. For example, the **/var** directory holds server data directories, such as **/var/www** for the Apache web server website files or **/var/named** for the DNS server. The **/tmp** directory is simply a directory to hold any temporary files programs may need to perform a particular task.

The **/var** directories are designed to hold data that changes with the normal operation of the Linux system. For example, spool files for documents that you are printing are kept here. A spool file is created as a temporary printing file and is removed after printing. Other files, such as system log files, are changed constantly. Table 15-4 lists the subdirectories of the **/var** directory

Directory	Description
/var/account	Processes accounting logs.
/var/cache	Holds application cache data for Man pages, web proxy data, fonts, or application-specific data.
/var/crash	Holds system crash dumps.
/var/games	Holds varying games data.
/var/lib	Holds state information for particular applications.
/var/local	Holds data that changes for programs installed in **/usr/local**.
/var/lock	Holds lock files that indicate when a particular program or file is in use.
/var/log	Holds log files such as **/var/log/messages** that contain all kernel and system program messages.
/var/mail	Holds user mailbox files.
/var/named	Holds DNS server domain configuration files.
/var/opt	Holds variable data for applications installed in **/opt**.
/var/run	Holds information about the system's running processes.
/var/spool	Holds applications' spool data such as that for mail, news, and printer queues, as well as `cron` and `at` jobs.
/var/tmp	Holds temporary files that should be preserved between system reboots.
/var/www	Holds web server website files.

Table 15-4: /var Subdirectories

The /proc File System

The **/proc** file system is a special file system that is generated in system memory. It does not exist on any disk. **/proc** contains files that provide important information about the state of your system.

File	Description
/proc/*num*	There is a directory for each process labeled by its number. **/proc/1** is the directory for process 1.
/proc/cpuinfo	Contains information about the CPU, such as its type, make, model, and performance.
/proc/devices	Lists the device drivers configured for the currently running kernel.
/proc/dma	Displays the DMA channels currently used.
/proc/filesystems	Lists file systems configured into the kernel.
/proc/interrupts	Displays the interrupts in use.
/proc/ioports	Shows the I/O ports in use.
/proc/kcore	Holds an image of the physical memory of the system.
/proc/kmsg	Contains messages generated by the kernel.
/proc/loadavg	Lists the system load average.
/proc/meminfo	Displays memory usage.
/proc/modules	Lists the kernel modules currently loaded.
/proc/net	Lists status information about network protocols.
/proc/stat	Contains system operating statistics, such as page fault occurrences.
/proc/uptime	Displays the time the system has been up.
/proc/version	Displays the kernel version.

Table 15-5: /proc Subdirectories and Files

For example, **/proc/cpuinfo** holds information about your computer's CPU processor, **/proc/devices** lists those devices currently configured to run with your kernel, **/proc/filesystems** lists the file systems, and **/proc** files are really interfaces to the kernel, obtaining information from the kernel about your system. Table 15-5 lists the **/proc** subdirectories and files. Like any file system, **/proc** has to be mounted. The **/etc/fstab** file will have a special entry for **/proc** with a file system type of proc and no device specified.

```
none    /proc    proc    defaults    0    0
```

Tip: You can use **sysctl**, the Kernel Tuning tool, to set proc file values you are allowed to change, like the maximum number of files, or turning on IP forwarding.

The sysfs File System: /sys

The **sysfs** file system is a virtual file system that provides the a hierarchical map of your kernel-supported devices such as PCI devices, buses, and block devices, as well as supporting kernel modules. The **classes** subdirectory will list all your supported devices by category, such as network and sound devices. With **sysfs** your system can easily determine the device file a particular device is associated with. This is very helpful for managing removable devices as well as dynamically configuring and managing devices as HAL and udev do. The **sysfs** file system is used by udev to dynamically generate needed device files in the **/dev** directory, as well as by HAL to manage removable device files and support as needed (HAL technically provides information only about devices, though it can use tools to dynamically change configurations as needed). The **/sys** file system type is **sysfs**. The **/sys** subdirectories organize your devices into different categories. The file system is used by **systool** to display a listing of your installed devices. The following example will list all your system devices:

```
systool
```

Like **/proc**, the **/sys** directory resides only in memory, but you still need to mount it in the **/etc/fstab** file.

```
none    /sys       sysfs    defaults   0       0
```

Device Files: /dev, udev, and HAL

To mount a file system, you have to specify its device name. The interfaces to devices that may be attached to your system are provided by special files known as *device files*. The names of these device files are the device names. Device files are located in the **/dev** directories and usually have abbreviated names ending with the number of the device. For example, **fd0** may reference the first floppy drive attached to your system. The prefix **sd** references both Serial ATA (SATA) and SCSI hard drives, so **sda2** would reference the second partition on the first SATA or SCSI hard drive. In most cases, you can use the `man` command with a prefix to obtain more detailed information about this kind of device. For example, `man sd` displays the Man pages for SCSI devices. A complete listing of all device names can be found in the **devices** file located in the **linux/doc/device-list** directory at the **http://kernel.org** website. Table 15-6 lists several of the commonly used device names.

udev and HAL

Device files are no longer handled in a static way; they are now dynamically generated as needed instead. Previously a device file was created for each possible device, leading to a very large number of device files in the **/etc/dev** directory. Now, your system will detect only those devices it uses and create device files for those only, giving you a much smaller listing of device files. The tool used to detect and generate device files is udev, user devices. Each time your system is booted, udev will automatically detect your devices and generate device files for them in the **/etc/dev** directory. This means that the **/etc/dev** directory and its files are recreated each time you boot. It is a dynamic directory, no longer static. To manage these device files, you need to use udev configuration files located in the **/etc/udev** and **/lib/udev** directories. This means that udev is able to also dynamically manage all removable devices; udev will generate and configure devices files for removable devices as they are attached, and then remove these files when the devices are removed. In this sense, all devices are now considered hotplugged, with fixed devices simply being hotplugged devices that are never removed.

Note: Most new systems use only Serial ATA (SATA) hard drives and CD/DVD drives. These will have the prefix **sd** and **scd**. The older IDE drives with their **hd** prefix are rarely used now.

As **/etc/dev** is now dynamic, any changes you would make manually to the **/etc/dev** directory will be lost when you reboot. This includes the creation of any symbolic links such as **/dev/cdrom** that many software applications use. Instead, such symbolic links have to be configured using udev rules listed in configuration files located in the **/etc/udev/rules.d** and the

/lib/udev/rules.d directories. Default rules are already in place for symbolic links, but you can create rules of your own. See Chapter 17 for more details.

Device Name	Description
fd	Floppy disks
hd	IDE hard drives (rarely used on new systems)
ht	IDE tape drives
js	Analog joysticks
lp	Printer ports
midi	Midi ports
md	RAID devices
nst	SCSI tape drives, no rewind
pty	Pseudoterminals (used for remote logins)
rd/c*n***d***n*	The directory that holds RAID devices is **rd**; **c***n* is the RAID controller and **d***n* is the RAID disk
sd	Serial ATA (SATA) and SCSI hard drives, SATA drives are standard on new systems.
scd	Serial ATA and SCSI CD/DVD-ROM drives
st	SCSI tape drives
tty	Terminals
ttyS	Serial ports
cdrecorder	Links to your CD-R or CD-RW device file, set in **/etc/udev/rules.d**
cdrom	Links to your CD-ROM device file, set in **/etc/udev/rules.d**
floppy	Links to your floppy device file, **/etc/udev/rules.d**
modem	Links to your modem device file, set in **/etc/udev/rules.d**
scanner	Links to your scanner device file, **/etc/udev/rules.d**
tape	Links to your tape device file, set in **/etc/udev/rules.d**

Table 15-6: Device Name Prefixes

In addition to udev, information about removable devices like CD-ROMs and floppy disks, along with cameras and USB printers, used by applications like the desktop to dynamically interface with them, is managed by a separate utility called the Hardware Abstract Layer (HAL). HAL allows a removable device like a USB printer to be recognized no matter what particular connections it may be using. For example, you can attach a USB printer in one USB port at one time and then switch it to another later.

HAL has a key impact on the **/etc/fstab** file used to manage file systems. No longer are entries maintained in the **/etc/fstab** file for removable devices like your CD-ROMs. These devices are managed directly by HAL using its set of storage callouts like **hal-system-storage-mount** to mount a device or **hal-system-storage-eject** to remove one. In effect you now have to use the HAL device information files to manage your removable file systems. Should you want to bypass HAL and manually configure a CD-ROM device, you simply place an entry for it in the **/etc/fstab** file.

Floppy, USB, and Hard Disk Device Names

The device name for your floppy drive is **fd0**; it is located in the directory **/dev**. **/dev/fd0** references your floppy drive. If you have more than one floppy drive, additional drives are represented by **fd1**, **fd2**, and so on. USB drives are set up similarly, beginning with **usb1**, like **/dev/usb1**.

All hard drives (SCSI, SATA, and IDE) use the prefix **sd**. The prefix for a hard disk is followed by a letter that labels the hard drive and a number for the partition. For example, **sda2** references the second partition on the first hard drive, where the first hard drive is referenced with the letter **a**, as in **sda**. The device **sdb3** refers to the third partition on the second hard drive (**sdb**). On an SATA/IDE hard disk devices, Linux supports up to four primary hard disk partitions, numbered 1 through 4. You are allowed any number of logical partitions. You can use **df** to display your hard disk partitions, which will list their device names.

RAID devices use the prefix **md**. RAID devices numbered from 0, like floppy drives. Device **md0** references the first RAID device, and **md1** references the second.

Storage Identification: UUID

Though the device name of a hard disk is denoted with the **sd** prefix, it is often referenced by other IDs. These are listed in the **/dev/disk** directory in the subdirectories **by_id**, **by_ path**, and **by_uuid**.

> **by_id**   Identifies the disk by vendor, model, and serial number

> **by_path**   Identifies by the device interface, like PCI.

> **by_uuid**   Identifies by the hard disk's UUID

All the entries in these directories are symbolic links to the associated device names. A hard disk device UUID is actually a link to its device name, like **/dev/sda2**. Use the **ls** command with the **-l** option to see the links.

```
ls -l /dev/disk/by_uuid
```

Ubuntu uses a Universal Unique IDentifier (UUID) to reference a hard disk instead of its device name. Systems now support hotplugged hard disks like USB external drives whose device name could change, as drives are added and removed. The UUID will uniquely identify the drive, insuring it is always correctly referenced. In the /etc/fstab file, used to mount drives, hard disk partitions are always referenced using their UUID, not their device name.

For hard disks already connected to your system when your system was installed, a UUID was generated and listed in the **/dev/disk/by_uuid** directory. If you know the device name of your hard disk, you can find out the UUID by listing the contents of the /dev/disk/by_uuid directory with the ls -l command.

```
ls -l /dev/disk/by_uuid
```

For a particular device you can use the **vol_id** command with --uuid option and the device name.

```
sudo vol_id --uuid /dev/sda2
```

Once you know the UUID you can use it to mount the hard drive. Entries in the GRUB **menu.lst** file will use UUIDs for boot partitions, and entries in the **/etc/fstab** file will use UUIDs to automatically mount hard disk partitions.

You can also use UUIDs for other devices like LVM volumes. LVM volumes will have their own device directory and device name.

```
sudo vol_id --uuid /dev/mymedia/myvideo
```

If you create a new Linux partition, you should generate a UUID for it so that it can be mounted by UUID. Use the uuidgen command with the device name to generate a UUID for the partition. The **uuidgen** command outputs the UUID to the standard output. It does not place it on the disk. For that you use the **tune2fs** command with the **-U** option which adds the UUID. The **tune2fs -U** command takes as its arguments the UUID and the device name. In the following example, the UUID is generated by the **uuidgen** command (backquotes) and applied to the **/dev/sdd3** partition.

```
tune2fs -U `uuidgen /dev/sdd3`  /dev/sdd3
```

You can then use **vol_id --uuid** to display the UUID.

```
sudo vol_id --uuid /dev/sdd3
```

You also need to set the UUID as a symbolic link in the /dev/disk/by-uuid directory to the device name. The UUID is obtained by using a backquotes **vol_id --uuid** operation on the partition.

```
sudo ln -s  /dev/sdd3 /dev/disk/by-uuid/`vol_id -uuid /dev/sdd3`
```

Now you can use the new partition's UUID to reference it in mount operations.

UUIDs can be very complex and difficult to type. One option is to save the output of the vol_id -uuid operation to a file that you can then later edit to copy and paste the UUID to another file, like menu.lst or fstab.

```
sudo vol_id --uuid  /dev/sdd3 > sdd3uuid
```

Another faster option is to just open another terminal window, run the **vol_id --uuid** command with the device name, and then click and drag to select and copy the output UUID (Edit | Copy) from the terminal window to the file you are editing (like **/etc/fstab** edited in another terminal window with the **nano** editor, use the terminal window Edit | Paste entry).

DVD/CD-RW/ROM Devices

Most DVD/CD-RW/ROM devices are now either SATA or SCSI CD-ROM drives. They begin with prefix **scd** and are followed by a distinguishing number. For example, the name of a SATA/SCSI DVD/CD-RW drive could be **scd0** or **scd1**. The **scd** name is actually a link to the device file, usually **sr** for Serial ATA DVD/CD drives.

DVD/CD-RW/ROM devices are configured by HAL and managed by DeviceKit. HAL configures device information in the **storage.fdi** file in the policy configuration directory. To configure a DVD/CD-RW device, like adding user mount capability, you need to configure its entry in **storage.fdi** configuration file (see Chapter 17 for details). The actual task of listing and detecting the device is managed by DeviceKit. The GNOME Volume Manager uses DeviceKit, HAL, and udev to access removable media directly. Media are mounted by **gnome-mount**, a wrapper for accessing DeviceKit and udev, which performs the mount (**/etc/fstab** is no longer used).

Removable DVD/CD devices connected with a USB cable will have the device name of their USB connection.

Though now rarely in use, IDE DVD/CD-ROM devices are also supported. They have the old IDE prefix **hd**, and are identified by a following letter that distinguishes it from other IDE devices. For example, an IDE CD-ROM connected to your secondary IDE port may have the name **hdc**. An IDE CD-ROM connected as a slave to the secondary port may have the name **hdd**

Mounting File Systems

Attaching a file system on a storage device to your main directory tree is called *mounting* the device. The file system is mounted to an empty directory on the main directory tree. You can then change to that directory and access those files. If the directory does not yet exist, you have to create it. The directory in the file structure to which the new file system is attached is referred to as the *mountpoint*. For example, to access files on a CD-ROM, first you have to mount the CD-ROM.

Mounting fixed file systems like internal hard disks can normally be done only as the root user. This is a system administration task and should not usually be performed by a regular user. Removable media, though, like CD/DVD-ROMs and USB drives, are user mountable. Any user could mount a CD-ROM or USB drive.

When you install your Linux system and create the Linux partition on your hard drive, your system is automatically configured to mount your main file system whenever it starts. When your system shuts down, they are automatically unmounted. You have the option of unmounting any file system, removing it from the directory tree, and possibly replacing it with another, as is the case when you replace a CD-ROM.

Once a file system it actually mounted, an entry for it is made by the operating system in the **/etc/mstab** file. Here you will find listed all file systems currently mounted.

File System Information

The file systems on each storage device are formatted to take up a specified amount of space. For example, you may have formatted your hard drive partition to take up 3GB. Files installed or created on that file system take up part of the space, while the remainder is available for new files and directories.

Gnome System Monitor: File Systems tab

To find out how much space you have free on a file system, you can use the **df** command or, on the desktop, either the GNOME System Monitor, the Disk Usage Analyzer, or the KDE KDiskFree utility. KDiskFree displays a list of devices, showing how much space is free on each partition, and the percentage used.

For the GNOME System Monitor (System | Administration | System Monitor) , click the File Systems tab to display a list of the free space on your file systems (see Figure 15-1).   The

System Monitor will show the mount point (Directory), the file system type (Type), the amount of available space, and the amount of space used (Used) with a percentage graph.

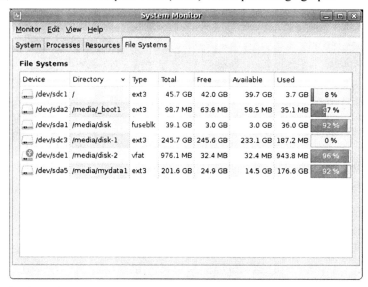

Figure 15-1: GNOME System Monitor, File Systems panel

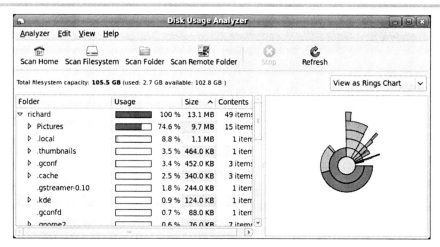

Figure 15-2: Disk Usage Analyzer, Applications | Accessories | Disk Usage Analyzer

Disk Usage Analyzer

The disk usage analyzer lets you see how much disk space is used and available on all your mounted hard disk partitions (see Figure 15-2). Applications | Accessories | Disk Usage Analyzer. It will also check all LVM and RAID arrays. Usage is shown in simple graph, letting you see how much overall space is available and where it is. You can scan your home directory (Scan Home), your entire file system (Scan Filesystem), a particular folder (Scan Folder), or a remote folder (Scan Remote Folder). When you scan a directory or the file system, disk usage for your directories is analyzed and displayed in the left pane along with a representational graph for the disk usage on the right pane. In the left listing, each files system is first shown with a graph for its usage, as well as its size and number of top-level directories and files. Then the directories are shown, along with their size and contents (files and directories).

On the right pane, the graph can be either a Ring Chart or a Treemap. The Ring Chart is the default. Choose the one you want from the View as drop down menu. For the Ring Chart, directories are show, starting with the top level directories at the center and moving out to the subdirectories. Passing your mouse over a section in the graph will display its directory name and disk usage, as well as all its subdirectories. The Treemap chart shows a box representation, with greater disk usage in larger boxes, and subdirectories encased within directory boxes.

df

The **df** command reports file system disk space usage. It lists all your file systems by their device names, how much disk space they take up, and the percentage of the disk space used, as well as where they are mounted. With the **-h** option, it displays information in a more readable format; such as measuring disk space in megabytes instead of memory blocks. The **df** command is also a safe way to obtain a listing of all your partitions, instead of using **fdisk** (because with **fdisk** you can erase partitions). **df** shows only mounted partitions, however, whereas **fdisk** shows all partitions.

```
$ df -h
Filesystem Size Used Avail Use% Mounted on
/dev/hda3   9.7G 2.8G 6.4G  31%   /
/dev/hda2   99M  6.3M 88M   7%    /boot
/dev/hda2   22G  36M  21G   1%    /home
/dev/hdc    525M 525M 0     100%  /media/disk
```

You can also use **df** to tell you to what file system a given directory belongs. Enter **df** with the directory name or **df** . for the current directory.

```
$ df .
Filesystem 1024-blocks Used Available Capacity Mounted on
/dev/hda3 297635 169499 112764 60% /
```

e2fsck and fsck

To check the consistency of the file system and repair it if it is damaged, you can use file system checking tools. **fsck** checks and repairs a Linux file system. **e2fsck** is designed to support **ext2** and **ext3** file systems, whereas the more generic **fsck** also works on any other file systems. The **ext2** and **ext3** file systems are the file systems normally used for Linux hard disk partitions and floppy disks. Linux file systems are normally **ext3**, which you use **e2fsck** to check. **fsck** and **e2fsck** take as their argument the device name of the hard disk partition that the file system uses.

```
fsck    device-name
```

Before you check a file system, be sure that the file system is unmounted. **e2fsck** should not be used on a mounted file system. To use **e2fsck**, enter e2fsck and the device name that references the file system. The **-p** option automatically repairs a file system without first requesting approval from the user for each repair task. The following examples check the disk in the floppy drive and the primary hard drive:

```
# e2fsck /dev/fd0
# e2fsck /dev/hda1
```

With **fsck**, the **-t** option lets you specify the type of file system to check, and the **-a** option automatically repairs systems, whereas the **-r** option first asks for confirmation. The **-A** option checks all systems in the **/etc/fstab** file.

Journaling

The **ext3** and ReiserFS file systems introduced journaling capabilities to Linux systems. Journaling provides for fast and effective recovery in case of disk crashes, instead of using **e2fsck** or **fsck**. With journaling, a log is kept of all file system actions, which are placed in a journal file. In the event of a crash, Linux only needs to read the journal file and replay it to restore the system to its previous (stable) state. Files that were in the process of writing to the disk can be restored to their original state. Journaling also avoids lengthy **fsck** checks on reboots that occur when your system suddenly loses power or freezes and has to be restarted physically. Instead of using **fsck** to manually check each file and directory, your system just reads its journal files to restore the file system.

Keeping a journal entails more work for a file system than a non-journal method. Though all journaling systems maintain a file system's directory structure (what is known as the *metadata*), they offer various levels of file data recovery. Maintaining file data recovery information can be time-consuming, slowing down the file system's response time. At the same time, journaling systems make more efficient use of the file system, providing a faster response time than the non-journal **ext2** file system.

There are other kind of journaling file systems you can use on Linux. These include ReiserFS, JFS, and XFS. ReiserFS, provides a completely reworked file system structure based on journaling (**namesys.com**). Most distributions also provide support for ReiserFS file systems. JFS is the IBM version of a journaling file system, designed for use on servers providing high throughput such as e-business enterprise servers (**http://jfs.sourceforge.net**). It is freely distributed under the GNU public license. XFS is another high-performance journaling system developed by Silicon Graphics (**http://oss.sgi.com/projects/xfs**). XFS is compatible with RAID and NFS file systems.

ext3 Journaling

Journaling is supported in the Linux kernel with **ext3**. The **ext3** file system is also fully compatible with the earlier **ext2** version it replaces. To create an **ext3** file system, you use the **mkfs.ext3** command. You can even upgrade **ext2** file systems to **ext3** versions automatically, with no loss of data or change in partitions. This upgrade just adds a journal file to an **ext2** file system and enables journaling on it, using the **tune2fs** command. Be sure to change the **ext2** file type to **ext3** in any corresponding **/etc/fstab** entries. The following example converts the **ext2** file system on **/dev/hda3** to an **ext3** file system by adding a journal file (**-j**).

```
tune2fs -j /dev/hda3
```

The **ext3** file system maintains full metadata recovery support (directory tree recovery), but it offers various levels of file data recovery. In effect, you are trading off less file data recovery for more speed. The **ext3** file system supports three options: **writeback**, **ordered**, and **journal**.

The default is **writeback**. The **writeback** option provides only metadata recovery, no file data recovery. The **ordered** option supports limited file data recovery, and the **journal** option provides for full file data recovery. Any files in the process of being changed during a crash will be recovered. To specify a ext3 option, use the **data** option in the **mount** command.

```
mount -t ext3 data=ordered /dev/sd1a  /mydata
```

ext4 file systems

The ext4 file system enhances the ext3 file system in terms of scalability and access methods. In includes the same journaling capabilities as ext3. The ext4 file system type is designed to handle very large files efficiently, supporting a much larger file size. Access methods now use extents instead of direct mapping, making access of large files much more efficient. Memory is allocated using Multiblock allocation with delayed allocation, making for faster writes and better fragmentation and performance. The ext3 file system, though, remains a very effective choice for systems managing many smaller files.

Some ext4 features are:

➤ Maximum file system size is now one Exabyte (1EiB)

➤ Maximum file size is 16 terabytes (16 TB)

➤ Unlimited subdirectories

➤ Increased performance for very large files

ReiserFS

Though journaling is often used to recover from disk crashes, a journal-based file system can do much more. The **ext3**, JFS, and XFS file systems only provide the logging operations used in recovery, whereas ReiserFS uses journaling techniques to completely rework file system operations. In ReiserFS, journaling is used to read and write data, abandoning the block structure used in traditional Unix and Linux systems. This gives it the capability to access a large number of small files very quickly, as well as use only the amount of disk space they need. However, efficiency is not that much better with larger files.

Btrfs

The **btrfs** file system is the next generation Linux file system, provided with Ubuntu 9.04 as a technology preview. It is still under heavy development. Like ext4, GRUB does not support booting from a btrfs file system. Install the **btrfs-tools** package to install the Btrfs file management commands like **mkfs.btrfs** for formatting and **btrfsck** for file system checking. To enable btrfs file system support use the boot option **icantbelieveitsnotbtr**.

Btrfs aims to provide support for both small and large files, as well as the very large file system structures used in data centers. For more information see:

```
http://btrfs.wiki.kernel.org/index.php/Main_Page
```

Mounting File Systems Automatically: /etc/fstab

File systems are mounted using the `mount` command. Although you can mount a file system directly with only a `mount` command, you can simplify the process by placing mount information in the **/etc/fstab** configuration file. Using entries in this file, you can have certain file systems automatically mounted whenever your system boots. For other file systems, you can specify configuration information, such as mount points and access permissions, which can be automatically used whenever you mount the file system. You needn't enter this information as arguments to a `mount` command as you otherwise must. For example, if you add a new hard disk partition to your Linux system, you can add mount information in the **/etc/fstab** file to have the partition automatically mounted on startup, and then unmounted when you shut down. Otherwise, you must mount and unmount the partition explicitly each time you boot up and shut down your system.

Both KDE and GNOME will also automatically mount any unmounted file system using their own file system detection and mount operations. On GNOME, the Gnome virtual file system (GVFS) will detect any unmounted and removable file systems and sue HAL and udev to mount them to the **/media** directory. Should you want a file system mounted to a different directory, you would have to place a mount entry for it in the **/etc/fstab** file, specifying that directory. LVM file systems have to be manually mounted with the **mount** command or **/etc/fstab** entries.

Automatic file system mounts with /etc/fstab

Though most file systems are automatically mounted for you, there may be instances where you need to have a file system mounted manually. Using the mount command you can do this directly, or you can specify the mount operation in the **/etc/fstab** file to have it mounted automatically. Ubuntu file systems are uniquely identified with their UUID (Universally Unique IDentifier). These are listed in the **/dev/disk/by-uuid** directory (or with the **sudo vol_id --uuid** command). In the **/etc/fstab** file, the file system partition device names are listed as a comment, and then followed by the actual file system mount operation using the UUID. The following example mounts the file system on partition **/dev/sdb2** to the **/media/mypics** directory as an **ext3** file system with default options (**defaults**).

```
# /dev/sdb2
UUID=b8c526db-cb60-43f6-b0a3-5c0054f6a64a   /media/mypics  ext3  defaults  0 2
```

As noted in the earlier section titled **Storage Identification: UUID**, you can open another terminal window, run the **vol_id --uuid** command with the device name, and then click and drag to select and copy the output UUID (Edit | Copy) from the terminal window to the file you are editing (like **/etc/fstab** edited in another terminal window with the GEdit editor, use the terminal window Edit | Paste entry). Once you have the UUID, add the mount point, file system type, and any options.

You can also identify your file system by giving it a label. You can use the **e2label** command to label an **ext2** or **ext3** file system (It is recommended though that you always use UUIDs to reference you hard drives). In the /etc/fstab file, you use the LABEL assignment to specify the lablel for the device.

```
LABEL=mydata2
```

In the following example, the Linux file system labeled **mydata2** is mounted to the **/mynewdata** directory as an **ext3** file system type.

```
LABEL=mydata2    /mynewdata        ext3        defaults            1 1
```

The label was created using the following command.

```
e2label   /dev/sdb3  mydata2
```

The sample **/etc/fstab** file is shown here.

/etc/fstab

```
# /etc/fstab: static file system information.
#
# <file system> <mount point>    <type>  <options>        <dump>  <pass>
proc            /proc            proc    defaults         0       0
# /dev/sda2
UUID=a179d6e6-b90c-4cc4-982d-a4cfcedea7df / ext3 defaults,errors=remount-ro 0 1
# /dev/sda1
UUID=48b96071-6284-4fe9-b364-503817cefb74  none  swap  sw      0 0
/dev/hdc        /media/cdrom0   udf,iso9660 user,noauto,exec   0 0
/dev/fd0        /media/floppy0  auto        rw,user,noauto,exec 0 0
# /dev/sdb2
UUID=b8c526db-cb60-43f6-b0a3-5c0054f6a64a /media/mypics  ext3 defaults 0 2
# /dev/sdb3
LABEL=mydata2    /mynewdata            ext3          defaults          1 1
```

Should you have to edit your **/etc/fstab** file, you can use the **gksu** command with the **gedit** editor on your desktop. In a terminal window (Applications | Accessories | Terminal) enter the following command. You will be first prompted to enter your password.

```
gksu gedit /etc/fstab
```

To mount manually, use the **mount** command and specify the type with the **-t ext3** option. Use the **-L** option to mount by label. List the file system first and then the directory name to which it will be mounted. For a NTFS partition you would use the type **ntfs**. The mount option has the format:

```
sudo mount -t type   file-system  directory
```

The following example mounts the file system with the label **newdata** to the **/mydata1** directory

```
sudo mount -t ext3 -L newdata   /mydata1
```

The next example used the UUID instead.

```
sudo mount -t ext3 -U 22dcf52f-0221-4d5a-acdd-e6e43561739d    /mydata1
```

Instead of typing out the UUID you could obtain it with **vol_id -uuid** in backquotes.

```
sudo mount -t ext3 -U `vol_id --uuid /dev/sdd3` /mydata1
```

HAL and fstab

To have Linux automatically mount the file system on your new hard disk partition, you need to add only its name to the **fstab** file, except in the case of removable devices like CD-ROMs and USB printers. Removable devices are managed by HAL, using the storage policy files located in **/usr/share/hal/fdi** and **/etc/hal/fdi** directories. The devices are automatically detected by the **haldaemon** service, and are managed directly by HAL using its set of storage callouts, such as **hal-system-storage-mount** to mount a device or **hal-system-storage-eject** to remove one. In effect you now have to use the HAL device information files to manage your removable file systems. If you want different options set for the device, you should create your own **storage-methods.fdi** file in the **30user** directory. The configuration is implemented using the XML language. Check the default storage file in **10osvendors/20-storage-methods.fdi** as well as samples in **/usr/share/doc/hal**version**/conf** directory. See Chapter 17 for examples of using HAL to set device options.

fstab Fields

An entry in an **fstab** file contains several fields, each separated from the next by a space or tab. These are described as the device, mountpoint, file system type, options, dump, and **fsck** fields, arranged in the sequence shown here:

```
<device> <mountpoint> <filesystemtype> <options> <dump> <fsck>
```

The first field is the name of the file system to be mounted. This entry can be either a device name, a device identifier (UUID), or a file system label. A label is specified by assigning the label name to the tag **LABEL**. For hard drives, the device identifier is used (UUID), normally a serial number. A device name usually begins with **/dev**, such as **/dev/sda3** for the third hard disk partition. Though you can use a device name, the method has become deprecated and no longer advisable. The next field is the directory in your file structure where you want the file system on this device to be attached. The third field is the type of file system being mounted. Table 15-7 provides a list of all the different types you can mount. The type for a standard Linux hard disk partition is **ext3**.

Type	Description
auto	Attempts to detect the file system type automatically
minux	Minux file systems (filenames are limited to 30 characters)
ext	Earlier version of Linux file system, no longer in use
ext4	New Linux file system format supporting long filenames and very large file sizes; includes journaling
ext3	Standard Linux file system supporting long filenames and large file sizes; includes journaling
ext2	Older standard Linux file system supporting long filenames and large file sizes; does not have journaling
xiaf	Xiaf file system
msdos	File system for MS-DOS partitions (16-bit)
vfat	File system for Windows 95, 98, and Millennium partitions (32-bit)
reiserfs	A ReiserFS journaling file system
xfs	A Silicon Graphics (SGI) file system
ntfs3g	Windows NT, XP Vista, and 2000 file systems with write capability, NTFS-3g

	project.
ntfs	Windows NT, XP, Vista, and 2000 file systems (affords read only access)
smbfs	Samba remote file systems, such as NFS
hpfs	File system for OS/2 high-performance partitions
nfs	NFS file system for mounting partitions from remote systems
nfs4	NFSv4 file system for mounting partitions from remote systems
umsdos	UMS-DOS file system
swap	Linux swap partition or swap file
sysv	Unix System V file systems
iso9660	File system for mounting CD-ROM
proc	Used by operating system for processes (kernel support file system)
sysfs	Used by operating system for devices (kernel support file system)
usbfs	Used by operating system for USB devices (kernel support file system)
devpts	Unix 98 Pseudo Terminals (ttys, kernel interface file system)
shmfs and **tmpfs**	Linux Virtual Memory, POSIX shared memory maintenance access (kernel interface file system)
adfs	Apple DOS file systems
affs	Amiga fast file systems
ramfs	RAM-based file systems
udf	Universal Disk Format used on CD/DVD-ROMs
ufs	Unix File System, found on Unix system (older format)

Table 15-7: File System Types

All file systems are uniquely identified with their UUID (Universally Unique IDentifier). These are listed in the **/dev/disk/by-uuid** directory (or with the **sudo vol_id --uuid** command). Ubuntu will use the UUID to identify any unlabeled file system. In the **/etc/fstab** file, the file system partition devices are listed as a comment, and then followed by the actual file system mount operation using the UUID.

If you did not installed using a Desktop CD (not the Alternate CD), then the system will be installed on a standard **ext3** partition. The next example shows an entry for the root system installed on a standard Linux hard disk partition (not LVM). This entry is mounted at the root directory, /, and has a file type of ext3. The device is referenced by a UUID identifier:

```
UUID=74fb43a1-0e77-47-8c4d-3ea63f87b4b    /    ext3    defaults    0    1
```

The following example shows a **LABEL** entry for the hard disk partition, where the label name is **mydata2**:

```
LABEL=mydata2    /mynewdata    ext3    defaults    0    1
```

LVM FIle Systems

If you installed on LVM partitions using the Ubuntu Alternate CD, your installation would use an LVM volume for the root partition.. A separate boot partitions will be set up that is not part of the LVM device. LVM devices cannot be used to boot a system. This is done from a regular **ext3** partition that is mounted to the **/boot** directory. The following example mounts the boot file system on partition identified as 81acc8a8-128a-4860-bae3-999bfee5e0f5 to the **/boot** directory as an **ext3** file system with default options (**defaults**).

```
UUID=81acc8a8-128a-4860-bae3-999bfee5e0f5     /boot   ext3   defaults   1  1
```

LVM file systems are already labeled. LVM file system device names are located in the **/dev** directory with a directory for the volume group and device names within that directory for each logical volume in that group. LVM volumes would be set up for your root and swap partitions, such as a LVM subdirectory in the **/dev** directory. As an example the LVM volume group **vg_richard8** would have an LVM directory **/dev/vg_richard8**. This directory would hold links for the root and swap volumes such as **lv_root** and **lv_swap**. These link to the actual device files in the **/dev/mapper** directory. The **lv_root** link references **/dev/mapper/vg-richard8-lv_root**. This is the reference used in the **/etc/fstab** file to mount the LVM root partition.

```
/dev/mapper/vg-richard8-lv_root      /          ext3      defaults      0   0
```

For any fresh installation (not an upgrade), Desktop or Alternate, any added LVM devices, like those used for additional storage, may have to be manually mounted. In this case, you would place an entry for the mount operation in the **/etc/fstab** file. The LVM device name is in the **/etc/fstab** file. In the following example, an LVM file system, **myvideo**, is mounted to the **/mymedia** directory. The logical volume **myvideo** is part of the logical group, **mymedia**, which is a directory it the **/dev** directory, **/dev/mymedia/myvideo**.

```
/dev/mymedia/myvideo            /mymedia   ext3     defaults     0  0
```

Instead of using the LVMs device name, you could use its UUID. Use the vol_id --uuid command to obtain the UUID and then copy and past it to the edited **fstab** file.

```
sudo vol_id --uuid /dev/mymedia/myvideo
```

The LVM volume could then be mounted with its UUID.

```
UUID=09db5d24-09db-458d-b193-aa8e6220d3de     /mymedia    ext3     defaults    0   0
```

Auto Mounts

The file system type for a floppy disk may differ depending on the disk you are trying to mount. For example, you may want to read a Windows-formatted floppy disk at one time and a Linux-formatted floppy disk at another time. For this reason, the file system type specified for the floppy device is **auto**. With this option, the type of file system formatted on the floppy disk is detected automatically, and the appropriate file system type is used.

```
/dev/fd0 /media/floppy auto  defaults,noauto  0 0
```

mount Options

The field after the file system type lists the different options for mounting the file system. The default set of options is specified by `defaults`, and specific options are listed next to each other separated by a comma (no spaces). The **defaults** option specifies that a device is read/write (**rw**), it is asynchronous (**async**), it is a block device (**dev**), that it cannot be mounted by ordinary users (**nouser**), and that programs can be executed on it (**exec**).

Removable devices like CD-ROMs and floppy disks are now managed by HAL, the Hardware Abstraction Layer. HAL uses its own configuration files to set the options for these devices. You can place your own entries in the **/etc/fstab** file for CD-ROMs to bypass HAL. This will, however, no longer let your CD-ROMs and DVD-ROMs be automatically detected.

Option	Description
async	Indicates that all I/O to the file system should be done asynchronously.
auto	Indicates that the file system can be mounted with the –a option. A mount –a command executed when the system boots, in effect, mounts file systems automatically.
defaults	Uses default options: rw, suid, dev, exec, auto, nouser, and async.
dev	Interprets character or block special devices on the file system.
group	Users that belong to the device's group can mount it
noauto	Indicates that the file system can only be mounted explicitly. The –a option does not cause the file system to be mounted.
exec	Permits execution of binaries.
owner	Allow user that is the owner of device to mount file system.
nouser	Forbids an ordinary (that is, nonroot) user to mount the file system.
fscontext	Provide SELinux security context to those file systems without one.
remount	Attempts to remount an already-mounted file system. This is commonly used to change the mount flags for a file system, especially to make a read-only file system writable.
ro	Mounts the file system as read-only.
rw	Mounts the file system as read/write.
suid	Allows set-user-identifier or set-group-identifier bits to take effect.
sync	Indicates that all I/O to the file system should be done synchronously.
user	Enables an ordinary user to mount the file system. Ordinary users always have the following options activated: noexec, nosuid, and nodev.
nodev	Does not interpret character or block special devices on the file system.
noexec	Does not allow execution of binaries on the mounted file systems.
nosuid	Does not allow set-user-identifier or set-group-identifier bits to take effect.

Table 15-8: Mount Options for File Systems

In a HAL configuration, a CD-ROM has **ro** and **noauto** options. **ro** specifies that the device is read-only, and **noauto** specifies it is not automatically mounted. The **noauto** option is used with both CD-ROMs and floppy drives, so they won't automatically mount, because you don't know if you have anything in them when you start up. At the same time, the HAL entries for both the CD-ROM and the floppy drive can specify where they are to be mounted when you decide to mount them. The users option allows any user to mount the system, useful for removable devices. The group option allows only users belonging to the device's group to mount it. The **fscontext** option is used by SELinux.

Boot and Disk Check

The last two fields of an **fstab** entry consist of integer values. The first one is used by the **dump** command to determine if a file system needs to be dumped, backing up the file system. The second value is used by **fsck** to see if a file system should be checked at reboot, and in what order with other file systems. If the field has a value of 1, it indicates a boot partition, and 2 indicates other partitions. The 0 value means **fsck** needn't check the file system.

Partition Labels: e2label

For **ext2** and **ext3** partitions, you can change or add a label with the **e2label** tool or **tune2fs** with the **-L** option. Specify the device and the label name. If you change a label, be sure to change corresponding entries in the **/etc/fstab** file. Just use **e2label** with the device name to find out what the current label is. In the next example, the user changes the label of the **/dev/hda3** device to **TURTLE**:

```
e2label /dev/hda3  TURTLE
```

Windows Partitions

Windows partitions attached to your system are automatically detected and mounted in the **/media** directory using the ntfs-3g drivers.

You can however manually mount Windows file systems if you wish. For Server systems you may have to do this. You can mount MS-DOS; Windows 95/98/Me onto your Linux file structure, just as you would mount any Linux file system. You have to specify the file type of **vfat** for Windows 95/98/Me and **msdos** for MS-DOS. Windows XP, Vista, NT, and 2000 use the **ntfs** file type. To have your manual mounts performed automatically, you need to add an entry for your Windows partitions in your **/etc/fstab** file and give it the **defaults** option or be sure to include an **auto** option. You make an entry for each Windows partition you want to mount and then specify the device name for that partition, followed by the directory in which you want to mount it. The next example shows a Windows 95/98/ME partition (**vfat**) entry for an **/etc/fstab** file. Notice the last entry in the **/etc/fstab** file example is an entry for mounting a Windows partition.

```
/dev/hda1 /mnt/windows vfat defaults 0 0
```

For Windows Vista, XP, NT, and 2000, you would specify the **ntfs** type. This file type is recognized by the **ntfs3g** kernel module which is automatically loaded. It detects all your NTFS drives.

```
/dev/sda2 /mnt/windows ntfs defaults 0 0
```

As with Linux partitions it is preferable that you use the partitions UUID. Use the **sudo vol_id --uuid** command to obtain the UUID for the Windows partition. Copy and paste from a terminal window or redirect to a file so you can read in the UUID to the **/etc/fstab** file when you edit it.

```
sudo vol_id --uuid  /dev/sda2 > mysda2uuid
cat mysda2uuid
   00203D81203D7EAA
```

You and then mount the Windows device with its uuid.

```
UUID=00203D81203D7EAA  /mnt/windows  ntfs   defaults  0  0
```

Mounting File Systems Manually: mount and umount

You can also mount or unmount any file system using the **mount** and **umount** commands directly (notice that **umount** lacks an *n*). The mount operations discussed in the preceding sections use the **mount** command to mount a file system. Normally, file systems can be mounted on hard disk partitions only by the root user, whereas CD-ROMs and floppy disks can be mounted by any user. Table 15-9 lists the different options for the **mount** command.

The mount Command

The **mount** command takes two arguments: the storage device through which Linux accesses the file system, and the mountpoint directory in the file structure to which the new file system is attached. The *mountpoint* is the directory on your main directory tree where you want the files on the storage device attached. The *device* is a special device file that connects your system to the hardware device. The syntax for the **mount** command is as follows:

```
mount device mountpoint
```

Mount Option	Description
-f	Fakes the mounting of a file system. Use it to check if a file system can be mounted.
-v	Verbose mode. mount displays descriptions of the actions it is taking. Use with -f to check for any problems mounting a file system, -fv.
-w	Mounts the file system with read/write permission.
-r	Mounts the file system with read-only permission.
-n	Mounts the file system without placing an entry for it in the **mstab** file.
-t type	Specifies the type of file system to be mounted. See Table 15-7 for valid file system types.
-a	Mounts all file systems listed in **/etc/fstab**.
-o option-list	Mounts the file system using a list of options. This is a comma-separated list of options following -o. See Table 15-8 for a list of the options.

Table 15-9: The mount Command options

As noted previously, device files are located in the **/dev** directories and usually have abbreviated names ending with the number of the device. For example, **fd0** may refer to the first floppy drive attached to your system. The following example mounts a hard disk in the first (**hdc2**) to the **/mystuff** directory. The mountpoint directory needs to be empty. If you already have a file system mounted there, you will receive a message that another file system is already mounted there and that the directory is busy. If you mount a file system to a directory that already has files and subdirectories in it, those will be bypassed, giving you access only to the files in the mounted file system. Unmounting the file system, of course, restores access to the original directory files. Mounting internal hard disk partitions requires administrative access, use the **sudo** command.

```
sudo mount /dev/hdc2 /mystuff
```

For any partition with an entry in the **/etc/fstab** file, you can mount the partition using only the mount directory specified in its `fstab` entry; you needn't enter the device filename. The `mount` command looks up the entry for the partition in the **fstab** file, using the directory to identify the entry and, in that way, find the device name. For example, to mount the **/dev/hdc2** partition in the preceding example, the `mount` command only needs to know the directory it is mounted to—in this case, **/mnt/mystuff**.

```
sudo mount /mnt/mystuff
```

If you are unsure about the type of file system that a disk holds, you can mount it specifying the `auto` file system type with the `-t` option. Given the **auto** file system type, `mount` attempts to detect the type of file system on the disk automatically. This is useful if you are manually mounting a floppy disk whose file system type you are unsure of (HAL also automatically detects the file system type of any removable media, including floppies).

```
mount -t auto /dev/fd0 /media/floppy
```

The umount Command

If you want to replace one mounted file system with another, you must first explicitly unmount the one already mounted. Say you have mounted a floppy disk, and now you want to take it out and insert a new one. You must unmount that floppy disk before you can insert and mount the new one. You unmount a file system with the `umount` command. The `umount` command can take as its argument either a device name or the directory where it was mounted. Here is the syntax:

```
umount device-or-mountpoint
```

The following example unmounts the floppy disk wherever it is mounted:

```
umount /dev/fd0
```

Using the example in which the device is mounted on the **/mydir** directory, you can use that directory to unmount the file system:

```
sudo umount /mydir
```

One important constraint applies to the `umount` command: you can never unmount a file system in which you are currently working. If you change to a directory within a file system that you then try to unmount, you receive an error message stating that the file system is busy. For example, suppose a CD-ROM is mounted on the **/media/disk** directory, and then you change to that **/media/disk** directory. If you decide to change CD-ROMs, you first have to unmount the current one with the `umount` command. This will fail because you are currently working in the directory in which it is mounted. You have to leave that directory before you can unmount the CD-ROM.

```
$ sudo mount /dev/hdc /media/disk
$ cd /media/disk
$ umount /media/disk
     umount: /dev/hdc: device is busy
$ cd /root
$ umount /media/disk
```

Tip: If other users are using a file system you are trying to unmount, you can use the `lsof` or `fuser` command to find out who they are.

Managing CD/DVD Discs, USB Drives, and Floppy disks

When you mount a CD/DVD disc, USB drive, or floppy disk, you cannot then simply remove it to insert another one in the drive. You first have to unmount it, detaching the file system from the overall directory tree. In fact, the CD/DVD drive remains locked until you unmount it. Once you unmount a CD/DVD disc, you can then take it out and put in another one, which you then must mount before you can access it. When changing several CD/DVD disc or floppy disks, you are continually mounting and unmounting them. For a CD-ROM, instead of using the `umount` command, you can use the `eject` command with the device name or mountpoint, which will unmount and then eject the CD-ROM from the drive.

To mount a CD/DVD disc, USB drive, or floppy disk, all you have to do is insert it into the drive. HAL will detect it and mount it automatically in the **/media/disk** directory.

If, instead, you want to manually mount the drive from the command line with the `mount` command, you will have to first decide on a directory to mount it to (create it if it does not exist). The **/media/disk** directory is created dynamically when a disk is inserted and deleted when the disk is removed. To manually mount a disk, use the `mount` command, the device name, like **/dev/cdrom**, and the directory it is mounted to.

```
# mount /dev/cdrom   /media/cdrom1
```

If you want to manually unmount the drive, say from the command line, you can use the `unmount` command and the name of the directory it is mounted on.

```
# umount /media/cdrom1
```

Or if mounted by HAL, you could use

```
# umount /media/disk
```

When you burn a CD, you may need to create a CD image file. You can access such an image file from your hard drive, mounting it as if it were another file system (even ripped images could be mounted in this way). For this, you use the `loop` option, specifying an open loop device such as **/dev/loop0**. If no loop device is indicated, `mount` will try to find a open one. The file system type is `iso9660`, a CD-ROM ISO image file type.

```
# mount -t iso9660 -o loop=/dev/loop0 image-file mount-directory
```

To mount the image file **mymusic.cdimage** to the **/mnt/mystuff** directory and make it read-only, you would use

```
# mount -t iso9660 -o ro,loop=/dev/loop0 mymusic.cdimage /mnt/mystuff
```

Once the image file is mounted, you can access files on the CD-ROM as you would in any directory.

Tip: You use `mkisofs` to create a CD-ROM image made up from your files or another CD-ROM.

Mounting Hard Drive Partitions: Linux and Windows

You can mount either Linux or Windows hard drive partitions with the `mount` command. However, it is much more practical to have them mounted automatically using the **/etc/fstab** file as described previously. The Linux hard disk partitions you created during installation are already automatically mounted for you. As noted previously, to mount a Linux hard disk partition, enter the `mount` command with the device name of the partition and the directory to which you want to mount it. IDE hard drives use the prefix **hd**, and SCSI hard drives use the prefix **sd**. The next example mounts the Linux hard disk partition on **/dev/hda4** to the directory **/mnt/mydata**.

```
# mount -t ext3 /dev/hda4 /mnt/mydata
```

Mounting DVD/CD disk Images

Mounting a DVD/CD disc image is also performed with the mount command, but requires the use of a loop device. You can use the `loop` option, specifying an open loop device such as **/dev/loop0**. If no loop device is indicated, `mount` will try to find a open one. The file system type is `iso9660`, a CD-ROM ISO image file type.

```
mount -t iso9660 -o loop=/dev/loop0 image-file mount-directory
```

In the following example, the **mydoc.iso** is mounted to the **/media/cdrom** directory as a file system of type `iso9660`. Be sure to unmount it when you finish. The image can be mounted to an empty directory on your system.

```
mount -t iso9660 -o ro,loop=/dev/loop0 mydocuments.iso /media/mycdrom
```

Creating File Systems: mkfs, mke2fs, mkswap, parted, and fdisk

Linux provides a variety of tools for creating and managing file systems, letting you add new hard disk partitions, create CD images, and format floppies. To use a new hard drive, you will first have to partition it and then create a file system on it. You can use either `parted` or `fdisk` to partition your hard drive. It may be easier and safer, though, to use the GUI front ends for parted, GParted and QTParted. Both provide clear graphics and an easy to use interface for managing, creating, and removing file systems.

To create the file system on the partitions, you can use the `mkfs` command in a terminal window, which is a front end for various file system builders. For swap partitions, you use a special tool, `mkswap`, and to create file systems on a CD-ROM, you use the `mkisofs` tool. Linux partition and file system tools are listed in Table 15-10.

Tool	Description
fdisk	Menu-driven program that creates and deletes partitions.
cfdisk	Screen-based interface for fdisk.
parted	Manages GNU partition.
QTParted	KDE GUI interface for Parted, partitioning and file system creation.
GParted	GNOME GUI interface for Parted, partitioning and file system creation.
mkfs	Creates a file system on a partition or floppy disk using the specified file system type. Front end to formatting utilities.
mke2fs	Creates an **ext2** file system on a Linux partition; use the -j option to create an **ext3** file system.
mkfs.ext3	Creates an **ext3** file system on a Linux partition.
mkfs.ext2	Creates an **ext2** file system on a Linux partition.
mkfs.reiserfs	Creates a ReiserFS journaling file system on a Linux partition (links to mkreiserfs).
mkfs.bfs	Creates a SCO bfs file system on a Linux partition.
mkfs.msdos	Creates a DOS file system on a given partition.
mkfs.vfat	Creates a Windows 16-bit file system on a given partition (Windows 95/98/Me).
mkfs.cramfs	Creates a CRAMFS compressed flash memory file system, read-only (used for embedded devices).
mkswap	Sets up a Linux swap area on a device or in a file.
mkdosfs	Creates an MS-DOS file system under Linux.
mkisofs	Creates an ISO CD-ROM disk image.
dumpe2fs	Displays lower-level block information for a file system.
resize2fs	Extends the size of a partition, using unused space currently available on a disk.
hdparm	IDE hard disk tuner, sets IDE hard disk features.
tune2fs	Tunes a file system, setting features such as the label, journaling, and reserved block space.

Table 15-10: Linux Partition and File System Creation Tools

Parted and GParted

Most users will use the **parted** (**http://gnu.org/software/parted**) to manage hard disk partitions, create new ones, and delete old ones. Unlike **fdisk**, Parted also lets you resize partitions. To use **parted** on the partitions in a given hard drive, none of the partitions on that drive can be in use. This means that if you want to use **parted** on partitions located on that same hard drive as your kernel, you have to boot your system in rescue mode and choose not to mount your system files. For any other hard drives, you only need to unmount their partitions and turn your swap space off with the **swapoff** command.

Note: QTParted works in much the same way as GParted. You will need to have
       supporting KDE libraries installed. A left sidebar shows available disks. It also
       uses a graphical display and expandable tree for partitions. See
       http://qtparted.sourceforge.net for more information.

GParted, The GNOME Partition Editor

Parted can be used in its original command line interface from a terminal window, or with
a desktop interface like GNOME's GParted or KDE's QTParted. Most users will prefer the
GNOME GParted (GNOME Partition Editor) interface which provides an easy to use graphical
display for all your partitions (see Figure 15-3). GParted is part of the main Ubuntu repository, and
accessible as System | Administration | GParted. GParted can create most file system partitions,
including Linux ext3 and reiserfs, as well as Windows NTFS and vfat, and MAC hfs. GParted
makes use of supporting software like e2fsprogs for ext3 partitions and ntfsprogs for NTFS
partitions, both installed with the desktop disc. See **http://gparted.sourceforge.net** for more
information. Keep in mind that both GParted and QTParted, though proven reliable, are still under
development. The command line tools such as parted and fdisk remain the primary partition tools.

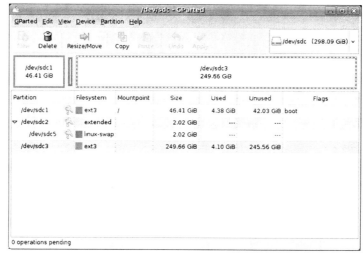

Figure 15-3: GParted

A graphical display shows the partitions on a selected hard disk, showing you the partition
labels and device names, as well as the proportional size of each. You use a drop-down menu in the
top upper-right to select a particular disk on your system. The disk will be identified with its
device name, like **/dev/sda**, and its size. The lower part of the GParted window shows the hard
disk partitions for the selected drives in an expandable tree. Each partition's file system,
mountpoint, and size are shown. The amount of space used and any flags like whether the disk is
bootable, are also displayed. From the View menu you can choose to display information about the
selected device, and list the tasks to be applied.

You can create, resize, format, and delete partitions. Free space will be listed as
unallocated space. Mounted partitions show a lock icon on their entries. If you want to perform

any action on those partitions, you have to first unmount them. Right-click on the partition entry and choose Unmount from the pop-up menu.

To create a partition click on the New button. This will open a Create new partition window where you can specify the partitions size, whether it is primary or extended, and its file system type.

To perform any operations on partitions, right-click the partition entry to display a pop-up menu where you can choose these tasks. You can also select the entry and then choose a task form the Partition menu. The Format entry expands to another sub menu listing all the supported file system types, like ntfs or ext3. Deleting a partition will remove it permanently (Delete button), losing all data. You can resize a partition to a larger size if there is space available on either side. A partition can be reduced if there is unused space within the partition. A resize window shows the new space open to either side and lets you change size from either end.

You can also all disk labels and add flags. To change a disk label, select Set DiskLabel from the Device menu. A disk label names the partition, allowing your system to reference it by its label name instead of using its device name. This is helpful for removable devices whose device name may change, but labels will not. The flags indicate partition use like boot for bootable partition, **lvm** for one that supports an lvm file system and **raid** for a member of a raid array.

Once you have finished making changes, click the Apply button to have those changes take effect. Nothing will have actually changed until you click the Apply button.

The parted command

Alternatively you can use the parted command in a Terminal window to manage partitions. You can then start Parted with the **parted** command and the device name of the hard disk you want to work on. Alternatively you can use GParted on GNOME or QTParted on KDE. The following example starts **parted** for the hard disk **/dev/hda**.

```
parted  /dev/hda
```

Use the **print** command to list all your partitions. The partition number for each partition will be listed in the first column under the Minor heading. The Start and End columns list the beginning and end positions that the partition uses on the hard drive. The numbers are in megabytes, starting from the first megabyte to the total available. To create a new partition, use the **mkpart** command with either **primary** or **extended**, the file system type, and the beginning and end positions. You can create up to three primary partitions and one extended partition (or four primary partitions if there is no extended partition). The extended partition can, in turn, have several logical partitions. Once you have created the partition, you can later use **mkfs** to format it with a file system. To remove a partition, use the **rm** command and the partition number. To resize a partition, use the **resize** command with the partition number and the beginning and end positions. You can even move a partition using the **move** command. The **help** command lists all commands.

fdisk

To start **fdisk**, enter **fdisk** on the command line with the device name of the hard disk you are partitioning. This brings up an interactive program you can use to create your Linux partition. Be careful using Linux **fdisk**. It can literally erase entire hard disk partitions and all the data on those partitions if you are not careful. The following command invokes **fdisk** for creating partitions on the **hdb** hard drive.

```
fdisk   /dev/hdb
```

Command	Action
a	Toggle a bootable flag
l	List known partition types
m	List commands
n	Add a new partition
p	Print the partition table
q	Quit without saving changes
t	Change a partition's system ID
w	Write table to disk and exit

Table 15-11: Commonly Used fdisk Commands

The partitions have different types that you need to specify. Linux **fdisk** is a line-oriented program. It has a set of one-character commands that you simply press on the keyboard. You may then be prompted to type in certain information and press ENTER. If you run into trouble during the **fdisk** procedure, you can press Q at any time, and you will return to the previous screen without any changes having been made. No changes are actually made to your hard disk until you press W. This should be your very last command; it makes the actual changes to your hard disk and then quits **fdisk**, returning you to the installation program. Table 15-11 lists the commonly used **fdisk** commands.

Perform the following steps to create a Linux partition.

➢ Press N to define a new partition; you will be asked if it is a primary partition.

➢ Press P to indicate that it is a primary partition. Linux supports up to four primary partitions.

➢ Enter the partition number for the partition you are creating and enter the beginning cylinder for the partition (this is the first number in parentheses at the end of the prompt).

➢ You are then prompted to enter the last cylinder number. You can either enter the last cylinder you want for this partition or enter a size. For example, you can enter the size as **+1000M** for 1GB, preceding the amount with a + sign. Bear in mind that the size cannot exceed your free space.

➢ You then specify the partition type. The default type for a Linux partition is 83. If you are creating a different type of partition, such as a swap partition, press T to indicate that this is the type you want.

➢ Enter the partition number, such as 82 for a swap partition.

➢ When you are finished, press W to write out the changes to the hard disk, and then press ENTER to continue.

mkfs

Once you create your partition, you have to create a file system on it. To do this, use the `mkfs` command to build the Linux file system and pass the name of the hard disk partition as a parameter. You must specify its full pathname with the `mkfs` command. Table 15-12 lists the options for the `mkfs` command. For example, the second partition on the first hard drive has the device name **/dev/hdb1**. You can now mount your new hard disk partition, attaching it to your file structure. The next example formats that partition:

```
# mkfs -t ext3 /dev/hdb1
```

The `mkfs` command is really just a front end for several different file system builders. A *file system builder* performs the actual task of creating a file system. Linux supports various file system builders, including several journaling file systems and Windows file systems. The name of a file system builder has the prefix `mkfs` and a suffix for the name of the type of file system. For example, the file system builder for the **ext3** file system is `mkfs.ext3`. For ReiserFS file systems, it is `mkfs.reiserfs` (link to **mkreiserfs** which is part of reiser-utils package). For Windows 16-bit file systems (95/98/Me), it is `mkfs.vfat`.

Some of these file builders are just other names for traditional file system creation tools. For example, the `mkfs.ext2` file builder it just another name for the **mke2fs** ext2 file system creation tool, and `mkfs.msdos` is the **mkdosfs** command. As **ext3** is an extension of **ext2**, the command `mkfs.ext3` simply invokes **mke2fs**, the tool for creating **ext2** and **ext3** file systems, and directs it to create an **ext3** file system (using the `-j` option). Any of the file builders can be used directly to create a file system of that type. Options are listed before the device name. The next example is equivalent to the preceding one, creating an **ext3** file system on the **sdb1** device:

```
mkfs.ext3 /dev/sdb1
```

Option	Description
Blocks	Specifies number of blocks for the file system. There are 1440 blocks for a 1.44MB floppy disk.
`-t` *file-system-type*	Specifies the type of file system to format. The default is the standard Linux file system type, **ext3**.
file-system-options	Options for the type of file system specified. Listed before the device name, but after the file system type.
`-V`	Verbose mode. Displays description of each action `mkfs` takes.
`-v`	Instructs the file system builder program that `mkfs` invokes to show actions it takes.
`-c`	Checks a partition for bad blocks before formatting it (may take some time).
`-l` *filename*	Reads a list of bad blocks.

Table 15-12: The mkfs Options

The syntax for the `mkfs` command is as follows. You can add options for a particular file system after the type and before the device. The block size is used for file builders that do not detect the disk size.

```
mkfs options [-t type] file-sysoptions device size
```

Tip: Once you have formatted your disk, you can label it with the **e2label** command.

The same procedure works for floppy disks. In this case, the **mkfs** command takes as its argument the device name. It uses the **ext2** file system (the default for **mkfs**), because a floppy is too small to support a journaling file system.

```
# mkfs /dev/fd0
```

mkswap

If you want to create a swap partition, you first use **fdisk** or **parted** to create the partition, if it does not already exist, and then you use the **mkswap** command to format it as a swap partition. **mkswap** formats the entire partition unless otherwise instructed. It takes as its argument the device name for the swap partition.

```
mkswap /dev/sdb2
```

You then need to create an entry for it in the **/etc/fstab** file so that it will be automatically mounted when your system boots.

CD-ROM and DVD ROM Recording

Recording data to DVD/CD discs on Linux is now handled directly by the GNOME and KDE desktops. Simple drag and drop operations on an blank DVD/CD disc lets you burn the disc. You can also use GNOME and KDE CD recording applications such as Brasero on GNOME and KOnCD to create your DVD/CDs easily. All are front ends to the **mkisofs** and **cdrecord** tool. s To record DVDs on DVD writers, you can use **cdrecord** for DVD-R/RW drives and the DVD+RW tools for DVD+RW/R drives. If you want to record CD-ROMs on a DVD writer, you can just use **cdrecord**. application with many options. .

The **cdrecord** application currently works only on DVD-R/RW drives; it is part of the dvdrtools package. If you want to use DVD+RW/R drives, use the DVD+RW tools such as **growisofs** and **dvd+rw-format**. Some DVD+RW tools are included in the dvd+rw-tools package. Check the DVD+RW tools website for more information, **http://fy.chalmers.se/~appro/linux/DVD+RW.**

With the **mkisofs** command, you can create a CD image file, which you can then write to a CD-R/RW write device. Once you create your CD image file, you can write it to a CD-write device, using the **cdrecord** or **cdwrite** application.

mkisofs

To create a CD image, you first select the files you want on your CD. Then you can use **mkisofs** to create an ISO CD image of them.

You may need to include several important options with **mkisofs** to create a data CD properly. The **-o** option is used to specify the name of the CD image file. This can be any name you want to give it. The **-R** option specifies RockRidge CD protocols, and the **-J** option provides for long Windows 95/98/ME or XP names. The **-r** option, in addition to the RockRidge protocols (**-R**), sets standard global permissions for your files, such as read access for all users and no write access because the CD-ROM is read-only. The **-T** option creates translation tables for filenames for use on systems that are not RockRidge compliant. The **-U** option provides for relaxed filenames that are not standard ISO compliant, such as long filenames, those with more than one period in their name, those that begin with a period such as shell configuration files, and ones that use lowercase characters (there are also separate options for each of these features if you just want to use a few of them). Most RPM and source code package names fall in this category. The **-iso-level** option lets you remove ISO restrictions such as the length of a filename. The **-V** option sets the volume label (name) for the CD. Finally, the **-v** option displays the progress of the image creation.

The last argument is the directory that contains the files for which you want to make the CD image. For this, you can specify a directory. For example, if you are creating a CD-ROM to contain the data files in the **mydocs** directory, you would specify that directory. This top directory will not be included, just the files and subdirectories in it. You can also change to that directory and then use **.** to indicate the current directory.

If you were creating a simple CD to use on Linux, you would use **mkisofs** to first create the CD image. Here the verbose option will show the creation progress, and the **-V** option lets you specify the CD label. A CD image called **songs.iso** is created using the file located in the **newsong** directory:

```
mkisofs -v -V "Goodsongs" -o moresongs.iso  newsongs
```

If you also wanted to use the CD on a Windows system, you would add the **-r** (RockRidge with standard global file access) and **-J** (Joliet) options:

```
mkisofs -v -r -J -V "Goodsongs" -o moresongs.iso  newsongs
```

You need to include certain options if you are using filenames that are not ISO compliant, such as ones with more than 31 characters or ones that use lowercase characters. The **-U** option lets you use completely unrestricted filenames, whereas certain options like **-L** for the unrestricted length will release specific restrictions only. The following example creates a CD image called **mydoc.iso** using the files and subdirectories located in the **mdoc** directory and labels the CD image with the name "Greatdocs":

```
mkisofs -v -r -T -J -U -V "Greatdocs" -o mydocuments.iso   mydocs
```

Mounting Disk Images

Once you have created your CD image, you can check to see if it is correct by mounting it as a file system on your Linux system. In effect, to test the CD image, you mount it to a directory and then access it as if it were simply another file system.

On GNOME you can use the Archive Mounter. Right-click on the disk image file and select the Archive Mounter. The image will be mounted and accessible as a file system.

To manually mount using the **mount** command, requires the use of a loop device. Specify the loop device with the **loop** option as shown in the next example. Here the **mydoc.iso** is mounted to the **/media/cdrom** directory as a file system of type **iso9660**. Be sure to unmount it when you finish.

```
mount -t iso9660 -o ro,loop=/dev/loop0 mydocuments.iso /media/cdrom
```

Bootable CD-ROMs

If you are creating a bootable CD-ROM, you need to indicate the boot image file to use and the boot catalog. With the **-c** option, you specify the boot catalog. With the **-b** option, you specify the boot image. The *boot image* is a boot disk image, like that used to start up an installation procedure. For example, on the Ubuntu CD-ROM, the boot image is **isolinux/isolinux.bin**, and the boot catalog is **isolinux/boot.cat** (you can also use **images/boot.img**. and **boot.cat**). Copy those files to your hard disk. The following example creates a bootable CD-ROM image using Ubuntu distribution files located on the DVD/CD-ROM drive.

```
mkisofs -o Ubuntu9.iso -b isolinux/isolinux.bin -c isolinux/boot.cat \
  -no-emul-boot -boot-load-size 4 -boot-info-table \
 -v -r -R -T -J -V "Ubuntu9"  /media/cdrom
```

cdrecord

Once **mkisofs** has created the CD image file, you can use Nautilus (the GNOME file manager) to directly burn an ISO image to a CD/DVD write disk. On the command line interface, you could, instead, use **cdrecord** to write it to a CD/DVD write disc. There is a command called **dvdrcecord**, but this is just a script that calls **cdrecord**, which now writes to both DVD and CD media. If you have more than one CD-writer device, you should specify the DVD/CD-R/RW drive to use by indicating its device name. In this example, the device is an IDE CD-R located at **/dev/sdc**. The **dev=** option is used to indicate this drive. The final argument for **cdrecord** is the name of the CD image file.

```
cdrecord  dev=/dev/sdc  mydocuments.iso
```

In this example, a SCSI rewritable CD-RW device with the device **/dev/scd0** is used.

```
cdrecord  dev=/dev/scd0  mydocuments.iso
```

If you are creating an audio CD, use the **-audio** option, as shown here. This option uses the CD-DA audio format:

```
cdrecord  dev=/dev/sdc -audio moresongs.iso
```

Tip: The **dummy** option for **cdrecord** lets you test the CD writing operation for a given image.

dvd+rw Tools

The primary dvd+rw tool is **growisofs**, with which you create DVD+RW/R disks. Two other minor supporting tools are also included, a formatter, dvd+rw-format, and a compatibility tool, dvd+rw-booktype. See the dvd+rw-tools page in **/usr/share/doc** for detailed instructions.

The **growisofs** tool functions like the **mkisofs** tool, except that it writes directly to the DVD+RW/R disc, rather than to an image. It has the same options as **mkisofs**, with a few exceptions, and is actually a front end to the **mkisofs** command. There is, of course, no **-o** option for specifying a disk image. You specify the DVD device instead. For example, to write the contents of the **newsongs** directory to a DVD+RW disc, you would use **growisofs** directly.

```
rowisofs -v -V "Goodsongs" -Z /dev/sdc  newsongs
```

The device is specified by its name, usually **/dev/scd0** for the first SCSII device or **/dev/sdc** for the first secondary IDE drive. Recall that IDE DVD writers are configured as SCSI devices when your system boots up. `growisofs` provides a special **-z** option for burning an initial session. For multi-sessions (DVD-RW), you can use the `mkisofs` **-M** option. If you want to reuse a DVD-RW disc, just overwrite it. You do not have to reformat it.

To burn an ISO image file to the disc, use the **-z** option and assign the ISO image to the device.

```
growisofs -v -V "Goodsongs" -Z /dev/sdc=moresongs.iso
```

Though `growisofs` will automatically format new DVD+RW discs, the dvd+rw tools also include the dvd+rw-format tool for explicitly performing formats only. You use dvd+rw-format tool only to explicitly format new DVD+RW (read/write) discs, preparing them for writing. This is done only once, and only for DVD+RW discs that have never been used before. DVD+R discs do not need any formatting.

The dvd+rw-booktype tool sets the compatibility setting for older DVD-ROM readers that may not be able to read DVD+RW/R discs.

Mono and .NET Support

With Mono, Linux now provides .NET support, along with .NET applications like the Beagle desktop search tool and the F-Spot photo management tool. Mono provides an open source development environment for .NET applications. The Mono project is an open source project supported by Novell that implements the .NET framework on Unix, Linux, and OS X systems. Currently Mono 1.2 and 2.0 are offered. .1.2 corresponds generally with .NET 1.1 features, and 2.0 with .NET 2.0. See **http://mono-project.com** for detailed information.

Mono is implemented on Linux using several components. These include the basic Mono .NET application, including Mono tools like the Mono certification manager (**certmgr**), the Global Assemblies Cache Manager tool (**gacutil**) for making assemblies available at runtime, and mcs, the Mono C# compiler. There are several additional tools for distinct features like visual basic support, SQL database queries, and .NET Web support. The Mono language testing tool, NUnit, is also included.

Configuration is found in the **/etc/mono/config** file, which is an XML-like file that maps dynamic link library (DLL) references to Linux libraries. The **/etc/mono** file also contains configuration files for 1.0 and 2.0 versions of Mono. Mono is installed in **/usr/lib/mono**. In the corresponding 1.0 and 2.0 directories you will find the DLL and EXE .NET support assemblies for different Mono applications. Other directories will hold .NET DLLs and configuration for several applications and services, including Evolution, D-Bus, and GTK.

Local configuration information and runtime applications are placed in the user's **.config** directory.

16. LVM and RAID

Logical Volume Manager

Creating LVMs during Installation

system-config-lvm

LVM Tools: using the LVM commands

Using LVM to replace drives

LVM Example for multiple hard drives

Configuring RAID Devices

Motherboard RAID Support: dmraid

Linux Software RAID Levels

RAID Devices and Partitions: md and fd

RAID Administration: mdadm

Creating and Installing RAID Devices

With onset of cheap, efficient, and very large hard drives, even simple home systems may employ several hard drives. The use of multiple hard drives opens up opportunities for ensuring storage reliability as well as more easily organizing access to your hard disks. Linux provides two methods for better managing your hard disks: Logical Volume Management (LVM) and Redundant Arrays of Independent Disks (RAID). LVM is a method for organizing all your hard disks into logical volumes, letting you pool the storage capabilities of several hard disks into a single logical volume. Your system then sees one large storage device, and you do not have to micromanage each underlying hard disk and its partitions. LVM is perhaps the most effective way to add hard drives to your system, creating a large accessible pool of storage. RAID is a way of storing the same data in different places on multiple hard disks. These multiple hard drives are treated as a single hard drive. They include recovery information that allows you to restore your files should one of the drives fail. The two can be mixed, implementing LVM volumes on RAID arrays. LVM provides flexibility, and RAID can provide data protection.

With LVM you no longer have to keep track of separate disks and their partitions, trying to remember where files are stored on what partitions located in what drive. Partitions and their drives are combined into logical file systems that you can attach to your system directory tree. You can have several logical file systems, each with their own drives and/or partitions.

In a system with several hard drives with both LVM and RAID you can combine the hard drives into one logical file system that accesses the storage as one large pool. Files are stored in a single directory structure, not on directories on a particular partition. Instead of mounting file systems for each individual hard drive, there is only one file system to mount for all the hard drives. LVM has the added advantage of letting you implement several logical file systems on different partitions across several hard drives.

RAID is best suited to desktops and servers that hold multiple hard drives and require data recovery. The most favored form of RAID, RAID 5, requires a minimum of three hard drives. RAID, with the exception of RAID 0, provides the best protection against hard drive failure and is considered a necessity for storage-intensive tasks such as enterprise, database, and Internet server operations. It can also provide peace of mind for smaller operations, providing recovery from hard disk failure. Keep in mind that there are different forms of RAID, each with advantages and weaknesses. RAID 0 provides no recovery capabilities at all. After setting up a RAID array, you can implement LVM volumes on the array.

In comparison to LVM, RAID can provide faster access for applications that work with very large files, such as multimedia, database, or graphics applications. But for normal operations, LVM is just as efficient as RAID. LVM, though, requires running your Linux system and configuring it from your Linux operating system. RAID, which is now supported at the hardware level on most computers, is easier to set up, especially a simple RAID 0 operation that merely combines hard drives into one drive.

Logical Volume Manager (LVM)

For easier hard disk storage management, you can set up your system to use the Logical Volume Manager (LVM), creating LVM partitions that are organized into logical volumes to which free space is automatically allocated. Logical volumes provide a more flexible and powerful way of dealing with disk storage, organizing physical partitions into logical volumes in which you can easily manage disk space. Disk storage for a logical volume is treated as one pool of memory, though the volume may in fact contain several hard disk partitions spread across different hard disks. Adding a new LVM partition merely increases the pool of storage accessible to the entire system. The original LVM package was developed for kernel 2.4. The current LVM2 package is used for kernel 2.6. Check the LVM HOWTO at **http://tldp.org** for detailed examples.

Note: On Ubuntu, you can use Red Hat's **system-config-lvm** tool to manage your LVM devices with a simple GUI interface, but be careful if you have Windows partitions or RAID devices.

LVM Structure

In an LVM structure, LVM physical partitions, also known as *extents,* are organized into logical groups, which are in turn used by logical volumes. In effect, you are dealing with three different levels of organization. At the lowest level, you have physical volumes. These are physical hard disk partitions that you create with partition creation tools such as **parted** or **fdisk**. The partition type will be a Linux LVM partition, code **8e**. These physical volumes are organized into logical groups, known as volume groups that operate much like logical hard disks. You assign collections of physical volumes to different logical groups.

Once you have your logical groups, you can then create logical volumes. Logical volumes function much like hard disk partitions on a standard setup. For example, on the **turtle** group volume, you could create a **/var** logical volume, and on the **rabbit** logical group, you could create **/home** and **/projects** logical volumes. You can have several logical volumes on one logical group, just as you can have several partitions on one hard disk.

You treat the logical volumes as you would any ordinary hard disk partition. You create a file system on one with the **mkfs** command, and then you can mount the file system to use it with the **mount** command. The Linux file system type could be **ext3**.

Storage on logical volumes is managed using what are known as extents. A logical group defines a standard size for an extent, say 4MB, and then divides each physical volume in its group into extents of that size. Logical volumes are, in turn, divided into extents of the same size, which are then mapped to the physical volumes.

Logical volumes can be linear, striped, or mirrored. The mirror option will create a mirror copy of a logical volume, providing a restore capability. The striped option lets you automatically distribute your logical volume across several partitions as you would a RAID device. This adds better efficiency for very large files but is complicated to implement. As on a RAID device, stripe sizes have to be consistent across partitions and, as LVM partitions can be of any size, the stripe sizes have to be carefully calculated. The simplest approach is to use a linear implementation, much like a RAID 0 device, treating the storage as one large ordinary drive, with storage accessed sequentially.

There is one restriction and recommendation for logical volumes. The boot partition cannot be part of a logical volume. You still have to create a separate hard disk partition as your boot partition with the **/boot** mountpoint in which your kernel and all needed boot files are installed. In addition, it is recommended that you not place your root partition on a logical volume. Doing so can complicate any needed data recovery. This is why a default partition configuration for many distributions, set up during installation, will include a separate **/boot** partition of 100MB of type **ext3**, whereas the root and swap partitions will be installed on logical volumes. There will be two partitions, one for the logical group (LVM physical volume, **pv**) holding both swap and root volumes, and another for the boot partition (**ext3**). The logical volumes will in turn both be **ext3** file systems.

Creating LVM volumes during installation

If you install your system using the Alternate install CD, you will have the option to create LVM partition during the install procedure. Create an LVM physical partition on your hard disk. Once you have created the LVM physical partition, you create your logical volumes. You first need to assign the LVM physical partitions to volume groups, which are essentially logical hard drives. Once the volume groups are created, you are ready to create your logical volumes. You can create several logical volumes within each group. The logical volumes function like partitions. You will have to specify a file system type and mountpoint for each logical volume you create, and you need at least a swap and root volume. The file system type for the swap volume is swap, and for the root volume it's a standard Linux file system type like **ext3**.

system-config-lvm

The system-config-lvm tool provides a GUI interface for managing your Logical Volume Manager. With it you can obtain information about your logical and physical volumes, as well as perform simple tasks such as deleting and extending logical volumes, or migrating and removing physical volumes. It remains to date the best GUI tool available for managing LVM. It is well worth the effort to install it on Ubuntu should you use LVM extensively.

The system-config-lvm tool is now available on the Ubuntu Universe repository. It is a Red Hat Linux and Fedora Linux system configuration tool, made available for use on Ubuntu. You can download and install it using the Synaptic Package Manager. You can access is from Applications | System Tools | Logical Volume Management.

Warning: There is a warning that system-config-lvm will not recognize Windows partitions and RAID devices, and instead lists them as uninitialized disks. It will let you accidently erase Windows partitions or RAID devices should you select them for use in an LVM device. If you have Windows partitions or RAID devices on your system, make sure you know the hard disk devices they use, so you do not select them for use in LVM devices.

Using system-config-lvm

As, previously noted, you can invoke system-config-lvm from its menu entry under System | Administration | Logical Volume Management. You can also enter **system-config-lvm** in a terminal window. system-config-lvm will display a window showing your logical and physical volumes, a graphical representation of a selected volume or volume group, and information about the selected volumes. Figure 16-1 shows two volume groups, **VolGroup00** and **mymedia.** In this example, the **mymedia** volume group has one logical volume called **myvideo**, which in turn has two physical volumes, **sdb1** and **sdd1**. These are the **b** and **d** SATA drives.

Selecting a physical volume displays buttons with options to extend the volume group or remove physical volumes, selecting a particular partition allows you to migrate a particular volume or remove it from the group. When extending a volume group, you will be presented with a list of possible partitions to choose from.

Selecting a logical group displays buttons to create or remove the volume, and selecting a particular volume in that group permits you to remove the logical volume or edit its properties. A logical volume's properties will let you specify its file system type, size, and logical volume name. When adding a new logical volume, you can use properties to set the name, size, and file system type, formatting it appropriately. Space permitting, you can even resize current volumes.

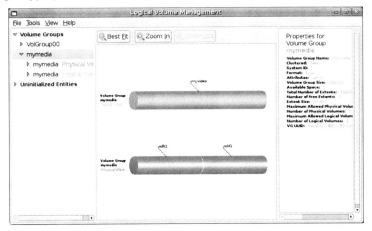

Figure 16-1: system-config-lvm on Ubuntu, System | Administration | Logical Volume Management

The uninitialized entries are partitions that do not belong to any volume. The boot partition cannot belong to a volume group, it cannot be a logical volume. Be sure to leave it alone. For other uninitialized partitions, you can select their entries and initialize them to add them to a volume group. Use the Initialize Block Device entry in the Tools menu. All non-LVM volumes will be listed as unitialized volumes, including those already used for Windows, RAID, and standard Linux partitions. Be sure to know which partitions are in use and be careful not to select them for use in an LVM group, otherwise you will wipe out all data on those partitions.

If you have the free space on a logical group you can create a new logical volume. First select the logical group entry on the left-hand pane. A Create New Logical Volume button will appear which you can click to open up a new dialog where you can create a new logical volume (see Figure 16-2). There are entries for the volume name (LV name), the size (LV size), the file system you want it formatted with, and where you want it mounted (Mount point). You also have the option of specifying the size of the extents, though the default normally works well. You can specify whether a logical volume should be linear, mirrored, or striped. These features are similar to the linear, mirrored, or striped implementations used in RAID devices. Normally you would choose the linear implementation, which is the default.

To extend the size of a volume using free space in the volume group, select the volume group and the Edit properties button will appear which you can then click. This open the same window as displayed in Figure 16-2. You can then use the slider on the volume size (Size) to increase the size of the volume. When you click OK, system-config-lvm will unmount your volume group and then resize the volume and check the file system, extending the size while preserving your original data. This capability is a major advantage for LVM devices. Hard disk partitions are fixed, whereas LVM logical disks can easily be expanded. To expand a hard disk partition, you had to destroy the old one and create a new, larger one that in turn was also fixed. With LVM you just add more storage. The logical structure is separated from the physical implementation.

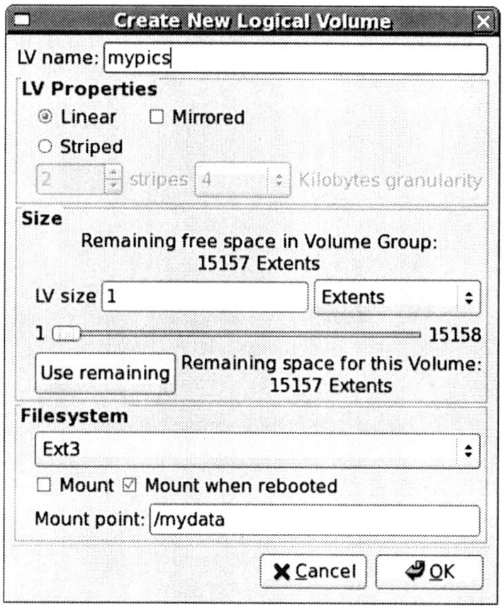

Figure 16-2: Creating a new logical volume

LVM Tools: Using the LVM Commands

You can use the collection of LVM tools to manage your LVM volumes, adding new LVM physical partitions and removing current ones (see Table 16-1). These are available from the Ubuntu main repository. You can use these tools in a terminal window to manage and create your LVM volumes. A GUI LVM tool like system-config-lvm, is actually a GUI interfaces for the LVM tools. You can either use LVM tools directly or use the **lvm** command to generate an interactive shell from which you can run LVM commands. Man pages are available for all the LVM commands. LVM maintains configuration information in the **/etc/lvm/lvm.conf** file, where you can configure LVM options such as the log file, the configuration backup directory, or the directory for LVM devices (see the **lvm.conf** Man page for details).

Displaying LVM Information

You can use the **pvdisplay**, **vgdisplay**, and **lvdisplay** commands to show detailed information about a physical partition, volume groups, and logical volumes. **pvscan**, **vgscan**, and **lvscan** list your physical, group, and logical volumes.

Managing LVM Physical Volumes with the LVM commands

A physical volume can be any hard disk partition or RAID device. A RAID device is seen as a single physical volume. You can create physical volumes either from a single hard disk or from partitions on a hard disk. On very large systems with many hard disks, you would more likely use an entire hard disk for each physical volume.

You would first use a partition utility like **fdisk**, **parted**, or **gparted** to create a partition of the LVM partition type (**8e**). Then you can initialize the partition as a physical volume using the **pvcreate** command.

To initialize a physical volume on an entire hard disk, you use the hard disk device name, as shown here:

```
pvcreate /dev/sdc
```

This will initialize one physical partition, **pv**, called **sdc1** on the **sdc** hard drive (the third Serial ATA drive, c).

If you are using a particular partition on a drive, you create a new physical volume using the partition's device name, as shown here:

```
pvcreate /dev/sda3
```

To initialize several drives, just list them. The following create two physical partitions, sdc1 an sdd1.

```
pvcreate /dev/sdc /dev/sdd
```

You could also use several partitions on different hard drives. This is a situation in which your hard drives each hold several partitions. This condition occurs often when you are using some partitions on your hard drive for different purposes like different operating systems, or if you want to distribute your Logical group across several hard drives. To initialize these partitions at once, you simply list them.

```
pvcreate /dev/sda3 /dev/sdb1 /dev/sdb2
```

Once you have initialized your partitions, you have to create LVM groups on them.

Managing LVM Groups

Physical LVM partitions are used to make up a volume group. You can manually create a volume group using the **vgcreate** command and the name of the group along with a list of physical partitions you want in the group.

If you are then creating a new volume group to place these in, you can include them in the group when you create the volume group with the **vgcreate** command. The volume group can use one or more physical partitions. The default install configuration described previously used only one physical partition for the **VolGroup00**. In the following example, a volume group called **mymedia** that is made up two physical volumes, **sdc** and **sdd**.

```
vgcreate mymedia /dev/sdc /dev/sdd
```

The previous example sets up a logical group on two serial ATA hard drives, each with its own single partition. Alternatively, you can set up a volume group to span partitions on several hard drives. If you are using partitions for different functions, this approach gives you the flexibility for using all the space available across multiple hard drives. The following example creates a group called **mygroup** consisting of three physical partitions, **/dev/sda3**, **/dev/sdb2**, and **/dev/sdb4**:

```
vgcreate mygroup /dev/sda3 /dev/sdb2 /dev/sdb4
```

Command	Description
lvm	Open an interactive shell for executing LVM commands.
lvmdiskscan	Scan all disks for LVM physical partitions.
lvdisplay	Display detailed information about logical volumes
lvcreate	create logical volumes
lvrename	rename a logical volume
lvchange	Modify a logical volume
lvextend	Extend the size of a logical volume
lvreduce	Reduce the size of a logical volume
lvremove	Remove logical volumes
lvs	List logical volumes with detailed information
lvresize	Change the size of a logical Volume
lvscan	Scan system for logical volumes
pvdisplay	Display detailed information about LVM physical partitions
pvchange	Modify an LVM physical partition
pvcreate	create LVM physical partitions
pvmove	Move content of an LVM physical partition to another partition
pvremove	Delete LVM physical partitions.
pvs	List physical partitions with detailed information
pvresize	Resize a physical partition
pvscan	Scan system for physical partitions
vgdisplay	Display detailed information about volume groups
vgexport	Activate a volume group
vgimport	Make an exported volume group known to a new system. Useful for moving an activated volume group from one system to another.
vgmerge	Combine volume groups
vgreduce	Remove physical partitions from a volume group
vgremove	Delete a volume group
vgs	List volume groups with detailed information
vgslit	Split a volume group
vgscan	Scan system for volume groups
vgck	Check volume groups
vgrename	Rename a volume group

vgcfgbackup	Backup volume group configuration (metadata)
vgcfgrestore	Restore volume group configuration (metadata)

Table 16-1: LVM commands

If you to later want to add a physical volume to a volume group you use the **vgextend** command. The **vgextend** command adds a new partition to a logical group. In the following example, the partition **/dev/sda4** is added to the volume group **mygroup**. In effect, you are extending the size of the logical group by adding a new physical partition.

```
vgextend mygroup  /dev/sda4
```

To add an entire new drive to a volume group you would follow a similar procedure. The following example adds a fifth serial ATA hard drive, **sde**, first creating a physical volume on it and then adding that volume, sde, to the **mymedia** volume group.

```
pvcreate /dev/sde
vgextend mymedia /dev/sde
```

To remove a physical partition, first remove it from its logical group. You may have to use the **pmove** command to move any data off the physical partition. Then use the **vgreduce** command to remove it from its logical group.

You can remove a entire volume group by first deactivating it with **vgchange -a n** and then using the **vgremove** command.

Activating Volume Groups

Whereas in a standard file system structure, you mount and unmount hard disk partitions, with an LVM structure, you activate and deactivate entire volume groups. The group volumes are inaccessible until you activate them with the **vgchange** command with the **-a** option. To activate a group, first reboot your system, and then enter the **vgchange** command with the **-a** option and the **y** argument to activate the logical group (an **n** argument will deactivate the group).

```
vgchange -a  y  mygroup
```

Managing LVM Logical Volumes

To create logical volumes, you use the **lvcreate** command and then format your logical volume using the standard formatting command like **mkfs.ext3**.

With the **-n** option you specify the volume's name, which functions like a hard disk partition's label. You use the **-L** or **--size** options to specify the size of the volume. Use a size suffix for the measure, **G** for Gigabyte, **M** for megabyte, and **K** for kilobytes. There are other options for implementing features such as whether to implement a linear, striped, or mirrored volume, or to specify the size of the extents to use. Usually the defaults work well. The following example creates a logical volume named **projects** on the **mygroup** logical group with a size of 20GB.

```
lvcreate -n projects  -L 20GB mygroup
```

The following example sets up a logical volume on the **mymedia** volume group that is 540GB in size. The **mymedia** volume group is made up of two physical volumes, each on 320GB hard drives. In effect the two hard drives are logically seen as one.

```
lvcreate -n myvideos  -L 540GB mymedia
```

Once you have created your logical volume, you then have to create a file system to use on it. The following creates an **ext3** file system on the **myvideos** logical volume.

```
mkfs.ext3 myvideos
```

You could also use:

```
mkfs -t ext3 myvideos
```

With **lvextend**, you can increase the size of the logical volume if there is unallocated space available in the volume group.

Should you want to reduce the size of a logical volume you use the **lvreduce** command, indicating the new size. Be sure to first reduce the size of any file systems (**ext3**) on the logical volume, using the **resize2fs** command.

To rename a logical volume use the **lvrename** command. If you want to completely remove a logical volume, you can use the **lvremove** command.

You can remove a logical volume with the **lvremove** command. With **lvextend**, you can increase the size of the logical volume, and **lvreduce** will reduce its size.

Steps to create a new LVM group and volume

> **Physical Partition**   First create a physical partition on your hard drive. You can use GParted, QTparted, or fdisk with the disk device name to create the partition. For example, to use fdisk to create a new partition on a new hard drive, whose device name is **/etc/sde**, you would enter:

```
fdisk /etc/sde
```

Then, in the fdisk shell, use the fdisk **n** command to create a new partition, set it as a primary partition (**p**), and make it the first partition. If you plan to use the entire hard drive for your LVM, you would need only one partition that would cover the entire drive.

Then use the **t** command to set the partition type to 8E. The 8E type is the LVM partition type. To make your changes, enter **w** to write changes to the disk.

> **Physical Volume**   Next create a physical volume (pv) on the new and empty LVM partition, using the **pvcreate** command and the device name.

```
pvcreate /dev/sde
```

> **Volume Group**   Then create your volume group with **vgcreate** command, with the volume group name and the hard disk device name.

```
vgcreate mynewgroup  /dev/sde
```

Be sure the volume group is activated. Use the **vgs** command to list it. If not listed, use the following command to activate it.

```
vgchange -a  y  mynewgroup
```

> **Logical Volume**   Then create a logical volume or volumes for the volume group, using the **lvcreate** command. The **--size** or **-L** options determines the size and the **--name** option

specifies the name. To find out the available free space use the **vgs** command. You can have more than one logical volume in a volume group, or just one if you prefer. A logical volume is conceptually similar to logical volumes in a extended partition on Windows systems.

```
lvcreate --size --name mynewvol1
```

> **Format the Logical volume**. You then use the **mkfs** command with the **-t** option to format the logical volume. On Ubuntu, the logical volume will be listed in a directory for the LVM group, within the /dev directory, **/dev/mynewgroup/mynewvol1**. This is a link to the **/dev/mapper** directory that actually holds the device file prefix with the volume group name, **/dev/mapper/mynewgroup-mynewvol1**.

```
mkfs -t ext3 /dev/mapper/mynewgroup-mynewvol1
```

Steps to add a new drive to a LVM group and volume

> **Physical Partition**   First create a physical partition on your hard drive. You can use GParted, QTparted, or fdisk with the disk device name to create the partition. For the type specify LVM (**8E**).

> **Physical Volume**   Next create a physical volume (pv) on the new and empty LVM partition, using the pvcreate command and the device name.

```
pvcreate /dev/sdf
```

> **Add to Logical Group**   Use the vgextend command to add the new physical volume to your existing logical group (LG).

```
vgextend  mynewgroup  /dev/sdf
```

> **Add to Logical Volume**   Then you can use then create new logical volumes in the new space, or expand the size of a current logical volume. To expand the size of a logical volume to the new space, first umount the logical volume. Then use the **lvextend** command to expand to the space on the new hard drive that is now part the same logical group. With no size specified, the entire space on the new hard drive will be added.

```
umount /dev/mynewgroup/mynewvol1
lvextend /dev/mynewgroup/mynewvol  /dev/sdf
```

Use the **-L** option to specify a particular size, **-L +250G** . Be sure to add the + sign to have the size added to the current logical volume size. To find out the available free space, use the **vgs** command.

> **Add to file system**   Then use the **resize2fs** command to extend the linux file system (ext3) on to logical volume to include the new space, formatting it. Unless you specify a size (second parameter), then all the available unformatted space is used.

```
resize2fs /dev/mynewgroup/mynewvol1
```

LVM Device Names: /dev/mapper

The **device-mapper** driver is used by LVM to set up tables for mapping logical devices to hard disk. The device name for a logical volume is kept in the **/dev/mapper** directory and has the format *logical group –logical volume*. In addition, there will be a corresponding device folder for the logical group, which will contain logical volume names. These device names are links to the **/dev/mapper** names. For example, the **mypics** logical volume in the **mymedia** logical group has the device name, **/dev/mapper/mymedia-mypics**. There will be a corresponding folder called **/dev/mymedia**. The device name **/dev/mymedia/mypics** is a link to the **/dev/mapper/mymedia-mypics** device name. You can just as easily use the link as shown in this chapter, as the original device name. The snapshot device described later in this chapter would have the device name **/dev/mapper/mymedia-mypicssnap1** with the link device name being **/dev/mymedia/mypicssnap**.

Note: You can back up volume group meta data (configuration) using the **vgcfgbackup** command. This does not backup your logical volumes (no content). Meta data backups are stored in **/etc/lvm/backup**, and can be restored using **vgcfgrestore**. You may need to restore your volume if you are using the same upgraded system on a new computer hardware.

Using LVM to replace drives

LVM can be very useful when you need to replace an older hard drive with a new one. Hard drives are expected to last about six years on the average. You could want to replace the older drive with a larger one (hard drive storage sizes double every year or so). Replacing drives is easy for additional hard drives. To replace a boot drive is much more complicated.

To replace the drive, simply incorporate the new drive to your logical volume (see Steps to add a new drive to an LVM group and volume). The size of your logical volume will increase accordingly. You can use the **pmove** command to move data from the old drive to the new one. Then, issue commands to remove the old drive (**vgreduce**) from the volume group. From the user and system point of view, no changes are made. Files from your old drive will still be stored in the same directories, though the actual storage will be implemented on the new drive.

Replacement with LVM become more complicated if you want to replace your boot drive, the hard drive from which your system starts up and which holds your linux kernel. The boot drive contains a special boot partition and the master boot record. The boot partition cannot be part of any LVM volume. You would first have to create a boot partition on the new drive using a partition tool such as Parted or fdisk, labeling it as boot. The boot drive is usually very small, about 200 MB. Then mount the partition on your system, copy the contents of your **/boot** directory to it. Then you add the remainder of the disk to your logical volume and logically remove the old disk, copying the contents of the old disk to the new one. You would still have to boot with linux rescue DVD (or install DVD in rescue mode), and issue the **grub-install** command to install the master boot record on your new drive. You can then boot from the new drive.

LVM Example for Multiple Hard Drives

With hard drives becoming cheaper and the demand for storage increasing, many systems now use multiple hard drives. To manage multiple hard drives, partitions on each used to have to be individually managed, unless you implemented a RAID system. RAID allows you to treat several hard disks as one storage device, but there are restrictions on the size and kinds of devices you can combine. Without RAID, each hard drive had to be managed separately, with files having to fit into remaining storage as the drives filled up.

With LVM, you no longer have such restrictions. You can combine hard disks into a single storage device. This method is also flexible, letting you replace disks without losing any data, as well adding new disks to automatically increase your storage (or replace smaller disks with larger ones).

For example, say you want to add two hard disks to your system, but you want to treat the storage in both logically instead of having to manage partitions in each. LVM lets you treat the combined storage of both hard drives as one giant pool. In effect, two 500GB drives can be treated as one 1 terabyte storage device.

In the following example, the Linux system makes use of three hard drives. The Linux system and boot partitions are on the first hard drive, **sda**. Added to this system are two hard drives, **sdc** and **sdd**, which will make up an LVM storage device to be added to the system.

Using system-config-lvm

Using the example in Figure 16-3, the steps involved in creating and accessing logical volumes are described in following commands. In this example there are two hard disk drives that will be combined into one LVM drives. The hard drives are Serial ATA drives identified on the systems as **sdc** and **sdd**. Each drive is first partitioned with a single LVM physical partitions. On system-config-lvm, the drives will be listed as uninitialized. Select them and initialize them to create the physical partitions on the hard disks. In this example, the partitions **sdc** and **sdd** are created.

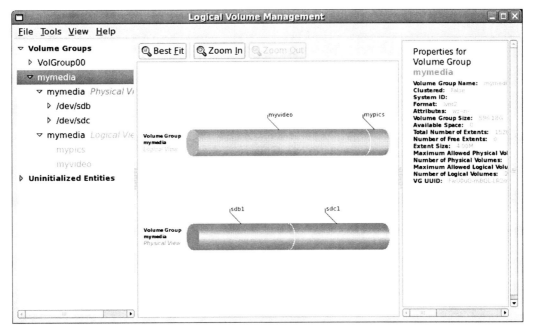

Figure 16-3: Logical Volume Management with two hard drives using system-config-lvm

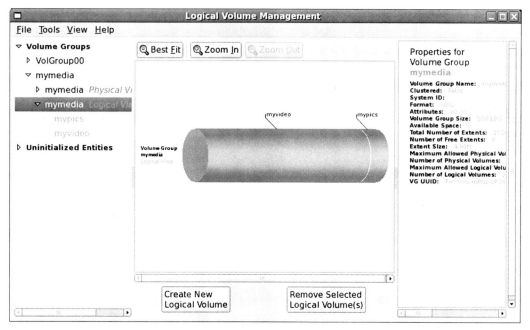

Figure 16-4: Logical volumes with system-config-lvm

You then create then volume group, and then create your logical volumes (see Figure 16-4). For logical volumes, select the logical group entry on the left hand pane. Then Click on the Create New Logical Volume. This opens up a new window with a panel for creating a new Logical volume . Figure 16-4 shows the **myvideo** and **mypics** logical volumes which are part of the mymedia logical group.

Using LVM commands

Using the LVM commands you can achieve the same effect. Each drive is first partitioned with a single LVM physical partition. Use a partition creation tool like `fdisk` or `parted` to create the physical partitions on the hard disks **sdc** and **sdd**.

You first initialize the physical volumes on the **sdc** and **sdd** drives with the `pvcreate` command. The **sda1** and **sda2** partitions in the **sda** entry are reserved for the boot and root partitions and are never initialized.

```
pvcreate /dev/sdc /dev/sdd
```

You then create the logical groups you want, using the `vgcreate` command. In this case there are one logical group, **mymedia**. The **mymedia** group uses **sdc** and **sdd**. If you create a physical volume later and want to add it to a volume group, you would use the `vgextend` command.

```
vgcreate mymedia  /dev/sdc /dev/sdd
```

You can now create the logical volumes in each volume group, using the `lvcreate` command. In this example two logical volumes are created, one for **myvideos** and another for **mypics**. The corresponding `lvcreate` commands are shown here:

```
lvcreate  -n myvideo  -l 540GB   mymedia
lvcreate  -n mypics   -l 60GB    mymedia
```

Then you can activate the logical volumes. Reboot and use **vgchange** with the **-a y** option to activate the logical volumes.

```
vgchange -a y mymedia
```

You can now create the file systems for each logical volume.

```
mkfs.ext3 myvideo
mkfs.ext3 mypics
```

Then you can mount the logical volumes. In this example they are mounted to subdirectories of the same name in **/mydata**, **/mydate/mypics** and **/mydata/myvideo**.

```
mount -t ext3 /dev/mymedia/mypics   /mydata/mypics
mount -t ext3 /dev/mymedia/myvideo  /mydata/myvideo
```

LVM Snapshots

A snapshot records the state of the logical volume at a designated time. It does not create a full copy of data on the volume, just changes since the last snapshot. A snapshot defines the state of the data at a given time. This allows you to backup the data in a consistent way. Also, should you need to restore a file to its pervious version, you can use the snapshot of it. Snapshots are treated as logical volume and can be mounted, copied, or deleted.

To create a snapshot you use the lvcreate command with the -s option. In this example the snapshot is given the name mypics-snap1 (**-n** option). You need to specify the full device name for the logical group you want to create the snapshot for. Be sure there is enough free space available in the logical group for the snapshot. In this example, the snapshot logical volume is created in the **/dev/mymedia** logical group. It could just a s easily be created in any other logical group. Although a snapshot normally uses very little space, you have to guard against overflows. If the snapshot is allocated same size as the original, it will never overflow For systems where little of the original data changes, the snapshot can be very small. The following example allocate one third the size of the original (60GB).

```
 lvcreate  -s -n mypics-snap1 -l 20GB /dev/mymedia
```

You can then mount the snapshot as you would any other file system.

```
mount /dev/mymedia/mypics-snap1 /mysnaps
```

To delete a snapshot you use the lvremove command, removing it like you would any logical volume.

```
lvremove  -f /dev/mymedia/mypics-snap1
```

Snapshots are very useful for making backups, while a system is still active. You can sue tar or dump to backup the mounted snapshot to a disk or tape. All the data form the original logical volume will be included, along with the changes noted by the snapshot.

Snapshots also allows you to perform effective undo operations. You can create snapshot of a logical volume. Then unmount the original and mount the snapshot in its place. Any changes you make will be performed on the snapshot, not the original. Should problems occur, unmount the snapshot and then mount the original. This restores the original state of your data. You could also do this using several snapshots, restoring to a previous snapshot. With this procedure, you could test new software on a snapshot, without endangering your original data. The software would be operating on the snapshot, not the original logical volume.

You can also use them as alternative versions of a logical volume. You can read and write to a snapshot. A write will change only the snapshot volume, not the original, creating, in effect, a alternate version.

Configuring RAID Devices

RAID is a method of storing data across several disks to provide greater performance and redundancy. In effect, you can have several hard disks treated as just one hard disk by your operating system. RAID then efficiently stores and retrieves data across all these disks, instead of having the operating system access each one as a separate file system. Lower-level details of storage and retrieval are no longer a concern of the operating system. This allows greater flexibility in adding or removing hard disks, as well as implementing redundancy in the storage system to provide greater reliability. With RAID, you can have several hard disks that are treated as one virtual disk, where some of the disks are used as real-time mirrors, duplicating data. You can use RAID in several ways, depending upon the degree of reliability you need. When you place data on multiple disks, I/O operations can overlap in a balanced way, improving performance. Because having multiple disks increases the mean time between failures (MTBF), storing data redundantly also increases fault tolerance.

RAID can be implemented on a hardware or software level. On a hardware level, you can have hard disks connected to a RAID hardware controller, usually a special PC card. Your operating system then accesses storage through the RAID hardware controller. Alternatively, you can implement RAID as a software controller, letting a software RAID controller program manage access to hard disks treated as RAID devices. The software version lets you use hard disks as RAID disks. Linux uses the MD driver, supported in the 2.4 kernel, to implement a software RAID controller. Linux software RAID supports several levels (linear, 0, 1, 4, 5, 6 and 10), whereas hardware RAID supports more. Hardware RAID levels, such as 7–10, provide combinations of greater performance and reliability.

Tip: Before you can use RAID on your system, make sure it is supported on your kernel, along with the RAID levels you want to use. If not, you will have to reconfigure and install a RAID module for the kernel. Check the Multi-Driver Support component in your kernel configuration. You can specify support for any or all of the RAID levels.

Motherboard RAID Support: dmraid

With kernel 2.6, hardware RAID devices are supported with the Device-Mapper Software RAID support tool (**dmraid**), which currently supports a wide range of motherboard RAID devices. Keep in mind that many "hardware" RAID devices are, in effect, really software RAID (fakeraid). Though you configure them in the motherboard BIOS, the drivers operate as software, like any other drivers. In this respect they could be considered less flexible than a Linux software RAID solution, and they could also depend directly on vendor support for any fixes for updates.

The **dmraid** driver will map your system to hardware RAID devices such as those provided by Intel, Promise, and Silicon Magic, and often included on motherboards. The dmraid tool uses the device-mapper driver to set up a virtual file system interface, just as is done for LVM drives. The RAID device names will be located in **/dev/mapper**.

You use your BIOS RAID configuration utility to set up your RAID devices as instructed by your hardware documentation. During a Linux installation, the RAID devices are automatically detected and the dmraid module is loaded, selecting the appropriate drivers.

With the **dmraid** command you can detect and activate RAID devices. The following command displays your RAID devices:

```
dmraid -r
```

To list currently supported devices, use **dmraid** with the **-l** option.

```
dmraid -l
```

The dmraid tool is improved continually and may not work well with some RAID devices.

RAID Level	Capability	Description
Linear	Appending	Treats RAID hard drives as one virtual drive with no striping, mirroring, or parity reconstruction.
0	Striping	Implements disk striping across drives with no redundancy.
1	Mirroring	Implements a high level of redundancy. Each drive is treated as mirror for all data.
4	Parity	Implements data reconstruction capability using parity information, kept on a separate disk.
5	Distributed parity	Implements data reconstruction capability using parity information. Parity information is distributed across all drives, instead of using a separate drive as in RAID 4. Requires at least three hard drives.
6	Distributed parity	Implements data reconstruction capability using dual distributed parity information. Dual sets of parity information are distributed across all drives. Can be considered an enhanced form of RAID 5.
10	Striping and Mirroring	Implements a high level of redundancy with striping. Also know as 1+0
Multipath	Multiple access to devices	Supports multiple access to the same device.

Table 16-2: Linux Software RAID Levels

Linux Software RAID Levels

Linux software RAID can be implemented at different levels, depending on whether you want organization, efficiency, redundancy, or reconstruction capability. Each capability corresponds to different RAID levels. For most levels, the size of the hard disk devices should be the same. For mirroring for RAID 1, disks of the same size are required, and for RAID 5 they are recommended. Linux software RAID supports several levels, as shown in Table 16-2. RAID 5 requires at least three hard drives. In addition, FAULTY raid level is provided for testing purposes.

Linear

The *linear* level lets you simply organize several hard disks into one logical hard disk, providing a pool of continuous storage. Instead of being forced to set up separate partitions on each hard drive, in effect you have only one hard drive. The storage is managed sequentially. When one hard disk fills up, the next one is used. In effect, you are *appending* one hard disk to the other. This level provides no recovery capability. If you have a hard disk RAID array containing two 80GB disks, after you use up the storage on one, you will automatically start on the next.

RAID 0: Striping

For efficiency, RAID stores data using disk *striping,* where data is organized into standardized stripes that can be stored across the RAID drives for faster access (level 0). RAID 0 also organizes your hard disks into common RAID devices but treats them like single hard disks, storing data randomly across all the disks. If you had a hard disk RAID array containing two 80GB disks, you could access them as one 160GB RAID device.

RAID 1: Mirroring

RAID level 1 implements redundancy through *mirroring.* In mirroring, the same data is written to each RAID drive. Each disk has a complete copy of all the data written, so that if one or more disks fail, the others still have your data. Though extremely safe, redundancy can be very inefficient and consumes a great deal of storage. For example, on a RAID array of two 80GB disk drives, one disk is used for standard storage and the other is a real-time backup. This leaves you with only 80GB for use on your system. Write operations also have to be duplicated across as many mirrored hard disks as are used by the RAID array, slowing down operations.

RAID 4: Parity

Though it is not supported due to overhead costs, RAID 4, like RAID 5, supports a more compressed form of recovery using parity information instead of mirrored data. With RAID 4, parity information is kept on a separate disk, while the others are used for data storage, much like in a linear model.

RAID 5 and 6: Distributed Parity

As an alternative to mirroring, data can be reconstructed using *parity information* in case of a hard drive crash. Parity information is saved instead of full duplication of the data. Parity information takes up the space equivalent of one drive, leaving most of the space on the RAID drives free for storage. RAID 5 combines both striping and parity (see RAID 4), where parity information is distributed across the hard drives, rather than in one drive dedicated to that purpose. This allows the use of the more efficient access method, striping. With both striping and parity,

RAID 5 provides both fast access and recovery capability, making it the most popular RAID level used. For example, a RAID array of four 80GB hard drives would be treated as one 320GB hard drive with part of that storage (80 GB) used to hold parity information, leaving 240GB free. RAID 5 does require at least three hard drives.

RAID 6 operates the same as RAID 5, but it uses dual sets of parity information for the data, providing even greater restoration capability.

RAID 10: Striping and Mirroring

RAID 10, also known as RAID 1+0, combines both striping and mirroring (RAID 0 and 1). This provides both redundancies and fast access.

Tip: Many distributions also allow you to create and format RAID drives during installation. At that time, you can create your RAID partitions and devices.

Multipath

Though not actually a RAID level, Multipath allows for multiple access to the same device. Should one controller fail, another can be used to access the device. In effect, you have controller-level redundancy. Support is implemented using the **mdadmd** daemon. This is started with the mdadmd service script.

```
sudo /etc/init.d/mdadmd start
```

RAID Devices and Partitions: md and fd

A RAID device is named an **md** and uses the MD driver. These devices are already defined on your Linux system in the **/etc/dev** directory, starting with **md0**: **/dev/md0** is the first RAID device, and **/dev/md1** is the second, and so on. Each RAID device, in turn, uses hard disk partitions, where each partition contains an entire hard disk. These partitions are usually referred to as RAID disks, whereas a RAID device is an array of the RAID disks it uses.

When creating a RAID partition, you should set the partition type to be **fd**, instead of the 83 for the standard Linux partition. The **fd** type is that used by RAID for automatic detection.

Booting from a RAID Device

Usually, as part of the installation process, you can create RAID devices from which you can also boot your system. Your Linux system will be configured to load RAID kernel support and automatically detect your RAID devices. The boot loader will be installed on your RAID device, meaning on all the hard disks making up that device.

Most Linux distributions do not support booting from RAID 5, only RAID 1. This means that if you want to use RAID 5 and still boot from RAID disks, you will need to create at least two (or more if you want) RAID devices using corresponding partitions for each device across your hard disks. One device would hold your **/boot** partition and be installed as a RAID 1 device. This RAID 1 device would be the first RAID device, **md0**, consisting of the first partition on each hard disk. The second RAID device, **md1**, could then be a RAID 5 device and would consist of corresponding partitions on the other hard disks. Your system could then boot from the RAID 1 device but use the RAID 5 device.

If you do not create RAID disks during installation but instead create them later and want to boot from them, you will have to make sure your system is configured correctly. The RAID devices need to be created with persistent superblocks, and support for the RAID devices has to be enabled in the kernel. On Linux distributions, this support is enabled as a module. Difficulties occur if you are using RAID 5 for your / (root) partition. This partition contains the RAID 5 module, but to access the partition, you have to already load the RAID 5 module. To work around this limitation, you can create a RAM disk in the **/boot** partition that contains the RAID 5 module. Use the `mkinitrd` command to create the RAM disk and the `--with` option to specify the module to include.

```
mkinitrd --preload raid5 --with=raid5 raid-ramdisk 2.6.24-10
```

RAID Administration: mdadm

You use the **mdadm** tool to manage and monitor RAID devices. The **mdadm** tool is an all-purpose means of creating, monitoring, administering, and fixing RAID devices. You can run commands directly to create and format RAID disks. It also runs as a daemon to monitor and detect problems with the devices.

The **mdadm** tool has seven different modes of operation, each with its own set of options, including monitor with the `-f` option to run it as a daemon, or create with the `-l` option to set a RAID level for a disk. Table 16-3 lists the different modes of operation. Check the **mdadm** Man page for a detailed listing of the options for each mode.

Creating and Installing RAID Devices

If you created your RAID devices and their partitions during the installation process, you should already have working RAID devices. Your RAID devices will be configured in the **/etc/mdadm.conf** file, and the status of your RAID devices will be listed in the **/proc/mdstat** file. You can manually start or stop your RAID devices with the `raidstart` and `mdadm` commands. The `-a` option operates on all of them, though you can specify particular devices if you want.

Mode	Description
assemble	Assembles RAID array from devices.
build	Builds array without per-device superblocks.
create	Builds array with per-device superblocks.
manage	Manages array devices, adding or removing disks.
misc	Performs specific operations on a device, such as making it read only.
monitor	Monitors arrays for changes and act on them (used for RAID 1, 4, 5, 6).
grow	Changes array size, as when replacing smaller devices with larger ones.

Table 16-3: mdadm Modes

To create a new RAID device manually for an already-installed system, follow these steps:

➢ Make sure that your kernel supports the RAID level you want for the device you are creating.

> ➤ If you have not already done so, create the RAID disks (partitions) you will use for your RAID device.

> ➤ Create your RAID device with `mdadm` command in the build or create mode. The array will also be activated.

> ➤ Alternatively, you can configure your RAID device (**/dev/md**_n_) in the **/etc/mdadm.conf** file, specifying the RAID disks to use, and then use the `mdadm` command specifying the RAID device to create.

> ➤ Create a file system on the RAID device (`mkfs`) and then mount it.

Adding a Separate RAID File System

If you just want to add a RAID file system to a system that already has a standard boot partition, you can dispense with the first RAID 1 partition. Given three hard disks to use for the RAID file system, you just need three partitions, one for each disk, **/dev/sda1 ,/dev/sdc1,** and **/dev/sdb1**.

```
ARRAY /dev/md0   devices=/dev/sda1, /dev/sdc1, /dev/sdb1  level=5 num-devices=2
```

You then create the array with the following command:

```
mdadm -C /dev/md0 -n3 /dev/sda1 /dev/sdc1 /dev/sdb1 -l5
```

You can then format and mount your RAID device.

Creating Hard Disk Partitions: fd

To add new RAID devices or to create them in the first place, you need to manually create the hard disk partitions they will use and then configure RAID devices to use those partitions. To create a hard disk partition for use in a RAID array, use `fdisk` or `parted` and specify `fd` as the file system type. You invoke `fdisk` or `parted` with the device name of the hard disk you want to create the partition on. Be sure to specify `fd` as the partition type. The following example invokes `fdisk` for the hard disk **/dev/sdc** (the first hard disk on the secondary IDE connection):

```
fdisk /dev/sdc
```

Though technically partitions, these hard disk devices are referred to as disks in RAID configuration documentation and files.

Note: You can also use gparted or qtparted to create your hard disk partitions. These tools provide a GUI interface for `parted` (Applications | System Tools menu).

Configuring RAID: /etc/mdadm.conf

Once you have your disks, you then need to configure them as RAID devices. RAID devices are configured in the **/etc/mdadm.conf** file, with options as shown in Table 16-4. This file will be used by the `mdadm` command in the create mode to create the RAID device. In the **/etc/mdadm.conf** file, you create both DEVICE and ARRAY entries. The DEVICE entries list the RAID devices. The ARRAY entries list the RAID arrays and their options. This example implements a simple array on two disks. Serial ATA drives are used.

Directive or Option	Description
`DEVICE` *devices-list*	Partitions and drives used for RAID devices.
`ARRAY`	ARRAY configuration section for a particular RAID device.
`level=`*num*	The RAID level for the RAID device, such as 0, 1, 4, 5, and −1 (linear).
`devices=`*disk-device-list*	The disk devices (partitions) that make up the RAID array.
`num-devices=`*count*	Number of RAID devices in an array. Each RAID device section must have this directive. The maximum is 12.
`spare-group=`*name*	Text name for a spare group, whose devices can be used for other arrays.
`auto=`*option*	Automatically create specified devices if they do not exist. You can create traditional nonpartitioned (`yes` or `md` option) or the newer partitionable arrays (`mdp` or `part` option). For partitionable arrays the default is 4, which you can change.
`super-minor`	Minor number of the array superblock, same as md device number.
`uuid=`*UUID-number*	UUID identifier stored in array superblock, used to identify the RAID array. Can be used to reference an array in commands.
`MAILADDR`	Monitor mode, mail address where alerts are sent.
`PROGRAM`	Monitor mode, program to run when events occur.

Table 16-4: mdadm.conf Options

```
DEVICE  /dev/sda1 /dev/sdb1
```

You can list more than one device for a DEVICE entry, as well as have separate DEVICE entries. You can also specify multiple devices using file matching symbols, like *, ?, and []. The following specifies all the partitions on **sda** drive as RAID devices:

```
DEVICE  /dev/ sda*  /dev/sdb1
```

For an **ARRAY** entry, you specify the name of the RAID device you are configuring, such as **/dev/md0** for the first RAID device. You then add configuration options such as **devices** to list the partitions that make up the array, **level** for the RAID level, and **num-devices** for the number of devices. The following example configures the RAID array **/dev/md0** as three disks (partitions) using **/dev/sdb1**, **/dev/sdc1**, and **/dev/sdd1** and is configured for RAID 5 (**level=5**).

```
ARRAY /dev/md0   devices=/dev/sdb1, /dev/sdc1, /dev/sdd1  level=5 num-devices=3
```

Creating a RAID Array

You can create a RAID array either using options specified with the **mdadm** command or using configurations listed in the **/etc/mdadm.conf** file. Use of the **/etc/mdadm.conf** file is not required, though it does make RAID creation more manageable, especially for large or complex arrays. Once you have created your RAID devices, your RAID device will be automatically activated. The following command creates a RAID array, **/dev/md1**, using three devices, **/dev/sdb1** ,**/dev/sdc1**, and **/dev/sdd1**, at level 5.

```
mdadm --create /dev/md1 --raid-devices=3 /dev/sdb1 /dev/sdc1 /dev/sdd1 --level=5
```

Each option has a corresponding short version, as shown in Table 16-5. The same command is shown here with single-letter options.

```
mdadm -C /dev/md1 -n3 /dev/sdb1 /dev/sdc1 /dev/sdd1 -l5
```

mdadm --create Option	Description
-n --raid-devices	Number of RAID devices
-l --level	RAID level
-C --create	Create mode
-c --chunk	Chunk (stripe) size in powers of 2; default is 64KB
-x --spare-devices	Number of spare devices in the array
-z --size	Size of blocks used in devices, by default set to the smallest device if not the same size
-p --parity	The parity algorithm; left-symmetric is used by default

Table 16-5: The mdadm --create Options

If you have configured your RAID devices in the **/etc/mdadm.conf** file, you use the mdadm command in the create mode to create your RAID devices. mdadm takes as its argument the name of the RAID device, such as **/dev/md0** for the first RAID device. It then locates the entry for that device in the **/etc/mdadm.conf** file and uses that configuration information to create the RAID file system on that device. You can specify an alternative configuration file with the -c option, if you wish. mdadm operates as a kind of mkfs command for RAID devices, initializing the partitions and creating the RAID file systems. Any data on the partitions making up the RAID array will be erased.

```
mdadm --create /dev/md0
```

Creating Spare Groups

Linux software RAID now allows RAID arrays to share their spare devices. This means that if arrays belong to the same spare group, a device that fails in one array can automatically use the spare in another array. Spare devices from any array can be used in another as needed. You set the spare group that an array belongs to with the --spare-group option. The mdadm monitoring mode will detect a failed device in an array and automatically replace it with a spare device from arrays in the same spare group. The first command in the next example creates a spare drive called **/dev/sde1** for the **/dev/md0** array and labels it **mygroup**. In the second command, array **/dev/md1** has no spare drive but belongs to the same spare group as array **/dev/md0**. Should a drive in **/dev/md1** fail, it can automatically use the spare device, **/dev/sde1**, from **/dev/md0**. The following code lines are really two lines, each beginning with mdadm:

```
mdadm --create /dev/md0 --raid-devices=3 /dev/sda1 /dev/sdc1 /dev/sdd1-x
       /dev/sde1 --level=1 --spare-group=mygroup
mdadm --create /dev/md1 --raid-devices=2 /dev/sdf2 /dev/sdg2 --level=1
       --spare-group=mygroup
```

Creating a File System

Once the RAID devices are activated, you can create file systems on the RAID devices and mount those file systems. The following example creates a standard Linux file system on the **/dev/md0** device:

```
mkfs -t ext3 /dev/md0
```

In the following example, the user then creates a directory called **/myraid** and mounts the RAID device there:

```
mkdir /myraid
mount /dev/md0 /myraid
```

If you plan to use your RAID device for maintaining your user directories and files, you mount the RAID device as your **/home** partition. Such a mounting point might normally be used if you created your RAID devices when installing your system. To transfer your current home directories to a RAID device, first back them up on another partition, and then mount your RAID device, copying your home directories to it.

Managing RAID Arrays

You can manage RAID arrays with the **mdadm** manage mode operations. In this mode you can add or remove devices in arrays, as well as mark ones as failed. The **--add** option lets you add a device to an active array, essentially a hot swap operation.

```
mdadm /dev/md0 --add /dev/sde1
```

To remove a device from an active array, you first have to mark it as failed with the **--fail** option and then remove it with **--remove**.

```
mdadm /dev/md0 --fail /dev/sdb1 --remove /dev/sdb1
```

Starting and Stopping RAID Arrays

To start an already existing RAID array, you use **mdadm** with the assemble mode (newly created arrays are automatically started). To do so directly on the command line requires that you also know what devices make up the array, listing them after the RAID array.

```
mdadm -A /dev/md1 /dev/sdf1  /dev/sdg1
```

It is easier to configure your RAID arrays in the **/etc/mdadm.conf** file. With the scan option, **-s**, **mdadm** will then read array information from the **/etc/mdadm.conf** file. If you do not specify a RAID array, all arrays will be started.

```
mdadm -s /dev/md0
```

To stop a RAID array, you use the **-s** option.

```
mdadm -S /dev/md0
```

Monitoring RAID Arrays

As a daemon, **mdadm** is started and stopped using the **mdmonitor** service script in **/etc/init.d**. This invokes **mdadm** in the monitor mode, detecting any problems that arise and logging reports as well as taking appropriate action.

```
service mdadm start
```

You can monitor devices directly by invoking **mdadm** with the monitor mode.

```
mdadm --monitor /dev/md0
```

Monitor-related options can be set in the **/etc/mdadm.conf** file. MAILADDR sets the mail address where notification of RAID events are sent. PROGRAM sets the program to use if events occur.

If you decide to change your RAID configuration or add new devices, you first have to deactivate your currently active RAID devices. To deactivate a RAID device, you use the **mdadm** command in the misc mode. Be sure to close any open files and unmount any file systems on the device first.

```
umount /dev/md0
mdadm -S /dev/md0
```

17. Devices

The sysfs File System: /sys

The proc File System: /proc

udev: Device Files

Hardware Abstraction Layer: HAL

Manual Devices

Installing and Managing Terminals and Modems

Input Devices

Installing Sound, Network, and Other Cards

PCMCIA Devices

Modules

All devices, such as printers, terminals, and CD-ROMs, are connected to your Linux operating system through special files called *device files.* Such files contain all the information your operating system needs to control the specified device. This design introduces great flexibility. The operating system is independent of the specific details for managing a particular device; the specifics are all handled by the device file. The operating system simply informs the device what task it is to perform, and the device file tells it how. If you change devices, you have to change only the device file, not the whole system.

To install a device on your Linux system, you need a device file for it, software configuration such as that provided by a configuration tool, and kernel support—usually supplied by a module or support that is already compiled and built into the kernel. Device files are not handled in a static way. They are dynamically generated as needed by udev and managed by the Hardware Abstraction Layer (HAL). B a device file was created for each possible device, leading to a very large number of device files in the **/etc/dev** directory. Now, your system will detect only those devices it uses and create device files for those only, giving you a much smaller listing of device files. Both udev and HAL are hotplug systems, with udev used for creating devices and HAL designed for providing information about them, as well as managing the configuration for removable devices such as those with file systems such as those for USB card readers and CD-ROMs.

Resource	Description
/sys	The sysfs file system listing configuration information for all the devices on your system
/proc	An older process file system listing kernel information, including device information
http://kernel.org/pub/linux/docs/device-list/devices.txt	Linux device names
http://kernel.org/pub/linux/utils/kernel/hotplug/udev.html	The udev website
/etc/udev	The udev configuration directory
http://freedesktop.org/wiki/Software/hal	The HAL website
/etc/hal	The HAL configuration directory
/usr/share/hal/fdi	The HAL device information files, for configuring HAL information support and policies
/etc/hal/fdi	The HAL system administrator's device information files

Table 17-1: Device Resources

Managing devices in Ubuntu is at the same time easier but much more complex. You now have to use udev and HAL to configure devices, though much of this is now automatic. Device information is maintained in a special device file system called sysfs located at **/sys**. This is a virtual file system like **/proc** and is used to keep track of all devices supported by the kernel. Several of the resources you might need to consult and directories you may have to use are listed in Table 17-1.

The sysfs File System: /sys

The system file system is designed to hold detailed information about system devices. This information can be used by hotplug tools like udev to create device interfaces as they are needed. Instead of having a static and complete manual configuration for a device, the sysfs system maintains configuration information about the device, which is then used as needed by the hotplugging system to create device interfaces when a device is attached to the system. More and more devices are now removable, and many are meant to be attached temporarily (cameras, for example). Instead of maintaining separate static and dynamic methods for configuring devices, Linux distributions make all devices structurally hotplugged.

The sysfs file system is a virtual file system that provides the a hierarchical map of your kernel-supported devices such as PCI devices, buses, and block devices, as well as supporting kernel modules. The **class** subdirectory will list all your supported devices by category, such as net and sound devices. With sysfs your system can easily determine the device file a particular device is associated with. This is very helpful for managing removable devices as well as dynamically managing and configuring devices as HAL and udev do. The sysfs file system is used by udev to dynamically generate needed device files in the **/dev** directory, as well as by HAL to manage removable device files as needed. The **/sys** file system type is sysfs. The **/sys** subdirectories organize your devices into different categories. The file system is used by **systool** to display a listing of your installed devices. The tool is part of the **sysfsutils** package (Universe respository). The following example will list all your system devices.

```
systool
```

Like **/proc**, the **/sys** directory resides only in memory, but it is still mounted in the **/etc/fstab** file.

File	Description
/proc/devices	Lists the device drivers configured for the currently running kernel
/proc/dma	Displays the DMA channels currently used
/proc/interrupts	Displays the IRQs (interrupts) in use
/proc/ioports	Shows the I/O ports in use
/proc/pci	Lists PCI devices
/proc/asound	Lists sound devices
/proc/ide	Directory for IDE devices
/proc/net	Directory for network devices

Table 17-2: /proc Device Information Files

The proc File System: /proc

The **/proc** file system is an older file system that was used to maintain information about kernel processes, including devices. It maintains special information files for your devices, though many of these are now supported by the sysfs file system. The **/proc/devices** file lists your installed character and block devices along with their major numbers. Intetrrupts requests (IRQs), direct memory access channels (DMAs), and I/O ports currently used for devices are listed in the

interrupts, **dma**, and **ioports** files, respectively. Certain files list information covering several devices, such as **pci**, which lists all your PCI devices, and **sound**, which lists all your sound devices. The **sound** file lists detailed information about your sound card. Several subdirectories, such as **net**, **ide**, and **scsi**, contain information files for different devices. Certain files hold configuration information that can be changed dynamically, such as the IP packet forwarding capability and the maximum number of files. You can change these values with the **sysctl** tool or by manually editing certain files. Table 17-2 lists several device-related **/proc** files.

udev: Device Files

Devices are hotpluggable, meaning they can be easily attached and removed. Their configuration is dynamically detected and does not rely on manual administrative settings. The hotplug tool used to detect device files is udev, user devices. Each time your system is booted, udev automatically detects your devices and generates device files for them in the **/etc/dev** directory. This means that the **/etc/dev** directory and its files are recreated each time you boot. It is a dynamic directory, no longer static. udev uses a set of rules to direct how device files are to be generated, including any corresponding symbolic links. These are located in the **/etc/udev/rules.d** file. You can find out more about udev at http://**kernel.org/pub/linux/utils/kernel/hotplug/udev.html**.

As part of the hotplug system, udev will automatically detect kernel devices that are added or removed from the system. When the device interface is first created, its corresponding **sysfs** file is located and read, determining any additional attributes such as serial numbers and device major and minor numbers that can be used to uniquely identify the device. These can be used as keys in udev rules to create the device interface. Once the device is created, it is listed in the udev database, which keeps track of currently installed devices.

If a device is added, udev is called by hotplug. It checks the sysfs file for that device for the major and minor numbers, if provided. It then uses the rules in its rules file to create the device file and any symbolic links to create the device file in **/dev**, with permissions specified for the device in the udev permissions rules.

As **/etc/dev** is now dynamic, any changes you make manually to the **/etc/dev** directory will be lost when you reboot. This includes the creation of any symbolic links you might create manually, such as **/dev/cdrom** that many software applications use. Instead, such symbolic links have to be configured in the udev rules files, located in the **/etc/udev/rules.d** directory. Default rules are already in place for symbolic links, but you can create rules to add your own.

udev Configuration

The configuration file for udev is **/etc/udev/udev.conf**. Here are set global udev options such as the logging level. The udev tool uses the udev **rules.d** files to dynamically create your device files. Be very careful in making any changes, particularly to rules file locations. Support for all devices on your system relies on these rules. The default **udev.conf** file is shown here and supports entries only for the location of the device files (**udev_root**) and the logging priority (**udev_log**).

```
# udev.conf
# The initial syslog(3) priority: "err", "info", "debug" or its
# numerical equivalent. For runtime debugging, the daemons internal
# state can be changed with: "udevadm control --log_priority=<value>".
udev_log="err"
```

You use the **udevadm** command to obtain information about devices and to set options for the **udev** server, primarily options used in debugging. The **udevadm** control command has options to set the log priority, stop processing events, set environment variables, and set the number or maximum events allowed. **udevadm** takes as its argument a command, which in turn may have options. The commands are listed in Table 17-3.

Command	Description
info *options*	Queries udev database for device information
settle *options*	Watch udev device queue
control *options instructions*	Set options for udev events
monitor *options*	Display udev events
test *options devpath*	Simulate udev event for testing and debugging
version	Udev version
help	List udev commands and description
trigger *options*	Request device events

Table 17-3: udevman commands

Device Names and udev Rules: /etc/udev/rules.d

The name of a device file is designed to reflect the task of the device. Printer device files begin with **lp** for "line print." Because you can have more than one printer connected to your system, the particular printer device files are distinguished by two or more numbers or letters following the prefix **lp**, such as **lp0**, **lp1**, **lp2**. The same is true for terminal device files, which begin with the prefix **tty**, for "teletype."; they are further distinguished by numbers or letters such as **tty0**, **tty1**, **ttyS0**, and so on. You can obtain a complete listing of the current device filenames and the devices for which they are used from the **kernel.org** website at **http://kernel.org/pub/linux/docs/device-list/devices.txt**.

With udev, device names are determined dynamically by rules listed in the udev rules files. These are located in **/etc/udev/rules.d**. The rules files that you will find in this directory are generated by your system during installation. You should never edit them. If you need to add rules of your own, you should create your own rules file. The rules files are named, beginning with a number to establish priority. They are read sequentially, with the first rules overriding any conflicting later ones. All rules files have a **.rules** extension.

The **/etc/udev/rules.d** directory hold specialized rules for your installation that you can configure. The **/lib/udev/rules.d** directory holds system rules, including default rules, which you do not modify. The rules files that you will find in the **/lib/udev/rules.d** directory are generated by your system during installation. You should never edit them. If you need to add rules of your own, you should create your own rules file, or carefully edit the rules files in the **/etc/udev/rules.d** directory.

/etc/udev/rules.d

In the **/etc/udev/rules.d** directory, rules have been distributed among a variety of different rules files which can be modified. Network device rules are held in the **70-persistent-net.rules** file, and the rules for DVD/CD devices are held in the **70-persistent-cd.rules** file. These rules files can be modified by adding additional rules. You should be careful when performing any modifications, making sure your rules are correct.

To customize your setup, you can create your own separate rules files in **/etc/udev/rules.d**. In your rules file you would normally define only symlinks, using SYMLINK keys alone, as described in the following sections. These set up symbolic links to devices, letting you access them with other device names. NAME keys are used to create the original device interface, a task usually left to udev.

/lib/udev/rules.d

Default rules for your devices are placed by udev in the rules files in the **/lib/udev/rules.d/** directory. These rules have been provided for your Ubuntu distribution and are designed specifically for it. You should never modify these rules. They will always be overwritten on update. Many of the rules files are set up for more specialized devices like **45-libmtp8.rules** for music players, **85-pcmcia.rules** for PCMCIA devices, and **40-alsa.rules** for the sound driver.

Though you never edit these files, though you can check them to see how device naming is handled. These files will create device files using the official kernel names. These names are often referenced directly by applications that expect to find devices with these particular names, such as **lp0** for a printer device

udev rules

In an udev rules file, each line maps a device attribute to a device name, as well as specifying any symbolic names (links). Attributes are specified using keys, of which there may be more than one. If all the keys match a device, then the associated name is used for it and a device file of that name will be generated. An assignable key, like NAME for the device name or SYMLINK for a symbolic name, is use to assign the matched value. Instead of listing a device name, a program or script may be specified instead to generate the name. This is often the case for DVD/CD-ROM devices, where the device name could be a dvdwriter, cdwriter, cdrom, or dvdrom.

Each line maps a device attribute to a device name, as well as specifying any symbolic names (links). Attributes are specified using keys, of which there may be more than one. If all the keys match a device, then the associated name is used for it and a device file of that name will be generated. An assignable key, like NAME for the device name or SYMLINK for a symbolic name, is use to assign the matched value. Instead of listing a device name, a program or script may be specified instead to generate the name. This is often the case for DVD/CD-ROM devices, where the device name could be a dvdwriter, cdwriter, cdrom, or dvdrom.

The rules consist of a comma-separated list of fields. A field consists of a matching or assignable key. The matching keys use the == and != operators to compare for equality and inequality.   The *, ?, and [] operators can match any characters, any single character, or a class of characters, just as in the shell.   The assignable keys can use the =, +=, and := operators to assign values. The = operator assigns a single value, the += appends the value to those already assigned, and the := operator makes an assignment final, preventing later changes. The udev keys are listed in Table 17-4. Check the udev Man page for detailed descriptions.

Matching Keys	Description
ACTION	Match the event action
DEVPATH	Match the device path
ENV{*key*}	Match an environment variable value
BUS	Match the bus type of the device. (The sysfs device bus must be able to be determined by a "device" symlink.)
DRIVER	Match the device driver name.
ID	Match the device number on the bus, for instance, the PCI bus ID.
KERNEL	Match the kernel device name.
PROGRAM	Use an external program to determine the device. This key is valid if the program returns successful. The string returned by the program may be additionally matched with the RESULT key.
RESULT	Match the returned string of the last PROGRAM call. This key may be used in any following rule after a PROGRAM call.
SUBSYSTEM	Match the device subsystem.
SYSFS{{*filename*}}	Match the sysfs device attribute, for instance, a label, vendor, USB serial number, SCSI UUID, or file system label.
Assignable Keys	**Description**
NAME	The name of the node to be created, or the name the network interface should be renamed to.
OWNER, GROUP, MODE	The permissions for the device.
PLACE	Match the location on the bus, such as the physical port of a USB device.
ENV{*key*}	Export variable to environment
IMPORT{*type*}	Import results of a program, contents of a text file, or stored keys in a parent device. The type can be **program**, **file**, or **parent**.
SYMLINK	The name of the symbolic link (symlink) for the device.
RUN	Add program to list of programs to be run by device

Table 17-4: udev Rule keys

These examples are similar to the default rules set up by udev in **/lib/udev/rules.d**. You can find many of these rules listed in the **50-udev-default.rules** file. Be careful never to modify any of the files in the **/lib/udev/rules.d** directory.

The key fields such as KERNEL support pattern matching to specify collections of devices. For example, mouse* will match all devices beginning with the pattern "mouse". The following field uses the KERNEL key to match on all mouse devices as listed by the kernel:

```
KERNEL=="mouse*"
```

The next key will match on all printer devices numbered **lp0** through **lp9**. It uses brackets to specify a range of numbers or characters, in this case 0 through 9, **[0-9]**:

```
KERNEL=="lp[0-9]*"
```

The NAME, SYMLINK, and PROGRAM fields support string substitution codes similar to the way printf codes work. Such a code is preceded by a % symbol. The code allows several possible devices and names to be referenced in the same rule. Table 17-5 lists the supported codes.

Substitution Code	Description
%n	The kernel number of the device
%k	The kernel name for the device
%M	The kernel major number
%m	The kernel minor number
%p	The device path
%b	The device name matched from the device path
%c	The string returned by a PROGRAM field (can't be used in a PROGRAM field)
%s {*filename*}	Content of sysfs attribute
%E{*key*}	Value of environment variable
%N	Name of a temporary device node, to provide access before real node is created
%%	Quotes the % character in case it is needed in the device name

Table 17-5: udev Substitution Codes

Rules use a KERNEL key to designate devices. The KERNEL key is followed by either a NAME key to specify the device filename or a SYMLINK key to set up a symbolic link for a device file. The following rule uses a KERNEL key to match on all mouse devices as listed by the kernel. Corresponding device names are placed in the **/dev/input** directory, and the name used is the kernel name for the device (**%k**):

```
KERNEL=="mouse*",  NAME="input/%k"
```

A default rule for mice can be found in the **/lib/udev/ruled.d/50-udev-default.rules** file. It covers mouse and mice devices. The MODE is 0640, which is discussed in later sections.

```
KERNEL=="mouse*|mice|event*", NAME="input/%k", MODE="0640"
```

The following rule uses both a SUBSYSTEMS key and a KERNEL key to set up device files for USB printers, whose kernel names will be used to create device files in **/dev/usb**:

```
SUBSYSTEMS=="usb", KERNEL=="lp[0-9]*", NAME="usb/%k"
```

Symbolic Links

Certain device files are really symbolic links bearing common device names that are often linked to the actual device file used. A *symbolic link* is another name for a file that is used like a shortcut, referencing that file. Common devices like printers, CD-ROM drives, hard drives, SCSI devices, and sound devices, along with many others, will have corresponding symbolic links. For example, a **/dev/cdrom** symbolic link links to the actual device file used for your CD-ROM. If your CD-ROM is an IDE device, it may use the device file **hdc**. In this case, **/dev/cdrom** is a link to **/dev/hdc**. In effect, **/dev/cdrom** is another name for **/dev/hdc**. Serial ATA DVD/CD drives will be linked to **scd** devices, such as **scd0** for the first Serial ATA CD/DVD drive. If your drive functions both as a CD and DVD writer and reader, you will have several links to the same device. In this case the links **cdrom**, **cdrw**, **cdwriter**, **dvd**, **dvdrw**, and **dvdwriter** will all link to the same CD/DVD RW-ROM device.

A **/dev/modem** link file also exists for your modem. If your modem is connected to the second serial port, its device file will be **/dev/ttyS1**. In this case, **/dev/modem** will be a link to that device file. Applications can then use **/dev/modem** to access your modem instead of having to know the actual device file used. Table 17-6 lists commonly used device links.

Symbolic links are created by udev using the SYMLINK field. The symbolic links for a device can be listed either with the same rule creating a device file (NAME key) or in a separate rule that will specify only a symbolic link. The inclusion of the NAME key does not have to be specific, if the default device name is used. The + added to the = symbol will automatically create the device with the default name, not requiring an explicit NAME key in the rule. The following rule is for USB printers. It includes both the default name, and implied NAME key creating the device (+), and a symbolic link, **usb%k**. The **%k** will add the kernel device name to the symbolic link. The rule can be found in the **/lib/udev/rules.d/50-udev-default.rules** file.

```
SUBSYSTEM=="usb", KERNEL=="lp*", NAME="usb/%k", SYMLINK+="usb%k", GROUP="lp"
```

Link	Description
cdrom	Link to your CD-ROM device file, set in **/etc/udev/rules.d**
dvd	Link to your DVD-ROM device file, set in **/etc/udev/rules.d**
cdwriter	Link to your CD-R or CD-RW device file, set in **/etc/udev/rules.d**
dvdwriter	Link to your DVD-R or DVD-RW device file, set in **/etc/udev/rules.d**
modem	Link to your modem device file, set in **/etc/udev/rules.d**
floppy	Link to your floppy device file, set in **/etc/udev/rules.d**
tape	Link to your tape device file, set in **/etc/udev/rules.d**
scanner	Link to your scanner device file, set in **/etc/udev/rules.d**
mouse	Link to your mouse device file, set in **/etc/udev/rules.d**
tape	Link to your tape device file, set in **/etc/udev/rules.d**

Table 17-6: Device Symbolic Links

Should you want to create more than one symbolic link for a device, you can list them in the SYMLINK field. The following creates two symbolic links, one **cdrom** and another named **cdrom-** with the kernel name attached (**%k**).

```
SYMLINK+="cdrom cdrom-%k"
```

In the **70-persistent-cd.rules** files you will find several SYMLINK fields for optical devices, one of which is shown here.

```
SYMLINK+="dvd"
```

Symbolic links for CD/DVD aliases are generated for you automatically using a rules generator file, **75-cd-aliases-generator**. You should not have to create any symbolic links for CD/DVD aliases, including removable ones (such as USB/Firewire).

If you want to create more than one symbolic link for a device, you can list them in the SYMLINK key. Should you decide to set up a separate rule that specifies just a symbolic link, the symbolic link will be kept on a list awaiting the creation of its device. This also allows you to add other symbolic links for a device in other rules files. This situation can be confusing because symbolic links can be created for devices that are not yet generated. The symbolic links will be defined and held until needed, when the device is generated. This is why you could have many more SYMLINK rules than NAME rules in udev that actually set up device files. In the case of removable devices, they will not have a device name generated until they are connected.

In most cases you will only need symbolic links for devices using the official symbolic names. Most of these are already defined for you. Should you need to create just a symbolic link, you can create a SYMLINK rule for it. However, a new SYMLINK rule needs to be placed before the name rules that name that device. The SYMLINK rules for a device are read by udev and kept until a device is named. Then those symbolic names can be used for that device. You can have as many symbolic links for the same device as you want, meaning that you could have several SYMLINK rules for the same device. When the NAME rule for the device is encountered, the previous SYMLINK keys are simply appended.

Most standard symbolic names are already defined in the rules files, such as **scd%n** for the for a SCSI CD-ROM device. In the following example, the device is referenced by its KERNEL key and the symbolic link is applied with SYMLINK key.:

```
SUBSYSTEM=="block", KERNEL=="sr[0-9]*", SYMLINK+="scd%n", GROUP="cdrom"
```

Persistent Rules

The default name rules will provide names for your devices using the official symbolic names reserved for them, for instance, lp$n$ for printer, where n is the number of the printer. For fixed devices, such as fixed printers, this is normally adequate. However, for removable devices, such as USB printers that may be attached in different sequences at different times to USB ports, the names used may not refer to the same printer. For example, if you have two USB printers, an Epson and Canon, and you attach the Epson first and the Canon second, the Epson will be given the name **usb/lp0** and the Canon will have the name **usb/lp1**. If, however, you later detach them and reattach the Canon first and the Epson second, then the Canon will have the name **usb/lp0** and the Epson will have **usb/lp1**. The particular device needs to be correctly identified no matter what connection it is attached to.

To always correctly identify a device, udev uses persistent names. The rules for these names are held in the persistent names files. Currently there are persistent rule files for storage, tape, input, cd, and network devices. The input device persistent rules are held in the **60 - persistent-input.rules** and the storage rules are in **60-persistent-storage.rules**. Persistent rules for network devices are **70-persistent-net.rules**, and CD/DVD devices are in **70-persistent-cd.rules** file

Generated Rules

Devices can have their rules determined using generator rules files. These generator rules make use of udev scripts and programs in the **/lib/udev** directory to identify the devices. Network device rules are determined using a generator files. Entries for persistent rules files for network devices are created by their generator rules. Any additional rules you want to set up for network devices also be placed in the network persistent rules file. You have to add a generated field, ENV{GENERATED} = "1", at the end of any of your own rules.

The persistent rules file for network interfaces is **/lib/udev/75--persistent-net-generator.rules** and the persistent network interface file is **/etc/udev/70-persistent-net.rules**. The generator rules file determines the MAC address of the network device and then invokes the **write_net_rules** script in **/lib/udev** to determine the rule. The rule is placed in the **70-persistent-net.rules** file. You will find an entries here for your Ethernet connections, such as **eth0**.

Symbolic links (aliases) for CD/DVD devices are also created by a generator rules file, **/lib/udev/75-cd-aliases-generator**. This file is run for devices that have no rule for persistent names. These rules are placed in the **/etc/udev/70-persistent-cd.rules** file. For USB and Firewire connected CD/DVDs, the generator file invokes the **write_cd_rules** script with the **by-id** option to uniquely identify the CD/DVD device using its device id like a serial number or model. Other CD/DVDs have symbolic names generated using just the **write_cd_rules** program with no option which defaults to a by-path option. This option identifies the device by its path name on the system, useful for fixed attached CD/DVD devices.

Program Keys, IMPORT{program} keys, and /lib/udev

The PROGRAM, RUN, and IMPORT keys can be used to specify and run external scripts or programs needed to set up or manage devices. The PROGRAM keys is used for scripts that set up devices, and the RUN key to run programs on devices already set up. RUN programs are usually executed when a device is removed or attached. The IMPORT key is designed to import results or file content into a rules file. It can also be used to run programs to generate rules for devices. The IMPORT and PROGRAM keys normally use udev callouts that return device values like serial numbers or perform rule generation tasks (see Table 17-7).

The PROGRAM scripts and programs used to set up devices can be found in the **/lib/udev** directory. These include **write_cd_rules** for setting up CD/DVD-RW/ROM symlinks, **create_floppy_devices** for floppy drives, and various ID scripts for determining the serial number of a device like **usb_id**, **vol_id**, and **cdrom_id**.

The rules in the **75-cd-aliases-generator.rules** file in the **/lib/udev/rules.d** directory are used to generate symlinks for CD/DVD-ROMs that are not covered by any previous rules. They are designed for CD/DVD devices that are frequently being removed and attached at different connections. These rules, including the following one, will invoke the **write_cd_rules** script in the **/lib/udev** directory, using the PROGRAM key.

```
ACTION=="add", SUBSYSTEM=="block", ENV{ID_CDROM}=="?*", ENV{GENERATED}!="?*",
PROGRAM="write_cd_rules", SYMLINK+="%c"
```

The **write_cd_rules** script will generate a rule in the appropriate rules file in the **/etc/udev/rules.d** directory. These rules files are editable (unlike those in the **/lib/udev/rules.d** directory).

The IMPORT command will import the results of a program or the content of file into the rule file. The IMPORT options are **program** for a program to run, or **file** for the contents of a file to read. In some cases it used primarily to run a script to generate rules. IMPORT operation are used to determine the serial number of a removable device using scripts like **ata_id**. Attached devices will have serial numbers accessible in the **/dev/disk/by-id** directory. An entry from the **60-persistent-storage.rules** file for IDE hard disks is shown here:

```
KERNEL=="hd*[!0-9]", IMPORT{program}="ata_id --export $tempnode"
```

An IMPORT operation is used for persistent network devices, the rules in the **75-persistent-net-gnerator.rules** file uses the **write_net_rules** script to generate rules. This script both write rules to the **/etc/udev/ruled.d/70-peristent-net.rules** file.

```
# write rule
DRIVERS=="?*", IMPORT{program}="write_net_rules"
```

For hotplug network connections, the **60-net.rules** file will run a rule to run the **net.hotplug** script using the RUN key.

```
SUBSYSTEM=="net", RUN+="/etc/sysconfig/network-scripts/net.hotplug"
```

udev callout	Description
`ata_id`	Callout script to return a serial number for a ATA storage device
`bluetooth_serial`	Callout script for a Bluetooth serial device
`cdrom_id`	Callout script to return a serial number for a CD/DVD-ROM device
`scsi_id`	Callout script to return a serial number for a SCSI storage device
`path_id`	Callout script to generate a unique path name for a device
`ata_id`	Callout script to return a serial number for a ATA storage device
`usb_id`	Callout script to return a serial number for a USB device
`vol_id`	Callout script to return a serial number for a Volume storage device
`create_floppy_devices`	Create a floppy device
`rename_device`	Rename a device
`write_cd_rules`	Write persistent CD/DVD-RW/ROM rules
`write_net_rules`	Write persistent network device rules

Table 17-7: Udev callouts (scripts), /lib/udev

Creating udev Rules

If you want to create rules of your own, you can place them in a separate rules file in the **/etc/udev/rules.d** directory (though you can edit the rules files already in that directory). The NAME rules that name devices are read lexically, where the first NAME rule will take precedence over any later ones. Only the first NAME rule for a device will be used. Later NAME rules for that same device will be ignored. Keep in mind that a SYMLINK rule with a += includes a NAME rule for the default device, even though the NAME key is not explicitly shown.

Since rules are being created that are meant to replace the default rules, they would have to be run first. To do this, you would place them in a rules file that begins with a very low number, say 10. Rules files are read in lexical order, with the lower numbers read first. You could create a file called **10-user.rules** in the **/etc/udev/rules.d** directory. Here you would place your own rules. Conversely, if you wanted rules that would run only if the defaults failed for some reason, you would use a rules file numbered higher, like **90-mydefaults.rules**. For example, a user could set up a canon-pr rule to replace the default printer rule for that printer. The new user canon-pr rule would be placed in a **10-user.rules** file to be executed before the printer rules file, thereby taking precedence. The default printer rule (shown here) would not be applied to the Canon printer.

```
SUBSYTEM="usb", KERNEL="lp*", NAME="usb/%k"
```

SYMLINK Rules

In most cases, you will only need to create symbolic links for devices, using the official name. You can also create rules that just create symbolic links. However, these need to be placed before the name rules that name the devices. These SYMLINK rules are read by udev and kept until a device is named. Then all the symbolic names will be used for that device. You can have as many symbolic links for the same device as you want, meaning that you could have several SYMLINK rules for the same device. When the NAME rule for the device is encountered, the previous SYMLINK keys are simply appended.

Most standard symbolic names are already defined, such as audio for the audio device. In the following example, the device is referenced by its KERNEL key and the symbolic link is applied with SYMLINK key. The NAME key for the default device is implied'

If you always know the name for a device, you can easily add a SYMLINK rule. For example, if you know your DVD-ROM is attached to the first secondary IDE connection (**sdc**), you can create a symbolic name of your own choosing with a SYMLINK rule. In the next example a new symbolic link, **mydvdrom**, is created for the DVD-ROM on the **/dev/sdc** device.

```
KERNEL="sdc", SYMLINK="mydvdrom"
```

For a SYMLINK rule to be used, it must occur before a NAME rule that names the device. You should place these rules in a file that will precede the other rules files, such as **10-user.rules**.

Manually Creating Persistent Names: udevinfo

The default udev rules will provide names for your devices using the official symbolic names reserved for them, for instance, lp*n* for printer, where *n* is the number of the printer. For fixed devices, such as fixed printers, this is normally adequate. However, for removable devices, such as USB printers, that may be attached in different sequences at different times to USB ports, the names used may not refer to the same printer. For example, if you have two USB printers, an

Epson and Canon, and attach the Epson first and the Canon second, the Epson will be given the name **usb/lp0** and the Canon will have the name **usb/lp1**. If, however, you later detach them and reattach the Canon first and the Epson second, then the Canon will have the name **usb/lp0** and the Epson will have **usb/lp1**. If you want the Epson to always have the same symbolic name, say **epson-pr**, and likewise the Canon, as in **canon-pr**, you would have to create your own rule for detecting these printers and giving them your own symbolic names.

The key task in creating a persistent name is to use unique information to identify the device. You then create a rule that references the device with the unique information, identifying it, and then name it with an official name but giving it a unique symbolic name. You can then use the unique symbolic name, like **canon-pr**, to always reference just that printer and no other, when it is plugged in. In this example, unique information such as the Canon printer serial number is used to identify the Canon printer. It is next named with the official name, **usb/lp0** or **usb/lp1**, depending on whether another printer was plugged in first, and then it is given a unique symbolic name, **canon-pr**, which will reference that official name, whatever it may be. Keeping the official name, like **lp0**, preserves standard access to the device as used by many applications.

You use **/sys** file system information about the device to detect the correct device to reference with the symbolic link. Unique **/sys** device information such as the vendor serial number or the vendor name can be used to uniquely reference the device. To obtain this information, you need to first query the **/sys** file system. You do this with the `udevinfo` command.

First you will need to know where the device is located in the **/sys** file system. You plug in your device, which will automatically configure and name it, using the official name. For example, plugging in the USB printer will create a **/dev/usb/lp0** device name for it. You can use this device name to find out where the USB printer information is in **/sys**. Use the `udevinfo` command with the `-q path` option to query for the **/sys** pathname, and add the `-n` option with the device's full pathname to identify the device you are searching for. The following command will display the **/sys** path for the printer with the device name **lp0**. In this case, the device is in the **class** subdirectory under **usb**. The path will assume **/sys**.

```
udevinfo -q path -n  /dev/usb/lp0
  /class/usb/lp0
```

One you have the device's **/sys** path, you can use that path to display information about it. Use the `udevinfo` command again with the `-a` option to display all information about the device and the `-p` option to specify its path in the **/sys** file system. The listing can be extensive, so you should pipe the output to `less` or redirect it to a file.

```
udevinfo -a  -p  /sys/class/usb/lp0 | less
```

Some of the key output to look for is the bus used and information such as the serial number, product name, or manufacturer, as shown here. Look for information that uniquely identifies the device, such as the serial number. Some devices will support different buses, and the information may be different for each. Be sure to use the information for that bus when setting up your keys in the udev rule.

```
BUS="usb"
ATTRS{serial}="300HCR"
ATTRS{manufacturer}="Canon"
ATTRS{idproduct}="1074"
ATTRS{product}="S330"
```

You can use much of this information in an ATTRS key in an udev rule to identify the device. The ATTRS key (attributes) is used to obtain **/sys** information about a device. You use the ATTRS key with the field you want referenced placed in braces. You can then match that field to a value to reference the particular device you want. Use the = sign and a valid field value to match against. Once you know the **/sys** serial number of a device, you can use it in ATTRS keys in udev rules to uniquely reference the device. The following key checks the serial number of the devices field for the Canon printer's serial number:

```
ATTRS{serial}=="300HCR"
```

A user rule can now be created for the Canon printer.

In another rules file you can add your own symbolic link using **/sys** information to uniquely identify the printer and name the device with its official kernel name. The first two keys, BUS and ATTRS, specify the particular printer. In this case the serial number of the printer is used to uniquely identify it. The NAME key will name the printer using the official kernel name, always referenced with the **%k** code. Since this is a USB printer, its device file will be placed in the **usb** subdirectory, **usb/%k**. Then the SYMLINK key defines the unique symbolic name to use, in this case **canon-pr** in the **/dev/usb** directory.

```
SUBSYSTEM="usb", ATTRS{serial}="300HCR", NAME="usb/%k", SYMLINK="usb/canon-pr"
```

The rules are applied dynamically in real time. To run a new rule, simple attach your USB printer (or detach and reattach). You will see the device files automatically generated.

Permission and Owner Fields: MODE, GROUP, OWNER

Additional fields provide ownership and permission attributes for devices. The MODE field is used to specify permissions, the OWNER to specify the user the owns the device (usually the root user). The GROUP field lets you add the device to a group that can then be used to control access.

The MODE field is a octal bit permission setting, the same as used for file permissions. Usually this is set to 660, owner and group read/write permission. Pattern matching is supported with the *****, **?**, and **[]** operators. The following example sets mouse devices to the owner read/write owner and group read permissions, 0640:

```
KERNEL=="mouse*|mice|event*", NAME="input/%k", MODE="0640"
```

The floppy device (**fd**) entry specifies a **floppy** group.

```
KERNEL=="fd[01]*", GROUP="floppy"
```

Parallel printer devices (**parport**) are assigned to the **lp** group.

```
KERNEL=="parport[0-9]*", GROUP="lp"
```

Tape devices (**pt** and **ntp**) use the **disk** group.

```
KERNEL==""pt[0-9]*|npt[0-9]*", GROUP="disk"
```

The default settings set the OWNER and GROUP to root with owner read/write permissions (600).

```
KERNEL=="*",  OWNER="root" GROUP="root", MODE="0600"
```

Hardware Abstraction Layer: HAL

The purpose of the Hardware Abstraction Layer (HAL) is to abstract the process of applications accessing devices. Applications should not have to know anything about a device, even its symbolic name. The application should just have to request a device of a certain type, and then a service, such as HAL, should provide what is available. Device implementation becomes hidden from applications.

HAL makes devices easily available to desktops and applications using a D-BUS (device bus) structure. Device are managed as objects that applications can easily access. The D-BUS service is provided by the HAL daemon, **haldaemon**. Interaction with the device object is provided by the **www.freedesktop.org** HAL service.

HAL is an information service for devices. The HAL daemon maintains a dynamic database of connected hardware devices. This information can be used by specialized callout programs to maintain certain device configuration files. This is the case with the managing removable storage devices. HAL will invoke the specialized callout programs that will use HAL information to dynamically manage devices. Removable devices like CD-ROM discs or USB card readers are managed by specialized callouts with HAL information, detecting when such items are attached. The situation can be confusing. Callout programs perform the actual tasks, but HAL provides the device information. For example, though the callout hal-system-storage-mount mounts a device, the options and mountpoints used for CD-ROM entries are specified in HAL device information files that set policies for storage management.

Note: No longer are entries maintained in the */etc/fstab* file for removable devices like your CD-ROMs. These devices are managed directly by HAL using it set of storage callouts like **hal-storage-mount** to mount a device or **hal-storage-eject** to remove one. In effect you now have to use the HAL device information files to manage your removable file systems.

HAL is a software project of **www.freedesktop.org**, which specializes in open source desktop tools. Check the latest HAL specification documentation at **http://freedesktop.org** (search on **HAL**) for detailed explanations of how HAL works (the **specifications** link on the HAL page, Latest HAL Specification). The documentation is very detailed and complete. Also download and install the **hal-docs** package. In the **/usr/share/doc/hal*** directory you will find detailed documentation for HAL specifications (**spec/hal-spec.html**), as well and a general overview. Use your browser to read the **hal-spec.html** page (the version number, **0.5.12**, will change with HAL updates).

```
file:///usr/share/doc/hal-0.5.12/spec/hal-spec.html
```

The HAL Daemon and HAL tools

The HAL daemon, **hald**, is run as the **haldaemon** process. Information provided by the HAL daemon for all your devices can be displayed using the HAL tools such as **lshal** to list your HAL devices and **hal-get-property** to display a certain property of a device. The **hal-get-property** tool used the **--udi** option to obtain a device's Unique Device Identifier and the **--key** option for the name of the property.

The **hal-set-property** uses the **--udi** and **--key** options. You can set property values with options like **--string, --bool, --int**, and add values with options like **--strlist-post**. use the **--remove** option to remove a property.

The **hal-find-by-property** lets you search for a HAL device by searching device properties. The **--string** option lets you provide a pattern to search for in the HAL device property fields. The **--key** option will search on a name. The UIDs for matching devices are output. The hal-find-by-capability lets you search for a HAL device based on device capabilities. The **--capability** option lets you provide a pattern to search for. The UIDs for matching devices are displayed.

For removable media, HAL will continually poll for the device in order to quickly detect it when inserted or attached. This can cause problems if the device configuration is corrupted, as well as apply addition overhead for managing the device. Should you have difficulties with a removable media device, you can disable polling for it with hal-disable-polling. The **--udi** option uses the UDI to reference the device. You can also use the **--enable-polling** option to restore polling.

The **lock-out** tool let you control HAL locks manually. It is useful only for software that does not use HAL already. The **--run** option specifies the program to be run.

Tool	Description
`lshal`	Display HAL devices
`hal-get-property`	Retrieve a device property for the HAL database
`hal-set-property`	Set a device property for the HAL database
`hal-find-by-property`	Search for a device on the property fields
`hal-find-by-capability`	Search for a device based on a capability
`hal-disable-polling`	Disable polling for removable media.

HAL Configuration: /etc/hal/fdi, and /usr/share/hal/fdi

Information about devices and policies to manage devices are held in device information files in the **/etc/hal/fdi** and **/usr/share/hal/fdi** directories. These directories are where you set properties such as options that are to be used for CD-ROMs in **/etc/fstab**.

The implementation of HAL on Linux configures storage management by focusing on storage methods for mountable volumes, instead of particular devices. Volume properties define actions to take and valid options that can be used. Special callouts perform the actions directly, such as **hal-storage-mount** to mount media, or **hal-storage-eject** to remove it.

Device Information Files: fdi

HAL properties for these devices are handled by device information files (fdi) in the **/usr/share/hal/fdi** and **/etc/hal/fdi** directories. The **/usr/share/hal/fdi** directory is used for configurations provided by the distribution, whereas **/etc/hal/fdi** is used for setting user administrative configurations. In both are listed subdirectories for the different kinds of information that HAL manages, such as **policy**, whose subdirectories have files with policies for how to manage devices. The files, known as device information files, have rules for obtaining information about devices, as well as rules for detecting and assigning options for removable devices. The device information files have the extension **.fdi**, as in **storage-methods.fdi**. For example, the **policy** directory has two subdirectories: **10osvendor** and **20thirdpary**. The **10osvendor** holds the fdi files that have policy rules for managing removable devices on Linux (10osvendor replaces 90defaultpolicy in earlier HAL versions). This directory holds the **20-storage-methods.fdi** policy file used for storage devices. Here you will find the properties that specify options for removable storage devices such as CD-ROMs. The directories begin with numbers; lower numbers are read first. Unlike with udev, the last property read will override any previous property settings, so priority is given to higher-numbered directories and the fdi files they hold. This is why the default policies are in **10osvendor**, whereas the user policies, which override the defaults, are in a higher-numbered directory like **30user**, as are third-party policies, **20thirdpolicy**.

Three device information file directories set up in the device information file directories, each for different kinds of information: information, policy, and preprobe:

> **Information**   For information about devices.

> **Policy**   For setting policies such as storage policies. The default policies for a storage device are in a **20-storage-methods.fdi** file in the **policy/10osvendor** directory.

> **Preprobe**   Handles difficult devices such as unusual drives or drive configurations, for instance, those in **preprobe/10osvendor/10-ide-drives.fdi**. This contains information needed even before the device is probed.

> Within these subdirectories are still other subdirectories indicating where the device information files come from, such as **vendor**, **thirdparty**, or **user**, and their priority. Certain critical files are listed here:

> **information/10freedesktop**   Information provided by **freedesktop.org**

> **policy/10osvendor**   Default policies (set by system administrator and OS distribution)

> **preprobe/10usevendor**   Preprobe policies for difficult devices

Properties

Information for a device is specified with a *property* entry. Such entries consist of a key/value pair, where the key specifies the device and its attribute, and the value is the value for that attribute. There are many kinds of values, such as Boolean true/false, string values such as those use to specify directory mountpoints, or integer values.

Properties are classified according to metadata, physical connection, function, and policies. Metadata provides general information about a device, such as the bus it uses, its driver, or its HAL ID. Metadata properties begin with the key info, as in info.bus. Physical properties describe physical connections, namely the buses used. The IDE, PCI, and SCSI bus information is listed in ide, pci, and scsi keys. The usb_device properties are used for the USB bus; an example is **usb_device.number**.

The functional properties apply to specific kinds of devices. Here you will find properties for storage devices, such as the `storage.cdrom` keys that specify if an optical device is writable capabilities. For example, the `storage.cdrom.cdr` key set to true will specify that an optical drive can write to CD-R discs.

The volume properties are used for devices that can be mounted, like CD discs or USB drives.

Methods and properties can indicate how devices are to be handled. Methods are, in effect, the directives that callout programs will use to carry out tasks. Methods for storage media are handled using Volume properties, specifying methods (callouts) to use. Volume properties can specify device options like file system type and mount options. HAL uses scripts in the **/usr/libexec** directory to actually manage media. The following abbreviated entries come from the **20-storage-methods.fdi** policy file. The first specifies the action to take and the second the callout script to execute, **hal-storage-mount**.

```
<append key="Volume.method_names" type="strlist">Mount</append>
<append key="Volume.method_execpaths" type="strlist">hal-storage-mount</append>
```

Mount options are designated using **volume.mount.valid_options** as shown here for ro (read only). Options that will be used will be determined when the mount callout is executed.

```
<append key="volume.mount.valid_options"type="strlist">ro</append>
```

Several of the commonly used volume methods and properties are listed in Table 17-8.

Property	Description
volume.method_names	Action to be taken
volume.method.execpath	Callout script to be run for a device
volume.mount_point (*string*)	The preferred mountpoint for the storage device
volume.method.argnames (*string*)	Set of arguments to use for a file system
volume.mount.valid_options (*strlist*)	Default mount options for volumes, where *strlist* can be any mount option, such as **ro** or **exec**

Table 17-8: HAL Volume properties and methods.

Device Information File Directives

Properties are defined in directives listed in device information files. As noted, device information files have **.fdi** extensions. A directive is encased in greater- and less-than symbols. There are three directives:

> **merge** Merges a new property into a device's information database

> **append** Appends or modifies a property for that device already in the database

> The **match** Tests device information values

A directive includes a type attribute designating the type of value to be stored, such as string, bool, int, and double. The **copy_property** type copies a property. The following discussion of the **storage-methods.fdi** file shows several examples of merge and match directives.

storage.fdi

The **20-storage-methods.fdi** file in the **/usr/share/hal/fdi/policy/10osvendor** directory lists the policies for your removable storage devices. Here is where your options for storage volumes (e.g., CD-ROM) entries are actually specified. The file is organized in sections beginning with particular types of devices to standard defaults. Keys are used to define options, such as **volume.mount.valid_options**, which will specify a mount option for a storage device such as a CD-ROM. Keys are used to specify exceptions like hotplugged devices.

The **20-storage-methods.fdi** file begins with default properties and then lists those for specific kinds of devices. Unless redefined in a later key, the default will remain in effect. The options you will see listed for the default storage volumes will apply to CD-ROMs. For example, the **noexec** option is set as a valid default. The following sets **noexec** as a default mount option for a storage device. There are also entries for **ro** and **quiet**. The append operation adds the policy option.

```
<append key="volume.mount.valid_options"type="strlist">noexec</append>
```

The default mountpoint root directory for storage devices is now set by the mount callout script, **hal-storage-mount**. Currently this is **/media**. The default mountpoint is disk. HAL will try to use the Volume property information to generate a mountpoint.

The following example manages blank disks. Instead of being mounted, such disks can only be ejected. To determine possible actions, HAL uses **method_names**, **method_signatures**, and **method_execpaths** for the Volume properties (the org.freedesktop.Hal prefix for the keys has been removed from this example to make it more readable, as in **org.freedesktop.Hal.Volume.method_names**).

```
<match key="volume.disc.is_blank" bool="true">

<append key="info.interfaces"type="strlist">Volume</append>
<append key="Volume.method_names" type="strlist">Eject</append>
<append key="Volume.method_signatures" type="strlist">as</append>
<append key=" Volume.method_argnames" type="strlist">extra_options</append>
<append key="Device.Volume.method_execpaths" type="strlist">hal-storage-eject</append>

</match>
```

After dealing with special cases, the file system devices are matched as shown here:

```
<match key="volume.fsusage" string="filesystem">
```

Storage devices to ignore like recovery partitions are specified.

```
    <!-- ASUS ships some desktop with a recovery partition -->
<match key="volume.label" string="PQSERVICE">
<merge key="volume.ignore" type="bool">true</merge>
</match>
```

Then the actions to take and the callout script to use are specified such as the one for Unmount that uses **hal-storage-mount**.

```
<append key="Device.Volume.method_names" type="strlist">Mount</append>
<append key="Device.Volume.method_signatures" type="strlist">ssas</append>
<append key="Volume.method_argnames" type="strlist">mount_point fstype extra_options</append>
<append key="Device.Volume.method_execpaths" type="strlist">hal-storage-mount</append>
```

Options are then specified with Volume.mount.valid_options, starting with defaults and continuing with special cases, like **ext3** shown here.

```
<!-- allow these mount options for ext3 -->
```

```
<match key="volume.fstype" string="ext3">
<append key="volume.mount.valid_options" type="strlist">acl</append>
<append key="volume.mount.valid_options" type="strlist">user_xattr</append>
<append key="volume.mount.valid_options"type="strlist">data=</append>
 </match>
```

HAL Callouts

Callouts are programs invoked when the device object list is modified or when a device changes. As such, callouts can be used to maintain system-wide policy (that may be specific to the particular OS) such as changing permissions on device nodes, managing removable devices, or configuring the networking subsystem. There are three different kinds of callouts for devices, capabilities, and properties. *Device* callouts are run when a device is added or removed. *Capability* callouts add or remove device capabilities, and *property* callouts add or remove a device's property. Callouts are implemented using **method** property rules, such as the one that invokes the **hal-storage-eject** callout when CD/DVD-ROMs are removed as shown here:

```
<append key="org.freedesktop.Hal.Device.Volume.method_execpaths" type="strlist">hal-storage-
eject</append>
```

Callouts are placed in the **/usr/libexec** directory with the HAL callouts prefixed with **hal-**. . Here you will find many of storage callouts used by HAL such as **hal-storage-eject** and **hal-storage-mount**. The **gnome-mount** tool used for mounting CD/DVD disk on the Gnome desktop uses the HAL callouts.

Manual Devices

You can, if you wish, create device file interfaces manually yourself using the **MAKEDEV** or **mknod** commands. **MAKEDEV** is a script that can create device files for known fixed devices like attached hard disks. Check the **MAKEDEV** man page for details.

Linux implements several types of devices, the most common of which are block and character. A *block device,* such as a hard disk, transmits data a block at a time. A *character device,* such as a printer or modem, transmits data one character at a time, or rather as a continuous stream of data, not as separate blocks. Device driver files for character devices have a *c* as the first character in the permissions segment displayed by the **ls** command. Device driver files for block devices have a *b.* In the next example, **lp0** (the printer) is a character device and **sda1** (the hard disk) is a block device:

```
# ls -l sda1 lp0
brw-rw---- 1 root disk 3, 1 Jan 30 02:04 sda1
crw-rw---- 1 root lp   6, 0 Jan 30 02:04 lp0
```

The device type can be either *b, c, p,* or *u.* The *b* indicates a block device, and *c* is for a character device. The *u* is for an unbuffered character device, and the *p* is for a FIFO (first in, first out) device. Devices of the same type often have the same name; for example, serial interfaces all have the name **ttyS**. Devices of the same type are then uniquely identified by a number attached to the name. This number has two components: the major number and the minor number. Devices may have the same major number, but if so, the minor number is always different. This major and minor structure is designed to deal with situations in which several devices may be dependent on one larger device, such as several modems connected to the same I/O card. All the modems will have the same major number that references the card, but each modem will have a unique minor number. Both the minor and major numbers are required for block and character devices (*b, c,* and *u*). They are not used for FIFO devices, however.

Valid device names along with their major and minor numbers are listed in the **devices.txt** file located in the **/Documentation** directory for the kernel source code, **/usr/src/linux-**
*ver***/Documentation**. When you create a device, you use the major and minor numbers as well as the device name prefix for the particular kind of device you are creating. Most of these devices are already created for you and are listed in the **/etc/dev** directory.

Though the MAKEDEV command is preferable for creating device files, it can only create files for which it is configured. For devices not configured for use by MAKEDEV, you will have to use the mknod command. This is a lower-level command that requires manual configuration of all its settings. With the mknod command you can create a device file in the traditional manner without any of the configuration support that MAKEDEV provides.

The mknod command can create either a character or block-type device. The mknod command has the following syntax:

```
mknod options device device-type major-num minor-num
```

As most devices are automatically generated by udev created easily by MAKEDEV, you will rarely if ever need to use mknod. As a simple example, creating a device file with mknod for a printer port is discussed here. Linux systems usually provide device files for printer ports (**lp0–2**). As an example, you can see how an additional port could be created manually with the mknod command. Printer devices are character devices and must be owned by the root and daemon. The permissions for printer devices are read and write for the owner and the group, 660. The major device number is set to 6, while the minor device number is set to the port number of the printer, such as 0 for LPT1 and 1 for LPT2. Once the device is created, you use chown to change its ownership to the **root** user, since only the administrator should control it. Change the group to **lp** with the chgrp command.

Most devices belong to their own groups, such as **disks** for hard disk partitions, **lp** for printers, **floppy** for floppy disks, and **tty** for terminals. In the next example, a printer device is made on a fourth parallel port, **lp3**. The **-m** option specifies the permissions—in this case, 660. The device is a character device, as indicated by the c argument following the device name. The major number is 6, and the minor number is 3. If you were making a device at **lp4**, the major number would still be 6, but the minor number would be 4. Once the device is made, the chown command then changes the ownership of the parallel printer device to **root**. For printers, be sure that a spool directory has been created for your device. If not, you need to make one. Spool directories contain files for data that varies according to the device output or input, like that for printers or scanners.

As with all manual devices, the device file has to be placed in the **/etc/udev/devices** directory; udev will later put it in **/dev**.

```
# mknod -m 660 /etc/udev/devices/lp3 c 6 3
# chown root /etc/udev/devices/lp3
# chgrp lp /etc/udev/devices/lp3
```

Installing and Managing Terminals and Modems

In Linux, several users may be logged in at the same time. Each user needs his or her own terminal through which to access the Linux system, of course. The monitor on your PC acts as a special terminal, called the *console,* but you can add other terminals through either the serial ports on your PC or a special multiport card installed on your PC. The other terminals can be standalone terminals or PCs using terminal emulation programs. For a detailed explanation of terminal installation, see the **Term-HOWTO** file in **/usr/share/doc/HOWTO** or at the Linux Documentation Project site (**http://tldp.org**). A brief explanation is provided here.

Serial Ports

The serial ports on your PC are referred to as COM1, COM2, COM3, and COM4. These serial ports correspond to the terminal devices **/dev/ttyS0** through **/dev/ttyS3**. Note that several of these serial devices may already be used for other input devices such as your mouse and for communications devices such as your modem. If you have a serial printer, one of these serial devices is already used for that. If you installed a multiport card, you have many more ports from which to choose. For each terminal you add, udev will create the appropriate character device on your Linux system. The permissions for a terminal device are normally 660. *Terminal devices* are character devices with a major number of 4 and minor numbers usually beginning at 64.

Note: Terminal devices are managed by your system using the `mingetty` program. When your system starts, it sets up a set of connected terminals using TTY upstart files in the /etc/event.d directory, like tty1. These runs the mingetty program with the terminal device name, like **tty1**.

terminfo and /etc/event.d Files

The **/etc/inittab** file is no longer used to hold instructions for your system on how to manage terminal devices. Instead separate files in the **/etc/event.d** directory are uses, one for each terminal. The files are named with the **tty** prefix, like **tty1**.

The files have four basic components: an ID, a runlevel, an action, and a process. Terminal devices are identified by ID numbers, beginning with 1 for the first device. The runlevel at which the terminal operates is usually 1. The action is usually respawn, which means to run the process continually. The process is a call to the `mingetty`, `mgetty`, or `agetty` with the terminal device name.

The **/etc/terminfo** and **/usr/share/terminfo** directories holds the specification files for different terminal types. These are the different types of terminals users could use to log in to your system. It replaces the older **/etc/termcap** file. See the terminfo man page for more details.

tset

When a user logs in, having the terminal device initialized using the `tset` command is helpful. Usually the `tset` command is placed in the user's **.profile** file and is automatically executed whenever the user logs in to the system. You use the `tset` command to set the terminal type and any other options the terminal device requires. A common entry of `tset` for a **.profile** file follows. The `-m dialup:` option prompts the user to enter a terminal type. The type specified here is a default type that is displayed in parentheses. The user presses ENTER to choose the default. The prompt looks like this: `TERM=(vt100)?`.

```
eval 'tset -s -Q -m dialup:?vt00'
```

Note: Input devices, such as mice and keyboards, are displayed on several levels. Initial detection is performed during installation where you select the mouse and keyboard types. Keyboard and mice will automatically be detected by HAL. You can perform detailed configuration with your desktop configuration tools, such as the GNOME or KDE mouse configuration tools. On GNOME, select System | Preferences | Mouse to configure your mouse. There is a Keyboard entry on that same menu for keyboards.

Sound, Network, and Other Cards

Support for most devices is provided in the form of kernel modules that can be dynamically loaded into the kernel. For example, drivers for an AC97 sound card are in the module **snd-ac97-codec.ko**. Loading this module makes your sound card accessible to Linux. Most Linux distributions automatically detect the cards installed on your system and load the needed modules. Sound, network, and other devices are installed automatically by HAL and udev. The needed kernel module is selected and loaded for you. If you change sound cards, the new card is automatically detected. You could also load modules you need manually, removing an older conflicting one. Installing support for a card is usually a simple matter of loading a module that includes the drivers for it. Device files for most devices are already set up for you in the **/dev** directory by **udev**.

Sound and Video Devices

Sound devices are now automatically detected and configured by HAL and udev. Some sound cards may require more specialized support.

For the 2.4 kernel, most Linux sound drivers were developed as part of the Open Sound System (OSS) and freely distributed as OSS/Free. These are installed as part of Linux distributions. The OSS device drivers are intended to provide a uniform API for all Unix platforms, including Linux. They support Sound Blaster– and Windows Sound System–compatible sound cards (ISA and PCI).

The Advanced Linux Sound Architecture (ALSA) replaced OSS in the 2.6 Linux kernel; it aims to be a better alternative to OSS, while maintaining compatibility with it. ALSA provides a modular sound driver, an API, and a configuration manager. ALSA is a GNU project and is entirely free; its Web site at **www.alsa-project.org** contains extensive documentation, applications, and drivers. Currently available are the ALSA sound driver, the ALSA Kernel API, the ALSA library to support application development, and the ALSA manager to provide a configuration interface for the driver. ALSA evolved from the Linux Ultra Sound Project.

A video device will have the name **/dev/video0**. Supporting kernel modules are loaded automatically. Digital Video Broadcast (DVB) devices like TV tuner cards are located in the **/dev/dvb** directory. Device names begin with **adapter**, starting with **adapter0**.

PCMCIA Devices

PCMCIA devices are card readers commonly found on laptops to connect devices like modems or wireless cards, though they are becoming standard on many desktop systems as well. The same PCMCIA device can support many different kinds of devices, including network cards, modems, hard disks, and Bluetooth devices.

PCMCIA support is now managed by udev and HAL. You no longer use the **cardmgr/pcmcia** service. PCMCIA devices are now considered hotplugged devices managed by HAL and udev directly. Card information and control is now managed by **pccardctl**. The PCMCIA udev rules are listed in **/etc/udev/rules.d/60-pcmcia.rules**, which automatically probes and install cards. Check **www.kernel.org/pub/linux/utils/kernel/pcmcia/pcmcia.html** for more information.

You can obtain information about a PCMCIA device with the **pccardctl** command, as well as manually eject and insert a device. The **status**, **config**, and **ident** options will display the device's socket status and configuration, and the identification of the device. The **insert** and **eject** options will let you add and remove a device. The **cardinfo** command also provides device information.

It is not advisable to hot-swap IDE or SCSI devices. For these you should first manually shut down the device using the **pccardctl** command.

```
pccardctl eject
pccardctl scheme home
```

DKMS

DKMS is the Dynamic Kernel Module Support originally developed by DELL. DKMS enabled device drivers can be automatically generated whenever your kernel is updated. This is helpful for proprietary drivers like the Nvidia and ATI proprietary graphics drivers (the X11 open source drivers, Xorg, are automatically included with the kernel package). In the past, whenever you updated your kernel, you also had to download and install a separate proprietary kernel module complied just for that new kernel. If the module was not ready, then you could not use a proprietary driver. To avoid this problem, DKMS was developed with uses the original proprietary source code to create new kernel modules as they are needed. When you install a new kernel, DKMS then detects the new configuration and compiles a compatible proprietary kernel module for your new kernel. This action is fully automatic and entirely hidden from the user.

On Ubuntu 9.04 both the Nvidia and ATI proprietary graphics drivers are DKMS enable packages that are managed and generated by the DKMS service. The generated kernel modules are placed in the **/lib/modules/***kernel-version***/kernel/updates** directory. When you install either graphics proprietary package, their source code in downloaded and used to create a graphics drivers for use by your kernel. The source code is placed in the **/usr/src** directory.

The DKMS configuration files and build locations for different DKMS enabled software are located in subdirectories in the **/var/lib/dkms** directory. The subdirectories will have the module name like fglrx for the ATI proprietary driver and nvdia for the Nvidia drivers. Within this directory will be version subdirectories for different driver releases like **8.543** for ATI or **177.80** for Nvidia. A source link accesses the source code files in the **/etc/src** directory for that driver version. The **build** subdirectory contains configured source and support files like patches, used to actually generate the kernel module. Both include the **dkms.conf** configuration file for that software package. The compiled module will be located in the version directory and have the extension **.ko**, as in **fglrx.ko**.

DKMS configuration files are located in the **/etc/dkms** directory. The **/etc/dkms/framework.conf** file holds DKMS variable definitions for directories DKMS uses like the source code and kernel module directories. The **/etc/init.d/dkms_autoinstaller** is a script the runs the DKMS operations to generate and install a kernel module. DKMS removal and install directives for kernel updates are maintained in the **/etc/kernel** directory.

Should DKMS fail to install and update automatically, you can perform the update manually using the **dkms** command. The **dkms** command with the **build** action will create the kernel module, and then the **dkms** command with the install action will install module to the appropriate kernel module directory. The **-m** option specifies the module you want to build and the **-k** option is the kernel version (use **uname -r** to display your current kernel version). Drivers like Nvidia and ATI release new versions regularly (ATI every month). You use the **-v** option to specify the driver version you want. See the man page for **dkms** for full details.

```
sudo dkms build -m fglrx -v 8.543 -k 2.6.27-7-generic
sudo dkms install -m fglrx -v 8.543 -k 2.6.27-7-generic
```

Modules

The Linux kernel employs the use of modules to support different operating system features, including support for various devices such as sound and network cards. In many cases, you do have the option of implementing support for a device either as a module or by directly compiling it as a built-in kernel feature, which requires you to rebuild the kernel. A safer and more robust solution is to use modules. *Modules* are components of the Linux kernel that can be loaded as needed. To add support for a new device, you can now simply instruct a kernel to load the module for that device. In some cases, you may have to recompile only that module to provide support for your device. The use of modules has the added advantage of reducing the size of the kernel program as well as making your system more stable. The kernel can load modules in memory only as they are needed. Should a module fail, only the module stops running, and it will not affect the entire system.

Kernel Module Tools

The modules your system needs are determined during installation, according to the kind of configuration information you provided and the automatic detection performed by your Linux distribution. For example, if your system uses an Ethernet card whose type you specified during installation, the system loads the module for that card. You can, however, manually control what modules are to be loaded for your system. In effect, this enables you to customize your kernel whatever way you want. The 2.6 Linux kernel includes the Kernel Module Loader (Kmod), which has the capability to load modules automatically as they are needed. Kernel module loading support must also be enabled in the kernel, though this is usually considered part of a standard configuration. In addition, several tools enable you to load and unload modules manually. The Kernel Module Loader uses certain kernel commands to perform the task of loading or unloading modules.

Command	Description
`lsmod`	Lists modules currently loaded.
`insmod`	Loads a module into the kernel. Does not check for dependencies.
`rmmod`	Unloads a module currently loaded. Does not check for dependencies.
`modinfo`	Displays information about a module: `-a` (author), `-d` (description), `-p` (module parameters), `-f` (module filename), `-v` (module version).
`depmod`	Creates a dependency file listing all other modules on which the specified module may rely.
`modprobe`	Loads a module with any dependent modules it may also need. Uses the file of dependency listings generated by `depmod`: `-r` (unload a module), `-l` (list modules).

Table 17-9: Kernel Module Commands

The `modprobe` command is a general-purpose command that calls `insmod` to load modules and `rmmod` to unload them. These commands are listed in Table 17-9. Options for particular modules, general configuration, and even specific module loading can specified in the **/etc/modprobe.d** files. You can use this file to automatically load and configure modules. You can also specify modules to be loaded at the boot prompt or in **menu.lst**.

Module Files and Directories: /lib/modules

The filename for a module has the extension **.ko**. Kernel modules reside in the **/lib/modules/**version directory, where *version* is the version number for your current kernel with the extension generic. The directory for the 2.6.24-10-generic kernel is **/lib/modules/2.6.28-14-generic**. As you install new kernels on your system, new module directories are generated for them. One method to access the directory for the current kernel is to use the `uname -r` command to generate the kernel version number. This command needs to have back quotes.

```
cd /lib/modules/`uname -r`
```

In this directory, modules for the kernel reside in the **/kernel** directory. Within the **/kernel** directory are several subdirectories, including the **/drivers** directory that holds subdirectories for modules like network drivers and video drivers. These subdirectories serve to categorize your modules, making them easier to locate. For example, the **kernel/drivers/net** directory holds modules for your Ethernet cards, and the **kernel/drivers/video** directory contains video card modules.

Specialized modules are placed in the ubuntu directory instead of the kernel directory. These include the sound drivers. The ALSA sound driver are located at /lib/modules/2.6.24-17/ubuntu/sound/alsa-drivers

Managing Modules with modprobe and /etc/modules

There are several commands you can use to manage modules. The `lsmod` command lists the modules currently loaded into your kernel, and `modinfo` provides information about particular modules. Though you can use the `insmod` and `rmmod` commands to load or unload modules directly, you should use only `modprobe` for these tasks. Often, however, a given module requires other modules to be loaded.

To have a module loaded automatically at boot, you simply place the module name in the **/etc/modules** file. Here you will also find entries for **fuse** and **lp**.   You can use this file to force loading a needed module that may not be detected by udev or HAL. This can be particularly true for specialized vendor kernel modules you may need to download, compile, and install.

The depmod Command

Instead of manually trying to determine what modules a given module depends on, you use the `depmod` command to detect the dependencies for you. The `depmod` command generates a file that lists all the modules on which a given module depends. The `depmod` command generates a hierarchical listing, noting what modules should be loaded first and in what order they will load. Then, to load the module, you use the `modprobe` command using that file. `modprobe` reads the file generated by `depmod` and loads any dependent modules in the correct order, along with the module you want. You need to execute `depmod` with the **-a** option once, before you ever use `modprobe`. Entering `depmod` **-a** creates a complete listing of all module dependencies. This command creates a file called **modules.dep** in the module directory for your current kernel version, **/lib/modules/**version.

```
depmod -a
```

The modprobe Command

To install a module manually, you use the `modprobe` command and the module name. You can add any parameters the module may require. The following command installs the Intel high definition sound module. `modprobe` also supports the use of the * character to enable you to use a pattern to select several modules. This example uses several values commonly used for sound cards. Use the values recommended for your sound card on your system. Most sound card drivers are supported by the ALSA project. Check their website to find what driver module is used for your card.

```
modprobe  snd-hda-intel
```

To discover what parameters a module takes, you can use the `modinfo` command with the **-p** option.

You can use the **-l** option to list modules and the **-t** option to look for modules in a specified subdirectory. Sound modules are located in the /lib/modules/2.6.version-generic/ubuntu directory, where version is the kernel version like 2.6.24-17. Sound modules are arranged in different subdirectories according to the driver and device interface they use, such as **pci**, **isa**, or **usb**. Most internal sound cards use **pci**. Within the interface directory, there may be further directories like emu10k1 used for the Creative Audigy cards and hda for high definition drivers. In the next example, the user lists all modules in the **sound/alsa-driver/pci/hda** directory:

```
# modprobe -l -t sound/pci/hda
/lib/modules/ 2.6.24-17-generic/ubuntu/sound/alsa-driver/sound/pci/hda/snd-hda-
intel.ko
```

Options for the `modprobe` command are placed in the **/etc/modprobe.d** directory.

The insmod Command

The `insmod` command performs the actual loading of modules. Both `modprobe` and the Kernel Module Loader make use of this command to load modules. Though `modprobe` is preferred, because it checks for dependencies, you can load or unload particular modules individually with `insmod` and `rmmod` commands. The `insmod` command takes as its argument the name of the module, as does `rmmod`. The name can be the simple base name, like `snd-ac97-codec` for the **snd-ac97-codec.ko** module. You can specify the complete module filename using the **-o** option. Other helpful options are the **-p** option, which lets you probe your system first to see if the module can be successfully loaded, and the **-n** option, which performs all tasks except actually loading the module (a dummy run). The **-v** option (verbose) lists all actions taken as they occur. In those rare cases where you may have to force a module to load, you can use the **-f** option. In the next example, `insmod` loads the **snd-ac97-codec.ko** module:

```
# insmod -v snd-ac97-codec
```

The rmmod Command

The `rmmod` command performs the actual unloading of modules. It is the command used by `modprobe` and the Kernel Module Loader to unload modules. You can use the `rmmod` command to remove a particular module as long as it is not being used or required by other modules. You can remove a module and all its dependent modules by using the **-r** option. The **-a** option removes all unused modules. With the **-e** option, when `rmmod` unloads a module, it saves any persistent data (parameters) in the persistent data directory, usually **/var/lib/modules/persist**.

The modprobe.d directory

Module loading can require system renaming as well as specifying options to use when loading specific modules. Even when removing or installing a module, certain additional programs may have to be run or other options specified. These parameters can be set in files located in an **/etc/modprobe.d** directory, like alsa-base.conf (ALSA sound), **blacklist.conf** (module name conflicts), and **dkms.conf** (DKMS module generation). Configuration for **modprobe** supports four actions: alias, options, install, and remove.

> **alias** *module name*   Provides another name for the module, used for network and sound devices.

> **options** *module options*   Specifies any options a particular module may need.

> **install** *module commands*   Uses the specified commands to install a module, letting you control module loading.

> **remove** *module commands*   Specifies commands to be run when a module is unloaded.

> **include** *config-file*   Additional configuration files.

> **blacklist** *module*   Ignore any internal aliases that given module may define for itself. This allows you to use only aliases defined by modprobe. Also avoids conflicting modules where two different modules may have the same alias defined internally. Default blacklist entries are held in one or more blacklist files in the **/etc/modprobe.d** directory. Their names begin with the term **blacklist**. Use the **modinfo** command to list a module's internal aliases.

Among the more common entries are aliases used for network protocols in the **aliases** file. Actual network devices are now managed by udev in the **70-persistent-net.rules** file, not by modprobe aliases.

Installing New Modules from Vendors: Driver Packages

Often you may find that your hardware device is not supported by current Linux modules. In this case you may have to download drivers from the hardware vendor or open source development group to create your own driver and install it for use by your kernel.

The drivers could be in DEB or compressed archives. The process for installing drivers differs, depending on how a vendor supports the driver. Different kinds of packages are listed here:

➢ **Deb packages**   Some support sites will provide drivers already packaged in Deb files for direct installation.

➢ **Drivers compiled in archives**   Some sites will provide drivers already compiled for your distribution but packaged in compressed archives. In this case a simple install operation will place the supporting module in the **modules** directory and make if available for use by the kernel.

➢ **Source code**   Other sites provide just the source code, which, when compiled, will detect your system configuration and compile the module accordingly.

➢ **Scripts with source code**   Some sites will provide customized scripts that may prompt you for basic questions about your system and then both compile and install the module.

For drivers that come in the form of compressed archives (**tar.gz** or **tar.bz2**), the compile and install operations normally make use a Makefile script operated by the **make** command. A simple install usually just requires running the following command in the driver's software directory:

```
make install
```

In the case of sites that supply only the source code, you may have to perform both configure and compile operations as you would for any software.

```
./configure
make
make install
```

For packages that have no install option, compiled or source, you will have to manually move the module to the kernel module directory, **/lib/modules/***version,* and use **depmod** and **modprobe** to load it (see the preceding section).

If a site gives you a customized script, you just run that script. For example, the Marvel gigabit LAN network interfaces found on many motherboards use the SysKonnect Linux drivers held in the **skge.o** module. The standard kernel configuration will generate and install this module. But if you are using a newer motherboard, you may need to download and install the latest Linux driver. For example, some vendors may provide a script, **install.sh**, that you run to configure, compile, and install the module.

```
./install.sh
```

Installing modules from Ubuntu module source packages

Some specialized devices do not have kernel modules to support them. They may, however, have Ubuntu Linux source packages with files that can be compiled and installed as modules on your system. These packages with have the suffix **-source**. To compile and install these modules you use the module assistant, **module-assistant**, available in the modules-assistant package. Also be sure that the headers package for your kernel is installed.

```
sudo apt-get modules-assistant
sudo apt-get install linux-headers-version
```

You install the module source package you want to compile. This example uses the source package for Broadcom drivers.

```
apt-get install  bcm570-source
```

Then use the **m-a** command with the **build** option to compile the kernel module and place it in a DEB package that you can then install.

```
module-assistant build   bcm570-source
```

For **module-assistant**, you can use the short form, **m-a**.

```
m-a build   bcm570-source
```

The DEP package will be placed in the **/usr/src** directory. You can use the **install** option to install it.

```
m-a install   bcm570-source
```

Installing New Modules from the Kernel

The source code for your Linux kernel contains an extensive set of modules, of which not all are actually used on your system. The kernel binaries provided by most distributions come with a extensive set of modules already installed. If, however, you install a device for which kernel support is not already installed, you will have to configure and compile the kernel module that provides the drivers for it. This involves using the kernel source code to select the module you need from a list in a kernel configuration tool, and then regenerating your kernel modules with the new module included. Then the new module is copied into the module library, installing it on your system. You can also enter it a file in the **/etc/modules** directory with any options, or use **modprobe** to install it manually.

Download the Ubuntu source code version of the kernel (see Chapter 7). Install to a local user directory. Change that local kernel directory. Then use the **make** command with the **gconfig** or **menuconfig** argument to display the kernel configuration menus, invoking them with the following commands. The **make gconfig** command starts an X Window System interface that needs to be run on your desktop from a terminal window.

```
make gconfig
```

Using the menus select the modules you need. Make sure each is marked as a module, clicking the Module check box in **gconfig** or typing **m** for **menuconfig**. Once the kernel is configured, save it and exit from the configuration menus. Then you compile the modules, creating the module binary files with the following command:

```
make modules
```

This places the modules in the kernel source modules directory. You can copy the one you want to the kernel modules directory, **/lib/modules/**version**/kernel**, where version is the version number of your Linux kernel. A simpler approach is to reinstall all your modules, using the following command. This copies all the compiled modules to the **/lib/modules/**version**/kernel** directory:

```
make modules_install
```

18. Archives, Compression, and Backups

Archives are used to back up files or to combine them into a package, which can then be transferred as one file over the Internet or posted on an FTP site for easy downloading. The standard archive utility used on Linux and Unix systems is tar, for which several GNOME and KDE front ends exist. You can choose from among several compression programs, including GNU zip (gzip), Zip, bzip, and compress. Table 18-1 lists the commonly used archive and compressions applications.

Applications	Description
tar	Archive creation and extraction **www.gnu.org/software/tar/manual/tar.html**
FileRoller (Archive Manager)	GNOME front end for tar and gzip/bzip2
gzip	File, directory, and archive compression **www.gnu.org/software/gzip/manual/**
bzip2	File, directory, and archive compression **www.gnu.org/software/gzip/manual/**
zip	File, directory, and archive compression

Table 18-1: Archive and Compression Applications

Backup operations have become an important part of administrative duties. Several backup tools are provided on Linux systems, including Amanda and the traditional dump/restore tools, as well as the **rsync** command for making individual copies. Anaconda provides server-based backups, letting different systems on a network back up to a central server. BackupPC provides network and local backup using configured rsync and tar tools. The dump tools let you refine your backup process, detecting data changed since the last backup. Table 18-2 lists websites for Linux backup tools.

Website	Tools
`http://rsync.samba.org`	rsync remote copy backup
`www.amanda.org`	Amanda network backup
`http://dump.sourceforge.net`	dump and restore tools
`http://backuppc.sourceforge.net`	BackupPC network or local backup using configured rsync and tar tools.

Table 18-2 Backup Resources

Archiving and Compressing Files with File Roller

GNOME provides the File Roller tool (Applications | Accessories | Archive Manager) that operates as a GNOME front end to archive and compress files, letting you perform Zip, gzip, tar, and bzip2 operation using a graphical interface. You can examine the contents of archives, extract the files you want, and create new compressed archives. When you create an archive, you determine its compression method by specifying its filename extension, such as **.gz** for gzip or **.bz2** for bzip2. You can select the different extensions from the File Type menu or enter the extension yourself. To both archive and compress files, you can choose a combined extension like .tar.bz2, which both archives with tar and compresses with bzip2. Click Add to add files to your archive. To extract files from an archive, open the archive to display the list of archive files. You can then click Extract to extract particular files or the entire archive.

Tip: File Roller can also be use to examine the contents of an archive file easily. From the file manager, right-click the archive and choose Open With Archive Manager. The list of files and directories in that archive will be displayed. For subdirectories, double-click their entries. This method also works for RPM software files, letting you browse all the files that make up a software package.

Archive Files and Devices: tar

The tar utility creates archives for files and directories. With tar, you can archive specific files, update them in the archive, and add new files as you want to that archive. You can even archive entire directories with all their files and subdirectories, all of which can be restored from the archive. The tar utility was originally designed to create archives on tapes. (The term "tar" stands for tape archive. However, you can create archives on any device, such as a floppy disk, or you can create an archive file to hold the archive.) The tar utility is ideal for making backups of your files or combining several files into a single file for transmission across a network (File Roller is a GNOME interface for tar). For more information on tar, check the man page or the online man page at **www.gnu.org/software/tar/manual/tar.html**.

Note: As an alternative to tar, you can use pax, which is designed to work with different kinds of Unix archive formats such as cpio, bcpio, and tar. You can extract, list, and create archives. The pax utility is helpful if you are handling archives created on Unix systems that are using different archive formats.

Displaying Archive Contents

Both file managers in GNOME and the KDE have the capability to display the contents of a tar archive file automatically. The contents are displayed as though they were files in a directory. You can list the files as icons or with details, sorting them by name, type, or other fields. You can even display the contents of files. Clicking a text file opens it with a text editor, and an image is displayed with an image viewer. If the file manager cannot determine what program to use to display the file, it prompts you to select an application. Both file managers can perform the same kinds of operations on archives residing on remote file systems, such as tar archives on FTP sites. You can obtain a listing of their contents and even read their readme files. The Nautilus file manager (GNOME) can also extract an archive. Right-click the Archive icon and select Extract.

Creating Archives

On Linux, tar is often used to create archives on devices or files. You can direct tar to archive files to a specific device or a file by using the **f** option with the name of the device or file. The syntax for the **tar** command using the **f** option is shown in the next example. The device or filename is often referred to as the archive name. When creating a file for a tar archive, the filename is usually given the extension **.tar**. This is a convention only and is not required. You can list as many filenames as you want. If a directory name is specified, all its subdirectories are included in the archive.

```
$ tar optionsf archive-name.tar directory-and-file-names
```

   To create an archive, use the **c** option. Combined with the **f** option, **c** creates an archive on a file or device. You enter the **c** option before and right next to the **f** option. No dash precedes a tar option. Table 18-3 lists the different options you can use with tar. In the next example, the directory **mydir** and all its subdirectories are saved in the file **myarch.tar**. In this example, the **mydir** directory holds two files, **mymeeting** and **party**, as well as a directory called **reports** that has three files: **weather**, **monday**, and **friday**.

```
$ tar cvf myarch.tar mydir
mydir/
mydir/reports/
mydir/reports/weather
mydir/reports/monday
mydir/reports/friday
mydir/mymeeting
mydir/party
```

Extracting Archives

   The user can later extract the directories from the tape using the **x** option. The **xf** option extracts files from an archive file or device. The tar extraction operation generates all subdirectories. In the next example, the **xf** option directs **tar** to extract all the files and subdirectories from the tar file **myarch.tar**:

```
$ tar xvf myarch.tar
mydir/
mydir/reports/
mydir/reports/weather
mydir/reports/monday
mydir/reports/friday
mydir/mymeeting
mydir/party
```

   You use the **r** option to add files to an already-created archive. The **r** option appends the files to the archive. In the next example, the user appends the files in the **mydocs** directory to the **myarch.tar** archive. Here, the directory **mydocs** and its files are added to the **myarch.tar** archive:

```
$ tar rvf myarch.tar mydocs
mydocs/
mydocs/doc1
```

Updating Archives

   If you change any of the files in your directories you previously archived, you can use the **u** option to instruct tar to update the archive with any modified files. The **tar** command compares the time of the last update for each archived file with those in the user's directory and copies into the archive any files that have been changed since they were last archived. Any newly created files in these directories are also added to the archive. In the next example, the user updates the **myarch.tar** file with any recently modified or newly created files in the **mydir** directory. In this case, the **gifts** file was added to the **mydir** directory.

```
tar uvf myarch.tar mydir
mydir/
mydir/gifts
```

If you need to see what files are stored in an archive, you can use the **tar** command with the **t** option. The next example lists all the files stored in the **myarch.tar** archive:

```
tar tvf myarch.tar
drwxr-xr-x root/root 0 2000-10-24 21:38:18 mydir/
drwxr-xr-x root/root 0 2000-10-24 21:38:51 mydir/reports/
-rw-r--r-- root/root 22 2000-10-24 21:38:40 mydir/reports/weather
-rw-r--r-- root/root 22 2000-10-24 21:38:45 mydir/reports/monday
-rw-r--r-- root/root 22 2000-10-24 21:38:51 mydir/reports/friday
-rw-r--r-- root/root 22 2000-10-24 21:38:18 mydir/mymeeting
-rw-r--r-- root/root 22 2000-10-24 21:36:42 mydir/party
drwxr-xr-x root/root 0 2000-10-24 21:48:45 mydocs/
-rw-r--r-- root/root 22 2000-10-24 21:48:45 mydocs/doc1
drwxr-xr-x root/root 0 2000-10-24 21:54:03 mydir/
-rw-r--r-- root/root 22 2000-10-24 21:54:03 mydir/gifts
```

Note: To backup files using several CD/DVD-ROMs, you would first create a split archive, one consisting of several files, using the -M option, the multi-volume option. The tape size for an ISO DVD would be specified with the tape-length option, --tape-length=2294900.

Compressing Archives

The **tar** operation does not perform compression on archived files. If you want to compress archived files, you can instruct tar to invoke the gzip utility to compress them. With the lowercase **z** option, tar first uses gzip to compress files before archiving them. The same **z** option invokes gzip to decompress them when extracting files.

```
$ tar czf myarch.tar.gz mydir
```

To use bzip instead of gzip to compress files before archiving them, you use the **j** option. The same **j** option invokes bzip to decompress them when extracting files.

```
$ tar cjf myarch.tar.bz2 mydir
```

A difference exists between compressing individual files in an archive and compressing the entire archive as a whole. Often, an archive is created for transferring several files at once as one tar file. To shorten transmission time, the archive should be as small as possible. You can use the compression utility gzip on the archive tar file to compress it, reducing its size, and then send the compressed version. The person receiving it can decompress it, restoring the tar file. Using gzip on a tar file often results in a file with the extension **.tar.gz**. The extension **.gz** is added to a compressed gzip file. The next example creates a compressed version of **myarch.tar** using the same name with the extension **.gz**:

```
$ gzip myarch.tar
$ ls
$ myarch.tar.gz
```

Commands	Execution
`tar` *options files*	Backs up files to tape, device, or archive file.
`tar` *options*f *archive_name filelist*	Backs up files to a specific file or device specified as *archive_name*. *filelist*; can be filenames or directories.
Options	
`c`	Creates a new archive.
`t`	Lists the names of files in an archive.
`r`	Appends files to an archive.
`U`	Updates an archive with new and changed files; adds only those files modified since they were archived or files not already present in the archive.
`--delete`	Removes a file from the archive.
`w`	Waits for a confirmation from the user before archiving each file; enables you to update an archive selectively.
`x`	Extracts files from an archive.
`m`	When extracting a file from an archive, no new timestamp is assigned.
`M`	Creates a multiple-volume archive that may be stored on several floppy disks.
`f` *archive-name*	Saves the tape archive to the file archive name, instead of to the default tape device. When given an archive name, the `f` option saves the tar archive in a file of that name.
`f` *device-name*	Saves a tar archive to a device such as a floppy disk or tape. **/dev/fd0** is the device name for your floppy disk; the default device is held in **/etc/default/tar-file**.
`v`	Displays each filename as it is archived.
`z`	Compresses or decompresses archived files using gzip.
`j`	Compresses or decompresses archived files using bzip2.

Table 18-3: File Archives: `tar`

Instead of retyping the **tar** command for different files, you can place the command in a script and pass the files to it. Be sure to make the script executable. In the following example, a simple **myarchprog** script is created that will archive filenames listed as its arguments.

myarchprog

```
tar  cvf  myarch.tar  $*
```

A run of the **myarchprog** script with multiple arguments is shown here:

```
$ myarchprog mydata preface
mydata
preface
```

Archiving to Tape

If you have a default device specified, such as a tape, and you want to create an archive on it, you can simply use **tar** without the **f** option and a device or filename. This can be helpful for making backups of your files. The name of the default device is held in a file called **/etc/default/tar**. The syntax for the **tar** command using the default tape device is shown in the following example. If a directory name is specified, all its subdirectories are included in the archive.

```
$ tar option directory-and-file-names
```

In the next example, the directory **mydir** and all its subdirectories are saved on a tape in the default tape device:

```
$ tar c mydir
```

In this example, the **mydir** directory and all its files and subdirectories are extracted from the default tape device and placed in the user's working directory:

```
$ tar x mydir
```

Note: There are other archive programs you can use such as cpio, pax, and shar. However, tar is the one most commonly used for archiving application software.

File Compression: gzip, bzip2, and zip

Two common reasons for reducing the size of a file are to save space and, if you are transferring the file across a network, to save transmission time. You can effectively reduce a file size by creating a compressed copy of it. Anytime you need the file again, you decompress it. Compression is used in combination with archiving to enable you to compress entire directories and their files at once. Decompression generates a copy of the archive file, which can then be extracted, generating a copy of those files and directories. File Roller provides a GNOME interface for these tasks. For more information on gzip, check the man page or the online man page at **www.gnu.org/software/gzip/manual/**. For bzip2 also check its man page or the online documentation at **www.bzip.org/docs.html**.

Compression with gzip

Several compression utilities are available for use on Linux and Unix systems. Most software for Linux systems uses the GNU gzip and gunzip utilities. The gzip utility compresses files, and gunzip decompresses them. To compress a file, enter the command **gzip** and the filename. This replaces the file with a compressed version of it with the extension **.gz**.

```
$ gzip mydata
$ ls
mydata.gz
```

To decompress a gzip file, use either **gzip** with the **-d** option or the command **gunzip**. These commands decompress a compressed file with the **.gz** extension and replace it with a decompressed version with the same root name but without the **.gz** extension. When you use gunzip, you needn't even type in the **.gz** extension; **gunzip** and **gzip -d** assume it. Table 20-8 lists the different gzip options.

```
$ gunzip mydata.gz
$ ls
mydata
```

Option	Execution
-c	Sends compressed version of file to standard output; each file listed is separately compressed: `gzip -c mydata preface > myfiles.gz`

-d	Decompresses a compressed file; or you can use gunzip:
	`gzip -d myfiles.gz`
	`gunzip myfiles.gz`

-h	Displays help listing.
-l *file-list*	Displays compressed and uncompressed size of each file listed: `gzip -l myfiles.gz.`
-r *directory-name*	Recursively searches for specified directories and compresses all the files in them; the search begins from the current working directory. When used with `gunzip`, compressed files of a specified directory are uncompressed.
-v *file-list*	For each compressed or decompressed file, displays its name and the percentage of its reduction in size.
-num	Determines the speed and size of the compression; the range is from −1 to −9. A lower number gives greater speed but less compression, resulting in a larger file that compresses and decompresses quickly. Thus −1 gives the quickest compression but with the largest size; −9 results in a very small file that takes longer to compress and decompress. The default is −6.

Table 18-4: The `gzip` Options

Tip: On your desktop, you can extract the contents of an archive by locating it with the file manager and double-clicking it. You can also right-click and choose Open with Archive Manager. This will start the File Roller application, which will open the archive, listing its contents. You can then choose to extract the archive. File Roller will use the appropriate tools to decompress the archive (bzip2, zip, or gzip) if compressed, and then extract the archive (tar).

You can also compress archived tar files. This results in files with the extensions **.tar.gz**. Compressed archived files are often used for transmitting extremely large files across networks.

```
$ gzip myarch.tar
$ ls
myarch.tar.gz
```

You can compress tar file members individually using the **tar z** option that invokes gzip. With the **z** option, tar invokes gzip to compress a file before placing it in an archive. Archives with members compressed with the **z** option, however, cannot be updated, nor is it possible to add to them. All members must be compressed, and all must be added at the same time.

The compress and uncompress Commands

You can also use the `compress` and `uncompress` commands to create compressed files. They generate a file that has a **.Z** extension and use a different compression format from gzip. The `compress` and `uncompress` commands are not that widely used, but you may run across **.Z** files occasionally. You can use the `uncompress` command to decompress a **.Z** file. The gzip utility is the standard GNU compression utility and should be used instead of `compress`.

Compressing with bzip2

Another popular compression utility is **bzip2**. It compresses files using the Burrows-Wheeler block-sorting text compression algorithm and Huffman coding. The command line options are similar to gzip by design, but they are not exactly the same. (See the bzip2 Man page for a complete listing.) You compress files using the `bzip2` command and decompress with `bunzip2`. The `bzip2` command creates files with the extension **.bz2**. You can use `bzcat` to output compressed data to the standard output. The `bzip2` command compresses files in blocks and enables you to specify their size (larger blocks give you greater compression). As when using gzip, you can use bzip2 to compress tar archive files. The following example compresses the **mydata** file into a bzip compressed file with the extension **.bz2**:

```
$ bzip2 mydata
$ ls
mydata.bz2
```

To decompress, use the `bunzip2` command on a bzip file:

```
$ bunzip2 mydata.bz2
```

Using Zip

Zip is a compression and archive utility modeled on PKZIP, which was used originally on DOS systems. Zip is a cross-platform utility used on Windows, Mac, MS-DOS, OS/2, Unix, and Linux systems. Zip commands can work with archives created by PKZIP and can use Zip archives. You compress a file using the `zip` command. This creates a Zip file with the **.zip** extension. If no files are listed, `zip` outputs the compressed data to the standard output. You can also use the − argument to have `zip` read from the standard input. To compress a directory, you include the `-r` option. This example archives and compresses a file:

```
$ zip mydata
$ ls
mydata.zip
```

The next example archives and compresses the **reports** directory:

```
$ zip -r reports
```

A full set of archive operations is supported. With the `-f` option, you can update a particular file in the Zip archive with a newer version. The `-u` option replaces or adds files, and the `-d` option deletes files from the Zip archive. Options also exist for encrypting files, making DOS-to-Unix end-of-line translations and including hidden files.

To decompress and extract the Zip file, you use the `unzip` command.

```
$ unzip mydata.zip
```

Individual Backups: archive and rsync

You can back up and restore particular files and directories with archive tools like `tar`, restoring the archives later. For backups, `tar` is usually used with a tape device. To automatically schedule backups, you can schedule appropriate `tar` commands with the **cron** utility. The archives can be also compressed for storage savings. You can then copy the compressed archives to any medium, such as a DVD disc, a floppy, or tape. On GNOME you can use File Roller (Archive Manager) to create archives easily (Applications | Accessories | Archive Manager). The Archive Manager menu entry is not initially displayed, use System | Preferences | Main Menu to have it displayed on the Applications | Accessories menu.

File Roller also supports LZMA compression, a more efficient and faster compression method. On Archive Manager, when creating a new archive, select "Tar compressed with lzma (.tar.lzma)" ad the Archive type. When choosing Create Archive from Nautilus file manager window on selected files. On the Create Archive dialog, choose the **.lzma** file type for just compression, and the **.tar.lzma** type for a compressed archive.

If you want to remote-copy a directory or files from one host to another, making a particular backup, you can use **rsync**, which is designed for network backups of particular directories or files, intelligently copying only those files that have been changed, rather than the contents of an entire directory. In archive mode, it can preserve the original ownership and permissions, providing corresponding users exist on the host system. The following example copies the **/home/george/myproject** directory to the **/backup** directory on the host **rabbit**, creating a corresponding **myproject** subdirectory. The **-t** specifies that this is a transfer. The remote host is referenced with an attached colon, **rabbit:**.

```
rsync -t /home/george/myproject   rabbit:/backup
```

If, instead, you wanted to preserve the ownership and permissions of the files, you would use the **-a** (archive) option. Adding a **-z** option will compress the file. The **-v** option provides a verbose mode.

```
rsync -avz  /home/george/myproject   rabbit:/backup
```

A trailing slash on the source will copy the contents of the directory, rather than generating a subdirectory of that name. Here the contents of the **myproject** directory are copied to the **george-project** directory.

```
rsync -avz  /home/george/myproject/   rabbit:/backup/george-project
```

The **rsync** command is configured to use SSH remote shell by default. You can specify it or an alternate remote shell to use with the **-e** option. For secure transmission you can encrypt the copy operation with ssh. Either use the **-e ssh** option or set the **RSYNC_RSH** variable to ssh.

```
rsync -avz -e ssh  /home/george/myproject   rabbit:/backup/myproject
```

As when using **rcp**, you can copy from a remote host to the one you are on.

```
rsync -avz  lizard:/home/mark/mypics/  /pic-archive/markpics
```

You can also run rsync as a server daemon. This will allow remote users to sync copies of files on your system with versions on their own, transferring only changed files rather than entire directories. Many mirror and software FTP sites operate as rsync servers, letting you update files without have to download the full versions again. Configuration information for rsync as a server is kept in the **/etc/rsyncd.conf** file. On Ubuntu, rsync as a server is managed through **xinetd**, using the **/etc/xinetd.d/rsync** file, which starts **rsync** with the --daemon option. In the **/etc/services** file, it is listed to run on port 873.

Tip: Though it is designed for copying between hosts, you can also use **rsync** to make copies within your own system, usually to a directory in another partition or hard drive. In fact there are eight different ways of using **rsync**. Check the **rsync** Man page for detailed descriptions of each.

BackupPC

BackupPC provides an easily managed local or network backup of your system or hosts on a system using configured rsync or tar tools. There is no client application to install, just configuration files. BackupPC can back up hosts on a network, including servers, or just a single system. Data can be backed up to local hard disks or to network storage such as shared partitions or storage servers. You can configure BackupPC using your Web page configuration interface. This is the host name of your computer with the /backuppc name attached, like **http://rabbit.turtle.com/backuppc**. Detailed documentation is installed at **/usr/share/doc/BackupPC**. You can find out more about BackupPC at **http://backuppc.sourceforge.net**.

BackupPC uses both compression and detection of identical files to significantly reduce the size of the backup, allowing several hosts to be backed up in limited space. Once an initial backup is performed, BackupPC will only back up changed files, reducing the time of the backup significantly.

BackupPC has its own service script with which you start the BackupPC service, **/etc/init.d/backuppc**. Configuration files are located at **/etc/BackupPC**. The **config.pl** file holds BackupPC configuration options and the hosts file lists hosts to be backed up.

You can use services-admin to have BackupPC start automatically. Check the "Remote Backup Server (backuppc)" entry. BackupPC has its own service script with which you start, stop, and restart the BackupPC service manually, **/etc/init.d/backuppc**.

```
sudo service backuppc start
```

When you first install BackupPC, an install screen will display information you will need to access your BackupPC tool. This includes the URL to use, the user name, and a password. Be sure to write down the user name and password. The URL is simply your computer name with **/backuppc** attached. The user name is **backuppc**. You can change the password with the **htpassword** command. The password is kept in the **/etc/backuppc/htpasswd** file in an encrypted format.

```
sudo htpassword /etc/backuppc/htpasswd  backuppc
```

To access BackupPC, start your browser and enter your URL (computer name with /backuppc) and then the backuppc user name with the password when prompted for authorization. The general welcome and status screen is displayed. The left sidebar has two sections titled Hosts and Server. The Server section has links for BackupPC server configuration. Host Summary will display host backup status.

BackupPC server configuration

To add other hosts, click on the Server Edit Hosts link on the left sidebar to open a page where you add or modify hosts (see Figure 18-1). Here you can add new hosts, change users, and add new users. Host entries are saved to the **/etc/backuppc/hosts** file. Click the Save button to finish.

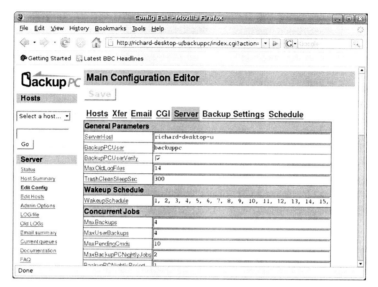

Figure 18-1: BackupPC Configuration

The Server Edit Config link opens a page with tabbed panels for all your server configuration options. The page opens to the Server panel, but you can also access the Hosts panel to add new users, Xfer to specify the backup method, and the Backup Settings to set backup options. The Server panel will control features like the host name of the server and the user name to provide access. On the Xfer panel you can configure different backup methods: archive (gzip), rsync, rsyncd, smb (Samba), tar. The Schedule panel sets the periods for full and incremental backups.

BackupPC host backup and configuration

The Hosts pop-up menu is located on the sidebar in the Hosts section. Here you choose the host to perform backup and restores on. The localhost entry will access your own computer. When you select a host, a new section will appear on the sidebar above the Host section, labeled with that host name, like localhost. In this section will be links for the host Home page, Browse backups, logs, and an Edit Config link to configure the backup for that host,

The host home page will list backups and display buttons for full and incremental backups. Click on the Start Full Backup to perform a full backup, and Start Incre Backup for an incremental backup (changed data only). You will be prompted for confirmation before the backup begins.

To select files to restore, you click the Browse backups link to display a tree of possible files and directories to restore. Select the ones you want or just click the Select All checkbox choose the entire backup. Then click on Restore Backup. A Restore page then lets you choose from three kinds of backup: a direct restore, Zip archive, or tar archive. For a direct restore you can have BackupPC either overwrite your current files with the restored ones, or save them to a specified directory where you can later choose which ones to use. The Zip and Tar restore options create archive files that hold your backup. You can then later extract and restore files form the archive.

The Edit Config link open a page of tabbed panels for your host backup configuration. On the Xfer panel you can decide on the type of backup you want to perform. You can choose from archive (zip), tar, rsync, rsyncd, and smb (Samba). Here you can set specific settings like the destination directory for a zip archive or the Samba share to access for an smb backup. The Schedule panel is where you specify the backup intervals for full and incremental backups.

BackupPC uses both compression and detection of identical files to significantly reduce the size of the backup, allowing several hosts to be backed up in limited space. Once an initial backup is performed, BackupPC will only back up changed files using incremental backups, reducing the time of the backup significantly.

Amanda

To back up hosts connected to a network to a central backup server, you can use the Advanced Maryland Automatic Network Disk Archiver (Amanda) to archive hosts (Universe repository). Amanda uses tar tools to back up all hosts to a single host operating as a backup server. Backup data is sent by each host to the host operating as the Amanda server, where they are written out to a backup medium such as tape. With an Amanda server, the backup operations for all hosts become centralized in one server, instead of each host having to perform its own backup. Any host that needs to restore data simply requests it from the Amanda server, specifying the file system, date, and filenames. Backup data is copied to the server's holding disk and from there to tapes. Detailed documentation and updates are provided at **amanda.org**. For the server, be sure to install the amanda-server package, and for clients you use the amanda-clients package. Ubuntu also provides an Amanda-common package for documentation, shared libraries, and Amanda tools.

Amanda is designed for automatic backups of hosts that may have very different configurations, as well as operating systems. You can back up any host that supports GNU tools, including Mac OS X and Windows systems connected through Samba.

Amanda Commands

Amanda has its own commands corresponding to the common backup tasks, beginning with "am," such as **amdump**, **amrestore**, and **amrecover**. The commands are listed in Table 18-5. The **amdump** command is the primary backup operation.

The **amdump** command performs requested backups; it is not designed for interactive use. For an interactive backup, you use an archive tool like tar directly. The **amdump** is placed within a **cron** instruction to be run at a specified time. If, for some reason, **amdump** cannot save all its data to the backup medium (tape or disk), it will retain the data on the holding disk. The data can then later be directly written with the with the **amflush** command.

You can restore particular files as well as complete systems with the **amrestore** command. With the **amrecover** tool, you can select from a list of backups.

Command	Description
amdump	Perform automatic backups for the file systems listed in the disklist configuration file.
amflush	Directly back up data from the holding disk to a tape.
amcleanup	Clean up if there is a system failure on the server.
amrecover	Select backups to restore using an interactive shell.
amrestore	Restore backups, either files or complete systems.
amlabel	Label the backup medium for Amanda.
amcheck	Check the backup systems and files as well as the backup tapes before backup operations.
amadmin	Back up administrative tasks.
amtape	Manage backup tapes, loading and removing them.
amverify	Check format of tapes.
amverifyrun	Check the tapes from the previous run, specify the configuration directory for the backup.
amrmtape	Remove a tape from the Amanda database, used for damaged tapes.
amstatus	Show the status of the current Amanda backup operation.

Table 18-5: Amanda Commands

Amanda Configuration

Configuration files are placed in **/etc/amanda** and log and database files in **/var/lib/amanda**. These are created automatically when you install Amanda. You will also need to create a directory to use as a holding disk where backups are kept before writing to the tape. This should be on a file system with very large available space, enough to hold the backup of your largest entire host.

/etc/amanda

Within the **/etc/amanda** directory are subdirectories for the different kind of backups you want to perform. Each directory will contain its own **amanda.conf** and **disklist** file. By default a daily backup directory is created called **DailySet1**, with a default **amanda.conf** and a sample **disklist** file. To use them, you will have to edit them to enter your system's own settings. For a different backup configuration, you can create a new directory and copy the **DailySet1** **amanda.conf** and **disklist** files to it, editing them as appropriate. When you issue Amanda commands like amdump to perform backups, you will use the name of the **/etc/amanda** subdirectory to indicate the kind of backup you want performed.

```
amdump DailySet1
```

The **/etc/amanda** directory also contains a sample **cron** file, **crontab.sample**, that shows how a **cron** entry should look.

amanda.conf

The **amanda.conf** file contains basic configuration parameters such as the tape type and logfile as well as holding file locations. In most cases you can just use the defaults as listed in the **DailySet1/amanda.conf** file. The file is commented in detail, telling you what entries you will have to change. You will need to set the tapedev entries to the tape device you use, and the tape type entry for your tape drive type. In the holding disk segment, you will need to specify the partition and the directory for the holding disk you want to use. See the amanda Man page and documentation for detailed information on various options.

disklist

The **disklist** file is where you specify the file systems and partitions to be backed up. An entry lists the host, the partition, and the dump-type. The possible dump-types are defined in **amanda.conf**. The dump-types set certain parameters such as the priority of the backup and whether to use compression or not. The comp-root type will back up root partitions with compression and low priority, whereas the always-full type will back up an entire partition with no compression and the highest priority. You can define other dump-types in **amanda.conf** and use them for different partitions.

Backups will be performed in the order listed; be sure to list the more important ones first. The **disklist** file in **DailySet1** provides detailed examples.

Enabling Amanda on the Network

To use Amanda on the network, you need to run two servers on the Amanda server as well as an Amanda client on each network host. Access must be enabled for both the clients and the server.

Amanda Server

The Amanda server runs through **xinetd**, using **xinetd** service files located in **/etc/xinetd.d**. The two service files are **amidxtape** and **amandaidx**. Then restart the **xinetd** daemon to have it take immediate effect.

For clients to be able to recover backups from the server, the clients' hostnames must be placed in the **.amandahosts** file in the server's Amanda users' directory, **/var/lib/amanda**. On the server, **/var/lib/amanda/.amandahosts** will list all the hosts that are backed up by Amanda.

Amanda Hosts

Each host needs to allow access by the Amanda server. To do this, you place the hostname of the Amanda server in each client's **.amandahosts** dot file. This file is located in the client's Amanda user home directory, **/var/lib/amanda**.

Each host needs to run the Amanda client daemon, **amanda**, which also runs under **xinetd**. The **/etc/xinetd.d/amanda** configuration file is used to control enabling Amanda.

Tip: If your server and hosts have firewalls, you will need to allow access through the ports that Amanda uses, usually 10080, 10082, and 10083.

Using Amanda

Backups are performed by the amdump command.

```
amdump DailySet1
```

An amdump command for each backup is placed in the Amanda **crontab** file. It is helpful to run an amcheck operation to make sure that a tape is ready.

```
0 16 * * 1-5 /usr/sbin/amcheck -m DailySet1
45 0 * * 2-6 /usr/sbin/amdump DailySet1
```

Before you can use a tape, you will have to label it with amlabel. Amanda uses the label to determine what tape should be used for a backup. Log in as the Amanda user (not root) and label the tape so that it can be used.

```
amlabel DailySet DailySet1
```

A client can recover a backup using amrecover. This needs to be run as the root user, not as the Amanda user. The amrecover command works through an interactive shell much like ftp, letting you list available files and select them to restore. Within the amrecover shell, the ls command will list available backups, the **add** command will select one, and the extract operation will restore it. The lcd command lets you change the client directory; amrecover will use **DailySet1** as the default, but for other configurations you will need to specify their configuration directory with the -c option. Should you have more than one Amanda server, you can list the one you want with the -t option.

```
amrecover -C DailySet1
```

To restore full system backups, you use the amrestore command, specifying the tape device and the hostname.

```
amrestore  /dev/rmt1  rabbit
```

To select certain files, you can pipe the output to a recovery command such as restore (discussed in the next section).

```
amrestore -p /dev/rmt1  rabbit mydir  | restore  -ibvf 2 -
```

Backups with dump and restore

You can back up and restore your system with the dump and restore utilities (Universe repository, **dump** package). dump can back up your entire system or perform incremental backups, saving only those files that have changed since the last backup. dump supports several options for managing the backup operation, such as specifying the size and length of storage media (see Table 18-6).

Note: Several disk dump tools are also available. The diskdumpfmt command can be used to format tapes for use by dump. diskdumpctl registers a dump partition with the system. savecore saves a **vmcore** file from the data in a dump partition. Dumped cores can be read by the **crash** tool. Check the **crash** Man page for details.

Option	Description
-0 through -9	Specifies the dump level. A dump level 0 is a full backup, copying the entire file system (see also the -h option). Dump level numbers above 0 perform incremental backups, copying all new or modified files new in the file system since the last backup at a lower level. The default level is 9.
-B *records*	Lets you specify the number of blocks in a volume, overriding the end-of-media detection or length and density calculations that dump normally uses for multivolume dumps.
-a	Lets dump bypass any tape length calculations and write until an end-of-media indication is detected. Recommended for most modern tape drives and is the default.
-b *blocksize*	Lets you specify the number of kilobytes per dump record. With this option, you can create larger blocks, speeding up backups.
-d *density*	Specifies the density for a tape in bits per inch (default is 1,600BPI).
-h *level*	Files that are tagged with a user's nodump flag will not be backed up at or above this specified level. The default is 1, which will not back up the tagged files in incremental backups.
-f *file/device*	Backs up the file system to the specified file or device. This can be a file or tape drive. You can specify multiple filenames, separated by commas. A remote device or file can be referenced with a preceding hostname, *hostname:file*.
-k	Uses Kerberos authentication to talk to remote tape servers.
-M *file/device*	Implements a multivolume backup, where the *file* written to is treated as a prefix and the suffix consisting of a numbered sequence from 001 is used for each succeeding file, *file*001, *file*002, and so on. Useful when backup files need to be greater than the Linux **ext3** 2GB file size limit.
-n	Notifies operators if a backup needs operator attention.
-s *feet*	Specifies the length of a tape in feet. dump will prompt for a new tape when the length is reached.
-S	Estimates the amount of space needed to perform a backup.
-T *date*	Allows you to specify your own date instead of using the **/etc/dumpdates** file.
-u	Writes an entry for a successful update in the **/etc/dumpdates** file.
-W	Detects and displays the file systems that need to be backed up. This information is taken from the **/etc/dumpdates** and **/etc/fstab** files.
-w	Detects and displays the file systems that need to be backed up, drawing only on information in **/etc/fstab**.

Table 18-6: Options for dump

The dump Levels

The dump utility uses *dump levels* to determine to what degree you want your system backed up. A dump level of 0 will copy file systems in their entirety. The remaining dump levels perform incremental backups, backing up only files and directories that have been created or modified since the last lower-level backup. A dump level of 1 will back up only files that have changed since the last level 0 backup. The dump level 2, in turn, will back up only files that have changed since the last level 1 backup (or 0 if there is no level 1), and so on up to dump level 9. You can run an initial complete backup at dump level 0 to back up your entire system and then run incremental backups at certain later dates, backing up only the changes since the full backup.

Using dump levels, you can devise certain strategies for backing up a file system. It is important to keep in mind that an incremental backup is run on changes from the last lower-level backup. For example, if the last backup was 6 and the next backup was 8, then the level 8 will back up everything from the level 6 backup.

The sequence of the backups is important. If there were three backups with levels 3, then 6, and then 5, the level 5 backup would take everything from the level 3 backup, not stopping at level 6. Level 3 is the next-*lower*-level backup for level 5, in this case. This can make for some complex incremental backup strategies. For example, if you want each succeeding incremental backup to include all the changes from the preceding incremental backups, you can run the backups in descending dump level order. Given a backup sequence of 7, 6, and 5, with 0 as the initial full backup, 6 would include all the changes to 7, because its next lower level is 0. Then 5 would include all the changes for 7 and 6, also because its next lower level is 0, making all the changes since the level 0 full backup. A simpler way to implement this is to make the incremental levels all the same. Given an initial level of 0, and then two backups both with level 1, the last level 1 would include all the changes from the backup with level 0, since level 0 is the next *lower* level—not the previous level 1 backup.

Recording Backups

Backups are recorded in the **/etc/dumpdates** file. This file will list all the previous backups, specifying the file system they were performed on, the dates they were performed, and the dump level used. You can use this information to restore files from a specified backup. Recall that the **/etc/fstab** file records the dump level as well as the recommended backup frequency for each file system. With the **-w** option, dump will analyze both the **/etc/dumpdates** and **/etc/fstab** files to determine which file systems need to be backed up. The dump command with the **-w** option just uses **/etc/fstab** to report the file systems ready for backup.

Operations with dump

The dump command takes as its arguments the dump level, the device it is storing the backup on, and the device name of the file system that is being backed up. If the storage medium (such as a tape) is too small to accommodate the backup, dump will pause and let you insert another. dump supports backups on multiple volumes. The u option will record the backup in the **/etc/dumpdates** file. In the following example, an entire backup (dump level 0) is performed on the file system on the **/dev/hda3** hard disk partition. The backup is stored on a tape device, **/dev/tape**.

```
dump -0u -f /dev/tape /dev/hda5
```

Note: You can use the mt command to control your tape device; mt has options to rewind, erase, and position the tape. The rmt command controls a remote tape device.

The storage device can be another hard disk partition, but it is usually a tape device. When you installed your system, your system most likely detected the device and set up **/dev/tape** as a link to it (just as it did with your CD-ROMs). If the link was not set up, you have to create it yourself or use the device name directly. Tape devices can have different device names, depending on the model or interface. SCSI tape devices are labeled with the prefix **st**, with a number attached for the particular device: **st0** is the first SCSI tape device. To use it in the dump command, just specify its name.

```
dump -0u -f /dev/st0 /dev/hda5
```

Should you need to back up to a device located on another system on your network, you have to specify that hostname for the system and the name of its device. The hostname is entered before the device name and delimited with a colon. In the following example, the user backs up file system **/dev/hda5** to the SCSI tape device with the name **/dev/st0** on the **rabbit.mytrek.com** system:

```
dump -0u -f rabbit.mytrek.com:/dev/st0 /dev/hda5
```

The dump command works on one file system at a time. If your system has more than one file system, you will need to issue a separate dump command for each.

Tip: You can use the system **cron** utility to schedule backups using dump at specified times.

Recovering Backups

You use the restore command either to restore an entire file system or to just retrieve particular files. restore will extract files or directories from a backup archive and copy them to the current working directory. Make sure you are in the directory you want the files restored to when you run restore. restore will also generate any subdirectories as needed, and it has several options for managing the restore operation

To recover individual files and directories, you run restore in an interactive mode using the **-i** option. This will generate a shell with all the directories and files on the tape, letting you select the ones you want to restore. When you are finished, restore will then retrieve from a backup only those files you selected. This shell has its own set of commands that you can use to select and extract files and directories. The following command will generate an interactive interface listing all the directories and files backed up on the tape in the **/dev/tape** device:

```
restore -ivf /dev/tape
```

This command will generate a shell encompassing the entire directory structure of the backup. You are given a shell prompt and can use the cd command to move to different directories and the ls command to list files and subdirectories. You use the add command to tag a file or directory for extraction. Should you later decide not to extract it, you can use the delete command to remove it from the tagged list. Once you have selected all the items you want, you enter the extract command to retrieve them from the backup archive. To quit the restore shell, you enter quit. The help command will list the restore shell commands.

If you need to restore an entire file system, use **restore** with the **-r** option. You can restore the file system to any blank formatted hard disk partition of adequate size, including the file system's original partition. If may be advisable, if possible, to restore the file system on another partition and check the results.

Restoring an entire file system involves setting up a formatted partition, mounting it to your system, and then changing to its top directory to run the **restore** command. First you should use **mkfs** to format the partition where you are restoring the file system, and then mount it onto your system. Then you use **restore** with the −**r** option and the −**f** option to specify the device holding the file system's backup. In the next example, the user formats and mounts the **/dev/hda5** partition and then restores on that partition the file system backup, currently on a tape in the **/dev/tape** device.

```
mkfs /dev/hda5
mount /dev/hda5 /mystuff
cd /mystuff
restore -rf /dev/tape
```

To restore from a backup device located on another system on your network, you have to specify that hostname for the system and the name of its device. The hostname is entered before the device name and delimited with a colon. In the following example, the user restores a file system from the backup on the tape device with the name **/dev/tape** on the **rabbit.mytrek.com** system:

```
restore -rf rabbit.mytrek.com:/dev/tape
```

19. Printing

Editing Printer Configuration

Printer Classes

Adding New Printers Manually

Remote Printers

Ubuntu Printers remotely accessed from Windows

Print services have become an integrated part of every Linux system. They allow you to use any printer on your system or network. Once treated as devices attached to a system directly, printers are now treated as network resources managed by print servers. In the case of a single printer attached directly to a system, the networking features become transparent and the printer appears as just one more device. On the other hand, you could easily use a print server's networking capability to let several systems use the same printer. Although printer installation is almost automatic on most Linux distributions, it helps to understand the underlying process. Printing sites and resources are listed in Table 19-1.

CUPS

The Common Unix Printing System (CUPS) provides printing services. It is freely available under the GNU Public License. Though it is now included with most distributions, you can also download the most recent source-code version of CUPS from **cups.org**, which provides detailed documentation on installing and managing printers. CUPS is based on the Internet Printing Protocol (IPP), which was designed to establish a printing standard for the Internet (for more information, see **pwg.org/ipp**). Whereas the older line printer (LPD)based printing systems focused primarily on line printers, an IPP-based system provides networking, PostScript, and web support. CUPS works like an Internet server and employs a configuration setup much like that of the Apache web server. Its network support lets clients directly access printers on remote servers, without having to configure the printers themselves. Configuration needs to be maintained only on the print servers.

Resource	Description
cups.org	Common Unix Printing System
pwg.org/ipp	Internet Printing Protocol
sourceforge.net/projects/lprng	LPRng print server (Universe repository)

Table 19-1: Print Resources

CUPS is the primary print server for most Linux distributions. With **libgnomecups**, GNOME now provides integrated support for CUPS, allowing GNOME-based applications to directly access CUPS printers.

Once you have installed your printers and configured your print server, you can print and manage your print queue using print clients. There are a variety of printer clients available for the CUPS server, GNOME print manager, the CUPS configuration tool, and various line printing tools like `lpq` and `lpc`. These are described in further detail later in this chapter. The CUPS configuration tool is a web-based configuration tool that can also manage printers and print jobs (open your browser and enter the URL **http://localhost:631**). A web page is displayed with entries for managing jobs, managing printers, and administrative tasks. Select the Manage Jobs entry to remove or reorder jobs you have submitted.

Check the Ubuntu Server Guide | File Servers | CUPS - Print Server for basic configuration.

```
https://help.ubuntu.com/9.04/serverguide/C/cups.html
```

Note: Line Printer, Next Generation (LPRng) was the traditional print server for Linux and Unix systems, but it has since been dropped from many Linux distributions. You can find out more about LPRng at **sourceforge.net/projects/lprng**.

Printer Devices and Configuration

Before you can use any printer, you first have to install it on a Linux system on your network. A local printer is installed directly on your own system. This involves creating an entry for the printer in a printer configuration file that defines the kind of printer it is, along with other features such as the device file and spool directory it uses. On CUPS, the printer configuration file is **/etc/cups/printers.conf**. Installing a printer is fairly simple: determine which device file to use for the printer and the configuration entries for it.

Tip: If you cannot find the drivers for your printer, you may be able to download them from OpenPrinting database at **linux-foundation.org/en/OpenPrinting**. The site maintains an extensive listing of drivers.

Printer Device Files

Linux dynamically creates the device names for printers that are installed. USB-connected printers will have a Hardware Abstract Layer (HAL) device connection. HAL is designed for removable devices that can easily be attached to other connections and still be recognized. For older printers connected to a particular port dedicated device files will be generated. As an example, for parallel printers, the device names will be **lp0**, **lp1**, and **lp2**, depending on how many parallel printers are connected. The number used in these names corresponds to a parallel port on your PC; **lp0** references the LPT1 parallel port and **lp1** references the LPT2 parallel port. Serial printers will use serial ports, referenced by the device files like **ttyS0**, **ttyS1**, **ttyS2**, and so on.

Printer URI (Universal Resource Identifier)

Printers can be local or remote. Both are referenced using Universal Resource Identifiers (URI). URIs support both network protocols used to communicate with remote printers, and device connections used to reference local printers.

Remote printers are referenced by the protocol used to communicate with it, like **ipp** for the Internet Printing Protocol used for Unix network printers, **smb** for the Samba protocol used for Windows network printers, and **lpd** for the older LPRng Unix servers. Their URIs are similar to a Web URL, indicating the network address of the system the printer is connected to.

```
ipp://mytsuff.com/printers/queue1
smb://guest@lizard/myhp
```

For attached local printers, especially older ones, the URI will use the device connection and the device name. The **usb:** prefix is used for USB printers, **parallel:** for older printers connected to a parallel port, **serial:** for printers connected to a serial port, and **scsi:** for SCSI connected printers.

In the CUPS **/etc/cups/printers.conf** file the DeviceURI entry will reference the URI for a printer. For USB printers, the URI is usually uses **usb:**.

```
DeviceURI usb://Canon/S330
```

Spool Directories

When your system prints a file, it makes use of special directories called *spool directories.* A *print job* is a file to be printed. When you send a file to a printer, a copy of it is made and placed in a spool directory set up for that printer. The location of the spool directory is obtained from the printer's entry in its configuration file. On Linux, the spool directory is located at **/var/spool/cups** under a directory with the name of the printer. For example, the spool directory for the myepson printer would be located at **/var/spool/cups/myepson**. The spool directory contains several files for managing print jobs. Some files use the name of the printer as their extension. For example, the myepson printer has the files **control.myepson**, which provides printer queue control, and **active.myepson** for the active print job, as well as **log.myepson,** which is the log file.

Server script

A cups startup script is installed in the **/etc/rc.d/init.d** directory. You can start, stop, and restart CUPS using the **service** command and the cups script or **admin-services** (System | Administration | Services). When you make changes or install printers, be sure to restart CUPS to have your changes take effect. You can use the following command:

```
sudo service cups restart
```

Installing Printers

There are several tools available for installing CUPS printers. The easiest method is to use Ubuntu system-config-printer tool on a desktop system. Alternatively you can use the CUPS Web browser-based configuration tools, included with the CUPS software (will work with **lynx** command line browser). Finally you can just edit the CUPS printer configuration files directly.

Configuring Printers on the Desktop with system-config-printer

The primary printing configuration tool on the Ubuntu desktop is system-config-printer (System | Administration | Printing). Any printer will be automatically detected when you first attached it. If the driver is not available, a Missing printer driver notification will be displayed. If the driver is not available, a Missing printer driver notification will be displayed (see Figure 19-1).

Figure 19-1: Printer detection notification

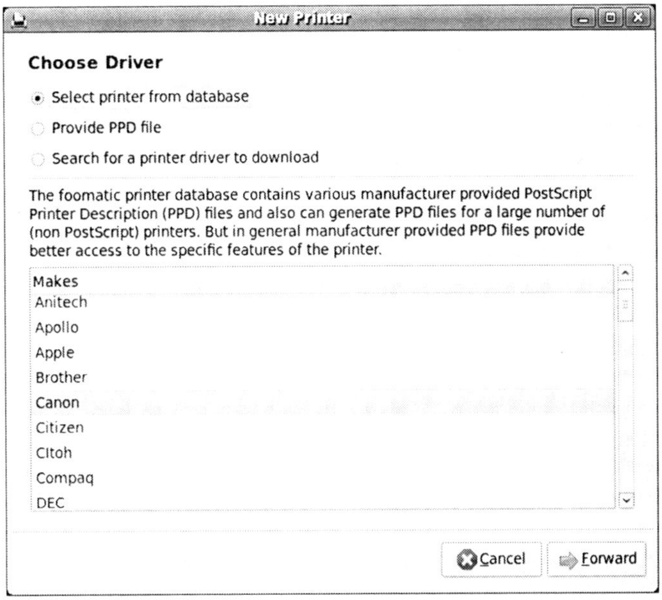

Figure 19-2: Choose Printer driver for missing driver

A New Printer dialog opens where you can choose how to locate your driver (see Figure 19-2).

The tool used to configure printers is system-config-printer. Though printers are automatically detected when attached, you can also modify your configuration as well as add access to remote printers on your network. You can start system-config-printer by selecting the Printing entry in the System | Administration menu.

The Printer configuration window displays icons for installed printers (see Figure 19-3). The menu bar has menus for Server configuration and selection, Printer features like its properties and the print queue, printer groups, and viewing printers by group and discovered printers. A toolbar has buttons for adding new printers manually and refreshing print configuration. A Filter search box lets you display only printers matching a search pattern. Click on the broom icon in the search box to clear the pattern. Clicking on the Looking glass icon in the File search box will display a pop-up menu that will let you search on Name, Description, Location, and Manufacturer/Model. You can save searches as a search group. You can also use the search results to create a printer group.

Figure 19-3: system-config-printer tool

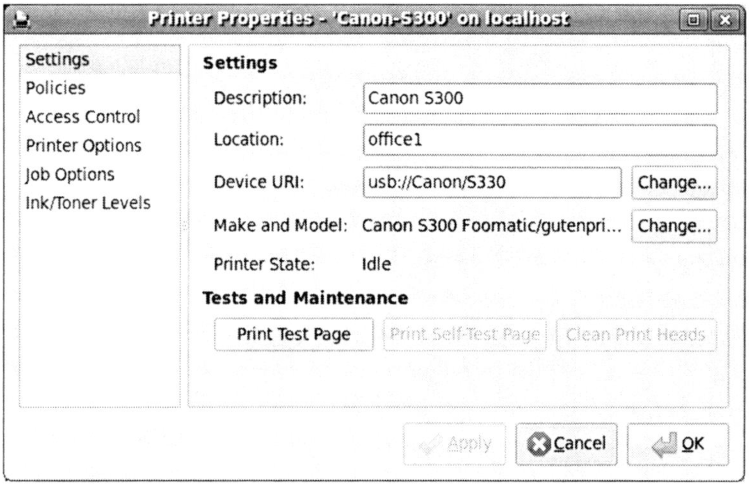

Figure 19-4: Printer properties window

To see the printer settings such as printer and job options, access controls, and policies, double-click on the printer icon or right-click and select Properties. The Printer Properties window opens up with five panes: Settings, Policies, Access Control, Printer Options, and Job Options (see Figure 19-4). These are the same as those used in Ubuntu 8.04.

The Printer configuration window Printer menu lets you rename the printer, enable or disable it, and make it a shared printer. Select the printer icon and then click the Printer menu (see Figure 19-5). The Delete entry will remove a printer configuration. Use the Set As Default entry to make the printer a system-wide or personal default printer.

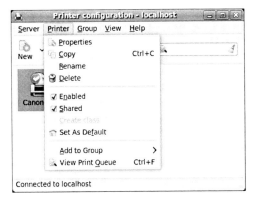

Figure 19-5: Printer configuration window Printer menu

Figure 19-6: Printer icon menu

The Printer icon menu is accesses by right-clicking on the printer icon (see Figure 19-6). It adds entries for accessing the printer properties and viewing the print queue. If the printer is already a default, there is no Set As Default entry. The properties entry opens the printer properties window for that printer.

The View Print Queue entry opens the Document print status window listing jobs for that printer. You can change the queue position as well as stop or delete jobs (see Figure 19-7). From the job menu you can cancel, hold (stop), release (restart), or reprint a print job. Reprint is only available if you have set the preserve jobs option in the printer settings Advanced dialog. You can also authenticate a job. From the View menu you can choose to display just printed jobs and refresh the queue.

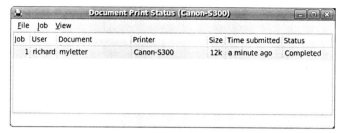

Figure 19-7: Printer queue

To check the server settings, select Settings from the Server menu. This opens a new window showing the CUPS printer server settings (see Figure 19-8). The Advanced button opens a window for job history and browser server options. If you want to allow reprinting, then select the "Preserve job files (allow reprinting)" option.

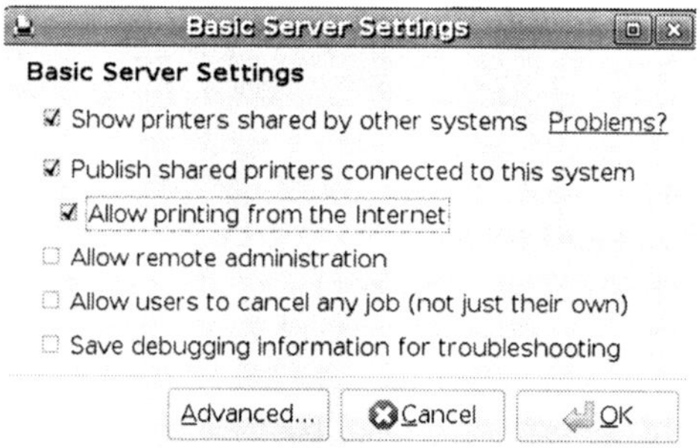

Figure 19-8: Server Settings

Figure 19-9: Selecting a CUPS server

To select a particular CUPS server, select the Connect entry in the Server menu. This opens a "Connect to CUPS Server" window with a drop down menu listing all current CUPS servers from which to choose (see Figure 19-9).

Editing Printer Configuration with system-config-printer

To edit an installed printer, double click its icon in the Printer configuration window, or right-click and select the Properties entry. This opens a Printer Properties window for that printer. A sidebar lists configuration panes. Click on one to display that pane. There are configuration entries for Settings, Policies, Access Control, Printer Options, and Job Control (see Figure 19-10).

Once you have made your changes, you can click Apply to save your changes and restart the printer daemon. You can test your printer with a PostScript, A4, or ASCII test sheet selected from the Test menu.

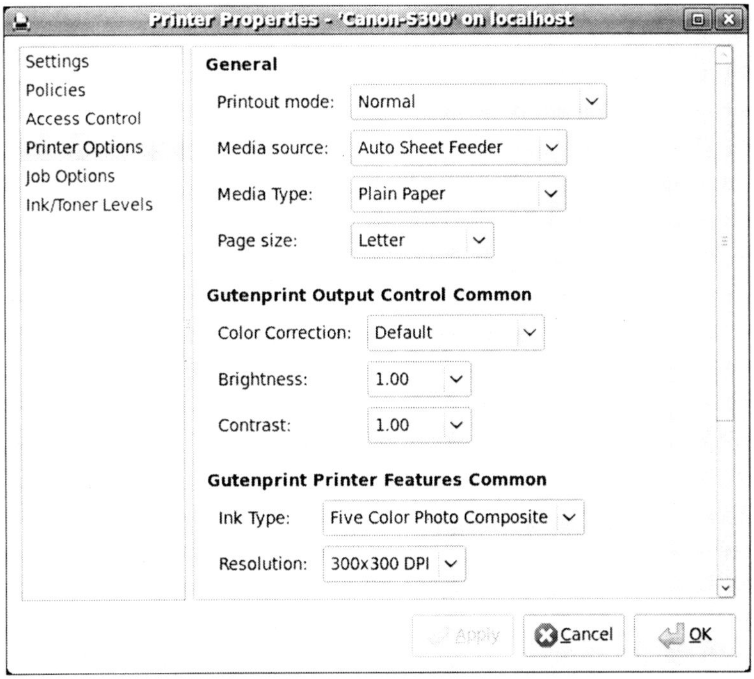

Figure 19-10: Printer Options pane

On the Settings pane you can change configuration settings like the driver and the printer name, enable or disable the printer, or specify whether to share it or not (see Figure 19-4). Should you need to change the selected driver, click on the Change button next to the Make and Model entry. This will open printer model and driver windows like those described in the Add new printer manually section. There you can specify the model and driver you want to use, even loading your own driver.

The Policies pane lets you specify a start and end banner, as well as an error policy which specifies whether to retry or abort the print job, or stop the printer should an error occur. The Access Control pane allows you to deny access to certain users.

The Printer Options pane is where you set particular printing features like paper size and type, print quality, and the input tray to use (see Figure 19-11).

On the Job Options pane you can select default printing features (see Figure 19-8). A pop-up menu provides a list of printing feature categories to choose from. You then click the Add button to add the category, selecting a particular feature from a pop-up menu. You can set such features as the number of copies (copies); letter, glossy, or A4-sized paper (media); the kind of document, for instance, text, PDF, PostScript, or image (document format); and single- or double-sided printing (sides).The Ink/Toner Levels pane will display Ink or Toner levels for supported printers, along with status messages.

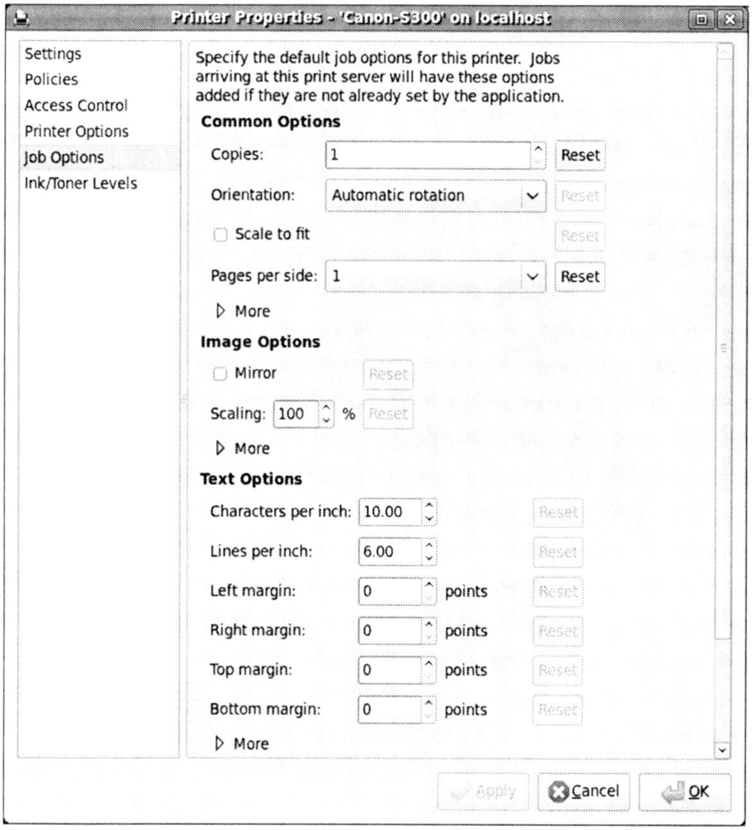

Figure 19-11: Jobs Options pane

Default System-wide and Personal Printers

To make printer the default printer, either right-click on the printer icon and select "Set As Default", or single click on the printer icon and then from the Printer configuration window's Printer menu select the "Set As Default" entry (see Figure 19-5 and 19-6). A Set Default Printer dialog open with options for setting the system-wide default or setting the personal default (see Figure 19-12). The system-wide default printer is the default for your entire network served by your CUPS server, not just your local system.

Figure 19-12: Set Default Printer dialog

The system-wide default printer will have a green check mark emblem on its printer icon in the Printer configuration window.

Should you wish to use a different printer yourself as your default printer, you can designate it as your personal default. To make a printer your personal default, select the entry "Set as my personal default printer" in the Set Default Printer dialog. A personal emblem, a heart, will appear on the printer's icon in the Printer configuration window. In Figure 19-13, the S300-windows printer is the system-wide default, whereas the S330 printer is the personal default.

Figure 19-13: System-wide and personal default printers

If you have more than one printer on your system, you can make one the default by clicking Make Default Printer button in the printer's properties Settings pane.

Printer Classes

The Class entry in the New menu lets you create a printer class. You can access the New menu from the Server menu or from the New button. This feature lets you select a group of printers to print a job instead of selecting just one. That way, if one printer is busy or down, another printer can be automatically selected to perform the job. Installed printers can be assigned to different classes. When you click the Class entry in the New menu, a New Class window opens. Here you can enter the name for the class, any comments, and the location (your host name is entered by default). The next screen lists available printers on right side (Other printers) and the printers you assigned to the class on the left side (Printers in this class). Use the arrow button to add or remove printers to the class. Click Apply when finished. The class will appear under the Local Classes heading on the main system-config-printer window. Panes for a selected class are much the same as for a printer, with a members pane instead of a print control pane. In the Members pane you can change what printers belong to the class

Adding New Printers Manually

Printers are normally detected automatically, though in the case of older printers and network printers, you may need to add the printer manually. In this case click the New button and select Printer. A New Printer window opens up displaying series of dialog boxes where you select the connection, model, drivers, and printer name with location.

On the Select Device screen, you select the appropriate printer connection information. Connected local printer brands will already be listed by name, such as Canon. For remote printers you specify the type of network connection, like Windows printers via Samba for printers connected to a Windows system, AppSocket/HP Direct for HP printers connected directly to your network. The Internet Printing Protocol (ipp) for printers on Linux and Unix systems on your network. These connections are displayed under the Network Printer heading. Click the pointer to display them.

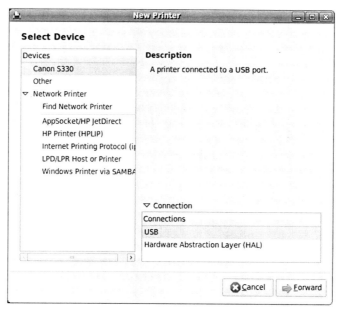

Figure 19-14: Selecting a new printer connection

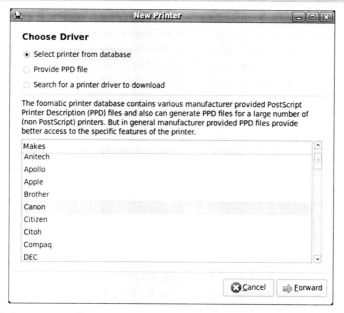

Figure 19-15: Printer manufacturer for new printers

For most connected printers, your connection is usually determined by the device hotplug services udev and HAL, which now manage all devices. Printers connected to your local system will be first entries on the list. A USB printer will simply be described as a USB printer, using the usb URI designation (see Figure 19-14 and 19-4).

For an older local printer, you will need to choose the port the printer is connected to, such as LPT1 for the first parallel port used for older parallel printers, or Serial Port #1 for a printer connected to the first serial port. For this example an older parallel printer will be set up, LPT #1.

A search will then be conducted for the appropriate driver, including downloadable drivers. If the driver is found, the Choose Driver screen is then displayed with the appropriate driver manufacturer already selected for you. You need only click the forward button. On the next screen, also labeled Choose Driver, the printer models and drivers files will be listed and the appropriate one already selected for you. Just click the Forward button. The Describe Printer screen is then displayed where you can enter the Printer Name, Description, and Location. These are ways you can personally identify a printer. Then click Apply.

If you printer driver is not detected or detected incorrectly, then, on the Choose Driver screen you have the options to choose the driver yourself from the database, from a PPD driver file of your own, or from your own search of the OpenPrinting online repository. The selection display will change according to which option you choose.

The database option will list possible manufacturers. Use your mouse to select the one you want.

The search option will display a search box for make and model. Enter both the make (printer manufacturer) and part of the model name (See figure 3-15). The search results will be available in the Printer model drop down menu. Select the one you want.

The PPD file option simply displays a file location button that when clicked, open a Select file dialog you can use to locate your PPD file on your system.

Figure 19-16: Searching for a printer driver from the OpenPrinting repository

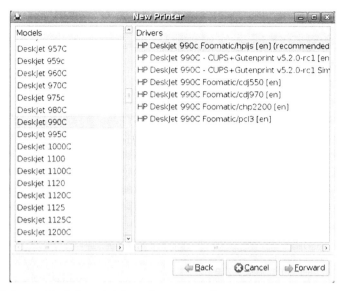

Figure 19-17: Printer Model and driver for new printers using local database

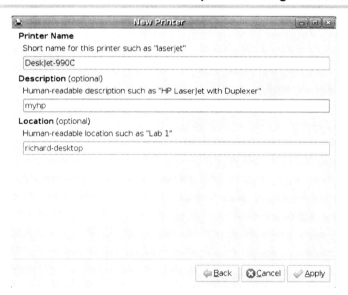

Figure 19-18: Printer Name and Location for new printers

Instead of manually selecting the driver, you can try to search for it on OpenPrinting repository (see Figure 19-16). Click the Search for a printer driver to download entry. Enter the printer name and model and click the Search button. From the pop up menu labeled Printer model, select the driver for your printer. Then click Forward.

If you are selecting a printer from the database, then, on the next screen you select that manufacturer's model along with its driver (see Figure 19-17). For some older printer, though the driver can be located on the online repository, you will still choose it from the local database (the drivers are the same). The selected drivers for your printer will be listed. You can find out more about the printer and driver by clicking the Printer and Driver buttons at the bottom of the screen. Then click the Forward button.

You then enter in your printer name and location (see Figure 19-18). These will be entered for you using the printer model and your system's host name. You can change the printer name to anything you want. When ready, click Apply.

You then see an icon for your printer displayed in the Printer configuration window. You are now ready to print.

Note: KDE 4 provides a printer configuration interface for CUPS. Access it on the System Settings Advanced tab, or from Applications | System | Printer Configuration). Configuration is similar to system-config-printer.

CUPS Web Browser-based configuration tool

One of the easiest ways to configure and install printers with CUPS is to use the CUPS configuration tool, which is a web browser–based configuration tool. To start the web interface, enter the following URL into your web browser:

```
http://localhost:631
```

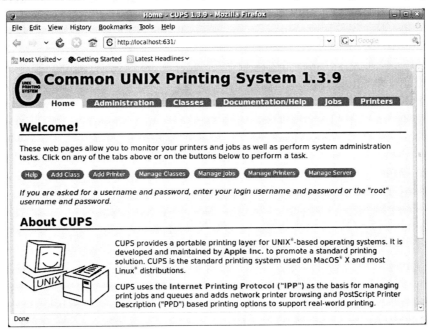

Figure 19-19: CUPS Web-based Configuration Tool

You can also use this CUPS configuration interface with a command line Web browser like **lynx** (install **lynx** first). This allows you to configure a printer from the command line interface. Use the ENTER key to display menus and make selections, and arrow keys to navigate.

```
lynx localhost:631
```

This opens the Home screen for the CUPS Web interface. There are tabs for various sections, as well as buttons for specialized tasks like adding printers (see Figure 19-19). Tabs including Administration, Classes, Documentation, Jobs, and Printers. You can manage and add printers. The Printers tab will list installed printers with buttons for accessing their print queues, printer options, and job options, among others. The Jobs tab lists your print jobs and lets you manage them.

When you try to make any changes for the first time during the session, you will first be asked to enter the administrator's username (your user name) and password (your user password), just as you would for the **sudo** command.

The Administration tab displays segments for Printers, Classes, Jobs, and the Server (see Figure 19-20). The server section is where you allow printer sharing. Buttons allow you to view logs and change settings.

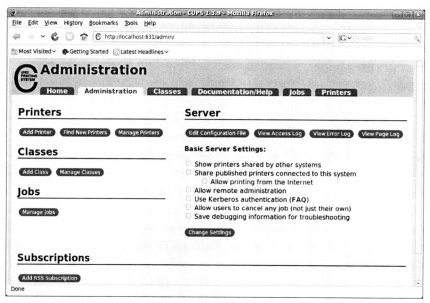

Figure 19-20: CUPS Web-based Administration tab

With the CUPS configuration tool, you install a printer on CUPS through a series of Web pages, each of which requests different information. To install a printer, click the Add Printer button either on the Home page or the Administration page. A page is displayed where you enter the printer name and location (see Figure 19-21). The location is the host to which the printer is connected. The procedure is similar to **system-config-printer**. Subsequent pages will prompt you to enter the device, make and model of the printer, and the driver, which you select from available listings.

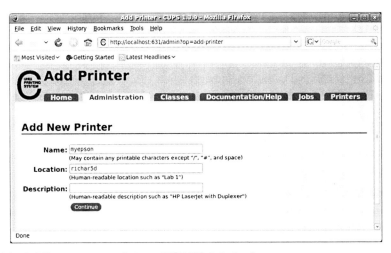

Figure 19-21: Adding a new printer: CUP Web Interface

Once you have added the printer, you can configure it. Clicking the Printers tab or the Manage Printers button in the Administration page. The Printers page will list your installed printers (see Figure 19-22). For each printer, a list of buttons lets you perform certain tasks, including button. You can stop the printer, configure its printing, modify its installation, and even delete the printer. Clicking the Set Printer Options button displays a page on the Administration tab where you can configure how your printer prints, by specifying the resolution or paper size.

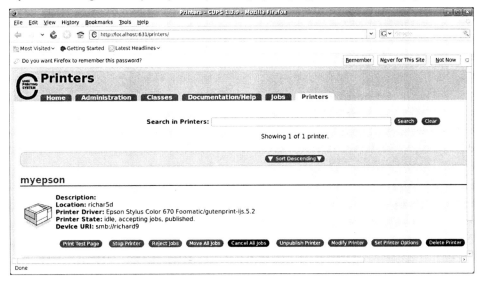

Figure 19-22: CUPS Printers: CUP Web interface

Note: You can perform all administrative tasks from the command line using the `lpadmin` command. See the CUPS documentation for more details.

Configuring Remote Printers on CUPS

To install a remote printer that is attached to a Windows system or another Linux system running CUPS, you specify its location using special URL protocols. For another CUPS printer on a remote host, the protocol used is **ipp**, for Internet Printing Protocol, whereas for a Windows printer, it would be **smb**. Older Unix or Linux systems using LPRng would use the **lpd** protocol.

Configuring Remote Printers on the Desktop with system-config-printer

To install a remote printer that is attached to a Windows system or another Linux system running CUPS, you specify its location using URI protocols. For a locally attached USB printer, the USB URI is uses, **usb**. For another CUPS printer on a remote host, the protocol used is **ipp**, for Internet Printing Protocol, whereas for a Windows printer, it would be **smb**. Older UNIX or Linux systems using LPRng would use the **lpd** protocol.

You can also use system-config-printer to set up a remote printer on Linux, UNIX, or Windows networks. When you add a new printer or edit one, the New Printer/Select Connection dialog will list possible remote connection types. When you select a remote connection entry, a pane will be displayed where you can enter configuration information.

For a remote Linux or UNIX printer, select either Internet Printing Protocol (**ipp**), which is used for newer systems, or LPD/LPR Host or Printer, which is used for older systems. Both panes display entries for the Host name and the Printer name. For the Host name, enter the hostname for the system that controls the printer. For the Printer name, enter the device name on that host for the printer. The LPD/LPR dialog also has a probe button for detecting the printer.

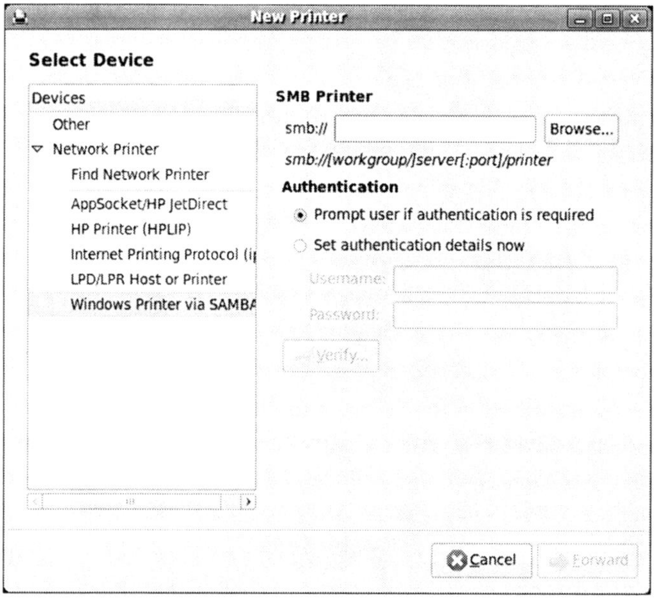

Figure 19-23: Selecting a Windows printer

For an Apple or HP jet direct printer on your network, select the AppSocket/HP jetDirect entry. You are prompted to enter the IP address and printer name.

A "Windows printer via Samba" is one located on a Windows network (see Figure 19-23). You need to specify the Windows server (host name or IP address), the name of the share, the name of the printer's workgroup, and the username and password. The format of the printer SMB URL is shown on the SMP Printer pane. The share is the hostname and printer name in the **smb** URI format *//workgroup/hostname/printername.* The workgroup is the windows network workgroup that the printer belongs to. On small networks there is usually only one. The hostname is the computer where the printer is located. The username and password can be for the printer resource itself, or for access by a particular user. The pane will display a box at the top where you can enter the share host and printer name as a **smb** URI.

Figure 19-24: SMB Browser, selecting a remote windows printer

You can click the Browse button to open a SMB Browser window, where you can select the printer from a listing of Windows hosts on your network (see Figure 19-24). For example, if your Windows network is WORKGROUP, then the entry WORKGROUP will be shown, which you can then expand to list all the Windows hosts on that network (if your network is MSHOME, then that is what will be listed).

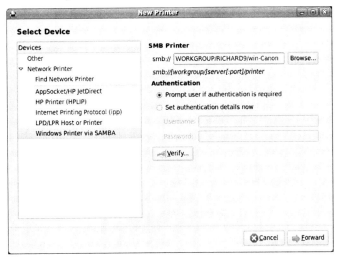

Figure 19-25: Remote windows printer connection configuration

When you make your selection, the corresponding URL will show up in the **smb://** box (See Figure 19-25). If you are using the Firestarter firewall, be sure to turn it off before browsing a Windows workgroup for a printer, unless already configured to allow Samba access. Also on the pane, you can enter in any needed Samba authentication, if required, like user name or password. Check "Authentication required" to allow you to enter the Samba Username and Password.

You then continue with install screens for the printer model, driver, and name. Once installed, you can then access the printer properties just as you would any printer (see Figure 19-26).

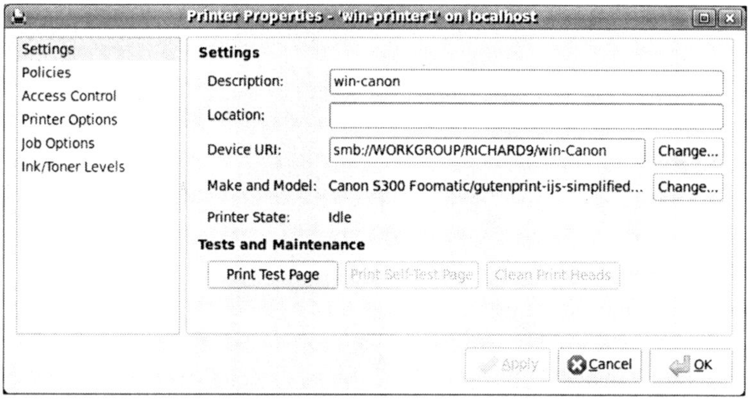

Figure 19-26: Remote Windows printer Settings

To access an SMB shared remote printer, you need to install Samba and have the Server Message Block services enabled using the smb and nmb daemons. The Samba service will be enabled by default. The service is enabled by checking the Windows Folders entry in the Gnome Services tool (System | Administration | Services). Printer sharing must, in turn, be enabled on the Windows network.

Configuring remote printers manually

In the **printers.conf** file, for a remote printer, the DeviceURI entry, instead of listing the device, will have an Internet address, along with its protocol. For example, a remote printer on a CUPS server (**ipp**) would be indicated as shown here (a Windows printer would use the **smb** protocol):

```
DeviceURI ipp://mytsuff.com/printers/queue1
```

For a Windows printer, you first need to install, configure, and run Samba. (CUPS uses Samba to access Windows printers.) When you install the Windows printer on CUPS, you specify its location using the URL protocol **smb**. The user allowed to log in to the printer is entered before the hostname and separated from it by an @ sign. On most configurations, this is the **guest** user. The location entry for a Windows printer called **myhp** attached to a Windows host named **lizard** is shown here. Its Samba share reference would be **//lizard/myhp**:

```
DeviceURI smb://guest@lizard/myhp
```

To enable CUPS on Samba, you also have to set the printing option in the **/etc/samba/smb.conf** file to **cups**, as shown here:

```
printing = cups
printcap name = cups
```

To enable CUPS to work with Samba, you have to link the **smbspool** to the CUPS **smb** spool directory:

```
ln -s /usr/bin/smbspool    /usr/cups/backend/smb
```

Note: To configure a shared Linux printer for access by Windows hosts, you need to configure it as a SMB shared printer. You do this with Samba.

Ubuntu Printers remotely accessed from Windows

On a Windows system, like Windows XP, you can use the Add Printer Wizard to locate a shared printer on a Linux system (see Figure 19-27). Locate the Ubuntu system, click on it, and the shared printers on the Ubuntu system will be listed.

Tip: If the Windows driver for your printer on your Windows system should fail, you could just attach printer to an Ubuntu system and use the Linux drivers, even remotely accessing the printer from your Windows system.

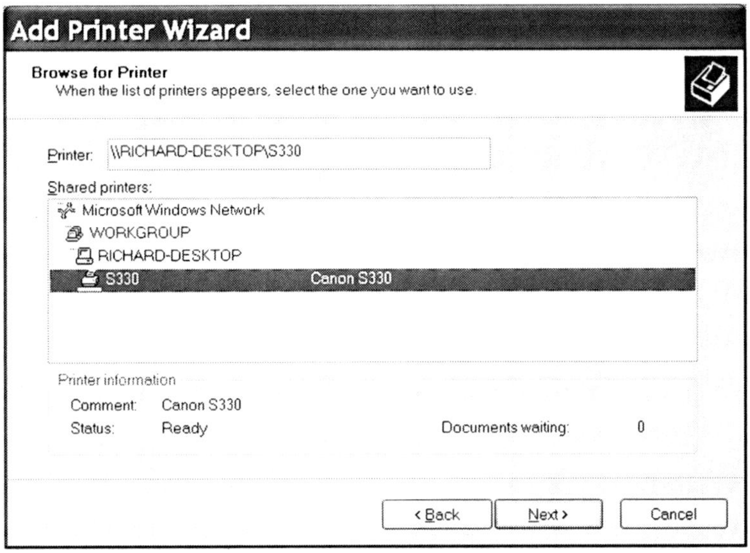

Figure 19-27: Remote Linux printer selection on Windows

CUPS Printer Classes

CUPS features a way to let you select a group of printers to print a job instead of selecting just one. That way, if one printer is busy or down, another printer can be automatically selected to perform the job. Such groupings of printers are called *classes*. Once you have installed your printers, you can group them into different classes. For example, you may want to group all inkjet printers into one class and laser printers into another, or you may want to group printers connected to one specific printer server in their own class. To create a class, select Classes on the Administration page and enter the name of the class. You can then add printers to it.

CUPS Configuration files

CUPS configuration files are placed in the **/etc/cups** directory. These files are listed in Table 19-2. The **classes.conf**, **printers.conf**, and **client.conf** files can be managed by the web interface. The **printers.conf** file contains the configuration information for the different printers you have installed. Any of these files can be edited manually, if you wish.

Filename	Description
classes.conf	Contains configurations for different local printer classes
client.conf	Lists specific options for specified clients
cupsd.conf	Configures the CUPS server, **cupsd**
printers.conf	Contains printer configurations for available local printers

Table 19-2: CUPS Configuration Files

cupsd.conf

The CUPS server is configured with the **cupsd.conf** file located in **/etc/cups**. You must edit configuration options manually; the server is not configured with the web interface. Your installation of CUPS installs a commented version of the **cupsd.conf** file with each option listed, though most options will be commented out. Commented lines are preceded with a **#** symbol. Each option is documented in detail. The server configuration uses an Apache web server syntax consisting of a set of directives. As with Apache, several of these directives can group other directives into blocks.

For a detailed explanation of cupsd.conf directives check the CUPS documentation for cupsd.conf. You can also reference this documentation from the Documentation page on the CUPS browser-based administration tool, **http://localhost:631**.

```
http://www.cups.org/documentation.php/doc-1.4/ref-cupsd-conf.html
```

The cupsd.conf file begins with setting the log level to warning.

```
LogLevel warning
```

The administrator group is then referenced, **lpadmin**. CUPS set up the **lpadmin** group for you when you installed the server.

```
SystemGroup lpadmin
```

The Listen directives are sets the machine and socket on which to receive connections. These are set by default to the local machine, localhost port 631. If you are using a dedicated network interface for connecting to a local network, you would add the network card's IP address, allowing access from machines on your network.

```
# Only listen for connections from the local machine.
Listen localhost:631
Listen /var/run/cups/cups.sock
```

Browsing directives allows your local printers to be detected on your network, enabling them to be shared. For shared printing, the Browsing directive is set to on (it is set to Off by default). A BrowseOrder of allow, deny will deny all browse transmissions, then first check the

BrowseAllow directives for exceptions. A reverse order (deny, allow) does the opposite, accepting all browse transmissions, and then first check for those denied by BrowseDeny directives. The default **cupsd.conf** file has a BrowseOrder allow, deny directive followed by a BrowseAllow directive which is set to **all**. To limit this to a particular network, use the IP address of the network instead of **all**. The BrowseAddress directive will make your local printers available as shared printers on the specified network. It is set to @LOCAL to allow access on your local network. You can add other BrowseAddress directives to allow access by other networks.

```
# Show shared printers on the local network.
Browsing On
BrowseOrder allow,deny
BrowseAllow all
BrowseAddress @LOCAL
```

CUPS supports both Basic and Digest forms of authentication, specified in the `AuthType` directive. Basic authentication uses a user and password. For example, to use the web interface, you are prompted to enter the root user and the root user password. Digest authentication makes use of user and password information kept in the CUPS **/etc/cups/passwd.md5** file, using MD5 versions of a user and password for authentication. In addition, CUPS also supports a BasicDigest and Negotiate authentication. BasicDigest will use the CUPS md5 password file for basic authentication. Negotiate will use Kerberos authentication. The default authentication type is set using the DefaultAuthType directive, set to Basic.

```
# Default authentication type, when authentication is required...
DefaultAuthType Basic
```

Location Directives

Certain directives allow you to place access controls on specific locations. These can be printers or resources, such as the administrative tool or the spool directories. Location controls are implemented with the `Location` directive. There are several Location directives that control access. The first controls access to the server root directory,/. The Order allow, deny entry activates restrictions on access by remote systems. If there are no following Allow or Deny entries then the default is to deny all. There is an implied Allow localhost with the Order allow, deny directive, always giving access to the local machine. In effect, access here is denied to all system, allowing access only by the local system.

```
# Restrict access to the server...
<Location />
  Order allow,deny
</Location>
```

The `Location` directive also restricts administrative access, the **/admin** resource, adding a requirement for encryption. The **Order allow,deny** directive denies access to all systems, except for the local machine.

```
# Restrict access to the admin pages...
<Location /admin>
  Encryption Required
  Order allow,deny
</Location>
```

Allow from and **Deny from** directives can permit or deny access from specific hosts and networks. If you wanted to just allow access to a particular machine, you would use an Allow from directive with the machine's IP address. CUPS also uses **@LOCAL** to indicate you local network, and **IF**(*name*) for a particular network interface (*name* is the device name of the interface) used to access a network. Should you want to allow administrative access by all other systems on your local network, you can add the **Allow from @LOCAL**. If you add an **Allow** directive, you also have to explicitly add the **Allow localhost** to insure access by your local machine.

```
# Restrict access to the admin pages...
<Location /admin>
  Encryption Required
  Allow from localhost
  Allow from @LOCAL
  Order allow,deny
</Location>
```

The following entry would allow access from a particular machine.

```
Allow From 192.168.0.5
```

The next location directive restricts access to the CUPS configuration files, **/admin/conf**. The **AuthType default** directive refers to the default set by DefaultAuthType.

The **Require user** directive references the **SystemGroup** directive, **@SYSTEM**. Only users from that group are allowed access.

```
# Restrict access to configuration files...
<Location /admin/conf>
  AuthType Default
  Require user @SYSTEM
  Order allow,deny
</Location>
```

Default Operation Policy: Limit Directives

A default operation policy is then defined for access to basic administration, printer, print job, and owner operations. The default operation policy section begins with the **<Policy default>** directive. Limit directives are used to implement the directives for each kind of operation. Job operations covers task like sending a document, restarting a job, suspending a job, and restarting a job. Administrative tasks include modifying a printer configuration, deleting a printer, managing printer classes, and setting the default printer. Printer operations govern tasks like pausing a printer, enable or disable a printer, and shutting down a printer. The owner operations consist of just canceling a job and authenticating access to a job.

See the CUPS documentation on managing operations policies for more details.

```
http://www.cups.org/documentation.php/doc-1.4/policies.html
```

On all the default **Limit** directives, access is allowed only by the local machine (localhost), **Order allow,deny**.

Both the administrative and printer **Limit** directives are set to the **AuthType default** and limited to access by an administrative users, **Require user @SYSTEM**. The administrative directive is shown here.

```
# All administration operations require an administrator to authenticate...
<Limit CUPS-Add-Modify-Printer CUPS-Delete-Printer CUPS-Add-Modify-Class CUPS-
Delete-Class CUPS-Set-Default>
  AuthType Default
  Require user @SYSTEM
  Order deny,allow
</Limit>
```

Both the job related and owner Limit directives require either owner or administrative authentication, **Require user @OWNER @SYSTEM**. The **Owner Limit** directive is shown here.

```
# Only the owner or an administrator can cancel or authenticate a job...
<Limit Cancel-Job CUPS-Authenticate-Job>
  Require user @OWNER @SYSTEM
  Order deny,allow
</Limit>
```

For all other tasks, **<Limit All>**, access is restricted to the local machine (localhost).

```
<Limit All>
 Order deny,allow
</Limit>
```

The `AuthClass` directive can be used within a **Limit** directive to specify the printer class allowed access. The `System` class includes the root, sys, and system users.

cupsctl

You can use the `cupsctl` command to modify your cupsd.conf file, rather than editing the file directly. Check the **cupsctl** Man page for details. The `cupsctl` command with no options will display current settings.

```
cupstctl
```

The changes you can make with this command are limited turning off remote administration or disabling shared printing. The major options you can set are:

> ➢ **remote-admin**   Enable or disable remote administration

> ➢ **remote-any**   Enable or disable remote printing

> ➢ **remote-printers**   Enable or disable the display of remote printers

> ➢ **share-printers**   Enable or disable sharing of local printers with other systems

printers.conf

Configured information for a printer will be stored in the **/etc/cups/printers.conf** file. You can examine this file directly, even making changes. Here is an example of a printer configuration entry. The `DeviceURI` entry specifies the device used, in this case a USB printer managed by HAL. It is currently idle, with no jobs:

```
# Printer configuration file for CUPS
# Written by cupsd
<Printer mycannon>
Info Cannon s330
Location
DeviceURI usb://Canon/S330
State Idle
StateTime 1166554036
Accepting Yes
Shared Yes
JobSheets none none
QuotaPeriod 0
PageLimit 0
KLimit 0
OpPolicy default
ErrorPolicy retry-job
</Printer>
```

CUPS Command Line Print Clients

Once a print job is placed on a print queue, you can use any of several print clients to manage the printing jobs on your printer or printers, such as Klpq, the GNOME Print Manager, and the CUPS Printer Configuration tool for CUPS. You can also use several command line print CUPS clients. These include the **lpr**, **lpc**, **lpq**, and **lprm** commands. With these clients, you can print documents, list a print queue, reorder it, and remove print jobs, effectively canceling them. For network connections, CUPS features an encryption option for its commands, **-E**, to encrypt print jobs and print information sent of a network. Table 19-3 shows various printer commands.

Note: The command line clients have the same name, and much the same syntax, as the older LPR and LPRng command line clients used in Unix and older Linux systems.

lpr

The **lpr** client submits a job, and **lpd** then takes it in turn and places it on the appropriate print queue; **lpr** takes as its argument the name of a file. If no printer is specified, then the default printer is used. The **-P** option enables you to specify a particular printer. In the next example, the user first prints the file **preface** and then prints the file **report** to the printer with the name **myepson**:

```
$ lpr preface
$ lpr -P myepson report
```

lpc

You can use **lpc** to enable or disable printers, reorder their print queues, and re-execute configuration files. To use **lpc**, enter the command **lpc** at the shell prompt. You are then given an **lpc>** prompt at which you can enter **lpc** commands to manage your printers and reorder their jobs. The **status** command with the name of the printer displays whether the printer is ready, how many print jobs it has, and so on. The **stop** and **start** commands can stop a printer and start it back up. The printers shown depend on the printers configured for a particular print server. A printer configured on CUPS will only show if you have switched to CUPS.

```
$ lpc
lpc> status myepson
myepson:
 printer is on device 'usb' speed -1
 queuing is enabled
 printing is enabled
 1 entry in spool area
```

Printer Management	Description
GNOME Print Manager	GNOME print queue management tool (CUPS).
CUPS Configuration Tool	Prints, manages, and configures CUPS.
lpr *options file-list*	Prints a file, copies the file to the printer's spool directory, and places it on the print queue to be printed in turn. -P *printer* prints the file on the specified printer.
lpq *options*	Displays the print jobs in the print queue. -P *printer* prints the queue for the specified printer. -l prints a detailed listing.
lpstat *options*	Displays printer status.
lprm *options printjob-id* or *printer*	Removes a print job from the print queue. You identify a particular print job by its number as listed by lpq. -P *printer* removes all print jobs for the specified printer.
lpc	Manages your printers. At the lpc> prompt, you can enter commands to check the status of your printers and take other actions.

Table 19-3: CUPS Print Clients

lpq and lpstat

You can manage the print queue using the lpq and lprm commands. The lpq command lists the printing jobs currently on the print queue. With the -P option and the printer name, you can list the jobs for a particular printer. If you specify a username, you can list the print jobs for that user. With the -l option, lpq displays detailed information about each job. If you want information on a specific job, simply use that job's ID number with lpq. To check the status of a printer, use lpstat.

```
$ lpq
myepson is ready and printing
Rank    Owner   Jobs  File(s)         Total Size
active  chris   1     report          1024
```

lprm

The `lprm` command enables you to remove a print job from the queue, erasing the job before it can be printed. The `lprm` command takes many of the same options as `lpq`. To remove a specific job, use `lprm` with the job number. To remove all printing jobs for a particular printer, use the `-P` option with the printer name. `lprm` with no options removes the job printing currently. The following command removes the first print job in the queue (use `lpq` to obtain the job number):

```
lprm 1
```

CUPS Command Line Administrative Tools

CUPS provides command line administrative tools like `lpadmin`, `lpoptions`, `lpinfo`, `enable`, `disable`, `accept`, and `reject`. The `enable` and `disable` commands start and stop print queues directly, whereas the `accept` and `reject` commands start and stop particular jobs. The `lpinfo` command provides information about printers, and `lpoptions` lets you set printing options. The `lpadmin` command lets you perform administrative tasks like adding printers and changing configurations. CUPS administrative tools are listed in Table 19-4.

Administration Tool	Description
`lpadmin`	CUPS printer configuration
`lpoptions`	Sets printing options
`cupsenable`	Activates a printer
`cupsdisable`	Stops a printer
`accept`	Allows a printer to accept new jobs
`reject`	Prevents a printer from accepting print jobs
`lpinfo`	Lists CUPS devices available

Table 19-4: CUPS Administrative Tools

lpadmin

You can use the `lpadmin` command to either set the default printer or configure various options for a printer. You can use the `-d` option to specify a particular printer as the default destination. Here `myepson` is made the default printer:

```
lpadmin -d myepson
```

The `-p` option lets you designate a printer for which to set various options. The following example sets printer description information:

```
lpadmin -p myepson  -D  Epson550
```

Certain options let you control per-user quotas for print jobs. The `job-k-limit` option sets the size of a job allowed per user, `job-page-limit` sets the page limit for a job, and `job-quota-period` limits the number of jobs with a specified time frame. The following command set a page limit of 100 for each user:

```
lpadmin -p myepson  -o job-page-limit=100
```

User access control is determined with the –u option with an **allow** or **deny** list. Users allowed access are listed following the **allow**: entry, and those denied access are listed with a **deny**: entry. Here access is granted to **chris** but denied to **aleina** and **larisa**.

```
lpadmin -p myepson -u allow:chris  deny:aleina,larisa
```

Use **all** or **none** to permit or deny access to all or no users. You can create exceptions by using **all** or **none** in combination with user-specific access. The following example allows access to all users except **justin**:

```
lpadmin -p myepson  -u allow:all  deny:justin
```

lpoptions

The **lpoptions** command lets you set printing options and defaults that mostly govern how your print jobs will be printed. For example, you can set the color or page format to be used with a particular printer. Default settings for all users are maintained by the root user in the **/etc/cups/lpoptions** file, and each user can create their own configurations, which are saved in their **.lpoptions** files. The –**l** option lists current options for a printer, and the –**p** option designates a printer (you can also set the default printer to use with the –**d** option).

```
lpoptions -p myepson -l
```

Printer options are set using the –**o** option along with the option name and value, –**o** *option=value*. You can remove a printer option with the –**r** option. For example, to print on both sides of your sheets, you can set the **sides** option to **two-sided**:

```
lpoptions -p myepson -o sides=two-sided
```

To remove the option, use –**r**.

```
lpoptions -p myepson -r sides
```

To display a listing of available options, check the standard printing options in the CUPS Software Manual at **cups.org**.

cupsenable and cupsdisable

The **cupsenable** command starts a printer, and the **cupsdisable** command stops it. With the –**c** option, you can cancel all jobs on the printer's queue, and the –**r** option broadcasts a message explaining the shutdown.

```
cupsdisable myepson
```

These are CUPS versions of the Sytem V **enable** and **disable** commands, renamed to avoid conflicts.

accept and reject

The **accept** and **reject** commands let you control access to the printer queues for specific printers. The **reject** command prevents a printer from accepting jobs, whereas **accept** allows new print jobs.

```
reject myepson
```

The Man pages for accept and reject are **cupsaccept** and **cupsreject**. These names are also links to the **accept** and **reject** commands, allowing you to use them instead.

lpinfo

The **lpinfo** command is a handy tool for letting you know what CUPS devices and drivers are available on your system. Use the **-v** option for devices and the **-m** option for drivers.

```
lpinfo -m
```

20. Network Connections

Ubuntu will automatically detect and configure your network connections with Network Manager. Should the automatic configuration either fail or be incomplete for some reason, you can also use Network Manager to perform a manual configuration. On GNOME, NetworkManager is accessed using a GNOME applet or from the System | Preferences | Network Configuration menu entry. On KDE you use KNetworkManager. In addition your network will also need a firewall. UFW (with the Gufw interface) or Firestarter is recommended. You may also connect to a network with Windows computer. To access them you use the Samba server. To access shared directories and printers on other Linux and UNIX computers on your network, you can use the NFS. For dial-up service, you can use NetworkManager, If you are working from a command line interface, you can use WvDial. Table 20-1 lists several different network configuration tools.

Network Information: Dynamic and Static

If you are on a network, you may need to obtain certain information to configure your interface. Most networks now support dynamic configuration using either the older Dynamic Host Configuration Protocol (DHCP) or the new IPv6 Protocol and its automatic address configuration. In this case, you need only check the DHCP entry in most network configuration tools. If your network does not support DHCP or IPv6 automatic addressing, you will have to provide detailed information about your connection. Such connections are known as static connections, whereas DCHP and IPv6 connections are dynamic. In a static connection, you need to manually enter your connection information such as your IP address and DNS servers, whereas in a dynamic connection this information is automatically provided to your system by a DHCP server or generated by IPv6 when you connect to the network. For DHCP, a DHCP client on each host will obtain the information from a DHCP server serving that network. IPv6 generates its addresses directly from the device and router information such as the device hardware MAC address.

Network Configuration Tool	Description
Network Manager	Automates wireless and standard network connection, selection, and notification (System | Preferences | Network Connections). Used for all network connections including LAN, wireless, broadband, VPN, and DSL.
network-manager-kde	KDE version of NetworkManager
gnome-network-admin	Older GNOME network configuration tool (Universe repository).
ufw	Sets up a network firewall.
Gufw	GNOME interface for UFW firewall
Firestarter	Sets up a network firewall.
wvdial	PPP modem connection, enter on a command line.
pand	Implements the Bluetooth Personal Network.

Table 20-1: Ubuntu Network Configuration Tools

In addition, if you are using a DSL dynamic, ISDN, or modem connection, you will also have to supply provider, login, and password information, whether your system is dynamic or static. You may also need to supply specialized information such as DSL or modem compression methods, dialup number, or wireless channels to select.

You can obtain most of your static network information from your network administrator or from your ISP (Internet service provider). You would need the following information:

The device name for your network interface   For LAN and wireless connections, this is usually an Ethernet card with the name **eth0** or **eth1**. For a modem, DSL, or ISDN connection, this is a PPP device named **ppp0** (**ippp0** for ISDN). Virtual private network (VPN) connections are also supported.

Hostname   Your computer will be identified by this name on the Internet. Do not use localhost; that name is reserved for special use by your system. The name of the host should be a simple word, which can include numbers, but not punctuation such as periods and backslashes. The hostname includes both the name of the host and its domain. For example, a hostname for a machine could be **turtle**, whose domain is **mytrek.com**, giving it a hostname of **turtle.mytrek.com**.

Domain name   This is the name of your network.

The Internet Protocol (IP) address assigned to your machine   This is needed only for static Internet connections. Dynamic connections use the DHCP protocol to automatically assign an IP address for you. Every host on the Internet is assigned an IP address. Traditionally, this address used an IPv4 format consisting of a set of four numbers, separated by periods, which uniquely identifies a single location on the Internet, allowing information from other locations to reach that computer. Networks are now converting to the new IP protocol version 6, IPv6, which uses a new format with a much more complex numbering sequence.

Your network IP address   Static connections only. This address is usually similar to the IP address, but with one or more zeros at the end.

The netmask   Static connections only. This is usually 255.255.255.0 for most networks. If, however, you are part of a large network, check with your network administrator or ISP.

The broadcast address for your network, if available (optional)   Static connections only. Usually, your broadcast address is the same as your IP address with the number 255 added at the end.

The IP address of your network's gateway computer   Static connections only. This is the computer that connects your local network to a larger one like the Internet.

Name servers   Static connections only. The IP address of the name servers your network uses. These enable the use of URLs.

NIS domain and IP address for an NIS server   Necessary if your network uses an NIS server (optional).

User login and password information   Needed for dynamic DSL, ISDN, and modem connections.

Network Manager (desktop network configuration)

Network Manager will automatically detect your network connections, both wired and wireless. Network Manager makes use the automatic device detection capabilities of udev and HAL to configure your connections. Should you instead need to configure your network connections manually, you still use Network Manager, selecting the manual options and entering the required network connection information. Network Manager operates as a daemon with the name NetworkManager. It will automatically scan for both wired and wireless connections.

Ubuntu 9.04 uses an enhanced version of Network Manager which can also manually configure any network connection, replacing GNOME's network-admin. Ubuntu uses Network Manager to configure all your network connections. This includes wired, wireless, and all manual connections. The network-admin tool has been dropped. Network Interface Connection (NIC cards) hardware is detected using HAL. Information provided by Network Manager is made available to other applications over D-Bus.

Network Manager is designed to work in the background, providing status information for your connection and switching from one configured connection to another as needed. For initial configuration, it detects as much information as possible about the new connection. It operates as a GNOME Panel applet, monitoring your connection, and can work on any Linux distribution.

Network Manager is user specific. When a user logs in, sets up the network connection preferred by that user, though wired connections will be started automatically. The user preferred wireless connections will be start up.

Network Manager applet and options menu

Basic desktop network connection operations are discussed in Chapter 3.

Network Manager will display a Network applet icon to the right on the top panel. The Network Manager applet icon will vary according to the type of connection. An Ethernet (wired) connection will display two computer monitors, one in front of the other. A wireless connection will display a staggered bar graph (see Figure 20-1). If the connection is not active, a red x will appear on the icon. When Network Manager is detecting possible wireless connections, it will display a rotating connection image. If you have both a wired and wireless connection, and the wired connection is active, the wired connection image (double monitor) will be used.

Figure 20-1: Network Manager wired, wireless, and detection icons.

Figure 20-2: Network Manager options

Right-click to have the option of editing your connection, shutting off your connection (Enable Networking and Enable Wireless), or to see information about the connection (see Figure 20-2). A computer with both wired and wireless connections will have entries to Enable Networking and Enable Wireless. Selecting Enable Wireless will disconnected only the wireless connections, leaving the wired connection active. The Enable Wireless checkbox will be come unchecked and a message will be displayed telling you that your wireless connection is disconnected. Selecting Enable Networking will disable your wired connection, along with any wireless connections. Do this to work offline, without any network access.

A computer with only a wired network device (no wireless) will only show an Enable Networking entry, as shown here. Selecting it sill disconnect you from any network access, allowing you to work offline.

Network Manager manual configuration for all network connections

For any wired network connection that Network Manager automatically connects to, a configuration entry will be placed for it in the Network Connections Wired tab. The Auto eth0 connection in this example will have an Auto eth0 entry in the Network Connections window Wired tab. Clicking on it displays an "Editing Wired Connection" window that holds all the configuration information for that network connection.

When you connect to a wireless network for the first time, a configuration entry will be made for the wireless connection in the Wireless tab of the Network Connections tool.

Should you need to edit any network connection, wired or wireless, you right-click on the Network Manager icon and select Edit Network Connections (see Figure 20-2). You can also select System | Preferences | Network Connections. This opens Network Manager's Network Connections window as shown in Figure 20-3. Established connections will be listed, with Add, Edit, and Delete buttons for adding, editing, and removing network connections. Your current network connections should already be listed, having been automatically detected by udev and HAL. In the Figure 20-3 a wired Ethernet connection referred to as **Auto eth0** is listed, the first Ethernet connection. This is an automatic configuration set up by Network Manager when it automatically connected to the wired network.

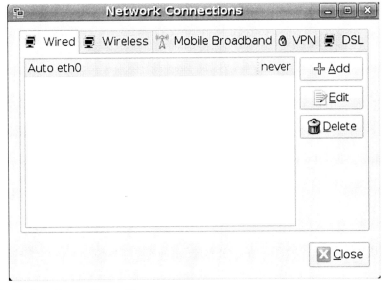

Figure 20-3: Network configuration

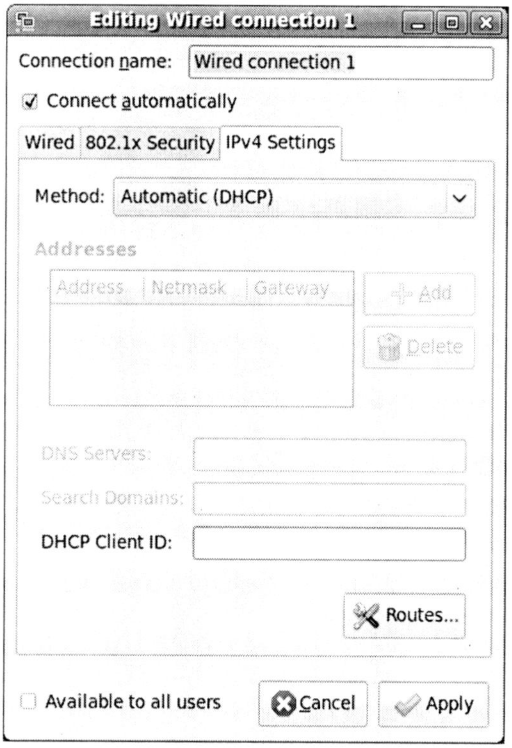

Figure 20-4: DHCP Wired Configuration

On the Network Connections window there are three tabs: Wired, Wireless, Mobile Broadband, VPN, and DSL.

> **Wired**: The wired connection is used for the standard IPv4 and IPv6 Ethernet connections, featuring support for DHCP and manual Ethernet settings.

> **Wireless**: The Wireless tab is where you enter in wireless configuration data like your ESSID, password, and encryption method.

> **Mobile Broadband**: The mobile broadband tab is the wireless 3G configuration, with selection for the service you are using.

> **VPN**: The VPN tab lets you specify a virtual private network. Be sure VPN support is installed on your system.

> **DSL**: The DSL tab lets you set up a direct DSL connection.

Each tab will list their configured network connections. Click on the ADD or EDIT buttons to configure a new network connection of that type, or edit an existing one.

All configuration dialogs will display an option at the bottom of the dialog to allow you to make your configuration available to all users (this replaces the "System setting" option use in previous versions). In effect, this option implements a system wide network connection configuration.

Figure 20-5: Manual Wired Configuration

Wired Configuration

To edit a wired connection, select the connection and click the EDIT buttons on the Wired tab. This opens an Editing window as shown in Figure 20-4.

The ADD button is used to add a new connection and opens a similar window, with no settings. The Wired tab lists the MAC hardware address and the MTU. The MTU is usually set to automatic. Figure 20-4 shows the standard default configuration for a wired Ethernet connection using DHCP. Connect automatically will set up the connection when the system starts up.

There are three tabs, Wired, 8.02.1x Security, and IPv4 Settings.

The IPv4 Setting tab lets you select the kind of wired connection you have. The options are:

> **Automatic (DHCP)**: DHCP connection. Address information is blocked out.

> **Automatic (DHCP) addresses only**: DHCP that lets you specify your DNS server addresses.

> **Manual**: Enter your IP, network, and gateway addresses along with your DNS server addresses and your network domain name.

> ➤ **Link-local only**: IPv6 private local network (like IPv4 192.18.0 addresses). All address entries are blocked out.

> ➤ **Shared to other computers**: All address entries are blocked out.

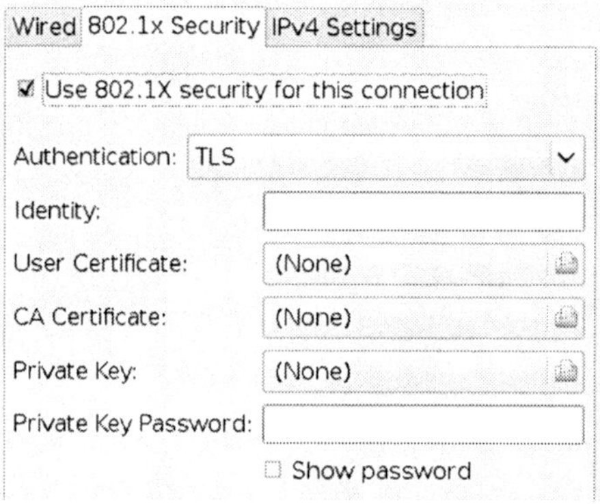

Figure 20-6: 802.1 Security Configuration

Figure 20-7: Wireless configuration

Figure 20-5 shows the manual configuration entries for a wired Ethernet connection. Click the Add button to enter the IP address, network mask, and gateway address. Then enter the address for the DNS servers and your network search domains.

The Routes button will open a window where you can manually enter any network routes.

The 802.1 tab allows you to configure 802.1 security, if your network supports it (see Figure 20-6).

Wireless Configuration

For wireless connections, you click ADD or EDIT on the Network Connections window's Wireless tab. The Editing Wireless connection window opens with tabs for your wireless information, security, and IPv4 settings (See Figure 20-7). On the Wireless tab you specify your SSID, along with your Mode and MAC address.

Figure 20-8: Wireless Security: WEP and WPA

On the Wireless Security tab you enter your wireless connection security method (see Figure 20-8). The commonly used method, WEP, is supported, along with WPA personal. The WPA personal method only requires a password. More secure connections like Dynamic WEP and Enterprise WPA are also supported. These will require much more configuration information like authentication methods, certificates, and keys.

On the IPv4 Settings tab you enter your wireless connection's network address settings. This tab is the same as the IPv4 Setting on the Wired connection (see Figures 20-5 and 20-6). You have the same options: DHCP, DHCP with DNS addresses, Manual, Link-local only, and Shared.

DSL Configuration

For a direct DSL connection, you click ADD or EDIT on the Network Connections window's DSL tab. The DSL connection window will open, showing tabs for DSL configuration and for wired, PPP, and IPv4 network connections. On the DSL tab you enter your DSL user name, service provider, and password (see Figure 20-9). A wired connection only requires a MAC address and MTU byte amount. The PPP tab is the same as that used for Mobile Broadband, and IPv4 is the same as that used for Wired, Wireless, and Mobile Broadband.

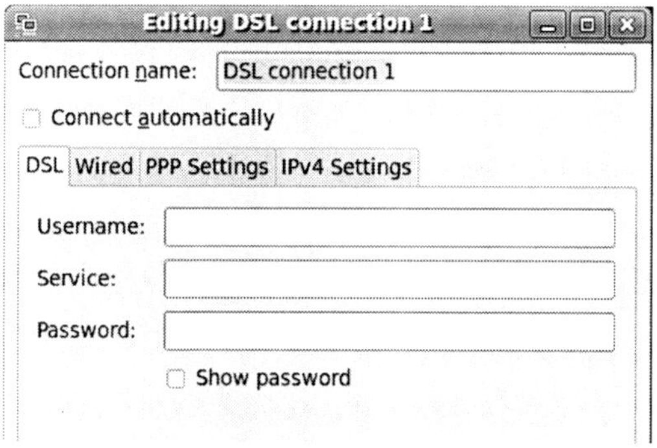

Figure 20-9: DSL manual configuration

Mobile Broadband: 3G Support

To set up a Mobile Broadband 3G connections, you select the Mobile Broadband tab in the Network Connections window, and click the ADD or EDIT button. A 3G wizard will start up to help you set up the appropriate configuration for your particular 3G service (see Figure 20-10).

The 3G wizard thin displays a Service Provider window with possible 3G service providers (see Figure 20-11).

Figure 20-10: 3G Wizard

The providers are organized by country, with the country you selected for your time zone initially displayed.

To see other countries, click on the expand arrow. A Country list will be displayed.

Figure 20-11: 3G Provider Listings

As you select a country, its available 3G services are displayed in the Provider listing (see Figure 20-12).Once you have made your selection, you are asked to verify it. You can give the selection label a different name if you wish (see Figure 20-13).

Figure 20-12: 3G Country listing

Once a service is selected, you can further edit the configuration by clicking its entry in the Mobile Broadband tab and clicking the EDIT button. The Editing window opens with tabs for

Mobile Broadband, PPP, IPv4 settings. On the Mobile Broadband panel you can enter your number, user name, and password. Advance options including the APN, Network, type, PIN, and PUK (see Figure 20-14). The APN should already be entered.

Figure 20-13: 3G provider verification

Figure 20-14: 3G configuration

PPP Configuration

For either Wireless Broadband or DSL connections you can also specify PPP information. The PPP tab is the same for both (See Figure 20-15). There are sections Authentication, Compression, and the Echo options. Check what features are supported by your particular PPP connection. For Authentication, click the Configure button to open a dialog listing possible authentication methods. Check the ones you connection supports.

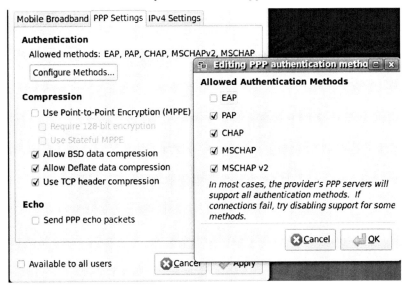

Figure 20-15: PPP Configuration

Network Manager VPN

The VPN Connection entry submenu will list configured VPN connection for easy access. The Configure VPN entry will open Network Manager to the VPN tab where you can then add, edit, or delete VPN connections. The Disconnect VPN entry will end the current active VPN connection. The VPN tab will not be active until you first install VPN software, like **openvpn**.

Network Manager wireless router, using your wireless connection as a wireless router.

You can also set up your wireless connection as a wireless router for your own wireless network. The "Create New Wireless Network" entry will open a dialog letting you set up your computer as a wireless router that other computers can connect to (see Figure 20-16). Enter a Network name, select the kind of wireless security you want to use, and enter a password for accessing the network. You will be prompted to enter your keyring password.

The wireless network you created will not perform any SSID broadcasting. You access it through the "Connect to Hidden Wireless network" entry on the Network Manager menu. This opens the "Hidden wireless network" window (see Figure 20-16). Your new wireless network will be listed in the Connection drop-down menu. When you select it, the network name and security information is displayed.

Figure 20-16: Create New Wireless Network and connect as Hidden network

Note: You could also use the **network-admin** tool (gnome-network-admin package), used in previous Ubuntu releases, to configure your network. This package is no longer supported by Ubuntu (no updates), though it is available on the Universe repository. If you choose to install it, you can access as System | Administration | Network.

Command Line Manual Network Configuration: /etc/network/interfaces

To configure your network manually from your command line interface, you can edit a set of configuration files to enter your network information. Interface information like your IP, gateway, and network addresses are placed in the **/etc/network/interfaces** file. See the **interfaces** Man page for more details. You can edit this file with administrative access directly.

```
sudo vi /etc/network/interfaces
```

You many have already entered this connection information during installation. If not, or if the information has changed, you can edit the **/etc/network/interfaces** file and make the changes.

Use the **iface** command to specify the different addresses. If your connection is static, meaning it has a specific IP address and gateway, the iface command would indicate a static connection. The **iface** command takes as its arguments the device name (**eth0** for first Ethernet device), the protocol used for the connection (**inet** for IPv4 and **inet6** for IPv6), and the type of connection (**static** for a device with an assigned IP address, and **dhcp** for one dynamically assigned by a DHCP server). The addresses are then listed for address, network, broadcast, gateway, and netmask.

```
iface eth0 inet static
       address  192.168.0.5
       netmask  255.255.255.0
       gateway  10.0.0.3
       network  192.168.0.0
       broadcast  192.168.0.255
```

The **auto** entry will list all your network interface devices that would be automatically activated when the system boots. It lists your network devices. You will always have an **lo** device which is your system's localhost interface.

```
auto lo eth0
```

To identify your IP address with your host name, without having to rely on a DNS server, place an entry for it in the **/etc/hosts** file. An entry consists of an IP address, the full host/domain name (Fully Qualified Domain Name) and any aliases.

```
192.168.0.5  rabbit.mytrek.com   myrabbit
```

After you make your changes, be sure to restart networking.

```
sudo service networking restart
```

If you decide to change the system's host name, be sure to edit **/etc/hostname** file and enter the new hostname. The change will become permanent on the next reboot. You can use the **hostname** command to make the change immediately, but a permanent change requires editing the **/etc/hostname** file.

If you change your DNS servers, edit the **/etc/resolv.conf** file to enter the names of the new DNS servers. Precede the DNS entry with nameserver.

/etc/resolv.conf

```
nameserver 192.168.0.7
```

Command Line PPP Access: wvdial

If, for some reason, you have been unable to set up a modem connection on your Desktop, you may have to set it up from the command line interface. For a dial-up PPP connection, you can use the wvdial dialer, which is an intelligent dialer that not only dials up an ISP service but also performs login operations, supplying your username and password.

The wvdial program first loads its configuration from the **/etc/wvdial.conf** file. In here, you can place modem and account information, including modem speed and serial device, as well as ISP phone number, username, and password. The **wvdial.conf** file is organized into sections, beginning with a section label enclosed in brackets. A section holds variables for different parameters that are assigned values, such as `username = chris`. The default section holds default values inherited by other sections, so you needn't repeat them. Table 20-2 lists the wvdial variables.

You can use the wvdialconf utility to create a default **wvdial.conf** file for you automatically; wvdialconf will detect your modem and set default values for basic features. You can then edit the **wvdial.conf** file and modify the Phone, Username, and Password entries with your ISP dial-up information. Remove the preceding semicolon (**;**) to unquote the entry. Any line beginning with a semicolon is ignored as a comment.

```
$ wvdialconf
```

Variable	Description
Inherits	Explicitly inherits from the specified section. By default, sections inherit from the [Dialer Defaults] section.
Modem	The device wvdial should use as your modem. The default is **/dev/modem**.
Baud	The speed at which wvdial communicates with your modem. The default is 57,600 baud.
Init1...Init9	Specifies the initialization strings to be used by your modem; wvdial can use up to 9. The default is "ATZ" for Init1.
Phone	The phone number you want wvdial to dial.
Area Code	Specifies the area code, if any.
Dial Prefix	Specifies any needed dialing prefix—for example, 70 to disable call waiting or 9 for an outside line.
Dial Command	Specifies the dial operation. The default is "ATDT".
Login	Specifies the username you use at your ISP.
Login Prompt	If your ISP has an unusual login prompt, you can specify it here.
Password	Specifies the password you use at your ISP.
Password Prompt	If your ISP has an unusual password prompt, you can specify it here.
Force Address	Specifies a static IP address to use (for ISPs that provide static IP addresses to users).
Auto Reconnect	If enabled, wvdial attempts to reestablish a connection automatically if you are randomly disconnected by the other side. This option is on by default.

Table 20-2: Variables for wvdial

You can also create a named dialer. This is helpful if you have different ISPs you log in to. The following example shows the **/etc/wvdial.conf** file:

To start wvdial, enter the command **wvdial**, which then reads the connection configuration information from the **/etc/wvdial.conf** file; wvdial dials the ISP and initiates the PPP connection, providing your username and password when requested.

```
$ wvdial
```

You can set up connection configurations for any number of connections in the **/etc/wvdial.conf** file. To select one, enter its label as an argument to the `wvdial` command, as shown here:

```
$ wvdial myisp
```

Command Line Manual Wireless Configuration

NetworkManager will automatically detect and configure your wireless connections. However, you can manually configure your connections with wireless tools like Network Manager (wireless properties), KNetworkManager, and ifwconfig.

Wireless configuration makes use of the same set of Wireless Extensions. The Wireless Tools package is a set of network configuration and reporting tools for wireless devices installed on a Linux system (**wireless-tools**). They are currently supported and developed as part of the Linux Wireless Extension and Wireless Tools Project, an open source project maintained by Hewlett-Packard. Wireless Tools consists of the configuration and report tools listed here:

Tool	Description
iwconfig	Sets the wireless configuration options basic to most wireless devices.
iwlist	Displays current status information of a device.
iwspy	Sets the list of IP addresses in a wireless network and checks the quality of their connections.
iwpriv	Accesses configuration options specific to a particular device.

iwconfig

The `iwconfig` command works much like `ifconfig`, configuring a network connection. You can run `iwconfig` directly on a command line, specifying certain parameters. Added parameters let you set wireless-specific features such as the network name (nwid), the frequency or channel the card uses (freq or channel), and the bit rate for transmissions (rate). See the `iwconfig` Man page for a complete listing of accepted parameters. Some of the commonly used parameters are listed in Table 20-3.

For example, to set the channel used for the wireless device installed as the first Ethernet device, you would use the following, setting the channel to 2:

```
iwconfig eth0 channel 2
```

You can also use `iwconfig` to display statistics for your wireless devices, just as `ifconfig` does. Enter the `iwconfig` command with no arguments or with the name of the device. Information such as the name, frequency, sensitivity, and bit rate is listed. Check also **/proc/net/wireless** for statistics.

Parameter	Description
essid	A network name
freq	The frequency of the connection
channel	The channel used
nwid or domain	The network ID or domain
mode	The operating mode used for the device, such as Ad Hoc, Managed, or Auto. Ad Hoc = one cell with no access point, Managed = network with several access points and supports roaming, Master = the node is an access point, Repeater = node forwards packets to other nodes, Secondary = backup master or repeater, Monitor = only receives packets
sens	The sensitivity, the lowest signal level at which data can be received
key or enc	The encryption key used
frag	Cut packets into smaller fragments to increase better transmission
bit or rate	Speed at which bits are transmitted. The auto option automatically falls back to lower rates for noisy channels
ap	Specify a specific access point
power	Power management for wakeup and sleep operations

Table 20-3: Commonly Used Parameters

iwpriv

The **iwpriv** command works in conjunction with **iwconfig**, allowing you set options specific to a particular kind of wireless device. With **iwpriv**, you can also turn on roaming or select the port to use. You use the *private-command* parameter to enter the device-specific options. The following example sets roaming on:

```
iwpriv eth0 roam on
```

iwspy

Your wireless device can check its connection to another wireless device it is receiving data from, reporting the quality, signal strength, and noise level of the transmissions. Your device can maintain a list of addresses for different devices it may receive data from. You use the **iwspy** tool to set or add the addresses that you want checked. You can list either IP addresses or the hardware versions. A **+** sign will add the address, instead of replacing the entire list:

```
iwspy eth0 +192.168.2.5
```

To display the quality, signal, and noise levels for your connections, you use the **iwspy** command with just the device name:

```
iwspy eth0
iwlist eth0 freq
```

iwlist

To obtain more detailed information about your wireless device, such as all the frequencies or channels available, you use the `iwlist` tool. Using the device name with a particular parameter, you can obtain specific information about a device, including the frequency, access points, rate, power features, retry limits, and encryption keys used. You can use iwlist to obtain information about faulty connections. The following example will list the frequencies used on the **eth0** wireless device.

```
iwlist eth0 freq
```

GNOME Network Tools: gnome-nettool

For the GNOME desktop, the **gnome-nettool** utility provides a GNOME interface for entering the `ping` and `traceroute` commands as well as Finger, Whois, and Lookup for querying users and hosts on the network (see Figure 20-17). The **gnome-nettool** utility is installed by default and is accessible from System | Administration | Network Tools. Whois will provide domain name information about a particular domain, and Lookup will provide both domain name and IP addresses. It also includes network status tools such as **netstat** and **portscan**. The first panel, Devices, describes your connected network devices, including configuration and transmission information about each device, such as the hardware address and bytes transmitted. Both IPv4 and IPv6 host IP addresses will be listed.

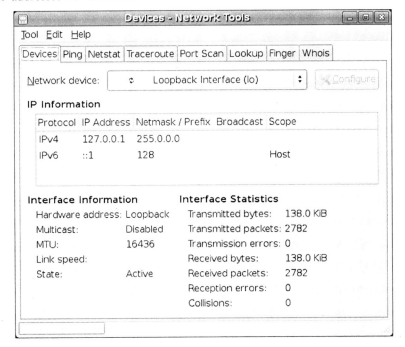

Figure 20-17: Gnome network tool

Network Information: ping, finger, traceroute, and host

You can use the `ping`, `finger`, `traceroute`, and `host` commands to find out status information about systems and users on your network. The `ping` command is used to check if a remote system is up and running. You use `finger` to find out information about other users on your network, seeing if they are logged in or if they have received mail; `host` displays address information about a system on your network, giving you a system's IP and domain name addresses; and `traceroute` can be used to track the sequence of computer networks and systems your message passed through on its way to you. Table 20-4 lists various network information tools.

Network Information Tools	Description
`ping`	Detects whether a system is connected to the network.
`finger`	Obtains information about users on the network.
`who`	Checks what users are currently online.
`whois`	Obtains domain information.
`host`	Obtains network address information about a remote host.
`traceroute`	Tracks the sequence of computer networks and hosts your message passes through.
`ethereal`	Protocol analyzer to examine network traffic.
`gnome-nettool`	GNOME interface for various network tools including ping, finger, and traceroute.
`mtr` and `xmtr`	My traceroute combines both ping and traceroute operations (Traceroute on System Tools menu).

Table 20-4: Network Tools

ping

The `ping` command detects whether a system is up and running. `ping` takes as its argument the name of the system you want to check. If the system you want to check is down, `ping` issues a timeout message indicating a connection could not be made. The next example checks to see if **www.ubuntu.com** is up and connected to the network:

```
$ ping www.ubuntu.com
PING www.ubuntu.com (91.189.94.8) 56(84) bytes of data.
64 bytes from jujube.canonical.com (91.189.94.8): icmp_seq=1 ttl=48 time=609 ms
64 bytes from jujube.canonical.com (91.189.94.8): icmp_seq=2 ttl=48 time=438 ms
64 bytes from jujube.canonical.com (91.189.94.8): icmp_seq=3 ttl=48 time=568 ms
^C
--- www.ubuntu.com ping statistics ---
4 packets transmitted, 3 received, 25% packet loss, time 3554ms
rtt min/avg/max/mdev = 438.939/539.125/609.885/72.824 ms
```

You can also use `ping` with an IP address instead of a domain name. With an IP address, `ping` can try to detect the remote system directly without having to go through a domain name server to translate the domain name to an IP address. This can be helpful for situations where your network's domain name server may be temporarily down and you want to check if a particular remote host on your network is connected.

```
# ping 209.132.177.50
```

Note: A `ping` operation could also fail if `ping` access is denied by a network's firewall.

finger and who

You can use the **finger** command to obtain information about other users on your network and the **who** command to see what users are currently online on your system. The **who** and **w** commands lists all users currently connected, along with when, how long, and where they logged in. The **w** command provides more detailed information. It has several options for specifying the level of detail. The **who** command is meant to operate on a local system or network; **finger** can operate on large networks, including the Internet, though most systems block it for security reasons.

Note: Ethereal is a protocol analyzer that can capture network packets and display detailed information about them. You can detect what kind of information is being transmitted on your network as well as its source and destination. Ethereal is used primarily for network and server administration.

host

With the **host** command, you can find network address information about a remote system connected to your network. This information usually consists of a system's IP address, domain name address, domain name nicknames, and mail server. This information is obtained from your network's domain name server. For the Internet, this includes all systems you can connect to over the Internet.

The **host** command is an effective way to determine a remote site's IP address or URL. If you have only the IP address of a site, you can use **host** to find out its domain name. For network administration, an IP address can be helpful for making your own domain name entries in your **/etc/host** file. That way, you needn't rely on a remote domain name server (DNS) for locating a site.

```
# host gnomefiles.org
gnomefiles.org has address 67.18.254.188
gnomefiles.org mail is handled by 10 mx.zayda.net.

# host 67.18.254.188
188.254.18.67.in-addr.arpa domain name pointer gnomefiles.org.
```

traceroute

Internet connections are made through various routes, traveling through a series of interconnected gateway hosts. The path from one system to another could take different routes, some of which may be faster than others. For a slow connection, you can use **traceroute** to check the route through which you are connected to a host, monitoring the speed and the number of intervening gateway connections a route takes. The **traceroute** command takes as its argument the hostname or IP addresses for the system whose route you want to check. Options are available for specifying parameters like the type of service (**-t**) or the source host (**-s**). The **traceroute** command will return a list of hosts the route traverses, along with the times for three probes sent to each gateway. Times greater than five seconds are displayed with an asterisk, *.

```
traceroute rabbit.mytrek.com
```

You can also use the mtr or xmtr tools to perform both ping and traces (Traceroute on the System Tools menu).

ubuntu

Part 4: Shells

Shells

Working with Files and Directories

Shell Scripts and Programming

Shell Configuration

21. Shells

The Command Line

History

Filename Expansion: *, ?, [ ]

Standard Input/Output and Redirection

Pipes

Jobs

The *shell* is a command interpreter that provides a line-oriented interactive and non-interactive interface between the user and the operating system. You enter commands on a command line; they are interpreted by the shell and then sent as instructions to the operating system (the command line interface is accessible from Gnome and KDE through a Terminal windows – Applications/Accessories menu). You can also place commands in a script file to be consecutively executed much like a program. This interpretive capability of the shell provides for many sophisticated features. For example, the shell has a set of file expansion characters that can generate filenames. The shell can redirect input and output, as well as run operations in the background, freeing you to perform other tasks.

Shell	Web Site
`www.gnu.org/software/bash`	BASH Web site with online manual, FAQ, and current releases
`www.gnu.org/software/bash/manual/bash.html`	BASH online manual
`www.zsh.org`	Z shell Web site with referrals to FAQs and current downloads.
`www.tcsh.org`	TCSH Web site with detailed support including manual, tips, FAQ, and recent releases
`www.kornshell.com`	Korn shell site with manual, FAQ, and references

Table 21-1: Linux Shells

Several different types of shells have been developed for Linux: the Bourne Again shell (BASH), the Korn shell, the TCSH shell, and the Z shell. All shells are available for your use, although the BASH shell is the default. You only need one type of shell to do your work. Ubuntu Linux includes all the major shells, although it installs and uses the BASH shell as the default. If you use the command line shell, you will be using the BASH shell unless you specify another. This chapter discusses the BASH shell, which shares many of the same features as other shells.

You can find out more about shells at their respective Web sites as listed in Table 21-1. Also, a detailed online manual is available for each installed shell. Use the **man** command and the shell's keyword to access them, **bash** for the BASH shell, **ksh** for the Korn shell, **zsh** for the Z shell, and **tsch** for the TSCH shell. For example, the command **man bash** will access the BASH shell online manual.

Note: You can find out more about the BASH shell at **http://gnu.org/software/bash**. A detailed online manual is available on your Linux system using the **man** command with the **bash** keyword.

The Command Line

The Linux command line interface consists of a single line into which you enter commands with any of their options and arguments. From GNOME or KDE, you can access the command line interface by opening a terminal window. Should you start Linux with the command line interface, you will be presented with a BASH shell command line when you log in.

By default, the BASH shell has a dollar sign (**$**) prompt, but Linux has several other types of shells, each with its own prompt (like **%** for the C shell). The root user will have a different prompt, the **#**. A shell *prompt,* such as the one shown here, marks the beginning of the command line:

```
$
```

You can enter a command along with options and arguments at the prompt. For example, with an **-l** option, the **ls** command will display a line of information about each file, listing such data as its size and the date and time it was last modified. In the next example, the user enters the **ls** command followed by a **-l** option. The dash before the **-l** option is required. Linux uses it to distinguish an option from an argument.

```
$ ls -l
```

If you wanted only the information displayed for a particular file, you could add that file's name as the argument, following the **-l** option:

```
$ ls -l mydata
-rw-r--r-- 1 chris weather 207 Feb 20 11:55 mydata
```

Tip: Some commands can be complex and take some time to execute. When you mistakenly execute the wrong command, you can interrupt and stop such commands with the interrupt key—CTRL-C.

You can enter a command on several lines by typing a backslash just before you press ENTER. The backslash "escapes" the ENTER key, effectively continuing the same command line to the next line. In the next example, the **cp** command is entered on three lines. The first two lines end in a backslash, effectively making all three lines one command line.

```
$ cp -i \
mydata \
/home/george/myproject/newdata
```

You can also enter several commands on the same line by separating them with a semicolon (**;**). In effect the semicolon operates as an execute operation. Commands will be executed in the sequence they are entered. The following command executes an **ls** command followed by a **date** command.

```
$ ls ; date
```

You can also conditionally run several commands on the same line with the **&&** operator. A command is executed only if the previous one is true. This feature is useful for running several dependent scripts on the same line. In the next example, the **ls** command is run only if the **date** command is successfully executed.

```
$ date && ls
```

TIP: Command can also be run as arguments on a command line, using their results for other commands. To run a command within a command line, you encase the command in back quotes, see Values from Linux Commands later in this chapter.

Movement Commands	Operation
CTRL-F, RIGHT-ARROW	Move forward a character
CTRL-B, LEFT-ARROW	Move backward a character
CTRL-A or HOME	Move to beginning of line
CTRL-E or END	Move to end of line
ALT-F	Move forward a word
ALT-B	Move backward a word
CTRL-L	Clear screen and place line at top
Editing Commands	**Operation**
CTRL-D or DEL	Delete character cursor is on
CTRL-H or BACKSPACE	Delete character before the cursor
CTRL-K	Cut remainder of line from cursor position
CTRL-U	Cut from cursor position to beginning of line
CTRL-W	Cut previous word
CTRL-C	Cut entire line
ALT-D	Cut the remainder of a word
ALT-DEL	Cut from the cursor to the beginning of a word
CTRL-Y	Paste previous cut text
ALT-Y	Paste from set of previously cut text
CTRL-Y	Paste previous cut text
CTRL-V	Insert quoted text, used for inserting control or meta (Alt) keys as text, such as CTRL-B for backspace or CTRL-T for tabs
ALT-T	Transpose current and previous word
ALT-L	Lowercase current word
ALT-U	Uppercase current word
ALT-C	Capitalize current word
CTRL-SHIFT-_	Undo previous change

Table 21-2: Command Line Editing Operations

Command Line Editing

The BASH shell, which is your default shell, has special command line editing capabilities that you may find helpful as you learn Linux (see Table 21-2). You can easily modify commands you have entered before executing them, moving anywhere on the command line and inserting or deleting characters. This is particularly helpful for complex commands.

You can use the CTRL-F or RIGHT ARROW key to move forward a character, or the CTRL-B or LEFT ARROW key to move back a character. CTRL-D or DEL deletes the character the cursor is on, and CTRL-H or BACKSPACE deletes the character before the cursor. To add text, you use the arrow keys to move the cursor to where you want to insert text and type the new characters. You can even cut words with the CTRL-W or ALT-D key and then use the CTRL-Y key to paste them back in at a different position, effectively moving the words. As a rule, the CTRL version of the command operates on characters, and the ALT version works on words, such as CTRL-T to transpose characters and ALT-T to transpose words. At any time, you can press ENTER to execute the command. For example, if you make a spelling mistake when entering a command, rather than reentering the entire command, you can use the editing operations to correct the mistake. The actual associations of keys and their tasks, along with global settings, are specified in the **/etc/inputrc** file.

The editing capabilities of the BASH shell command line are provided by Readline. Readline supports numerous editing operations. You can even bind a key to a selected editing operation. Readline uses the **/etc/inputrc** file to configure key bindings. This file is read automatically by your **/etc/profile** shell configuration file when you log in. Users can customize their editing commands by creating an **.inputrc** file in their home directory (this is a dot file). It may be best to first copy the **/etc/inputrc** file as your **.inputrc** file and then edit it. **/etc/profile** will first check for a local **.inputrc** file before accessing the **/etc/inputrc** file. You can find out more about Readline in the BASH shell reference manual at **www.gnu.org/manual/bash**.

Command and Filename Completion

The BASH command line has a built-in feature that performs command line and file name completion. Automatic completions can be effected using the TAB key. If you enter an incomplete pattern as a command or filename argument, you can then press the TAB key to activate the command and filename completion feature, which completes the pattern. Directories will have a / attached to their name. If more than one command or file has the same prefix, the shell simply beeps and waits for you to enter the TAB key again. It then displays a list of possible command completions and waits for you to add enough characters to select a unique command or filename.

For situations where you know there are likely multiple possibilities, you can just press the ESC key instead of two TABs. In the next example, the user issues a `cat` command with an incomplete filename. When the user presses the TAB key, the system searches for a match and, when it finds one, fills in the filename. The user can then press ENTER to execute the command.

```
$ cat pre tab
$ cat preface
```

Note: The configuration and directives for completing commands are held in the **/etc/bash_completion** file, which also invokes more specialized configurations in the **/etc/bash_completion.d** directory. The **bash_completion** file includes directives that check whether the user has administrative permission to run or access certain commands or files. If the user does not have permission, a reminder to use **sudo** is issued. Administrators can modify the completion directives as they wish.

The automatic completions also work with the names of variables, users, and hosts. In this case, the partial text needs to be preceded by a special character, indicating the type of name. A listing of possible automatic completions follows:

➤ Filenames begin with any text or /.

➤ Shell variable text begins with a $ sign.

➤ User name text begins with a ~ sign.

➤ Host name text begins with a @.

➤ Commands, aliases, and text in files begin with normal text.

Variables begin with a **$** sign, so any text beginning with a dollar sign is treated as a variable to be completed. Variables are selected from previously defined variables, like system shell variables. User names begin with a tilde (~). Host names begin with a @ sign, with possible names taken from the **/etc/hosts** file. For example, to complete the variable HOME given just $HOM, simply press the TAB key.

```
$ echo $HOM <tab>
$ echo $HOME
```

If you entered just an H, then you could enter two tabs to see all possible variables beginning with H. The command line is redisplayed, letting you complete the name.

```
$ echo $H <tab> <tab>
$HISTCMD $HISTFILE $HOME $HOSTTYPE HISTFILE  $HISTSIZE $HISTNAME
$ echo $H
```

Command (CTRL-R for listing possible completions)	Description
TAB	Automatic completion
TAB TAB or ESC	List possible completions
ALT-/, CTRL-R-/	Filename completion, normal text for automatic
ALT-$, CTRL-R-$	Shell variable completion, $ for automatic
ALT-~, CTRL-R-~	User name completion, ~ for automatic
ALT-@, CTRL-R-@	Host name completion, @ for automatic
ALT-!, CTRL-R-!	Command name completion, normal text for automatic

Table 21-3: Command Line Text Completion Commands

You can also specifically select the kind of text to complete, using corresponding command keys. In this case, it does not matter what kind of sign a name begins with.

For example, the ALT-~ will treat the current text as a user name. ALT-@ will treat it as a host name, and ALT-$, as a variable. ALT-! will treat it as a command. To display a list of possible completions, use the CTRL-X key with the appropriate completion key, as in CTRL-X-$ to list possible variable completions. See Table 21-3 for a complete listing.

History

The BASH shell keeps a list, called a *history list,* of your previously entered commands. You can display each command, in turn, on your command line by pressing the UP ARROW key. The DOWN ARROW key moves you down the list. You can modify and execute any of these previous commands when you display them on your command line.

Tip: The capability to redisplay a previous command is helpful when you've already executed a command you had entered incorrectly. In this case, you would be presented with an error message and a new, empty command line. By pressing the UP ARROW key, you can redisplay your previous command, make corrections to it, and then execute it again. This way, you would not have to enter the whole command again.

History Events

In the BASH shell, the *history utility* keeps a record of the most recent commands you have executed. The commands are numbered starting at 1, and a limit exists to the number of commands remembered—the default is 500. The history utility is a kind of short-term memory, keeping track of the most recent commands you have executed. To see the set of your most recent commands, type **history** on the command line and press ENTER. A list of your most recent commands is then displayed, preceded by a number.

```
$ history
1 cp mydata today
2 vi mydata
3 mv mydata reports
4 cd reports
5 ls
```

Each of these commands is technically referred to as an event. An *event* describes an action that has been taken—a command that has been executed. The events are numbered according to their sequence of execution. The most recent event has the highest number. Each of these events can be identified by its number or beginning characters in the command.

Tip: The ability to redisplay a command is helpful when you've already executed a command you entered incorrectly. In this case, you are presented with an error message and a new, empty command line. By pressing the UP ARROW key, you can redisplay the incorrect command, make corrections to it, and then execute it again. This way, you do not have to enter the whole command again.

The history utility lets you to reference a former event, placing it on your command line and so you can execute it. The easiest way to do this is to use the UP ARROW and DOWN ARROW keys to place history events on your command line, one at a time. You needn't display the list first with **history**. Pressing the UP ARROW key once places the last history event on your command line. Pressing it again places the next history event on the command line. Pressing the DOWN ARROW key places the previous event on the command line.

You can use certain control and meta keys to perform other history operations like searching the history list. A meta key is the ALT key, and the ESC key on keyboards that have no ALT key. The ALT key is used here. ALT-< will move you to the beginning of the history list; ALT-N will search it. CTRL-S and CTRL-R will perform incremental searches, display matching commands as you type in a search string. Table 21-4 lists the different commands for referencing the history list.

Tip: If more than one history event matches what you have entered, you will hear a beep, and you can then enter more characters to help uniquely identify the event.

You can also reference and execute history events using the ! history command. The ! is followed by a reference that identifies the command. The reference can be either the number of the event or a beginning set of characters in the event. In the next example, the third command in the history list is referenced first by number and then by the beginning characters:

```
$ !3
mv mydata reports
$ !mv my
mv mydata reports
```

History Commands	Description
CTRL-N or DOWN ARROW	Moves down to the next event in the history list
CTRL-P or UP ARROW	Moves up to the previous event in the history list
ALT-<	Moves to the beginning of the history event list
ALT->	Moves to the end of the history event list
ALT-N	Forward Search, next matching item
ALT-P	Backward Search, previous matching item
CTRL-S	Forward Search History, forward incremental search
CTRL-R	Reverse Search History, reverse incremental search
fc *event-reference*	Edits an event with the standard editor and then executes it **Options** -l List recent history events; same as **history** command -e *editor event-reference* Invokes a specified editor to edit a specific event
History Event References	
! *event num*	References an event with an event number
! !	References the previous command
! *characters*	References an event with beginning characters
! ?*pattern*?	References an event with a pattern in the event
! -*event num*	References an event with an offset from the first event
! *num*-*num*	References a range of events

Table 21-4: History Commands and History Event References

You can also reference an event using an offset from the end of the list. A negative number will offset from the end of the list to that event, thereby referencing it. In the next example, the fourth command, `cd mydata`, is referenced using a negative offset, and then executed. Remember that you are offsetting from the end of the list—in this case, event 5—up toward the beginning of the list, event 1. An offset of 4 beginning from event 5 places you at event 2.

```
$ !-4
vi mydata
```

To reference the last event, you use a following !, as in !!. In the next example, the command !! executes the last command the user executed—in this case, `ls`:

```
$ !!
ls
mydata today reports
```

History Event Editing

You can also edit any event in the history list before you execute it. In the BASH shell, you can do this two ways: You can use the command line editor capability to reference and edit any event in the history list. You can also use a history `fc` command option to reference an event and edit it with the full Vi editor. Each approach involves two different editing capabilities. The first is limited to the commands in the command line editor, which edits only a single line with a subset of Emacs commands. At the same time, however, it enables you to reference events easily in the history list. The second approach invokes the standard Vi editor with all its features, but only for a specified history event.

With the command line editor, not only can you edit the current command, you can also move to a previous event in the history list to edit and execute it. The CTRL-P command then moves you up to the prior event in the list. The CTRL-N command moves you down the list. The ALT-< command moves you to the top of the list, and the ALT-> command moves you to the bottom. You can even use a pattern to search for a given event. The slash followed by a pattern searches backward in the list, and the question mark followed by a pattern searches forward in the list. The **n** command repeats the search.

Once you locate the event you want to edit, you use the Emacs command line editing commands to edit the line. CTRL-D deletes a character. CTRL-F or the RIGHT ARROW moves you forward a character, and CTRL-B or the LEFT ARROW moves you back a character. To add text, position your cursor and type in the characters you want.

If you want to edit an event using a standard editor instead, you need to reference the event using the `fc` command and a specific event reference, such as an event number. The editor used is the specified by the shell in the **FCEDIT** or **EDITOR** variable. This serves as the default editor for the `fc` command. You can assign to the **FCEDIT** or **EDITOR** variable a different editor if you want, such as Emacs instead of Vi. The next example edits the fourth event, `cd reports`, with the standard editor and then executes the edited event:

```
$ fc 4
```

You can select more than one command at a time to be edited and executed by referencing a range of commands. You select a range of commands by indicating an identifier for the first command followed by an identifier for the last command in the range. An identifier can be the command number or the beginning characters in the command. In the next example, the range of commands 2–4 is edited and executed, first using event numbers and then using beginning characters in those events:

```
$ fc 2 4
$ fc vi c
```

The `fc` command uses the default editor specified in the `FCEDIT` special variable. If `FCEDIT` is not defined, it checks for the `EDITOR` variable. If neither is defined it uses Vi, which is usually used. If you want to use the Emacs editor instead, you use the `-e` option and the term `emacs` when you invoke `fc`. The next example edits the fourth event, `cd reports`, with the Emacs editor and then executes the edited event:

```
$ fc -e emacs 4
```

Configuring History: HISTFILE and HISTSAVE

The number of events saved by your system is kept in a special system variable called `HISTSIZE`. By default, this is usually set to 500. You can change this to another value by simply assigning a new value to `HISTSIZE`. In the next example, the user changes the number of history events saved to *10* by resetting the `HISTSIZE` variable:

```
$ HISTSIZE=10
```

The actual history events are saved in a file whose name is held in a special variable called `HISTSIZE`. By default, this file is the **.bash_history** file. You can change the file in which history events are saved, however, by assigning a new filename to the `HISTSIZE` variable. In the next example, the value of `HISTSIZE` is displayed. Then a new filename is assigned to it, **newhist**. History events are then saved in the **newhist** file.

```
$ echo $HISTFILE
.bash_history
$ HISTFILE="newhist"
$ echo $HISTFILE
newhist
```

Filename Expansion: *, ?, [ ]

Filenames are the most common arguments used in a command. Often you may know only part of the filename, or you may want to reference several filenames that have the same extension or begin with the same characters. The shell provides a set of special characters that search out, match, and generate a list of filenames. These are the asterisk, the question mark, and brackets (`*`, `?`, `[]`). Given a partial filename, the shell uses these matching operators to search for files and expand to a list of filenames found. The shell replaces the partial filename argument with the expanded list of matched filenames. This list of filenames can then become the arguments for commands such as `ls`, which can operate on many files. Table 21-5 lists the shell's file expansion characters.

Matching Multiple Characters

The asterisk (`*`) references files beginning or ending with a specific set of characters. You place the asterisk before or after a set of characters that form a pattern to be searched for in filenames.

Common Shell Symbols	Execution
ENTER	Execute a command line.
;	Separate commands on the same command line.
`command`	Execute a command.
$ (command)	Execute a command.
[ ]	Match on a class of possible characters in filenames.
\	Quote the following character. Used to quote special characters.
		Pipe the standard output of one command as input for another command.
&	Execute a command in the background.
!	Reference history command.
File Expansion Symbols	**Execution**
*	Match on any set of characters in filenames.
?	Match on any single character in filenames.
[ ]	Match on a class of characters in filenames.
Redirection Symbols	**Execution**
>	Redirect the standard output to a file or device, creating the file if it does not exist and overwriting the file if it does exist.
>!	The exclamation point forces the overwriting of a file if it already exists.
<	Redirect the standard input from a file or device to a program.
>>	Redirect the standard output to a file or device, appending the output to the end of the file.
Standard Error Redirection Symbols	**Execution**
2>	Redirect the standard error to a file or device.
2>>	Redirect and append the standard error to a file or device.
2>&1	Redirect the standard error to the standard output.

Table 21-5: Shell Symbols

If the asterisk is placed before the pattern, filenames that end in that pattern are searched for. If the asterisk is placed after the pattern, filenames that begin with that pattern are searched for. Any matching filename is copied into a list of filenames generated by this operation.

In the next example, all filenames beginning with the pattern "doc" are searched for and a list generated. Then all filenames ending with the pattern "day" are searched for and a list is generated. The last example shows how the * can be used in any combination of characters.

```
$ ls
doc1 doc2 document docs mydoc monday tuesday
```

```
$ ls doc*
doc1 doc2 document docs
$ ls *day
monday tuesday
$ ls m*d*
monday
$
```

Filenames often include an extension specified with a period and followed by a string denoting the file type, such as **.c** for C files, **.cpp** for C++ files, or even **.jpg** for JPEG image files. The extension has no special status and is only part of the characters making up the filename. Using the asterisk makes it easy to select files with a given extension. In the next example, the asterisk is used to list only those files with a **.c** extension. The asterisk placed before the **.c** constitutes the argument for **ls**.

```
$ ls *.c
calc.c main.c
```

You can use * with the **rm** command to erase several files at once. The asterisk first selects a list of files with a given extension, or beginning or ending with a given set of characters, and then it presents this list of files to the **rm** command to be erased. In the next example, the **rm** command erases all files beginning with the pattern "doc":

```
$ rm doc*
```

Caution: Use the * file expansion character carefully and sparingly with the **rm** command. The combination can be dangerous. A misplaced * in an **rm** command without the -i option could easily erase all the files in your current directory. The -i option will first prompt the user to confirm whether the file should be deleted.

Matching Single Characters

The question mark (**?**) matches only a single incomplete character in filenames. Suppose you want to match the files **doc1** and **docA**, but not the file **document**. Whereas the asterisk will match filenames of any length, the question mark limits the match to just one extra character. The next example matches files that begin with the word "doc" followed by a single differing letter:

```
$ ls
doc1 docA document
$ ls doc?
doc1 docA
```

Matching a Range of Characters

Whereas the * and ? file expansion characters specify incomplete portions of a filename, the brackets ([]) enable you to specify a set of valid characters to search for. Any character placed within the brackets will be matched in the filename. Suppose you want to list files beginning with "doc", but only ending in *1* or *A*. You are not interested in filenames ending in *2* or *B,* or any other character. Here is how it's done:

```
$ ls
doc1 doc2 doc3 docA docB docD document
$ ls doc[1A]
doc1 docA
```

You can also specify a set of characters as a range, rather than listing them one by one. A dash placed between the upper and lower bounds of a set of characters selects all characters within that range. The range is usually determined by the character set in use. In an ASCII character set, the range "a-g" will select all lowercase alphabetic characters from *a* through *g,* inclusive. In the next example, files beginning with the pattern "doc" and ending in characters *1* through *3* are selected. Then, those ending in characters *B* through *E* are matched.

```
$ ls doc[1-3]
doc1 doc2 doc3
$ ls doc[B-E]
docB docD
```

You can combine the brackets with other file expansion characters to form flexible matching operators. Suppose you want to list only filenames ending in either a **.c** or **.o** extension, but no other extension. You can use a combination of the asterisk and brackets: *** [co].** The asterisk matches all filenames, and the brackets match only filenames with extension **.c** or **.o**.

```
$ ls *.[co]
main.c  main.o  calc.c
```

Matching Shell Symbols

At times, a file expansion character is actually part of a filename. In these cases, you need to quote the character by preceding it with a backslash (\) to reference the file. In the next example, the user needs to reference a file that ends with the **?** character, **answers?**. The **?** is, however, a file expansion character and would match any filename beginning with "answers" that has one or more characters. In this case, the user quotes the **?** with a preceding backslash to reference the filename.

```
$ ls answers\?
answers?
```

Placing the filename in double quotes will also quote the character.

```
$ ls "answers?"
answers?
```

This is also true for filenames or directories that have white space characters like the space character. In this case you could either use the backslash to quote the space character in the file or directory name, or place the entire name in double quotes.

```
$ ls My\ Documents
My Documents
$ ls "My Documents"
My Documents
```

Generating Patterns

Though not a file expansion operation, {} is often useful for generating names that you can use to create or modify files and directories. The braces operation only generates a list of names. It does not match on existing filenames. Patterns are placed within the braces and separated with commas. Any pattern placed within the braces will be used to generate a version of the pattern, using either the preceding or following pattern, or both. Suppose you want to generate a list of names beginning with "doc", but only ending in the patterns "ument", "final", and "draft". Here is how it's done:

```
$ echo doc{ument,final,draft}
document docfinal docdraft
```

Since the names generated do not have to exist, you could use the {} operation in a command to create directories, as shown here:

```
$ mkdir {fall,winter,spring}report
$ ls
fallreport springreport winterreport
```

Standard Input/Output and Redirection

The data in input and output operations is organized like a file. Data input at the keyboard is placed in a data stream arranged as a continuous set of bytes. Data output from a command or program is also placed in a data stream and arranged as a continuous set of bytes. This input data stream is referred to in Linux as the *standard input,* while the output data stream is called the *standard output.* There is also a separate output data stream reserved solely for error messages, called the *standard error* (see the section "Redirecting and Piping the Standard Error: >&, 2>" later in this chapter).

Because the standard input and standard output have the same organization as that of a file, they can easily interact with files. Linux has a redirection capability that lets you easily move data in and out of files. You can redirect the standard output so that, instead of displaying the output on a screen, you can save it in a file. You can also redirect the standard input away from the keyboard to a file, so that input is read from a file instead of from your keyboard.

When a Linux command is executed that produces output, this output is placed in the standard output data stream. The default destination for the standard output data stream is a device—in this case, the screen. *Devices,* such as the keyboard and screen, are treated as files. They receive and send out streams of bytes with the same organization as that of a byte-stream file. The screen is a device that displays a continuous stream of bytes. By default, the standard output will send its data to the screen device, which will then display the data.

For example, the `ls` command generates a list of all filenames and outputs this list to the standard output. Next, this stream of bytes in the standard output is directed to the screen device. The list of filenames is then printed on the screen. The `cat` command also sends output to the standard output. The contents of a file are copied to the standard output, whose default destination is the screen. The contents of the file are then displayed on the screen.

Redirecting the Standard Output: > and >>

Suppose that instead of displaying a list of files on the screen, you would like to save this list in a file. In other words, you would like to direct the standard output to a file rather than the screen. To do this, you place the output redirection operator, the greater-than sign (`>`), followed by the name of a file on the command line after the Linux command. Table 21-6 lists the different ways you can use the redirection operators. In the next example, the output of the `ls` command is redirected from the screen device to a file:

```
$ ls -l *.c > programlist
```

Command	Execution
ENTER	Execute a command line.
;	Separate commands on the same command line.
command *opts args*	Enter backslash before carriage return to continue entering a command on the next line.
` `command` `	Execute a command.
Special Characters for Filename Expansion	**Execution**
*	Match on any set of characters.
?	Match on any single characters.
[]	Match on a class of possible characters.
\	Quote the following character. Used to quote special characters.
Redirection	**Execution**
command > filename	Redirect the standard output to a file or device, creating the file if it does not exist and overwriting the file if it does exist.
command < filename	Redirect the standard input from a file or device to a program.
command >> filename	Redirect the standard output to a file or device, appending the output to the end of the file.
command 2> filename	Redirect the standard error to a file or device
command 2>> filename	Redirect and append the standard error to a file or device
command 2>&1	Redirect the standard error to the standard output in the Bourne shell.
command >& filename	Redirect the standard error to a file or device in the C shell.
Pipes	**Execution**
*command	command*	Pipe the standard output of one command as input for another command.

Table 21-6: The Shell Operations

The redirection operation creates the new destination file. If the file already exists, it will be overwritten with the data in the standard output. You can set the `noclobber` feature to prevent overwriting an existing file with the redirection operation. In this case, the redirection operation on an existing file will fail. You can overcome the `noclobber` feature by placing an exclamation point after the redirection operator. You can place the `noclobber` command in a shell configuration file to make it an automatic default operation. The next example sets the `noclobber` feature for the BASH shell and then forces the overwriting of the **oldarticle** file if it already exists:

```
$ set -o noclobber
$ cat myarticle >! oldarticle
```

Although the redirection operator and the filename are placed after the command, the redirection operation is not executed after the command. In fact, it is executed before the command. The redirection operation creates the file and sets up the redirection before it receives any data from the standard output. If the file already exists, it will be destroyed and replaced by a file of the same name. In effect, the command generating the output is executed only after the redirected file has been created.

In the next example, the output of the `ls` command is redirected from the screen device to a file. First the `ls` command lists files, and in the next command, `ls` redirects its file list to the **listf** file. Then the `cat` command displays the list of files saved in **listf**. Notice the list of files in **listf** includes the **listf** filename. The list of filenames generated by the `ls` command includes the name of the file created by the redirection operation—in this case, **listf**. The **listf** file is first created by the redirection operation, and then the `ls` command lists it along with other files. This file list output by `ls` is then redirected to the **listf** file, instead of being printed on the screen.

```
$ ls
mydata intro preface
$ ls > listf
$ cat listf
mydata intro listf preface
```

Tip: Errors occur when you try to use the same filename for both an input file for the command and the redirected destination file. In this case, because the redirection operation is executed first, the input file, because it exists, is destroyed and replaced by a file of the same name. When the command is executed, it finds an input file that is empty.

You can also append the standard output to an existing file using the `>>` redirection operator. Instead of overwriting the file, the data in the standard output is added at the end of the file. In the next example, the **myarticle** and **oldarticle** files are appended to the **allarticles** file. The **allarticles** file will then contain the contents of both **myarticle** and **oldarticle**.

```
$ cat myarticle >> allarticles
$ cat oldarticle >> allarticles
```

The Standard Input

Many Linux commands can receive data from the standard input. The standard input itself receives data from a device or a file. The default device for the standard input is the keyboard. Characters typed on the keyboard are placed in the standard input, which is then directed to the Linux command. Just as with the standard output, you can also redirect the standard input, receiving input from a file rather than the keyboard. The operator for redirecting the standard input is the less-than sign (`<`). In the next example, the standard input is redirected to receive input from the **myarticle** file, rather than the keyboard device (use CTRL-D to end the typed input). The contents of **myarticle** are read into the standard input by the redirection operation. Then the `cat` command reads the standard input and displays the contents of **myarticle**.

```
$ cat < myarticle
hello Christopher
How are you today
$
```

You can combine the redirection operations for both standard input and standard output. In the next example, the `cat` command has no filename arguments. Without filename arguments, the `cat` command receives input from the standard input and sends output to the standard output. However, the standard input has been redirected to receive its data from a file, while the standard output has been redirected to place its data in a file.

```
$ cat < myarticle > newarticle
```

Pipes: |

You may encounter situations in which you need to send data from one command to another. In other words, you may want to send the standard output of a command to another command, rather than to a destination file. Suppose you want to send a list of your filenames to the printer to be printed. You need two commands to do this: the `ls` command to generate a list of filenames and the `lpr` command to send the list to the printer. In effect, you need to take the output of the `ls` command and use it as input for the `lpr` command. You can think of the data as flowing from one command to another. To form such a connection in Linux, you use what is called a *pipe*. The *pipe operator* (|, the vertical bar character) placed between two commands forms a connection between them. The standard output of one command becomes the standard input for the other. The pipe operation receives output from the command placed before the pipe and sends this data as input to the command placed after the pipe. As shown in the next example, you can connect the `ls` command and the `lpr` command with a pipe. The list of filenames output by the `ls` command is piped into the `lpr` command.

```
$ ls | lpr
```

You can combine the `pipe` operation with other shell features, such as file expansion characters, to perform specialized operations. The next example prints only files with a **.c** extension. The `ls` command is used with the asterisk and ".c" to generate a list of filenames with the **.c** extension. Then this list is piped to the `lpr` command.

```
$ ls *.c | lpr
```

In the preceding example, a list of filenames was used as input, but what is important to note is that pipes operate on the standard output of a command, whatever that might be. The contents of whole files or even several files can be piped from one command to another. In the next example, the `cat` command reads and outputs the contents of the **mydata** file, which are then piped to the `lpr` command:

```
$ cat mydata | lpr
```

Many Linux commands generate modified output. For example, the `sort` command takes the contents of a file and generates a version with each line sorted in alphabetic order. The `sort` command works best with files that are lists of items. Commands such as `sort` that output a modified version of its input are referred to as *filters*. Filters are often used with pipes. In the next example, a sorted version of **mylist** is generated and piped into the `more` command for display on the screen. Note that the original file, **mylist**, has not been changed and is not itself sorted. Only the output of `sort` in the standard output is sorted.

```
$ sort mylist | more
```

The standard input piped into a command can be more carefully controlled with the standard input argument (**-**). When you use the dash as an argument for a command, it represents the standard input.

Redirecting and Piping the Standard Error: >&, 2>

When you execute commands, an error could possibly occur. You may enter the wrong number of arguments, or some kind of system error could take place. When an error occurs, the system issues an error message. Usually such error messages are displayed on the screen, along with the standard output. Linux distinguishes between standard output and error messages, however. Error messages are placed in yet another standard byte stream, called the *standard error.* In the next example, the **cat** command is assigned as its argument the name of a file that does not exist, **myintro**. In this case, the **cat** command simply issues an error:

```
$ cat myintro
cat : myintro not found
$
```

Because error messages are in a separate data stream from the standard output, error messages still appear on the screen for you to see even if you have redirected the standard output to a file. In the next example, the standard output of the **cat** command is redirected to the file **mydata**. However, the standard error, containing the error messages, is still directed to the screen.

```
$ cat myintro > mydata
cat : myintro not found
$
```

You can redirect the standard error, as you can the standard output. This means you can save your error messages in a file for future reference. This is helpful if you need a record of the error messages. Like the standard output, the standard error has the screen device for its default destination. However, you can redirect the standard error to any file or device you choose using special redirection operators. In this case, the error messages will not be displayed on the screen.

Redirection of the standard error relies on a special feature of shell redirection. You can reference all the standard byte streams in redirection operations with numbers. The numbers *0, 1,* and *2* reference the standard input, standard output, and standard error, respectively. By default, an output redirection, **>**, operates on the standard output, *1*. You can modify the output redirection to operate on the standard error, however, by preceding the output redirection operator with the number *2*. In the next example, the **cat** command again will generate an error. The error message is redirected to the standard byte stream represented by the number *2*, the standard error.

```
$ cat nodata 2> myerrors
$ cat myerrors
cat : nodata not found
$
```

You can also append the standard error to a file by using the number *2* and the redirection append operator (**>>**). In the next example, the user appends the standard error to the **myerrors** file, which then functions as a log of errors:

```
$ cat nodata 2>> myerrors
```

Jobs: Background, Kills, and Interruptions

In Linux, you not only have control over a command's input and output, but also over its execution. You can run a job in the background while you execute other commands. You can also cancel commands before they have finished executing. You can even interrupt a command, starting it again later from where you left off. Background operations are particularly useful for long jobs. Instead of waiting at the terminal until a command has finished execution, you can place it in the background. You can then continue executing other Linux commands. You can, for example, edit a file while other files are printing. The background commands, as well as commands to cancel and interrupt jobs, are listed in Table 21-7.

Background Jobs	Execution
%*jobnum*	References job by job number, use the jobs command to display job numbers.
%	References recent job.
%*string*	References job by an exact matching string.
%?*string*?	References job that contains unique string.
%--	References job before recent job.
&	Execute a command in the background.
fg %*jobnum*	Bring a command in the background to the foreground or resume an interrupted program.
bg	Place a command in the foreground into the background.
CTRL-Z	Interrupt and stop the currently running program. The program remains stopped and waiting in the background for you to resume it.
notify %*jobnum*	Notify you when a job ends.
kill %*jobnum*	
kill *processnum*	Cancel and end a job running in the background.
jobs	List all background jobs.
ps -a	List all currently running processes, including background jobs.
at *time date*	Execute commands at a specified time and date. The time can be entered with hours and minutes and qualified as A.M. or P.M.

Table 21-7: Job Management Operations

Running Jobs in the Background

You execute a command in the background by placing an ampersand (**&**) on the command line at the end of the command. When you place a job in the background, a user job number and a system process number are displayed. The user job number, placed in brackets, is the number by which the user references the job. The system process number is the number by which the system identifies the job. In the next example, the command to print the file **mydata** is placed in the background:

```
$ lpr mydata &
[1]   534
$
```

You can place more than one command in the background. Each is classified as a job and given a name and a job number. The command **jobs** lists the jobs being run in the background. Each entry in the list consists of the job number in brackets, whether it is stopped or running, and the name of the job. The + sign indicates the job currently being processed, and the - sign indicates the next job to be executed. In the next example, two commands have been placed in the background. The **jobs** command then lists those jobs, showing which one is currently being executed.

```
$ lpr intro &
[1]   547
$ cat *.c > myprogs &
[2]   548
$ jobs
[1]   +   Running   lpr intro
[2]   -   Running   cat *.c > myprogs
$
```

Referencing Jobs

Normally, jobs are referenced using the job number, preceded by a **%** symbol. You can obtain this number with the **jobs** command, which will list all background jobs, as shown in the preceding example. In addition you can also reference a job using an identifying string (see Table 10-7). The string must be either an exact match or a partial unique match. If there is no exact or unique match, you will receive an error message. Also, the % symbol itself without any job number references the recent background job. Followed by a -- it references the second previous background job. The following example brings job 1 in the previous example to the foreground:

```
fg %lpr
```

Job Notification

After you execute any command in Linux, the system tells you what background jobs, if you have any running, have been completed so far. The system does not interrupt any operation, such as editing, to notify you about a completed job. If you want to be notified immediately when a certain job ends, no matter what you are doing on the system, you can use the **notify** command to instruct the system to tell you. The **notify** command takes a job number as its argument. When that job is finished, the system interrupts what you are doing to notify you the job has ended. The next example tells the system to notify the user when job 2 has finished:

```
$ notify %2
```

Bringing Jobs to the Foreground

You can bring a job out of the background with the foreground command, **fg**. If only one job is in the background, the **fg** command alone will bring it to the foreground. If more than one job is in the background, you must use the job's number with the command. You place the job number after the **fg** command, preceded with a percent sign. A **bg** command also places a job in the background. This command is usually used for interrupted jobs. In the next example, the second job is brought back into the foreground. You may not immediately receive a prompt again because the second command is now in the foreground and executing. When the command is finished executing, the prompt appears and you can execute another command.

```
$ fg %2
cat *.c > myprogs
$
```

Canceling Jobs

If you want to cancel a job running in the background, you can force it to end with the **kill** command. The **kill** command takes as its argument either the user job number or the system process number. The user job number must be preceded by a percent sign (**%**). You can find out the job number from the **jobs** command. In the next example, the **jobs** command lists the background jobs; then job 2 is canceled:

```
$ jobs
[1]  +  Running  lpr intro
[2]  -  Running  cat *.c > myprogs
$ kill %2
```

Suspending and Stopping Jobs

You can suspend a job and stop it by pressing CTRL-Z. This places the job to the side until it is restarted. The job is not ended; it merely remains suspended until you want to continue. When you're ready, you can continue with the job either in the foreground or the background using the **fg** or **bg** command. The **fg** command restarts a suspended job in the foreground. The **bg** command places the suspended job in the background.

At times, you may need to place a job currently running in the foreground into the background. However, you cannot move a currently running job directly into the background. You first need to suspend it with CTRL-Z and then place it in the background with the **bg** command. In the next example, the current command to list and redirect .c files is first suspended with CTRL-Z. Then that job is placed in the background:

```
$ cat *.c > myprogs
^Z
$ bg
```

Note: You can also use CTRL-Z to stop currently running jobs such as Vi, suspending them in the background until you are ready to resume them. The Vi session remains a stopped job in the background until resumed with the **bg** command.

Ending Processes: ps and kill

You can also cancel a job using the system process number, which you can obtain with the **ps** command. The **ps** command will display your processes, and you can use a process number to end any running process. The **ps** command displays a great deal more information than the **jobs** command. The next example lists the processes a user is running. The PID is the system process number, also known as the process ID. TTY is the terminal identifier. TIME is how long the process has taken so far. COMMAND is the name of the process.

```
$ ps
PID     TTY     TIME     COMMAND
523     tty24   0:05     sh
567     tty24   0:01     lpr
570     tty24   0:00     ps
```

You can then reference the system process number in a kill command. Use the process number without any preceding percent sign. The next example kills process 567:

```
$ kill 567
```

Check the **ps** man page for more detailed information about detecting and displaying process information. To just display a process ID number use the output options **-o pid=**. Combining the **ps** command with the **-C** option lets you display just the process ID for a particular command. If more than one process exists for that command, such as multiple bash shells, then all the PIDs will be displayed.

```
$ ps -C lpr -o pid=
567
```

For unique commands, those you know have only one process running, you can safely combine the previous command with the **kill** command to end the process on one line. This avoids interactively having to display and enter the PID to kill the process. The technique can be useful for non-interactive operations such as **cron** and helpful for ending open-ended operations such as video recording. In the following example, a command using just one process, **getatsc**, is ended in a single **kill** operation. The **getatsc** commandis an HDTV recording command. Backquotes are used first to execute the **ps** command to obtain the PID. (See "Values from Linux Commands" later in the chapter.)

```
kill `ps -C getatsc -o pid=`
```

22. Shells: Files and Directories

Linux Files

The File Structure

Listing, Displaying, and Printing Files: ls, cat, more, less, and lpr

Managing Directories: mkdir, rmdir, ls, cd, pwd

File and Directory Operations: find, cp, mv, rm, ln

Filters and Regular Expressions

Searching Files: grep

In Linux, all files are organized into directories that, in turn, are hierarchically connected to each other in one overall file structure. A file is referenced not according to just its name, but also according to its place in this file structure. You can create as many new directories as you want, adding more directories to the file structure. The Linux file commands can perform sophisticated operations, such as moving or copying whole directories along with their subdirectories. You can use file operations such as `find`, `cp`, `mv`, and `ln` to locate files and copy, move, or link them from one directory to another. Desktop file managers, such as Konqueror and Nautilus used on the KDE and GNOME desktops, provide a graphical user interface to perform the same operations using icons, windows, and menus (see Chapters 3). This chapter will focus on the commands you use in the shell command line to manage files, such as `cp` and `mv`. However, whether you use the command line or a GUI file manager, the underlying file structure is the same.

Note: Linux also allows you to mount and access file systems used by other operating systems such as Unix or Windows. Linux itself supports a variety of different file systems such as ext2, ext3, and ReiserFS.

Linux Files

You can name a file using any letters, underscores, and numbers. You can also include periods and commas. Except in certain special cases, you should never begin a filename with a period. Other characters, such as slashes, question marks, or asterisks, are reserved for use as special characters by the system and should not be part of a filename. Filenames can be as long as 256 characters. Filenames can also include spaces, though to reference such filenames from the command line, be sure to encase them in quotes. On a desktop like GNOME or KDE you do not need quotes.

You can include an extension as part of a filename. A period is used to distinguish the filename proper from the extension. Extensions can be useful for categorizing your files. You are probably familiar with certain standard extensions that have been adopted by convention. For example, C source code files always have an extension of **.c**. Files that contain compiled object code have an **.o** extension. You can, of course, make up your own file extensions. The following examples are all valid Linux filenames. Keep in mind that to reference the last of these names on the command line, you would have to encase it in quotes as "New book review":

```
preface
chapter2
9700info
New_Revisions
calc.c
intro.bk1
New book review
```

Special initialization files are also used to hold shell configuration commands. These are the hidden, or dot, files, which begin with a period. Dot files used by commands and applications have predetermined names, such as the **.mozilla** directory used to hold your Mozilla data and configuration files. Recall that when you use `ls` to display your filenames, the dot files will not be displayed. To include the dot files, you need to use `ls` with the `-a` option.

The `ls -l` command displays detailed information about a file. First the permissions are displayed, followed by the number of links, the owner of the file, the name of the group the user belongs to, the file size in bytes, the date and time the file was last modified, and the name of the file. Permissions indicate who can access the file: the user, members of a group, or all other users. Permissions are discussed in detail later in this chapter. The group name indicates the group permitted to access the file object. The file type for **mydata** is that of an ordinary file. Only one link exists, indicating the file has no other names and no other links. The owner's name is **chris**, the same as the login name, and the group name is **weather**. Other users probably also belong to the **weather** group. The size of the file is 207 bytes, and it was last modified on February 20 at 11:55 A.M. The name of the file is **mydata**.

If you want to display this detailed information for all the files in a directory, simply use the **ls -l** command without an argument.

```
$ ls -l
-rw-r--r-- 1 chris weather 207 Feb 20 11:55 mydata
-rw-rw-r-- 1 chris weather 568 Feb 14 10:30 today
-rw-rw-r-- 1 chris weather 308 Feb 17 12:40 monday
```

All files in Linux have one physical format—a byte stream. A *byte stream* is just a sequence of bytes. This allows Linux to apply the file concept to every data component in the system. Directories are classified as files, as are devices. Treating everything as a file allows Linux to organize and exchange data more easily. The data in a file can be sent directly to a device such as a screen because a device interfaces with the system using the same byte-stream file format as regular files.

This same file format is used to implement other operating system components. The interface to a device, such as the screen or keyboard, is designated as a file. Other components, such as directories, are themselves byte-stream files, but they have a special internal organization. A directory file contains information about a directory, organized in a special directory format. Because these different components are treated as files, they can be said to constitute different *file types*. A character device is one file type. A directory is another file type. The number of these file types may vary according to your specific implementation of Linux. Five common types of files exist, however: ordinary files, directory files, first-in first-out pipes, character device files, and block device files. Although you may rarely reference a file's type, it can be useful when searching for directories or devices. Later in the chapter, you'll see how to use the file type in a search criterion with the **find** command to search specifically for directory or device names.

Although all ordinary files have a byte-stream format, they may be used in different ways. The most significant difference is between binary and text files. Compiled programs are examples of binary files. However, even text files can be classified according to their different uses. You can have files that contain C programming source code or shell commands, or even a file that is empty. The file could be an executable program or a directory file. The Linux **file** command helps you determine what a file is used for. It examines the first few lines of a file and tries to determine a classification for it. The **file** command looks for special keywords or special numbers in those first few lines, but it is not always accurate. In the next example, the **file** command examines the contents of two files and determines a classification for them:

```
$ file monday reports
monday: text
reports: directory
```

If you need to examine the entire file byte by byte, you can do so with the **od** (octal dump) command which performs a dump of a file. By default, it prints every byte in its octal representation. However, you can also specify a character, decimal, or hexadecimal representation. The od command is helpful when you need to detect any special character in your file or if you want to display a binary file.

The File Structure

Linux organizes files into a hierarchically connected set of directories. Each directory may contain either files or other directories. In this respect, directories perform two important functions. A *directory* holds files, much like files held in a file drawer, and a directory connects to other directories, much as a branch in a tree is connected to other branches. Because of the similarities to a tree, such a structure is often referred to as a *tree structure*.

The Linux file structure branches into several directories beginning with a root directory, /. Within the root directory, several system directories contain files and programs that are features of the Linux system. The root directory also contains a directory called **/home** which contains the home directories of all the users in the system. Each user's home directory, in turn, contains the directories the user has made for their own use. Each of these can also contain directories. Such nested directories branch out from the user's home directory.

Note: The user's home directory can be any directory, though it is usually the directory that bears the user's login name. This directory is located in the directory named **/home** on your Linux system. For example, a user named **dylan** will have a home directory called **dylan** located in the system's **/home** directory. The user's home directory is a subdirectory of the directory called **/home** on your system.

Home Directories

When you log in to the system, you are placed within your home directory. The name given to this directory by the system is the same as your login name. Any files you create when you first log in are organized within your home directory. Within your home directory, however, you can create more directories. You can then change to these directories and store files in them. The same is true for other users on the system. Each user has a home directory, identified by the appropriate login name. Users, in turn, can create their own directories.

You can access a directory either through its name or by making it your working directory. Each directory is given a name when it is created. You can use this name in file operations to access files in that directory. You can also make the directory your working directory. If you do not use any directory names in a file operation, the working directory will be accessed. The working directory is the one from which you are currently working. When you log in, the working directory is your home directory, usually having the same name as your login name. You can change the working directory by using the cd command to designate another directory as the working directory.

Pathnames

The name you give to a directory or file when you create it is not its full name. The full name of a directory is its *pathname*. The hierarchically nested relationship among directories forms paths, and these paths can be used to identify and reference any directory or file uniquely or absolutely. Each directory in the file structure can be said to have its own unique path. The actual name by which the system identifies a directory always begins with the root directory and consists of all directories nested below that directory.

In Linux, you write a pathname by listing each directory in the path separated from the last by a forward slash. A slash preceding the first directory in the path represents the root. The pathname for the **chris** directory is **/home/chris**. The pathname for the **reports** directory is **/home/chris/reports**. Pathnames also apply to files. When you create a file within a directory, you give the file a name. The actual name by which the system identifies the file, however, is the filename combined with the path of directories from the root to the file's directory. As an example, the pathname for **monday** is **/home/chris/reports/monday** (the root directory is represented by the first slash). The path for the **monday** file consists of the root, **home**, **chris**, and **reports** directories and the filename **monday**.

Directory	Function
/	Begins the file system structure, called the *root.*
/home	Contains users' home directories.
/bin	Holds all the standard commands and utility programs.
/usr	Holds those files and commands used by the system; this directory breaks down into several subdirectories.
/usr/bin	Holds user-oriented commands and utility programs.
/usr/sbin	Holds system administration commands.
/usr/lib	Holds libraries for programming languages.
/usr/share/doc	Holds Linux documentation.
/usr/share/man	Holds the online Man files.
/var/spool	Holds spooled files, such as those generated for printing jobs and network transfers.
/sbin	Holds system administration commands for booting the system.
/var	Holds files that vary, such as mailbox files.
/dev	Holds file interfaces for devices such as the terminals and printers (dynamically generated by udev, do not edit).
/etc	Holds system configuration files and any other system files.

Table 22-1: Standard System Directories in Linux

Pathnames may be absolute or relative. An *absolute pathname* is the complete pathname of a file or directory beginning with the root directory. A *relative pathname* begins from your working directory; it is the path of a file relative to your working directory. The working directory is the one you are currently operating in. Using the previous example, if **chris** is your working directory, the relative pathname for the file **monday** is **reports/monday**. The absolute pathname for **monday** is **/home/chris/reports/monday**.

The absolute pathname from the root to your home directory can be especially complex and, at times, even subject to change by the system administrator. To make it easier to reference, you can use a special character, the tilde (~), which represents the absolute pathname of your home directory. In the next example, from the **thankyou** directory, the user references the **monday** file in the home directory by placing a tilde and slash before **monday**:

```
$ pwd
/home/chris/letters/thankyou
$ cat ~/monday
raining and warm
$
```

You must specify the rest of the path from your home directory. In the next example, the user references the **monday** file in the **reports** directory. The tilde represents the path to the user's home directory, **/home/chris**, and then the rest of the path to the **monday** file is specified.

```
$ cat ~/reports/monday
```

System Directories

The root directory that begins the Linux file structure contains several system directories. The system directories contain files and programs used to run and maintain the system. Many contain other subdirectories with programs for executing specific features of Linux. For example, the directory **/usr/bin** contains the various Linux commands that users execute, such as **lpl**. The directory **/bin** holds system level commands. Table 22-1 lists the basic system directories.

Listing, Displaying, and Printing Files: ls, cat, more, less, and lpr

One of the primary functions of an operating system is the management of files. You may need to perform certain basic output operations on your files, such as displaying them on your screen or printing them. The Linux system provides a set of commands that perform basic file-management operations, such as listing, displaying, and printing files, as well as copying, renaming, and erasing files. These commands are usually made up of abbreviated versions of words. For example, the **ls** command is a shortened form of "list" and lists the files in your directory. The **lpr** command is an abbreviated form of "line print" and will print a file. The **cat**, **less**, and **more** commands display the contents of a file on the screen. Table 22-2 lists these commands with their different options. When you log in to your Linux system, you may want a list of the files in your home directory. The **ls** command, which outputs a list of your file and directory names, is useful for this. The **ls** command has many possible options for displaying filenames according to specific features.

Displaying Files: cat, less, and more

You may also need to look at the contents of a file. The **cat** and **more** commands display the contents of a file on the screen. The name **cat** stands for *concatenate.*

```
$ cat mydata
computers
```

The **cat** command outputs the entire text of a file to the screen at once. This presents a problem when the file is large because its text quickly speeds past on the screen. The **more** and **less** commands are designed to overcome this limitation by displaying one screen of text at a time. You can then move forward or backward in the text at your leisure. You invoke the **more** or

less command by entering the command name followed by the name of the file you want to view (**less** is a more powerful and configurable display utility).

`$ less mydata`

When **more** or **less** invoke a file, the first screen of text is displayed. To continue to the next screen, you press the F key or the SPACEBAR. To move back in the text, you press the B key. You can quit at any time by pressing the Q key.

Command or Option	Execution
`ls`	This command lists file and directory names.
`cat` *filenames*	This filter can be used to display a file. It can take filenames for its arguments. It outputs the contents of those files directly to the standard output, which, by default, is directed to the screen.
`more` *filenames*	This utility displays a file screen by screen. Press the SPACEBAR to continue to the next screen and **q** to quit.
`less` *filenames*	This utility also displays a file screen by screen. Press the SPACEBAR to continue to the next screen and **q** to quit.
`lpr` *filenames*	Sends a file to the line printer to be printed; a list of files may be used as arguments. Use the **-P** option to specify a printer.
`lpq`	Lists the print queue for printing jobs.
`lprm`	Removes a printing job from the print queue.

Table 22-2: Listing, Displaying, and Printing Files

Printing Files: lpr, lpq, and lprm

With the printer commands such as **lpr** and **lprm**, you can perform printing operations such as printing files or canceling print jobs (see Table 22-2). When you need to print files, use the **lpr** command to send files to the printer connected to your system. In the next example, the user prints the **mydata** file:

`$ lpr mydata`

If you want to print several files at once, you can specify more than one file on the command line after the **lpr** command. In the next example, the user prints out both the **mydata** and **preface** files:

`$ lpr mydata preface`

Printing jobs are placed in a queue and printed one at a time in the background. You can continue with other work as your files print. You can see the position of a particular printing job at any given time with the **lpq** command, which gives the owner of the printing job (the login name of the user who sent the job), the print job ID, the size in bytes, and the temporary file in which it is currently held.

If you need to cancel an unwanted printing job, you can do so with the `lprm` command, which takes as its argument either the ID number of the printing job or the owner's name. It then removes the print job from the print queue. For this task, `lpq` is helpful, for it provides you with the ID number and owner of the printing job you need to use with `lprm`.

Managing Directories: mkdir, rmdir, ls, cd, pwd

You can create and remove your own directories, as well as change your working directory, with the `mkdir`, `rmdir`, and `cd` commands. Each of these commands can take as its argument the pathname for a directory. The `pwd` command displays the absolute pathname of your working directory. In addition to these commands, the special characters represented by a single dot, a double dot, and a tilde can be used to reference the working directory, the parent of the working directory, and the home directory, respectively. Taken together, these commands enable you to manage your directories. You can create nested directories, move from one directory to another, and use pathnames to reference any of your directories. Those commands commonly used to manage directories are listed in Table 22-3.

Creating and Deleting Directories

You create and remove directories with the `mkdir` and `rmdir` commands. In either case, you can also use pathnames for the directories. In the next example, the user creates the directory **reports**. Then the user creates the directory **articles** using a pathname:

```
$ mkdir reports
$ mkdir /home/chris/articles
```

You can remove a directory with the `rmdir` command followed by the directory name. In the next example, the user removes the directory **reports** with the `rmdir` command:

```
$ rmdir reports
```

To remove a directory and all its subdirectories, you use the `rm` command with the `-r` option. This is a very powerful command and could easily be used to erase all your files. You will be prompted for each file. To simply remove all files and subdirectories without prompts, add the `-f` option. The following example deletes the **reports** directory and all its subdirectories:

```
rm -rf reports
```

Displaying Directory Contents

You have seen how to use the `ls` command to list the files and directories within your working directory. To distinguish between file and directory names, however, you need to use the `ls` command with the `-F` option. A slash is then placed after each directory name in the list.

```
$ ls
weather reports articles
$ ls -F
weather reports/ articles/
```

The `ls` command also takes as an argument any directory name or directory pathname. This enables you to list the files in any directory without first having to change to that directory. In the next example, the `ls` command takes as its argument the name of a directory, **reports**. Then the `ls` command is executed again, only this time the absolute pathname of **reports** is used.

```
$ ls reports
monday tuesday
$ ls /home/chris/reports
monday tuesday
$
```

Command	Execution
mkdir *directory*	Creates a directory.
rmdir *directory*	Erases a directory.
ls -F	Lists directory name with a preceding slash.
ls -R	Lists working directory as well as all subdirectories.
cd *directory name*	Changes to the specified directory, making it the working directory. **cd** without a directory name changes back to the home directory: **$ cd reports**
pwd	Displays the pathname of the working directory.
directory name / filename	A slash is used in pathnames to separate each directory name. In the case of pathnames for files, a slash separates the preceding directory names from the filename.
..	References the parent directory. You can use it as an argument or as part of a pathname. **$ cd ..** **$ mv ../larisa oldarticles**
.	References the working directory. You can use it as an argument or as part of a pathname. **$ ls .**
~ / *pathname*	The tilde is a special character that represents the pathname for the home directory. It is useful when you need to use an absolute pathname for a file or directory: **$ cp monday ~/today**

Table 22-3: Directory Commands

Moving Through Directories

The `cd` command takes as its argument the name of the directory to which you want to change. The name of the directory can be the name of a subdirectory in your working directory or the full pathname of any directory on the system. If you want to change back to your home directory, you only need to enter the `cd` command by itself, without a filename argument.

```
$ cd reports
$ pwd
/home/chris/reports
```

Referencing the Parent Directory

A directory always has a parent (except, of course, for the root). For example, in the preceding listing, the parent for **reports** is the **chris** directory. When a directory is created, two entries are made: one represented with a dot (.), and the other with double dots (. .). The dot represents the pathnames of the directory, and the double dots represent the pathname of its parent directory. Double dots, used as an argument in a command, reference a parent directory. The single dot references the directory itself.

You can use the single dot to reference your working directory, instead of using its pathname. For example, to copy a file to the working directory retaining the same name, the dot can be used in place of the working directory's pathname. In this sense, the dot is another name for the working directory. In the next example, the user copies the **weather** file from the **chris** directory to the **reports** directory. The **reports** directory is the working directory and can be represented with the single dot.

```
$ cd reports
$ cp /home/chris/weather .
```

The . . symbol is often used to reference files in the parent directory. In the next example, the **cat** command displays the **weather** file in the parent directory. The pathname for the file is the . . symbol (for the parent directory) followed by a slash and the filename.

```
$ cat ../weather
raining and warm
```

Tip: You can use the **cd** command with the . . symbol to step back through successive parent directories of the directory tree from a lower directory.

File and Directory Operations: find, cp, mv, rm, ln

As you create more and more files, you may want to back them up, change their names, erase some of them, or even give them added names. Linux provides you with several file commands that enable you to search for files, copy files, rename files, or remove files (see Tables 11-5). If you have a large number of files, you can also search them to locate a specific one. The commands are shortened forms of full words, consisting of only two characters. The **cp** command stands for "copy" and copies a file, **mv** stands for "move" and renames or moves a file, **rm** stands for "remove" and erases a file, and **ln** stands for "link" and adds another name for a file, often used as a shortcut to the original. One exception to the two-character rule is the **find** command, which performs searches of your filenames to find a file. All these operations can be handled by the GUI desktops, like GNOME and KDE.

Searching Directories: find

Once you have a large number of files in many different directories, you may need to search them to locate a specific file, or files, of a certain type. The **find** command enables you to perform such a search from the command line. The **find** command takes as its arguments directory names followed by several possible options that specify the type of search and the criteria for the search; it then searches within the directories listed and their subdirectories for files that meet these criteria. The **find** command can search for a file by name, type, owner, and even the time of the last update.

```
$ find directory-list -option criteria
```

Tip: From the GNOME desktop you can use the "Search" tool in the Places menu to search for files. From the KDE Desktop you can use the find tool in the file manager.

The **-name** option has as its criteria a pattern and instructs **find** to search for the filename that matches that pattern. To search for a file by name, you use the **find** command with the directory name followed by the **-name** option and the name of the file.

```
$ find directory-list -name filename
```

The **find** command also has options that merely perform actions, such as outputting the results of a search. If you want **find** to display the filenames it has found, you simply include the **-print** option on the command line along with any other options. The **-print** option is an action that instructs **find** to write to the standard output the names of all the files it locates (you can also use the **-ls** option instead to list files in the long format). In the next example, the user searches for all the files in the **reports** directory with the name **monday**. Once located, the file, with its relative pathname, is printed.

```
$ find reports -name monday -print
reports/monday
```

The **find** command prints out the filenames using the directory name specified in the directory list. If you specify an absolute pathname, the absolute path of the found directories will be output. If you specify a relative pathname, only the relative pathname is output. In the preceding example, the user specified a relative pathname, **reports**, in the directory list. Located filenames were output beginning with this relative pathname. In the next example, the user specifies an absolute pathname in the directory list. Located filenames are then output using this absolute pathname.

```
$ find /home/chris -name monday -print
/home/chris/reports/monday
```

Tip: Should you need to find the location of a specific program or configuration file, you could use **find** to search for the file from the root directory. Log in as the root user and use **/** as the directory. This command searched for the location of the **more** command and files on the entire file system: **find / -name more -print**.

Searching the Working Directory

If you want to search your working directory, you can use the dot in the directory pathname to represent your working directory. The double dots would represent the parent directory. The next example searches all files and subdirectories in the working directory, using the dot to represent the working directory. If you are located in your home directory, this is a convenient way to search through all your own directories. Notice the located filenames are output beginning with a dot.

```
$ find . -name weather -print
./weather
```

Command or Option	Execution
`find`	Searches directories for files according to search criteria. This command has several options that specify the type of criteria and actions to be taken.
`-name` *pattern*	Searches for files with the *pattern* in the name.
`-lname` *pattern*	Searches for symbolic link files.
`-group` *name*	Searches for files belonging to the group *name*.
`-gid` *name*	Searches for files belonging to a group according to group ID.
`-user` *name*	Searches for files belonging to a user.
`-uid` *name*	Searches for files belonging to a user according to user ID.
`-size` *numc*	Searches for files with the size *num* in blocks. If **c** is added after *num*, the size in bytes (characters) is searched for.
`-mtime` *num*	Searches for files last modified *num* days ago.
`-newer` *pattern*	Searches for files modified after the one matched by *pattern*.
`-context` *scontext*	Searches for files according to security context (SE Linux).
`-print`	Outputs the result of the search to the standard output. The result is usually a list of filenames, including their full pathnames.
`-type` *filetype*	Searches for files with the specified file type. File type can be **b** for block device, **c** for character device, **d** for directory, **f** for file, or **l** for symbolic link.
`-perm` *permission*	Searches for files with certain permissions set. Use octal or symbolic format for permissions.
`-ls`	Provides a detailed listing of each file, with owner, permission, size, and date information.
`-exec` *command*	Executes command when files found.

Table 22-4: The `find` Command

You can use shell wildcard characters as part of the pattern criteria for searching files. The special character must be quoted, however, to avoid evaluation by the shell. In the next example, all files (indicated with the asterisk) with the **.c** extension in the **programs** directory are searched for and then displayed in the long format using the **-ls** action:

```
$ find programs -name '*.c' -ls
```

Locating Directories

You can also use the `find` command to locate other directories. In Linux, a directory is officially classified as a special type of file. Although all files have a byte-stream format, some files, such as directories, are used in special ways. In this sense, a file can be said to have a file type. The `find` command has an option called **-type** that searches for a file of a given type. The **-type** option takes a one-character modifier that represents the file type. The modifier that represents a directory is a **d**. In the next example, both the directory name and the directory file type are used to search for the directory called **travel**:

```
$ find /home/chris -name travel -type d -print
/home/chris/articles/travel
$
```

File types are not so much different types of files as they are the file format applied to other components of the operating system, such as devices. In this sense, a device is treated as a type of file, and you can use **find** to search for devices and directories, as well as ordinary files. Table 22-4 lists the different types available for the **find** command's **-type** option.

You can also use the find operation to search for files by ownership or security criteria, like those belonging to a specific user or those with a certain security context. The **-user** option lets to locate all files belonging to a certain user. The following example lists all files that the user **chris** has created or owns on the entire system. To list those just in the users' home directories, you would use **/home** for the starting search directory. This would find all those in a user's home directory as well as any owned by that user in other user directories.

```
$ find / -user chris -print
```

Copying Files

To make a copy of a file, you simply give **cp** two filenames as its arguments (see Table 22-5). The first filename is the name of the file to be copied—the one that already exists. This is often referred to as the *source file*. The second filename is the name you want for the copy. This will be a new file containing a copy of all the data in the source file. This second argument is often referred to as the *destination file*. The syntax for the **cp** command follows:

```
$ cp source-file destination-file
```

In the next example, the user copies a file called **proposal** to a new file called **oldprop**:

```
$ cp proposal oldprop
```

You could unintentionally destroy another file with the **cp** command. The **cp** command generates a copy by first creating a file and then copying data into it. If another file has the same name as the destination file, that file is destroyed and a new file with that name is created. By default Ubuntu configures your system to check for an existing copy by the same name (**cp** is aliased with the **-i** option). To copy a file from your working directory to another directory, you only need to use that directory name as the second argument in the **cp** command. In the next example, the **proposal** file is overwritten by the **newprop** file. The **proposal** file already exists.

```
$ cp newprop proposal
```

You can use any of the wildcard characters to generate a list of filenames to use with **cp** or **mv**. For example, suppose you need to copy all your C source code files to a given directory. Instead of listing each one individually on the command line, you could use an ***** character with the **.c** extension to match on and generate a list of C source code files (all files with a **.c** extension). In the next example, the user copies all source code files in the current directory to the **sourcebks** directory:

```
$ cp *.c sourcebks
```

If you want to copy all the files in a given directory to another directory, you could use * to match on and generate a list of all those files in a cp command. In the next example, the user copies all the files in the **props** directory to the **oldprop** directory. Notice the use of a **props** pathname preceding the * special characters. In this context, **props** is a pathname that will be appended before each file in the list that * generates.

```
$ cp props/* oldprop
```

You can, of course, use any of the other special characters, such as ., ?, or []. In the next example, the user copies both source code and object code files (**.c** and **.o**) to the **projbk** directory:

```
$ cp *.[oc] projbk
```

When you copy a file, you may want to give the copy a different name than the original. To do so, place the new filename after the directory name, separated by a slash.

```
$ cp filename directory-name/new-filename
```

Moving Files

You can use the **mv** command either to rename a file or to move a file from one directory to another. When using **mv** to rename a file, you simply use the new filename as the second argument. The first argument is the current name of the file you are renaming. If you want to rename a file when you move it, you can specify the new name of the file after the directory name. In the next example, the **proposal** file is renamed with the name **version1**:

```
$ mv proposal version1
```

As with **cp**, it is easy for **mv** to erase a file accidentally. When renaming a file, you might accidentally choose a filename already used by another file. In this case, that other file will be erased. The **mv** command also has an **-i** option that checks first to see if a file by that name already exists.

You can also use any of the special characters to generate a list of filenames to use with **mv**. In the next example, the user moves all source code files in the current directory to the **newproj** directory:

```
$ mv *.c newproj
```

If you want to move all the files in a given directory to another directory, you can use * to match on and generate a list of all those files. In the next example, the user moves all the files in the **reports** directory to the **repbks** directory:

```
$ mv reports/* repbks
```

Note: The easiest way to copy files to a CD-R/RW or DVD-R/RW disc is to use the built-in Nautilus burning capability. Just insert a blank disk, open it as a folder, and drag and drop files on to it. You will be prompted automatically to burn the files.

Copying and Moving Directories

You can also copy or move whole directories at once. Both **cp** and **mv** can take as their first argument a directory name, enabling you to copy or move subdirectories from one directory into another (see Table 22-5). The first argument is the name of the directory to be moved or copied, while the second argument is the name of the directory within which it is to be placed. The same pathname structure used for files applies to moving or copying directories.

You can just as easily copy subdirectories from one directory to another. To copy a directory, the **cp** command requires you to use the **-r** option. The **-r** option stands for "recursive." It directs the **cp** command to copy a directory, as well as any subdirectories it may contain. In other words, the entire directory subtree, from that directory on, will be copied. In the next example, the **travel** directory is copied to the **oldarticles** directory. Now two **travel** subdirectories exist, one in **articles** and one in **oldarticles**.

```
$ cp -r articles/travel oldarticles
$ ls -F articles
/travel
$ ls -F oldarticles
/travel
```

Command	Execution
cp *filename filename*	Copies a file. **cp** takes two arguments: the original file and the name of the new copy. You can use pathnames for the files to copy across directories:
cp -r *dimame dimame*	Copies a subdirectory from one directory to another. The copied directory includes all its own subdirectories:
mv *filename filename*	Moves (renames) a file. The **mv** command takes two arguments: the first is the file to be moved. The second argument can be the new filename or the pathname of a directory. If it is the name of a directory, then the file is literally moved to that directory, changing the file's pathname:
mv *dimame dimame*	Moves directories. In this case, the first and last arguments are directories:
ln *filename filename*	Creates added names for files referred to as links. A link can be created in one directory that references a file in another directory:
rm *filenames*	Removes (erases) a file. Can take any number of filenames as its arguments. Literally removes links to a file. If a file has more than one link, you need to remove all of them to erase a file:

Table 22-5: File Operations

Erasing Files and Directories: the rm Command

As you use Linux, you will find the number of files you use increases rapidly. Generating files in Linux is easy. Applications such as editors, and commands such as **cp**, easily create files. Eventually, many of these files may become outdated and useless. You can then remove them with the **rm** command. The **rm** command can take any number of arguments, enabling you to list several filenames and erase them all at the same time. In the next example, the user erases the file **oldprop**:

```
$ rm oldprop
```

Be careful when using the `rm` command, because it is irrevocable. Once a file is removed, it cannot be restored (there is no undo). With the `-i` option, you are prompted separately for each file and asked whether to remove it. If you enter **y**, the file will be removed. If you enter anything else, the file is not removed. In the next example, the `rm` command is instructed to erase the files **proposal** and **oldprop**. The `rm` command then asks for confirmation for each file. The user decides to remove **oldprop,** but not **proposal**.

```
$ rm -i proposal oldprop
Remove proposal? n
Remove oldprop? y
$
```

Links: the ln Command

You can give a file more than one name using the `ln` command. You might want to reference a file using different filenames to access it from different directories. The added names are often referred to as *links*. Linux supports two different types of links, hard and symbolic. *Hard* links are literally another name for the same file, whereas *symbolic* links function like shortcuts referencing another file. Symbolic links are much more flexible and can work over many different file systems, whereas hard links are limited to your local file system. Furthermore, hard links introduce security concerns, as they allow direct access from a link that may have public access to an original file that you may want protected. Links are usually implemented as symbolic links.

Symbolic Links

To set up a symbolic link, you use the `ln` command with the `-s` option and two arguments: the name of the original file and the new, added filename. The `ls` operation lists both filenames, but only one physical file will exist.

```
$ ln -s original-file-name added-file-name
```

In the next example, the **today** file is given the additional name **weather**. In this case, **weather** is just another name for the **today** file.

```
$ ls
today
$ ln -s today weather
$ ls
today weather
```

You can give the same file several names by using the `ln` command on the same file many times. In the next example, the file **today** is given both the names **weather** and **weekend**:

```
$ ln -s today weather
$ ln -s today weekend
$ ls
today weather weekend
```

If you list the full information about a symbolic link and its file, you will find the information displayed is different. In the next example, the user lists the full information for both **lunch** and **/home/george/veglist** using the `ls` command with the `-1` option. The first character in the line specifies the file type. Symbolic links have their own file type, represented by an **l**. The file type for **lunch** is **l**, indicating it is a symbolic link, not an ordinary file. The number after the term "group" is the size of the file. Notice the sizes differ. The size of the **lunch** file is only four bytes. This is because **lunch** is only a symbolic link—a file that holds the pathname of another file—and a pathname takes up only a few bytes. It is not a direct hard link to the **veglist** file.

```
$ ls -l lunch /home/george/veglist
lrw-rw-r-- 1 chris group 4 Feb 14 10:30 lunch
-rw-rw-r-- 1 george group 793 Feb 14 10:30 veglist
```

To erase a file, you need to remove only its original name (and any hard links to it). If any symbolic links are left over, they will be unable to access the file. In this case, a symbolic link would hold the pathname of a file that no longer exists.

Hard Links

You can give the same file several names by using the `ln` command on the same file many times. To set up a hard link, you use the `ln` command with no `-s` option and two arguments: the name of the original file and the new, added filename. The `ls` operation lists both filenames, but only one physical file will exist.

```
$ ln original-file-name added-file-name
```

In the next example, the **monday** file is given the additional name **storm**. It is just another name for the **monday** file.

```
$ ls
today
$ ln monday storm
$ ls
monday storm
```

To erase a file that has hard links, you need to remove all its hard links. The name of a file is actually considered a link to that file—hence the command `rm` that removes the link to the file. If you have several links to the file and remove only one of them, the others stay in place and you can reference the file through them. The same is true even if you remove the original link—the original name of the file. Any added links will work just as well. In the next example, the **today** file is removed with the `rm` command. However, a link to that same file exists, called **weather**. The file can then be referenced under the name **weather**.

```
$ ln today weather
$ rm today
$ cat weather
The storm broke today
and the sun came out.
$
```

Filters and Regular Expressions

Filters are commands that read data, perform operations on that data, and then send the results to the standard output. Filters generate different kinds of output, depending on their task. Some filters generate information only about the input, other filters output selected parts of the input, and still other filters output an entire version of the input, but in a modified way. Some filters are limited to one of these, while others have options that specify one or the other. You can think of a filter as operating on a stream of data—receiving data and generating modified output. As data is passed through the filter, it is analyzed, screened, or modified.

The data stream input to a filter consists of a sequence of bytes that can be received from files, devices, or the output of other commands or filters. The filter operates on the data stream, but it does not modify the source of the data. If a filter receives input from a file, the file itself is not modified. Only its data is read and fed into the filter.

The output of a filter is usually sent to the standard output. It can then be redirected to another file or device, or piped as input to another utility or filter. All the features of redirection and pipes apply to filters. Often data is read by one filter and its modified output piped into another filter.

Note: Data could easily undergo several modifications as it is passed from one filter to another. However, it is always important to realize the original source of the data is never changed.

Many utilities and filters use patterns to locate and select specific text in your file. Sometimes, you may need to use patterns in a more flexible and powerful way, searching for several different variations on a given pattern. You can include a set of special characters in your pattern to enable a flexible search. A pattern that contains such special characters is called a *regular expression*. Regular expressions can be used in most filters and utilities that employ pattern searches such as **sed**, **awk**, **grep**, and **egrep**.

Tip: Although many of the special characters used for regular expressions are similar to the shell file expansion characters, they are used in a different way. Shell file expansion characters operate on filenames. Regular expressions search text.

You can save the output of a filter in a file or send it to a printer. To do so, you need to use redirection or pipes. To save the output of a filter to a file, you redirect it to a file using the redirection operation (**>**). To send output to the printer, you pipe the output to the **lpr** utility, which then prints it. In the next command, the **cat** command pipes its output to the **lpr** command, which then prints it.

```
$ cat complist | lpr
```

All filters accept input from the standard input. In fact, the output of one filter can be piped as the input for another filter. Many filters also accept input directly from files, however. Such filters can take filenames as their arguments and read data directly from those files.

Searching Files: grep

The **grep** and **fgrep** filters search the contents of files for a pattern. They then tell you in what file the pattern was found and print the lines in which it occurred in each file. Preceding each line is the name of the file in which the line is located. The **grep** command can search for only one pattern, whereas **fgrep** can search for more than one pattern at a time.

The **grep** filter takes two types of arguments. The first argument is the pattern to be searched for; the second argument is a list of filenames, which are the files to be searched. You enter the filenames on the command line after the pattern. You can also use special characters, such as the asterisk, to generate a file list.

```
$ grep pattern filenames-list
```

If you want to include more than one word in the pattern search, you enclose the words within single quotation marks. This is to quote the spaces between the words in the pattern. Otherwise, the shell would interpret the space as a delimiter or argument on the command line, and `grep` would try to interpret words in the pattern as part of the file list. In the next example, `grep` searches for the pattern *text file*:

```
$ grep 'text file' preface
A text file in Linux
text files, changing or
```

If you use more than one file in the file list, `grep` will output the name of the file before the matching line. In the next example, two files, **preface** and **intro**, are searched for the pattern *data*. Before each occurrence, the filename is output.

```
$ grep data preface intro
 preface: data in the file.
 intro: new data
```

As mentioned earlier, you can also use shell file expansion characters to generate a list of files to be searched. In the next example, the asterisk file expansion character is used to generate a list of all files in your directory. This is a simple way of searching all of a directory's files for a pattern.

```
$ grep data *
```

The special characters are often useful for searching a selected set of files. For example, if you want to search all your C program source code files for a particular pattern, you can specify the set of source code files with `*.c`. Suppose you have an unintended infinite loop in your program and you need to locate all instances of iterations. The next example searches only those files with a **.c** extension for the pattern *while* and displays the lines of code that perform iterations:

```
$ grep while *.c
```

Regular Expressions

Regular expressions enable you to match possible variations on a pattern, as well as patterns located at different points in the text. You can search for patterns in your text that have different ending or beginning letters, or you can match text at the beginning or end of a line. The regular expression special characters are the circumflex, dollar sign, asterisk, period, and brackets: `^`, `$`, `*`, `.`, `[]`. The circumflex and dollar sign match on the beginning and end of a line. The asterisk matches repeated characters, the period matches single characters, and the brackets match on classes of characters. See Table 22-6 for a listing of the regular expression special characters.

Note: Regular expressions are used extensively in many Linux filters and applications to perform searches and matching operations. The Vi and Emacs editors and the `sed`, `diff`, `grep`, and `gawk` filters all use regular expressions.

Suppose you want to use the long-form output of `ls` to display just your directories. One way to do this is to generate a list of all directories in the long form and pipe this list to `grep`, which can then pick out the directory entries. You can do this by using the `^` special character to specify the beginning of a line. Remember, in the long-form output of `ls`, the first character indicates the file type. A **d** represents a directory, an **l** represents a symbolic link, and an **a** represents a regular file. Using the pattern `'^d'`, `grep` will match only on those lines beginning with a *d*.

```
$ ls -l | grep '^d'
drwxr-x---  2  chris 512 Feb 10 04:30  reports
drwxr-x---  2  chris 512 Jan 6  01:20  letters
```

Character	Match	Operation
^	Start of a line	References the beginning of a line
$	End of a line	References the end of a line
.	Any character	Matches on any one possible character in a pattern
*	Repeated characters	Matches on repeated characters in a pattern
[]	Classes	Matches on classes of characters (a set of characters) in the pattern

Tab;e 22-6: Regular Expression Special Characters

23. Shell Scripts and Programming

Shell Variables

Environment Variables

Control Structures

A shell script combines Linux commands in such a way as to perform a specific task. The different kinds of shells provides many programming tools that you can use to create shell programs. You can define variables and assign values to them. You can also define variables in a script file and have a user interactively enter values for them when the script is executed. The shell provides loop and conditional control structures that repeat Linux commands or make decisions on which commands you want to execute. You can also construct expressions that perform arithmetic or comparison operations. All these shell programming tools operate in ways similar to those found in other programming languages, so if you're already familiar with programming, you might find shell programming simple to learn.

The BASH, TCSH, and Z shells are types of shells. You can have many instances of a particular kind of shell. A *shell,* by definition, is an interpretive environment within which you execute commands. You can have many environments running at the same time, of either the same or different types of shells; you have several shells running at the same time that are of the BASH shell type, for example.

This chapter will cover the basics of creating a shell program using the BASH and TCSH shells, the shells used on most Linux systems. You will learn how to create your own scripts, define shell variables, and develop user interfaces, as well as learn the more difficult task of combining control structures to create complex programs. Tables throughout the chapter list shell commands and operators, while numerous examples show how they are implemented.

Usually, the instructions making up a shell program are entered into a script file that can then be executed. You can even distribute your program among several script files, one of which will contain instructions on how to execute others. You can think of variables, expressions, and control structures as tools you use to bring together several Linux commands into one operation. In this sense, a shell program is a new and complex Linux command that you have created.

The BASH shell has a flexible and powerful set of programming commands that allows you to build complex scripts. It supports variables that can be either local to the given shell or exported to other shells. You can pass arguments from one script to another. The BASH shell has a complete set of control structures, including loops and if statements as well as case structures, all of which you'll learn about as you read this book. All shell commands interact easily with redirection and piping operations that allow them to accept input from the standard input or send it to the standard output. Unlike the Bourne shell, the first shell used for UNIX, BASH incorporates many of the features of the TCSH and Z shells. Arithmetic operations in particular are easier to perform in BASH.

Shell Variables

Within each shell, you can enter and execute commands. You can further enhance the capabilities of a shell using shell variables. A shell variable lets you hold data that you can reference over and over again as you execute different commands within a shell. For example, you can define a shell variable to hold the name of complex filename. Then, instead of retyping the filename in different commands, you can reference it with the shell variable.

You define variables within a shell, and such variables are known as *shell variables.* Some utilities, such as the Mail utility, have their own shells with their own shell variables. You can also create your own shell using *shell scripts.* You have a user shell that becomes active as soon as you log in. This is often referred to as the *login shell.* Special system-level parameter variables are defined within this login shell. Shell variables can also be used to define a shell's environment.

Note: Shell variables exist as long as your shell is active—that is, until you exit the shell. For example, logging out will exit the login shell. When you log in again, any variables you may need in your login shell must be defined again.

Definition and Evaluation of Variables: =, $, set, unset

You define a variable in a shell when you first use the variable's name. A variable's name may be any set of alphabetic characters, including the underscore. The name may also include a number, but the number cannot be the first character in the name. A name may not have any other type of character, such as an exclamation point, an ampersand, or even a space. Such symbols are reserved by the shell for its own use. Also, a variable name may not include more than one word. The shell uses spaces on the command line to distinguish different components of a command such as options, arguments, and the command name.

You assign a value to a variable with the assignment operator (=). You type the variable name, the assignment operator, and then the value assigned. Do not place any spaces around the assignment operator. The assignment operation `poet = Virgil`, for example, will fail. (The C shell has a slightly different type of assignment operation.) You can assign any set of characters to a variable. In the next example, the variable `poet` is assigned the string `Virgil`:

```
$ poet=Virgil
```

Once you have assigned a value to a variable, you can then use the variable name to reference the value. Often you use the values of variables as arguments for a command. You can reference the value of a variable using the variable name preceded by the `$` operator. The dollar sign is a special operator that uses the variable name to reference a variable's value, in effect evaluating the variable. Evaluation retrieves a variable's value, usually a set of characters. This set of characters then replaces the variable name on the command line. Wherever a `$` is placed before the variable name, the variable name is replaced with the value of the variable. In the next example, the shell variable `poet` is evaluated and its contents, `Virgil`, are used as the argument for an `echo` command. The `echo` command simply echoes or prints a set of characters to the screen.

```
$ echo $poet
Virgil
```

You must be careful to distinguish between the evaluation of a variable and its name alone. If you leave out the `$` operator before the variable name, all you have is the variable name itself. In the next example, the `$` operator is absent from the variable name. In this case, the `echo` command has as its argument the word *poet*, and so prints out *poet*:

```
$ echo poet
poet
```

The contents of a variable are often used as command arguments. A common command argument is a directory pathname. It can be tedious to retype a directory path that is being used over and over again. If you assign the directory pathname to a variable, you can simply use the evaluated variable in its place. The directory path you assign to the variable is retrieved when the variable is evaluated with the `$` operator. The next example assigns a directory pathname to a variable and then uses the evaluated variable in a copy command. The evaluation of `ldir` (which is

$ldir) results in the pathname **/home/chris/letters**. The copy command evaluates to `cp myletter /home/chris/letters`.

```
$ ldir=/home/chris/letters
$ cp myletter $ldir
```

You can obtain a list of all the defined variables with the **set** command. If you decide you do not want a certain variable, you can remove it with the **unset** command. The **unset** command undefines a variable.

Variable Values: Strings

The values that you assign to variables may consist of any set of characters. These characters may be a character string that you explicitly type in or the result obtained from executing a Linux command. In most cases, you will need to quote your values using either single quotes, double quotes, backslashes, or back quotes. Single quotes, double quotes, and backslashes allow you to quote strings in different ways. Back quotes have the special function of executing a Linux command and using its results as arguments on the command line.

Quoting Strings: Double Quotes, Single Quotes, and Backslashes

Variable values can be made up of any characters. However, problems occur when you want to include characters that are also used by the shell as operators. Your shell has certain metacharacters that it uses in evaluating the command line. A space is used to parse arguments on the command line. The asterisk, question mark, and brackets are metacharacters used to generate lists of filenames. The period represents the current directory. The dollar sign, $, is used to evaluate variables, and the greater-than and less-than characters , > <, are redirection operators. The ampersand is used to execute background commands and the bar pipes output. If you want to use any of these characters as part of the value of a variable, you first need to quote them. Quoting a metacharacter on a command line makes it just another character. It is not evaluated by the shell.

You can use double quotes, single quotes, and backslashes to quote such metacharacters. Double and single quotes allow you to quote several metacharacters at a time. Any metacharacters within double or single quotes are quoted. A backslash quotes the single character that follows it.

If you want to assign more than one word to a variable, you need to quote the spaces separating the words. You can do so by enclosing all the words within double quotes. You can think of this as creating a character string to be assigned to the variable. Of course, any other metacharacters enclosed within the double quotes are also quoted.

In the following first example, the double quotes enclose words separated by spaces. Because the spaces are enclosed within double quotes, they are treated as characters, not as delimiters used to parse command line arguments. In the second example, double quotes also enclose a period, treating it as just a character. In the third example, an asterisk is also enclosed within the double quotes. The asterisk is considered just another character in the string and is not evaluated.

```
$ notice="The meeting will be tomorrow"
$ echo $notice
The meeting will be tomorrow

$ message="The project is on time."
```

```
$ echo $message
The project is on time.

$ notice="You can get a list of files with ls *.c"
$ echo $notice
You can get a list of files with ls *.c
```

Double quotes, however, do not quote the dollar sign, the operator that evaluates variables. A $ operator next to a variable name enclosed within double quotes will still be evaluated, replacing the variable name with its value. The value of the variable will then become part of the string, not the variable name. There may be times when you want a variable within quotes to be evaluated. In the next example, the double quotes are used so that the winner's name will be included in the notice.

```
$ winner=dylan
$ notice="The person who won is $winner"
$ echo $notice
The person who won is dylan
```

On the other hand, there may be times when you do not want a variable within quotes to be evaluated. In that case you have to use the single quotes. Single quotes suppress any variable evaluation and treat the dollar sign as just another character. In the next example, single quotes prevent the evaluation of the winner variable.

```
$ winner=dylan
$ result='The name is in the $winner variable'
$ echo $result
The name is in the $winner variable
```

If, in this case, the double quotes were used instead, an unintended variable evaluation would take place. In the next example, the characters "$winner" are interpreted as a variable evaluation.

```
$ winner=dylan
$ result="The name is in the $winner variable"
$ echo $result
The name is in the dylan variable
```

You can always quote any metacharacter, including the $ operator, by preceding it with a backslash. The use of the backslash is to quote ENTER keys (newlines). The backslash is useful when you want to both evaluate variables within a string and include $ characters. In the next example, the backslash is placed before the $ in order to treat it as a dollar sign character: \$. At the same time the variable $winner is evaluated because the double quotes that are used do not quote the $ operator.

```
$ winner=dylan
$ result="$winner won \$100.00"
$ echo $result
dylan won $100.00
```

Quoting Commands: Single Quotes

There are, however, times when you may want to use single quotes around a Linux command. Single quotes allow you to assign the written command to a variable. If you do so, you can then use that variable name as another name for the Linux command. Entering in the variable name preceded by the $ operator on the command line will execute the command. In the next example, a shell variable is assigned the characters that make up a Linux command to list files, `'ls -F'`. Notice the single quotes around the command. When the shell variable is evaluated on the command line, the Linux command it contains will become a command line argument, and it will be executed by the shell.

```
$ lsf='ls -F'
$ $lsf
mydata /reports /letters
$
```

In effect you are creating another name for a command, like an alias.

Values from Linux Commands: Back Quotes

Although you can create variable values by typing in characters or character strings, you can also obtain values from other Linux commands. To assign the result of Linux command to a variable, you first need to execute the command. If you place a Linux command within back quotes (`) on the command line, that command is first executed and its result becomes an argument on the command line. In the case of assignments, the result of a command can be assigned to a variable by placing the command within back quotes first to execute it. The back quotes can be thought of as an expression consisting of a command to be executed whose result is then assigned to the variable. The characters making up the command itself are not assigned. In the next example, the command `ls *.c` is executed and its result is then assigned to the variable `listc`. `ls *.c`, which generates a list of all files with a **.c** extension. This list of files is then assigned to the `listc` variable.

```
$ listc=`ls `*.c`
$ echo $listc
main.c prog.c lib.c
```

Keep in mind the difference between single quotes and back quotes. Single quotes treat a Linux command as a set of characters. Back quotes force execution of the Linux command. There may be times when you accidentally enter single quotes when you mean to use back quotes. In the following first example, the assignment for the `lscc` variable has single quotes, not back quotes, placed around the `ls *.c` command. In this case, `ls *.c` are just characters to be assigned to the variable `lscc`. In the second example, back quotes are placed around the `ls *.c` command, forcing evaluation of the command. A list of filenames ending in **.c** is generated and assigned as the value of `lscc`.

```
$ lscc='ls *.c'
$ echo $lscc
ls *.c

$ lscc=`ls *.c`
$ echo $lscc
main.c  prog.c
```

Shell Scripts: User-Defined Commands

You can place shell commands within a file and then have the shell read and execute the commands in the file. In this sense, the file functions as a shell program, executing shell commands as if they were statements in a program. A file that contains shell commands is called a *shell script*.

You enter shell commands into a script file using a standard text editor such as the Vi editor. The **sh** or **.** command used with the script's filename will read the script file and execute the commands. In the next example, the text file called **lsc** contains an **ls** command that displays only files with the extension **.c**:

lsc

```
ls *.c
```

A run of the **lsc** script is shown here:

```
$ sh lsc
main.c calc.c
$ . lsc
main.c calc.c
```

Executing Scripts

You can dispense with the **sh** and **.** commands by setting the executable permission of a script file. When the script file is first created by your text editor, it is given only read and write permission. The **chmod** command with the **+x** option will give the script file executable permission. Once it is executable, entering the name of the script file at the shell prompt and pressing ENTER will execute the script file and the shell commands in it. In effect, the script's filename becomes a new shell command. In this way, you can use shell scripts to design and create your own Linux commands. You need to set the permission only once.

In the next example, the **lsc** file's executable permission for the owner is set to on. Then the **lsc** shell script is directly executed like any Linux command.

```
$ chmod u+x lsc
$ lsc
main.c calc.c
```

You may have to specify that the script you are using is in your current working directory. You do this by prefixing the script name with a period and slash combination, as in **./lsc**. The period is a special character representing the name of your current working directory. The slash is a directory pathname separator. The following example shows how to execute the **lsc** script:

```
$ ./lsc
main.c calc.c
```

Script Arguments

Just as any Linux command can take arguments, so also can a shell script. Arguments on the command line are referenced sequentially starting with 1. An argument is referenced using the **$** operator and the number of its position. The first argument is referenced with **$1**, the second, with **$2**, and so on. In the next example, the **lsext** script prints out files with a specified extension.

The first argument is the extension. The script is then executed with the argument **c** (of course, the executable permission must have been set).

lsext

```
ls *.$1
```

A run of the **lsext** script with an argument is shown here:

```
$ lsext c
main.c calc.c
```

In the next example, the commands to print out a file with line numbers have been placed in an executable file called **lpnum**, which takes a filename as its argument. The **cat** command with the **-n** option first outputs the contents of the file with line numbers. Then this output is piped into the **lpr** command, which prints it. The command to print out the line numbers is executed in the background.

lpnum

```
cat -n $1 | lpr &
```

A run of the **lpnum** script with an argument is shown here:

```
$ lpnum mydata
```

You may need to reference more than one argument at a time. The number of arguments used may vary. In **lpnum**, you may want to print out three files at one time and five files at some other time. The **$** operator with the asterisk, **$***, references all the arguments on the command line. Using **$*** enables you to create scripts that take a varying number of arguments. In the next example, **lpnum** is rewritten using **$*** so that it can take a different number of arguments each time you use it:

lpnum

```
cat -n $* | lpr &
```

A run of the **lpnum** script with multiple arguments is shown here:

```
$ lpnum mydata preface
```

Environment Variables and Subshells: export and setenv

When you log in to your account, your Linux system generates your user shell. Within this shell, you can issue commands and declare variables. You can also create and execute shell scripts. However, when you execute a shell script, the system generates a subshell. You then have two shells, the one you logged in to and the one generated for the script. Within the script shell you can execute another shell script, which will then have its own shell. When a script has finished execution, its shell terminates and you enter back to the shell from which it was executed. In this sense, you can have many shells, each nested within the other.

Variables that you define within a shell are local to it. If you define a variable in a shell script, then, when the script is run, the variable is defined with that script's shell and is local to it. No other shell can reference it. In a sense, the variable is hidden within its shell.

To illustrate this situation more clearly, the next example will use two scripts, one of which is called from within the other. When the first script executes, it generates its own shell. From within this shell, another script is executed which, in turn, generates its own shell. In the next example, the user first executes the **dispfirst** script, which displays a first name. When the **dispfirst** script executes, it generates its own shell and then, within that shell, it defines the `firstname` variable. After it displays the contents of `firstname`, the script executes another script: **displast**. When **displast** executes, it generates its own shell. It defines the `lastname` variable within its shell and then displays the contents of `lastname`. It then tries to reference `firstname` and display its contents. It cannot do so because `firstname` is local to **dispfirst's** shell and cannot be referenced outside it. An error message is displayed indicating that for the **displast** shell, `firstname` is an undefined variable.

dispfirst

```
firstname="Charles"

echo "First name is $firstname"

displast
```

displast

```
lastname="Dickens"

echo "Last name is $lastname"
echo "$firstname $lastname"
```

The run of the **dispfirst** script is shown here:

```
$ dispfirst
First name is Charles
Last name is Dickens
 Dickens
sh: firstname: not found
```

If you want the same value of a variable used both in a script's shell and a subshell, you can simply define the variable twice, once in each script, and assign it the same value. In the previous example, there is a `myfile` variable defined in **dispfile** and in **printfile**. The user executes the **b** script, which first displays the list file with line numbers. When the **dispfile** script executes, it generates its own shell and then, within that shell, it defines the `myfile` variable. After it displays the contents of the file, the script then executes another script **printfile**. When **printfile** executes, it generates its own shell. It defines its own `myfile` variable within its shell and then sends a file to the printer.

What if you want to define a variable in one shell and have its value referenced in any subshell? For example, what if you want to define the `myfile` variable in the **dispfile** script and have its value, "List", referenced from within the **printfile** script, rather than explicitly defining another variable in **printfile**? Since variables are local to the shell they are defined in, there is no way you can do this with ordinary variables. However, there is a type of variable called an *environment variable* that allows its value to be referenced by any subshells. Environment variables constitute an environment for the shell and any subshell it generates, no matter how deeply nested.

dispfile

```
myfile="List"

echo "Displaying $myfile"
pr -t -n $myfile
```

printfile

```
printfile

myfile="List"

echo "Printing $myfile"
lp $myfile &
```

The run of the **dispfile** script is shown here:

```
$ dispfile
Displaying List
1 screen
2 modem
3 paper
Printing List
```

You can define environment variables in the three major types of shells: Bourne, Korn, and C. However, the strategy used to implement environmental variables in the Bourne and Korn shells is very different from that of the C shell. In the Bourne and Korn shells, environmental variables are exported. That is to say, a copy of an environmental variable is made in each subshell. In a sense, if the `myfile` variable is exported, a copy is automatically defined in each subshell for you. In the C shell, on the other hand, an environmental variable is defined only once and can be directly referenced by any subshell.

Shell Environment Variables

In the Bourne, BASH, and Korn shells, an environment variable can be thought of as a regular variable with added capabilities. To make an environment variable, you apply the `export` command to a variable you have already defined. The `export` command instructs the system to define a copy of that variable for each new shell generated. Each new shell will have its own copy of the environment variable. This process is called *exporting variables*.

In the next example, the variable `myfile` is defined in the **dispfile** script. It is then turned into an environment variable using the `export` command. The `myfile` variable will consequently be exported to any subshells, such as that generated when **printfile** is executed.

dispfile

```
myfile="List"
export myfile

echo "Displaying $myfile"
pr -t -n $myfile

printfile
```

printfile

```
echo "Printing $myfile"
lp $myfile &
```

The run of the **dispfile** script is shown here:

```
$ dispfile
Displaying List
1 screen
2 modem
3 paper
Printing List
```

When **printfile** is executed it will be given its own copy of `myfile` and can reference that copy within its own shell. You no longer need to explicitly define another `myfile` variable in **printfile**.

It is a mistake to think of exported environment variables as global variables. A new shell can never reference a variable outside of itself. Instead, a copy of the variable with its value is generated for the new shell. You can think of exported variables as exporting their values to a shell, not themselves. For those familiar with programming structures, exported variables can be thought of as a form of call-by-value.

Control Structures

You can control the execution of Linux commands in a shell script with control structures. Control structures allow you to repeat commands and to select certain commands over others. A control structure consists of two major components: a test and commands. If the test is successful, then the commands are executed. In this way, you can use control structures to make decisions as to whether commands should be executed.

Two different kinds of control structures are used: *loops*, which repeat commands, and *conditions*, which execute commands when certain conditions are met. The BASH shell has three loop control structures—**while**, **for**, and **for-in**—and two condition structures—**if** and **case**. The control structures have as their test the execution of a Linux command. All Linux commands return an exit status after they have finished executing. If a command is successful, its exit status will be 0. If the command fails for any reason, its exit status will be a positive value referencing the type of failure that occurred. The control structures check to see whether the exit status of a Linux command is 0 or some other value. In the case of the **if** and **while** structures, if the exit status is a 0 value, the command was successful and the structure continues.

Test Operations

With the `test` command, you can compare integers and strings, and even perform logical operations. The command consists of the keyword `test` followed by the values being compared, separated by an option that specifies what kind of comparison is taking place. The option can be thought of as the operator, but it is written, like other options, with a minus sign and letter codes. For example, `-eq` is the option that represents the equality comparison. Two string operations, however, actually use an operator instead of an option. When you compare two strings for equality, you use the equal sign (=). For inequality you use `!=`. Table 23-1 lists some of the commonly used options and operators used by `test`. The syntax for the `test` command is shown here:

```
test value -option value
test string = string
```

Integer Comparisons	Function
-gt	Greater-than
-lt	Less-than
-ge	Greater-than-or-equal-to
-le	Less-than-or-equal-to
-eq	Equal
-ne	Not-equal
String Comparisons	
-z	Tests for empty string
=	Equal strings
!=	Not-equal strings
Logical Operations	
-a	Logical AND
-o	Logical OR
!	Logical NOT
File Tests	
-f	File exists and is a regular file
-s	File is not empty
-r	File is readable
-w	File can be written to, modified
-x	File is executable
-d	Filename is a directory name

Table 23-1: BASH Shell Test Operators

The next example compares two integer values to determine whether they are equal. In this case, the equality option, `-eq`, should be used. The exit status of the `test` command is examined to determine the result of the test operation. The shell special variable **$?** holds the exit status of the most recently executed Linux command.

```
$ num=5
$ test $num -eq 10
$ echo $?
1
```

Instead of using the keyword **test** for the **test** command, you can use enclosing brackets. The command **test $greeting = "hi"** can be written as

```
$ [ $greeting = "hi" ]
```

Similarly, the command **test $num -eq 10** can be written as

```
$ [ $num -eq 10 ]
```

The brackets themselves must be surrounded by white space: a space, TAB, or ENTER. Without the spaces, the code is invalid.

Conditional Control Structures

The BASH shell has a set of conditional control structures that allow you to choose what Linux commands to execute. Many of these are similar to conditional control structures found in programming languages, but there are some differences. The **if** condition tests the success of a Linux command, not an expression. Furthermore, the end of an **if-then** command must be indicated with the keyword **fi**, and the end of a **case** command is indicated with the keyword **esac**. The condition control structures are listed in Table 23-2.

The **if** structure places a condition on commands. That condition is the exit status of a specific Linux command. If a command is successful, returning an exit status of 0, then the commands within the **if** structure are executed. If the exit status is anything other than 0, the command has failed and the commands within the **if** structure are not executed. The **if** command begins with the keyword **if** and is followed by a Linux command whose exit condition will be evaluated. The keyword **fi** ends the command.

The **elsels** script in the next example executes the **ls** command to list files with two different possible options, either by size or with all file information. If the user enters an **s**, files are listed by size; otherwise, all file information is listed.

elsels

```
echo Enter s to list file sizes,
echo        otherwise all file information is listed.
echo -n "Please enter option: "
read choice
if [  "$choice" = s  ]
    then
        ls -s
    else
        ls -l
fi
echo Good-bye
```

Condition Control Structures: if, else, elif, case	Function
if *command* **then** *command* **fi**	**if** executes an action if its test command is true.

if *command* **then**
 command
else
 command
fi
	if-else executes an action if the exit status of its test command is true; if false, the **else** action is executed.

if *command* **then**
 command
elif *command* **then**
 command
else
 command
fi
	elif allows you to nest **if** structures, enabling selection among several alternatives; at the first true **if** structure, its commands are executed and control leaves the entire **elif** structure.

case *string* **in** *pattern*) *command;;* **esac**	**case** matches the string value to any of several patterns; if a pattern is matched, its associated commands are executed.
command **&&** *command*	The logical AND condition returns a true 0 value if both commands return a true 0 value; if one returns a nonzero value, then the AND condition is false and also returns a nonzero value.
command || *command*	The logical OR condition returns a true 0 value if one or the other command returns a true 0 value; if both commands return a nonzero value, then the OR condition is false and also returns a nonzero value.
! *command*	The logical NOT condition inverts the return value of the command.
Loop Control Structures: while, until, for, for-in, select	
while *command* **do** *command* **done**	**while** executes an action as long as its test command is true.
until *command* **do** *command* **done**	**until** executes an action as long as its test command is false.
for *variable* **in** *list-values* **do** *command* **done**	**for-in** is designed for use with lists of values; the variable operand is consecutively assigned the values in the list.

for *variable* **do** *command* **done**	**for** is designed for reference script arguments; the variable operand is consecutively assigned each argument value.
select *string* **in** *item-list* **do** *command* **done**	**select** creates a menu based on the items in the *item-list*; then it executes the command; the command is usually a **case**.

Table 23-2:BASH Shell Control Structures

A run of the program follows:

```
$ elsels
Enter s to list file sizes,
otherwise all file information is listed.
Please enter option: s
total 2
     1 monday     2 today
```

Loop Control Structures

The **while** loop repeats commands. A **while** loop begins with the keyword **while** and is followed by a Linux command. The keyword **do** follows on the next line. The end of the loop is specified by the keyword **done**. The Linux command used in **while** structures is often a test command indicated by enclosing brackets.

The **for-in** structure is designed to reference a list of values sequentially. It takes two operands: a variable and a list of values. The values in the list are assigned one by one to the variable in the **for-in** structure. Like the **while** command, the **for-in** structure is a loop. Each time through the loop, the next value in the list is assigned to the variable. When the end of the list is reached, the loop stops. Like the **while** loop, the body of a **for-in** loop begins with the keyword **do** and ends with the keyword **done**. The **cbackup** script makes a backup of each file and places it in a directory called **sourcebak**. Notice the use of the * special character to generate a list of all filenames with a **.c** extension.

cbackup

```
for backfile in *.c
do
     cp $backfile sourcebak/$backfile
 echo $backfile
done
```

A run of the program follows:

```
$ cbackup
io.c
lib.c
main.c
$
```

The **for** structure without a specified list of values takes as its list of values the command line arguments. The arguments specified on the command line when the shell file is invoked become a list of values referenced by the `for` command. The variable used in the `for` command is set automatically to each argument value in sequence. The first time through the loop, the variable is set to the value of the first argument. The second time, it is set to the value of the second argument.

24. Shell Configuration

Shell Configuration Files

Configuration Directories and Files

Aliases

Controlling Shell Operations

Environment Variables and Subshells: export

Configuring Your Shell with Shell Parameters

Four different major shells are commonly used on Linux systems: the Bourne Again shell (BASH), the AT&T Korn shell, the TCSH shell, and the Z shell. The BASH shell is an advanced version of the Bourne shell, which includes most of the advanced features developed for the Korn shell and the C shell. TCSH is an enhanced version of the C shell, originally developed for BSD versions of UNIX. The AT&T UNIX Korn shell is open source. The Z shell is an enhanced version of the Korn shell. Although their UNIX counterparts differ greatly, the Linux shells share many of the same features. In UNIX, the Bourne shell lacks many capabilities found in the other UNIX shells. In Linux, however, the BASH shell incorporates all the advanced features of the Korn shell and C shell, as well as the TCSH shell. All four shells are available for your use, though the BASH shell is the default.

Command	Description
`bash`	BASH shell, **/bin/bash**
`bsh`	BASH shell, **/bin/bsh** (link to **/bin/bash**)
`sh`	BASH shell, **/bin/sh** (link to **/bin/bash**)
`tcsh`	TCSH shell, **/usr/tcsh**
`csh`	TCSH shell , **/bin/csh** (link to **/bin/tcsh**)
`ksh`	Korn shell, **/bin/ksh** (also added link **/usr/bin/ksh**)
`zsh`	Z shell, **/bin/zsh**

Table 24-1: Shell Invocation Command Names

The BASH shell is the default shell for most Linux distributions. If you are logging in to a command line interface, you will be placed in the default shell automatically and given a shell prompt at which to enter your commands. The shell prompt for the BASH shell is a dollar sign (**$**). In the GUI interface, such as GNOME or KDE, you can open a terminal window that will display a command line interface with the prompt for the default shell (BASH). Though you log in to your default shell or display it automatically in a terminal window, you can change to another shell by entering its name. Entering **tcsh** invokes the TCSH shell, **bash** the BASH shell, **ksh** the Korn shell, and **zsh** the Z shell. You can leave a shell by pressing CTRL-D or using the **exit** command. You only need one type of shell to do your work. Table 24-1 shows the different commands you can use to invoke different shells. Some shells have added links you can use to invoke the same shell, like **sh** and **bsh**, which link to and invoke the **bash** command for the BASH shell.

This chapter describes common features of the BASH shell, such as aliases, as well as how to configure the shell to your own needs using shell variables and initialization files. The other shells share many of the same features and use similar variables and configuration files.

Though the basic shell features and configurations are shown here, you should consult the respective online manuals and FAQs for each shell for more detailed examples and explanations.

Shell Initialization and Configuration Files

Each type of shell has its own set of initialization and configuration files. The TCSH shell uses **.login**, **.tcshrc**, and **.logout** files in place of **.profile**, **.bashrc**, and **.bash_logout**. The Z shell has several initialization files: **.zshenv**, **.zlogin**, **.zprofile**, **.zschrc**, and **.zlogout**. See Table 24-2 for a listing. Check the Man pages for each shell to see how they are usually configured. When you install a shell, default versions of these files are automatically placed in the users' home directories. Except for the TCSH shell, all shells use much the same syntax for variable definitions and assigning values (TCSH uses a slightly different syntax, described in its Man pages).

Filename	Function
BASH Shell	
.profile	Login initialization file
.bashrc	BASH shell configuration file
.bash_logout	Logout name
.bash_history	History file
/etc/profile	System login initialization file
/etc/bashrc	System BASH shell configuration file
/etc/profile.d	Directory for specialized BASH shell configuration files
/etc/bash_completion	Completion options for applications
TCSH Shell	
.login	Login initialization file
.tcshrc	TCSH shell configuration file
.logout	Logout file
Z Shell	
.zshenv	Shell login file (first read)
.zprofile	Login initialization file
.zlogin	Shell login file
.zshrc	Z shell configuration file
.zlogout	Logout file
Korn Shell	
.profile	Login initialization file
.kshrc	KORN shell configuration file

Table 24-2: Shell Configuration Files

Configuration Directories and Files

Applications often install configuration files in a user's home directory that contain specific configuration information, which tailors the application to the needs of that particular user. This may take the form of a single configuration file that begins with a period, or a directory that contains several configuration files. The directory name will also begin with a period. For example, Mozilla installs a directory called **.mozilla** in the user's home directory that contains configuration files. On the other hand, many mail applications uses a single file called **.mailrc** to hold alias and feature settings set up by the user, though others like Evolution also have their own, **.evolution**. Most single configuration files end in the letters **rc**. **FTP** uses a file called **.netrc**. Most newsreaders use a file called **.newsrc**. Entries in configuration files are usually set by the application, though you can usually make entries directly by editing the file. Applications have their own set of special variables to which you can define and assign values. You can list the configuration files in your home directory with the `ls -a` command.

Aliases

You use the `alias` command to create another name for a command. The `alias` command operates like a macro that expands to the command it represents. The alias does not literally replace the name of the command; it simply gives another name to that command. An `alias` command begins with the keyword `alias` and the new name for the command, followed by an equal sign and the command the alias will reference.

Note: No spaces should be placed around the equal sign used in the `alias` command.

In the next example, `list` becomes another name for the `ls` command:

```
$ alias list=ls
$ ls
mydata today
$ list
mydata today
$
```

If you want an alias to be automatically defined, you have to enter the alias operation in a shell configuration file. On Ubuntu, aliases are defined in either the user's **.bashrc** file or in a **.bash_aliases** file. To use a **.bash_aliases** file, you have to first uncomment the commands in the .bashrc file that will read the **.bash_aliases** file. Just edit the **.bashrc** file and remove the preceding # so it appears like the following:

```
if [ -f ~/.bash_aliases ]; then
    . ~/.bash_aliases
fi
```

You can also place aliases in the **.bashrc** file directly. Some are already defined, though commented out. You can edit the **.bashrc** file and remove the # comment symbols from those lines to activate the aliases.

```
# some more ls aliases
alias ll='ls -l'
alias la='ls -A'
alias l='ls -CF'
```

Aliasing Commands and Options

You can also use an alias to substitute for a command and its option, but you need to enclose both the command and the option within single quotes. Any command you alias that contains spaces must be enclosed in single quotes as well. In the next example, the alias `lss` references the `ls` command with its `-s` option, and the alias `lsa` references the `ls` command with the `-F` option. The `ls` command with the `-s` option lists files and their sizes in blocks, and `ls` with the **-F** option places a slash after directory names. Notice how single quotes enclose the command and its option.

```
$ alias lss='ls -s'
$ lss
mydata 14   today  6   reports  1
$ alias lsa='ls -F'
$ lsa
mydata today reports/
$
```

Aliases are helpful for simplifying complex operations. In the next example, `listlong` becomes another name for the `ls` command with the **-l** option (the long format that lists all file information), as well as the **-h** option for using a human-readable format for file sizes. Be sure to encase the command and its arguments within single quotes so that they are taken as one argument and not parsed by the shell.

```
$ alias listlong='ls -lh'
$ listlong
-rw-r--r--   1 root   root   51K  Sep  18  2008 mydata
-rw-r--r--   1 root   root   16K  Sep  27  2008 today
```

Aliasing Commands and Arguments

You may often use an alias to include a command name with an argument. If you execute a command that has an argument with a complex combination of special characters on a regular basis, you may want to alias it. For example, suppose you often list just your source code and object code files—those files ending in either a **.c** or **.o**. You would need to use as an argument for `ls` a combination of special characters such as ***.[co]**. Instead, you can alias `ls` with the **.[co]** argument, giving it a simple name. In the next example, the user creates an alias called `lsc` for the command `ls.[co]`:

```
$ alias lsc='ls *.[co]'
$ lsc
main.c main.o lib.c lib.o
```

Aliasing Commands

You can also use the name of a command as an alias. This can be helpful in cases where you should use a command only with a specific option. In the case of the **rm**, **cp**, and **mv** commands, the **-i** option should always be used to ensure an existing file is not overwritten. Instead of always being careful to use the **-i** option each time you use one of these commands, you can alias the command name to include the option. In the next example, the **rm**, **cp**, and **mv** commands have been aliased to include the **-i** option:

```
$ alias rm='rm -i'
$ alias mv='mv -i'
$ alias cp='cp -i'
```

The **alias** command by itself provides a list of all aliases that have been defined, showing the commands they represent. You can remove an alias by using the **unalias** command. In the next example, the user lists the current aliases and then removes the `lsa` alias:

```
$ alias
lsa=ls -F
list=ls
rm=rm -i
$ unalias lsa
```

Controlling Shell Operations

The BASH shell has several features that enable you to control the way different shell operations work. For example, setting the `noclobber` feature prevents redirection from overwriting files. You can turn these features on and off like a toggle, using the `set` command. The `set` command takes two arguments: an option specifying on or off and the name of the feature. To set a feature on, you use the –o option, and to set it off, you use the +o option. Here is the basic form:

```
$ set -o feature          turn the feature on
$ set +o feature          turn the feature off
```

Features	Description

$ set -+o *feature*	BASH shell features are turned on and off with the `set` command; –o sets a feature on and +o turns it off:
	$ set -o noclobber *set noclobber on*
	$ set +o noclobber *set noclobber off*

ignoreeof	Disables CTRL-D logout
noclobber	Does not overwrite files through redirection
noglob	Disables special characters used for filename expansion: *, ?, ~, and []

Table 24-3: BASH Shell Special Features

Three of the most common features are `ignoreeof`, `noclobber`, and `noglob`. Table 24-3 lists these different features, as well as the `set` command. Setting `ignoreeof` enables a feature that prevents you from logging out of the user shell with CTRL-D. CTRL-D is not only used to log out of the user shell, but also to end user input entered directly into the standard input. CTRL-D is used often for the Mail program or for utilities such as `cat`. You can easily enter an extra CTRL-D in such circumstances and accidentally log yourself out. The `ignoreeof` feature prevents such accidental logouts. In the next example, the `ignoreeof` feature is turned on using the `set` command with the –o option. The user can then log out only by entering the `logout` command.

```
$ set -o ignoreeof
$ CTRL-D
Use exit to logout
$
```

Environment Variables and Subshells: export

When you log in to your account, Linux generates your user shell. Within this shell, you can issue commands and declare variables. You can also create and execute shell scripts. When you execute a shell script, however, the system generates a subshell. You then have two shells, the one you logged in to and the one generated for the script. Within the script shell, you can execute another shell script, which then has its own shell. When a script has finished execution, its shell terminates and you return to the shell from which it was executed. In this sense, you can have many shells, each nested within the other. Variables you define within a shell are local to it. If you define a variable in a shell script, then, when the script is run, the variable is defined with that script's shell and is local to it. No other shell can reference that variable. In a sense, the variable is hidden within its shell.

You can define environment variables in all types of shells, including the BASH shell, the Z shell, and the TCSH shell. The strategy used to implement environment variables in the BASH shell, however, is different from that of the TCSH shell. In the BASH shell, environment variables are exported. That is to say, a copy of an environment variable is made in each subshell. For example, if the **EDITOR** variable is exported, a copy is automatically defined in each subshell for you. In the TCSH shell, on the other hand, an environment variable is defined only once and can be directly referenced by any subshell.

Shell Variables	Description
BASH	Holds full pathname of BASH command
BASH_VERSION	Displays the current BASH version number
GROUPS	Groups that the user belongs to
HISTCMD	Number of the current command in the history list
HOME	Pathname for user's home directory
HOSTNAME	The hostname
HOSTTYPE	Displays the type of machine the host runs on
OLDPWD	Previous working directory
OSTYPE	Operating system in use
PATH	List of pathnames for directories searched for executable commands
PPID	Process ID for shell's parent shell
PWD	User's working directory
RANDOM	Generates random number when referenced
SHLVL	Current shell level, number of shells invoked
UID	User ID of the current user

Table 24-4: Shell Variables, Set by the Shell

In the BASH shell, an environment variable can be thought of as a regular variable with added capabilities. To make an environment variable, you apply the **export** command to a variable you have already defined. The **export** command instructs the system to define a copy of that variable for each new shell generated. Each new shell will have its own copy of the environment variable. This process is called *exporting variables.* To think of exported environment variables as global variables is a mistake. A new shell can never reference a variable outside of itself. Instead, a copy of the variable with its value is generated for the new shell.

Configuring Your Shell with Shell Parameters

When you log in, Linux will set certain parameters for your login shell. These parameters can take the form of variables or features. See the previous section "Controlling Shell Operations" for a description of how to set features. Linux reserves a predefined set of variables for shell and system use. These are assigned system values, in effect, setting parameters. Linux sets up parameter shell variables you can use to configure your user shell. Many of these parameter shell variables are defined by the system when you log in. Some parameter shell variables are set by the shell automatically, and others are set by initialization scripts, described later. Certain shell variables are set directly by the shell, and others are simply used by it. Many of these other variables are application specific, used for such tasks as mail, history, or editing. Functionally, it may be better to think of these as system-level variables, as they are used to configure your entire system, setting values such as the location of executable commands on your system, or the number of history commands allowable. See Table 24-4 for a list of those shell variables set by the shell for shell-specific tasks; Table 24-5 lists those used by the shell for supporting other applications.

A reserved set of keywords is used for the names of these system variables. You should not use these keywords as the names of any of your own variable names. The system shell variables are all specified in uppercase letters, making them easy to identify. Shell feature variables are in lowercase letters. For example, the keyword HOME is used by the system to define the HOME variable. HOME is a special environment variable that holds the pathname of the user's home directory. On the other hand, the keyword noclobber is used to set the noclobber feature on or off.

Shell Parameter Variables

Many of the shell parameter variables automatically defined and assigned initial values by the system when you log in can be changed, if you wish. Some parameter variables exist whose values should not be changed, however. For example, the HOME variable holds the pathname for your home directory. Commands such as cd reference the pathname in the HOME shell variable to locate your home directory. Some of the more common of these parameter variables are described in this section.

Other parameter variables are defined by the system and given an initial value that you are free to change. To do this, you redefine them and assign a new value. For example, the PATH variable is defined by the system and given an initial value; it contains the pathnames of directories where commands are located. Whenever you execute a command, the shell searches for it in these directories. You can add a new directory to be searched by redefining the PATH variable yourself, so that it will include the new directory's pathname.

Still other parameter variables exist that the system does not define. These are usually optional features, such as the EXINIT variable that enables you to set options for the Vi editor. Each time you log in, you must define and assign a value to such variables. Some of the more common parameter variables are SHELL, PATH, PS1, PS2, and MAIL. The SHELL variable holds the pathname of the program for the type of shell you log in to. The PATH variable lists the different directories to be searched for a Linux command. The PS1 and PS2 variables hold the prompt symbols. The MAIL variable holds the pathname of your mailbox file. You can modify the values for any of these to customize your shell.

Note: You can obtain a listing of the currently defined shell variables using the `env` command. The `env` command operates like the `set` command, but it lists only parameter variables.

Using Initialization Files

You can automatically define parameter variables using special shell scripts called initialization files. An *initialization file* is a specially named shell script executed whenever you enter a certain shell. You can edit the initialization file and place in it definitions and assignments for parameter variables. When you enter the shell, the initialization file will execute these definitions and assignments, effectively initializing parameter variables with your own values. For example, the BASH shell's **.profile** file is an initialization file executed every time you log in. It contains definitions and assignments of parameter variables. However, the **.profile** file is basically only a shell script, which you can edit with any text editor such as the Vi editor; changing, if you wish, the values assigned to parameter variables.

In the BASH shell, all the parameter variables are designed to be environment variables. When you define or redefine a parameter variable, you also need to export it to make it an environment variable. This means any change you make to a parameter variable must be accompanied by an **export** command. You will see that at the end of the login initialization file, **.profile**, there is usually an **export** command for all the parameter variables defined in it.

Your Home Directory: HOME

The `HOME` variable contains the pathname of your home directory. Your home directory is determined by the parameter administrator when your account is created. The pathname for your home directory is automatically read into your `HOME` variable when you log in. In the next example, the `echo` command displays the contents of the `HOME` variable:

```
$ echo $HOME
/home/chris
```

The `HOME` variable is often used when you need to specify the absolute pathname of your home directory. In the next example, the absolute pathname of **reports** is specified using `HOME` for the home directory's path:

```
$ ls $HOME/reports
```

Command Locations: PATH

The `PATH` variable contains a series of directory paths separated by colons. Each time a command is executed, the paths listed in the `PATH` variable are searched one by one for that command. For example, the `cp` command resides on the system in the directory **/bin**. This directory path is one of the directories listed in the `PATH` variable. Each time you execute the `cp` command, this path is searched and the `cp` command located. The system defines and assigns `PATH` an initial set of pathnames. In Linux, the initial pathnames are **/bin** and **/usr/bin**.

Shell Variables	Description

BASH_VERSION	Displays the current BASH version number
CDPATH	Search path for the **cd** command
EXINIT	Initialization commands for Ex/Vi editor
FCEDIT	Editor used by the history **fc** command.
GROUPS	Groups that the user belongs to
HISTFILE	The pathname of the history file
HISTSIZE	Number of commands allowed for history
HISTFILESIZE	Size of the history file in lines
HOME	Pathname for user's home directory
IFS	Interfield delimiter symbol
IGNOREEOF	If not set, EOF character will close the shell. Can be set to the number of EOF characters to ignore before accepting one to close the shell (default is 10)
INPUTRC	Set the **inputrc** configuration file for Readline (command line). Default is current directory, **.inputrc**. Most Linux distributions set this to **/etc/inputrc**
KDEDIR	The pathname location for the KDE desktop
LOGNAME	Login name
MAIL	Name of specific mail file checked by Mail utility for received messages, if MAILPATH is not set
MAILCHECK	Interval for checking for received mail
MAILPATH	List of mail files to be checked by Mail for received messages
HOSTTYPE	Linux platforms, such as i686, x86_64, or ppc
PROMPT_COMMAND	Command to be executed before each prompt, integrating the result as part of the prompt
HISTFILE	The pathname of the history file
PS1	Primary shell prompt
PS2	Secondary shell prompt
SHELL	Pathname of program for type of shell you are using
TERM	Terminal type
TMOUT	Time that the shell remains active awaiting input
USER	Username
UID	Real user ID (numeric)

Table 24-5: System Environment Variables Used by the Shell

The shell can execute any executable file, including programs and scripts you have created. For this reason, the **PATH** variable can also reference your working directory; so if you want to execute one of your own scripts or programs in your working directory, the shell can locate it. No spaces are allowed between the pathnames in the string. A colon with no pathname specified references your working directory. Usually, a single colon is placed at the end of the pathnames as an empty entry specifying your working directory. For example, the pathname **//bin:/usr/bin:** references three directories: **/bin**, **/usr/bin**, and your current working directory.

```
$ echo $PATH
/bin:/usr/sbin:
```

You can add any new directory path you want to the **PATH** variable. This can be useful if you have created several of your own Linux commands using shell scripts. You can place these new shell script commands in a directory you create and then add that directory to the **PATH** list. Then, no matter what directory you are in, you can execute one of your shell scripts. The **PATH** variable will contain the directory for that script, so that directory will be searched each time you issue a command.

You add a directory to the **PATH** variable with a variable assignment. You can execute this assignment directly in your shell. In the next example, the user **chris** adds a new directory, called **bin**, to the **PATH**. Although you could carefully type in the complete pathnames listed in **PATH** for the assignment, you can also use an evaluation of **PATH**—**$PATH**—in its place. In this example, an evaluation of **HOME** is also used to designate the user's home directory in the new directory's pathname. Notice the last colon, which specifies the working directory:

```
$ PATH=$PATH:$HOME/mybin:
$ export PATH
$ echo $PATH
/bin:/usr/bin::/home/chris/mybin
```

If you add a directory to **PATH** yourself while you are logged in, the directory will be added only for the duration of your login session. When you log back in, the login initialization file, **.profile**, will again initialize your **PATH** with its original set of directories. The **.profile** file is described in detail a bit later in this chapter. To add a new directory to your **PATH** permanently, you need to edit your **.profile** file and find the assignment for the **PATH** variable. Then, you simply insert the directory, preceded by a colon, into the set of pathnames assigned to **PATH**.

Specifying the BASH Environment: BASH_ENV

The **BASH_ENV** variable holds the name of the BASH shell initialization file to be executed whenever a BASH shell is generated. For example, when a BASH shell script is executed, the **BASH_ENV** variable is checked and the name of the script that it holds is executed before the shell script. The **BASH_ENV** variable usually holds **$HOME/.bashrc**. This is the **.bashrc** file in the user's home directory. (The **.bashrc** file is discussed later in this chapter.) You can specify a different file if you wish, using that instead of the **.bashrc** file for BASH shell scripts.

Configuring the Shell Prompt

The **PS1** and **PS2** variables contain the primary and secondary prompt symbols, respectively. The primary prompt symbol for the BASH shell is a dollar sign (**$**). You can change the prompt symbol by assigning a new set of characters to the **PS1** variable. In the next example, the shell prompt is changed to the **->** symbol:

```
$ PS1='->'
-> export PS1
->
```

The following table lists the codes for configuring your prompt:

Prompt Codes	Description
\!	Current history number
\$	Use $ as prompt for all users except the root user, which has the # as its prompt
\d	Current date
\#	History command number for just the current shell
\h	Hostname
\s	Shell type currently active
\t	Time of day in hours, minutes, and seconds.
\u	Username
\v	Shell version
\w	Full pathname of the current working directory
\W	Name of the current working directory
\\	Displays a backslash character
\n	Inserts a newline
\[\]	Allows entry of terminal specific display characters for features like color or bold font
\nnn	Character specified in octal format

You can change the prompt to be any set of characters, including a string, as shown in the next example:

```
$ PS1="Please enter a command: "
Please enter a command: export PS1
Please enter a command: ls
mydata /reports
Please enter a command:
```

The **PS2** variable holds the secondary prompt symbol, which is used for commands that take several lines to complete. The default secondary prompt is **>**. The added command lines begin with the secondary prompt instead of the primary prompt. You can change the secondary prompt just as easily as the primary prompt, as shown here:

```
$ PS2="@ "
```

Like the TCSH shell, the BASH shell provides you with a predefined set of codes you can use to configure your prompt. With them you can make the time, your username, or your directory pathname a part of your prompt. You can even have your prompt display the history event number of the current command you are about to enter. Each code is preceded by a \ symbol: \w represents the current working directory, \t the time, and \u your username; \! will display the next history event number. In the next example, the user adds the current working directory to the prompt:

```
$ PS1="\w $"
/home/dylan $
```

The codes must be included within a quoted string. If no quotes exist, the code characters are not evaluated and are themselves used as the prompt. **PS1=\w** sets the prompt to the characters \w, not the working directory. The next example incorporates both the time and the history event number with a new prompt:

```
$ PS1="\t \! ->"
```

The default BASH prompt is \s-\v\$ to display the type of shell, the shell version, and the $ symbol as the prompt. Some distributions have changed this to a more complex command consisting of the user name, the hostname, and the name of the current working directory. A sample configuration is shown here. A simple equivalent is show here with @ sign in the hostname and a $ for the final prompt symbol. The home directory is represented with a tilde (~).

```
$ PS1="\u@\h:\w$"
richard@turtle.com:~$
```

Ubuntu also includes some complex prompt definitions in the **.bashrc** file to support color prompts and detect any remote user logins.

Specifying Your News Server

Several shell parameter variables are used to set values used by network applications, such as web browsers or newsreaders. **NNTPSERVER** is used to set the value of a remote news server accessible on your network. If you are using an ISP, the ISP usually provides a Usenet news server you can access with your newsreader applications. However, you first have to provide your newsreaders with the Internet address of the news server. This is the role of the **NNTPSERVER** variable. News servers on the Internet usually use the NNTP protocol. **NNTPSERVER** should hold the address of such a news server. For many ISPs, the news server address is a domain name that begins with **nntp**. The following example assigns the news server address **nntp.myservice.com** to the **NNTPSERVER** shell variable. Newsreader applications automatically obtain the news server address from **NNTPSERVER**. Usually, this assignment is placed in the shell initialization file, **.profile**, so that it is automatically set each time a user logs in.

```
NNTPSERVER=news.myservice.com
export NNTPSERVER
```

Configuring Your Login Shell: .profile

The **.profile** file is the BASH shell's login initialization file. It is a script file that is automatically executed whenever a user logs in. The file contains shell commands that define system environment variables used to manage your shell. They may be either redefinitions of system-defined variables or definitions of user-defined variables. For example, when you log in, your user shell needs to know what directories hold Linux commands. It will reference the **PATH** variable to find the pathnames for these directories. However, first, the **PATH** variable must be assigned those pathnames. In the **.profile** file, an assignment operation does just this. Because it is in the **.profile** file, the assignment is executed automatically when the user logs in.

.profile

```
# ~/.profile: executed by the command interpreter for login shells.
# This file is not read by bash(1), if ~/.bash_profile or ~/.bash_login
# exists.
# see /usr/share/doc/bash/examples/startup-files for examples.
# the files are located in the bash-doc package.

# the default umask is set in /etc/profile
#umask 022

# if running bash
if [ -n "$BASH_VERSION" ]; then
    # include .bashrc if it exists
    if [ -f "$HOME/.bashrc" ]; then
        . "$HOME/.bashrc"
    fi
fi

# set PATH so it includes user's private bin if it exists
if [ -d "$HOME/bin" ] ; then
    PATH="$HOME/bin:$PATH"
fi
```

Exporting Variables

Any new parameter variables you may add to the **.profile** file, will also need to be exported, using the **export** command. This makes them accessible to any subshells you may enter. You can export several variables in one **export** command by listing them as arguments. The **.profile** file contain no variable definitions, though you can add ones of your own. In this case, the **.profile** file would have an **export** command with a list of all the variables defined in the file. If a variable is missing from this list, you may be unable to access it. The **.bashrc** file contain a definition of the **HISTCONTROL** variable, which is then exported. You can also combine the assignment and **export** command into one operation as shown here for **NNTPSERVER**:

```
export NNTPSERVER=news.myservice.com
```

Variable Assignments

A copy of the standard **.profile** file, provided for you when your account is created, is listed in the next example. Notice how **PATH** is assigned. **PATH** is a parameter variable the system has already defined. **PATH** holds the pathnames of directories searched for any command you enter. The assignment **PATH="$PATH:$HOME/bin"** has the effect of redefining **PATH** to include your **bin** directory within your home directory so that your **bin** directory will also be searched for any commands, including ones you create yourself, such as scripts or programs.

Should you want to have your current working directory searched also, you can use any text editor to add another PATH line in your **.profile** file **PATH="$PATH:"**. You would insert a colon : after **PATH**. In fact, you can change this entry to add as many directories as you want to search. Making commands automatically executable in your current working directory could be a security risk, allowing files in any directory to be executed, instead of in certain specified directories. An example of how to modify your **.profile** file is shown in the following section.

```
PATH="$PATH:"
```

Editing Your BASH Profile Script

Your **.profile** initialization file is a text file that can be edited by a text editor, like any other text file. You can easily add new directories to your **PATH** by editing **.profile** and using editing commands to insert a new directory pathname in the list of directory pathnames assigned to the **PATH** variable. You can even add new variable definitions. If you do so, however, be sure to include the new variable's name in the **export** command's argument list. For example, if your **.profile** file does not have any definition of the **EXINIT** variable, you can edit the file and add a new line that assigns a value to **EXINIT**. The definition **EXINIT='set nu ai'** will configure the Vi editor with line numbering and indentation. You then need to add **EXINIT** to the **export** command's argument list. When the **.profile** file executes again, the **EXINIT** variable will be set to the command **set nu ai**. When the Vi editor is invoked, the command in the **EXINIT** variable will be executed, setting the line number and auto-indent options automatically.

.profile

```
# ~/.profile: executed by the command interpreter for login shells.
# This file is not read by bash(1), if ~/.bash_profile or ~/.bash_login
# exists.
# see /usr/share/doc/bash/examples/startup-files for examples.
# the files are located in the bash-doc package.

# the default umask is set in /etc/profile
#umask 022

# if running bash
if [ -n "$BASH_VERSION" ]; then
    # include .bashrc if it exists
    if [ -f "$HOME/.bashrc" ]; then
        . "$HOME/.bashrc"
    fi
fi

# set PATH so it includes user's private bin if it exists
if [ -d "$HOME/bin" ] ; then
    PATH="$HOME/bin:$PATH"
fi

HISTSIZE=30
NNTPSERVER=news.myserver.com
EXINIT='set nu ai'
PS1="\w \$"
export PATH HISTSIZE EXINIT PS1 NNTPSERVER
```

In the following example, the user's **.profile** has been modified to include definitions of **EXINIT** and redefinitions of **PATH**, **PS1**, and **HISTSIZE**. The **PATH** variable has the ending colon added to it that specifies the current working directory, enabling you to execute commands that may be located in either the home directory or the working directory. The redefinition of **HISTSIZE** reduces the number of history events saved, from 1,000 defined in the system's **.profile** file, to 30.

The redefinition of the PS1 parameter variable changes the prompt to just show the pathname of the current working directory. Any changes you make to parameter variables within your **.profile** file override those made earlier by the system's **.profile** file. All these parameter variables are then exported with the **export** command.

Manually Re-executing the .profile script

Although the **.profile** script is executed each time you log in, it is not automatically re-executed after you make changes to it. The **.profile** script is an initialization file that is executed *only* whenever you log in. If you want to take advantage of any changes you make to it without having to log out and log in again, you can re-execute the **.profile** script with the dot (.) command. The **.profile** script is a shell script and, like any shell script, can be executed with the . command.

```
$ . .profile
```

Alternatively, you can use the **source** command to execute the **.profile** initialization file or any initialization file such as **.login** used in the TCSH shell or **.bashrc**.

```
$ source .profile
```

System Shell Profile Script

Your Linux system also has its own profile file that it executes whenever any user logs in. This system initialization file is simply called **profile** and is found in the **/etc** directory, **/etc/profile**. This file contains parameter variable definitions the system needs to provide for each user. On Ubuntu, the **/etc/profile** script checks the /etc/profile.d directory for any shell configuration scripts to run, and then runs the **/etc/bash.baschrc** script, which performs most of the configuration tasks.

The number of configuration settings needed for different applications would make the **/etc/profile** file much too large to manage. Instead, application task-specific aliases and variables are placed in separate configuration files located in the **/etc/profile.d** directory. There are corresponding scripts for both the BASH and C shells. The BASH shell scripts are run from **/etc/profile** with the following commands. A for loop sequentially acceses eash script and executes it with the dot (.) operator.

```
for i in /etc/profile.d/*.sh; do
  if [ -r $i ]; then
    . $i
  fi
done
```

For a basic install, you will have only the **gvfs-bash-completion.sh** script. As you install other shells and application there may be more. The **/etc/profile.d** scripts are named for the kinds of tasks and applications they configure. Files run by the BASH shell end in the extension **.sh**, and those run by the C shell have the extension **.csh**. The **/etc/profile** script will also check first if the **PS1** variable is defined before running any **/etc/profile.d** scripts.

A copy of the system's **.profile** file follows

/etc/profile

```
# /etc/profile: system-wide .profile file for the Bourne shell (sh(1))
# and Bourne compatible shells (bash(1), ksh(1), ash(1), ...).

if [ -d /etc/profile.d ]; then
  for i in /etc/profile.d/*.sh; do
    if [ -r $i ]; then
      . $i
    fi
  done
  unset i
fi

if [ "$PS1" ]; then
  if [ "$BASH" ]; then
    PS1='\u@\h:\w\$ '
    if [ -f /etc/bash.bashrc ]; then
      . /etc/bash.bashrc
    fi
  else
    if [ "`id -u`" -eq 0 ]; then
      PS1='# '
    else
      PS1='$ '
    fi
  fi
fi

umask 022
```

Configuring the BASH Shell: .bashrc

The **.bashrc** scruot is a configuration file executed each time you enter the BASH shell or generate any subshells. If the BASH shell is your login shell, **.bashrc** is executed along with your **.profile** script when you log in. If you enter the BASH shell from another shell, the **.bashrc** script is automatically executed, and the variable and alias definitions it contains will be defined. If you enter a different type of shell, the configuration file for that shell will be executed instead. For example, if you were to enter the TCSH shell with the **tcsh** command, the **.tcshrc** configuration file would be executed instead of **.bashrc**.

The User .bashrc BASH Script

The **.bashrc** shell configuration file is actually executed each time you generate a BASH shell, such as when you run a shell script. In other words, each time a subshell is created, the **.bashrc** file is executed. This has the effect of exporting any local variables or aliases you have defined in the **.bashrc** shell initialization file. The **.bashrc** file usually contains the definition of aliases and any feature variables used to turn on shell features. Aliases and feature variables are locally defined within the shell. But the **.bashrc** file defines them in every shell. For this reason, the **.bashrc** file usually holds aliases and options you want defined for each shell. As an example of how you can add your own aliases and options, aliases for the **rm**, **cp**, and **mv** commands and the shell **noclobber** and **ignoreeof** options have been added. For the root user **.bashrc**, the **rm**, **cp**, and **mv** aliases have already been included in the root's **.bashrc** file.

The **.bashrc** file will check for aliases in a **.bash_aliases** file and run **/etc/bash_completion** for command completion directives.

The **.bashrc** file will set several features including history, prompt, alias, and command completion settings. The **HISTCONTROL** directive is defined to ignore duplicate commands.

```
# don't put duplicate lines in the history. See bash(1)
# for more options export HISTCONTROL=ignoredups
# ... and ignore same successive entries.
export HISTCONTROL=ignoreboth
```

Several commands then define the shell prompt, beginning with **PS1=**. The code for reading the user's **.bash_aliases** script is included. Possible aliases are also provided. Both are commented. You can remove the comment symbols, **#**, to activate them.

```
# Alias definitions.
# You may want to put all your additions into a separate file like
# ~/.bash_aliases, instead of adding them here directly.
# See /usr/share/doc/bash-doc/examples in the bash-doc package.

#if [ -f ~/.bash_aliases ]; then
#    . ~/.bash_aliases
#fi

# some more ls aliases
#alias ll='ls -l'
#alias la='ls -A'
#alias l='ls -CF'
```

The **.bash_completion** file is then read to set up command completion options:

```
# enable programmable completion features (you don't need to enable
# this, if it's already enabled in /etc/bash.bashrc and /etc/profile
# sources /etc/bash.bashrc).
if [ -f /etc/bash_completion ]; then
    . /etc/bash_completion
fi
```

You can add any commands or definitions of your own to your **.bashrc** file. If you have made changes to **.bashrc** and you want them to take effect during your current login session, you need to re-execute the file with either the **.** or the **source** command:

```
$ . .bashrc
```

The System /etc/bash.bashrc BASH Script

Ubuntu also has a system **bashrc** file executed for all users, called **bash.bashrc**. Currently the **/etc/bash.bashrc** file sets the default shell prompt, as well as instructions for checking whether a user is authorized to use a command. The bash.bashrc file is shown here:

```
# set a fancy prompt (non-color, overwrite the one in /etc/profile)
PS1='${debian_chroot:+($debian_chroot)}\u@\h:\w\$ '

# sudo hint
if [ ! -e $HOME/.sudo_as_admin_successful ]; then
    case " $(groups) " in *\ admin\ *)
    if [ -x /usr/bin/sudo ]; then
      cat <<-EOF
      To run a command as administrator (user "root"), use "sudo <command>".
      See "man sudo_root" for details.

      EOF
    fi
    esac
fi

# if the command-not-found package is installed, use it
if [ -x /usr/lib/command-not-found ]; then
    function command_not_found_handle {
                if [ -x /usr/lib/command-not-found ]; then

                /usr/bin/python /usr/lib/command-not-found -- $1
                return $?
    else

                return 127
      }
fi
```

The BASH Shell Logout File: .bash_logout

The **.bash_logout** file is also a configuration file, but it is executed when the user logs out. It is designed to perform any operations you want to occur whenever you log out. Instead of variable definitions, the **.bash_logout** file usually contains shell commands that form a kind of shutdown procedure—actions you always want taken before you log out. One common logout command is to clear the screen and then issue a farewell message.

As with **.profile**, you can add your own shell commands to **.bash_logout**. In fact, the **.bash_logout** file is not automatically set up for you when your account is first created. You need to create it yourself, using the Vi or Emacs editor. You could then add a farewell message or other operations. The default **.bash_logout** file includes instructions to invoke the **clear_console** command to clear the screen.

.bash_logout

```
# ~/.bash_logout: executed by bash(1) when login shell exits.
# when leaving the console clear the screen to increase privacy

    if [ "$SHLVL" = 1 ]; then
          [ -x /usr/bin/clear_console ] && /usr/bin/clear_console -q
    fi
```

As with **.profile**, you can add your own shell commands to **.bash_logout**. The root user **.bash_logout** file includes instructions to invoke the **clear** command to clear the screen. In the next example, the user has added an echo command in the **.bash_logout** file.

Appendix A: Getting Ubuntu

The Ubuntu Linux distribution installs a professional-level and very stable Linux system along with the KDE and GNOME GUI interfaces, flexible and easy-to-use system configuration tools, an extensive set of Internet servers, a variety of different multimedia applications, and thousands of Linux applications of all kinds. You can find recent information about Ubuntu at **www.ubuntu.com**.

Most Ubuntu software is available for download from the Ubuntu repository. Install disks are available also, either as smaller desktop only installs, or larger server installs. You normally use the Ubuntu Desktop Live CD to install Ubuntu. Ubuntu distribution strategy relies on install disks with a selected collection of software that can be later updated and enhanced from the very large collection of software on the Ubuntu repository. This means that the collection of software in an initial installation can be relatively small. Software on the Ubuntu repository is also continually updated, so any installation will likely have to undergo extensive updates from the repository.

With smaller install disks, you can quickly download and burn an Ubuntu install image. The Desktop Live CD is available from the GetUbuntu page on the Ubuntu Web site. There are 32 bit and 64 bit versions for all current releases. The release covered in this book is the 9.04 release, Jaunty Jackalope.

www.ubuntu.com/getubuntu

In addition, there are Server and Alternate versions as well as an Install DVD. These you can download ISO images for all versions directly from the following site.

http://releases.ubuntu.com/jaunty

This site also includes the torrents for the versions, letting you use a BitTorrent client to download the CD or DVD image. Torrents are also listed at:

http://torrent.ubuntu.com

You can also use Jigdo to download an image from various mirrors at once, switching to the fastest as their access loads change.

Also, there are several editions of Ubuntu that you can download from the respective edition Web site. Edubuntu and Kubuntu are available at **http://releases.ubuntu.com**. The others can be downloaded from **http://cdimages.ubuntu.com**.

> ➤ **www.edubuntu.org** Educational version

> ➤ **www.xubuntu.org**   Xfce desktop version

> ➤ **www.kubuntu.org**   KDE desktop version

> ➤ **http://wiki.ubuntu.com/Gobuntu** Open Source only version

The Ubuntu Network Remix image (UNR) is a USB image designed for use on netbook PCs. The UNR can operate like a Live USB image. It is designed for netbook PCs with up to 10 inch screens and a minimum 256MB RAM. The image file is named **ubuntu-9.04-netbook-remix-i386.img**. The UNR is available at **http://releases.ubuntu.com/jaunty** and at **http://www.ubuntu.com/getubuntu/download-netbook**. You use USB Imagewriter (**usb-imagewriter** package) to burn it on Ubuntu. For details see:

```
https://help.ubuntu.com/community/Installation/FromImgFiles
```

Install/Live DVD and MID USB images

The Install/Live DVD and MID USB file images are available either as a torrent files or full image files at **http://cdimages.ubuntu.com** under the **releases/jaunty/release** directory.

```
http://cdimages.ubuntu.com/releases/jaunty/release/
```

The Install/Live DVD image file is a large file, about 4.3 GB.

Ubuntu also provides a Low-Power Intel Architecture MID USB image for handheld devices using the Intel Atom and A1xx processors. This is a Live CD image that can be burned to a USB drive, which can then be run on the handheld directly from the USB drive. The MID USB image is available from **http://releases.ubuntu.com** as **ubuntu-9.04-mid-lpia.img**.

Additional editions

Additional community supported editions are also available like Kubuntu-4 with KDE release 4, mythbuntu for MythTV, and UbuntuStudio with image development software. You can download these, along with the other editions from

```
http://cdimages.ubuntu.com
```

Once you have the install image, you will need to burn it to a DVD or CD disk, which you can then use to install your system.

If you are a first time user, you may want to first run the Live CD to see how Ubuntu operates, before you decide to install. The Live-CD can run from system memory.

```
http://help.ubuntu.com
```

Using BitTorrent

You can use any FTP or Web client, such as gFTP or Firefox, to download the CD image files. The DVD image, though, is a very large file that can take a long time to download, especially if the FTP site is very busy or if your have a slow Internet connection. An alternative for such very large files is to use BitTorrent. BitTorrent is a safe distributed download operation that is ideal for large files, letting many participants download and upload the same file, building a torrent that can run very fast for all participants. The BitTorrent files are located both at **http://releases.ubuntu.com**.

You will first need to install the BitTorrent client. Transmission is the default BitTorrent client installed on GNOME by Ubuntu (Applications | Internet | Transmission). For KUbuntu you can use Ktorrent. There are other several BitTorrent clients available such as **azureus, rtorrent,** and the original **bittorrent**.

Jigdo

The preferred method for downloading large DVD ISO images is Jigdo (Jigsaw Download). Jigdo combines the best of both direct downloads and BitTorrent, while maximizing use of the download data for constructing various spins. In effect, Jigdo sets up a bittorrent download operation using just the Ubuntu mirror sites (no uploading). Jigdo automatically detects the mirror sites that currently provide the fastest download speeds and downloads your image file from them. Mirror sites accessed are switched as download speeds change. If you previously downloaded directly from mirrors, with Jigdo you no longer have to go searching for a fast download mirror site. Jigdo finds them for you.

See the Jigdo Download Howto page at **http://help.ubuntu.com** for more details.

```
https://help.ubuntu.com/community/JigdoDownloadHowto
```

Jigdo is available for the server and alternate CD/DVDs. It is not used for the desktop versions (32 or 64 bit).

For jigdo, first install the **jigdo-file** package and then run the **jigdo-lite** command in a terminal window. You will be prompted for a **.jigdo** file. You can provide the URL for the .jigdo file for the ISO image you want, or download the **.jigdo** file first and provide its path name. At the **http://releases.ubuntu.com** site you will find jigdo files for each ISO image, along with **.torrent** and **.iso** files. The jigdo file for an i386 server is:

```
ubuntu-9.04-server-i386.jigdo
```

Its full URL would be:

```
http://releases.ubuntu.com/releases/9.04/ubuntu-9.04-server-i386.jigdo
```

Jigdo organizes the download into central repository that can be combined into different spins. If you download the Ubuntu desktop CD, and then later the server CD, the data already downloaded for the desktop CD can be used to build the server CD, reducing the actual downloaded data significantly. You will be prompted to provide the location of any mounted CD or CD image.

You can also use jigdo, which provides a GNOME interface for using jigdo. Install the **jigdo** package and run the **jigdo** command in a terminal window.

ubuntu

Table Listing

Figure Listing

Index

LaVergne, TN USA
08 October 2009
160310LV00003B/12/P